Y0-BXG-151

Cookery the Australian Way

SHIRLEY CAMERON & SUZANNE RUSSELL

First Edition 1966 (Reprinted 11 times)
Second Edition 1974 (Reprinted 5 times)
Third Edition 1980 (Reprinted 8 times)
Fourth Edition 1987 (Reprinted 7 times)
Fifth Edition 1993 (Reprinted 4 times)
Sixth Edition published 1998 by
MACMILLAN EDUCATION AUSTRALIA PTY LTD
627 Chapel Street, South Yarra 3141
Reprinted 1999, 2000, 2001

Associated companies and representatives
throughout the world

National Library of Australia
cataloguing in publication data

Cameron, Shirley M.
Cookery the Australian way.
6th ed.
Includes index.
ISBN 0 7329 5042 2
1. Cookery. I. Russell, Suzanne M. II. Title.

641.5

Text design by Sergio Fontana
Page layout by Anne Stanhope
Illustrated by Stanley Wong
Index by Kathleen Gray
Cover design by Stephen Horsley Design
Cover photograph: *Australian Gourmet Traveller* (Australian Consolidated Press) (Haloumi salad)

Printed in Thailand

Contents

Acknowledgements

The authors would like to thank the many Home Economics teachers who provided information on changes to school curricula and suggestions that will assist teachers and students using the book in Home Economics classes.

The support of the Board, members and staff of the Victorian Home Economics and Textile Teachers' Association is gratefully acknowledged, particularly the assistance of Von Canty, Helen Colla, Jenny Dalman, Patsy Hanson, Glenys Heath, Jenny McComb, Kim Weston, Dianne West and Heather McKenzie.

The authors and publishers are grateful to the following for permission to reproduce copyright material:

The Australian Nutrition Foundation for permission to use The Healthy Eating Pyramid (Plate 1), The Healthy Eating Pyramid for Vegetarians (p. 5) and the Healthy Weight Range (p. 11); The Australian Meat and Livestock Corporation for Plates 6 and 7; The Australian Pork Corporation for Plate 8; Tim Lowe for the Australian bush food photographs on Plate 13; Hannah Yiu (Oriental Merchant Pty Ltd) for the Asian Vegetable photographs on Plate 12; the Commonwealth Department of Health and Family Services, Healthy Public Policy Unit, for The Australian Guide to Healthy Eating (Plate 2).

Food styling for the Healthy Eating Pyramid by Tania Letch, Consumer Sciences, Royal Melbourne Institute of Technology.

Food styling for Plates 3, 4, 9, 10, 11, 14 and 15 by Julie Ferguson.

Food photography for Plates 3, 4, 9, 10, 11, 14, 15 and 16 by Michael Carter.

Preface

The sixth edition of Cookery the Australian Way
is dedicated to Winifred Williams.

As society has changed so too has *Cookery The Australian Way*. The sixth edition continues to reflect the trends in healthy eating, the increased range of fruit and vegetables, the recognition of bush tucker and the ethnic diversity of our community.

As the foundation of successful cookery requires an understanding of ingredients and the appropriate use of equipment, a new section detailing this information has been included. At the end of each chapter tips for product quality and quality criteria have been added.

There are more recipes for finger foods and snacks reflecting the eating patterns of busy people. The vegetable section has been extended and the vegetarian chapter expanded as the growing awareness of the nutritional benefits of increasing our fruit and vegetable consumption becomes more evident. The meat chapter now includes many stir-fry recipes and other dishes that are cooked quickly. A detailed description of fruits available is given in the desserts chapter.

Preparation time has been given for many recipes to assist in planning when limited time is available. In the cake chapter recipes are now given in alphabetical order and ideas on the presentation of cakes are given after each recipe. Many new cake recipes have been provided, such as **Fresh fruit cake**, **Macadamia cake** and **Carrot and pumpkin cake**, while old favourites, such as **Lamingtons**, **Rich fruit cake** and **Patty cakes**, are still there.

Creative cooking can provide relaxation after hectic work days, and the aroma of homemade bread, fruit preserves and delicious desserts give a sense of satisfaction and family unity.

The concept of basic recipes with suggested variations in presentation and ingredients has been retained. The use of bold type in the book for the name of a dish denotes the presence of that recipe in this book. These references are followed by the relevant page numbers so that recipes can be located quickly and easily.

The authors trust you will find this sixth edition even more comprehensive and exciting than the previous editions and that you will use the recipes as a start to creating your own variations using the abundance of foods available in Australia.

I guessed the pepper; the soup was too hot!
I guessed the water; it dried in the pot!
I guessed the salt; and – what do you think?
We did nothing else the whole day but drink!

I guessed the sugar; the sauce was too sweet!
And so by my guessing I spoiled our treat;
And now I guess nothing, for cooking by guess
Is sure to result in a terrible mess.

1 Nutrition

'We are what we eat.'

In Australia we have a wide variety of foods available, and to assist in making healthy choices we can be guided by the Dietary Guidelines for Australians, the Healthy Eating Pyramid, the Australian Guide to Healthy Eating and the Five Food Groups.

Food is defined as any substance that, when taken into the body, provides energy and promotes growth and the maintenance of health. All foods are composed of nutrients. These nutrients are proteins, carbohydrates (including dietary fibre), fats, minerals, vitamins and water, each with a specific role and chemical composition.

Choosing a nutritionally balanced intake is important in assisting us to be fit, healthy and happy.

Why we eat

Hunger is the desire to eat caused by the body's need to take in food. The sensation of hunger is controlled by the hypothalamus in the brain and the usual reaction is an 'empty feeling' in the stomach. The hypothalamus reacts to the level of sugar in the blood and hunger can be delayed by eating a small amount of a food containing a simple carbohydrate, for example, an apple.

Appetite is influenced by the appeal certain foods or types of foods have for each of us. We can have an appetite or liking for particular foods, and not for others, even though we may be hungry. Appetite is determined by past experience and is influenced by the smell, texture, sight and particularly the taste of the food. Our taste buds, mainly found on the tongue, are able to differentiate between sweet, sour, salty and bitter tastes. We have the ability to control our appetite and thus we are able to eat less food if we wish to lose weight, or more food if we wish to gain weight.

To live and grow we all need the same nutrients, but for various reasons each of us needs different amounts of these nutrients, particularly those supplying energy. Our size, age, gender, amount of physical activity, genetic make-up, state of health and the interaction with other nutrients consumed influence the amount of the energy and the nutrients we need.

Geographic climate and season affect food intake. In colder climates and weather more energy is required to maintain body heat, therefore kilojoule intake is usually increased.

Changes in eating patterns

Cultural and social influences, including celebration and tradition, play a major part in our eating habits. Australians traditionally eat three meals a day: breakfast, lunch and dinner. However, the type of foods Australians consume has changed. These changes have been caused by many factors, including the following:

The influence of our expanding multicultural community has increased the range of foods available.

Technological developments and improved techniques in commercial food processing, including the development of new packaging materials, have made a wide variety of prepared and packaged foods available.

Temperature, time and atmosphere-controlled distribution systems have enabled most foods to be readily accessible across Australia.

The application of scientific research has not only increased the range of foods available but has also allowed the genetic and nutritional manipulation of the food supply.

Television, radio, print media and other forms of advertising have made us aware of the many types of foods available and influences our choices when purchasing foods.

The structure and social patterns of the family have altered, resulting in changed attitudes to eating and entertaining. The increasing number of working family members has meant less time is available for purchase and preparation of food and for formal entertaining. There has also been an increased involvement of family members in the purchase and preparation of food. Our climate is conducive to outdoor eating and the barbecue is a popular way of eating and entertaining.

The increased use of takeaway food shops, family restaurants and processed convenience foods has led to changed eating habits. Approximately 35% of meals in Australia are eaten away from the home.

A balanced food plan

The food nutrients interact with each other in the body and some are unable to function optimally unless they are in the presence of other nutrients. Each day the body requires certain amounts of each nutrient to function properly. The nutrients assist the body by:

- building and repairing body tissue – proteins

- providing a source of energy – carbohydrates and fats
- regulating body processes – vitamins, minerals and water
- assisting the passage of food through the digestive tract – carbohydrates in the form of fibre.

In Australia our usual meal pattern is three meals a day, but when planning food intake we should also remember drinks, fruit and other food eaten between meals. Some snack foods may be high in the energy-giving nutrients, such as carbohydrates and fats, but provide little of the other nutrients. These are referred to as energy-dense foods. However, with careful selection, snacks, such as low-fat cheese on wholemeal toast with fresh fruit, can make a nutritionally balanced contribution to our daily intake. Our activity level should be considered when planning food intake, including snacks.

Food selection models

Food selection models, such as the Dietary Guidelines, the Healthy Eating Pyramid, the Australian Guide to Healthy Eating and the Five Food Groups, should be used as guides to developing a balanced food plan that includes a variety of foods each day.

The Dietary Guidelines

The Dietary Guidelines were developed by the Commonwealth Department of Health and Community Services in 1982 with the aim of improving the health of all Australians.

- Enjoy a wide variety of nutritious foods.
- Eat plenty of bread and cereals (preferably wholegrain), vegetables (including legumes) and fruits.
- Eat a diet low in fat and, in particular, low in saturated fat.
- Maintain a healthy body weight by balancing physical activity and food intake.
- If you drink alcohol, limit your intake.
- Eat only a moderate amount of sugars and foods containing added sugars.
- Choose low-salt foods and use salt sparingly.
- Encourage and support breast feeding.

Guidelines on specific nutrients were added in 1992 in order to address the particular concerns of specific groups within the general population.

- Eat foods containing calcium. This is particularly important for girls and women.
- Eat foods containing iron. This applies particularly to girls, women, vegetarians and athletes.

The Dietary Guidelines for Children and Adolescents were developed by the National Health and Medical Research Council (NHMRC) in 1995 to show the different dietary requirements of those aged between birth and eighteen years. Children need appropriate food and physical activity to grow and develop normally, and their growth should be checked regularly.

- Enjoy a wide variety of nutritious foods.
- Eat plenty of breads, cereals, vegetables (including legumes) and fruits.
- Low-fat diets are not suitable for young children. For older children, a diet low in fat and in particular, low in saturated fat, is appropriate.

- Encourage water as a drink. Alcohol is not recommended for children.
- Eat only a moderate amount of sugars and foods containing added sugars.
- Choose low-salt foods.
- Encourage and support breastfeeding.

Healthy Eating Pyramid

The Healthy Eating Pyramid, developed by the Australian Nutrition Foundation (ANF), demonstrates how foods can be grouped according to their energy density and graphically reflects the proportions in which they should be consumed.

The bottom layer contains the foods we should eat most: fruits and vegetables, legumes, bread and cereals (preferably wholegrain). These are rich in vitamins, minerals and the complex carbohydrates (including fibre) and contain smaller amounts of proteins and fats. They are nutrient-dense rather than energy-dense.

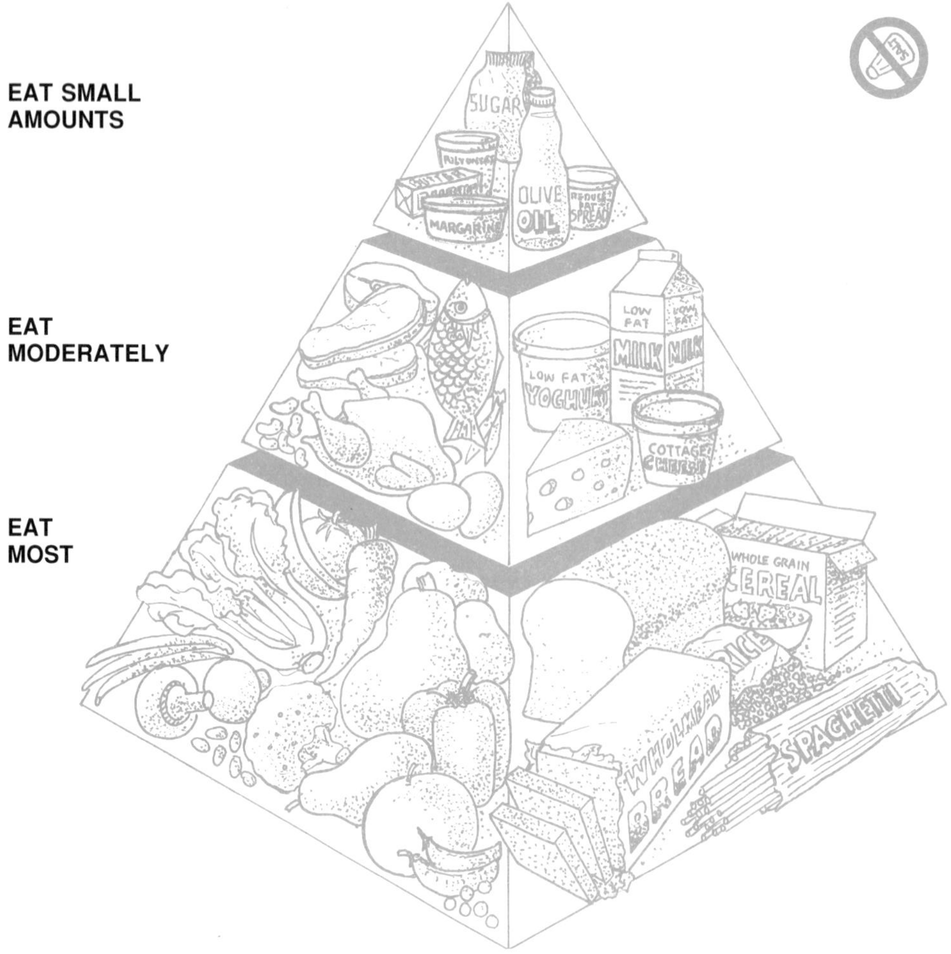

We should have a moderate amount of the foods from the middle section. These foods (milk, cheese, yoghurt, lean meat, poultry, fish, legumes, nuts and eggs) are rich in proteins, vitamins and minerals (especially iron and calcium). These foods are also nutrient-dense but many of them also contain moderate amounts of fat. Fat intake can be reduced by choosing the low-fat varieties of these foods such as skim milk, low-fat modified milk, low-fat yoghurt and low-fat cheeses.

The top layer contains those foods that we should eat in small amounts: fats, oils and sugars. Butter, cream, table margarine, dairy blend and oils are included in this group as they contain 80% or more fat, however, they provide valuable sources of the fat-soluble vitamins, A and D. Sugars include table sugar (sucrose), glucose, dextrose, fructose, lactose. Sugars and foods with a high sugar content, such as honey, confectionery and soft drinks, are high in energy-producing nutrients, but lack other nutrients. They are called energy-dense foods and contribute to dental cavities, obesity and diabetes. The pyramid also reflects that salt (sodium) should not be added to food.

Healthy Eating Pyramid for Vegetarians

The Healthy Eating Pyramid for Vegetarians was developed by the ANF in 1995 to assist lacto-ovo vegetarians select balanced and healthy meals.

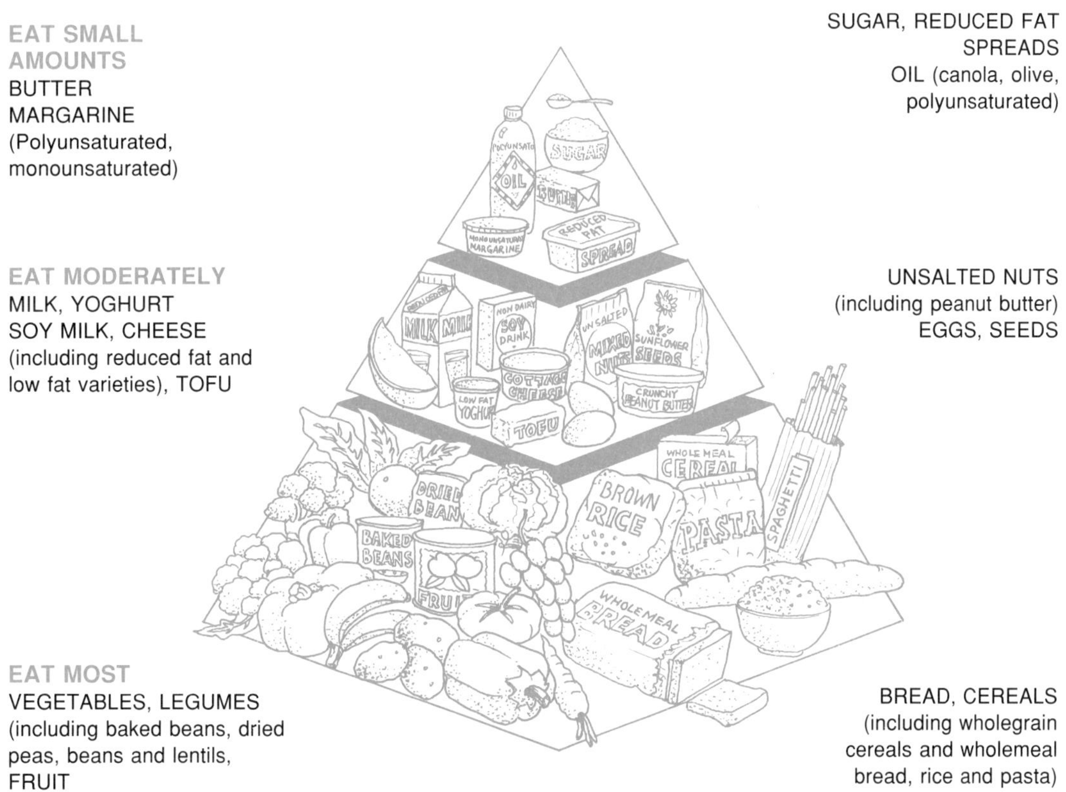

The Australian Guide to Healthy Eating

This model was developed for the Commonwealth Department of Health and Family Services by the Children's Health Development Foundation, Women's and Children's Hospital (South Australia) and the Faculty of Health and Behavioural Sciences, Deakin University (Victoria), and released in 1998. The foods in the circular guide are combined into five groups according to nutrient similarity. The area allocated to each group indicates the proportion in which each group should be consumed. (Also, see page opposite p. 11)

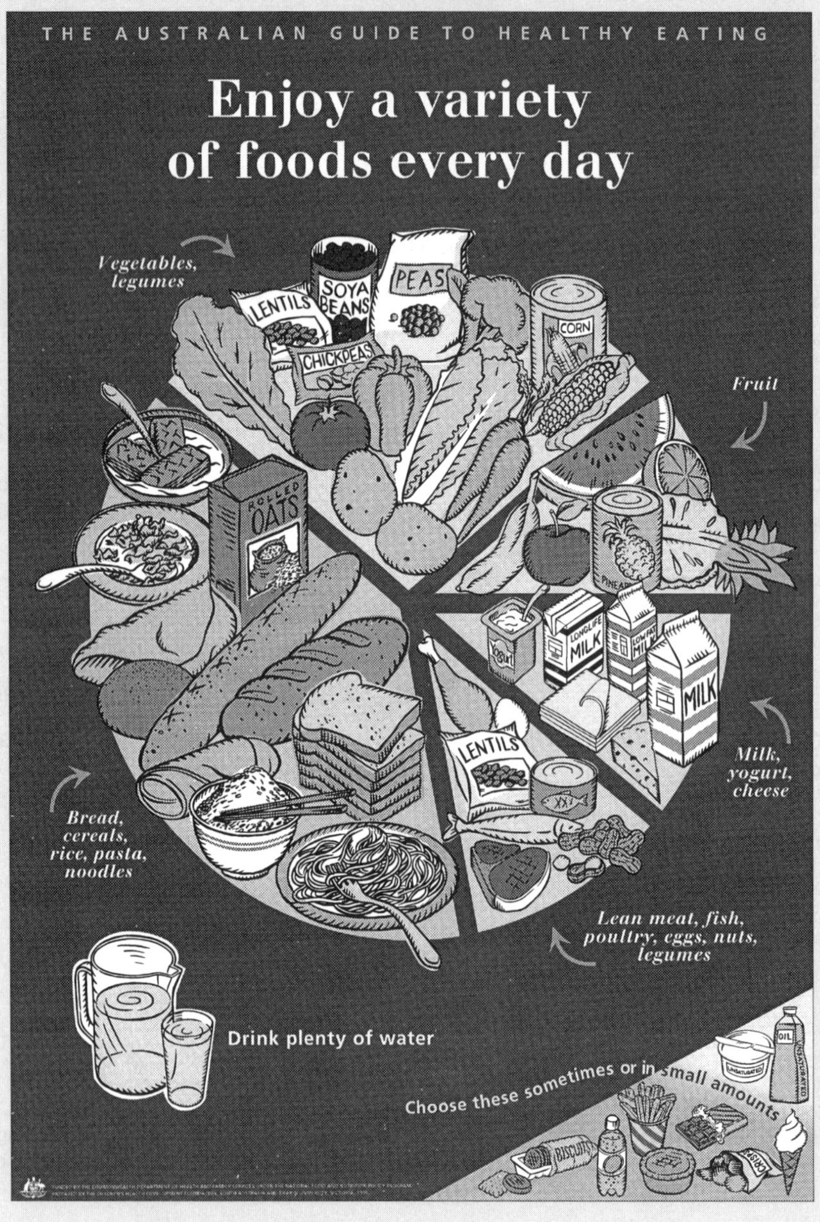

Five Food Groups

The Five Food Groups is another guide to help us plan our daily food intake. This guide emphasises the major nutrients present in each type of food. The following chart shows the Five Food Groups and the minimum amounts recommended daily for a healthy food intake.

The Five Food Groups	
Breads and cereals (preferably wholegrain)	Choose at least four servings e.g. 1 slice wholegrain bread 1/2 cup breakfast cereal 1/2 cup cooked pasta 1/2 cup cooked brown rice 
Fruit and vegetables	Choose at least seven servings (2 fruit and 5 vegetables), e.g. orange, apple tomato, potato, broccoli, lettuce and carrot 
Meat and meat equivalents	One serve, e.g. 75–100 g lean meat or poultry or fish or 1 egg or 1/4 cup nuts or cooked beans or lentils 
Milk and milk products	One serve, amount depends on stage in life cycle e.g. milk (300 mL adults, 600 mL children) or cheese (35 g adults, 70 g children) or yoghurt (300 mL adults, 600 mL children) 
Fats and oils	1 tablespoon margarine or butter or cream or dairy blend 

Energy requirements

Just as a car needs petrol to run, our bodies require energy to function and food is the source of this energy. Energy is required by the body in order to carry out its various functions and is measured in kilojoules (kJ).

If more food is eaten than the body requires for its activities, then we gain weight and if less food is eaten than required for activities, then we lose weight.

Recommended energy intakes for adolescents 14–18 years (MJ/day)

Age (years)	Males	Females
14–15	10.5–11.8	8.6–9.8
15–16	11.1–12.5	8.7–9.9
16–17	11.7–13.2	8.8–10.0
17–18	12.0–13.5	8.8–10.0

Source: FAO-WHO-UNI (1985)

Recommended energy intakes for adults aged 18–30 (MJ/day)

Height (cm)	Weight (kg)	Males	Females
150	50.6	–	7.2–8.3
160	57.6	9.1–10.4	7.9–9.0
170	65.0	9.8–11.2	8.5–9.7
180	72.9	10.5–12.0	9.2–10.5
190	81.2	11.2–12.8	9.9–11.2
200	90.0	12.0–13.7	–

Source: National Health and Medical Research Council (1985)

We don't all need the same amount of energy. There are many factors that influence the amount of energy each individual needs, including body size, age, activity level, gender, state of health, hereditary factors and growth rate.

The energy required by the body is used for:

- maintaining essential body processes such as breathing, digestion, heart beat, blood circulation, temperature regulation and muscle tone
- muscle action to enable physical activity such as running, walking and sitting
- growth.

When at rest the body uses just enough energy for the essential body processes. This is called the basal metabolic rate. It varies from person to person but on average is about 4 kJ per minute. Energy use rises to 12–15 kJ/minute for slow walking, 16–20 kJ/minute for swimming and over 25–30 kJ/minute for running.

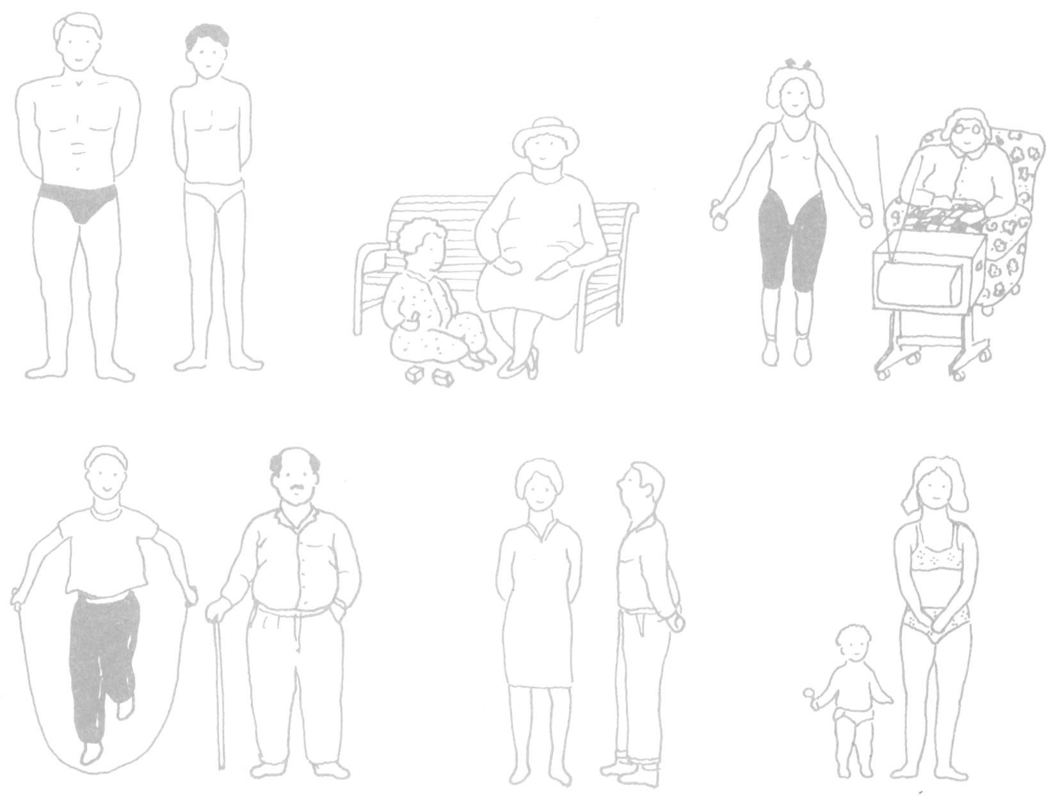

Food is broken down to produce energy. The energy is used immediately or is converted to glycogen and fat and stored, then used to produce energy as required. For every 30 kJ consumed above the body's requirements, approximately 1 gram of fat is added to body weight. If 30 kJ less than body needs is eaten then 1 gram of body fat is used to provide energy.

Energy expenditure varies according to a person's body weight and the amount of effort put into daily activities.

Energy expenditure

Activity	kJ use per minute	
	Female	*Male*
Sleep	4	5
Sitting	8	10
Slow walking, standing, light work	12	15
Physical work, vigorous playground activities, tennis	16	20
Energetic dancing, aerobics, running, swimming	25+	30+

Energy value of foods

The energy value of foods is measured in kilojoules (kJ). The foods we eat are acted on or metabolised in the body to produce energy, with each type of nutrient yielding a different kilojoule (kJ) or energy value. This can be expressed as kJ per gram as follows:

Fat = 37 kJ/g
Alcohol = 29 kJ/g
Protein = 17 kJ/g
Carbohydrate = 16 kJ/g

Water, fibre, minerals and vitamins have no kilojoule value, but are important in the metabolic processes and the utilisation of energy.

Food	Serve	Mass	kJ
Apple, raw	1	125 g	337
Banana	1	125 g	500
Biscuit – dry	3	12 g	200
– sweet	2	16 g	320
Bread – brown	2 slices	50 g	510
– white		46 g	470
Butter or margarine		20 g	580
Casserole	1 cup	250 g	1500
Carrots	1 small	60 g	100
Cornflakes	1 cup	30 g	473
Cheese sandwich	1	80 g	1150
Chiko roll	1	200 g	2800
Chocolate malted milk	1	345 mL	1360
Corn chips	1 pkt	60 g	1040
Doughnut	1	40 g	590
Egg, fried	1	60 g	410
Fish, fried	1 fillet	100 g	1000
Beefburger in bun	1	205 g	2360
Hot dog	1	115 g	1340
Lamb chop	1	100 g	1200
Lemonade	1 glass	250 mL	410
Lettuce leaves	2	20 g	20
Meat and salad	1	125 g	1160
Meat pie	1	163 g	2170
Milk	1 glass	250 mL	700
Muesli – toasted	1/2 cup	55 g	929
Orange juice	1 glass	250 mL	480
Pasta – boiled	1 cup	180 g	895
Peanuts		30 g	730
Pizza	1/4	130 g	1370
Potato – boiled	1	125 g	320
– chips	18–20	90 g	1010
White rice – boiled	1 cup	190 g	993
Sausage	2	100 g	1300
Steak		100 g	1000
Tomato	1	125 g	72
Yoghurt		200 g	830

THE HEALTHY EATING PYRAMID

EAT SMALL AMOUNTS

SUGAR
REDUCED-FAT SPREADS
OIL (canola, olive, polyunsaturated)

BUTTER
MARGARINE
(polyunsaturated, monounsaturated)

NO SALT

EAT MODERATELY

LEAN MEAT
EGGS
FISH
CHICKEN
NUTS

MILK
YOGHURT
CHEESE
(include the reduced-fat and low-fat varieties of dairy products)

EAT MOST

FRUIT
VEGETABLES
DRIED PEAS
BEANS
LENTILS

BREAD
CEREALS
(including wholegrain cereals and wholemeal bread, rice and pasta)

PLATE 1

PLATE 2

THE AUSTRALIAN GUIDE TO HEALTHY EATING

Enjoy a variety of foods every day

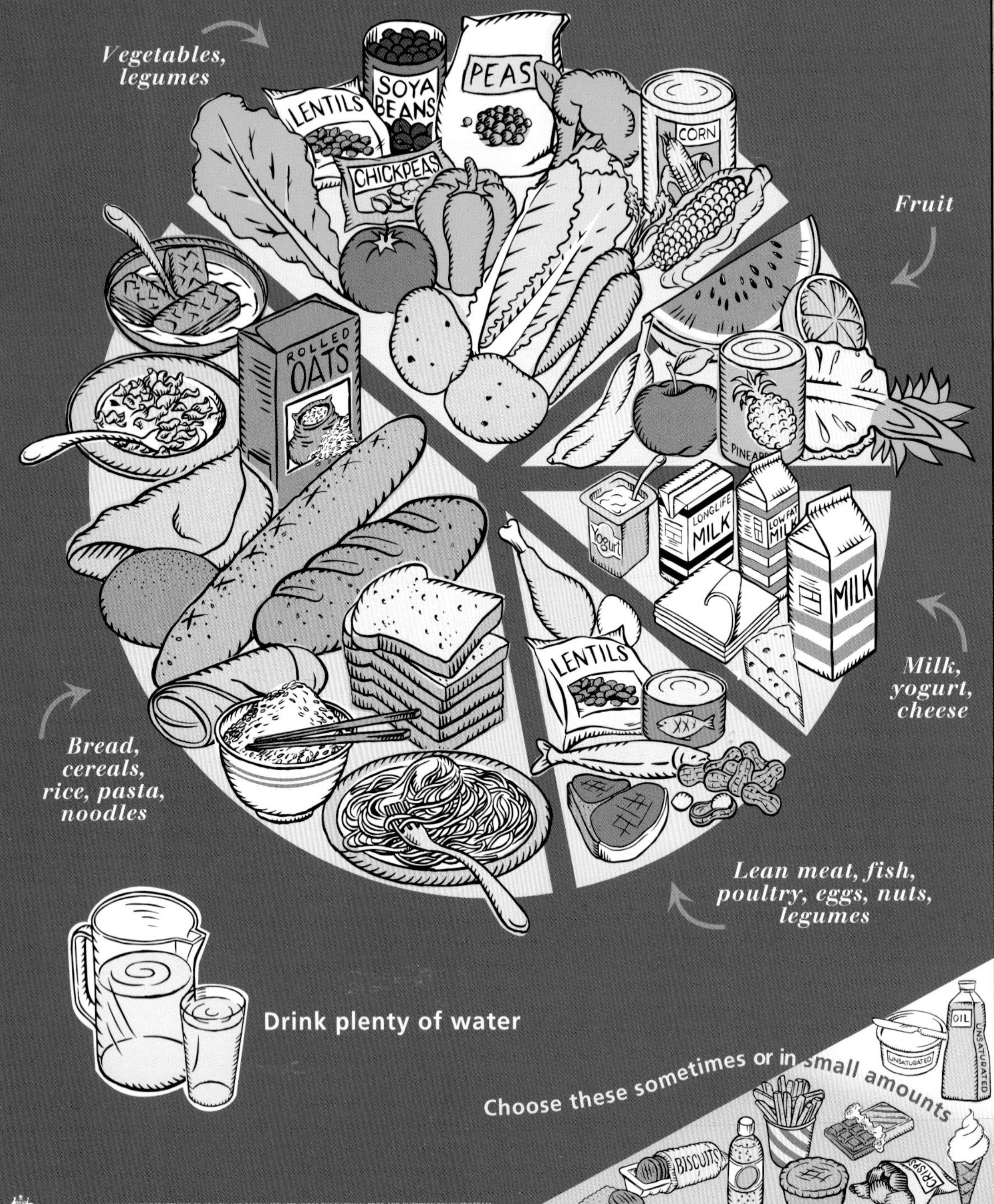

FUNDED BY THE COMMONWEALTH DEPARTMENT OF HEALTH AND FAMILY SERVICES UNDER THE NATIONAL FOOD AND NUTRITION POLICY PROGRAM.
PREPARED BY THE CHILDREN'S HEALTH DEVELOPMENT FOUNDATION, SOUTH AUSTRALIA AND DEAKIN UNIVERSITY, VICTORIA. 1998.

Control of body weight

Energy balance is an important aspect of health and can be defined as energy intake meeting energy used. If an individual has a lower energy intake than is required and the body stores are depleted, it can result in tissue wasting, slowing of body functions and inhibited growth and development. Excess energy intake can lead to increased fat stores, weight gain and obesity over a period of time.

Over the past few years Australians have tended to reduce their physical activity. Reliance on the car, television viewing and labour-saving devices means that we exercise less and therefore use less energy. This, combined with our traditional Western diet, which has been high in fats, sugar, salt and alcohol and low in fibre, is responsible for an increasing number of people being overweight. Many adults in Australia today increase their weight by 1 g per day. The diet-related conditions found in Australia include heart disease, non-insulin dependent diabetes, hypertension, bowel cancer and cirrhosis of the liver.

Body weight can be altered by increasing or decreasing the kilojoule or energy value of the total food intake and the amount of physical activity undertaken. When reducing body weight by increasing exercise and reducing the intake of high energy-value foods, it is important that the weight loss is gradual. Approximately 0.5 to 1 kg per week reduction is the suggested maximum weight loss.

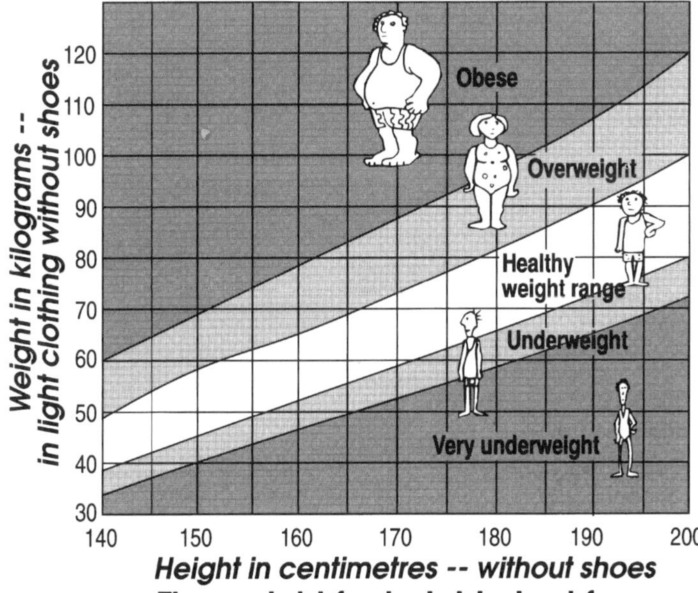

The weight for height chart for men and women from 18 years onwards.

Weight-control diets that do not include a variety of foods and thus a balance of nutrients, can lead to tiredness and the risk of vitamin and mineral deficiencies. This may be a long-term danger to health.

The ideal proportion of nutrient intake for energy is 50–55% from carbohydrates (40% from complex carbohydrates), 12–15% from proteins and 30–35% or less from fats.

Avoid diets that concentrate on a very limited range of foods, for example, high-protein or low-carbohydrate foods.

Follow the principles of the Healthy Eating Pyramid, the Australian Guide to Healthy Eating and the Dietary Guidelines for sensible and safe weight control.

Safe weight loss not only applies to those who are overweight or obese. Care needs to be taken to avoid those problems associated with excessive weight loss, for example, the eating disorders of anorexia nervosa and bulimia nervosa. These eating disorders are often associated with the misconception that excessive slimness and beauty, and acceptance by family and friends, go hand in hand. Anorexia nervosa and bulimia nervosa can lead to dental decay, amenorrhea, serious illness, emaciation and, in severe cases, death.

Daily nutrient requirements

The National Health and Medical Research Council has compiled tables listing recommended nutrient intakes and energy requirements: 'Dietary allowances for use in Australia', 1991. These are based on the Recommended Daily Intake (RDI), that is, the nutrients required by the body each day to provide sufficient energy for the basal metabolic rate and for physical activities. The amounts of each nutrient required are based on the reference man and reference woman, that is, a 'typical' Australian man and woman.

The reference man is twenty-five years of age. He is healthy, that is, he is free from disease and exhibits a 'normal' degree of physical fitness. He weighs 70 kg and lives in the warm temperate zone at a mean external annual temperature of 18°C. He consumes an adequate well-balanced diet; he neither gains nor loses weight. His activity is exemplified by the following average weekly schedule. On each working day, 8 hours of physical work; 4 hours of 'sedentary' activity; 2 hours of walking slowly on the level and at least 2 hours out of doors and, on each non-working day, the active pursuit of exercise and sport, not of the extremely strenuous variety. The degree of activity involved in occupation in light industry or general laboratory work would represent approximately his working activity.

The reference woman is a similarly healthy woman, aged twenty-five years, weighing 58 kg. She lives in the same environment as a reference man and is engaged in general household duties, including the care of small children, or in light industrial work. Non-working activities include slow walking for 2 hours and 2 hours spent out of doors. At times she engages in activities such as gardening and non-strenuous sports.

Dietary allowances for use in Australia

	Infants			Young children		Boys		
	0–6 mths		7–12 mths	1–3 yrs	4–7 yrs	8–11 yrs	12–15 yrs	16–18 yrs
	Breastfed	Bottlefed						
Vitamin A (ug retinol equivalents)	425	425	300	300	350	500	725	750
Thiamin (mg)	0.15	0.25	0.35	0.5	0.7	0.9	1.2	1.2
Riboflavin (mg)	0.4	0.4	0.6	0.8	1.1	1.4	1.8	1.9
Niacin (mg niacin equivalents)	4	4	7	10	12	15	20	21
Vitamin B6 (mg)	0.25	0.25	0.45	0.6–0.9	0.8–1.3	1.1–1.6	1.4–2.1	1.5–2.2
Total folate (ug)	50	50	75	100	100	150	200	200
Vitamin B12 (ug)	0.3	0.3	0.7	1.0	1.5	1.5	2.0	2.0
Vitamin C (mg)	25	25	30	30	30	30	30	40
Vitamin E (mg alpha tocopherol equivalents)	2.5	4.0	4.0	5.0	6.0	8.0	10.5	11.0
Zinc (mg)	3	3–6	4.5	4.5	6	9	12	12
Iron (mg)	0.5	3.0	9.0	6–8	6–8	6–8	10–13	10–13
Iodine (ug)	50	50	60	70	90	120	150	150
Magnesium (mg)	40	40	60	80	110	180	260	320
Calcium (mg)	300	500	550	700	800	800	1200	1000
Phosphorus (mg)	150	150	300	500	700	800	1200	1100
Selenium (ug)	10	10	15	25	30	50	85	85
Sodium (mmol)	6–12	6–12	14–25	14–50	20–75	26–100	40–100	40–100
(mg)	140–280	140–280	320–580	320–1150	460–1730	600–2300	920–2300	920–2300
Potassium (mmol)	10–15	10–15	12–35	25–70	40–100	50–140	50–140	50–140
(mg)	390–580	390–580	470–1370	980–2730	1560–3900	1950–5460	1950–5460	1950–5460
Protein (g)	*	2.0/kg body wt	1.6/kg body wt	14–18	18–24	27–38	42–60	64–70

Dietary allowances for use in Australia

	Girls			Men	Women				
	8–11 yrs	12–15 yrs	16–18 yrs	19–64 yrs	64 yrs	19–54 yrs	54+ yrs	Pregnant	Lactating
Vitamin A (ug retinol equivalents)	500	725	750	750	750	750	750	+0	+450
Thiamin (mg)	0.8	1.0	0.9	1.1	0.9	0.8	0.7	+0.2	+0.4
Riboflavin (mg)	1.3	1.6	1.4	1.7	1.3	1.2	1.0	+0.3	+0.5
Niacin (mg niacin equivalents)	15	18	16	19	16	13	11	+2	+5
Vitamin B6 (mg)	1.0–1.5	1.2–1.8	1.1–1.6	1.3–1.9	1.0–1.5	0.9–1.4	0.8–1.1	+0.1	+0.7–0.8
Total folate (ug)	150	200	200	200	200	200	200	+200	+150
Vitamin B12 (ug)	1.5	2.0	2.0	2.0	2.0	2.0	2.0	+1.0	+0.5
Vitamin C (mg)	30	30	30	40	40	30	30	+30	+45
Vitamin E (mg alpha tocopherol equivalents)	8.0	9.0	8.0	10.0	10.0	7.0	7.0	+0	+2.5
Zinc (mg)	9	12	12	12	12	12	12	+4	+6
Iron (mg)	6.8	10–13	10–13	7	7	12–16	5–7	+10–20	+0
Iodine (ug)	120	120	120	150	150	120	120	+30	+50
Magnesium (mg)	160	240	270	320	320	270	270	+30	+50
Calcium (mg)	900	1000	800	800	800	800	1000	+300	+400
Phosphorus (mg)	800	1200	1100	1000	1000	1000	1000	+200	+200
Selenium (ug)	50	70	70	85	85	70	70	+10	+15
Sodium (mmol)	26–100	40–100	40–100	40–100	40–100	40–100	40–100	+0	+0
(mg)	600–2300	920–2300	920–2300	920–2300	920–2300	920–2300	920–2300	+0	+0
Potassium (mmol)	50–140	50–140	50–140	50–140	50–140	50–140	50–140	+0	+0
(mg)	1950–5460	1950–5460	1950–5460	1950–5460	1950–5460	1950–5460	1950–5460	+0	+0
Protein (g)	27–39	44–55	57	55	55	45	45	+6	+16

Food nutrients

Each day the body requires certain amounts of each nutrient and the food selection models are based on the Recommended Daily Intake of nutrients.

Food composition tables (Metric Tables of Composition of Australian Foods) and computer programs (such as NUTTAB) can assist us in planning our nutrient intake.

Proteins

The name comes from the Greek word *proteois* and means 'to take first place', as an adequate amount of this nutrient is essential.

Chemical composition

Proteins are formed from simpler compounds called amino acids and vary because of different combinations, proportions and numbers of these amino acids in the protein molecule. There are 22 amino acids that normally occur in foods.

Functions

- Body building and repair, which includes the formation of muscles, bones and teeth, hair and nails and growth of these tissues.
- Assist in production of antibodies that act in body's systems of immunity against disease, e.g. globulin.
- Assist production of enzymes that aid metabolism, e.g. pepsin.
- Assist in production of hormones that regulate body functions, e.g. insulin.
- Assist in process of storing oxygen in the muscles for use during exercise, e.g. myoglobin.
- Assist in the blood clotting process where the protein fibrinogen is turned into insoluble fibrin as blood clots.
- A source of energy if the diet does not supply sufficient carbohydrates and fats to meet the individual's requirements, however, this is an expensive energy source.

Sources

The adult body can make some of the essential amino acids it requires, but there are 8 amino acids that the body needs but cannot make or cannot make in sufficient quantities. Children's bodies cannot make 9 of the essential amino acids. The body needs specific proportions of these amino acids – a lack of one means the others cannot be properly utilised. The following amino acids are those that must be provided in food for good health:

Phenylalanine	Tryptophan	Leucine
Valine	Threonine	Lysine
Methionine	Isoleucine	Histidine (children only)

The other essential amino acids can be manufactured or 'synthesised' within the human body.

Animal-based proteins, with the exception of gelatin, contain all the essential amino acids in the proportions needed by the body. These are found in animal foods including meat, fish, poultry, milk, eggs and cheese. They are sometimes referred to as 'complete proteins'.

Plant foods also contain protein. It is usually in smaller amounts than animal sources, although dried beans and peas, nuts and cereals are useful sources. Soya beans, although low in methionine, contain all the essential amino acids. All other plant proteins are missing one or more of the essential amino acids, but different vegetable and cereal foods can be served in the same meal to provide the full range of essential amino acids (see p. 5 for vegetarian diets). Plant proteins may be referred to as 'incomplete proteins'.

Requirements

The protein requirement for adults is 1 gram of protein per kilogram body weight, which allows for a wide safety margin. Increased amounts are required during pregnancy and lactation. Children require proportionately more protein, especially during stages of rapid growth. Excess protein consumption can contribute to weight gain as the protein not used by the body is converted to body fat.

Examples of proteins

Albumins e.g. egg albumin in egg white, lactalbumin in milk. They are soluble in water and coagulated by heat.

Casein found in milk and can be precipitated by the enzyme rennet. This property is used in the preparation of junket.

Collagen forms protein matrix in bones and teeth and connective tissue in the body. Forms gelatin after prolonged cooking in moist heat.

Globulins e.g. myosin in meat muscle; fibrin in blood and meat; legumin in peas, beans and lentils; ovoglobulin in egg white; lactoglobulin in milk. They are soluble in water and coagulated by heat.

Keratin found in hair and nails. It is insoluble in water.

Vitellin found in egg yolk.

Carbohydrates

Chemical composition

Carbohydrates or saccharides are compounds formed from molecules of sugar and are classified as simple or complex carbohydrates.

Monosaccharides are simple carbohydrates, consisting of single molecules. The three main monosaccharides are glucose, galactose and fructose, and these form the building blocks for the other carbohydrates. Monosaccharides are sweet, dissolve in water and are absorbed directly into the bloodstream in the body.

Disaccharides are simple carbohydrates, composed of two joined monosaccharides. Three of the most commonly occurring are sucrose or ordinary sugar (consists of a molecule of glucose and a molecule of fructose), lactose, found in milk (consists of a molecule of glucose and a molecule of galactose) and maltose, found in malt (consists of two glucose molecules). Disaccharides are broken down in the body during digestion into monosaccharides.

Polysaccharides are complex carbohydrates and are composed of large numbers of monosaccharide molecules and occur in foods as:

- starch, dextrins or glycogen, which are broken down in the body to glucose, fructose and galactose
- cellulose, which forms the cell walls of plants and is therefore found in all fruits, vegetables and wholegrain cereals. It is not readily digested by the body and is referred to as fibre, roughage or dietary fibre.

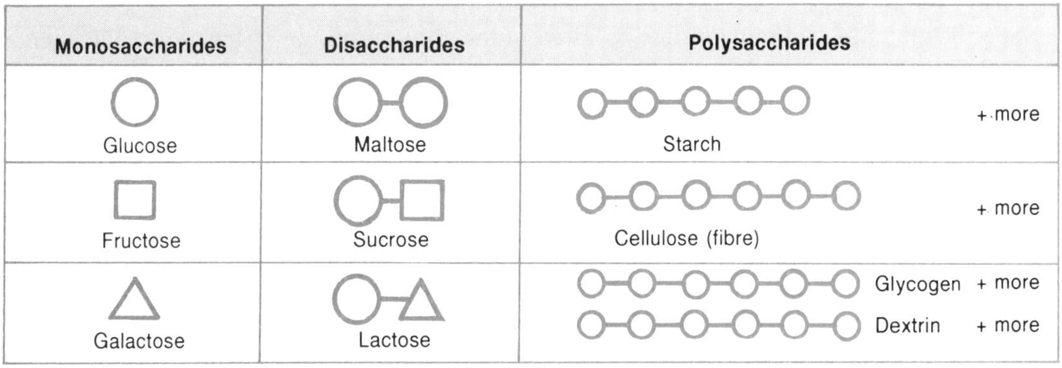

Monosaccharides	Disaccharides	Polysaccharides
○ Glucose	○-○ Maltose	○-○-○-○-○ Starch + more
□ Fructose	○-□ Sucrose	○-○-○-○-○-○ Cellulose (fibre) + more
△ Galactose	○-△ Lactose	○-○-○-○-○-○ Glycogen + more ○-○-○-○-○-○ Dextrin + more

Functions

- Carbohydrates (other than fibre) are a source of energy for the body and are required to maintain basal metabolic rate and for physical activity.
- Fibre, not readily digested by the body, is important because it stimulates the digestive system to move the food through the digestive tract.

Sources

Simple carbohydrates are found in sweet foods such as sugars, honey, jams, sweets and sweetened aerated drinks, as well as fruits, vegetables and cereals.

Complex carbohydrates are found in cereal foods such as breakfast cereals, bread, spaghetti and other pasta. Wheat, rice and fruits and vegetables provide polysaccharides as well as other nutrients to the body. Refining or milling cereals removes the cellulose and other nutrients, therefore wholegrain cereals have a higher complex carbohydrate value.

Requirements

In the highly industrialised nations, about one-half of the daily energy requirements of the body are obtained from carbohydrate foods. In developing countries, where a higher proportion of income is spent on food, carbohydrate foods supply a larger proportion of the energy required, and in Arctic areas, energy from an increased fat intake reduces the amount of carbohydrate required.

Complex carbohydrate foods are comparatively cheap, easily produced and stored, and are readily converted into energy in the body. In Australia, there is a tendency for many people to take in more simple carbohydrates than required by the body, especially in the form of sweet foods. The excess is stored as body fat and can lead to weight gain. Sweet foods are a contributing factor to dental caries and it is therefore best to ensure that only small amounts of the sweet foods and larger amounts of polysaccharides are used as the major energy source. In the Healthy Eating Pyramid the complex carbohydrate foods are in the Eat Most layer and sugar is in the Eat in Small Amounts layer.

Specific vitamins and minerals are required to metabolise carbohydrates to provide energy to the body.

Examples

Glucose is found in many foods on its own, for example, in fruit, or combined as a disaccharide or polysaccharide.

Sucrose or sugar is found in cane sugar, sugar beet and other foods. It is a disaccharide.

Pectin is a polysaccharide found in many 'firm ripe' fruits. It is necessary for the formation of a 'gel' in jam and jelly making.

Dextrin is a polysaccharide derived as a breakdown product of starch. When subjected to dry heat it becomes brown in colour with a characteristic taste, as in the outer surface of toast.

Glycogen is a polysaccharide present in small amounts in meat and liver. Glycogen is stored in the body in muscle tissue and in the liver, and is rapidly converted to glucose if extra energy is required.

Dietary fibre

Dietary fibre is made up of various complex carbohydrates, but unlike starch or glycogen, they cannot be digested by human enzymes. Although it is not digested or absorbed by the human body, dietary fibre's assistance in the prevention of ill health is essential and often overlooked.

Chemical composition

Dietary fibre consists of cellulose, lignin, pectins, gums, hellicellulose and non-cellulose wall polysaccharides that all come from the stems, leaves, seeds and roots of plants. Its effects on the human body relate not only to the chemical composition of the dietary fibre but also to the physical properties of the plants themselves.

Function

- Increases the bulk of the faeces thereby promoting the passage of food through the intestinal tract.
- Increases the movement of potentially carcinogenic substances through the intestinal tract unabsorbed.
- Protects against coronary heart disease, cardiovascular disease, gall bladder, diverticular and large bowel diseases and diabetes.
- Reduces blood cholesterol and helps maintains mineral balance.
- Relieves pressure on the bowels and promotes regularity, which reduces the likelihood of haemorrhoids, constipation and hiatus hernia.
- Helps with the treatment of obesity – dietary fibre creates a feeling of fullness without the added kilojoules of fats and other carbohydrates. Foods high in fibre are generally low in fat.
- Excess causes flatulence, diarrhoea and related problems.

Sources

Dietary fibre is found in all plant products, such as cereals, fruits and vegetables. Milling, refining, processing and cooking can reduce the amount of fibre present in the food eaten. Raw fruit and vegetables and unrefined cereals contain the highest proportions of dietary fibre.

Requirements

There is no absolute recommended daily intake of dietary fibre because it is difficult to measure the exact amount of fibre in foods consumed. Processing, cooking and storage of fruits, vegetables and cereals effect their physical structures to varying degrees, altering their affect on the intestinal tract. The guidelines for dietary fibre intake recommend increasing fresh and raw foods in the diet. A varied diet for adults should include seven serves of fruits and vegetables each day – about 30 g of dietary fibre.

Fats and oils

Fats are solid at room temperature and usually of animal origin, e.g. butter or lard. Oils are liquid at room temperature and usually are of vegetable origin, e.g. olive oil, peanut oil, canola oil or maize oil. Fats and oils are also called lipids.

Chemical composition and sources

Fat molecules consist of hydrogen, carbon and oxygen and are mainly found in foods in the form of triglycerides. Triglycerides are formed from a glycerol molecule attached to three fatty acids. A fatty acid is a chain of carbon atoms, each with hydrogen atoms attached by bonds. Fatty acids can be saturated, mono-unsaturated or polyunsaturated depending on the number of double bonds in the molecule.

All fats and oils (lipids) contain a mixture of saturated, mono-unsaturated and polyunsaturated fatty acids, and they are classified by the various amounts of the different fatty acids they contain.

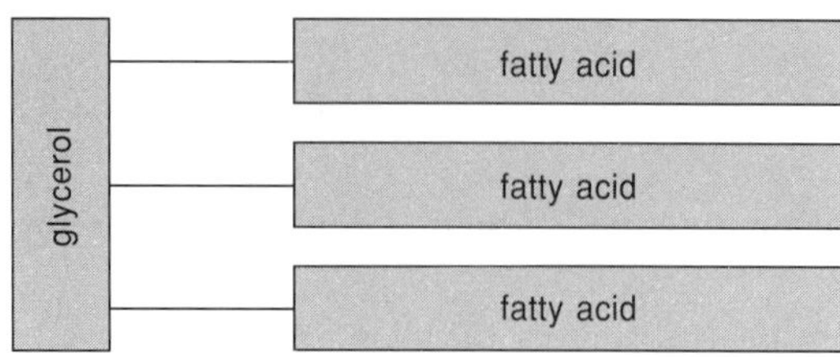

The level of saturation in a lipid depends on the relative amounts of saturated and unsaturated fatty acids. Usually those of animal origin have a higher proportion of saturated fatty acids than those of vegetable origin.

Saturated fats

When each carbon atom in the fatty acid chain is attached by a single bond to the next atom, and the molecule is unable to take up any more hydrogen atoms, it is saturated. All fats contain some saturated fatty acids, but animal fats such as those in butter, cheese and meat are our main dietary sources. Palm oil and coconut oil are the only vegetable oils that contain predominantly saturated fatty acids.

Role of cholesterol

Cholesterol is another type of lipid, but does not contain any fatty acids. In appearance it is a solid white waxy substance and is only produced by animals. High levels of cholesterol in our blood have been shown to be related to heart disease. Cholesterol is required by the body to maintain optimum health (it is necessary for steroid hormone production and vitamin D production), with about three-quarters of our daily needs of cholesterol made in the body and about one-quarter obtained from animal fats in our diet.

To a limited extent our metabolism automatically reduces the body's production when dietary cholesterol increases, however, hereditary factors, a stressful lifestyle and high saturated fat intake can affect this process. Cholesterol is transported through the blood vessels to and from the body cells in protein-fat particles, called lipoproteins. The two main lipoproteins involved are:

- **Low density lipoproteins (LDL)**, which transport cholesterol from the liver to the cells. Excess LDL-cholesterol particles can lead to a build-up of cholesterol on the walls of arteries, narrowing them and reducing the flow of blood to the heart, a disease called atherosclerosis.
- **High density lipoproteins (HDL)** Current research indicates the HDL removes cholesterol from the cell walls, returning it to the liver for processing, thus HDL is beneficial to health and its effectiveness is increased by exercise.

Saturated fats raise the level of LDL cholesterol in the blood. Therefore reducing the intake of saturated fats, through restricting the intake of animal fats, reduces the level of blood cholesterol.

Mono-unsaturated fats

If a fatty acid molecule contains one pair of adjacent carbon atoms connected by a double bond, the double bond can be broken and the molecule is able to take up two atoms of hydrogen. Mono-unsaturated fats can reduce blood cholesterol levels indirectly by displacing saturated fats from the diet. Food sources include olives and olive oils, peanut oil, nuts and avocados.

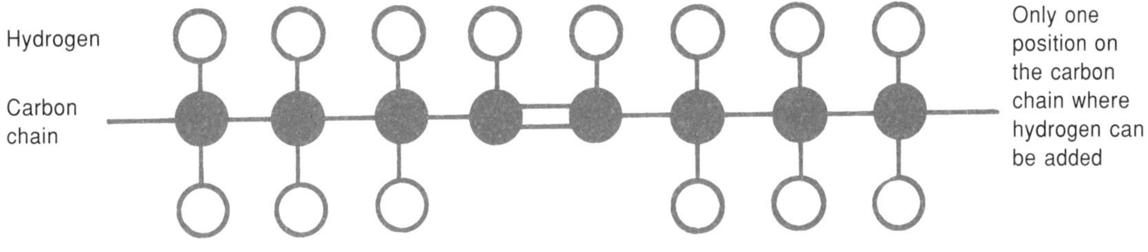

Monounsaturated fat

Polyunsaturated fats

When there is more than one double bond in the fatty acid chain, it is said to be polyunsaturated. Triglycerides rich in polyunsaturated fatty acids are usually liquid at room temperature and are in the form of oils. Food sources include maize, safflower, sunflower and soya bean oils, fish and nuts.

Omega-3 fats are a group of polyunsaturated fats found mainly in fish and some plant foods, such as linseed oil and canola oil. These fats have been shown to reduce the incidence of blocked arteries and may assist in reducing the incidence of atherosclerosis.

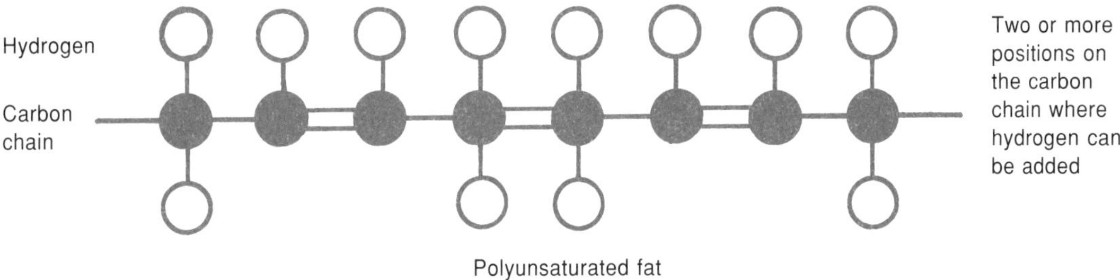

Polyunsaturated fat

Trans fats

In margarine manufacture some of the polyunsaturated fatty acids have some double bonds removed; the remaining carbon atoms then take up hydrogen and the molecule is altered to a 'trans structure'. The process is known as hydrogenation and results in solidified oils. The trans fatty acids formed still present the same health risks as saturated fatty acids, however, only some of the molecules are altered, therefore margarines still have a high proportion of polyunsaturated fats. The P/S ratio on the label of margarines refers to the proportion of polyunsaturated fatty acids to saturated fatty acids.

Functions

Fats and oils provide approximately twice as much energy per gram as protein and carbohydrate.

Some contain the fat-soluble vitamins A, D, E and K. During digestion, fatty acids are retained in the stomach for a longer period than protein and carbohydrate, hence they satisfy the appetite to a greater degree than other food nutrients. Flavours in meat and other foods are present in the fat component.

Requirements

Humans have a need for some essential fatty acids from polyunsaturated sources. It is recommended that approximately 30% of energy intake should be from fats, with no more than 10% coming from saturated fats. Children have a slightly higher need for fat compared with adults.

Australians tend to consume high amounts of saturated fats. We should endeavour to reduce our total amount of dietary fat, particularly saturated fat, to control blood cholesterol levels. Like many diet-related conditions, there is considerable difference in individual risk factors. Some people have a higher risk of developing heart disease than others due to the interplay of hereditary factors, environment, state of health and diet.

Vitamins

These are organic compounds that are present in small quantities in foods, and are essential for normal growth and health. Most cannot be synthesised by the human body and must be obtained from food. Some are synthesised by bacteria in the human alimentary tract. They assist in the metabolism of food in the body.

Vitamins were discovered in the 1920s, and because of the difficulty of isolating them and determining their chemical composition, they were identified by alphabetical letters. They have since been given names as their structure and functions have been established.

Vitamins A, D, E and K are fat-soluble, and when taken in excess, are retained in the fat in the body, resulting in hypervitaminosis, therefore caution must be exercised if vitamin supplements are taken regularly. Vitamins of the B complex, and vitamin C are water-soluble, and excess is excreted in the urine. Excess vitamin C may cause kidney damage, while excess vitamin B6 may cause nerve damage.

If the Dietary Guidelines are followed, vitamins will be supplied in quantities sufficient to meet daily requirements.

Vitamins

Characteristics	Functions	Deficiency/Excess	Sources
Retinol (vitamin A)			
Fat-soluble. Stable at normal cooking temperatures. Excess stored in liver.	• Required for healthy skin and tissue lining. • Assists in formation of bones and teeth. • Stimulates growth. • Improves vision in dim light.	**Deficiency** • Night blindness. • Dryness of eyes. • Stunted growth. • Dryness of skin.	Liver, whole milk, cream, butter, fish and fish oils, egg yolk, table margarine, cheese.
Carotene is converted to vitamin A in body.		**Possible excess symptoms** • Drowsiness. • Vomiting. • Headache. • Extensive skin peeling.	Carotene from carrots, green leafy vegetables, capsicum, yellow fruits, mangoes and pumpkins.
Vitamin B group ***Thiamine (vitamin B1)***			
Water-soluble: leached by washing and cooking. Destroyed by high temperatures. Availability to body reduced by alcohol.	Important for release of energy during the metabolism of carbohydrate.	**Deficiency** • Fatigue. • Stiffness in leg muscles. • Disturbed brain and nerve function. • Beri-beri.	Yeast extracts, wholegrain and enriched cereals, wheat germ, brown rice, legumes, nuts, egg yolk, meat-especially pork.
Riboflavin (vitamin B2)			
Water-soluble. Heat stable. Easily destroyed by sunlight. Removed in milling.	Required for energy metabolism.	**Deficiency** • Cracking and soreness at corners of mouth (cheilosis). • Sore inflamed tongue. Rash at junction of nose and face. • Fatigue. • Growth failure.	Yeast extract, milk, egg, liver, kidney, enriched cereals.
Niacin (vitamin B3)			
Water-soluble. Heat stable. Removed in milling.	Essential for production of energy.	**Deficiency** Dermatitis. Digestive disturbances, diarrhoea. Depression. Pellagra.	Synthesised from tryptophan in large intestine. Liver, meat, fish, peanuts, peanut butter, yeast extract, enriched cereals, wholegrain rice.

Vitamins

Characteristics	Functions	Deficiency/Excess	Sources
Pyridoxine (vitamin B6)			
Water-soluble. Heat stable.	Essential for metabolism of fat and protein. Essential for synthesis of non-essential to essential amino acids.	**Deficiency** • Anaemia. • Dermatitis. • Convulsive seizures, nerve damage. • Reduction of antibody production. (Deficiency is rare.)	Widely distributed in plant and animal tissues, meat, liver, vegetables, outer coats of cereals, e.g. bran.
Pantothenic acid			
Water-soluble. Destroyed by prolonged heating.	Necessary for many metabolic processes.	Although essential, no deficiencies have been observed.	Widely distributed in foods
Cobalamin (vitamin B12)			
Water-soluble. Stable during cooking. Affected by alcohol.	Necessary for release of red blood cells from bone marrow. Associated with protein metabolism.	**Deficiency** • Pernicious anaemia.	Animal tissues, e.g. meat, egg, fish, liver, kidney, milk. Vegetables do not contain B12.
Folic Acid			
Water soluble. Unstable to light and high temperatures.	Essential for metabolism. Related to function of cobalamin, vitamin C.	**Deficiency** Anaemia in pregnancy and old age and chronic alcoholics.	Widely distributed in foods. Synthesised by bacteria in intestine. Liver, kidney, yeast, mushrooms, root vegetables.
Biotin			
Water-soluble. Heat stable.	Necessary for metabolism.	Although essential, no deficiency signs have been observed.	Widely distributed in foods. Synthesised by bacteria in intestine.
Ascorbic acid (vitamin C)			
Water-soluble. Easily destroyed by air (oxidation), heat and light. Is not stored in the body.	Required for functioning of cells that form new tissue in healing of wounds. Necessary for formation of bones and teeth.	**Deficiency** • Easy bruising. • Excessive bleeding as blood clotting mechanism is impaired. Lowering of body's resistance to infection. **Excess** • Kidney stones may develop.	Citrus fruits and raw fruits especially berry and tropical fruits and vegetables such as green leafy vegetables and broccoli, capsicum, parsley and potato.

Vitamins

Characteristics	Functions	Deficiency/Excess	Sources
Cholecalciferol (vitamin D)			
Fat-soluble. Stable at ordinary cooking temperatures. Stored in liver, skin, brain, spleen and bones.	Assists in absorption of calcium from intestine. Assists in utilisation of calcium in bones.	**Deficiency** • Improperly formed teeth. • Malformation of bones. • Rickets. **Excess** • Calcification. • Dwarfing in children. • Kidney damage. • Hypercalcaemia.	Fish liver oil, table margarine, egg yolk, butter, milk, cheese. Formed by the action of sunlight on the skin.
Tocopherol (vitamin E)			
Fat-soluble. May be destroyed by light. Prevents oxidation of fats (rancidity).	Maintains healthy membranes.	Deficiency unlikely because of wide distribution in foods.	Eggs, vegetable oils, wheat germ, wholegrain cereals.
Vitamin K			
Fat-soluble. Stable to heat. Destroyed by acids and bases, light and oxygen. Antibiotics disturb production of vitamin K in large intestine.	Essential for normal clotting of blood.	**Deficiency** Tendency towards excessive bleeding may develop. Antibodies disturb its production in the large intestine.	Balanced diet provides adequate amounts. Produced by bacterial synthesis in large intestine.

Minerals

Minerals are found in the skeleton, as constituents of body fluids and as part of the cellular structure. Their main functions are to give rigidity to bones and teeth and to regulate the functioning of the body systems. Trace minerals are required in very small amounts. If the Dietary Guidelines are followed, minerals will be supplied in quantities sufficient to meet daily requirements.

Minerals

Characteristics	Functions	Deficiency/Excess	Sources
Phosphorus Present in skeleton. Intake should equal that of calcium.	With calcium it is major constituent of bones and teeth. Constituent of all body cells. Vital for food metabolism.	Diet is seldom, if ever, inadequate in this nutrient. Excess can lead to kidney disease.	Meat, liver, milk, cheese, egg, citrus fruits, flour, oatmeal.
Calcium The body contains more calcium than any other mineral. 99% is concentrated in bones, which act as a reservoir. See Concerns of the Australian diet p. 29.	With other minerals, mainly phosphorus, it forms bones and teeth. Assists normal contraction of heart muscles. Helps nerves respond to stimuli. Necessary for blood clot formation.	**Deficiency** • Osteoporosis. • Stunted growth. • Badly formed teeth. • Rickets. • Cramps. • Reduced ability of blood to clot.	Dairy products – milk and cheese, green leafy vegetables, canned fish, cereals. Adults may prefer to use calcium enriched skim milk.
Magnesium One of the major mineral constituents of the body. Present in all skeletal and soft tissue.	Constituent of teeth and bones. Plays a part in carbohydrate metabolism. Needed for activity of many enzymes.	**Deficiency** Severe muscular twitching may occur.	Widely distributed in foods, particularly milk, meats, vegetables and cereals.
Sodium Present mostly in blood plasma and fluids around cells. Lost from body in perspiration and urine. See Concerns of the Australian diet p. 29.	Necessary to maintain balance between fluids outside body cells. Required for muscle contraction.	Deficiency seldom seen. **Excess** • High blood pressure. • Oedema.	Widely distributed in foods.
Potassium Concentrated in body cells. Starvation diets can lead to decrease in absorption of vitamin K.	Necessary to maintain balance of fluids inside body cells. Maintains acid-base balance.	Deficiency unlikely unless there is preceding deficiency of sodium. **Excess** Can lead to kidney failure and heart disease.	Found in most foods mainly combined with protein: meat, milk, eggs, fish, wheat germ, leafy vegetables, fresh fruit, particularly bananas and citrus.

Minerals

Characteristics	Functions	Deficiency/Excess	Sources
Sulphur Found in all protein tissue in body.	Exact function not fully established. Thought to be related to protein nutrition because it occurs with amino acids.	Little is known about deficiency in humans, but may contribute to extreme protein malnutrition.	Cheese, lean meat, peanuts, lentils, wheat germ.
Iron Present in enzyme systems of every cell. 30% stored in liver, spleen and bone marrow. See Concerns of the Australian diet p. 29.	Important constituent of haemoglobin in red blood cells, hence responsible for transportation of oxygen throughout the body.	**Deficiency** Once absorbed is only slowly lost. Excess bleeding creates serious loss, causing anaemia, shown by pallor of skin, fatigue and breathlessness. **Excess** Liver damage.	Meat, liver, kidney, egg, dried fruits, wholegrain cereals, green vegetables, oysters.
Iodine Trace mineral. Widely distributed in body tissues but most localised in thyroid gland.	Necessary for correct functioning of thyroid gland situated in throat. This gland influences the rate of the body's metabolism, hence growth and body temperature.	**Deficiency** Physical and mental development of children may be retarded. May cause goitre (the swelling of thyroid gland).	Dairy products, sea foods, vegetables.
Fluorine Trace mineral.	Valuable in combating tooth decay in children. Helps strengthen bones.	**Deficiency** • Dental caries. **Excess** • Mottling of teeth.	Small amounts in most foods. Many water supplies and tooth pastes are artificially fluoridated.
Zinc Trace mineral. Present in most body tissues.	Assists in protein synthesis.	**Deficiency** • Poor growth. • Slow tissue healing after surgery and burns.	Found in most foods mainly combined with protein. Strict vegetarians may be at risk as zinc in vegetables is utilised less efficiently than zinc in meat.

Water

Water is essential for all living things, both animal and vegetable. It makes up approximately 70% of the mass of the human body, and it is present in all cells of the body. We may live without food for some weeks, but without water we quickly become exhausted through dehydration and die within days.

Functions

- Moistens the air we breathe as it passes over the mucous membranes of the nose.
- Forms the bulk of all body fluids such as blood, lymph and urine.
- Forms part of the secretions that digest food and is the solvent for transporting enzymes, food nutrients and other chemicals.
- Is the solvent for waste products removed from the body in perspiration, in urine from the kidneys and in faeces.
- Is given off in moist warm air from the lungs.

Sources

Some water is formed in the body during metabolism from hydrogen and oxygen in nutrients. Most solid food contains some water: biscuits about 10%; bread about 35%; meat about 70%; vegetables and fruits 90% or more. We should drink at least 6 glasses of water each day. Water is also obtained from milk, tea, coffee and fruit juice.

Water balance

The loss of water as urine, as perspiration, from the lungs and in the faeces must be replaced by a corresponding intake, which should be increased during strenuous work or exercise and in hot weather. The following indicates the approximate intake and loss of water:

Intake	all liquid drunk	1.6 L	**Loss**	urine	1.5 L
	water in food	0.7 L		perspiration	0.6 L
	metabolism of food	0.3 L		lungs	0.4 L
				faeces	0.1 L
		2.6 L			2.6 L

Concerns of the Australian diet

In this technologically advancing society, we are busier and place more demands on our bodies each day. We seem to find less time to eat properly but still expect our bodies to run effectively, which can lead to problems relating to the deficiency or excess of some vital nutrients.

Calcium and iron deficiency, sodium excess and obesity are four major concerns of current Australian food consumption patterns.

Calcium and iron are essential for the healthy growth of the human body and their major food sources are often omitted from our diets, leading to problems with osteoporosis and anaemia. Conversely, sodium and fats seem to be over consumed through the ready availability of high-salt and fat-based fast foods and convenience foods, leading to problems with hypertension and obesity.

Calcium intake

Calcium is required by the human body for the proper growth and development of bones, teeth, nerves and muscles. It is also an activator for some enzymes necessary for body functions. Bones are the reservoir for calcium in the body, and hormones regulate the movement of calcium from the bones into other body cells when required. This process occurs throughout life and adequate calcium intake is vital to help maintain this process.

Bone stores of calcium begin building up from infancy, peak at adolescence to middle age and depletion accelerates in the elderly. For women, the drop in the level of the hormone oestrogen at menopause increases the rate of bone calcium depletion, thus increasing the risk of developing osteoporosis. Osteoporosis occurs when there is a decrease in bone density, which may result in the bones becoming brittle and eventually leading to bone fractures. It is, however, important that everyone maintains an adequate calcium intake and has plenty of exercise throughout their life.

Sources include dairy products, fish and soya bean products. Green leafy vegetables contain calcium, however, oxalic acid and phytic acid affect absorption. The more oxalic acid and phytic acid present, the lower the rate of calcium absorption.

Factors affecting calcium absorption and storage in the body

	Factor	Requirement
Genetic	Menopause, age, oestrogen levels.	Possible hormone replacement therapy.
Physical	Exercise.	Increase.
	Appropriate body weight.	Maintain healthy weight range.
Food intake	Caffeine, alcohol, smoking.	Decreases absorption, limit intake.
	Vitamin D and phosphorous.	Essential for calcium absorption. Ensure adequate intake.
	Sodium, oxalic and phytic acid.	Decreases absorption, limit intake.

Iron intake

Iron deficiency is common in Australia. Iron is required by the body to combine with protein and copper to form the important blood component haemoglobin. Haemoglobin is used to transport oxygen from the lungs to all body tissues through the blood stream, without which body tissues could not function. Iron is also required to produce myoglobin, found in muscle tissue, to carry oxygen to be used in muscle contractions and is needed in enzymes and with other nutrients to assist in respiration.

Iron deficiency is known as anaemia. Signs of anaemia are shortness of breath, tiredness, lack of energy, coldness, pale skin, palpitations and susceptibility to infections. Anaemia results from blood loss, heavy periods, repeated pregnancies, inadequate dietary intake and poor absorption of iron. Those most at risk of suffering from anaemia are teenagers, pregnant women, women on 'fad' diets, some vegetarians, women in competitive sports, women with heavy periods and infants.

Teenagers, especially girls as they commence menstruating, run the risk of anaemia because they are still growing, often skip meals and may avoid foods high in iron. Pregnant women require extra iron, not only for their health but also for their baby. Women who suffer heavy blood losses from childbirth and then become pregnant again are at risk and often require iron supplements. Infants need extra iron in their diets from about six months of age because their own iron stores are depleting. Formulas, baby food and baby cereals are fortified with iron to maintain iron levels until the babies can eat other iron-rich foods. Men generally only suffer anaemia from heavy blood losses.

Factors affecting iron absorption

Increase	Decrease
Vitamin C	Antacids
Lean red meat	Tea, coffee
Fish, poultry	Soy protein
Normal stomach acidity	Dietary fibre

Sources

The best way to optimise iron absorption is to eat a variety of foods at each meal.

There are two types of iron present in foods and both are important:

Type I is haem iron and is found in flesh foods such as lean red meat, offal such as liver, kidney, heart and chicken and fish. Haem iron is effectively absorbed by the body.

Type II is non-haem iron and is found in plant foods such as wholegrain bread, cereals and cereal products (breakfast cereals are fortified with non-haem iron), dark green leafy vegetables, legumes, nuts, seeds and dried fruit. Non-haem iron is less effectively absorbed by the body, but with foods rich in vitamin C at the same meal, absorption is increased.

Sodium intake

Sodium is important in the maintenance of fluid levels and the control of blood pressure in the human body. Only small amounts of sodium are required. Sodium is present in our diet mainly in the form of sodium chloride, otherwise known as salt. Sodium is also present in sodium bicarbonate and monosodium glutamate (MSG).

Historically, salt was used as a preservative before refrigeration and processing techniques were introduced into our society, and we have developed a taste for salt not related to our biological needs. Foods such as meat, chicken, fish, eggs and milk contain small amounts of sodium and this is adequate for our dietary needs, yet most of the salt we eat is added in manufacturing processes and in foods eaten away from home, such as takeaway foods.

Sodium has been linked to several conditions such as hypertension (high blood pressure) and other complications that can be damaging to the human body. One in five Australians has hypertension and this increases to one in two elderly Australians. Decreasing salt intake has no adverse side effects.

Sodium in our diet comes from several sources: 10% is naturally found in food, 15% is from cooking or is added after cooking, and 75% is from foods prepared outside the home.

The amount of sodium, mainly salt, in our food intake should be reduced by carefully choosing the foods bought and eaten outside the home and by reducing use in the home.

Tips to reduce sodium intake

- Choose products labelled 'low salt', 'reduced salt' or 'no added salt'.
- Use herbs, spices, pepper, ginger, garlic, lemon or vinegar as flavouring in cooking instead of salt.
- Avoid putting salt on the table at meal times.
- Avoid giving infants and children salty foods because sodium in their diet can establish preferences for salty foods – this can set up poor habits for their future.

Obesity

Obesity is the result of energy intake being greater than energy expenditure over a long period of time. It is usually measured as 20% or over the desirable body weight for height (see chart p. 11). Obesity often has a psychosocial effect – the interrelationship between appearance and self-esteem.

Body fat occurs naturally and is very important in a healthy human body, where it occurs as fats in cell membranes and as fats. In men, this energy storage fat is usually located in the abdominal area and in women it is usually located in the gluteal-femoral area (buttocks and thighs).

Causes of obesity are not the same for everyone. They can be quite complex, just as the health risks linked to obesity can vary between people. Obesity may be caused by genetic make-up, by hormonal activity or by environmental factors. Environmental influences are the major cause and include high dietary fat intake, low levels of physical activity, increased hours watching television and increased alcohol consumption.

Obesity increases the risks of cardiovascular disease, hypertension, gall bladder disease, arthritis, gout, pulmonary dysfunction (lung disease), strokes, varicose veins and some cancers. Obesity can result in other complications, for example, orthopaedic abnormalities, insulin resistance leading to diabetes, abnormal lipid profile and obese children and adolescents often becoming obese adults.

Obesity reversal, or weight loss, requires a multiple approach including family involvement, dietary intervention and exercise. It does take time and the ideal weight loss is 0.5–1 kg per week. Fad or quick weight-loss diets often make big promises but do not produce the desired results. If weight loss is too rapid it does not give the body's metabolism time to adjust and as a person finishes the diet they put weight on again; they have not been taught how to permanently change to eating a balanced diet.

Reducing fat intake, eating a balanced diet and increasing energy expenditure are the best ways to lose weight. Obesity can be difficult to reverse and prevention seems to be more effective than the management of established obesity. Losing weight can reverse some of the complications associated with obesity so it is encouraged.

Ways to reduce fat in the diet

- Choose trimmed lean meat or cut away as much fat as possible.
- Put less margarine or butter on bread and toast, or better still none at all.
- Choose polyunsaturated oils and margarine.
- Choose raw fruit, vegetables or dried fruits as snacks.
- Shallow-fry foods or grill foods instead of deep frying.
- Reduce the amount of snacks between meals.
- Eat breakfast, with an emphasis on carbohydrates.
- Eat more complex carbohydrates and foods high in dietary fibre.
- Go for a walk instead of sitting down for a snack.
- Drink plenty of water – it gives a feeling of satiety (fullness) without the kilojoules.

Digestion and metabolism

Food is taken into the body through the mouth and passed along the gastrointestinal tract. As nutrients pass along they are digested, that is, physically and chemically broken down into chemically simpler compounds. Each part of the gastrointestinal tract has digestive juices containing enzymes that act on specific nutrients.

These chemically simpler compounds are then absorbed, mainly through the walls of the small intestine, into the lymphatic system or the bloodstream. Here, and in the cells, the compounds undergo the process of metabolism. Metabolism is the breaking up of the compounds

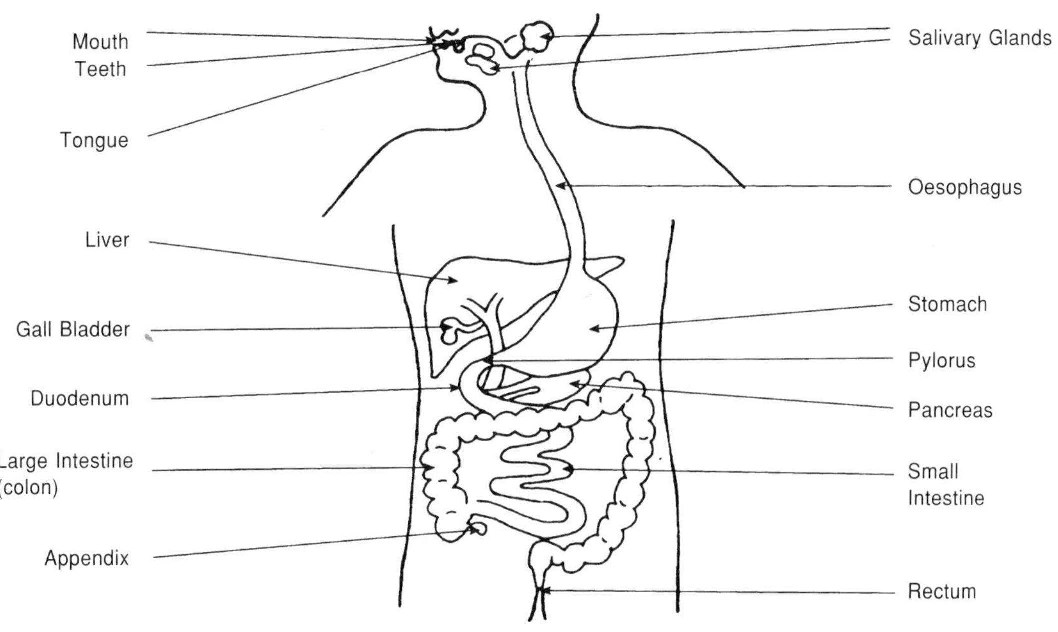

The Digestive System

into molecules and the oxidising of these to provide energy. They may also be rebuilt into other compounds for storage or for other uses. The residues and by-products are excreted from the body.

Digestion

Digestion is the physical and chemical breaking down of food into simpler compounds. The physical process begins in the mouth where food is moistened by saliva and broken up by chewing. The smaller food particles enable the digestive juices to mix with the food more easily. The tongue gathers the food into a ball, or bolus, and this is passed across the epiglottis (which covers the trachea or windpipe), through the oesophagus to the stomach. The food is moved along and churned by peristalsis, a series of muscular contractions of the walls of the gastrointestinal tract.

The stomach churns food for 1 to 2 hours, enabling the enzymes to mix with and act on the food, and then the food passes through the pylorus into the small intestine. The small intestine consists of the duodenum, where further digestion takes place, and the jejunum and ileum, where the last of the digestion takes place. The residue then moves into the large intestine or colon.

The chemical changes during digestion are brought about by the action of enzymes on the food. Proteins are broken down to peptides, then to amino acids. Carbohydrates are converted to disaccharides, then to monosaccharides (glucose, fructose and galactose). Fats pass through an emulsified stage to become fatty acids and glycerol.

Chemical changes during digestion

Nutrient	Changes	Enzyme
Mouth – enzyme is in saliva		
Protein	No change.	
Carbohydrate	Starches to maltose.	Amylases
Fats	No change.	
Stomach – enzymes are in gastric juice		
Protein	To peptides.	Proteases
Carbohydrate	Completion of salivary action.	
Fats	To emulsified fats.	Lipases
Small intestine – enzymes are in pancreatic and intestinal juices and bile		
Peptides	To amino acids.	Proteases
Carbohydrates	Maltose to glucose. Lactose to galactose and glucose. Sucrose to glucose and fructose.	Amylases
Emulsified fats	To fatty acids and glycerol.	Lipases

Absorption

The less complex products of digestion are absorbed through the walls of the small intestine, mainly the jejunum and the ileum. Water is absorbed through the walls of the colon.

The glucose, galactose, fructose and amino acids are absorbed directly into the bloodstream. The fatty acids and glycerol pass into the lymphatic system, then into the bloodstream. From here they undergo the process of metabolism.

Metabolism

Metabolism is the process of breaking down the absorbed compounds into single molecules consisting of carbon, hydrogen, oxygen and nitrogen, and the rebuilding of these into new compounds. During this process they may be oxidised to provide energy or combined together to form new compounds for storage or formation and repair of tissue.

The process of breaking down the compounds is known as catabolism, and the process of building the molecules up to compounds is called anabolism. Vitamins, minerals and water all play a part in metabolism.

The oxidation process uses oxygen breathed in by the lungs, releasing energy and producing carbon dioxide and water as the end products. For example, if glucose is oxidised, the following reaction takes place:

$$C_6H_{12}O_6 + 6O_2 \longrightarrow 6CO_2 + H_2O$$

(glucose) + (oxygen) energy (carbon dioxide) + (water)

Glucose, fructose and galactose are all broken down and oxidised in the same way. Some may be reconstituted to form glycogen and stored in the liver and muscles to be quickly converted to glucose when blood sugar levels fall. Excess glucose, galactose and fructose are rebuilt and stored as fat (adipose tissue) under the skin and around internal organs.

Fatty acids and glycerol are also broken down and oxidised. They may be rebuilt to form triglycerides and stored as fat.

Amino acids contain nitrogen in a form essential for the growth and repair of body tissue and the manufacture of hormones, enzymes and other secretions. As they are required by the body, they are removed from the bloodstream and rebuilt into the necessary compounds. Excess amino acids are broken down by enzymes as they pass through the liver. Urea is a by-product of this process and is excreted in the urine. Excess amino acids may also be oxidised to provide energy or stored as fat.

Excretion

Fibre and indigestible products are left after the process of digestion through the alimentary tract. They collect in the rectum and pass out of the body through the anus as faeces. During the process of metabolism, carbon dioxide is produced and passes out through the lungs. Excess minerals, vitamins, water and nitrogen are passed out as urine.

2 Ingredients and equipment

The foundation of successful cookery is the use of appropriate equipment and basic ingredients. The initial outlay for equipment can be small, with other items acquired over time to build up a range of durable and easily maintained food preparation equipment.

The variety of ingredients available to us increases every day, particularly those available in food markets and specialty delicatessens. Buy small quantities of new foods and then experiment to experience new tastes by varying old recipes.

Ingredients

Further information about some ingredients has been included in the following chapters:

- for fish varieties and quality factors see **Chapter 7 Fish** (p. 154)
- for meat cuts, varieties of poultry and quality factors see **Chapter 8 Meat and poultry** (p. 172)
- for descriptions and varieties of vegetables see **Chapter 9 Vegetables** (p. 227)
- for descriptions and varieties of fruits see **Chapter 12 Desserts and fruits** (p. 291)
- for information about legumes and cereals see **Chapter 5 Vegetarian dishes** (p. 112).

Cereal grains and flours

Cereal grains are the starchy part of grass crops grown for food and include wheat, rice, barley, rye, millet, maize or corn and oats. Buckwheat is technically not a grain, but because it is cooked and used in a similar manner it is usually included in any discussion on grains. The edible grain consists of the endosperm (mainly carbohydrate with a little protein), the germ or embryo (protein and a small amount of fat), surrounded by the husk or bran layer (consisting of cellulose or fibre and B vitamins). Milling or grinding reduces the grain to flour and usually removes some of the bran layer and the germ. Wholegrain cereals have the bran and germ left on the grain, and wholegrain or wholemeal flours have the bran and germ milled with the endosperm.

Cereal grains have a high proportion of starch, which is a carbohydrate. After milling and grinding, flour is produced and this may be used to thicken liquids, such as a sauce – this process is called gelatinisation. Starch does not dissolve in liquids, but absorbs liquid slowly on standing, swelling the starch cells. The absorption occurs at a faster rate on heating, eventually bursting the starch cells and allowing the water and starch molecules to form a gel. Each type of grain gels at a different temperature, and produces a gel of different texture, thickness, colour and stability.

Food value

Cereal grains are high in carbohydrate and low in fat. They are incomplete proteins as they do not contain all the essential amino acids. Wholegrain cereals and cereal products are good sources of dietary fibre, B group vitamins and a number of minerals.

Wheat

Wheat is the most commonly grown cereal in the Western world. The whole grains may be processed to make breakfast cereals; cracked, soaked, cooked and dried to make cracked wheat, kibbled wheat or bulgur; or milled to provide flour. The term 'flour' usually means 'wheat flour'.

The milling process involves separating the endosperm from the bran and germ and grinding it to a powdery flour. The number of parts by mass of flour that is produced from 100 parts of wheat is termed the extraction rate. The more bran and germ in the flour the higher the extraction rate, producing wholemeal flours. Lower extraction rates produce fine-textured whiter flours with a lower nutrient content. Australian wheat is milled to an average extraction rate of 76%.

There are seven marketing grades of Australian wheats; they are classified on variety and protein content. The term 'hard' is used as a reflection of their milling character, while low protein wheats are referred to as 'soft' as they offer less resistance to milling.

Prime hard is a high quality grade of varieties containing 13–15% protein. Used in specialty bread products that require a very high proportion of glutenin and gliadin, the proteins that

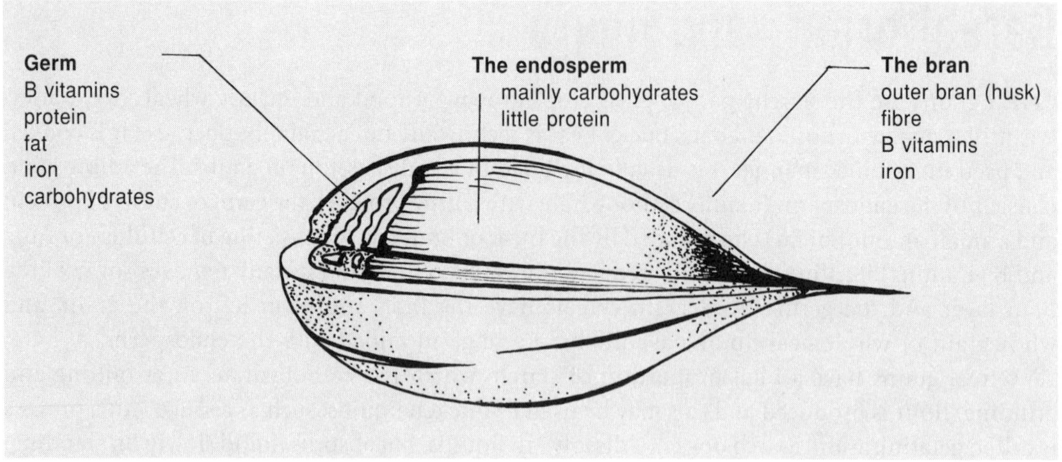

interact to form gluten when liquid is added. Gluten forms an elastic structure that sets during the baking of the bread or pasta and gives strength to the final product.

Hard varieties are suitable for the general range of breads that require a protein content of 11–14%.

Australian standard white is the category most Australian wheat falls into. It is used for making all-purpose flour and forms an important part of Australia's export crops.

Soft contains 10–12% protein and is used in cakes, biscuits and pastries where a fine texture is required.

Durum is a high protein variety containing more cellulose than other varieties. It absorbs less water and gives the structure and strength to pasta.

Special purpose medium contains protein with additional cellulose, used for noodles.

General purpose is a lower grade of wheat with a variable protein and water content.

Wheat flour products

Varieties and grades of wheat may be blended after milling to produce flours best suited for the purpose intended.

Plain flour is an all-purpose flour made from Australian standard white wheat or its equivalent. It does not contain any raising agent. The colour of flour may be whitened by the use of peroxide bleaches after the milling process. Unbleached flour has a cream colour.

Wholemeal flour has an extraction rate of over 95% and only the bran has been removed.

Wholegrain flour contains the whole of the grain and must have not less than 22% fibre.

Stoneground flour is prepared by crushing wholegrain wheat between milling stones, called querns. It retains most of the wholegrain and should be purchased in small quantities and used quickly as the fat content of the germ will become rancid over time.

Self-raising flour may be white, wholemeal or wholegrain flour and contains a raising agent. The raising agent may be bicarbonate of soda and an acid such as cream of tartar, or it may be an acid phosphate aerator (see Raising agents p. 42–43). The proportion of raising agent in self-raising flours is appropriate for scone making and most cakes.

Wheaten flour (sometimes made from wheat and sold as cornflour and should not be used in gluten-free diets) is a very fine wheat flour used for thickening.

Semolina is produced from the yellow coloured, hard endosperm extracted during the milling of durum wheat. It is used in pasta and gives a coarse texture and distinctive colour and flavour to cakes and breads.

Wheat germ and bran (sold separately) may be used in cooking and as breakfast cereals.

Bulgur is whole wheat grains that are commercially parboiled, dried and cracked between rollers. It is used to make tabouli and may be added to breads and cakes.

Couscous is made from wheat in Western countries. It originated in north Africa, where it is made from millet. The endosperm is steamed and cracked and used in savoury dishes to make traditional couscous dishes and other savoury dishes.

Cracked wheat consists of cracked pieces of grain and takes a considerable time to cook, depending on the size of the pieces.

'Instant' flours have been modified by partial cooking and drying to below 8% moisture. They are free-flowing and blend rapidly with liquids to produce smooth mixtures for use as thickeners and in sauces.

Gluten flour is commercially produced by mixing wheat flour to a dough, washing out the starch and drying the remaining mixture. This mixture contains 70% gluten, which is a protein. This is milled and sold as gluten flour and can be added to bread dough in the proportion of 2 tablespoons to 1 kg flour to give additional strength to the dough and allowing it to rise higher in the proving process.

Gluten-free flour is used in diets for those allergic to gluten. It is based on flours made from rice, millet or maize and may contain modified starches from other grains.

Wheat noodles are made from medium protein flour mixed with water to form a dough, then rolled into flat sheets, cut and stretched to form long strands. They may be dried before sale or sold as fresh noodles that require a shorter cooking time. The yellow Chinese-type wheat noodles gain their colour by the use of an alkaline salt in the mixture, differentiating them from the white Japanese type.

Pasta is made from durum wheat (14–16% protein) that has a yellow endosperm. The wheat is coarsely milled, mixed to a stiff dough, extruded into shapes and dried to form pasta, such as spaghetti, macaroni and rigatoni. It may be mixed with vegetables such as spinach to make green pasta or tomato to give a red colour. Wholegrain pasta is made from wholegrain wheat.

Rice

Rice has been the staple food in Eastern countries for many centuries. There are thousands of varieties grown, and, in general, these can be divided into two major groups, Indica and Japonica.

Rice in the Indica group is long grained and separates easily after cooking, and includes the Patna, basmati, jasmine or Thai rice and Carolina varieties. The Japonica group of rice is short grained and produces firm grains that stick together, and includes the arborio and calrose varieties.

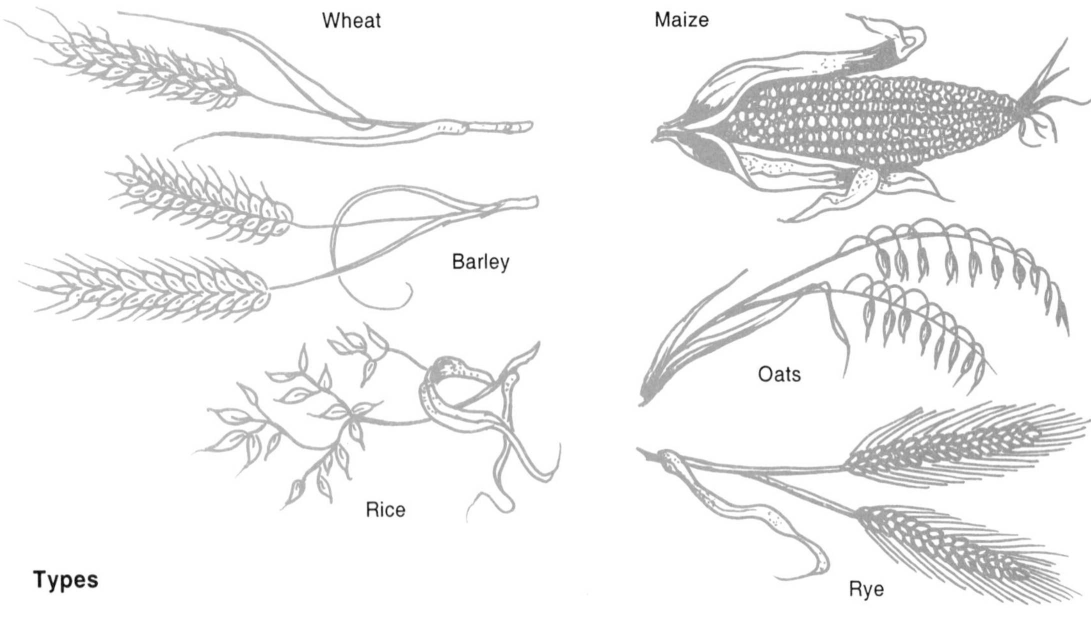

Types

Arborio is a short fat-grained rice that gives a creamy texture and is traditionally used for risotto as it can absorb four to five times its weight in liquid, compared to two to three times for other rice varieties.

Basmati is long-grain aromatic rice from Pakistan, used in pilafs.

Calrose is short-grain rice that is grown in Australia and is suited to Asian-style dishes and as a general-purpose rice.

Carolina has a firm texture when cooked and is used for fried rice and as an accompaniment to other dishes.

Jasmine or Thai rice has a fragrant perfume and is used in Asian and Indian dishes.

Brown rice has only the husk or hull removed, providing a good source of fibre from the bran and germ.

White rice has been milled and polished, removing the bran layers and the germ, giving a lower nutritive value and shorter cooking time.

Wild rice is not rice but the seed of an aquatic grass originating in North America. It was gathered by the Indians who cooked and used it in the same manner as rice. It has a long thin brown seed, with a firm texture and nutty flavour when cooked.

Rice products

Rice flour is ground rice and is used in crisp biscuits such as shortbread and as a thickener.

Quick-cooking rice has been commercially cooked and then dried.

Rice bran is the ground husk of the grain and is naturally sweet and high in fibre.

Rice cakes are made from wholegrain rice.

Rice noodles are made from rice flour and water dough and have a smooth texture.

Barley

Most of the barley grown in Australia is used for brewing beer. Some is used for animal feed, with only a very small amount being processed by the food industry. Pearl barley is the barley grain with the thick, hard, fibrous husk removed and can be used to thicken soups and casseroles and to make barley water.

Barley products

Malt extract is a thick, dark liquid used as a sweetener. The dried form is light in colour and used in milk drinks.

Rolled barley is used in mixed cereals such as muesli.

Corn or maize

Corn or maize is harvested as a cob. The grain kernels are attached, surrounded by brown silky threads covered with a green leafy husk. The husk and threads are removed and the kernels may be cooked and eaten as a vegetable (sweet corn) or milled to produce corn products.

Corn products

Cornflour is finely ground corn used for thickening liquids. It gives a more transparent finish than wheat flour and blends more easily. Check ingredient labels as some 'cornflour' sold in Australia is made from finely ground wheat flour and this must not be used in gluten-free diets.

Corn syrup or liquid glucose is chemically processed from cornflour.

Corn oil is extracted from the germ during processing.

Cornmeal is corn milled to a coarse granular texture and used for bread, tacos, polenta and corn chips.

Hominy grits are soaked, chemically treated and cracked corn kernels and are used, particularly in America, for breakfast dishes.

Popcorn is a variety of corn that bursts on heating.

Rye

Only about a quarter of the rye grown is processed into human food, the rest is used for animal feed and alcoholic beverage production. Rye is milled to produce a dark flour, which does not produce gluten, resulting in the denser, heavier rye breads.

Rye products

Dark or wholemeal rye flour is used to make pumpernickel breads.

Light rye flour has had the bran removed; the lighter the colour, the more bran has been removed. It is used for bread making and biscuits.

Millet and sorghum

Millet is a group of cereal grasses, of which sorghum is one. The tiny yellow grains are milled and used for flat breads, porridge and in gluten-free products.

Oats

During milling the hull is removed but not the germ. The oil in the germ becomes rancid if oats are stored for a long period.

Oat products

Rolled oats are the flattened large grains used in breakfast cereals.

Oatmeal is milled until it forms small particles, used in breads, breakfast cereals and muffins.

Oatbran is made from the fibrous layer under the husk, which is high in nutrients, particularly soluble fibre.

Buckwheat

Buckwheat is a tiny, hard, dark triangular fruit, used in the same way as a grain. It is milled and used, particularly in Eastern Europe, for pancakes and stuffings, and in Japan for making soba noodles.

Raising agents

Raising agents are added to ingredients or mixtures to produce gas bubbles that expand when moistened or heated and cause the mixture to rise. They are usually used in flour mixtures such as batters and doughs, and in some egg mixtures such as meringues.

Chemical reactions

Chemical reaction occurs when carbon dioxide gas is produced by the reaction of an acid and a carbonate in the presence of moisture. The process is accelerated by heat. Baking powder is a raising agent that operates using this reaction. It can be made by mixing 2 teaspoons cream of tartar with 1 teaspoon bicarbonate of soda and 1 teaspoon cornflour.

Baking powder may also be purchased. It contains a phosphate aerator and sodium bicarbonate mixed with finely ground flour to prevent moisture absorption. Baking powder is added to plain flour in the proportion of 1 tablespoon (10 g) baking powder to 2 cups (300 g) plain flour to make the equivalent of commercial self-raising flour.

Cream of tartar (acid) and bicarbonate of soda are used in some commercial self-raising flours. The reaction producing carbon dioxide begins as soon as the flour is moistened, thus mixtures made with cream of tartar and self-raising flour must be cooked immediately after mixing or the carbon dioxide gas will be lost.

PLATE 3

Shrimp and coriander triangles (p. 91),
Mini pizzas (p. 91),
Vietnamese spring rolls (p. 92),
Baby potatoes with crispy bacon (p. 86),
Oysters in the shell (p. 95).

PLATE 4

Spicy chickpea hotpot (p. 116),
Bok choy and ginger noodle stir-fry (p. 124),
Spinach ravioli with tomato and basil sauce (p. 122).

Phosphate aerators are used in most self-raising flours, as the acid and carbonate reaction is dependent on heat, thus the mixture can stand prior to cooking. These aerators have a distinctive taste in the final product.

Bicarbonate of soda may be mixed with a range of acid foods to produce carbon dioxide gas, including lemon or other acid fruit juices, sour milk or cream, treacle or golden syrup, jam, vinegar and dried fruits. As there is only a limited quantity of acid in the foods available for the chemical reaction, the amount of bicarbonate of soda required is small and an excess will cause yellowing of the mixture and a bitter flavour. The use of this raising agent usually darkens the mixture to a brown colour.

Biochemical reactions

Yeast is a living organism that is capable, under specific conditions, of fermenting and breaking down carbohydrates to produce carbon dioxide gas, which then acts as a raising agent (see **Chapter 17 Yeast breads and buns**).

Physical reactions

Beating or folding air into a mixture will cause the mixture to rise on heating. The air expands on heating and is trapped in the mixture causing it to rise.

- Air may be enclosed in a dough by folding and rolling, e.g. flaky pastry and rough puff pastry.
- Air may be beaten into a mixture of flour and a liquid, e.g. cake batters. The gluten in the flour is stretched by expanding air bubbles. The heat sets the gluten, and the cake, when baked, retains its expanded shape and light texture.
- Air may be beaten into egg white before this is added to the mixture, e.g. meringues, sponge cake. When air is beaten into egg white, the albumen, also a protein, is stretched and retains some of its expanded shape.
- A very moist light mixture such as choux pastry produces steam as it cooks. This steam produced from the heated moisture is trapped in the mixture and acts as a raising agent.

Fats and oils

Fats and oils contain a high proportion of the flavour components of food, and each is distinctive of its source, for example, olive oil from olives, meat fat or suet from meat. The flavour is imparted when combined with other foods, such as in salad dressings and in deep-frying. The term oil is usually used for those products that are liquid at room temperature, and fat for those that are solid at room temperature.

The term shortening may be used for all types of fats and oils that may be added to flour mixtures, or used for frying foods or making a roux.

Food value

Fats supply twice as many kilojoules per gram as do proteins and carbohydrates. The fat-soluble vitamins A and D are present in animal fats, and may be added to vegetable oil products, such as table margarine. Vitamins E and K are present in fats and oils. Fats and oils contain varying proportions of saturated and unsaturated fatty acids, with oils generally containing mainly unsaturated fatty acids and fats with more saturated fatty acids.

Butter

Butter is made from a minimum of 80% milk fat, that is the cream from cows' milk, with about 2% salt added. It contains a high proportion of saturated fatty acids.

Unsalted butter has no added salt.

Cultured butter (or Danish-type butter) has a culture added before churning. It may be unsalted or have approximately 1% added salt.

Clarified butter (or ghee) is butter fat that has been treated to precipitate the proteins and minerals and evaporate the moisture content.

Whipped butter has been beaten to incorporate air that softens the butter.

Margarine

Margarine is made from oils that have been partly hydrogenated (p. 45) to make them solid at room temperature. They may be used in the same way as butter. The maximum water content allowed is 16% and margarine may contain antioxidants and emulsifiers.

Table margarine has vitamins A and D added. Margarine labelled polyunsaturated must have not less than 40% unsaturated oil and not more than 20% saturated oil.

Vegetable oils

Oil is removed from the grains and seeds of plants by chemical extraction or by pressing. The chemical extraction process involves cracking, grinding, steaming, washing with solvent, bleaching and deodorising. The resulting product is usually cheaper, with less flavour, than the pressing method. In the pressing method, crushing rollers are used and then the mixture is either fed into a screw press for cold pressing or steam heated for hot pressing. Cold pressing gives the best flavour and is usually the more expensive oil. Virgin oil means the oil from the first pressing, as the mixture may be fed through the press several times to extract more oil each time.

Types of oils

Canola is popular for cooking and salad dressings as well as the manufacture of margarines and dairy-blend products. It has only 6% saturated fatty acids, one of the lowest ratios. It is particularly suited to frying as it has a smoke point of 225°C.

Coconut oil is one of the few vegetable oils that consists of saturated fatty acids. It is sold commercially as copha.

Corn or maize oil is used in frying and salad dressings. It is low in saturated fatty acids and is high in vitamin E.

Macadamia oil is used in salad dressings and has a distinctive nut flavour.

Olive oil is one of the most popular oils for salads and shallow frying. It is not suitable for deep frying as it develops a bitter flavour if heated several times. It is high in mono-unsaturated fatty acids.

Palm oil is used commercially for cooking many snack foods. It is comparatively cheap and is high in saturated fatty acids.

Peanut oil is used for cooking and in salad dressings.

Safflower oil has a high level of polyunsaturates and is used for cooking and salad dressings and in the production of margarine.

Sesame oil has a distinctive flavour and is used in Asian cooking.

Soya bean oil is bland in flavour and mainly used in processing.

Sunflower oil has a high level of polyunsaturates and is used in deep-frying and margarine production.

Walnut oil has a distinctive flavour and is used in salad dressings.

Blends of fats and oils

Butter, margarine and oils are blended to reduce the saturated fatty acid levels and give a product that is firm but not hard when kept in the refrigerator.

Dairy blend is a mixture of butter and vegetable oils with vitamins A and D and water. Depending on the proportions of butter and vegetable oils, it has the spreadability of margarine and the flavour of butter.

Fat substitutes

The trend towards reducing the fat content of foods has encouraged research into fat substitutes that can provide the mouth-feel and smooth texture of fats and oils, without the nutritional disadvantages. Carbohydrate-based fat substitutes include gums that are long-chain polymers, such as those used in oil-free salad dressings, and modified starches that are used in baked products. Protein-based substitutes are mainly used in dairy-type products such as ice-cream. More recent product development has led to synthetic sucrose polyester substances, which are undergoing trials prior to use in commercially sold products.

Meat fats

Suet is the fat around the kidneys and internal organs of sheep, ox and pig. Clarified fat is suet that has been 'rendered' or melted to allow moisture and solids to sink, then strained and allowed to set. It is sold commercially as dripping. Lard is clarified pig suet and is suitable for flaky pastries and bread making. Dripping is fat and meat juices collected from baking and grilling meat. It must be clarified before being used for frying.

Vinegar

Vinegars are produced during distillation processes, often as a by-product of wine and beer manufacture and are formed by the production of lactic acid. They have an acidic flavour and are used in salad dressings to give contrast to the smooth taste and texture of oils and in other dishes to give a tart, sharp flavour.

Balsamic vinegar is a dark-coloured liquid made from white grapes and aged for at least five years to give a strong, mellow flavour. It is expensive and used in salad dishes to give a distinctive, aromatic flavour.

Cider vinegar is made from the acetic acid produced when apples are fermented. It is light in colour and flavour.

Malt vinegar is usually brown and is produced during the fermentation of barley. It has a strong acid taste.

Rice vinegar is used in Chinese and Japanese cooking and is distilled from fermenting rice. It is mild in taste and slightly thicker than other vinegars.

White vinegar is the cheapest form of vinegar and is produced by mixing acetic acid and water. It has a strong acid taste with no other flavour.

Wine vinegar may be red or white and is produced through the introduction of a particular strain of bacteria that converts the alcohol to lactic acid.

Milk

Food value

Milk contains protein, fats, sugar, water, some vitamins and minerals. It is deficient in iron, vitamin C and fibre. Milk is high in sodium and has a high proportion of water to other nutrients.

Storage

Milk should be stored in a refrigerator in the container in which it is purchased. This retards the rapid growth of bacteria, but does not destroy them. Take note of the 'use-by' or 'best before' date on the container and use within the time. Sunlight will destroy the vitamin riboflavin, and may alter the flavour.

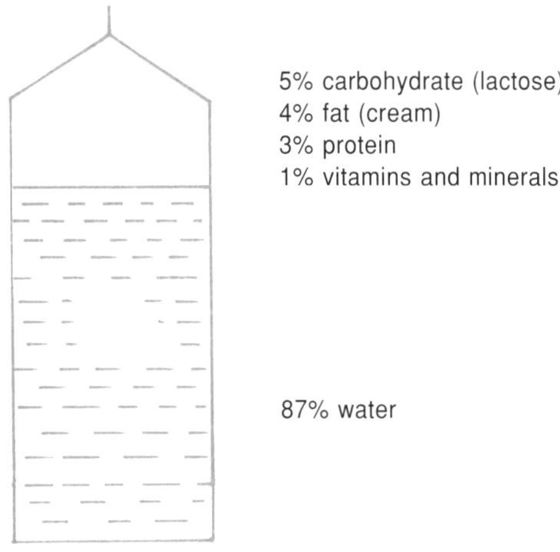

Milk products

Pasteurised milk is produced using the process called high-temperature-short-time (HTST). Milk is heated to 72°C for 15 seconds, then cooled rapidly to 4°C. This destroys most of the pathogenic bacteria present without altering the flavour, and the milk may be kept for several days in the refrigerator. The lactic acid bacteria that cause 'souring' are not destroyed.

UHT (ultra-high temperature treated) or long-life milk has been subjected to a temperature of not less than 135°C for 2–3 seconds and aseptically packed in hermetically sealed containers. May be stored without refrigeration for up to six months. After opening, store and use as for pasteurised milk.

Homogenised milk includes all UHT milk, evaporated milk and milk packed in cartons. In the homogenisation process the fat is divided into minute particles when the milk is forced through a small opening at high pressure, and the fat will not settle out from the milk.

Skim milk The milk fat content has been reduced; the percentage is stated on the label.

Modified milk The fat content varies from 15% to under 2%. These products have higher levels of calcium and lactose compared to skim milk.

Sweetened condensed milk Milk is heated to evaporate most of the water and 40% sucrose is added, which also acts as a preservative. If refrigerated, this milk will keep for some time after the can has been opened. It is available as full cream and skim milk sweetened condensed milk.

Evaporated milk (or unsweetened condensed milk) This is milk reduced by evaporation to 40% of original volume. It may be full cream or skim milk. It may be used instead of cream in some recipes, in ice-cream and to replace milk in custards. If chilled it may be whipped to increase its volume. After opening, store as for pasteurised milk.

Buttermilk is made by adding a culture to pasteurised skim milk and allowing it to stand for 12–14 hours at 14°C.

Full cream or skim milk powder may be prepared by drying whole or skim milk. Full cream milk powder may be reconstituted with water to make a substitute for fresh milk. Skim milk powder contains a high proportion of protein as the fat content has been reduced. It is useful for those on fat-reduced diets. In cookery, both types of dried milk may be added to recipes for bread, scones, cakes and puddings made using flour.

Cream

Cream consists of the fat particles that rise to the top of milk. It is very high in saturated fats – the proportion is stated on the label.

Pure or rich cream contains a minimum of 48% milk fat. It is thick enough not to require whipping. May be called triple cream.

Thickened cream contains a minimum of 35% milk fat. It is thickened with gelatine or vegetable gums to assist whipping. May be called double cream.

Reduced cream contains a minimum of 25% milk fat. It is a thin pouring cream.

Light cream contains a minimum of 18% milk fat. It is suitable to be served with coffee.

Extra light cream contains a minimum of 12% milk fat.

Sour or cultured cream is soured by the action of bacteria that produce lactic acid.

UHT or long-life cream is produced by same process as UHT milk. Refrigerate after opening.

Yoghurt

Yoghurt is a dairy product made by warming milk with selected strains of acid-producing bacteria. During the fermentation process, the milk sugars are broken down to release lactic acid, which coagulates the milk into a firm curd. The fat content of the milk controls the level of fat in the final product. Flavours are developed through the use of different bacteria, which give the tang or slightly acid taste to the natural yoghurts and through the use of fruit or other flavourings.

Cheese

Before the development of modern food technology, milk was best preserved by making it into cheese. Although each variety of cheese is made in a different way, the following basic steps are used in making all cheeses:

- The milk is pasteurised and warmed, and a bacterial culture is added to produce lactic acid.
- Rennet is added to form curd, which is then cut into small blocks to release the whey.
- The curd and whey are heated to shrink the curd and separate the whey.
- The curd is then treated in different ways to develop the characteristics of each particular variety of cheese.

Because 87% of milk is water it takes about 10 litres of milk to make 1 kg of cheese. Milk from cows, sheep and goats is made into cheese. Over 1000 different varieties of cheese have been developed and now many of these varieties are produced in Australia. These can be divided into fresh, soft, firm, and hard cheeses.

Fresh cheeses are made from the fresh curd as it is separated from the whey and is sold without further ripening. Varieties include cottage, creamed cottage and cream cheese. Ricotta cheese is made from whey. Mascarpone is a smooth triple cream cheese with a rich, slightly acidic taste.

Soft cheeses have a lower water content than fresh cheeses and are matured for varying periods according to variety. Some examples are blue vein and camembert, which are ripened by the action of moulds; fetta, a white Greek cheese that is matured in a brine solution; and mozzarella, a cheese with a soft, elastic texture.

Firm cheeses include varieties such as edam and gouda, originally from Holland, Swiss cheese with its characteristic large 'eyes', and samsoe and taffel from Denmark.

Hard cheeses have a lower moisture content and are matured for a longer time. They include the mild, semi-matured and matured cheddars, and Cheshire, originally from England. Hard grating cheeses are of Italian origin and include varieties such as parmesan, romano and pepato. All have a hard, granular texture that makes them ideal for grating.

Processed cheese is made by blending mild and more strongly flavoured cheeses with emulsifying agents and heating the blend. Processed cheese shows little or no change on storage at room temperature because the heat treatment kills the bacteria.

Sugars

The main sugar used in cookery is sucrose, a crystalline substance derived from the liquid extracted from sugar cane and sugar beet. There are several hundred different sugars, found as monosaccharides and disaccharides, in plants and animals (see Simple carbohydrates p. 16–18).

In Australia commercial sugar is processed from sugar cane. The sugar cane is cut, then pressed between large rollers to extract the juice. This is separated to remove particles of fibre and other solids, and then crystallised to form raw sugar. Raw sugar is treated and recrystallised in the refining process to produce a variety of sugar products.

Sugars are used to provide sweetening and as a preservative. They toughen cellulose and therefore retard the breaking up of fruits during cooking and slow down the freezing of foods.

Food value

Sugars are a readily digested form of carbohydrate and this provides energy. They provide no nutrients other than carbohydrates and should not be eaten in place of nutrient-dense foods. Sugar may promote dental caries by adhering to the teeth.

There is no significant nutritional difference between raw sugar and refined sugar products.

Sugar products

Brown sugar is semi-moist, golden brown, fine crystallised, refined sugar and gives extra flavour in a mixture.

Caster sugar is fine crystalline white sugar, used to give a smooth texture.

Coffee sugar is large, pale brown, slow-dissolving crystals of refined sugar.

Cube sugar is white sugar crystals moistened and pressed into moulds.

Glucose (sold as corn syrup) is a sugar in liquid form used for confectionery making.

Golden syrup is produced from sugar syrup that has been partially broken down into glucose and fructose. It is used as a flavouring ingredient.

Honey is produced by bees from the nectar of flowers and the flavour varies according to the plant. It has a high proportion of sugars and the nutrient value is the same as sugar.

Icing sugar is finely powdered white sugar, which absorbs moisture and becomes lumpy.

Icing sugar mixture is icing sugar to which cornflour has been added to prevent formation of lumps.

Lactose is a sugar found in milk and is used in commercial infant-feeding products.

Maple syrup is made by boiling and concentrating the sap of the sugar maple tree.

Raw sugar or demerara is refined to a stage where 2% ash remains, giving it colour and flavour.

Treacle is a dark brown syrup produced from the liquid remaining after the refined sugar has been crystallised and gives a strong flavour and dark colour to mixtures.

White granulated sugar is medium-sized crystalline sugar, used for most general purposes.

Sugar boiling

When syrup (sugar and water) is boiled the water evaporates, and the concentration and temperature rise. The temperature reached determines the consistency of the syrup when cooled.

To test temperature without a sugar thermometer: pour 1 teaspoon of syrup into a cup of cold water and observe the consistency as outlined below. For higher temperatures listen to the 'cracking' sound.

Consistency	Temperature	Use
Thread or fine strand	110–113°C	Spun sugar
Soft ball is formed	112–116°C	Fondant
Firm ball, slightly darker	118–120°C	Caramel
Hard ball, very hard	122–130°C	Marshmallow
Soft crack, makes slight cracking noise as it hits water	132–143°C	Butterscotch
Hard crack, loud cracking noise, darker	149–154°C	Toffee

Sorbitol and mannitol

These are sweet carbohydrates that are broken down slowly in the bloodstream and are used in diabetic diets. They cannot be used in cooking as they lose their sweetening power on heating.

Artificial sweeteners

Artificial or non-nutritive sweeteners have a strong market demand with many people wishing to reduce their energy intake. The artificial sweeteners in use in Australia are:

Saccharin was the first artificial sweetener to come onto the market. It is approximately 500 times sweeter than sugar, but leaves a bitter aftertaste.

Cyclamates are 30 times sweeter than sugar and are used in some 'table-top sweeteners' (placed 'on the table' for use in tea or coffee).

Aspartame is 200 times sweeter than sugar, but is unstable when heated, therefore it is not used in cooking or for heat-treated processed foods. Popular for soft drinks.

Acesulfame is similar in sweetening power to aspartame and is stable at high temperatures. The two are often used together.

Thaumatins are 2000 times sweeter than sugar but are expensive, unstable to heat and have an aftertaste.

Sucralose is a popular sweetener, sold as Splenda, and is 600 times sweeter than sugar. It is stable at high temperatures.

Alitame has a similar composition to aspartame, with a sweetening power 2000 times that of sugar. It is stable under most conditions and has a flavour close to sugar.

Eggs

Food value

An egg contains all of the essential food nutrients and is a valuable source of protein. The yolk consists mainly of fats, protein, water and minerals. The white contains protein (albumen), water and minerals.

Average percentage composition of hens' eggs

	Protein	Fat	Minerals	Water
Whole egg (excluding shell)	12	11	1	76
Yolk	17	30	1	52
White	10	0	0	90

Approximately 10% of the weight of an egg is shell, 60% white and 30% yolk.

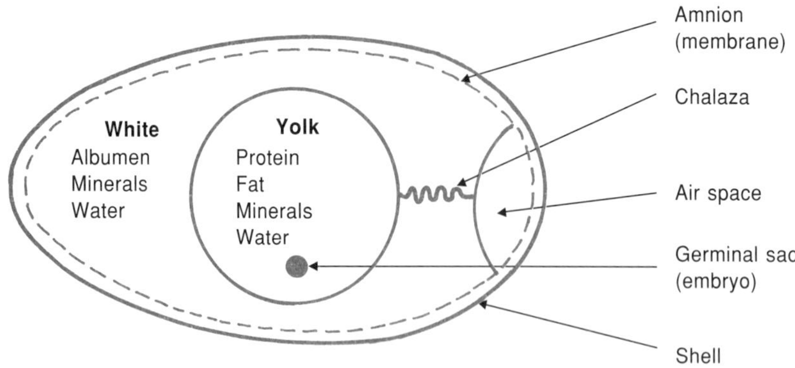

Structure of an egg

Tests for freshness

- Before removing the shell, place egg in a deep basin of water. A fresh egg sinks to the bottom, a stale egg produces sufficient gas to make it rise.
- The Haupt Test indicates the firmness of the yolk and white and therefore the age of the egg. Break an egg on to a saucer. In a fresh egg the yolk is bright and well-rounded, surrounded by thick white attached to the yolk. A fresh egg covers a relatively small area of the saucer. If the yolk is flat and the white is thin and spread out the egg is stale.

Types of eggs

Hens' eggs are generally sold in cartons based on the minimum mass of each egg in the carton. The carton sizes are 67 g, 61 g, 55 g and 49 g minimum size of egg. In this book we recommend the use of size 61 g eggs unless otherwise stated.

Free-range eggs are laid by hens that are not kept in small cages and are generally more expensive.

Quail eggs are approximately a third the size of hens' eggs and the shell is a green-fawn colour with dark spots. They are relatively expensive and used mainly for garnishing dishes. Cook for 3 minutes in simmering water.

Duck eggs are larger than hens' eggs with a stronger taste. They must be well cooked as they are more susceptible to microbiological contamination.

Uses of eggs

Thickening agents for example, in custards, sauces. When heated, egg proteins coagulate or thicken. Egg proteins have the ability to attract and hold large quantities of liquid, thus forming a gel. Egg white thickens at approximately 60°C and egg yolk solidifies at around 68°C. A beaten mixture coagulates at around 65°C. If heating is continued beyond this, the white becomes tough and shrinks and the yolk becomes dry and crumbly. This over-coagulation causes curdling.

Foaming agents for example, in sponges and soufflés. Egg white, when beaten, greatly increases volume by trapping and holding air. The air is trapped in bubbles surrounded by a thin elastic film of egg white. On heating the air expands and the protein in the egg white coagulates, trapping the air.

Emulsifying agents for example, in mayonnaise. The egg yolk proteins coat the oil droplets, creating an emulsion. This prevents the ingredients from separating, maintaining them as a smooth mixture.

Australian bush foods

Our early inhabitants had access to a wealth of foods growing abundantly in the Australian bush. It has taken many years for the potential of the flavours and nutrient value of these 'bush foods' to be recognised, but they are now being used in restaurants, sold in supermarkets and advertised in cooking programs on television.

Some of the bush food products available in Australia include the following:

Bunya nuts The shells must be boiled to release the nuts and these can then be used in desserts and confectionery, or as a thickener in casseroles.

Bush cucumber About the size of a date, with a bitter skin, but sweet minty cucumber flesh inside. Used in sauces and chutneys.

Bush tomato Earthy red-brown in colour with a dry, wrinkled appearance, about the diameter of a marble. Used in soups, sauces, casseroles, salads and chutneys.

Cumbungi The common bulrush, which can be used in a similar way to leeks.

Davidson plum Size of a ping pong ball, with dark purple skin and two small flat seeds surrounded by burgundy coloured flesh. Very sour and tangy, used to flavour meat.

Illawarra plum Similar to the cultivated plum, but much smaller in size, it is used in sauces and chutneys and can be pickled.

Kakadu plum A small green fruit with an apricot flavour, used in sauces and with fish and salads. High in Vitamin C.

Kurrajong grubs 4–6 cm long, they can be used in soups and stews.

Lemon myrtle leaf Used crushed to give a citrus flavour to meat and fish dishes.

Muntries Tiny pea-sized fruit with the taste of apples, used in salads and meat dishes.

Myrnong A tuber, which can be baked as a vegetable.

Native mint Strong peppery flavour, used in sauces and salad dressings.

Native pepperberries Small deep purple berries with strong pepper flavour, used in meat dishes.

Quandong Red fruits with a tart peach flavour, used in pies and jams.

Riberry Belongs to the lillipilli family. A spicy cinnamon-flavoured bright pinky-red berry.

Sour plum Deep purple sour plum, used in desserts and jams.

Warrigal greens A green vegetable that is prepared in a similar manner to silver beet or spinach.

Wattle seed Roasted and ground for use as a flavouring in ice-cream and other desserts.

Wild limes A native citrus that has a very sour taste. Used as a flavouring in meat dishes.

Wild rosella Bright crimson buds inside seed pods (remove the seed pods). The buds have a rhubarb-like taste and are used to flavour jams and chutneys.

Herbs

The leaves and other parts of plants used to give flavour to foods are called herbs. These usually grow in temperate climatic regions. Although most commonly used for savoury dishes such as soups, stews and casseroles, some herbs, such as bay leaf, are also added to sweet dishes and sauces made with milk.

Fresh herbs are preferable to dried herbs – these can be purchased or grown in your own garden. Herbs may be ground after drying. When dried, they must be stored in airtight containers.

The term 'fine herbs' means those with delicate flavours. They are basil, chervil (parsley type), rosemary and thyme.

The 'robust' or strongly flavoured herbs include mint, savory (mint flavour), sage, dill (faint caraway flavour) and many others.

Herb mixtures

Mixtures of herbs formulated for special uses are available for poultry seasoning, meat marinades and vegetable dishes. Salt is included in many mixtures.

Some herbs are available in several forms; for example, garlic may be bought fresh, it may be minced and sold in jars and it is also available as garlic powder and garlic salt.

Herbs commonly used

Basil Sweet basil flavour resembles cloves. Use with tomato dishes, soups and meat.

Bay leaf From the sweet bay tree. Use the whole leaf, either fresh or dried, and remove from food before serving. May be added to soups, stews, sauces and dishes prepared with milk.

Bouquet garni or cook's bunch A bunch of herbs, tied together with cotton or placed in a muslin bag so that it can be easily removed from the dish before serving. The herbs commonly used are 3 sprigs parsley, 1 sprig marjoram, 2 sprigs thyme, 1 bay leaf.

Chervil Resembles parsley in plant form and flavour. Use for cream soups, salads, egg and fish dishes.

Chives Small onion-type plant with a mild onion flavour. The chopped leaves are used as a flavour and garnish for salads, sandwiches, soups and savoury dishes.

Coriander Bright green leaves, similar in appearance to parsley, but with a distinctive flavour. It is used in many Asian dishes.

Dill Seed of a small herb and has a faint caraway flavour. It is used to flavour pickles, especially cucumber, for salads such as potato and coleslaw, and in sauces for steamed fish. Fresh dill leaves may also be used.

Fennel Has a mild aniseed flavour and is used mainly in Mediterranean countries to flavour seasonings and fish dishes.

Fenugreek Leguminous plant, similar to clover. It is used to flavour cheeses, as an ingredient of curry powder, and in some countries it is eaten, either boiled or raw, mixed with honey.

Garlic Plant of the onion family with a very strong odour and flavour. It is used in meat cookery, in chutneys and sauces, and in salads. A mild flavour of garlic may be imparted to a salad by rubbing the bowl with a cut clove of garlic.

Lemon grass Grass-like lemon-flavoured herb. Stems are used in mainly Asian and Indian cookery.

Marjoram Flavour is similar to thyme. It resembles thyme in appearance, but the leaves are a little larger and flatter.

Mint leaves and sprigs from the spearmint plant As the new shoots appear in spring, this is a traditional flavour for spring vegetables such as new potatoes and peas, and for roast spring lamb. It is also used in fruit drinks. When dried it can be used to flavour pea and lentil soups.

Oregano Resembles marjoram in plant form and flavour. Used in many dishes, particularly Mediterranean cookery.

Parsley The curly green leaves of this plant are used to flavour or garnish many savoury dishes. It may be dried but in this form loses much of its flavour and colour. Continental parsley has a larger flat leaf and is used in a similar way to the curly leafed variety.

Rosemary Comes from a small evergreen bush and has a pine-like fragrance and taste. It should be used fresh, in sprigs or finely chopped. Lamb, fish and poultry dishes may be flavoured with this herb.

Sage Leaves are dull green and slightly bitter. They may be combined with onion to flavour seasoning for roast pork and duck.

Savory Related to the mint family, but the leaves are smaller. It may be used for meat, chicken, egg dishes and to flavour sauces and salads.

Tarragon Has a faintly aniseed flavour, and is used to flavour vinegar and seafood dishes. The fresh and dried leaves are used.

Thyme The distinct and pleasant flavour of this small leafed herb makes it very popular for savoury dishes and seasonings.

Vietnamese mint Green with purple tinge. Hot pepper flavour.

Spices

Spices are obtained from aromatic plants that usually grow in tropical regions. Leaves, berries, seeds, stems and roots may be dried to give added flavour and variety to both sweet and savoury foods. These spices are usually sold in powdered form, and should be purchased in small quantities as they deteriorate more rapidly after grinding. They may be bought whole and ground with a mortar and pestle or coffee grinder.

Spice mixtures

A number of commercial mixtures of spices in addition to 'mixed spice' are available for special dishes such as marinades for meat and poultry. There are also mixtures suitable for seasoning forcemeat, for sauces, for vegetable dishes, biscuits and cakes.

Spices commonly used

Allspice (see Pimento).

Caraway seeds From a small plant grown in Europe and England that varies a little in colour in different countries. Used to flavour bread, cakes, cheeses and gravies.

Cardamom Small dark brown seeds and pods of reed-like plant, with a pleasant smell and hot pungent flavour. Used in sauces, soups and as an ingredient for curry powder. May be purchased ground.

Cayenne Hot bright red type of pepper made from small dried chillies. It originally came from the town of Cayenne in South America.

Cinnamon The bark of a tree, and is sold in stick form or ground. Used for cakes and sweet dishes.

Cloves Unopened flowers of a tropical plant. When whole they are used for chutneys, sauces and apple and pear dishes. Ground cloves may be used in cake and biscuits.

Coriander seeds Dried seed of a parsley-like plant. It is an ingredient of curry powder and some spice mixtures used for pickling fruit, vegetables and meat.

Cumin Seed of a plant used in the making of curry powder and to flavour vegetable dishes, soups, breads, biscuits and cheeses. It resembles caraway seed in appearance but not in flavour. May be purchased ground.

Curry powder A mixture of a great number of spices and herbs, the proportions of which may vary from country to country. It is used extensively in India and other Asian countries to flavour sauces for meat, vegetables, chicken, egg and fish dishes.

Galangal Large rhizome related to the ginger family, with a mild ginger flavour. Used in Asian and Indian dishes, curry pastes and Eastern European foods. Sold fresh and pickled.

Ginger Root-like rhizome of a tropical plant and may be sold fresh. After peeling it may be crystallised, preserved in syrup or dried and ground into a spice. It is used for cakes, biscuits, puddings and meat dishes.

Horseradish Root of a small plant, and has a sharp flavour that resembles mustard. It is best when grated fresh and made into a sauce to serve with roast beef. It may be purchased grated or dried and ground or as a sauce.

Mace Outer skin of nutmeg and has a similar flavour. It is used for savoury dishes.

Mixed spice A mixture of sweet spices used for cakes, puddings and similar dishes.

Mustard seeds Seeds of the mustard plant. They may be ground or mixed whole with other ingredients. They are used as a condiment with meats, or added to savoury dishes and sauces. Mustard seeds are also used in pickles.

Nutmeg Kernel of the fruit of a tropical tree and may be purchased whole or ground. Used to flavour cakes, biscuits, milk dishes and puddings.

Paprika Prepared from Hungarian capsicum or pepper. It is similar in colour to cayenne, but without its pungent flavour. It is used for savoury dishes.

Pepper Black pepper comes from the unripe berries, and white pepper from the ripe berries of the same tropical vine. Black pepper is stronger and is used in the making of pickles, chutneys and sauces. White pepper may be used in sauces as it gives a better appearance.

Peppercorns Whole berries from a specific pepper tree and used for soups, pickles and stews, or ground in a pepper mill at the table.

Pimento A berry that when ground is called 'allspice' because it is said to combine the flavours of cinnamon, cloves and nutmeg. Used whole for pickles and meat dishes.

Pimiento The Spanish name for bright red capsicums. They are usually bottled or canned and used as a garnish for hors d'oeuvres.

Poppyseeds Small dark-blue or black seeds of the white poppy. Used to sprinkle over bread before it is baked.

Saffron True saffron is made from the stigmas of the autumn crocus. It should be bright orange-red in colour, and is very expensive. A dull colour indicates old or inferior saffron. It has a bitter-sweet taste and is used mainly to flavour and colour soups, jellies and rice dishes.

Sesame seeds Have a nutty flavour and can be used in confectionery, in dishes containing chicken or vegetables, and in biscuits and bread. Also used to make pastes and cooking oils.

Turmeric Comes from a plant of the ginger family, but has a milder flavour. It is bright yellow and is used to colour pickles and dressings for salads.

Equipment

A relatively small range of equipment is required to prepare most recipes in this book (see photo opposite p. 379).

Food preparation utensils

- A set of cup and spoon measures enables accurate measurement of ingredients (see p. 70–71) and a set of scales is useful, but not necessary.
- A small vegetable knife and a 28 cm chef's knife are necessary equipment for food preparation. Other useful knives for basic cooking are a long serrated-edge knife for cutting bread and cakes, and a slim filleting knife used for boning and skinning fish. Good quality knives are expensive, but last a long time and are safer to use as they do not break under pressure. A good knife has a stainless steel blade that forms part of the handle, held in place by rivets through the handle. To use the chef's knife to best advantage, keep the tip of the knife on the chopping board and raise and lower the heel of the knife to cut the food. Knives should be sharpened regularly, preferably with a sharpening stone.
- Equipment for stirring, scraping, lifting and serving could include wooden and metal spoons, a spatula, egg slice, large fork, soup ladle.
- A hand whisk, rotary whisk or small electric beater can be used for beating egg whites or creaming butter and sugar.

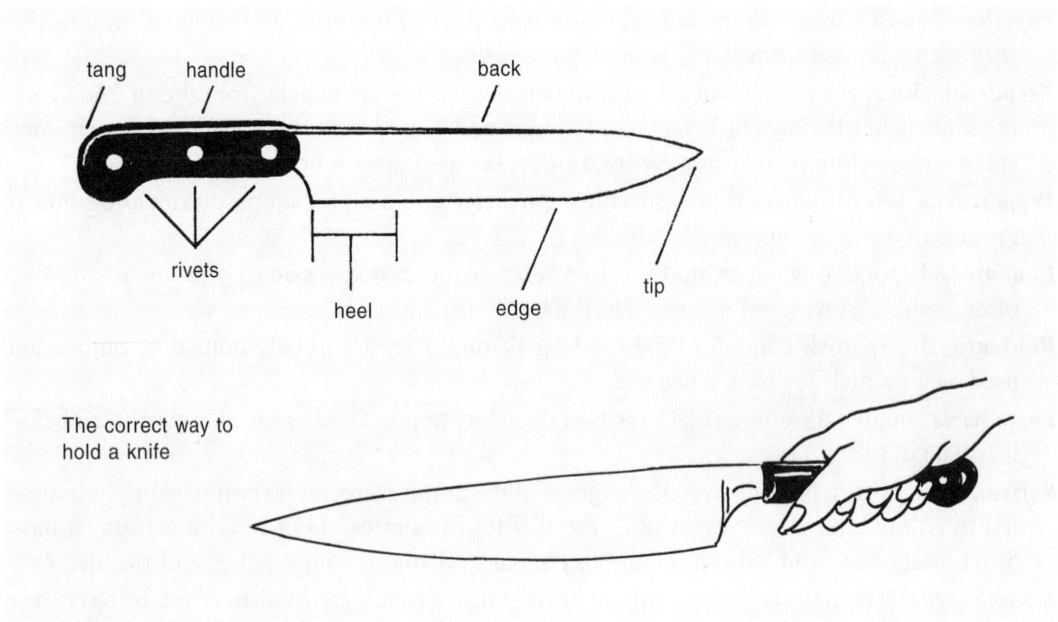

- Several bowls in small, medium and large sizes made from china, stainless steel or plastic are needed where the recipes have several steps.
- A colander can be used to drain solids from liquids and a sieve to make a puree.
- An electric food processor is useful for some recipes.

Cooking utensils

- A 26 cm non-stick frying pan, a small saucepan (less than 2 L), a medium saucepan (2 L to 3.5 L) and a large saucepan (over 3.5 L) are required for the recipes in this book. Stainless steel is the most durable material for saucepans and the more expensive type with a heavy base assists in preventing the food from burning.
- Baking dishes are deep-sided ovenproof trays for cooking meat and vegetables.
- Four-sided oven trays prevent liquids spilling out into the oven. Non-stick trays prevent sticking and are easier to clean.
- Ovenproof dishes can be used for both cooking and serving at the table. For the recipes in this book 2.5 L ovenproof dishes are suitable. Casseroles are ovenproof dishes with lids. Flame-proof casseroles can be used on top of the cooker over a gas flame or hotplate.
- Other equipment used in the book include a 22 cm pie dish (1 L), a 14 cm x 8 cm soufflé dish (1 L), a 22 cm quiche pan (1 L) and a wok or deep frying pan.
- For information on cake pans used in this book see p. 374–375 and for bread pans see p. 438.

3 Planning and presenting food

For most people, eating is a social occasion to be enjoyed. We choose foods we like, as well as foods that provide optimum nutrition. The way in which we prepare food will also influence the enjoyment and nutritional value of the food.

Purchase of food

Society is in a constant state of cultural and economic change and this influences family living and the foods we eat. Careful selection of food is important for the best results in cookery. The household food budget influences this selection – the less money available, the greater the need for spending it to the best nutritional advantage.

Changes affecting food management in the household

- Households with all adults working, providing increased income, but reducing shopping and food preparation time.
- Households with lower incomes, reducing the money available for food.
- The trend towards buying and preparing foods with a lower fat and sugar content.
- The popularity of 'natural' foods and foods grown and marketed as 'organic'.
- Changes to shopping hours and the types of shopping facilities.
- The increased use of takeaway and fast food outlets.
- The marketing and availability of 'convenience' foods.
- The release of new food preparation and cooking appliances on the market.

Strategies for meal planning

- Plan the week's meals in advance. Allow for some flexibility, such as use of leftovers, or an unexpected change in number of family members at home for a meal. This forward planning ensures the inclusion of foods essential for balanced meals, and allows for organised shopping. The purchase of foods in economical quantities saves time and money.
- After meals are planned, compile a list of foods to be purchased.
- If possible, shop in person and adhere fairly closely to the prepared list.
- Buy from clean well-managed shops where trade is brisk – rapid turnover ensures freshness.
- Buy foods in season, especially fruits and vegetables, for economy and better flavour and quality.
- Purchase foods from markets as they may be cheaper and fresher.
- Watch the trend in market prices, and take advantage of 'special' lines but only of foods required.
- Check weight and price when purchasing goods.
- When buying meat consider the proportionate amounts of muscle, bone and fat in comparison to the cost of meat.
- When shopping take an insulated container to transport frozen and perishable foods, or wrap them in several layers of newspaper.
- Buy only small quantities of untried foods until sure of the quality and family acceptability.
- Consider the cost of the packaged or prepared food against the cost of ingredients that may be purchased separately and combined at home.
- Read the information given on the label relating to mass, ingredients and date marking and consider the nutritive value of the food.
- Consider the time available for the purchase of foods and the preparation of meals in the home and compare the flavour of packaged food with food prepared in the home.
- Consider the possibility of using a combination of home-prepared and packaged foods to save time and labour, for example, packet or canned soup used as the basis for a casserole.
- If possible, keep a reserve of canned, packet and frozen foods for emergencies.
- Check accounts and cash-register dockets and keep receipts for reference. A record of expenditure could assist in future budgeting.

Food labelling

The following information is required by law on prepackaged foods:

- the product name
- the name and business address of manufacturer, packer, vendor or importer
- the country of origin and/or processing
- net weight or volume
- a statement of ingredients in descending order of their relative proportion by weight
- Food additives and substances not usually eaten as a food that are added to a processed food must be identified by coded numbers. Copies of additive numbers may be obtained from the Department of Health and Community Services. This enables those sensitive to an additive to avoid that food.
- Food with shelf life of less than two years must carry a date mark.

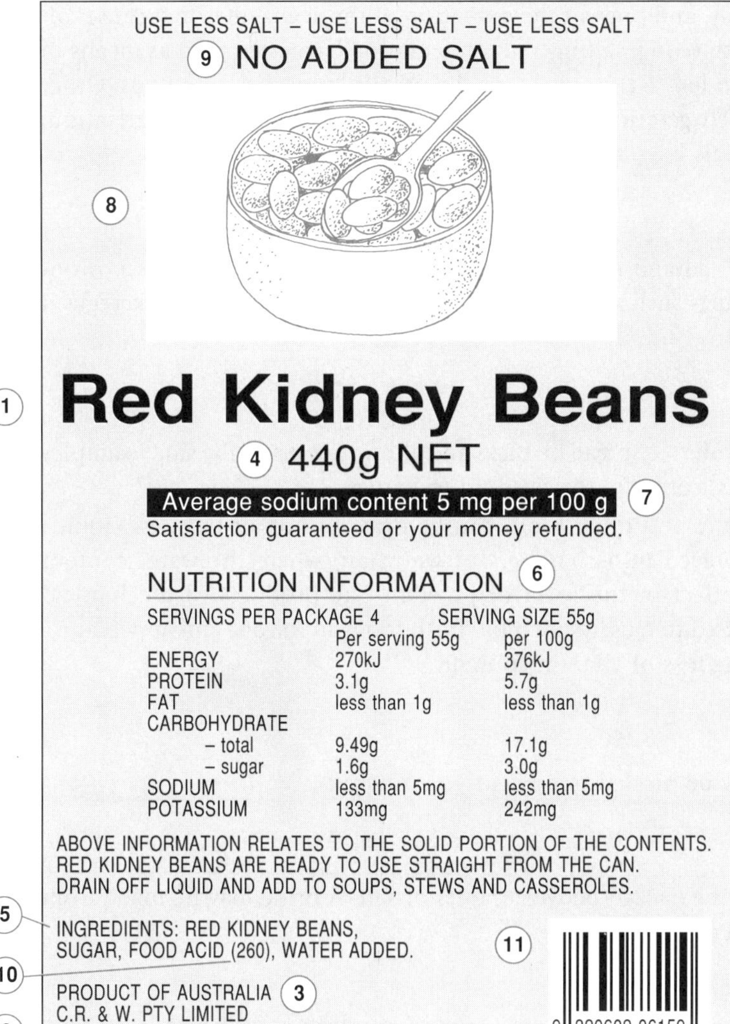

1 Name of product (required by law).

2 Name and business address of company (required by law).

3 Country of origin (required by law).

4 Net weight (required by law).

5 Ingredients in order of mass; water is situated last regardless of amount (required by law).

6 Nutrient panel.

7 This is a nutrient claim. If a nutrient claim is made, nutrition information must be provided in the form of a defined panel.

8 Illustrative or pictorial depictions must not be misleading or deceptive.

9 Nutrient claim.

10 Food additive number may be identified by code, number, by name or both.

11 Barcode for scanning at point of sale (optional).

Note that this label does not have a use-by date, as it is not required on canned food, which has a shelf life of over two years.

Convenience foods and commercial food processing

Ever since humans moved from being nomadic and began to cultivate the soil, people have endeavoured to find means of preserving food to ensure a wide range is available all year round. The range of preprepared and commercially processed foods, often called convenience foods, has increased rapidly.

Convenience foods are processed to reduce preparation in the home, provide combinations of flavours and textures, prevent the growth of undesirable micro-organisms such as yeasts, moulds and bacteria that cause rapid decay, and prevent the oxidation of those enzymes that cause 'off flavours' to develop. Sun-drying, smoking, salting and fermentation have been used as means of preservation for centuries, and modern technology uses the principles of these methods. Other methods such as dehydration, refrigeration, freezing, canning and bottling, pasteurisation, irradiation and the use of chemicals have also been developed.

Dry storage

Cereal grains are dry when harvested and may be stored for long periods in dry vermin-proof silos. Flour and other cereal products such as macaroni, spaghetti and breakfast foods keep well if stored in dry containers.

Dehydration

Sun-drying After harvesting, the fruits are spread on racks and allowed to dry in the sun. Examples of sun-dried fruits are sultanas, currants, apricots and tomatoes.

Mechanical dehydration Vegetables and other foods can be dried in hot air tunnels. Liquids such as milk and eggs are sprayed into chambers of warm air, where the water content evaporates and the solids collect in the form of powder. The products of mechanical dehydration may be reconstituted to closely resemble fresh foods in flavour and appearance. However, there is usually some loss of vitamin content.

Pickling

Onions and other vegetables may be pickled in an acid, e.g. vinegar.

Salting

Foods such as meat and fish may be packed between layers of salt. A brine may be made from salt and water instead of using layers of salt.

Sugar preservation

Fruits, either commercially canned or bottled, or home bottled, may be preserved in a syrup of sugar and water or fruit juice. When a very heavy syrup is used, fruits, ginger and citrus peel absorb a large amount of sugar. When allowed to dry, these become glacé fruits. If rolled in sugar they are called crystallised fruits. Jams, marmalades and jellies are also examples of fruits preserved by sugar.

Smoking

Fish and some meats such as bacon and hams are smoked and dried over slow-burning wood fires. This coagulates the protein on the outside, giving a distinctive colour and flavour.

Fermentation

By the action of yeast on sugar in fruit, the sugar is changed into alcohol, which is a preservative, e.g. wines.

Bacterial action

Used for cheese making. A coagulating enzyme, such as rennet, is added to milk to form a curd. A culture of harmless bacteria is added to produce lactic acid. After a short time, the curd is stirred and 'whey' (or water) is drained off. The curd or cheese can then be cut into blocks and matured for up to twelve months before sale.

Mechanical action

Churning coagulates the fat of milk allowing water and non-fat solids to drain off, thus producing butter.

Chemical preservatives

Some chemicals, such as sulphur dioxide, benzoic or acetic acid, stop bacterial action for a limited time. The use of chemical preservatives is rigidly controlled by law.

Sterilisation

Canned and bottled foods, such as fruits, vegetables, meats and fish, may be packed into cans or bottles with syrup, salt or oil, and then sterilised to destroy micro-organisms.

Pasteurisation

This is mainly used to preserve milk and some other liquids, for example, fruit juices. It destroys most of the pathogenic bacteria but gives only short-term preservation. The food keeps only a few days and must be refrigerated. For details on milk see p. 46–47.

Refrigeration

The temperature of food is kept below that required for rapid micro-organism growth. This temperature varies with different foods, but for optimum results the refrigerator should be kept between 2°C and 5°C. However, food does not keep indefinitely, and there is some loss of flavour and appearance.

Freezing

Food may be preserved by freezing the water within the cell, called 'combined water', and water surrounding the cell called 'free water'. A temperature of –18°C must be reached within a very short time. Rapid temperature reduction between –1°C and –5°C produces small crystals which ensure that the food, when thawed, retains its shape and is not 'mushy'. Freezing inhibits the growth of micro-organisms, although some survive and cause a gradual deterioration over several months. Processing, storage by manufacturers, transport in refrigerated vans, and retail refrigeration cabinets all require careful management to ensure that frozen foods are not kept too long and are never allowed to partially thaw and then be refrozen.

Freeze-drying

Foods are frozen and the temperature allowed to rise sufficiently for the ice crystals to sublimate, that is, to pass directly from the solid to the vapour state. This is a more expensive process than freezing. Foods available include instant coffee, spices and herbs. These foods may be stored at room temperature and are readily reconstituted with water. The reduction in weight makes these foods suitable for campers and hikers.

De-hydro freezing

Food, often fruit juices, is frozen slowly and the crystals of 'free water' are sieved off, while the 'combined water' is frozen. Fruit juice concentrates are processed in this way. They may be sold as a concentrate for dilution at home or reconstituted before sale.

Quick drying

Small particles of food, such as peas or beans, are dehydrated in a high direct temperature, usually above 75°C. As the high temperature denatures the protein, this process is suitable only for foods that are high in carbohydrate and low in protein.

Irradiation

Ionising gamma rays from a radioactive source such as Cobalt-60 are used in some countries to prolong the life of foods. Low-energy irradiation, usually not more than 10 kiloGrays, destroys many of the moulds and bacteria thus preserving the food. It can be used to inhibit the sprouting of potatoes and onions and prolong the shelf life of soft fruits, tropical fruits, spices and seafood. Irradiation may affect the colour, taste and texture of some foods. At the permitted level the food itself does not become radioactive.

Atmosphere-controlled ripening

Fruit and vegetables are stored in large sealed areas filled with inert gases to slow down the production of ethylene, which is produced when the fruit and vegetables ripen.

Modified-atmosphere packing

Packaging is flushed with nitrogen or carbon dioxide, which prevents the growth of spoilage organisms but not of pathogenic bacteria.

Cook-chill process

Food is cooked to reduce micro-organisms, then placed in flexible packaging and refrigerated. It has a limited shelf life of less than 21 days. If packaged under vacuum it is labelled 'sous vide'.

Kitchen safety

Burns, falls and cuts are accidents that may cause serious personal injury in the food preparation area, and great care should be taken to implement preventative safety measures.

Burns

Burns (from hot, dry surfaces) and scalds (from steam) can be prevented by using thick gloves or other padded implements to handle hot appliances. Take particular care of spitting oil during deep-frying and from steam escaping as lids are lifted from saucepans.

To treat an injured person run cold water over the burned or scalded area immediately. Remove any clothing or other items before swelling starts. Do not break any blisters. Burn spray or cream may be applied to reduce pain. Cover lightly with gauze and, if necessary, obtain medical assistance.

Falls

Falls are usually caused by wet and slippery floors, objects left lying on the floor or from climbing to reach high shelves. Prevention is the best approach. Spills on the floor should be cleaned immediately and signposted until dry. Cartons, food and appliances should be put away in their correct place immediately after use so that they do not pose a danger by being on the floor. Use a small step-ladder to reach equipment stored on high shelves.

Faulty electrical equipment may cause electric shock. Do not use appliances with wet hands or stand on a wet floor. Check equipment, cords and plugs regularly for frayed wires and have them repaired if necessary. Disconnect appliances before cleaning.

Cuts

Broken glass and knife cuts are common injuries in food preparation areas. Broken glass should be swept or vacuumed immediately. Dispose of any nearby food. Wipe over the surface with a damp disposable towel or cloth.

Store knives in a holder that protects and covers the blade. This prevents damage to the cutting edge and protects from inadvertent cuts. Use the correct knife for the job (p. 57) and sharpen knives regularly. Blades in food processors and other equipment, sharp edges on equipment and food slicers may also cause cuts.

If the cut is deep, quickly apply a tight bandage to slow the bleeding. Sit the injured person down to prevent them from falling and causing further injury and then obtain medical assistance.

For minor cuts, apply a tight bandage to slow bleeding. When bleeding has stopped, cover area with waterproof dressing. If the cut is on the hand wear a plastic glove if food is being handled.

After anyone has been treated for a cut in the food preparation area, wash the area and all equipment thoroughly with hot water and detergent and dispose of any food in the area.

Food safety

Food is a perishable commodity. It becomes contaminated with disease-causing (pathogenic) bacteria and moulds if it is not handled in a hygienic manner. Eating contaminated food may cause food poisoning, resulting in nausea, vomiting, abdominal pain and diarrhoea. The most common pathogenic bacteria are salmonella, staphylococcus and clostridium perfringens. Bacteria multiply when kept in moist warm conditions and produce a toxin, which causes food poisoning. This can occur when foods are kept warm (temperatures between 5°C and 60°C) for longer than two hours.

Personal hygiene

To prevent bacteria getting into food from soiled clothes or skin, anyone handling food must follow the basic rules of personal hygiene:

- Wear clean clothes in the food preparation area. Under health and safety legislation those who are preparing food in commercial premises are not permitted to wear the same clothes outside the workplace, as the clothes may bring disease-carrying organisms into the workplace.
- Hair should be clean and drawn back from the face. In commercial premises a head covering may have to be worn.
- Wash hands thoroughly in hot water with detergent before and after handling foods. Use extra care in washing hands after using the toilet, smoking, eating or using a handkerchief.
- Keep fingernails short and use a brush to clean under the nails.
- Remove jewellery from hands. If working in commercial food preparation area, all jewellery must be removed so that there is no risk of it falling into the food.
- Do not cough or sneeze in the food preparation area.
- Cover any cuts or abrasions with waterproof dressings to avoid bacterial contamination.
- Wear plastic gloves over any dressings on the hands. If working in commercial food preparation, plastic gloves must be worn at all times.

Workplace hygiene

- Ensure that all utensils and facilities are clean before using them. This helps to prevent disease-causing bacteria or other micro-organisms from coming into contact with food.
- Wash chopping boards in hot water with detergent each time a different food is prepared to prevent cross-contamination.
- Wipe down benches, floors and walls regularly with hot water and detergent to remove any food spills or splashes.
- Place rubbish in a covered container and dispose of regularly. Clean rubbish area often with hot water and detergent so that flies, mice, and other pests are not attracted to the area.

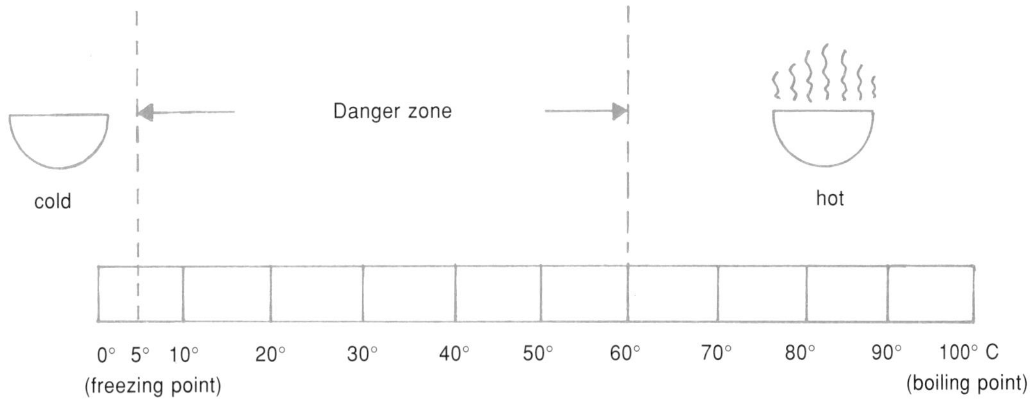

Food-holding temperatures

- Hot food prepared for serving must be stored at over 60°C to inhibit the growth of bacteria. Do not hold for more than two hours.
- Cold food prepared for serving must be kept at less than 5°C to inhibit the growth of bacteria. Do not hold for more than two hours.
- During preparation, food should be placed in the refrigerator between preparation stages.
- Frozen foods should be placed in the refrigerator to thaw slowly for up to 12 hours.

Storage of food

Long-life foods

Long-life foods such as flour, spaghetti, salt, sugar, spices, dried beans, peas, dried fruits, coffee beans and tea should be stored in clean, dry, clearly labelled and airtight containers. Canned foods should be stored in a dry area as moisture rusts cans. Bottled foods should be stored in a dark cupboard as light may affect the food.

Perishable foods

Perishable foods such as bread and cakes should be stored in clean containers in a cool dry place for 1–2 weeks. Breakfast cereals and biscuits keep for 3–4 weeks when stored in clean containers in a cool dry place. Potatoes and onions keep for 3–4 weeks in a cool, dark place where air can circulate.

Highly perishable or short-life foods

These foods should be stored in the refrigerator, between 2°C and 5°C. After the time indicated below, the growth of bacteria and moulds may cause deterioration in the texture and flavour of the food and the production of toxins causing food poisoning.

Storage of food

Highly perishable foods	Storage and time
Meat and poultry (fresh)	Place in container, loosely covered and in the coldest part of the refrigerator for up to 1 week.
Fish (fresh)	Scale and clean before storing for 1–2 days in a covered container in the coldest part of the refrigerator.
Milk and cream	Store in refrigerator for up to 1 week.
Fruits and vegetables	May be stored in refrigerator. Rockmelon, pineapple and strawberries must be placed in covered containers with well-fitting lids as flavour penetrates other foods. Store for up to 2 weeks.
Bacon	Wrap loosely and store in refrigerator for up to 2 weeks.
Cheese	Wrap to prevent drying and store in refrigerator up to 3 weeks.
Butter, margarine, dairy blend	Store in refrigerator in a separate container as these foods absorb other flavours. Store for up to 1 month.
Eggs	Store in refrigerator in carton or container for up to 2 weeks.

Frozen foods

The freezer should be kept at a temperature of –18°C. Some frozen foods have a longer storage life than others because of their composition, but the temperature of the unit also plays a major part in safe storage times.

Frozen food must not be allowed to thaw before being placed in a freezer unit, as this may reduce the quality and encourage the growth of pathogenic organisms. Bacteria are rendered dormant but are not destroyed by freezing, therefore careful handling and absolute cleanliness are essential.

Defrosting is necessary every 3–6 months, unless the unit is 'frost-free'. Arrange this when stocks are low. Pack frozen food into refrigerator or wrap well and return it to the unit as soon as possible.

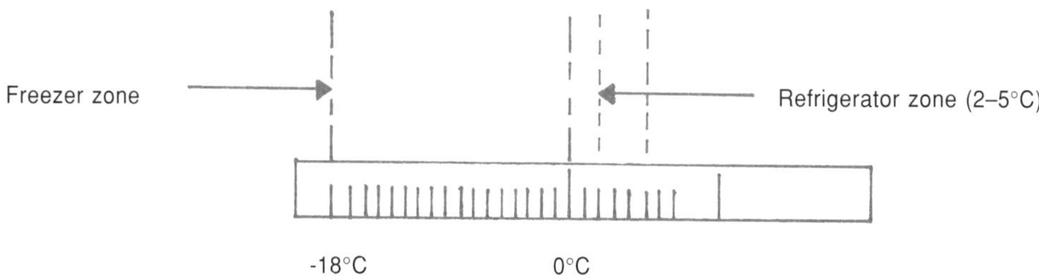

Frozen food and storage time	Preparation for use
Meat – 6 months	Steak and chops should be thawed in the refrigerator. Large pieces of meat should be thawed for 24 hours in refrigerator.
Poultry – 6 months	Must be completely thawed in refrigerator before cooking. This may take 24 hours or more for large turkeys, and is essential to ensure complete destruction of pathogenic organisms during cooking.
Fish – 3 months	Thaw before cooking.
Vegetables – 6 months	Do not thaw before cooking.
Fruit, cooked – 6 months	Thaw before use.
Pies – 3 months	May be frozen before or after cooking. Uncooked: partially thaw and allow longer cooking time. Cooked: thaw and warm through to heat filling and crisp the pastry.
Breads, cakes and sandwiches – 1 month	Wrap in foil or plastic food wrap. Before serving, place on cake cooler and thaw completely.
Ice-cream and ice blocks – 1 month	Serve directly from freezer.

Home freezing

- Fresh foods such as uncooked fruit, vegetables, fish, meat and poultry should be frozen as soon as possible.
- Vegetables should be blanched before freezing to destroy the enzymes that may produce 'off flavours', as their activity is only reduced by freezing and not destroyed.
- Salad vegetables with a high water content such as lettuce and celery should not be frozen as they do not retain their crispness when thawed.
- Baked foods such as cakes, pies, cooked meat and poultry, and casserole-type dishes should be frozen as soon as they have cooled.
- Foods must be wrapped to prevent freezer burn caused by oxidation. Plastic containers with snap-on lids, special freezer polythene bags and aluminium foil may be used. Expel as much air as possible and leave approximately 1 cm 'head space' to allow for expansion during freezing.
- Before packing, divide food into meal-sized units. Refreezing of unused portions reduces flavour and increases pathogenic organism activity, even to danger level in the case of meat, fish and vegetables.
- Round, square and tumbler-shaped containers to fit the available space may prove to be an economical investment. Colours may be used as additional identification.
- Mark food with date and contents.
- A record may be kept of all foods and their position in the freezer. Mark off quantity as used.

Measuring techniques

Careful measurement of ingredients is the foundation of successful cookery. Cups, measuring jugs, spoons and scales are used. Scales should be handled with care and adjusted at regular intervals.

Metric terms and abbreviations

gram	g	millilitre	mL	millimetre	mm
kilogram	kg	litre	L	centimetre	cm

Metric measures

- Australian Standard metric cup and fractional cups are used for dry ingredients. The capacity of the cup is 250 millilitres (mL). A set of 4 cups is necessary for measuring dry ingredients. This consists of 1 cup, $^1/_2$ cup, $^1/_3$ cup, $^1/_4$ cup.
- Australian Standard graduated jug and litre measures are used for liquid ingredients.
  250 mL jug = 250 millilitres (mL) = 1 metric cup
  1 litre (L) = 1000 millilitres = 4 metric cups
- Australian Standard spoons are used for liquid and dry ingredients and a set of 4 spoons is necessary.
  1 tablespoon = 20 millilitres (mL)
  1 teaspoon = 5 millilitres (mL)
  $^1/_2$ teaspoon = 2.5 millilitres (mL)
  $^1/_4$ teaspoon = 1.25 millilitres (mL)

Measuring techniques

Dry ingredients

1. Place measuring cup on bench with paper underneath it.
2. Spoon in the ingredients until the cup is slightly overfilled.
3. Do not shake or bang the measure.
4. Level off with a spatula.
5. Return excess to container.
6. Butter should be softened but not melted before it is measured by the cup.

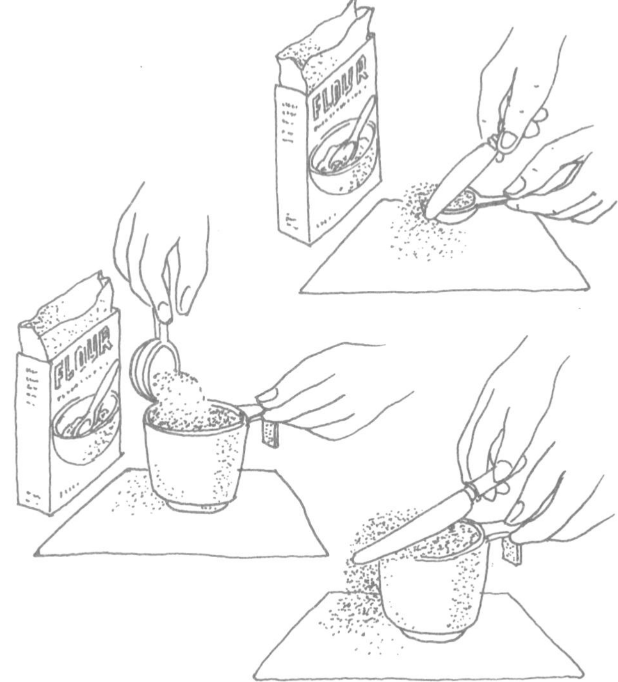

Liquid ingredients

1 Use graduated measuring jug.
2 Pour into measure, place on level surface and check at eye-level.
3 For spoon measures, keep spoon steady and fill to the brim.

Conversion from Imperial to Metric measures*

Imperial	Metric	Imperial	Metric
1/2 oz	is replaced by 15 grams	4 oz	is replaced by 125 grams
1 oz	is replaced by 30 grams	8 oz	is replaced by 250 grams
2 oz	is replaced by 60 grams	12 oz	is replaced by 375 grams
3 oz	is replaced by 90 grams	16 oz	is replaced by 500 grams (0.5 kg)

* Use only with scales – these do not apply to cup measures.

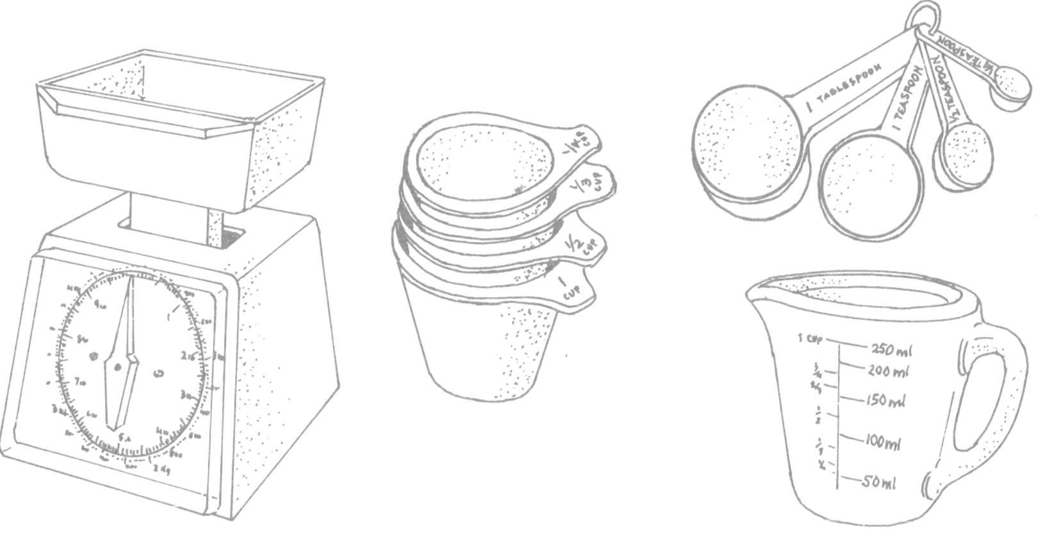

Food preparation processes

Aerate Incorporate air into a mixture.

Barbecue Cook food over open fire or other radiant heat or slowly on a revolving spit.

Bard Cover meat with pork fat.

Baste Spoon hot liquid over meat and vegetables while they are cooking.

Blanch Place food in boiling water, and bring quickly back to the boil, drain and plunge into ice-cold water to refresh and then drain.

Clarify Remove impurities from a food.

Concasse Peel, seed and dice tomato.

Deglaze Boil a small amount of wine or stock in the browned residue left after cooking in a frying or baking pan, to make a thin, tasty sauce.

Dice Cut food into small cubes.

Dredge Sprinkle food with a dry ingredient.

Flambé Cover food with alcoholic spirits and set alight briefly.

Garnish Decoration for food.

Glaze Brush liquid over pastry, scones, bread and buns to improve the appearance.

Lard Pull strips (called lardons) of pork through meat using a larding needle.

Parboil Partly cook food in boiling liquid.

Poach Cook in liquid just below boiling point.

Puree Mash, sieve or blend food in a food processor.

Reduce or reduction Concentrate a liquid by boiling and evaporating.

Refresh Place hot food in cold water to stop cooking process.

Render Melt scraps of fat.

Sauté Toss food gently with butter, margarine, dairy blend or oil and flavourings over heat.

Scald Heat liquid to boiling point, or to pour boiling liquid over food.

Scallop Arrange foods in layers in a casserole with sauce or liquid and then bake.

Score Cut narrow slits in the surface of food before cooking.

Sear Brown surface of meat quickly to coagulate the protein.

Segment Remove skin and pith from citrus fruits and cut out flesh between membranes.

Shred Cut into long narrow strips.

Sift Put dry ingredients through a strainer or sifter to remove lumps and to aerate them.

Simmer Bring a liquid to a temperature just below boiling point, approximately 85°C, and maintain that temperature for the period of cooking.

Snip Cut with scissors.

Steep Allow food to stand in liquid to extract the flavour.

Stir-fry Quickly fry pieces of food in a little oil, tossing over a high heat, usually in a wok.

Sterilise Heat in boiling water or steam to destroy living organisms.

Stew Simmer foods gently in sufficient liquid to cover.

Toss Mix ingredients lightly with a lifting motion.

Whip Beat food rapidly to incorporate air and increase volume.

Ovens and oven temperatures

There may be some variation in the accuracy of oven thermostats, as a precise adjustment is not always possible. An estimate must be made of the temperature variation, which is usually not more than 10°C.

To convert Fahrenheit to Celsius temperatures use a conversion chart or halve the cooking temperatures between 200°F and 450°F, e.g. 350°F is equivalent to 175°C.

Oven temperatures

Description	Thermostat Setting (°C)	Description	Thermostat Setting (°C)
Plate warming	60	Moderately hot	190
Cool	100–110	Hot	200
Slow	150–170	Very hot	220–240
Moderate	170–190		

Microwave cookery 

Microwave cooking is regulated by power, rather than by temperature. In this book there is a microwave symbol (shown above) at the beginning of recipes that are suitable for a microwave oven. The power required to cook the dish is also given, for example, 'microwave on high power for 3 minutes'.

Microwave radiation is a form of electromagnetic energy used to cook foods quickly in a microwave oven. Microwaves are reflected by some substances such as metal, pass through others such as glass, and are absorbed by liquid, and thus by foods containing liquid. Only when microwaves are absorbed does heating, and hence cooking, occur. Microwaves are colourless, odourless and tasteless. They do not affect the cell structure of food, or its appearance or taste any more than normal cooking.

Microwaves are generated when electrical energy passes through a vacuum tube device called a magnetron. Once converted, they form a random pattern within the oven cavity. Most ovens have a fan called a 'stirrer', which, being metal, reflects and distributes the microwaves throughout the oven cavity so that the food is hit by the microwaves from as many directions as possible to ensure even cooking. Some ovens have a turntable as well. Since metal reflects microwaves, it must not be used as a cooking vessel because it shields the food from the microwaves. This prevents cooking and creates the possibility of electric arcs that could damage the magnetron.

Microwaves pass through pottery, china, plastic, glass and paper, so these are ideal materials for containing the food that is to be cooked. Cooking occurs when the microwaves vibrate the water molecules in the food. The depth of penetration by the microwaves depends on the composition of the food, particularly the moisture content. Microwave ovens will not cook food that has a low moisture content. Since microwaves penetrate a short distance into the food before they are absorbed, the hottest part of the food is just below the surface. Thus the surface won't brown as it would in a conventional oven where maximum heat concentration is at the surface.

There are many variables in using microwaves, such as size and the thickness of the food portions, the size of the cooking dish, the arrangement of food on the dish. Allowance must be made for these.

Microwave cooking is particularly useful to people living alone, to busy people with little time to cook and to family members eating at different times. Microwave cooking is energy efficient.

Microwave safety guidelines and hints

- Never turn the oven on when it is empty.
- Do not interfere with the door or safety devices.
- Do not prop the door open.
- Do not clean with abrasive cleaners.
- Clean up any spilt food immediately, do not allow it to accumulate around the door. To assist in cleaning place a jug of water in the oven, heat, then wipe out oven.
- Use correct cookware, for example, ovenproof glass and ceramic dishes and microwave plastic ware.
- Most foods should be covered with plastic food wrap.
- Foods with high fat content can be placed on or covered with absorbent paper during cooking.
- Do not use metal dishes or dishes with metal trim or decoration as these cause arcing that may damage the magnetron.
- Do not secure plastic bags with ties that have metal in them.
- Aluminium foil reflects microwaves and so can be used to cover portions of food that cook more quickly, for example, the legs and wings of chicken. Do not cover more than one-third of the food with foil.
- Foods with casing or membrane around them should be pierced before heating to prevent them exploding in the oven, for example, egg yolks, brains and sausages.
- Whole eggs in the shells should not be cooked as they will explode.
- To convert conventional recipes reduce the cooking time, for example, a meat loaf that normally takes $1^1/_2$ hours to cook, takes only 30 minutes to cook in the microwave oven.
- Fillings in sausage rolls and other pastry foods become very hot, while the pastry, because of its lower water content does not become hot. Care must be taken when eating these hot foods.
- Extra colouring may be obtained from brown sugar, dark-coloured sauces or Parisian essence.

- Casseroles, which usually require long slow cooking, should have the liquid reduced by one-third as there is less evaporation.
- When cooking vegetables little or no salt is required as far less water is used.
- As food is cooked by power it is necessary to increase time with increased quantity, for example, 1 potato cooks in 3 minutes, 2 potatoes take 5 minutes, 3 potatoes take 7 minutes. There comes a point when cooking in a microwave oven is no longer faster.
- When food is removed from the microwave oven penetration of heat continues so food should be allowed to stand for approximately half cooking time – this is called 'standing time'.

Microwave cooking is very good for

- cooking fish, fruit and vegetables as they have a high water content
- defrosting and reheating food
- heating liquids such as soup and drinks
- making sauce in small quantities
- drying herbs, as the green colour is retained.

Microwave cooking is not good for

- browning and crisping food
- cooking cakes, as there is no colour change
- cooking pastry, as it will not crisp
- cooking foods with low water content

Planning and eating

Meal times are not only of value in satisfying hunger and supplying nutrients to the body, they also provide an opportunity for the members of the family group or household to spend time together. The ability to plan appetising and nutritious meals for the family and household is an important skill. As everyone has individual preferences and nutritional requirements, it is important that all members are involved in the planning of meals. As the time for meal preparation is often limited, it is frequently a cooperative venture with all members of the household assisting in some way.

When planning the menu, ensure that a variety of different foods are selected. Vary the tastes, textures and colours of the foods within a meal. Other factors to consider are individual preferences and nutritional requirements (see **Chapter 1 Nutrition**) and the household budget.

Breakfast or first meal of the day

An important although often overlooked meal of the day, breakfast not only 'breaks the fast' since the last meal, it also provides important energy and nutrients for a productive morning's work and play.

Breakfast should be easily and quickly prepared. The types of foods eaten at breakfast vary according to the season of the year and the amount of time available. See **Chapter 4 Savouries, starters, snacks and breakfast dishes** for some breakfast ideas.

Lunch

Lunch is often a light meal eaten in the middle of the day. Sandwiches or bread rolls with fillings are easy to prepare and pack and can provide variety (see p. 99). Homemade lunches and snacks are economical and have the advantage of giving us more control over the foods we choose to eat.

Plan lunch, keeping in mind the Dietary Guidelines, using a variety of fruits and vegetables (e.g. carrot and celery sticks, lettuce, tomato, fresh and dried fruits) and bread and cereals (e.g. rye bread, pocket bread, rice, crackers, noodles). A protein food should be included such as sliced meat, boiled egg, cheese, nuts, sardines or tuna.

Between-meal snacks that can be prepared in advance include simple packages of mixed dried fruits and nuts, fresh fruit, boiled eggs, popcorn, cheese sticks or wedges, celery sticks filled with ricotta cheese or peanut butter and wholemeal cakes and biscuits.

For dishes suitable for snacks and light lunches see **Chapter 4 Savouries, starters, snacks and breakfast dishes**.

Dinner

In many households, dinner is considered to be the main meal of the day. More time is taken with its planning, preparation and serving. The dishes served vary with the season of the year and the activities of the family. The other foods eaten during the day must be considered when planning dinner.

For many years the meal pattern in Australia included a main course of meat, fish or poultry served with accompanying vegetables followed by a dessert. This is becoming more flexible as the structure of both individual families and society change. Our expanding multicultural population has increased the range of foods available to us and broadened our concept of 'dinner'.

More people are consuming vegetable-based dishes as an alternative to the meat component of some or all of their meals. For vegetable-based dishes see **Chapter 5 Vegetarian dishes**.

Table preparation

The table or eating area should be prepared according to the type of meal being served and the occasion. For example, some meals may be suited to using glassware, tablecloth and china, while casual outdoor barbecues or family meals may be more practical and enjoyable using more durable tableware. Colour contrast and effects may be provided by decorations such as flowers and fruit.

Table setting

- A cloth or heat resistant mats may be used to protect the table surface.
- The cutlery is arranged in the order in which the pieces are to be used, commencing from the outside.
- Any table decoration such as fruit, candles, berries, nuts or flowers can be chosen to complement or accentuate the colour scheme. The arrangement should not obscure the view across the table.

Place setting for dinner

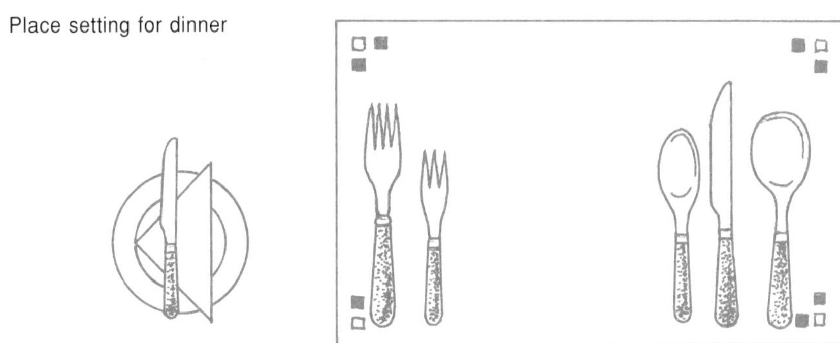

Table manners

Every family or household has its own expectations of 'good' manners. There is a great variety and contrast in what is considered correct in different families, depending on cultural background and individual family lifestyle. It is important to be aware of other peoples expectations, especially when eating out or in someone else's home.

A basic guide is to use cutlery or utensils according to the occasion. For example, a knife and fork at a formal dinner, chopsticks and a finger bowl at an Asian meal, a fork only for a buffet meal or party food, or fingers and a serviette at a casual barbecue.

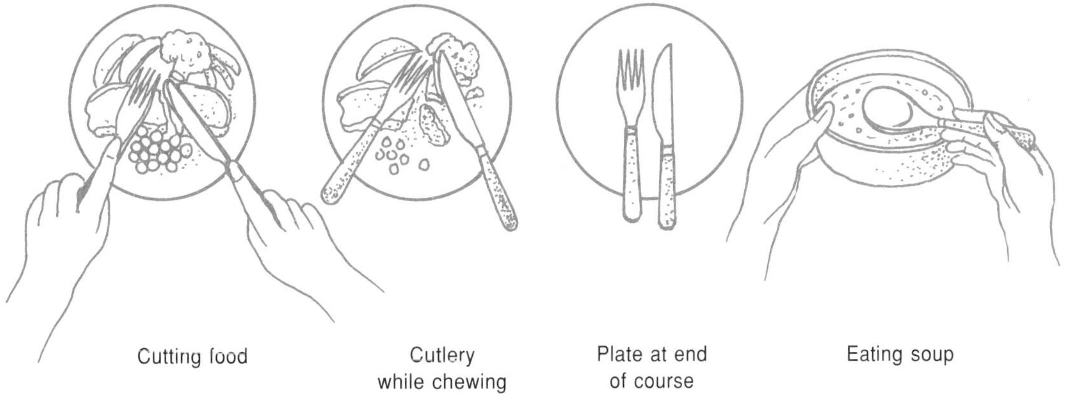

Cutting food — Cutlery while chewing — Plate at end of course — Eating soup

Entertaining

When preparing to entertain, time and thought must be given to planning the menu. Take into account the food preferences of the guests, the budget, experience in cooking, and the space and equipment available for cooking and serving.

Flavours and textures should be well combined, avoiding repetition of similar ingredients and flavours throughout the meal.

Invitations should inform the guests of the place, the occasion, the time and possible duration of the visit, thus indicating suitable attire. This information may be conveyed in a manner to suit the occasion: by telephone call, in a friendly note or in a formal invitation. The reply is given in the same manner as the invitation. After the visit, a note or a phone call to express the guest's thanks is a gesture the host will appreciate.

Much of today's entertaining is informal. Barbecues and buffet meals make fewer demands on the host than does a formal meal.

The 'buffet' meal or smorgasbord at which guests serve themselves is popular. Here, ease of eating and serving is an important factor. All items required for a particular course should be readily accessible and placed in the order in which they will be required, with cutlery and serviettes grouped near serving plates.

Orderly groupings of tableware contribute much to the finished effect. In selecting the menu, the dishes chosen should be such that they may be easily served and eaten with a fork when the diner is standing.

Catering for large groups

Preparing and serving foods for larger groups requires careful planning well in advance of the function. The caterer needs to prepare:

- a checklist of the necessary food and equipment
- a plan of action for preparation prior to the function
- an action sheet, with times, for the duration of the function.

Points to be checked include:

- the number of guests and age group. Older people will tend to eat less than teenagers.
- the budget allocation for the function, including food and drink, staff, equipment hire, decorations, entertainment and incidentals.
- the type of function. Is the food served to be finger foods, drinks and savouries or a substantial meal?
- pre-dinner arrangements. Are drinks and savouries to be served prior to dinner?
- the soft drink and alcoholic drink requirements. Is the caterer to provide the drinks?
- food and drink service. Will the guests be seated and served at tables, or will the guests serve themselves from a buffet and then sit at tables or stand up to eat?
- the theme of the occasion. Is it an event with specific food requirements, such as a cake that is to be served as the dessert? Will the caterer be required to organise entertainment, sound or other electronic systems. Is a special decor or colour scheme required?

- food preparation facilities. Are extra refrigeration, cooking and food-warming facilities required?
- availability of equipment. Will tables and table linen, chairs, china, cutlery, glassware and serving equipment need to be hired?
- dietary restrictions. Are there any guests with vegetarian, religious or other specific dietary needs?

Hints for catering

- Choose a menu with variety in colour, texture and taste of foods. Have some hot dishes and some cold to assist in effective use of equipment and last-minute preparation and service.
- Select dishes familiar to the cook that allow safe advance preparation. The larger the number of people, the more preparation should be carried out in advance.
- Keep foods refrigerated or frozen at all times when prepared in advance.
- Choose a colour scheme that can be co-ordinated through table linen, flowers and other decorations.
- **Develop an action plan** that lists all purchase requirements, gives details of the foods that can be prepared in advance and frozen or refrigerated, provides for setting the tables and preparing any flowers or other decorations and notes last-minute preparations in detail.
- Make a checklist of the equipment to be used by the guests, e.g. tables, chairs, tablecloths, serviettes, condiments, glasses, plates for each course, bread and butter plates, cups and saucers, serving bowls and dishes, knives, forks, spoons, sugar bowls, milk jugs, butter dishes, wine and water carafes, decorations.
- Prepare a list of foods and garnishes needed for each course and extras such as salt, pepper, bread or bread rolls and butter, tea, coffee, sugar, milk, wines, soft drinks and other beverages.
- Consider preparation and serving staff requirements, particularly for table service.
- If serving several courses at the tables, have at least one course with very little last-minute preparation, e.g. make the first course cold and in place prior to the guests coming to the table. This gives extra time for serving a hot main course.
- A buffet presentation, where guests serve themselves, reduces the workload. Ensure that hot dishes are very hot and cold dishes very cold. Set up the buffet so that guests pick up a plate first, then move along the table to serve from the serving dishes, picking up cutlery and serviettes at the end. If guests are then to sit at tables, the cutlery, serviettes and condiments can be set at the tables. Drinks and glasses can be on a separate serving table, placed on each table or served at the table.
- Provide iced water, with glasses, at each table or readily available.
- Employing a person to wash the dishes as the function is in progress will make the cleaning-up process considerably easier at the end, and will assist with order and space while food is being served.
- If tea and coffee are to be served, ensure that the preparation starts prior to the end of the meal, so that they are ready to serve soon after the last course is finished. Sugar and milk may be placed on the tables so that guests can serve themselves.

Quantities for catering

Savouries Allow 4 to 6 items per person if being served with drinks before dinner. For a finger food function of 1 1/2 to 2 hours, allow 10 to 12 items per person.

Soup Allow 200 mL per person.

Meat Allow 100–125 g per person uncooked or 75–100 g per person if cooked.

Poultry Allow 250 g per person if it contains bones. A number 12 chicken serves 4 people. A number 15 chicken serves 6 people. If there are no bones, 125 g per person is sufficient.

Fish Allow 150 g if whole, 125 g if cutlet with bone, or 100 g if boned fillet.

Casseroles Allow 200 mL per person if vegetables are also being served; 300–400 mL if casserole includes some vegetables, and potatoes, rice or other cereal are also being served; and 400–450 mL if all vegetables are included in the casserole dish.

Salads Allow 75–100 g per person of each salad, up to a total of 300 g if served with meat, fish or similar. 1 lettuce serves 10 people.

Vegetables Allow 75–100 g per person of each vegetable, up to a total of 300 g if the course is served with meat, fish or similar.

Sandwiches A 900 g sandwich loaf has approximately 28 slices of bread, making 56 points or triangles when made into sandwiches. Allow 200–250 g butter, margarine or dairy blend per loaf. Allow 40–50 g filling per 2 slices of bread (approximately 500 g per loaf), depending on type of filling.

Cakes A 24 cm deep springform pan provides 18 to 24 serves. See p. 374–375 for other sizes of pans.

Desserts Allow 175–200 g per person, depending on the richness and amount of garnish.

Fruit desserts Allow approximately 125 g prepared fruit per person and 20–30 mL cream.

Drinks When serving food with drinks, allow 2–3 drinks for a function lasting 1 hour, 3–4 drinks for 2 hours and 4–5 drinks for 3 hours. A 750 mL bottle of wine serves 5 to 6 drinks.

Tea Allow 3 g tea and 200 mL boiling water per person.

Coffee Allow 1.25 g instant coffee or 5 g coffee grounds and 200 mL water per person.

4 Savouries, starters, snacks and breakfast dishes

Savouries or hors d'oeuvres may be served prior to dinner, often with pre-dinner drinks, at parties or other social occasions. They should be small and easily eaten in the fingers such as **Cream cheese and olive savouries** or **Vietnamese spring rolls**.

Starters or appetisers are often served as the first course of a meal to stimulate the appetite. They are usually small serves of tasty food such as an **Avocado appetiser, Seafood cocktail** or **Minted pineapple**.

As our way of life in Australia becomes more informal we are tending to eat more between-meal snacks. These are often finger foods, that is, food that can be eaten without cutlery, and food that is quick to prepare, such as **Salad-filled pocket bread** or a **Ham and cheese croissant**.

Breakfast is an important meal as an 'energy starter' for the day. Breakfast dishes could include **Fruity porridge** or **French toast**.

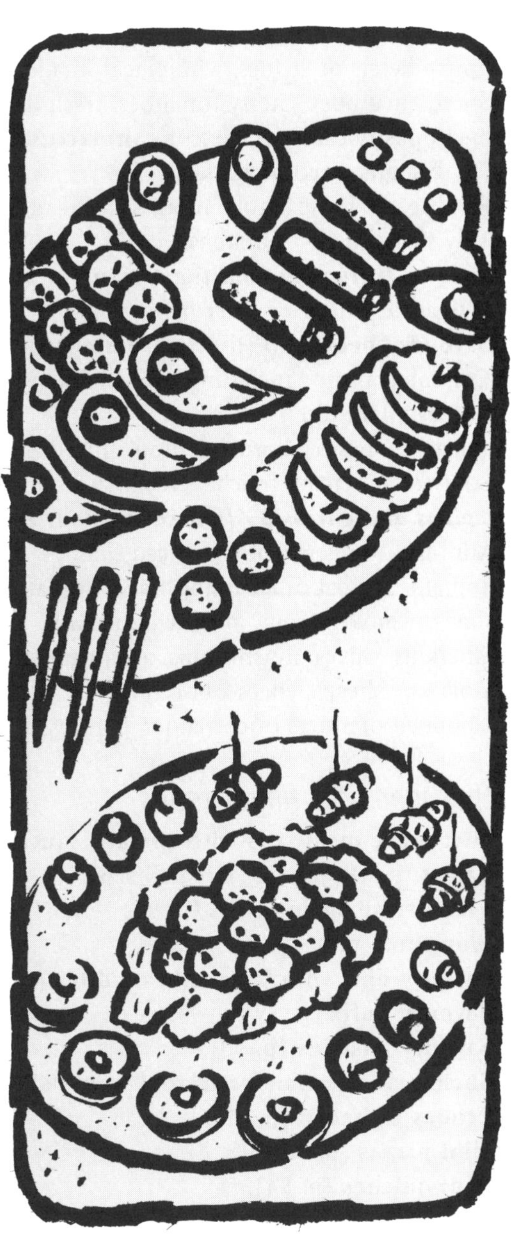

Savouries or hors d'oeuvres

Savouries or hors d'oeuvres are small tasty foods that can be picked up and eaten using the fingers. They may be served cold or hot, and are often set out on a platter in a colourful display.

Suggestions for savouries and hors d'oeuvres

Base (to hold the filling)

- Bread (fresh or toasted), for example, white, brown, pumpernickel, rye, herb.
- French bread stick, sliced.
- Tiny pikelets or scones, wholemeal, made with sour cream or fresh herbs.
- Sliced cucumber, cherry tomatoes, fresh dates, 4 cm-length celery sticks.
- Small pastry cases, made from **Shortcrust pastry** (p. 346) or **Cheese pastry** (p. 348).
- Dry biscuits or corn chips.
- Flat breads, for example, mountain bread, lavash, **Pocket bread** (p. 442), pita bread.
- Tiny steamed new potatoes.

Spread or filling (to hold the topping in place and add flavour)

- Margarine, butter or dairy blend.
- **Savoury cheese dip** (p. 85), **Hommus** (p. 87).
- Commercial dips including sun-dried tomato dip, sun-dried capsicum dip, smoked salmon dip, eggplant dip.
- Tapenade, pesto, skordalia, aioli, spiced plum sauce.
- Sour cream, crème fraiche, cream cheese, natural yoghurt, mayonnaise, mascarpone.

Toppings and garnishes (for extra colour and flavour)

- Mini-meatburgers, cooked sliced sausage, ham, fried crispy bacon pieces.
- Tomato, apricot or cucumber salsa, tomato or mango chutney.
- Caviar, smoked trout, anchovies, prawns, crabmeat, rollmops, canned mussels.
- Gherkins, olives, mushrooms, asparagus, finely sliced coleslaw, chopped chives.
- Goat's or sheep's cheese, bocconcini.
- Chopped or sprigs of coriander, parsley, dill, basil.

Other ideas for finger foods

- **Microwave meatballs with tomato sauce** (p. 184).
- **Satays** (p. 180), made in small size.
- **Vietnamese spring rolls** (p. 92).
- **Won tons** (p. 93).
- **Savoury dips** with **Vegetable crudités** (p. 87).
- **Savoury puffs** (p. 89).
- **Savoury pastries** (p. 90).
- **Shrimp and coriander triangles** (p. 91).
- **Prunes in bacon** (p. 93).
- **Mini pizzas** (p. 91).
- **Mini quiches** (p. 84).
- **Nachos** (p. 88).

CREAM CHEESE AND OLIVE SAVOURIES

A basic recipe for a finger food, served cold, using tasty toppings on a variety of bases. See p. 82 for further suggestions

Number: ***16 (allow 4 per person)***

Ingredients

16 crisp, dry biscuits *or* rounds of rye bread (approx. 4 cm diameter)

Spread

4 tablespoons (80 g) cream cheese
2 black olives, chopped

Garnish

16 black olive slices

Method

1. Mix cream cheese and chopped black olives.
2. Spread on each round of base.
3. Garnish with olive slices.

✦ SPICY TUNA AND CREAM CHEESE SAVOURIES ✦

Follow method for **Cream cheese and olive savouries**, using a base of 16 x 4 cm rounds of pumpernickel bread, a spread made from 100 g drained canned tuna, 1 tablespoon (20 g) tomato pesto, 1 teaspoon sweet chilli sauce and 2 chopped black olives, and garnish with black olive slices.

✦ SMOKED SALMON AND MASCARPONE ON WHOLEMEAL PIKELETS ✦

Follow method for **Cream cheese and olive savouries**, using a base of 16 tiny **Pikelets** (p. 370) made with wholemeal flour, 100 mL mascarpone mixed with 1 teaspoon of capers as the spread and smoked salmon slices as the topping, and garnish with sprigs of dill.

✦ OYSTER CANAPÉS WITH LIME MAYONNAISE ✦

Follow method for **Spicy tuna and cream cheese savouries**, using 16 x 4 cm rounds of fresh wholemeal bread as the base, 100 mL mayonnaise mixed with 1 teaspoon lime juice as the spread and fresh or smoked oysters as the topping, and garnish with tiny slices of lime.

✦ SARDINES AND SUN-DRIED TOMATO ON CHEESY FINGERS ✦

Follow method for **Cream cheese and olive savouries**, using 2 x 4 cm fingers of crisp-cooked **Cheese pastry** (p. 348) as the base, 5 tablespoons (100 g) tomato pesto as the spread and canned or cooked fresh sardines as the topping, and garnish with dried tomato pieces.

PÂTÉ AND MOUNTAIN BREAD PINWHEELS

Mountain bread is a thin flat bread that can be used as a base for a range of dips and fillings.

Number: **16**

Ingredients

1 sheet mountain bread
150 g pâté

Method

1. Spread pâté on mountain bread.
2. Roll up and cut into 1 cm slices.

AVOCADO PINWHEELS

Follow recipe for **Pâté and mountain bread pinwheels**. Use 4 slices fresh bread instead of mountain bread. Spread with 1 mashed avocado with black pepper and salt *or* with 250 g or 1 quantity **Guacamole** (p. 88). Roll up in plastic wrap and refrigerate for one hour prior to slicing into rounds.

MINI QUICHES

Number: **16**
Cooking utensil: patty pan tray
Preparation time: ***20 minutes***
Cooking time: ***35 minutes***
Oven temperature: ***190°C reduced to 180°C***

Ingredients

500 g (1 quantity) **Shortcrust pastry** (p. 346)
Filling
2 eggs, beaten
1 cup (250 mL) milk, warmed
1 rasher (80 g) bacon, finely chopped
2 spring onions, finely chopped

Method

1. Set oven to 190°C.
2. Roll out pastry to 5 mm thickness.
3. Using a 6 cm round cutter, cut 16 rounds and place in patty pans.
4. Cook at 190°C for 15 minutes.
5. Mix eggs, milk, bacon and spring onions. Pour some into each tart case.
6. Cook at 180°C for a further 20 minutes until mixture is just firm.

SALAMI AND TABOULI SAVOURY TARTLETS

Follow the method for **Mini quiches**. Omit filling ingredients. Cook patty pans for 20 minutes, cool and then fill with 1 cup (100 g) or 1/4 quantity **Tabouli** (p. 275) mixed with 50 g finely diced salami.

SAVOURY CHEESE DIP

Serves: 6

Ingredients

125 g cream cheese *or* ricotta cheese
$^1/_4$ cup (65 mL) mayonnaise *or* sour cream
2 teaspoons (10 mL) lemon juice
1 tablespoon chopped chives

Method

1 Mix all ingredients.
2 Can be stored in airtight container in refrigerator for 2–3 days.
3 Serve on platter with dry biscuits *or* **Vegetable crudités** (p. 87).

AVOCADO AND CHILLI DIP

Follow recipe for **Savoury cheese dip**. Add 1 mashed avocado, 1 teaspoon sweet chilli sauce, 20 g chopped dried tomato, 20 g chopped dried capsicum and 1 chopped spring onion.

SALMON AND SPRING ONION DIP

Follow recipe for **Savoury cheese dip**. Add 105 g can drained salmon and 1 sliced spring onion.

OYSTER DIP

Follow recipe for **Savoury cheese dip**, using mayonnaise. Add 100 g can drained and chopped smoked oysters and the juice of 1 lemon.

FRENCH ONION DIP

Follow recipe for **Savoury cheese dip**. Add 1 packet French onion soup mix mixed with $^1/_4$ cup (65 mL) milk.

SMOKED SALMON DIP

Follow recipe for **Savoury cheese dip**, using mayonnaise. Add 100 g chopped smoked salmon and the juice of 1 lemon.

ANTIPASTO

Originating in Italy as a dish served 'before the pasta', antipasto is a selection of savoury foods served at the beginning of a meal.

► *Serves:* 4

Ingredients

Choose 6–8 portions of food for each person from the following:

Oven-dried tomatoes (p. 488)
Oven-dried capsicums (p. 488)
sliced salami or cooked sausage
smoked, soused or pickled fish, shellfish or molluscs
gherkins, olives, pickled mushrooms, cauliflower, carrot, eggplant, grilled artichoke hearts
cheese, e.g. bocconcini

Method

1 Arrange on platter or individual plates.
2 Serve with crusty bread, foccacia or ciabatta.

APRICOT BITES

► *Number:* 16

Ingredients

16 dried apricot halves
80 g cream cheese
2 tablespoons (40 g) chopped crystallised ginger
16 pecan halves

Method

1 Mix cream cheese and ginger.
2 Fill dried apricots with mixture.
3 Top with pecan half.

BABY POTATOES WITH CRISPY BACON SAVOURIES

► *Number:* 16
► *Cooking utensil:* steamer

Preparation time: **15 minutes**
Cooking time: **15 minutes**

Ingredients

16 tiny new potatoes
Filling
4 tablespoons (80 mL) sour cream
2 tablespoons snipped chives
1 rasher (80 g) bacon, chopped and fried

Method

1 Steam potatoes until soft – about 15 minutes.
2 Cut cross in top, squeeze to open.
3 Mix sour cream and chives. Place in potatoes.
4 Garnish with bacon.

VEGETABLE CRUDITÉS

Serves: 8–10

Cooking utensil: large saucepan

Ingredients

2 carrots (250 g)
1 stalk (100 g) celery
1/2 red capsicum (75 g)
1/2 green capsicum (75 g)
1 zucchini (100 g)
100 g cauliflower florets
100 g broccoli florets
100 g button mushrooms
1 quantity **Savoury cheese dip** (p. 85)

Method

1. Cut carrot, celery, capsicum and zucchini into sticks approximately 1 cm x 1 cm x 8 cm.
2. Plunge vegetables (except mushrooms and celery) into boiling water for 20 seconds, drain and plunge into iced water. Drain.
3. Arrange vegetables on serving platter with **Savoury cheese dip**.

CUCUMBER AND YOGHURT DIP

Serves: 4

Ingredients

1 cucumber (125 g)
1 cup (250 g) natural yoghurt
1 clove (5 g) garlic, crushed
1 tablespoon chopped fresh mint
3 shakes pepper

Method

1. Wash and grate cucumber, place in sieve and press gently to remove excess moisture.
2. Mix all ingredients.
3. Place in bowl and serve with dry biscuits, crusty bread or other base, or with **Vegetable Crudités**.

HOMMUS

Serves: 6

Ingredients

1 cup (250 g) cooked chickpeas (p. 113)
  or 310 g can chickpeas
1/2 cup (125 g) tahini
3 shakes pepper
1 teaspoon olive oil
2 cloves (10 g) garlic, crushed
1/4 cup (65 mL) lemon juice

Method

1. Drain and rinse chickpeas.
2. Puree chickpeas in blender.
3. Add tahini, pepper, oil, garlic and lemon juice. Blend until smooth.
4. Serve with flat bread, fresh bread, **Vegetable crudités** or as a spread in sandwiches.

NACHOS

A popular Mexican dish that can be made hotter by increasing the amount of chilli used.

- *Serves:* 4
- *Cooking utensil:* saucepan, ovenproof dish
- *Preparation time:* **20 minutes**
- *Cooking time:* **20 minutes**
- *Oven temperature:* **180°C**

Ingredients

4 tomatoes (600 g), peeled and diced
440 g can red kidney beans, drained and rinsed
1 clove (5 g) garlic, crushed
1/2 small red chilli, finely chopped
2 spring onions, finely chopped
1 cup (250 g) **Guacamole** (see below)
250 g corn chips
1 cup (150 g) grated tasty cheese
1/2 cup (125 mL) sour cream

Method

1 Set oven to 180°C. Brush or spray ovenproof dish with oil.
2 In saucepan, cook tomato, kidney beans, garlic, chilli and spring onions for 10 minutes.
3 Place in ovenproof dish. Cover with corn chips and grated cheese.
4 Cook at 180°C for 10 minutes.
5 Spread **Guacamole** over top, swirl sour cream across top and serve.

GUACAMOLE

This can be served as a dip with fresh bread, corn chips or flat bread.

- *Serves:* 4

Ingredients

1 avocado, lightly mashed
1 spring onion, finely chopped
1/2 tomato (75 g), finely diced
1 tablespoon (20 mL) lemon juice
1 tablespoon (20 mL) sweet chilli sauce *or* 1 small chilli, finely chopped

Method

1 Mix all ingredients. Texture should be coarse and chunky.

SWEET CORN AND CAPSICUM SAVOURY PUFFS

This is a basic recipe for hot savoury puffs, filled with savoury foods mixed with a tasty white sauce. The fillings used in the pastry recipes following can also be used for the puffs. The cases may be purchased ready-made.

- *Number:* 24
- *Cooking utensil:* saucepan, oven tray
- *Heating time:* **5 minutes**
- *Oven temperature:* **150°C**

Ingredients

24 small **Choux pastry puffs** (p. 353)

Filling

1 tablespoon (20 g) butter

$1\frac{1}{2}$ tablespoons (15 g) plain flour

$\frac{1}{2}$ cup (125 mL) milk

1 cup (250 g) sweet corn kernels

$\frac{1}{2}$ green capsicum (65 g), finely chopped

Method

1. Make filling in saucepan: melt butter, add flour, cook 1 minute. Add milk slowly while stirring. Cook 1 minute.
2. Add sweet corn and capsicum and adjust flavour. Keep hot.
3. Cut tops off puffs and spoon in filling. Replace tops.
4. Place on oven tray and reheat at 150°C for 5 minutes.

✦ SALMON AND DILL SAVOURY PUFFS ✦

Follow recipe for **Sweet corn and capsicum savoury puffs**, replacing corn and capsicum with 250 g (1 cup) chopped cooked fresh, smoked or canned salmon, $\frac{1}{4}$ cup chopped dill and 2 tablespoons (40 mL) lemon juice. Garnish with dill sprigs.

✦ PRAWNS AND CHAMPIGNON SAVOURY PUFFS ✦

Follow recipe for **Sweet corn and capsicum savoury puffs**, replacing corn and capsicum with 250 g (1 cup) chopped cooked fresh or canned prawns, 50 g sliced champignons and 1 teaspoon (5 mL) fish sauce. Garnish with small pieces of lime.

CHICKEN AND CORIANDER SAVOURY PASTRIES

This is a basic recipe for hot savoury pastries and the fillings can be used in either the puffs or the pastries. The pastry cases may be bought, made from ready-made pastry, or prepared using the **Rough puff pastry** (p. 350) or **Puff pastry** (p. 350) recipes in **Chapter 13 Pastry**.

- *Number: 24*
- *Cooking utensil:* oven trays, saucepan
- *Cooking time: **15 minutes***
- *Oven temperature: 220°C*

Ingredients

500 g (1 quantity) **Rough puff pastry** (p. 350)
1 teaspoon (5 mL) milk
Filling
1 tablespoon (20 g) butter
1 1/2 tablespoons (15 g) plain flour
1/2 cup (125 mL) milk
1 cup (250 g) chopped cooked chicken
1/2 bunch coriander, chopped (save several sprigs for garnishing)

Method

1. Set oven at 220°C.
2. Roll pastry to 5 mm thickness and cut out 48 rounds 4 cm across.
3. Using 1 cm cutter, cut the centre out of 24 of these.
4. Place the 24 whole rounds (bases) on an oven tray and brush the tops lightly with water.
5. Place the 24 rings (sides) on the moistened pastry bases. Glaze with milk.
6. Place the 1 cm rounds (tops) on another tray. Glaze with milk.
7. Bake the pastries at 220°C near the top of the oven for 15 minutes. Cook the tops on the shelf beneath. Remove when golden brown.
8. Make filling in saucepan: melt butter, add flour, cook 1 minute. Add milk slowly while stirring. Cook 1 minute. Add chicken and coriander and adjust flavour. Keep hot.
9. Place filling in pastries. Place tops on and reheat at 150°C for 5 minutes.
10. Serve, garnished with coriander.

✦ ASPARAGUS BALSAMIC SAVOURY PASTRIES ✦

Follow recipe for **Chicken and coriander savoury pastries**, replacing chicken and coriander with 250 g (1 cup) chopped cooked or canned asparagus (retain 24 tiny pieces from tips for garnish) and 1 teaspoon (5 mL) balsamic vinegar. Garnish with asparagus tips.

SHRIMP AND CORIANDER TRIANGLES

- *Number:* **24**
- *Cooking utensil:* griller

Cooking time: **3–4 minutes**

Ingredients

6 slices toasted bread

Topping

300 g shrimps, shelled
2 tablespoons snipped chives
2 teaspoons crushed lemon grass
1 tablespoon chopped coriander
2 teaspoons (10 mL) fish sauce
2 teaspoons (10 mL) sweet chilli sauce
1 teaspoon (5 mL) lime *or* lemon juice
4 coriander sprigs for garnish

Method

1. Combine topping ingredients in food processor.
2. Remove crusts from toast.
3. Spread shrimp mixture on toast. Cut each slice into 4 triangles.
4. Place under griller, grill until brown.
5. Garnish with coriander sprigs and serve.

MINI PIZZAS

This recipe uses basic scone dough as the base for a tasty pizza topping.

- *Number:* **30–35**
- *Cooking utensil:* oven tray

Cooking time: **7–10 minutes**

- *Oven temperature:* **180°C**

Ingredients

1 tablespoon (20 g) butter, margarine *or* dairy blend
2 cups (300 g) self-raising flour
1/4 teaspoon salt
1 cup (250 mL) milk

Topping

1/2 cup (125 g) tomato paste *or* tapenade
2 cups (500 g) chopped savoury food, e.g. a selection from mushrooms, capsicum, pineapple, ham, salami, tomato, olives, anchovies and prawns
1 cup (120 g) grated cheese

Method

1. Set oven at 180°C. Brush or spray oven tray with oil.
2. Rub butter into flour and salt, using the fingertips.
3. Mix into a soft dough with the milk. Add more milk if required.
4. Turn on to a lightly floured board and knead until smooth.
5. Roll out 5 mm thick and cut into 6 cm rounds.
6. Spread each round thinly with tomato paste or tapenade.
7. Place savoury food on top and sprinkle with grated cheese.
8. Cook at 180°C for 7–10 minutes.

VIETNAMESE SPRING ROLLS

Number: 24

Cooking utensil: small frying pan

Ingredients

24 small round or square rice paper won ton wrappers

Filling

250 g pork mince
6 dried Chinese mushrooms, soaked, drained and chopped
50 g cellophane noodles, soaked, drained and chopped
1/4 cup chopped hot Vietnamese mint
1 carrot (125 g), grated
2 tablespoons (40 mL) sweet chilli sauce
2 spring onions, sliced
1 tablespoon (20 mL) fish sauce
1 cup (250 mL) vegetable oil

Dipping sauce

1 teaspoon (5 mL) fish sauce
1 teaspoon (5 mL) lemon juice
1 clove (5 g) garlic, crushed
1 red chilli, finely chopped

Method

1 Mix filling ingredients. Place 1 teaspoon filling in centre of rice paper.
2 Roll up, folding in the sides to make a parcel, moisten edges to hold. Repeat with remaining filling and rice papers.
3 Heat vegetable oil in frying pan, fry spring rolls for 8–10 minutes. Turn several times. Drain.
4 Mix dipping sauce ingredients and serve in separate bowl.

STEAMED VIETNAMESE SPRING ROLLS

Follow recipe for **Vietnamese spring rolls**, steaming for 25–30 minutes instead of frying. Serve with dipping sauce.

✦ WON TONS ✦

Follow recipe for **Vietnamese spring rolls**, replacing 125 g pork mince with 125 g chopped prawns. Place 1 teaspoon filling in centre of rice paper. Moisten rice paper near edge and gather over filling to centre, twist to seal. Fry 8–10 minutes or steam 25–30 minutes. Serve with dipping sauce.

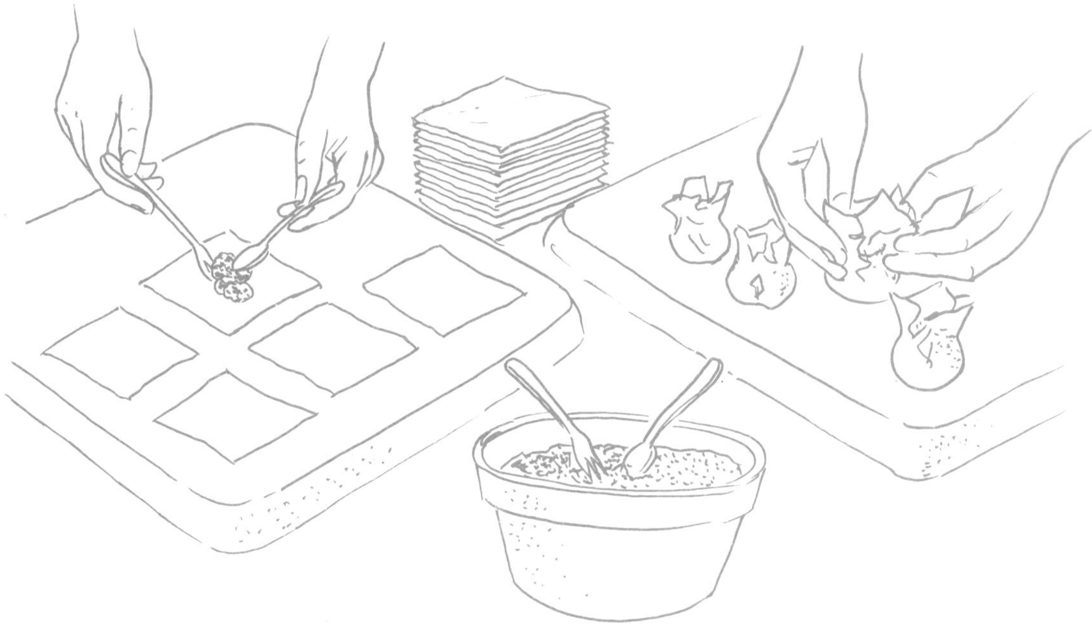

PRUNES IN BACON

- *Number:* ***36***
- *Cooking utensil:* 4-sided oven tray
- *Cooking time:* ***15 minutes***
- *Oven temperature:* ***180°C***

Ingredients

2 tablespoons (30 g) rice
2 tablespoons (40 g) chutney
3 shakes pepper
250 g pitted prunes
6 rashers (250 g) lean bacon
36 toothpicks
4 parsley sprigs

Method

1. Cook rice in boiling water 12 minutes. Strain and rinse.
2. Set oven at 180°C.
3. Mix rice, chutney and pepper. Place $^1/_2$ teaspoonfuls into the centre cavity of each prune.
4. Cut bacon into 3 cm x 8 cm strips and wrap one around each prune. Secure with a toothpick.
5. Bake at 180°C for 15 minutes.
6. Serve, garnished with parsley.

Starters and appetisers

Starters and appetisers are served as the first course in a formal dinner. They are usually light in texture and not too filling.

Suggestions for starters and appetisers

Chicken liver pâté (p. 96) on lettuce, served with rye bread.
Fresh, cooked asparagus (p. 231) on mesclun with **Mayonnaise** (p. 266).
Eggs mayonnaise (see below).
Curried eggs mayonnaise (see below).
Seafood cocktail (see opposite).
Oysters in the shell (p. 95).
Avocado appetiser (p. 96).
Avocado seafood (p. 96).
Salmon mousse (p. 97).
Grilled grapefruit (p. 97).
Mildura appetiser (p. 98).

EGGS MAYONNAISE

Serves: 8

Ingredients

4 eggs, hardboiled
2 tablespoons (40 mL) **Mayonnaise** (p. 266)
paprika in shaker
8 parsley sprigs

Method

1. Cut eggs in half lengthwise.
2. Remove yolks and press through coarse sieve over basin.
3. Mix yolks with mayonnaise.
4. Pipe or spoon mixture back into egg whites.
5. Decorate each with a shake of paprika.
6. Serve on platter, garnished with parsley.

CURRIED EGGS MAYONNAISE

Follow recipe for **Eggs mayonnaise**. Add 2 teaspoons curry powder *or* paste to egg yolk mixture.

SEAFOOD COCKTAIL

Serves: 4

Ingredients

500 g mixed seafood, e.g. crayfish, prawns, oysters, salmon
3 shakes pepper
2 tablespoons (40 mL) lemon juice
1/4 cup (65 mL) tomato sauce
1/4 cup (65 mL) cream
1 teaspoon (5 mL) Worcestershire sauce
1 teaspoon (5 mL) lemon juice
4 thin slices lemon

Method

1. Gently combine seafood, pepper and 2 tablespoons lemon juice. Chill for 30 minutes then place in 4 cocktail glasses or small dishes.
2. Mix tomato sauce, cream, Worcestershire sauce and 1 teaspoon lemon juice. Spoon over seafood.
3. Serve, garnished with lemon slices.

OYSTERS IN THE SHELL

Serves: 4

Ingredients

2 dozen oysters in shells
Sauce
1/4 cup (65 mL) tomato sauce
1/4 cup (65 mL) cream
1 teaspoon (5 mL) Worcestershire sauce
1 teaspoon (5 mL) lemon juice
4 cups crushed ice
4 lemon wedges
4 parsley sprigs
2 thin slices brown bread
2 teaspoons butter, margarine *or* dairy blend

Method

1. Keep oysters cool.
2. Mix sauce ingredients and chill for 1/2 hour.
3. Spread one cup of ice on each plate.
4. Place sauce in a tiny bowl (e.g. egg cup) in centre of each plate.
5. Arrange 6 oysters in their shells on the ice on each plate.
6. Spread bread with butter, sandwich together. Remove crusts from sandwiches and cut into quarters.
7. Garnish with lemon and parsley and serve with quartered sandwiches.

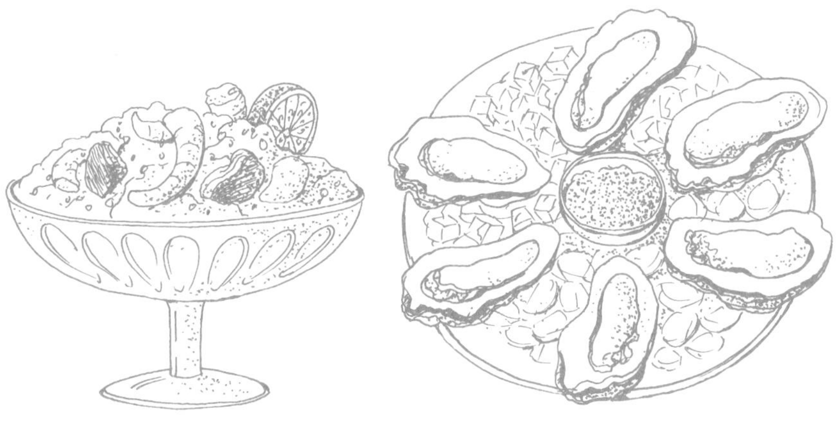

AVOCADO APPETISER

Serves: 4

Ingredients

2 avocados
2 teaspoons (10 mL) lemon juice
4 lettuce leaves
4 tablespoons (80 mL) **French dressing** (p. 266)

Method

1 Wash avocados, cut in half lengthwise and remove stone. Sprinkle with lemon juice.
2 Wash and dry lettuce leaves. Place on four plates.
3 Place avocados on lettuce and spoon over dressing.

AVOCADO SEAFOOD

Follow recipe for **Avocado appetiser**. Omit French dressing. Divide 250 g seafood between avocados and garnish each with 1 tablespoon (20 mL) **Mayonnaise** (p. 266) and 1 teaspoon caviar or small piece of seafood.

CHICKEN LIVER PÂTÉ

Serves: 4

Ingredients

250 g chicken liver
2 teaspoons (6 g) gelatine
1/2 cup (125 mL) water
1/2 teaspoon soy sauce
1/2 teaspoon Worcestershire sauce
1 onion (125 g), chopped
1 teaspoon (5 g) butter

Method

1 Place all ingredients in saucepan, bring to boil.
2 Simmer 7 minutes.
3 Mix thoroughly in blender.
4 Push through sieve.
5 Place in bowl or mould and refrigerate for 4 hours to set.
6 Serve with fingers of toast, dry biscuits or rye bread.

SALMON MOUSSE

Serve as an entree or lunch dish.

Serves: 4

Ingredients

1 tablespoon (12 g) gelatine
1/2 cup (125 mL) hot water
105 g can red salmon
1/2 cup (125 mL) sour cream
1 tablespoon (20 mL) lemon juice
2 spring onions, finely chopped
3 shakes pepper
6 lettuce leaves

Utensil: 4 x 1/2 cup moulds

Method

1. Dissolve gelatine in hot water.
2. Mix dissolved gelatine with salmon, sour cream, lemon juice, spring onions and pepper.
3. Pour into moulds, allow to set in refrigerator overnight.
4. Turn out onto lettuce leaves on plates.

GRILLED GRAPEFRUIT

Serves: 4

Ingredients

2 grapefruit
1 tablespoon (15 g) brown sugar
1/2 teaspoon mixed spice
2 glacé cherries

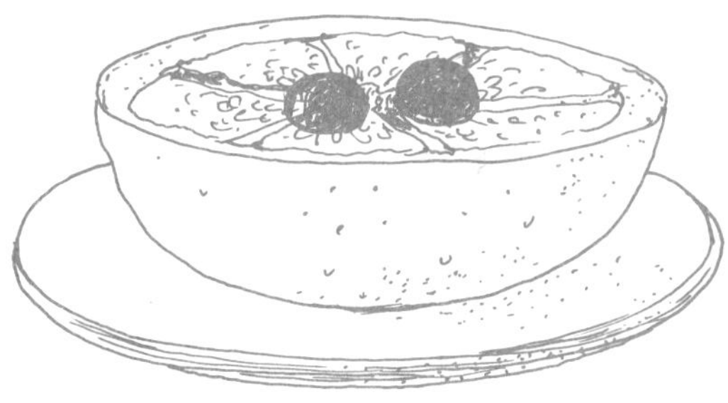

Method

1. Cut grapefruit in half. Discard centre core and pips.
2. Loosen pulp from pith and cut pulp into segments.
3. Spread top of each grapefruit with sugar and mixed spice.
4. Grill for 4 minutes or until lightly browned.
5. Garnish with half cherries.
6. Serve on small plates or dishes.

Microwave for 30 seconds on high power instead of grilling.

MINTED PINEAPPLE

Serves: 4

Ingredients

4 cups (600 g) prepared fresh pineapple, cut in 1 cm dice
1 tablespoon chopped fresh mint
2 glacé cherries
4 sprigs mint

Method

1. Mix pineapple and chopped mint. Chill for 30 minutes.
2. Serve in cocktail glasses or small dishes garnished with half cherries and mint sprigs.

MILDURA APPETISER

Serves: 2

Ingredients

1 orange
1 grapefruit
2 teaspoons (10 g) honey
1 glacé cherry

Method

1. Cut all peel and pith from orange and grapefruit.
2. Cut orange and grapefruit into segments, remove pips and membranes.
3. Place in small dishes, drizzle honey over fruit.
4. Serve garnished with half cherries.

Snacks

For many Australians, snacks form a substantial part of daily food intake, so it is important that snacks contribute to a well-balanced diet. Snack foods that contain some protein, fibre and not too much fat can also be served for lunch.

Snack suggestions

- **Sandwich** (p.99).
- Mountain bread with **Hommus** (p. 87).
- Pocket bread filled with **Coleslaw** (p. 270) or **Chicken salad** (p. 269).
- **Open Danish sandwich** (p. 105).
- **Sandwich loaf** (p. 104).
- **Ham and cheese croissant** (p. 101).
- **Omelette** (p. 108) rolled in mountain bread.
- **Baked potato with cheese filling** (p. 252).

Sandwiches

The Earl of Sandwich is given credit for inventing the sandwich when he ordered his dinner of roast beef to be served between slices of bread so that he could continue to play cards while he ate. Sandwiches can be large enough to make a substantial lunch or between-meal snack or served as a small savoury food. Slices of wholemeal, multigrain, herb or cheese bread, bread rolls, flat breads and pocket bread may be used. For extra flavour, spread filling with a little mayonnaise, mustard, cream cheese or pesto. A sandwich with a protein filling (such as meat, egg, fish, cheese, legumes) accompanied by salad vegetables makes a balanced meal. Wholemeal breads usually contain more fibre.

Suggestions for sandwich fillings

- Cottage cheese and crushed pineapple.
- Cream cheese and chopped crystallised ginger.
- Tuna and **Tabouli** (p. 275).
- Mixed bean salad and chutney.
- Chopped chicken and mango chutney.
- Cream cheese, sweet chilli sauce and canned salmon.
- Salami and **Tabouli** (p. 275).
- Tasty cheese with grated apple in yoghurt.
- Chopped hard-boiled eggs with mayonnaise and chopped black olives.
- Sliced tomato, basil and hommus.
- Sun-dried tomato, chopped celery, sliced white onion and cream cheese.
- **Bacon, lettuce and tomato sandwich** (p. 100).
- Sliced cucumber and grated carrot.
- **Chicken and avocado sandwich** (p. 100).
- **Meat loaf and chutney toasted sandwich** (p. 101).

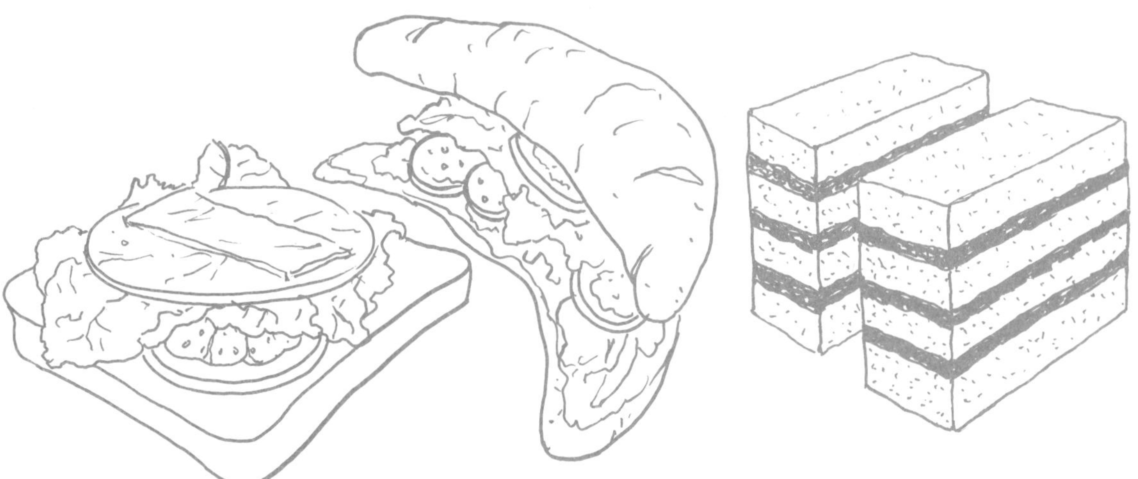

BACON, LETTUCE AND TOMATO SANDWICH

A popular sandwich, particularly when made with rye bread. You can leave out the butter to reduce fat.

Serves: **1**

Ingredients

2 slices bread
2 teaspoons (10 g) butter, margarine *or* dairy blend
2 teaspoons (10 g) **Mayonnaise** (p. 266)
2 lettuce leaves
Filling
1 thin bacon rasher (40 g), grilled
1 tomato (125 g), sliced

Method

1 Spread butter on one side of each slice of bread.
2 Spread mayonnaise over butter.
3 Place lettuce leaf on one slice.
4 Cut bacon in half and place piece on each lettuce leaf.
5 Place tomato slices on bacon. Freshly ground pepper may be added.
6 Place lettuce leaf on top, then other slice of bread, butter side down.
7 Cut in half and serve. May be garnished with a small gherkin and a pickled onion.

CHICKEN AND AVOCADO SANDWICH

Follow recipe for **Bacon, lettuce and tomato sandwich**, using pumpernickel bread. Replace bacon and tomato with 1/2 soft, ripe avocado and 1/2 cup (75 g) chopped cooked chicken.

CHEESE, CHIVE AND CELERY SANDWICH

Follow recipe for **Bacon, lettuce and tomato sandwich**. Replace bacon and tomato with a mixture of 50 g grated tasty cheese, 1 tablespoon snipped chives and 1 tablespoon finely diced celery.

MEAT LOAF AND CHUTNEY TOASTED SANDWICH

A hot toasted sandwich with a bowl of **Minestrone** (p. 152) or **Vegetable Soup** (p. 141) makes a nourishing lunch time meal in winter.

Ingredients

2 slices wholemeal bread

Filling

1 thick slice **Baked Meat Loaf** (p. 202) *or* 75 g cooked sausage
1 thick slice (30 g) tasty cheese
1 tablespoon (20 mL) tomato chutney
1 tablespoon (20 g) butter, margarine *or* dairy blend

Method

1. Spread chutney on one side of each slice of bread.
2. Add meat loaf and cheese to one slice and cover with other slice.
3. Melt butter in frying pan and fry sandwich over gentle heat for 5 minutes. Sandwich may also be toasted on both sides under griller and butter spread on outside when browned or a sandwich toaster may be used.
4. Cut in half and serve. May be garnished with halved cherry tomatoes.

HAM AND CHEESE CROISSANT

Serves: ***1***

Ingredients

1 croissant

Filling

2 slices Swiss cheese
1 slice (20 g) ham
1 tablespoon (5 g) alfalfa sprouts
1 cherry tomato (10 g)

Method

1. Cut croissant in half.
2. Stack cheese and ham on base of croissant. Cover with top.
3. Microwave for 30 seconds on medium power *or* heat in oven for 5 minutes at 180°C.
4. Serve, garnished with alfalfa sprouts and cherry tomato.

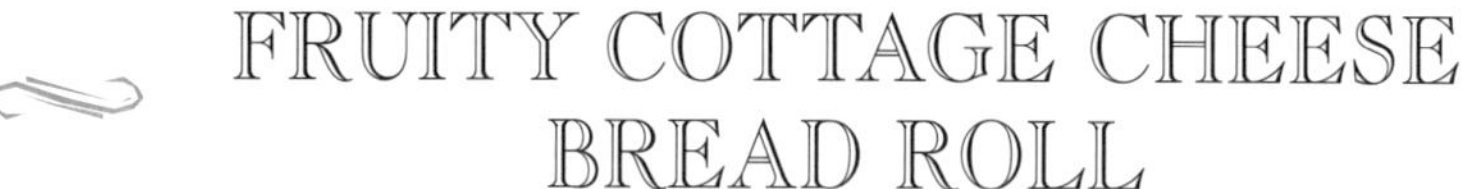

FRUITY COTTAGE CHEESE BREAD ROLL

This can be made using brioche, croissant or bagel instead of the bread roll. For larger quantities buy a French bread stick, fill (use 4 times the filling quantities) and then cut into manageable pieces. Low-fat cottage cheese reduces the fat level.

Ingredients

1 bread roll

Filling

3 tablespoons (60 g) cottage *or* cream cheese

1 tablespoon (20 g) diced dried fruits *or* 1 packet fruit medley

1 tablespoon (20 g) chopped walnuts *or* pecans

Method

1 Split bread roll.
2 Mix filling ingredients.
3 Spread with mixture and close two halves.

✦ CURRIED EGG BREAD ROLL ✦

Follow recipe for **Fruity cottage cheese bread roll**. Replace cheese, fruit and nuts with 1 mashed hard boiled egg with 1 teaspoon curry powder and 1 tablespoon (20 mL) **Mayonnaise** (p. 266). Bread may be spread with 2 teaspoons butter and the filling topped with a finely sliced lettuce leaf.

✦ BEEF AND PICKLE BREAD ROLL ✦

Follow recipe for **Fruity cottage cheese bread roll**. Replace cheese, fruit and nuts with 75 g sliced cooked beef, 1 tablespoon (20 g) mustard pickles, 1 sliced gherkin and 1 sliced pickled onion. Bread may be spread with 2 teaspoons butter and the filling topped with a lettuce leaf.

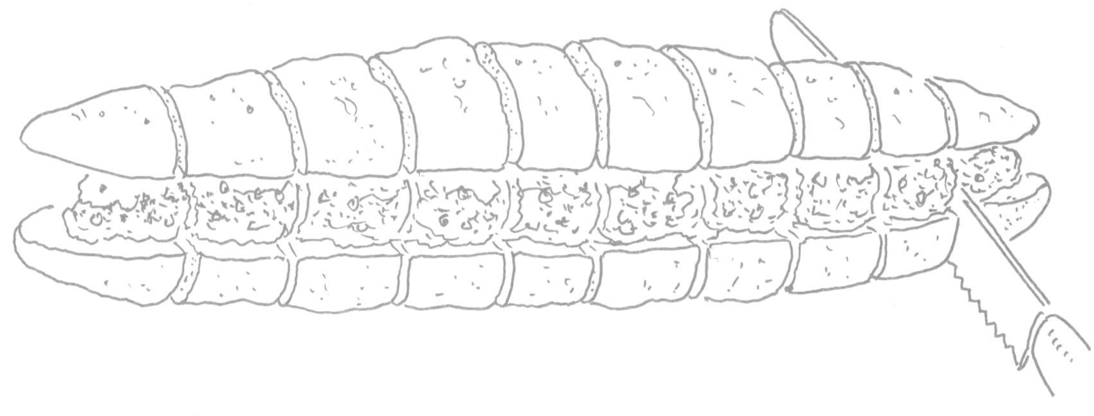

SALAD-FILLED POCKET BREAD

Many flat breads are suitable for use with sandwich fillings – they may be rolled up with meat slices, rolled around meat and vegetable fillings or folded into a parcel with salad fillings.

► *Serves:* **1**

Ingredients

1 slice flat bread, e.g. pita bread, mountain bread, pocket bread, lavash

Filling

1 small lettuce leaf, finely sliced
1 tablespoon (20 g) grated carrot
2 tablespoons alfalfa sprouts
1 spring onion, finely sliced
1 tablespoon (20 g) finely sliced celery
1 tablespoon (20 g) very finely sliced red cabbage
1 tablespoon (20 mL) **French dressing** (p. 266)

Method

1 Mix salad vegetables with dressing.
2 Place in pocket of bread or wrap as a parcel with bread.

COUNTRY CHICKEN LOAF

► *Serves:* **2**
► *Cooking utensil:* oven tray
► *Oven temperature:* **180°C**

Ingredients

2 round bread rolls
1 tablespoon (20 g) butter, melted

Filling

1/2 onion (65 g), chopped
1 tablespoon (20 g) butter
1 chicken breast (100 g), diced
1 tablespoon (15 g) plain flour
1 teaspoon (5 g) curry powder
1/4 cup (20 g) chopped mushrooms
1 tomato (125 g), chopped
1/2 cup (125 mL) hot water

Method

1 Set oven at 180°C.
2 Cut lid from rolls, scoop out centre and make into crumbs.
3 Brush inside of rolls with melted butter and bake at 180°C for 5 minutes.
4 Fry onion in 1 tablespoon butter in frying pan for 2 minutes.
5 Add chicken, fry until golden brown.
6 Add flour and curry powder, fry 1 minute.
7 Add mushrooms, tomato and crumbs.
8 Gradually add water, stir until thickened.
9 Spoon into bread cases and bake for 10 minutes at 180°C until crisp.

RIBBON SANDWICHES

Serves: **12**

Ingredients

12 slices square sandwich bread
fillings as in Method

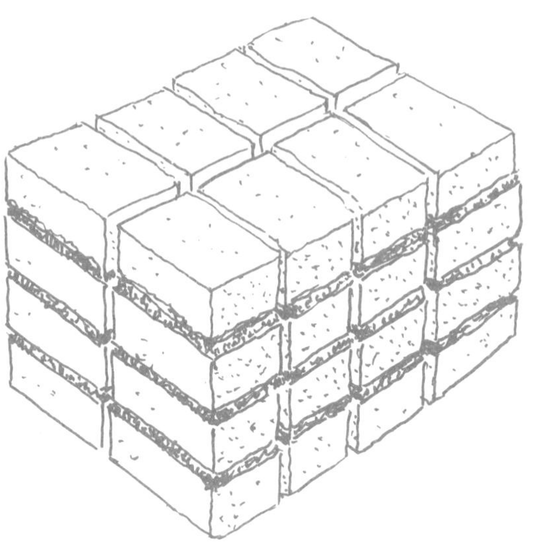

Method

1 Mix each filling separately:
   (a) Mix 100 g finely chopped ham with $^1/_4$ teaspoon mustard and 2 tablespoons (40 mL) **Mayonnaise** (p. 266).
   (b) Mix 3 hardboiled and mashed eggs with $^1/_2$ teaspoon curry powder, $^1/_2$ teaspoon chopped parsley, 2 tablespoons (40 mL) **Mayonnaise** (p. 266) and cayenne to taste.
   (c) Mix 105 g can red *or* pink salmon with 1 teaspoon (5 mL) lemon juice, 2 tablespoons (40 mL) **Mayonnaise** (p. 266) and pepper to taste.
2 Using $^1/_3$ of each filling and 4 slices of bread, make 3 sandwich stacks.
3 Cut off crusts, cut each stack into 8 rectangles.

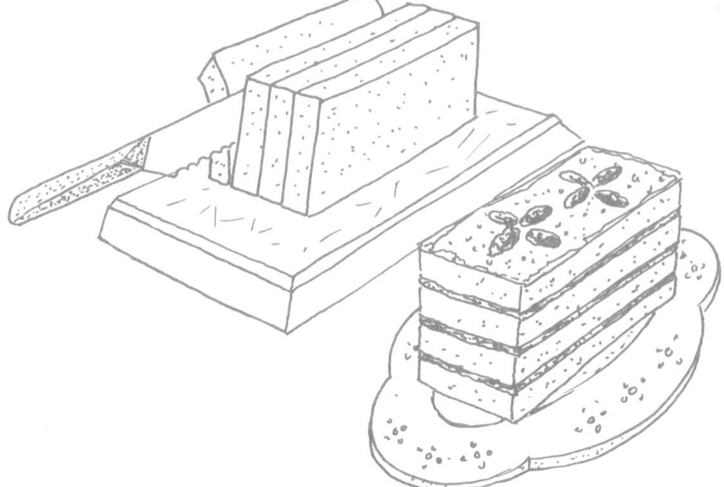

SANDWICH LOAF

Follow recipe for **Ribbon sandwiches**. Do not cut into rectangles, but assemble on serving dish into a loaf shape. Spread loaf with 250 g soft cream cheese and decorate with sliced gherkins and chopped walnuts. Cut into slices to serve.

CHICKEN AND MANGO OPEN DANISH SANDWICH

Serves: **1**

Ingredients

2 slices rye bread
1 tablespoon (20 mL) **Mayonnaise** (p. 266)
2 red lettuce leaves, e.g. radicchio
Topping
2 slices (100 g) cooked chicken
$^{1}/_{4}$ mango *or* 8 slices canned mango
8 young snow peas, strings removed

Method

1. Spread mayonnaise on one side of each slice of bread.
2. Place lettuce leaves on mayonnaise.
3. Place chicken on lettuce.
4. Cut mango into 8 slices lengthwise.
5. Blanch snow peas for 30 seconds in boiling water.
6. Alternate 4 mango slices and snow peas on each slice, overlapping slightly.

HAM AND TOMATO OPEN DANISH SANDWICH

Follow recipe for **Chicken and mango open Danish sandwich**.
Replace chicken, mango and snow peas with 100 g sliced ham, $^{1}/_{2}$ (75 g) sliced tomato and 50 g sliced Swiss cheese, and garnish with 1 finely sliced spring onion.

EGG AND ASPARAGUS OPEN DANISH SANDWICH

Follow recipe for **Chicken and mango open Danish sandwich**.
Replace chicken, mango and snow peas with 100 g fresh, lightly cooked asparagus spears, 1 tablespoon (20 mL) **Mayonnaise** (p. 266), 1 sliced hardboiled egg, and garnish with 1 finely sliced spring onion.

SALAMI AND TABOULI OPEN DANISH SANDWICH

Follow recipe for **Chicken and mango open Danish sandwich**.
Replace chicken, mango and snow peas with 100 g sliced salami, 50 g **Tabouli** (p.275) and 4 thin slices red capsicum.

ASPARAGUS ROLLS

These may also be made using sliced ham with mustard-flavoured mayonnaise.

Number: 8

Ingredients

8 thin slices fresh bread
1 tablespoon (20 mL) **Mayonnaise** (p. 266)
8 fresh asparagus spears, lightly cooked
8 shakes pepper
2 parsley sprigs

Method

1. Remove crusts from bread.
2. Spread mayonnaise on bread.
3. Place asparagus tip diagonally on each slice.
4. Roll up cornerwise. Press lightly. May be wrapped in plastic wrap and refrigerated for 1 hour to hold shape.

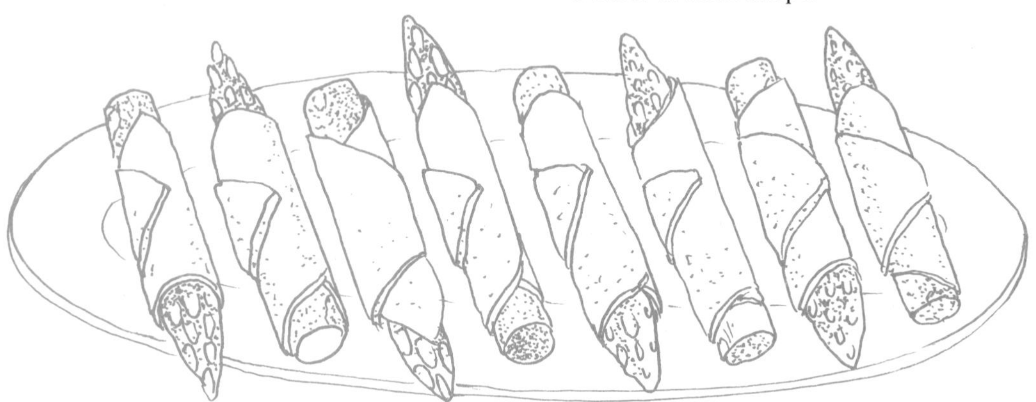

Breakfast dishes

Busy lifestyles call for quickly made, nutritious breakfasts.

Suggestions for breakfast

- Fresh or canned fruit (in juice) with yoghurt.
- Toasted English muffins with honey and banana.
- Blueberry muffin (warm frozen muffins for 2 minutes in the microwave oven on defrost).
- Rice cake with crunchy peanut butter topping and chopped dates.
- **French toast** (p. 107).
- **Poached egg** (p. 107).
- **Egg Benedict** (p. 107).
- **Scrambled egg** (p. 110).
- Scrambled egg placed in a hollowed out bread roll.
- **French omelette** (p. 109).
- **Fluffy or English omelette** (p. 108).
- **Porridge** (p. 110).
- **Fruity porridge** (p. 110).
- **Low-fat muesli** (p. 111).
- **Bircher-style muesli** (p. 111).

FRENCH TOAST

A quick and popular breakfast or snack which can be served with crispy bacon.

Serves: **1**

Ingredients

1 egg
2 tablespoons (40 mL) milk
4 shakes pepper
2 slices day-old bread
1 tablespoon (20 g) butter

Cooking utensil: frying pan

Method

1 Beat egg, milk and pepper.
2 Pour over bread on plate. Turn bread over.
3 Allow to stand 2–3 minutes to absorb egg.
4 Melt butter and fry bread until golden brown on both sides.

POACHED EGG

Serves: **1**

Ingredients

1 slice hot toast, buttered
1/2 teaspoon vinegar
1/4 teaspoon salt
1 egg
1 parsley sprig

Cooking utensil: saucepan *or* frying pan

Method

1 Boil 5 cm water in saucepan *or* frying pan. Add vinegar and salt.
2 Break egg into cup. Gently slide egg into saucepan.
3 Allow water to simmer gently for 2–3 minutes, until egg white is set.
4 Lift egg carefully, drain off water and place egg on toast.

EGG BENEDICT

Follow recipe for **Poached egg**. Omit toast. Serve egg on 1/2 muffin, toasted. Cover with 1 tablespoon **Hollandaise sauce** (p. 286). Place under griller to warm. Serve with **Bacon rolls** (p. 175) and garnish with capers.

FLUFFY OR ENGLISH OMELETTE

- *Serves:* **1**
- *Cooking utensil:* omelette pan *or* frying pan, griller

Cooking time: **5–10 minutes**

Ingredients

2 eggs
3 shakes pepper
2 tablespoons (40 mL) water
2 teaspoons (10 g) butter
1 parsley sprig
flavourings (see below)

Method

1. Prepare flavourings and keep hot. Warm serving plate.
2. Separate egg whites from yolks.
3. Add pepper and water to egg yolks and beat until creamy.
4. Beat egg whites until stiff, fold in yolks.
5. Melt butter in pan and pour in the egg mixture.
6. Cook slowly until brown underneath.
7. Place under hot griller and cook until top surface is set and nicely browned. Overcooking will shrink omelette.
8. Loosen edges of omelette from pan, and cut almost through centre with a sharp knife. With spatula, fold in half. Slip on to hot serving plate.
9. Flavouring may be added before omelette is folded in half or served on the plate beside the omelette.
10. Garnish and serve at once.

CHEESE OMELETTE

Add 1 tablespoon (10 g) grated cheese.

HERB OMELETTE

Add 1 teaspoon finely chopped herbs, e.g. thyme, marjoram *or* basil, to beaten eggs.

MUSHROOM OMELETTE

Add 50 g sautéed mushrooms *or* canned mushrooms.

TOMATO AND ONION OMELETTE

Cook 1 peeled and diced tomato (125 g), 1 chopped spring onion, 1/2 teaspoon salt, 2 teaspoons (10 g) butter, 6 shakes pepper and add to omelette.

SPANISH OMELETTE

To flavourings for **Tomato and onion omelette** add 1 tablespoon diced celery and 1 tablespoon diced capsicum. Cook as for **Tomato and onion omelette**. Pour mixture over omelette on serving plate.

✦ BACON OMELETTE ✦

Add 1 rasher (40 g) chopped fried bacon.

✦ CHICKEN OMELETTE ✦

Add 1/2 cup (75 g) diced cooked chicken and 1 teaspoon chopped parsley.

✦ HAM OMELETTE ✦

Add 1 tablespoon (15 g) chopped ham and 1/8 teaspoon mustard.

FRENCH OMELETTE

For flavourings, see Fluffy or English omelette varieties (above). Flavourings can be added to the omelette in a variety of ways: they may be added to the beaten eggs, sprinkled over the omelette while it is cooking, placed on one half of the cooked omelette before the other half is folded over, poured over the cooked omelette, or served as an accompaniment.

- *Serves:* ***1***
- *Cooking utensil:* omelette pan or frying pan
- *Cooking time:* ***5 minutes***

Ingredients

2 eggs
1/4 teaspoon salt
3 shakes pepper
2 tablespoons (40 mL) water
2 teaspoons (10 g) butter
1 parsley sprig
flavourings (see above)

Method

1. Prepare flavourings and keep hot. Warm serving plate.
2. Beat eggs slightly, add salt, pepper and water.
3. Heat butter in pan and pour in egg mixture. Cook over low heat. Stir gently with figure '8' movements until mixture commences to thicken. Allow to cook until set on top and golden brown on base.
4. When omelette has set, tilt the pan away from you, and loosen around the sides. Place flavourings on the half of the omelette away from the handle. Fold the other half of omelette over flavours as you tip omelette on to serving plate.
5. Garnish with parsley and serve at once.

SCRAMBLED EGG

► *Serves:* **1**

► *Cooking utensil:* small saucepan

Ingredients

1 slice hot toast, buttered
1 egg, beaten
1/8 teaspoon salt
1 shake pepper
2 tablespoons (40 mL) milk
1 teaspoon (5 g) butter
1/4 teaspoon chopped parsley

Method

1. Mix egg, salt, pepper and milk.
2. Melt butter in saucepan, add egg mixture.
3. Allow to thicken over gentle heat, stirring continuously. Do not overcook.
4. Pile on toast. Garnish with parsley and serve.

PORRIDGE

Porridge can be simmered, stirring continuously, in a saucepan for 4–10 minutes instead of using the microwave oven. Add a little extra water.

► *Serves:* **1**

Ingredients

1/2 cup (50 g) quick-cook rolled oats
1 cup (250 mL) water

Method

1. Microwave rolled oats and water for 2 minutes on medium power.
2. Serve with milk and 1 teaspoon honey *or* fruit yoghurt.

✦ FRUITY PORRIDGE ✦

Follow recipe for **Porridge**, replacing 1/2 cup milk with 1/2 cup fruit juice. Add 1/2 grated apple and 1 tablespoon sultanas.

LOW-FAT MUESLI

Serves: 2

Ingredients

1 cup (100 g) quick-cook rolled oats
1/4 cup 930 g) flaked almonds
2 tablespoons sultanas
1/4 cup (25 g) wheatgerm
1/2 cup (125 mL) rice bran

Method

1. Mix all ingredients.
2. Store in airtight container for not more than 1 month.
3. May be served with low-fat yoghurt or fresh fruit.

BIRCHER-STYLE MUESLI

To reduce fat content, use milk instead of cream.

Serves: 3

Ingredients

1 cup quick-cook rolled oats
1/4 cup hazelnuts, chopped
1 apple, grated
1/2 cup cream
2 tablespoons sultanas
juice and grated rind 1 lemon
juice and grated rind 1 orange

Method

1. Mix all ingredients to a creamy consistency.
2. Stand overnight in refrigerator.
3. Add milk if too stiff.
4. Keep in refrigerator. Use within 3 days.

5 Vegetarian dishes

Increasing numbers of Australians are choosing to make vegetable-based foods the focus of their diet and reduce their consumption of animal foods. The reasons for this may include cost, perceptions that these foods are healthier, or a preference for the taste and texture. Others may avoid animal products for religious or other dietary reasons.

In many regions of the world, fruits, vegetables, nuts, dried peas and beans (legumes) and cereal grains have always formed a major part of the diet.

Food value

Foods contain protein in a 'complete' or an 'incomplete' form (see p. 15–16). Those classified as complete protein foods contain all the essential amino acids. Vegetable-based foods are missing one or more essential amino acids. By combining foods from two or more of the different vegetable-based foods, that is, from the legumes group, the cereal grains group and the nuts group, all the essential amino acids are provided. Soya beans and their products, such as tofu, soy milk, soy flour, are the only vegetable-based foods containing all the essential amino acids. Iron is found in leafy-green vegetables and dried fruits. Yeast extract, cereal grains and nuts provide the B group vitamins. A major nutritional advantage of vegetarian meals is the high fibre, low kilojoule and low fat content of many dishes.

The three main types of vegetarian diets

Lacto-ovo-vegetarian includes eggs and dairy foods such as milk, cheese, butter and yoghurt.

Lacto-vegetarian includes dairy products such as milk, cheese, butter and yoghurt.

Vegan includes only vegetable products. A vegan diet is unsuitable for children as they have high energy and protein needs.

Cooking cereals and legumes

(to yield 2 cups)

Commodity	Amount	Cooking method
Beans – dried (e.g. soya, brown, navy, borlotti, cannellini, haricot, black eye)	1 cup (200 g)	Pour 1 litre (4 cups) water and 1 teaspoon salt over beans. Leave 6 hours (or overnight if possible). Drain. Bring to boil in fresh water, simmer 1–2 hours until tender. Drain.
Chickpeas	1 cup (200 g)	Pour 1 litre (4 cups) boiling water and 1/2 teaspoon salt over chickpeas. Leave 24 hours. Drain. Bring to boil in fresh water, simmer for 2–2 1/2 hours.
Couscous	1 cup (200 g)	Add to 500 mL (2 cups) boiling stock or water. Bring back to boil, remove from heat, cover and stand 5 minutes. Stir with fork.
Lentils	1 cup	Bring to boil in 1 litre (4 cups) water and 1/2 t
Noodles – fresh	1 1/2 cups (150 g)	Boil 1 litre (4 cups) water and 1/4 teaspoon salt. Add noodles, simmer 5 minutes. Drain.
Noodles – thick	1 1/2 cups (150 g)	Boil 1 litre (4 cups) water and 1/4 teaspoon salt. Add noodles, simmer 10 minutes. Drain.
Noodles – thin	1 1/2 cups (150 g)	Boil 1 litre (4 cups) water and 1/4 teaspoon salt. Add noodles, simmer 3 minutes. Drain.
Pasta – dried	1 1/2 cups (150 g)	Boil 1 litre (4 cups) water and 1/4 teaspoon salt. Add pasta, simmer 15 minutes. Drain.
Pasta – fresh	1 1/4 cups (150 g)	Boil 1 litre (4 cups) water and 1/4 teaspoon salt. Add pasta, simmer 5 minutes. Drain.
Pasta – wholemeal	1 1/2 cups (150 g)	Boil 1 litre (4 cups) water and 1/4 teaspoon salt. Add pasta, simmer 40 minutes. Drain.
Polenta	1 cup (150 g)	Mix into 1 L (4 cups) water or stock and 1/2 teaspoon salt, bring to boil, stirring continuously. Simmer 10 minutes, stirring regularly.
Rice – white	3/4 cup (150 g)	Boiling method: boil 1 litre (4 cups) water and 1/2 teaspoon salt. Add rice, simmer 12 minutes. Drain. Absorption method: place rice in a saucepan, just cover with cold water to 2cm above rice. Bring slowly to the boil, with lid on, and simmer 15–20 minutes, until cooked and all the water has been absorbed.
Rice – wholegrain (brown)	3/4 cup (150 g)	Boil 1 litre (4 cups) water and 1/2 teaspoon salt. Add rice, simmer 45 minutes. Drain. May be cooked by absorption method as in white rice.

BEAN BURGERS

- *Serves:* 4
- *Cooking utensil:* saucepan, frying pan

Preparation time: ***overnight and 1¼ hours***
Cooking time: ***10 minutes***

Ingredients

½ cup (100 g) black eye *or* soya beans, soaked overnight, *or* 310 g can
1 onion (125 g), finely chopped
1 tablespoon chopped fresh herbs
½ cup (60 g) grated cheese
2 tablespoons (20 g) wholemeal plain flour
1 tablespoon (20 mL) soy sauce
2 tablespoons (20 g) plain flour
3 tablespoons (60 mL) oil

Method

1. Cook soaked beans for 1 hour (p. 113) or drain and rinse canned beans.
2. Mash beans and add onion, herbs, cheese, wholemeal flour and soy sauce. A food processor may be used.
3. Form into 8 burgers and dip into flour.
4. Heat oil in frying pan.
5. Fry burgers gently for 10 minutes. Drain.
6. May be served with 500 mL (1 quantity) **Fresh tomato sauce** (p. 285).

CURRIED LENTIL PATTIES

These patties are delicious made with Dutch curry and rice soup mix, but check the list of ingredients for any meat products.

- *Serves:* 4
- *Cooking utensil:* saucepan, frying pan

Preparation time: ***overnight and 15 minutes***
Cooking time: ***10 minutes***

Ingredients

1 cup (200 g) red lentils
2 cups (500 mL) water
1 teaspoon (5 g) curry paste
1 packet (65 g) vegetable-based soup mix
2 tablespoons chopped parsley
2 tablespoons (20 g) wholemeal plain flour
2 tablespoons (40 mL) oil

Method

1. Wash lentils in strainer, place in saucepan with water. Bring to boil and simmer 15 minutes or until all the water is absorbed.
2. Add curry paste, soup mix and parsley to lentils.
3. Refrigerate for at least 30 minutes, overnight if possible.
4. Shape into patties and roll in flour.
5. Heat oil and fry 4–5 minutes on each side.

✦ LENTIL AND SILVER BEET PATTIES ✦

Follow recipe for **Curried lentil patties**. Add finely chopped stems and leaves of 4 stalks of silver beet, blanched 2 minutes in boiling water.

BEANS IN TOMATO SAUCE

Based on the traditional American dish 'Boston beans'.
The brown sugar may be replaced with molasses.

- *Serves:* 4
- *Cooking utensil:* saucepan

Preparation time: ***overnight and 15 minutes***
Cooking time: ***30 minutes***

Ingredients

1/2 cup (100 g) haricot *or* navy beans, soaked overnight, *or* 310 g can
1 onion (125 g), chopped
1 clove garlic (5 g), crushed
1 teaspoon (5 mL) oil
2 tomatoes (250 g), chopped
2 tablespoons (40 g) tomato paste
2 teaspoons (10 g) brown sugar
1 tablespoon (20 mL) vinegar
1 teaspoon (5 g) grain mustard

Method

1. Cook soaked beans for 25 minutes (p. 113) or drain and rinse canned beans.
2. Fry onion and garlic in oil until tender.
3. Add all other ingredients.
4. Stir until boiling. Simmer 30 minutes.

✦ BAKED BEANS IN TOMATO SAUCE ✦

Follow recipe for **Beans in tomato sauce**, using soaked beans. At step 4 place all ingredients in casserole (2.5 L) and bake in oven for 45 minutes at 180°C.

Non-Vegetarian Variation

✦ BEANS AND BACON IN TOMATO SAUCE ✦

Follow recipe for **Beans in tomato sauce**. At step 2 add 2 rashers (80 g) chopped bacon.

SPICY CHICKPEA HOTPOT

For a variation, use pumpkin or kumara instead of carrot.

- *Serves:* **4**
- *Cooking utensil:* large saucepan

Preparation time: **15 minutes**
Cooking time: **30 minutes**

Ingredients

$^3/_4$ cup (150 g) chickpeas, soaked 24 hours, *or* 425 g can
1 onion (125 g), chopped
2 tablespoons (40 mL) oil
1 tablespoon (15 g) plain flour
1 carrot (150 g), sliced
1 stalk celery (100 g), sliced
2 tablespoons (40 mL) tomato paste
1 tablespoon (20 mL) grain mustard
1 clove (5 g) garlic, crushed
2 tablespoons (40 mL) sweet chilli sauce
1 cup (250 mL) water
$^1/_2$ cup (75 g) fresh or frozen peas

Method

1. Cook soaked chickpeas for 2–2$^1/_2$ hours (p. 113) or drain and rinse canned chickpeas
2. Fry onion in oil.
3. Add flour and stir until brown. Remove from heat.
4. Add water slowly, bring to boil and add other ingredients, except green peas.
5. Simmer 20 minutes, add peas, cook further 10 minutes.

SPICY BORLOTTI BEAN HOTPOT

Follow recipe for **Spicy chickpea hotpot**. Replace chickpeas with $^3/_4$ cup (150 g) borlotti beans *or* 425 g can.

BYGAN DHAL

A traditional accompaniment to Indian dishes, particularly curries.

- *Serves:* 4
- *Cooking utensil:* saucepan, frying pan
- *Preparation time:* **20 minutes**
- *Cooking time:* **20 minutes**

Ingredients

$^1/_2$ cup (100 g) red lentils
1 cup (250 mL) water
1 eggplant (200 g)
$^1/_4$ teaspoon curry powder
$^1/_4$ teaspoon mustard
$^1/_2$ teaspoon salt
1 onion (125 g), finely chopped
1 tomato (125 g), diced
1 tablespoon (20 mL) oil
$^1/_2$ teaspoon lemon juice

Method

1. Bring water to boil, add lentils and cook gently for 5 minutes.
2. Cut eggplant into 2 cm dice (do not remove skin).
3. Add eggplant, curry powder, mustard and salt to lentils. Continue cooking until eggplant is tender, approximately 10 minutes.
4. Heat oil in frying pan. Fry onion until tender and lightly browned.
5. Stir onion and tomato into lentil mixture. Cook for 5 minutes. Add lemon juice. Should have consistency similar to porridge.

FELAFELS

A Middle Eastern dish often served with pita bread.

- *Serves:* 4
- *Cooking utensil:* saucepan, frying pan

Ingredients

1 cup (200 g) chickpeas, soaked 24 hours, *or* 425 g can
1 onion (125 g), chopped
2 tablespoons (40 g) tahini
$^1/_2$ cup chopped parsley
6 shakes pepper
$^1/_4$ cup (40 g) wholemeal plain flour
$^1/_2$ cup (75 g) sesame seeds
1 tablespoon (10 g) wholemeal plain flour, extra
1 tablespoon (20 mL) oil
250 mL *or* 1 quantity **Yoghurt dressing** (p. 267)

Method

1. Cook soaked chickpeas for 2–2$^1/_2$ hours (p. 113) *or* drain and rinse canned chickpeas.
2. Place chickpeas, onion, tahini, parsley, pepper, flour and sesame seeds in food blender or processor. Blend until smooth.
3. Shape spoonfuls of mixture into small balls. Roll in extra flour.
4. Heat oil in frying pan and fry for 2–3 minutes each side.
5. Serve with **Yoghurt dressing**.

TOFU SESAME STICKS

Serves: **4**
Cooking utensil: frying pan

Preparation time: ***Overnight and 15 minutes***
Cooking time: ***10 minutes***

Ingredients

300 g tofu (bean curd)
2 tablespoons (40 mL) teriyaki sauce
1 tablespoon (10 g) wholemeal plain flour
2 tablespoons (24 g) sesame seeds
1 tablespoon (20 mL) oil

Method

1. Cut tofu into 8 sticks and marinate in teriyaki sauce, overnight if possible, in refrigerator.
2. Combine flour and sesame seeds and coat tofu sticks.
3. Heat oil, fry tofu sticks until golden brown on each side.
4. Bring remaining marinade to boil and pour over tofu.

SWEET AND SOUR TOFU

Follow recipe for **Tofu sesame sticks**. Serve with 500 mL *or* 1 quantity of **Sweet and sour sauce** (p. 000).

POLENTA PIZZA WITH VEGETABLE TOPPING

Serves: **4**
Cooking utensil: saucepan, non-stick frying pan, griller

Preparation time: ***20 minutes and 1 hour refrigeration time***
Cooking time: ***25 minutes***

Ingredients

1/2 cup (75 g) polenta
2 cups (500 mL) water
2 tablespoons chopped parsley
1 egg
1 onion (125 g), chopped
2 tablespoons (40 mL) oil
1 tomato (125 g), chopped
2 zucchini (200 g), grated
8 olives, sliced
1/2 cup (60 g) grated cheese

Method

1. Cook polenta in water for 10 minutes, stirring continuously.
2. Add parsley and egg and spread in flat square dish 2 cm deep. Place in refrigerator for 1 hour to become firm.
3. Heat 1 tablespoon (20 mL) oil in saucepan, brown onion, add tomatoes and zucchini and simmer 15 minutes. Cool.
4. Cut polenta base into four. Heat 1 tablespoon (20 mL) oil in frying pan, fry polenta bases one at a time on one side and lift onto griller pan.
5. Place tomato mixture on top, garnish with olive slices and cheese and grill until brown.

HERBED POLENTA WITH TOMATO SAUCE

- *Serves:* ***4***
- *Cooking utensil:* saucepan, non-stick frying pan
- *Preparation time:* ***15 minutes and 1 hour refrigeration time***
- *Cooking time:* ***10 minutes***

Ingredients

1 cup (150 g) polenta
1 L (4 cups) water
2 tablespoons chopped fresh herbs *or* 1 teaspoon dried mixed herbs
1 tablespoon (20 mL) oil
300 g natural yoghurt
500 mL (1 quantity) **Fresh tomato sauce** (p. 285)

Method

1 Cook polenta in water for 10 minutes, stirring continuously.
2 Simmer 10 minutes, stirring regularly. Add herbs.
3 Spread in flat, square dish to 2 cm thickness. Place in refrigerator for 1 hour to become firm.
4 Cut into triangles for serving.
5 Heat oil in frying pan, fry triangles until lightly browned.
6 Serve polenta triangles with **Fresh tomato sauce**.

CARROT AND CASHEW LOAF

- *Serves:* ***4***
- *Cooking utensil:* medium loaf pan (1 L)
- *Preparation time:* ***25 minutes***
- *Cooking time:* ***45 minutes***
- *Oven temperature:* ***180°C***

Ingredients

1 cup (40 g) stale wholemeal breadcrumbs
2 carrots (300 g), grated
2 zucchini (200 g), grated
1 onion (125 g), chopped
1 cup (120 g) chopped cashew nuts
1 egg
1/2 cup (75 g) wholemeal self-raising flour
1 teaspoon (5 g) chopped ginger
2 tablespoons chopped parsley
1 tablespoon (20 mL) tahini

Method

1 Set oven at 180°C. Brush or spray loaf pan with oil and line base with baking paper.
2 Combine all ingredients.
3 Place in loaf pan.
4 Bake at 180°C for 45 minutes.
5 Serve hot or cold, cut into slices.

MACARONI CHEESE

For a variation, add a cup of cooked cauliflower florets to the cheese sauce.

- *Serves:* **4**
- *Cooking utensil:* saucepan, ovenproof dish

Preparation time: ***20 minutes***
Cooking time: ***15–20 minutes***
- *Oven temperature:* ***180°C***

Ingredients

1 1/2 cups (150 g) macaroni
1 tablespoon (20 g) butter
1 1/2 tablespoons (15 g) plain flour
1 teaspoon (5 g) mustard
1 1/4 cups (315 mL) milk
1 cup (120 g) grated tasty cheese
1/4 cup (25 g) dried breadcrumbs

Method

1. Set oven at 180°C. Brush or spray ovenproof dish with oil.
2. Cook macaroni in 1 L boiling water with 1/4 teaspoon salt for 12 minutes.
3. Make sauce: melt butter, add flour and cook 30 seconds. Remove from heat and add mustard then add milk gradually. Stir until boiling and add half the cheese.
4. Drain macaroni and mix with sauce.
5. Place in ovenproof dish. Mix remainder of cheese with breadcrumbs and sprinkle on top.
6. Bake in top of oven at 180°C for 15–20 minutes.

✦ MACARONI AND TOMATO CASSEROLE ✦

Follow recipe for **Macaroni cheese**. Cover macaroni mixture at step 3 with 1 sliced tomato (125 g) and 1 sliced onion (125 g) sautéed in 1 teaspoon (5 g) butter.

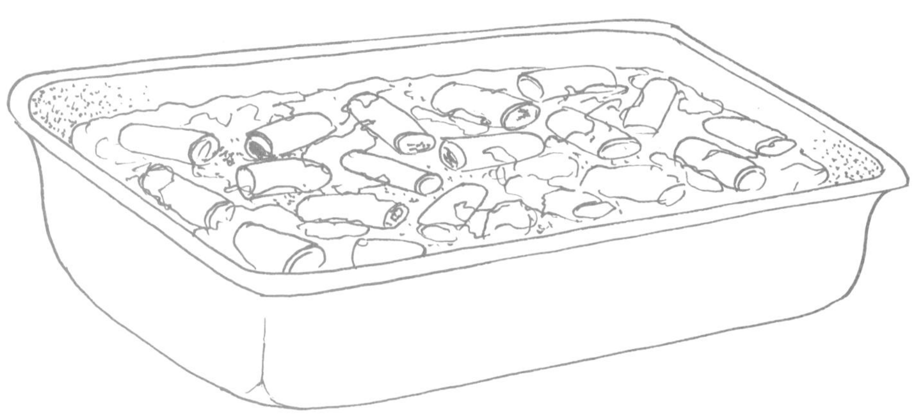

PASTA WITH PUMPKIN AND LEEK SAUCE

For a smooth, rich dish, replace half the cream with coconut milk or coconut cream.

- *Serves:* **4**
- *Cooking utensil:* large saucepan, medium saucepan

Preparation time: **15 minutes**
Cooking time: **20 minutes**

Ingredients

150 g pasta, e.g. tagliatelle, fettuccine
3 cups (400 g) diced butternut pumpkin
1 onion (125 g), chopped
1 clove garlic (5 g), crushed
1 tablespoon (20 mL) olive oil
1 leek (125 g), washed and sliced
1 tablespoon (20 g) curry paste
1 tablespoon (10 g) plain flour
1/4 cup (125 mL) milk
1/4 cup (125 mL) cream
1 tablespoon chopped coriander

Method

1. Cook pasta in 1 L boiling water with 1/4 teaspoon salt for 12–15 minutes.
2. Boil pumpkin for 10 minutes, until cooked but still firm.
3. Fry onion and garlic in oil until transparent, add leek, curry paste and flour, cook for a further 5 minutes.
4. Add milk, cream and pumpkin and bring to the boil slowly.
5. Drain pasta, place on serving plate and pour sauce over. Garnish with coriander.

FETTUCCINE MEDITERRANEAN

Spinach or tomato gives the fettuccine added flavour and colour.

- *Serves:* 4
- *Cooking utensil:* large saucepan

Ingredients

150 g fettuccine
1 tablespoon (20 mL) olive oil
1/2 onion (65 g), chopped
1 clove garlic (5 g), crushed
3 tomatoes (375 g)
2 tablespoons chopped fresh basil
4 green olives, sliced
4 black olives, sliced
1/4 cup (30 g) grated parmesan cheese

Preparation time: **15 minutes**
Cooking time: **20 minutes**

Method

1. Cook fettuccine in 1 L boiling water with 1/4 teaspoon salt for 12–15 minutes.
2. Fry onion and garlic in oil until transparent.
3. Peel and dice tomato, add to onion and cook 3 minutes. Add basil and half the olives.
4. Drain fettuccine, toss in tomato mixture, place on serving plate and serve garnished with cheese and olives.

✦ FETTUCCINE WITH MUSHROOMS ✦

Follow recipe for **Fettuccine Mediterranean**. Omit cheese, tomato, basil and olives. Add 2 cups (200 g) sliced mushrooms and 1/4 cup (65 mL) cream at step 3.

✦ SPINACH RAVIOLI WITH TOMATO AND BASIL SAUCE ✦

Follow recipe for **Fettuccine Mediterranean**. Replace fettucine with 300 g spinach-filled ravioli. Cook only five minutes.

Non-Vegetarian Variations

✦ FETTUCCINE WITH MORTADELLA ✦

Follow recipe for **Fettuccine Mediterranean**. Omit tomato. Add 250 g diced mortadella and 1/4 cup (65 mL) cream at step 4.

✦ FETTUCCINE WITH BACON ✦

Follow recipe for **Fettuccine Mediterranean**. Omit oil. Fry onion with 2 chopped (80 g) rashers bacon at step 2.

VEGETABLE LASAGNE

For variety use pumpkin, sweet potato, potato, ricotta cheese, spinach or cooked cannellini beans.

- *Serves:* **4**
- *Cooking utensil:* ovenproof dish *or* lasagne dish (2.5 L)

Ingredients

125 g instant lasagne
1 tablespoon (20 mL) oil
1 onion (125 g), chopped
1 clove garlic (5 g), crushed
2 cups (200 g) sliced mushrooms
4 tomatoes (500 g) *or* 420 g can, chopped
1 zucchini (100 g), grated
1 tablespoon (20 g) tomato paste
1 carrot (125 g), grated
3 shakes pepper
1 tablespoon chopped fresh basil
250 mL (1 quantity) **Cheese sauce** (p. 231)
1/2 cup (60 g) grated tasty cheese

- *Preparation time:* ***30 minutes***
- *Cooking time:* ***30–40 minutes***
- *Oven temperature:* ***180°C***

Method

1. Set oven at 180°C. Brush or spray casserole with oil.
2. Heat oil, sauté onion and garlic for 2 minutes.
3. Add mushrooms, tomatoes, zucchini, tomato paste, carrot, pepper and basil.
4. Stir over low heat for 20 minutes until sauce thickens.
5. Place a thin layer of vegetable sauce in dish, then a layer of lasagne. Repeat these layers, the top layer should be lasagne. Cover top layer with cheese sauce. Sprinkle with grated cheese.
6. Bake at 180°C for 30–40 minutes.

VEGETABLE TOFU LASAGNE

Follow recipe for **Vegetable lasagne**. Replace 75 g lasagne with 250 g tofu, drained and cut into 1 cm thick slices. Bake at 180°C for 25 minutes.

BOK CHOY AND GINGER NOODLE STIR-FRY

- *Serves:* 4
- *Cooking utensil:* large saucepan, wok

Preparation time: **15 minutes**
Cooking time: **30 minutes**

Ingredients

500 g vegetables, e.g. snow peas, capsicum, corn kernels, beans, celery
250 g bok choy *or* other Asian leaf and stem vegetable
2 tablespoons (40 g) chopped ginger
500 g thin egg noodles
2 teaspoons (10 mL) oil
1 onion (125 g), sliced
1 tablespoon (20 mL) sweet chilli sauce
1 tablespoon (20 mL) soy sauce

Method

1. Prepare vegetables and bok choy, cut into bite-sized pieces.
2. Cook noodles in boiling water for 3 minutes. Drain.
3. Heat oil in wok, fry onion for 1 minute.
4. Add vegetables and ginger, fry for 5 minutes.
5. Add noodles and sauces. Stir gently until heated through.

SPICY LENTIL NOODLES

- *Serves:* 4
- *Cooking utensil:* large saucepan

Preparation time: **15 minutes**
Cooking time: **30 minutes**

Ingredients

2 teaspoons (10 mL) oil
1 onion (125 g), finely chopped
425 g can tomatoes, chopped
½ cup (100 g) brown lentils
1 tablespoon (20 mL) sweet chilli sauce
1 teaspoon (5 mL) Worcestershire sauce
2 tablespoons (40 g) tomato paste
2 L (8 cups) water
300 g fresh *or* dried noodles
2 tablespoons (20 g) grated cheese

Method

1. Heat oil in saucepan.
2. Add onion and sauté until soft.
3. Add tomatoes, lentils, sauces and tomato paste.
4. Bring to the boil and simmer gently for 30 minutes until lentils are tender.
5. Cook noodles for 10 minutes (dried) or 5 minutes (fresh) (p. 113). Drain.
6. Add noodles to lentil mixture and mix gently.
7. Serve hot, sprinkled with grated cheese.

SAVOURY COUSCOUS

- *Serves:* ***4 as accompaniment***
- *Cooking utensil:* saucepan, frying pan

Preparation time: ***5 minutes***
Cooking time: ***10 minutes***

Ingredients

2 cups (500 mL) vegetable stock *or* water
1 cup (200 g) couscous
1 tablespoon (20 mL) oil
1 onion (125 g), diced
1/2 cup chopped fresh herbs

Method

1 Boil stock *or* water, add couscous, stir while bringing to boil.
2 Remove from heat and allow to stand, covered, for 5 minutes.
3 Heat oil and fry onion for 2 minutes, add couscous and herbs.
4 Stir gently with fork to heat through and serve as accompaniment to other dishes.

SAVOURY RICE

For a variety, add chopped spinach, leeks, or mushrooms with the onion, or nuts with the fresh herbs.

- *Serves:* ***4***
- *Cooking utensil:* saucepan, frying pan

Preparation time: ***10 minutes***
Cooking time: ***20 minutes***

Ingredients

1 cup (200 g) rice
1 tablespoon (20 mL) oil
1 onion (125 g), diced
1/2 cup chopped fresh herbs

Method

1 Cook rice in 1 L boiling water and 1/4 teaspoon salt for 12 minutes. Drain, rinse and cool.
2 Heat oil in frying pan, add onion and cook until transparent.
3 Add rice and herbs, stir gently to heat through.
4 Serve as accompaniment to other dishes.

FRIED RICE

For a non-vegetarian variation, add cooked minced steak, diced chicken, prawns or bacon.

- *Serves:* 4
- *Cooking utensil:* large saucepan, deep frying pan *or* wok

Preparation time: **10 minutes**
Cooking time: **20 minutes**

Ingredients

1 cup (200 g) rice
1 tablespoon (20 mL) oil
2 eggs, beaten
1 onion (125 g), chopped
1 clove (5 g) garlic, crushed
$^1/_2$ cup (50 g) beanshoots
$^1/_2$ cup (50 g) sliced mushrooms
1 tablespoon (20 mL) soy sauce
2 spring onions, chopped

Method

1 Cook rice in 1 L boiling water and $^1/_4$ teaspoon salt for 12 minutes. Drain, rinse and cool.
2 Heat 1 teaspoon oil in frying pan. Fry egg until set.
3 Lift egg and cut into small pieces.
4 Add remaining oil and fry onion and garlic until onion is transparent.
5 Add rice, beanshoots, soy sauce and egg pieces, stir gently. Cook 1 minute.
6 Garnish with spring onion and serve.

ROASTED TOMATO AND CAPSICUM RISOTTO

This may be made with 1/2 cup dry white wine added with the last of the stock.

- *Serves:* 4
- *Cooking utensil:* large saucepan, griller, 4-sided oven tray
- *Preparation time:* ***30 minutes***
- *Cooking time:* ***20 minutes***
- *Oven temperature:* ***200°C***

Ingredients

3 cups (750 mL) vegetable stock, boiling
1 red capsicum (125 g)
4 tomatoes (500 g)
1 onion (125 g), finely chopped
1 tablespoon (20 mL) olive oil
1 cup (200 g) arborio rice
1/8 teaspoon freshly ground black pepper
125 g mushrooms, sliced
1 tablespoon chopped coriander
50 g parmesan cheese shavings

Method

1. Set oven at 200°C.
2. Cut capsicum in half lengthwise, remove seeds, and grill skin-side up until blistered. Place in sealed plastic bag for 10 minutes. Peel and cut into strips.
3. Cut tomatoes in quarters, place skin side down on 4-sided oven tray and cook in oven at 200°C for 20 minutes. Cool.
4. Fry onion in oil for 5 minutes, add rice, stir over heat 1 minute.
5. Add 1 cup boiling stock and black pepper, stir while bringing quickly bring to boil. Add half of the capsicum, tomatoes, mushrooms and coriander.
6. Simmer until stock is absorbed, then add the remainder of the hot stock, 1/2 cup at a time, stirring until each addition is absorbed before adding the next. Stir continuously and cook until rice is tender but firm.
7. Stir in remaining capsicum, tomatoes and mushrooms.
8. Garnish with parmesan cheese and remaining coriander.

VEGETABLE STIR-FRY

Use a high heat and short cooking time to give the vegetables a bright colour and crispy texture.

- *Serves:* 4
- *Cooking utensil:* wok *or* deep frying pan

Ingredients

1 tablespoon (20 mL) oil
$^1/_2$ onion (65 g), sliced
1 stalk celery (100 g), sliced
60 g ($^1/_2$ cup) broccoli florets
60 g ($^1/_2$ cup) green beans, sliced
$^1/_2$ carrot (75 g) *or* $^1/_2$ red capsicum (75 g), sliced
50 g ($^1/_2$ cup) snow peas
$^1/_2$ Chinese cabbage *or* bok choy, sliced
50 g ($^1/_2$ cup) beanshoots
1 tablespoon (20 mL) soy sauce

- *Preparation time:* ***20 minutes***
- *Cooking time:* ***7 minutes***

Method

1 Heat oil in wok.
2 Add onion, stir for 1 minute.
3 Add remaining vegetables except beanshoots. Stir gently for 3 minutes.
4 Add beanshoots. Continue stirring for 1–2 minutes until crisp-cooked.
5 Add soy sauce and serve.

✦ HONEYED PUMPKIN STIR-FRY ✦

Follow recipe for **Vegetable stir-fry**. Omit broccoli and carrot or capsicum. Add $^1/_2$ cup pepito (roasted pumpkin seeds) at step 3. Add 300 g pumpkin cut into 2 cm dice, microwaved *or* steamed until firm but cooked, at step 4. Mix 1 tablespoon (20 mL) honey with soy sauce before adding.

VEGETABLE CURRY

For added flavour use kumara or pumpkin instead of potato.

- *Serves:* 4
- *Cooking utensil:* large saucepan

Preparation time: ***overnight and 1 hour***

Cooking time: ***25 minutes***

Ingredients

1/2 cup (100 g) red kidney beans, soaked overnight, *or* 310 g can
1 tablespoon (20 mL) oil
1 onion (125 g), chopped
1 tablespoon (20 g) curry paste
1 clove garlic (5 g), crushed
1 teaspoon (5 g) chopped ginger
2 potatoes (300 g), diced
125 g green beans, sliced
1 carrot (125 g), sliced
1 stalk celery (100 g), sliced
1 zucchini (100 g), sliced
1 cup (250 mL) water
2 tablespoons (20 g) coconut milk *or* cream
2 cups cooked rice (p. 113)

Method

1. Cook soaked beans for 1 hour (p. 113) or drain and rinse canned beans.
2. Heat oil and gently fry onion, garlic, ginger and spices until onion is tender.
3. Add all fresh vegetables and sauté for 5 minutes.
4. Add water, coconut milk *or* cream and drained beans, bring to boil and simmer 10 minutes.
5. Serve with cooked rice and curry accompaniments (p. 215).

VEGETABLE PASTIES

For a special occasion add 1/2 cup coarsely chopped macadamia nuts to the filling.

- *Number:* **6**
- *Cooking utensil:* 4-sided oven tray
- *Preparation time:* ***25 minutes***
- *Cooking time:* ***40–45 minutes***
- *Oven temperature:* ***200°C reduced to 180°C***

Ingredients

1 onion (125 g), chopped
1 potato (125 g), grated
1/2 carrot (75 g), diced
1/4 turnip, swede or sweet potato (30 g), diced
1/2 cup (100 g) shelled peas
1 tomato (125 g), chopped
1/2 teaspoon salt
6 shakes pepper
1 teaspoon chopped parsley
500 g (1 quantity) wholemeal **Shortcrust pastry** (p. 346)
6 parsley sprigs

Method

1. Set oven at 200°C. Brush or spray oven tray with oil.
2. Combine vegetables, salt, pepper and chopped parsley.
3. Divide pastry into 6 equal parts; knead each into a ball. Roll each piece into a round the size of a saucer (15 cm).
4. Place an equal portion of prepared mixture on each round, using all of the mixture.
5. Brush half way around the edges of the pastry with water, join edges together over the top of the mixture, pinch a small frill over the join and shape pasties into a crescent.
6. Place on oven tray and pierce top with fork. Glaze with milk.
7. Bake at 200°C for 10 minutes then at 180°C for 30–35 minutes, until golden brown.
8. Lift onto hot serving plate. Garnish with parsley sprigs and serve.

SPINACH CHEESE PARCELS

- *Number:* ***16***
- *Cooking utensil:* 4-sided oven tray
- *Preparation time:* ***15 minutes***
- *Cooking time:* ***25–30 minutes***
- *Oven temperature:* ***180°C***

Ingredients

250 g spinach, cooked and chopped
250 g fetta cheese
3 spring onions, chopped
2 eggs, beaten
250 g filo pastry (16 sheets)
1 tablespoon (20 g) butter, melted

Method

1. Set oven at 180°C. Brush or spray oven tray with oil.
2. Mix spinach, cheese, spring onions and eggs.
3. Fold 1 sheet filo pastry into 3, brush with melted butter.
4. Place 1 tablespoon filling at lower edge of pastry. Fold into small triangle. Continue to fold in triangles for length of the pastry.
5. Repeat to make 16 triangles.
6. Brush with melted butter.
7. Bake in oven at 180°C for 25–30 minutes.

KUMARA AND CORIANDER PARCELS

Follow recipe for **Spinach cheese puffs**. Omit spinach and cheese.
Use 250 g cooked kumara and cut into 1 cm dice and 250 g soft tofu cut into 1 cm dice.
Add 2 tablespoons chopped fresh coriander.

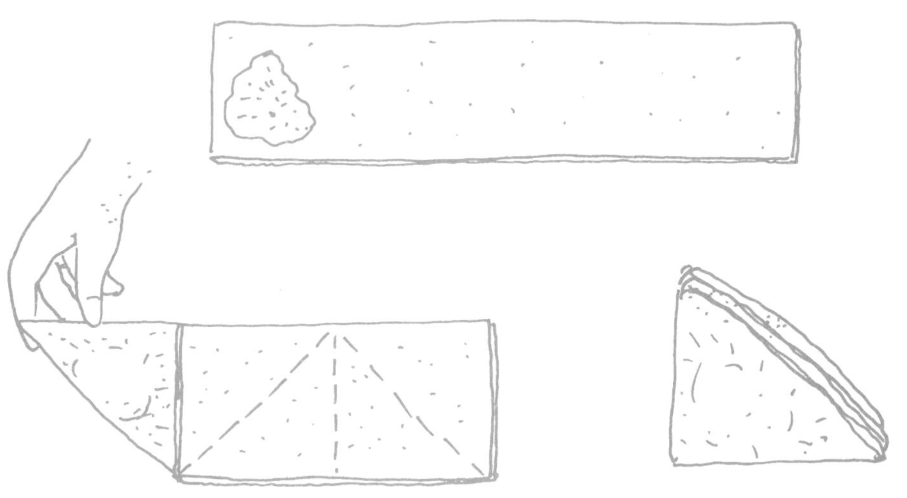

ZUCCHINI SLICE

This freezes well and is delicious in packed lunches.

- *Serves:* ***4 for meal or 16 slices***
- *Cooking utensil:* 20 cm square cake pan (2.5 L)
- *Preparation time:* ***20 minutes***
- *Cooking time:* ***40–45 minutes***
- *Oven temperature:* ***180°C***

Ingredients

1 onion (125 g), chopped
4 zucchini (400 g), grated
1 cup (150 g) self-raising flour
3 shakes pepper
3 eggs, beaten
1 cup (120 g) grated tasty cheese

Method

1. Set oven at 180°C. Brush or spray cake pan with oil.
2. Combine all ingredients except grated cheese.
3. Pour into cake pan. Sprinkle cheese on top.
4. Bake at 180°C for 40–45 minutes.
5. Cut into slices.

 Microwave on high power for 15 minutes.

CARROT AND ZUCCHINI SLICE

Replace 200 g of zucchini with 200 g grated carrot.

LEEK AND ZUCCHINI SLICE

Replace 200 g of zucchini with 200 g sliced leek.

TOMATO-TOPPED ZUCCHINI SLICE

Before cooking arrange 1 tomato (125 g), thinly sliced over top. Place 1 teaspoon (5 g) pesto on each tomato slice.

Non-Vegetarian Variations

ZUCCHINI AND BACON SLICE

Add 2 rashers (80 g) chopped bacon at step 3.

ZUCCHINI AND TUNA SLICE

Add 185 g can drained tuna at step 3.

QUICHE

Full-cream milk, not skim milk, must be used or the quiche will not set firm. For a richer quiche, replace 1/2 the milk with cream.

- *Serves:* **6**
- *Cooking utensil:* 22 cm quiche pan (1 L)
- *Preparation time:* ***15 minutes***
- *Cooking time:* ***25–30 minutes***
- *Oven temperature:* ***200°C reduced to 160°C***

Ingredients

250 g (1/2 quantity) **Shortcrust pastry** (p. 346) *or* 4–6 sheets filo pastry
6 spring onions, chopped
1 1/2 cups (250 mL) milk, warmed
4 eggs, beaten
3 shakes pepper
1 tomato (125 g), sliced
1/2 cup (60 g) grated cheese

Method

1. Set oven at 200°C.
2. Roll out pastry and line quiche pan (see p. 374–375), or line pan with filo pastry. Brush or spray filo pastry lightly with oil between layers.
3. Combine the spring onions, milk, eggs and pepper and pour into pastry base.
4. Place tomato slices on top and cover with grated cheese.
5. Bake 10 minutes at 200°C, then reduce temperature to 160°C and bake until set.
6. May be served hot or cold.

✦ ASPARAGUS QUICHE ✦

Follow recipe for **Quiche**. Half of the milk may be replaced by 250 g yoghurt. Omit tomato and arrange asparagus spears in a cartwheel pattern on top before baking.

✦ SPINACH QUICHE ✦

Follow recipe for **Quiche.** Half of the milk may be replaced by 250 g ricotta or low-fat cottage cheese. Add 1/2 cup blanched spinach and 1/4 teaspoon grated nutmeg to egg and milk mixture.

✦ LEEK AND CHEESE QUICHE ✦

Follow recipe for **Quiche**. Use Swiss cheese. Half of the milk milk may be replaced with cream. Blanch 1 sliced leek (125 g) in boiling water, drain and add to milk and egg mixture.

Non-Vegetarian Variations

✦ QUICHE LORRAINE ✦

Follow recipe for **Quiche**. Add 2 chopped rashers bacon (80 g) and 1 chopped onion (125 g).

QUICK CRUSTLESS QUICHE

- *Serves:* **6**
- *Cooking utensil:* 22 cm quiche pan (1 L)

Preparation time: ***20 minutes***
Cooking Time: ***35–40 minutes***
- *Oven temperature:* ***200°C reduced to 160°C***

Ingredients

4 eggs, beaten
$1\frac{1}{2}$ cups (375 mL) milk
$\frac{1}{2}$ cup (75 g) self-raising flour
1 zucchini (100 g), grated
1 carrot (125 g), grated
1 onion (125 g), diced
1 potato (150 g), grated
1 tablespoon chopped parsley
1 cup (120 g) grated tasty cheese

Method

1. Set oven at 200°C. Brush or spray quiche pan with oil.
2. Combine all ingredients except half cup of cheese.
3. Pour into quiche pan and sprinkle remaining cheese on top.
4. Bake 15 minutes at 200°C, then reduce temperature to 160°C. Bake 20–25 minutes until set.

Place in 22 cm microwave ring cake pan (1.75 L). Cover with plastic wrap and cook on medium power for 10–12 minutes.

EGG AND ONION PIE

- *Serves:* **6**
- *Cooking utensil:* saucepan, 22 cm pie dish (1 L)

Preparation time: ***15 minutes***
Cooking time: ***25–30 minutes***
- *Oven temperature:* ***200°C reduced to 160°C***

Ingredients

500 g (1 quantity) **Shortcrust pastry** (p. 346)
2 onions (250 g), sliced
1 teaspoon (5 mL) olive oil
6 eggs
6 spring onions, chopped
6 shakes pepper

Method

1. Set oven at 200°C.
2. Roll out pastry and line pie plate.
3. Sauté onions in oil for 7–10 minutes, until golden brown.
4. Break eggs into pastry case, sprinkle with spring onions and pepper. Slash egg yolks with a knife.
5. Cover pie with pastry. Glaze top with milk.
6. Bake 15 minutes at 200°C, then reduce temperature to 160°C and bake for a further 15 minutes.

Non-Vegetarian Variations

✦ EGG AND BACON PIE ✦

Follow recipe for **Egg and onion pie**. Replace onion with 2 rashers (80 g) chopped bacon.

SPANISH TORTILLA

A style of omelette, cut into wedges and served warm or cold.

► *Serves:* *4*

► *Cooking utensil:* non-stick frying pan, griller

Preparation time: ***15 minutes***

Cooking time: ***20 minutes***

Ingredients

1 cup (250 mL) milk
8 eggs, beaten
1 teaspoon salt
6 shakes pepper
2 potatoes (250 g), sliced
1 onion (125 g), sliced
1 tablespoon (20 mL) olive oil
4 sprigs parsley

Method

1. Sauté potatoes and onion in oil, 5–10 minutes (may be microwaved for 5 minutes on medium power).
2. Mix eggs, salt, pepper and pour over potatoes and onions. Cook gently until mixture sets.
3. Brown top under hot griller.
4. Allow to cool slightly, loosen mixture from pan and slide on to plate.
5. Cut into four wedges, garnish with parsley sprigs and serve warm or cold.

✦ FRITTATA ✦

The Italian version of tortilla, made with the addition of a green vegetable. Follow recipe for **Tortilla**, add 125 g lightly cooked broccoli florets, silver beet, green beans, zucchini *or* other green vegetable cut into bite-sized pieces at step 1.

CORN AND CHEESE ROULADE

- *Serves:* **4**
- *Cooking utensil:* Swiss roll cake pan (24 cm x 30 cm, 1 L)
- *Preparation time:* ***20 minutes***
- *Cooking time:* ***30 minutes***
- *Oven temperature:* ***170°C***

Ingredients

2 tablespoons (40 g) butter
3 tablespoons (30 g) plain flour
1 cup (250 mL) milk
3 eggs (61g), separated

Filling

1 cup (250 g) smooth ricotta cheese
210 g can corn kernels, drained
3 shakes pepper
1/4 cup (30 g) grated cheese

Method

1. Set oven at 170°C. Brush or spray Swiss roll cake pan with oil and line base with baking paper. Spread clean tea towel towel on bench.
2. Melt butter in small saucepan, stir in flour.
3. Add milk slowly, stirring continuously, while bringing to boil.
4. Remove from heat and beat in egg yolks. Cool.
5. Beat egg whites until stiff.
6. Fold egg yolk mixture into egg whites very lightly.
7. Pour into Swiss roll pan.
8. Bake for 30 minutes at 170°C. To test if cooked: press lightly with the finger in the centre of the cake – the impression should disappear at once.
9. Turn roulade onto tea towel, remove paper and trim crusts off sides. Quickly roll up in tea towel. Allow to stand for 2 minutes.
10. Make filling: mix ricotta cheese, corn kernels, pepper and cheese. Add a little cream if too thick to spread.
11. Unroll roulade. Spread with filling. Roll up.
12. Cut into 8 slices and serve.

TOMATO AND ZUCCHINI ROULADE

Follow recipe for **Corn and cheese roulade**. Omit corn. Add 2 tablespoons (40 g) tomato paste to milk mixture before beating in egg yolks. At step 8, mix filling with 1 cup (150 g) grated and sautéed zucchini in 1 teaspoon butter and 2 tablespoons (40 g) chopped semi-dried tomatoes. Use as filling.

SOUFFLÉ

Follow recipe for **Corn and cheese roulade**. Omit filling. At step 6 place mixture into 14 cm soufflé dish, brushed or sprayed with oil. Cook at 175°C for 30 minutes. Serve immediately soufflé comes out of oven. Serves 2.

CHEESE SOUFFLÉ

Follow recipe for **Corn and cheese roulade**. Omit filling. Add 1 cup (120 g) grated tasty cheese at step 4. At step 6 place mixture into 14 cm soufflé dish, brushed or sprayed with oil. Cook at 175°C for 30 minutes. Serve immediately soufflé comes out of oven. Serves 2.

Non-Vegetarian Variations

✦ SMOKED SALMON ROULADE ✦

Follow recipe for **Corn and cheese roulade**. Omit filling. At step 9 use 100 g smoked salmon mixed with 1 cup (250 mL) whipped sour cream as filling.

✦ HAM AND RICOTTA ROULADE ✦

Follow recipe for **Corn and cheese roulade**. Omit corn. Add 100 g chopped ham and 1 tablespoon (20 g) grain mustard to filling.

✦ CRABMEAT AND SPINACH ROULADE ✦

Follow recipe for **Corn and cheese roulade**. Omit corn and grated cheese. Add 105 g can crabmeat and 125 g cooked spinach to filling.

6 Soups

Soups may be served as a light meal or at the beginning of dinner. They provide contrast in flavour, colour and texture to other dishes of a meal. Soups are generally served hot but some varieties may be served chilled or iced.

A hearty thick soup such as **Corn Chowder** or **Minestrone** served with crusty bread makes a light meal, while a chilled soup such as **Vichyssoise** can be served as a refreshing first course.

Food value

Broth, stock soups and consommés provide very small amounts of minerals, protein and carbohydrates. The incomplete protein, gelatin, is obtained by simmering meat and bones in water and, when allowed to become cold, this gelatin sets the liquid to a jelly. Thick soups are richer in the food nutrients than thin soups and may contain a small amount of fat.

Classification of soups

Thin soups

Broths are made from water and contain diced meat, vegetables and cereal, garnished with chopped parsley, e.g. **Gravy broth**.

Stock soups are made from **Meat**, **Fish**, **Vegetable** or **Chicken stock**, the name being derived from the main ingredient used, e.g. **Chicken soup**.

Consommés or double broths are made from **Meat stock** that is flavoured and enriched by additional meat and vegetables and clarified with egg white and egg shells. The strained liquid should be crystal clear, well-flavoured and completely free from fat. Consommé may be served chilled. The name is derived from the garnish, e.g. **Julienne consommé**.

Thick Soups

Puree Soups are made from fresh or dried vegetables, pureed and thickened with blended flour or cornflour, e.g. **Pea soup**.

Cream soups are fresh vegetable, chicken or fish soups. The vegetable soups are pureed and take their name from the main vegetable, e.g. **Cream of asparagus soup**. They are thickened with roux or blended flour and enriched with milk or cream. If hot they can be served with croutons. Some may be served chilled, e.g. **Iced cucumber coup**.

Fish or seafood soup is made from **Fish stock**, thickened with roux or cereal. The name is derived from the fish or seafood used, e.g. **Oyster soup**.

Stock

Stock is obtained by simmering bones, meat, vegetables and flavours in water for several hours. The different types of stock include **Meat stock**, **Chicken stock**, **Vegetable stock** and **Fish stock**. Commercially prepared stock concentrates, such as beef or chicken in liquid, cube or powder form, may be used as a substitute for fresh stock. They usually have a high salt content and additional salt is not necessary.

Guidelines for making stock

- Use a heavy stockpot or saucepan with a tight-fitting lid.
- Use fresh meat, bones and vegetables. Potato or parsnip clouds the stock and cabbage gives an 'off' flavour.
- Bones from roast joints, scraps from meat and poultry cooked or uncooked and trimmings of vegetables may be added. Never add fat.
- Strain when cooked, as vegetables allowed to remain in the stock cause fermentation.
- When cool, lift fat from surface and keep stock in a refrigerator or freeze in 1 or 2 litre containers.

Using a pressure cooker

By using a pressure cooker it is possible to produce well-flavoured stock or soup in one-third of the normal time. Recipe booklets supplied by the pressure cooker manufacturers show the necessary modifications to the usual proportions and state time of pressure cooking. It is important to remember that the cooker should not be more than half full when all ingredients have been added. Thickening should be added after the pressure has been reduced.

MEAT STOCK

The basis of tasty soups and casseroles.

Cooking utensil: stockpot *or* large saucepan

Cooking time: ***2 hours***

Ingredients

1.5 kg beef and lamb bones
2 teaspoons (10 g) salt
2.5 L (10 cups) water
1 carrot (125 g), chopped
1 turnip (125 g), chopped
1 onion (125 g), chopped
2 stalks (200 g) celery, chopped
3 pimento (allspice)
bouquet garni
6 peppercorns

Method

1. Wash bones and remove any fat.
2. Put bones, salt and water into saucepan.
3. Bring slowly to the boil.
4. Add vegetables and flavourings and simmer for 2 hours.
5. Strain and allow to cool. Remove fat before using.
6. Keep in refrigerator or freeze.

✦ CHICKEN STOCK ✦

Follow recipe for **Meat stock**. Use chicken bones and giblets instead of meat. Cook for 1 hour.

✦ VEGETABLE STOCK ✦

Follow recipe for **Meat stock**. Omit bones. Use a variety of vegetables. Flavour with peppercorns, nutmeg and herbs. Simmer for 1 hour.

FISH STOCK

- *Cooking utensil:* saucepan
- *Cooking time:* ***20 minutes***

Ingredients

250 g fish bones and head
3 cups (750 mL) cold water
1 teaspoon salt
1 onion (125 g), chopped
1 stalk (100 g) celery, chopped
1 slice of lemon
3 parsley sprigs
2 peppercorns

Method

1. Wash bones and place in saucepan with water and salt.
2. Bring slowly to the boil.
3. Add vegetables and flavourings, simmer for 20 minutes.
4. Strain through a fine strainer.
5. Use for fish soups and sauces.

STOCK SOUP

- *Serves:* *4*
- *Cooking utensil:* saucepan
- *Cooking time:* ***10 minutes***

Ingredients

1 L (4 cups) **Meat** *or* **Chicken stock**
1 cup diced *or* julienne vegetables, e.g. onion, carrot, celery, turnip
1 teaspoon chopped parsley

Method

1. Heat stock, add vegetables and cook for 5 minutes until tender.
2. Taste and adjust flavours.
3. Serve garnished with parsley.

✦ CHICKEN SOUP ✦

Follow recipe for **Stock soup** using **Chicken stock** and adding 1/2 cup (75 g) diced chicken.

✦ FISH SOUP ✦

Follow recipe for **Stock soup** using **Fish stock** and adding 1/2 cup (75 g) diced fish.

CONSOMMÉ

Serves: **4**
Cooking utensil: large saucepan
Cooking time: ***30 minutes***

Ingredients

1 L (4 cups) **Meat stock** (p. 140)
1 egg white, lightly beaten
1 egg shell, crushed
125 g lean beef, thinly sliced
1/2 carrot (65 g), prepared and roughly diced
1/4 turnip (35 g), prepared and roughly diced
1/2 onion (65 g), prepared and roughly diced
piece celery (50 g), prepared and roughly diced
4 peppercorns
salt and pepper to taste

Method

1. Refrigerate stock until cold and remove all fat.
2. Place in saucepan.
3. Add egg whites, stir well. Add all other ingredients placing egg shells on surface.
4. Bring slowly to the boil. A 'raft' of egg shells, meat and vegetables should form on surface and trap the fine particles of meat and vegetables.
5. Reduce heat, cover and simmer very gently for 30 minutes. The 'raft' should remain intact until cooking is nearly finished.
6. Carefully lift out 'raft' and discard. Place coffee filter paper in strainer or funnel. Pour 1/2 cup boiling water through filter paper to clear any impurities. Discard water.
7. Strain consommé liquid slowly through filter paper. Repeat until liquid is clear.
8. Reheat and add suitable garnish before serving.

JULIENNE CONSOMMÉ

Follow recipe for **Consommé**. Prepare garnish of 1/2 cup (75 g) each of carrot, turnip and celery cut into match-like strips 4 cm long. Simmer in stock for 3 minutes. Strain and add to reheated consommé.

JARDINIERE CONSOMMÉ

Follow recipe for **Consommé**. Prepare garnish of 1/2 cup (75 g) each of carrot, turnip and celery cut into 1 cm cubes. Simmer in stock for 3 minutes. Strain and add to reheated consommé.

MACEDOINE CONSOMMÉ

Follow recipe for **Consommé**. Prepare garnish of 1/2 cup (75 g) each of carrot, turnip and celery cut into fancy shapes. Simmer in stock for 3 minutes. Strain and add to reheated consommé.

CHILLED CONSOMMÉ

Follow recipe for **Consommé**. After step 6, chill both consomme and cooked garnish and combine just before serving.

BROTH

► *Serves:* 4
► *Cooking utensil:* large saucepan *or* pressure cooker
Cooking time: $1^1/_4$ **hours**

Ingredients

250 g neck *or* shank of lamb
1.5 L (6 cups) water
1 teaspoon salt
6 shakes pepper
$^1/_4$ cup (50 g) pearl barley
$^1/_4$ carrot (35 g)
$^1/_4$ turnip (35 g)
$^1/_2$ onion (65 g)
1 stalk (100 g) celery
1 teaspoon chopped parsley

Method

1. Soak meat and bones in water with salt and pepper for 30 minutes if possible. Bring slowly to the boil.
2. Wash pearl barley and add as soon as soup is boiling. Simmer 1 hour.
3. Prepare and dice vegetables into 1 cm pieces. Add to soup and simmer for 15 minutes before serving.
4. Remove fat and bones, adjust flavour and consistency if necessary and serve some of each ingredient in each soup bowl. Garnish with chopped parsley.

✦ GRAVY BROTH ✦

Follow recipe for **Broth**. Omit lamb and pearl barley. Use 125 g gravy beef and $^1/_4$ cup (50 g) tapioca.

✦ COTTAGE BROTH ✦

Follow recipe for **Broth**. Omit pearl barley. Use $^1/_4$ cup (50 g) rice *or* oatmeal.

✦ CHICKEN BROTH ✦

Follow recipe for **Broth**. Omit lamb and pearl barley. Use chicken carcase *or* 250 g uncooked chicken. Add $^1/_4$ cup (50 g) rice at step 2 and simmer 30 minutes. Dice chicken into 1 cm pieces after cooking.

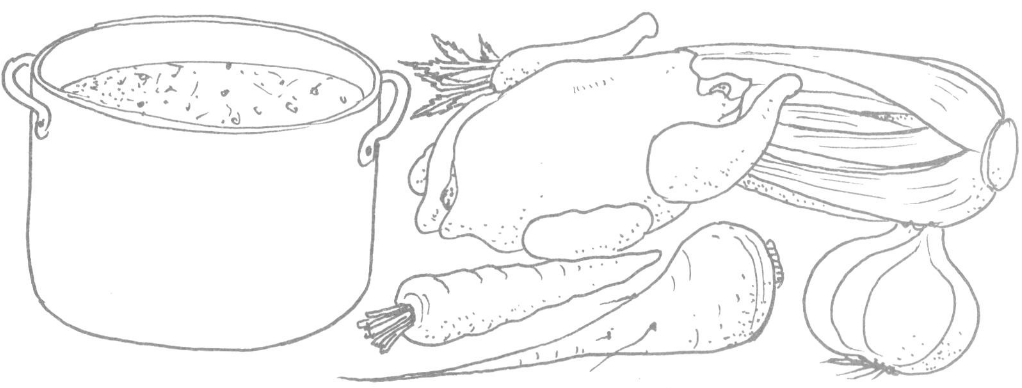

VEGETABLE CREAM SOUP

For extra richness 1/4 cup (190 mL) cream may be added.

- *Serves:* 4
- *Cooking utensil:* saucepan

Cooking time: ***30 minutes***

Ingredients

1 tablespoon (20 g) butter
1 rasher (40 g) bacon
2 cups (300 g) prepared and roughly diced main vegetable (see below)
1 cup (150 g) prepared and roughly diced flavouring vegetables (see below)
1 tablespoon (10 g) plain flour
3 shakes pepper
2 cups (500 mL) **Chicken stock** (p. 141)
3/4 cup (190 mL) milk
1/4 cup (65 mL) cream
12–18 **Croutons** (p. 153)

Method

1. Melt butter and sauté bacon and vegetables for 5 minutes. (Place lid on to 'sweat' vegetables but stir frequently.)
2. Remove from heat and stir in flour.
3. Add pepper, stock and stir until boiling. Simmer until vegetables are tender – approximately 20 minutes. Remove bacon.
4. Puree soup or use electric blender. Return soup to saucepan, add milk and reheat without boiling.
5. Adjust flavours and consistency if necessary and serve with croutons and suitable garnish.

✦ CREAM OF ASPARAGUS SOUP ✦

Follow recipe for **Vegetable cream soup**. Use 2 cups (300 g) asparagus as main vegetable and 1/2 cup (75 g) each of onion and celery as flavouring vegetables. Garnish with cooked asparagus tips, 2 cm long.

✦ CREAM OF CARROT or CRECY SOUP ✦

Follow recipe for **Vegetable cream soup**. Use 2 cups (300 g) carrot as main vegetable and 1/3 cup (50 g) each of onion, turnip and celery as flavouring vegetables. Add 1/8 teaspoon nutmeg at step 2.

✦ CREAM OF CAULIFLOWER or CRÈME DU BARRY SOUP ✦

Follow recipe for **Vegetable cream soup**. Use 2 1/2 cups (300 g) cauliflower as main vegetable and 1/3 cup (50 g) each of onion and celery as flavouring vegetables. Add 1 bay leaf at step 3, remove before pureeing. Garnish with 1/2 cup cooked cauliflower florets. May be served chilled.

✦ CREAM OF CELERY SOUP ✦

Follow recipe for **Vegetable cream soup**. Use 2 cups (300 g) celery as main vegetable and 1/2 cup (75 g) each of onion and turnip as flavouring vegetables. Garnish with 1 tablespoon chopped parsley *or* snipped chives.

✦ CREAM OF LEEK SOUP ✦

Follow recipe for **Vegetable cream soup**. Use 2 1/2 cups (300 g) leek as main vegetable and 1/2 cup (75 g) each of celery and turnip as flavouring vegetables. Garnish with 1 teaspoon yoghurt *or* grated cheese per serve.

✦ CREAM OF MUSHROOM ✦

Follow recipe for **Vegetable cream soup**. Use 3 cups (300 g) mushrooms as main vegetable and 1/2 cup (75 g) each of onion and celery as flavouring vegetables. Garnish with 1 teaspoon diced ham per serve.

✦ CREAM OF POTATO SOUP ✦

Follow recipe for **Vegetable cream soup**. Use 2 cups (300 g) potato as main vegetable and 1/2 cup (75 g) onion and celery as flavouring vegetables. Garnish with 1/2 cup (60 g) grated cheese and 1 tablespoon chopped parsley *or* 1/2 cup cooked sliced sausage.

✦ CREAM OF PUMPKIN or MARIANNE SOUP ✦

Follow recipe for **Vegetable cream soup**. Use 2 cups (300 g) pumpkin as main vegetable and 1/4 cup (30 g) each of celery, onion, carrot and turnip as flavouring vegetables. Add juice and grated rind of 1 orange *or* 1 tablespoon crushed lemongrass at step 4. The cream may be replaced with coconut milk.

✦ CREAM OF ZUCCHINI SOUP ✦

Follow recipe for **Vegetable cream soup**. Use 1 1/2 cups (300 g) zucchini as main vegetable (leave skin on) and 1/2 cup (75 g) each of celery and onion as flavouring vegetables. Add 1/8 teaspoon tarragon at step 3. Garnish with 1 teaspoon snipped chives *or* 1 teaspoon toasted almonds per serve.

✦ ICED CUCUMBER SOUP ✦

Follow recipe for **Vegetable cream soup**. Use 2 cups (300 g) cucumber as main vegetable (leave skin on) and 1/2 cup (75 g) onion as flavouring vegetable. Light sour cream may be used instead of cream. Garnish with 1 teaspoon snipped chives per serve. Chill before serving.

✦ VICHYSSOISE ✦

A chilled soup originally from France.

Follow recipe for **Vegetable cream soup**. Use 1 1/2 cups (225 g) potato, 1 cup (120 g) leeks and 1/2 cup (75 g) celery as main and flavouring vegetables. Add 1/8 teaspoon cayenne at step 3. Garnish with 1 teaspoon snipped chives per serve. Chill before serving.

PEA SOUP

A rich-flavoured winter soup. For a vegetarian soup use **Vegetable stock** (p. 141) and omit bacon bone.

Serves: 4
Cooking utensil: saucepan *or* pressure cooker
Cooking time: **30–40 minutes**

Ingredients

1/2 cup (100 g) split green peas
1 L (4 cups) **Meat stock** (p. 140) *or* water
6 shakes pepper
1/4 turnip (35 g)
2 stalks (200 g) celery
1/2 carrot (65 g)
1 onion (125 g)
1 sprig fresh mint *or* 1/4 teaspoon dried mint
1 piece bacon *or* bacon bone
1 tablespoon (10 g) plain flour
12 **Croutons** (p. 153)

Method

1. Rinse peas in strainer and place in stock.
2. Wash, peel and chop vegetables.
3. Place all ingredients, except flour and croutons, in saucepan.
4. Bring to the boil and simmer 30–40 minutes or until vegetables are tender.
5. Remove bacon bone and puree soup or use an electric blender. Return to saucepan.
6. Blend flour with 1/4 cup of cold water, add to soup.
7. Stir until boiling and simmer for 1 minute.
8. Adjust flavour and consistency if necessary. Serve with croutons.

BEAN SOUP

Follow recipe for **Pea soup**. Omit split peas. Use 1/2 cup (100 g) haricot *or* lima beans, soaked overnight if possible. Add 2 diced tomatoes (250 g) at step 2.

DUTCH PEA SOUP

Follow recipe for **Pea soup**. Add 2 cooked and sliced frankfurts *or* sausages at step 6.

LENTIL SOUP

Follow recipe for **Pea soup**. Omit split peas. Use 1/2 cup (100 g) red lentils. 1/2 teaspoon curry paste may be added at step 3.

LENTIL AND TOMATO SOUP

Follow recipe for **Pea soup**. Omit split peas. Use 1/2 cup (100 g) red lentils. Add 2 diced tomatoes (250 g) at step 3.

PEA AND TOMATO SOUP

Follow recipe for **Pea soup**. Add 2 diced tomatoes (250 g) at step 3.

SNAPPER SOUP

- *Serves:* 4
- *Cooking utensil:* saucepan

Cooking time: **10 minutes**

Ingredients

1 whole snapper (600 g)
1 tablespoon (20 g) butter
1 tablespoon (10 g) plain flour
2 cups (500 mL) **Fish stock** (see step 1)
3/4 cup (190 mL) milk
1/4 cup (65 mL) light cream
1 teaspoon lemon juice
1 teaspoon chopped parsley *or* dill

Method

1. Remove head, bones and skin and use to make **Fish stock** (p. 141).
2. Cut snapper flesh into 1 cm dice.
3. Melt butter in saucepan, stir in flour, add fish stock slowly and stir until boiling. Simmer 2 minutes.
4. Add fish, simmer 2 minutes.
5. Add milk and cream, reheat without boiling.
6. Add lemon juice, taste, adjust flavour and consistency.
7. Serve garnished with parsley *or* dill.

✦ CREAM OF OYSTER SOUP or OYSTER BISQUE ✦

Follow recipe for **Snapper soup**. Omit snapper. Add 12 oysters at step 3, simmer 1 minute.

✦ CREAM OF CRAYFISH SOUP or CRAYFISH BISQUE ✦

Follow recipe for **Snapper soup**. Omit snapper. Add 125 g diced crayfish *or* seafood extender at step 3, simmer 1 minute. Add 1 teaspoon tomato paste at step 4.

FRENCH ONION SOUP

- *Serves:* 4
- *Cooking utensil:* large saucepan

Cooking time: **1 hour**

Ingredients

4 onions (500 g)
2 tablespoons (40 g) butter
1 tablespoon (10 g) plain flour
1 L (4 cups) **Meat stock** (p. 140)
3 shakes pepper
4 slices French bread stick
4 tablespoons (40 g) grated cheese

Method

1. Peel and slice onions and fry slowly in butter until light brown (30 minutes).
2. Remove from heat and stir in flour. Blend thoroughly then add stock and mix well, add pepper.
3. Stir until boiling. Simmer 20 minutes.
4. Taste, adjust flavour and consistency if necessary.
5. Sprinkle cheese on bread, grill lightly.
6. Serve soup in bowl and place bread on top.

CORN CHOWDER

Serves: **6**
Cooking utensil: large saucepan
Cooking time: **20–25 minutes**

Ingredients

2 rashers (80 g) bacon, chopped
$^1/_2$ onion (65 g), chopped
1 stalk celery (100 g), cut into 1 cm dice
1 cup (150 g) diced potato
1 teaspoon salt
3 shakes cayenne
2 cups (500 mL) water
2 tablespoons (20 g) plain flour
2 cups (500 mL) milk
310 g can sweet corn kernels
1 tablespoon chopped capsicum
1 tablespoon chopped parsley
18 **Croutons** (p. 153)

Method

1. Lightly fry bacon, onion and celery. Do not brown.
2. Add potato, cook 1 minute.
3. Add seasoning and water. Cover and simmer for 10 minutes.
4. Blend flour with $^1/_4$ cup (65 mL) milk. Add remaining milk to vegetables.
5. Add blended flour, stir until boiling and cook 3 minutes.
6. Add corn, capsicum and parsley. Add salt and pepper to taste. Adjust the consistency to a thick soup, use a little cream if necessary.
7. Garnish with croutons and serve.

EGG AND LEMON SOUP

A Greek soup also known as Avgolemono.

Serves: **4**
Cooking utensil: saucepan
Cooking time: **15–20 minutes**

Ingredients

1 L (4 cups) **Chicken stock** (p. 141)
$^1/_4$ cup (50 g) rice
2 eggs
1 tablespoon (20 mL) lemon juice
2 teaspoons chopped fresh mint

Method

1. Bring stock to the boil, add rice. Cook 10–12 minutes until just tender. Reduce heat.
2. Beat eggs until frothy. Add lemon juice and stir in about 3 tablespoons hot stock. Slowly pour the mixture into stock, stirring continuously.
3. Heat slowly for about 2 minutes until mixture thickens slightly. Do not allow soup to boil or egg will curdle.
4. Adjust flavours, garnish with mint and serve at once.

BORSCH

A soup from Russia, combining sweet and sour flavours with the brilliant colour of beetroot.

- *Serves:* ***6***
- *Cooking utensil:* large saucepan

Cooking time: ***1 hour***

Ingredients

500 g beetroot
125 g minced beef
2 tomatoes (250 g), chopped
1 onion (125 g), chopped
1 L (4 cups) water
1 teaspoon salt
6 shakes pepper
1 tablespoon (20 mL) vinegar
1 teaspoon sugar
2 tablespoons (40 mL) sour cream

Method

1. Peel beetroot and grate on coarse grater.
2. Place minced beef, tomato, onion, water, salt and pepper in saucepan, bring to the boil and simmer 20 minutes.
3. Add vinegar, beetroot and sugar and simmer a further 20 minutes.
4. Taste, adjust flavour and consistency if necessary. Serve at once, garnished with sour cream.

GAZPACHO

A soup of Spanish origin served cold.

- *Serves:* ***4***

Ingredients

425 g can *or* 500 g tomatoes
1/4 capsicum (35 g)
1 cucumber (200 g)
1/4 onion (35 g)
1 clove (5 g) garlic, crushed
1 teaspoon (5 mL) olive oil
2 cups (500 mL) **Chicken stock** (p. 141)
1 tablespoon (20 mL) vinegar
1/2 teaspoon tabasco sauce
3 shakes pepper

Method

1. Finely chop tomatoes, capsicum, cucumber, onion.
2. Stir all ingredients together.
3. Taste and adjust seasoning if necessary.
4. Chill and serve.

SPICY ASIAN FISH SOUP

- *Serves:* 4
- *Cooking utensil:* large saucepan
- *Cooking time:* **10 minutes**

Ingredients

1 L (4 cups) **Fish stock** (p. 141) *or* water
1 tablespoon (20 mL) fish sauce
1 teaspoon (5 g) tamarind paste
1 tablespoon (20 mL) sweet chilli sauce
1 cup (100 g) beanshoots
100 g vermicelli *or* rice noodles
4 spring onions, chopped
200 g fish, diced, e.g. flathead
1 tomato (125 g), diced
1 tablespoon chopped fresh Vietnamese mint
1 tablespoon chopped fresh coriander

Method

1. Place all ingredients, except mint and coriander, in saucepan and bring to boil.
2. Simmer gently for 10 minutes. Add mint and coriander before serving.

VIETNAMESE PHO BO SOUP

Vietnamese soups are often a meal in themselves and are served for breakfast and lunch. Each diner is served with about 2 cups (500 mL) of soup in a large bowl.

- *Serves:* 4
- *Cooking utensil:* large saucepan
- *Cooking time:* **35 minutes**

Ingredients

500 g beef spare ribs
1.5 L (6 cups) water
1 teaspoon (5 g) chopped ginger
2 tablespoons (40 mL) fish sauce
1 onion (125 g), finely chopped
125 g fresh rice noodles *or* 75 g dried noodles
1/2 bunch coriander, chopped
2 spring onions, finely sliced
1 small red chilli, finely sliced
1 lime, cut into wedges

Method

1. Bring spare ribs, water, ginger, fish sauce and onion slowly to boil, simmer 30 minutes.
2. Lift out bones, remove meat, dice and return to saucepan.
3. Reheat to boiling point. If using dried noodles add and cook 2 minutes.
4. In each serving bowl place fresh noodles, coriander and spring onion. Pour hot liquid over.
5. Serve red chillies and lime wedges separately.

✦ PHO GA ✦

Follow recipe for **Vietnamese pho bo soup**. Omit beef.
At step 1 add 500 g chicken bones, with a small amount of chicken attached.

VIETNAMESE CRAB AND CORN SOUP

- *Serves:* *4*
- *Cooking utensil:* large saucepan

Cooking time: ***20 minutes***

Ingredients

1.5 L (6 cups) **Chicken stock** (p. 141)
1 onion (125 g), finely chopped
1 clove (5 g) garlic, crushed
210 g can crab meat
310 g can creamed sweet corn
1 tablespoon (10 g) plain flour
1 tablespoon (20 mL) water
1 egg, lightly beaten
2 spring onions, finely sliced
1/2 bunch coriander, chopped

Method

1. Bring chicken stock, onion and garlic to boil.
2. Add crab meat and sweet corn.
3. Mix flour and water, add to stock and simmer 1 minute.
4. Remove from heat, add egg, stirring gently to form threads in mixture.
5. Place in serving bowls and garnish with spring onions and coriander.

✦ VIETNAMESE CRAB AND ASPARAGUS SOUP ✦

Follow recipe for **Vietnamese crab and corn soup**. Omit sweet corn.
Use 200 g fresh, lightly cooked chopped asparagus at step 2.

MINESTRONE

This hearty soup is a meal in itself.

- *Serves:* **8**
- *Cooking utensil:* large saucepan

Cooking time: ***45 minutes***

Ingredients

$^1/_2$ leek (60 g), sliced
$^1/_2$ onion (75 g), chopped
$^1/_2$ rasher (20 g) bacon, chopped
1.5 L (6 cups) stock *or* water
3 shakes pepper
$^1/_2$ cup (75 g) diced carrot
$^1/_2$ cup (75 g) diced turnip
$^1/_2$ cup (75 g) diced potato
1 stalk (100 g) diced celery
$^1/_3$ cup (50 g) macaroni
$^1/_3$ cup (50 g) broken spaghetti
$^1/_2$ cup (50 g) shredded cabbage
2 tablespoons (40 g) tomato paste
325 g can cannellini *or* lima beans, drained
2 tablespoons (20 g) grated parmesan cheese

Method

1. Fry leek and onion with bacon, add stock, pepper, carrot, turnip, potato, celery, macaroni and spaghetti. Cook for 30 minutes.
2. Add cabbage, tomato paste and beans. Cook for 10 minutes.
3. Serve garnished with grated cheese.

CHICKEN AND LEEK SOUP

- *Serves:* **4**
- *Cooking utensil:* saucepan

Cooking time: ***25 minutes***

Ingredients

1 L (4 cups) **Chicken stock** (p. 141) *or* water
1 leek (250 g), thinly sliced
$^1/_4$ cup (50 g) rice
1 cup (150 g) diced cooked chicken
1 cup (250 mL) milk
1 tablespoon chopped parsley

Method

1. Place stock, leeks and rice in saucepan, bring to the boil and simmer for 15–20 minutes until rice is cooked.
2. Add chicken and milk and reheat without boiling.
3. Serve garnished with parsley.

CROUTONS

Serves: 4

Cooking utensil: frying pan

Ingredients

1 slice stale bread, 1 cm thick
4 tablespoons (80 mL) oil

Method

1. Remove crusts and cut bread into 1 cm cubes.
2. Heat oil in frying pan.
3. Fry cubes of bread until golden brown.
4. Drain on absorbent paper. Use as required.

MICROWAVE CROUTONS

Ingredients

$1\frac{1}{2}$ cups of bread cut into 1 cm cubes
$\frac{1}{2}$ teaspoon paprika
$\frac{1}{4}$ teaspoon garlic salt
$\frac{1}{4}$ teaspoon curry powder
2 teaspoons (10 mL) oil *or* spray oil
$\frac{1}{2}$ teaspoon dried parsley

Method

1. Place all ingredients into a microwave dish.
2. Spray with oil or add oil, shake to mix ingredients.
3. Microwave on high power (uncovered) for 4–5 minutes. Stir during cooking at 2 minute intervals.
4. Stand uncovered for 5 minutes to crisp.

7 Fish

Seafoods are an important part of the Australian diet. Consumption has increased due to the widespread promotion of the nutritional value of seafood and improvements in harvesting techniques which mean they reach the consumer in a fresh state.

Fish and shellfish are harvested from the sea, from freshwater sources such as rivers and lakes or through fish farming techniques. Developments in fish farming in Australia have increased the range and availability of fish and shellfish, such as trout, Atlantic salmon, yabbies, marron and oysters.

Seafoods are quickly cooked and ideal for busy people with limited time to prepare food, as well as for those looking for low-fat dishes. Fresh herbs, lightly cooked vegetables or salads can be served with fish, providing a wide variety of tastes and textures.

Food value

Seafood is a valuable source of the mineral iodine as well as calcium, potassium and iron. Fish is low in saturated fat and cholesterol, and oily fish is an excellent source of polyunsaturated oils and vitamin A. Crustaceans have a higher cholesterol content. The protein in fish is more easily digested as it has a high proportion of water to flesh. Omega 3 fatty acids, which have been shown to reduce the incidence of coronary heart disease, are also found in fish.

Purchase

In the following recipes several varieties of seafood are recommended as suitable. Many other varieties are available and may be substituted. Watch for seasonal availability, which influences the price. Although the names of fish have been officially agreed upon across Australia, they may still vary from one state to another.

Fresh fish Flesh is firm, gills are blood red and no unpleasant odour should be detected. Buy sufficient for one meal and cook as soon as possible after purchase, as the flesh deteriorates rapidly.

Frozen fish If purchased frozen, it keeps for approximately 3 months in a home freezer. Follow instructions on the label for storage, thawing and cooking. Fish is sometimes thawed by the retailer and repacked and may be labelled as 'thawed fish, previously frozen'. It must not be refrozen in the home freezer as bacteria develop each time it is thawed.

Molluscs Seafoods with a hard shell, e.g. oysters, clams, pipi. If purchased unopened, shell should be tightly clamped. Scallops and other shellfish are frequently sold after the shells have been removed, and the flesh may have been frozen. Odour and general appearance are the only guides to freshness and quality. Remove flesh after forcing shell open.

Crustacea Seafoods with an external skeleton, e.g. crabs, yabbies, crayfish. May be purchased cooked or raw. Raw prawns are labelled green prawns. The flesh becomes opaque during cooking. Shrimps, which are small prawns, can be used for some dishes. The flesh is removed after cooking.

Dried fish May be dried and salted or dried and smoked. It should be soaked in water before cooking to restore some of the moisture and remove excess salt.

Smoked fish Is smoked and partially dried, e.g. cod, trout. Smoked salmon is sugar cured. Bottled smoked saithe can be used as a flavouring or garnish.

Canned fish A wide variety of oily fish, shellfish and crustacea is available. The packing medium may be water, oil or a sauce. Some cheaper varieties, such as Australian salmon or tuna, are suitable for patties and casseroles, while others, such as red salmon and herrings in sauce, may be served cold with salads.

Fish roe The eggs of fish, such as sevruga, osietra and beluga caviar from the sturgeon, are expensive and used for garnishes and hors d'oeuvres. Tarama or salted mullet roe is canned in Australia and can be used as a less expensive substitute.

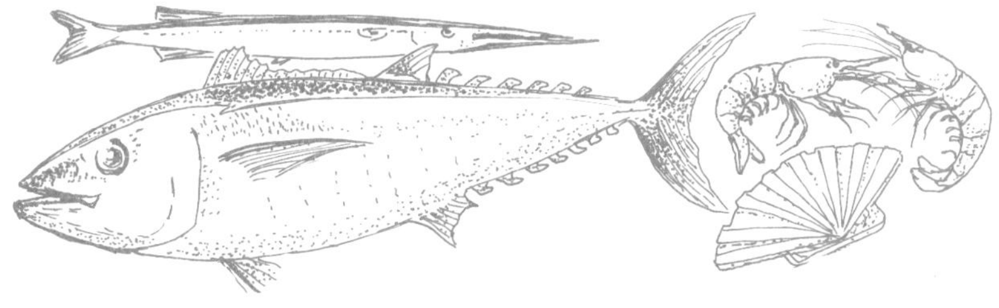

Preparation of fish

Fish is usually sold ready for cooking but there is always the fun of catching your own fish in which case the following preparation is necessary.

- Internal organs should be removed as soon as possible after catching. Scales are removed by scraping from the tail to the head. Loose scales are washed away under running water.
- Fins may be cut off with scissors.
- The skin may be removed. Place fillet skin downwards, slit at tail between the skin and flesh, then ease skin off with knife.
- Fillets (pieces without bones) are removed from both sides of the backbone. Place fish on board. With a sharp knife cut to backbone under the gill fin. Turn the blade of the knife and cut along the backbone to the tail. Turn fish over and repeat process on the other side.
- Cutlets, obtained from large fish, are slices cut through the backbone.

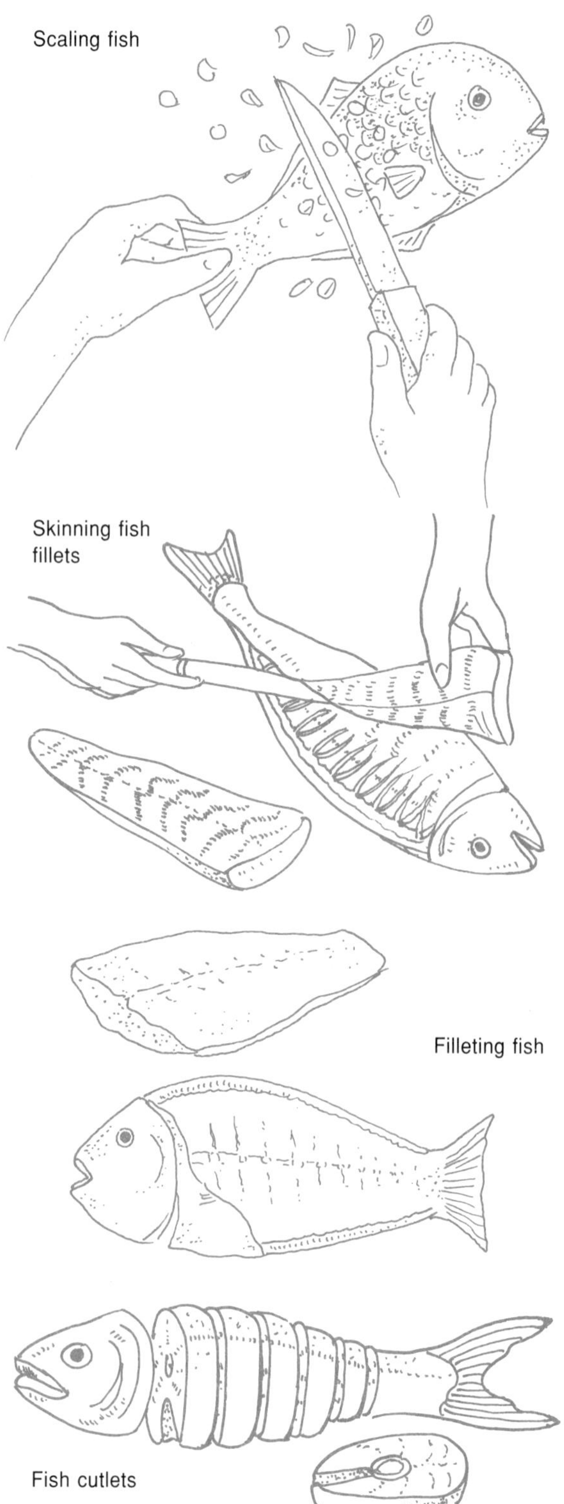

Guide to fish available in Australia

Fish	Use	Texture	Flavour	Cost
Abalone (shellfish)	Japanese cooking	Firm, white with black/green pigment	Delicate	***
Australian salmon	Bake or casserole	Soft	Strong, oily	*
Atlantic salmon	Bake, pan-fry, poach	Dark pink, firm	Delicate	***
Barramundi	Bake, pan-fry, poach	White, large flakes	Mild	***
Bream, black	Bake, grill, pan-fry, poach	Dry and flaky	Mild	**
Blue-eye or trevalla	Bake, pan-fry, poach	Firm, white when cooked	Mild	**
Blue grenadier	Bake, casserole	Pale pink, moist, very soft	Strong	**
Bug, e.g. Balmain, Moreton Bay	Use as for crab	Soft	Delicate, sweet	***
Boarfish	Bake, grill, poach	Firm, moist	Mild, sweet	**
Carp	Casserole	Dry, bony	Muddy taste	*
Crab, e.g. mud, blue swimmer (crustacea, usually cooked)	Salads, fish dishes	Soft	Delicate, sweet	***
Crayfish (crustacea, usually cooked)	Salads, special occasions	White, firm	Sweet, delicate	***
Cod, blue (smoked)	Poach	Coarse	Strong	*
Cod, Shetland (smoked)	Poach	Coarse	Strong	**
Dory, John	Pan-fry, poach	Fine, firm	Delicate	***
Dory, e.g. king, silver	Pan-fry, poach	Fine, firm	Delicate	**
Eel (often smoked)	Pan-fry	Firm, white	Strong, oily	*
Flathead	Bake, grill, pan-fry, soups	Dry, firm, flaky	Mild	*
Flake or shark	Bake, deep fry	Firm, white, boneless	Mild	*
Flounder	Grill or pan-fry whole	Firm, fine	Delicate	*
Garfish	Grill or pan-fry whole	Dry, firm, bony	Delicate, sweet	*
Gemfish	Bake, grill, pan-fry	Oily, pink, firm	Mild	*
Gurnard	Bake, casserole, pan-fry	Firm, slightly dry	Mild	*
Leatherjacket	Grill, pan-fry	Firm, white, few bones	Mild	*
Ling or rockling	Bake, grill, pan-fry	Moist, flaky, few bones	Delicate	*
Lobster (see crayfish)				
Luderick	Bake, pan-fry	Soft white	Mild	*
Marron (crustacea)	Grill, pan-fry, poach	Firm	Sweet, delicate	***

Cost * low cost ** medium cost *** high cost

Fish	Use	Texture	Flavour	Cost
Morwong	Bake, pan-fry	Dry, flaky	Mild	*
Mullet	Bake whole, casserole	Oily	Strong	*
Mulloway	Bake, grill, pan-fry	Firm, pink, slightly dry	Mild	**
Mussels (shellfish, may be smoked)	Poach, soups, casserole	Yellowish, soft	Mild	**
Orange roughy or deep sea perch	Bake, pan-fry, poach	White, firm, no bones	Mild	**
Oysters (shellfish)	Uncooked, grill	Soft	Delicate	***
Pike	Bake, pan-fry	Soft, white	Mild	*
Pipi (shellfish)	Poach, soups, casserole	Cream, soft	Very mild	**
Prawns (crustacea) If small, sold as shrimps	Pan-fry if raw (green prawns), salads, pan-fry if cooked	Firm, white with pink markings	Strong, sweet	***
Reef fish (e.g. sweetlip, coral)	Grill, pan-fry	White, moist, flaky	Delicate	***
Redfin	Grill, pan-fry	White, firm	Mild	*
Sardines or pilchards	Bake, pan-fry	Dark, oily	Strong	*
Scallops (shellfish)	Pan-fry, poach	White, soft, edible orange roe	Delicate	***
Sea perch	Bake, pan-fry	Pink, delicate	Mild	*
Snapper	Bake, grill, pan-fry, poach	Moist, flaky	Mild	**
Squid or calamari	Deep-fry, pan-fry	White, very firm	Mild	*
Tailor	Bake, pan-fry	Soft, slightly oily	Strong	**
Trevally	Bake, pan-fry	Firm, dry.	Mild	**
Trout	Grill or bake whole (if smoked, needs no cooking)	Pink, oily	Strong	**
Trumpeter	Bake, pan-fry	Pink, moist	Mild	**
Tuna, yellow fin	Bake, pan-fry, grill, sushi	Dark red, firm	Strong	***
Whiting, King George	Bake, grill, pan-fry, poach	Fine, white, some bones	Mild, sweet	***
Whiting, school	Bake, grill, pan-fry, poach	Fine, white, small bones	Mild	**
Yabbies (crustacea)	Grill, poach	Firm	Sweet, delicate	***
Whitebait or anchovies	Eaten whole, usually deep or pan-fried	Small with dark flesh	Strong	*

Cost * low cost ** medium cost *** high cost

Cooking

Seafoods cook more quickly than meat. The flesh is less fibrous and is formed in flakes separated by connective tissue. When the collagen in the connective tissue is converted to gelatin by heat, the flakes separate. As the gelatin (a protein) coagulates, the flesh turns white. Avoid overcooking as this tends to harden the protein and to make the flesh hard and dry.

Poaching Generally large, flaky fish are used, e.g. blue-eye, cod, ling. The fish is cooked in a liquid in a pan or in the microwave oven, and may be served with a sauce made from the cooking liquid. If cooked in the microwave oven, care must be taken not to overcook.

Grilling Suitable for small fish, which may be whole, in fillets or cutlets, e.g. snapper cutlets, trout, garfish. Cook under a hot griller or barbecue over a flame or hot coals.

Baking Usually whole fish of medium size are used, such as bream, mullet, and baked in a medium-heat oven. May be filled with seasoning to add flavour.

Deep frying Cutlets or fillets of fish, such as flake and flathead, may be coated with batter or egg and breadcrumbs, then deep fried in oil for a short time. Fat or oil used for frying fish should be kept only for this purpose as some fish flavours may be absorbed during cooking.

Sousing This involves marinating the fish in vinegar, which acts on the protein and whitens the flesh.

Pan-frying or sautéing Shallow frying quickly in oil, butter, margarine or dairy blend, e.g. prawns, flathead, orange roughy. May be served with a sauce.

POACHED FISH IN LEMON SAUCE

- *Fish suitable:* snapper, bream, orange roughy
- *Serves:* **4**
- *Cooking utensil:* frying pan
- *Preparation time:* ***20 minutes***
- *Cooking time:* ***10 minutes***

Ingredients

4 cutlets (500 g) *or* fillets (400 g) fish
1 tablespoon (20 g) butter
1½ tablespoons (15 g) cornflour
½ cup (125 mL) milk
zest and juice of 1 lemon
3 shakes pepper
4 lemon wedges

Method

1. Place approximately 2 cm water in frying pan with 1 teaspoon lemon juice, bring to boil.
2. Place fish in water, and then simmer very gently until flesh is white and flakes easily – approximately 10 minutes.
3. Lift carefully onto hot serving plate and keep hot. Retain ½ cup cooking liquid.
4. Make sauce: melt butter, add cornflour, stirring until smooth. Stir in milk and ½ cup cooking liquid. Stir until boiling. Cook 1 minute. Add lemon zest, juice and pepper.
5. Pour sauce over fish and serve garnished with lemon wedges.

Microwave for 3–4 minutes on high power.

BAKED FISH

- *Fish suitable:* mullet, flathead, snapper, trout, bream, sea perch
- *Serves: 4*
- *Cooking utensil:* ovenproof dish
- *Preparation time:* ***25 minutes***
- *Cooking time:* ***30–40 minutes***
- *Oven temperature:* ***180°C***

Ingredients

1 whole fish (600 g)
1 tablespoon chopped parsley
1 cup (30 g) fresh breadcrumbs
1 onion (125 g), chopped
$^1/_2$ teaspoon lemon zest
3 shakes pepper
1 tablespoon (20 g) butter *or* spray oil
lemon wedges

Method

1. Set oven at 180°C. Brush or spray ovenproof dish with oil.
2. Prepare fish: scale, clean body cavity, remove eyes and fins, and remove head if desired.
3. Mix parsley, breadcrumbs, onion, lemon zest and pepper. Sprinkle half of the mixture in ovenproof dish.
4. Place fish in dish and sprinkle with remainder of breadcrumb mixture. Dot with butter or spray lightly with oil.
5. Cover with foil or lid. Bake for 10 minutes at 180°C.
6. Remove lid or foil and continue to bake until flesh is white and flakes easily (20–30 minutes).
7. Serve on a hot dish, garnish with lemon.

Note: Fish may be filled with breadcrumb mixture and fastened with skewer.

Microwave for 3–4 minutes on high power.

BAKED SARDINES

- *Serves: 4*
- *Cooking utensil:* ovenproof dish
- *Preparation time:* ***10 minutes***
- *Cooking time:* ***10 minutes***
- *Oven temperature:* ***200°C***

Ingredients

400 g fresh sardine fillets
zest and juice of 1 lemon
2 spring onions, sliced
1 clove (5 g) garlic, chopped
1 tablespoon chopped parsley
3 shakes pepper
4 lemon slices

Method

1. Set oven at 200°C. Brush or spray ovenproof dish with oil.
2. Place sardines in ovenproof dish.
3. Combine lemon zest and juice, spring onions, garlic, parsley, pepper and sprinkle over sardines.
4. Bake at 200°C for 10 minutes.
5. Serve garnished with lemon slices.

MEDITERRANEAN FISH

- *Fish suitable:* gemfish, blue grenadier, ling, school whiting
- *Serves:* ***1***

Ingredients

1 teaspoon (5 mL) olive oil
$^1/_2$ onion (65 g), thinly sliced
1 tomato (125 g), diced
$^1/_2$ capsicum (65 g), sliced
1 fillet *or* cutlet (100 g) fish
4 olives
1 tablespoon chopped fresh basil

- *Cooking utensil:* frying pan with lid
- *Preparation time:* ***10 minutes***
- *Cooking time:* ***12–15 minutes***

Method

1 Heat oil, add onion and sauté until transparent. Add tomato and capsicum, sauté for 1–2 minutes.
2 Add fish and place half of vegetables on top of fish. Cook with lid on for 5 minutes.
3 Turn fish, placing other half vegetables on top. Add olives and basil. Cook for a further 7–10 minutes, until flesh of fish is white.

GRILLED FISH

- *Fish suitable:* mullet, whiting, flounder, garfish, leatherjacket
- *Serves:* ***4***

Ingredients

4 whole fish (600 g) *or* 4 fillets (400 g) fish
1 teaspoon (5 mL) olive oil
1 tablespoon (20 g) butter
$^1/_2$ teaspoon lemon juice
2 shakes pepper
1 teaspoon chopped parsley
4 lemon wedges
4 parsley sprigs

- *Cooking utensil:* griller *or* barbecue
- *Preparation time:* ***20 minutes***
- *Cooking time:* ***10–15 minutes***

Method

1 Turn on griller *or* barbecue.
2 Prepare fish: scale and clean. Make two cuts near shoulder of whole fish.
3 Brush with olive oil.
4 Cook for 5 minutes on either side. Brush with olive oil while cooking.
5 Combine butter, lemon juice, pepper and chopped parsley and divide into four.
6 When flesh of fish is white and flakes easily, lift onto serving plates.
7 Serve with butter mixture and garnish with lemon wedges and parsley sprigs.

Microwave for 5–6 minutes on medium power.

GRILLED MARINATED FISH

- *Fish suitable:* blue-eye, flathead, snapper, gemfish
- *Serves:* 4
- *Cooking utensil:* griller *or* barbecue
- *Preparation time:* ***15 minutes and 1 hour to marinate***
- *Cooking time:* ***10 minutes***

Ingredients

4 cutlets (500 g) *or* fillets (400 g) fish
1 tablespoon (20 mL) olive oil
2 tablespoons (40 mL) dry sherry
2 teaspoons (10 g) brown sugar
1 tablespoon (20 g) chopped ginger
1 onion (125 g), chopped
2 tablespoons (40 mL) soy sauce

Method

1. Place fish in large flat dish.
2. Combine remaining ingredients and pour over fish.
3. Cover fish and refrigerate for one hour, turning after 30 minutes.
4. Place fish under hot griller *or* on barbecue for 5 minutes on each side, brushing with marinade during cooking.

BARBECUE FISH IN FOIL

- *Fish suitable:* flake, blue grenadier, green prawns, flathead, boarfish
- *Serves:* 2
- *Cooking utensil:* griller *or* barbecue, 2 pieces foil, approximately 30 cm square
- *Preparation time:* ***20 minutes***
- *Cooking time:* ***8–10 minutes***

Ingredients

2 cutlets (250 g) *or* fillets (200 g) fish
2 tablespoons (40 mL) satay sauce
4 lettuce leaves
2 spring onions, sliced

Method

1. Spread satay sauce on each piece of fish.
2. Microwave lettuce leaves 30 seconds *or* dip into boiling water for 30 seconds. Rinse leaves in cold water.
3. Place a leaf on each piece of foil. Put fish on leaf, cover with spring onions. Place other leaf over, fold and seal foil.
4. Place on barbecue *or* under hot griller. Cook 8–10 minutes.
5. Remove foil and leaves, serve fish with salad *or* cooked vegetables.

FISH IN WINE SAUCE

- *Fish suitable:* John Dory, gemfish, orange roughy, barramundi, King George whiting
- *Serves:* 4
- *Cooking utensil:* frying pan
- *Preparation time:* ***10 minutes***
- *Cooking time:* ***5 minutes***

Ingredients

4 cutlets (500 g) *or* fillets (400 g) fish
2 tablespoons (20 g) plain flour
2 teaspoons (10 mL) oil
1/2 onion (65 g), finely sliced
1/4 cup (65 mL) stock *or* white wine
1/3 cup (85 mL) light cream
2 tablespoons chopped parsley

Method

1. Coat fish in flour.
2. Heat oil, fry onion until transparent.
3. Add fish and fry until flesh is white. Be careful not to break fish.
4. Add stock and cream, gently stir until hot.
5. Serve garnished with parsley.

FISH IN MUSHROOM SAUCE

Follow recipe for **Fish in wine sauce**. Add 1 cup (100 g) sliced mushroom with onions.

FISH VERONIQUE

Follow recipe for **Fish in wine sauce**. Add 1 cup (150 g) seedless grapes at step 4.

TROUT ALMONDINE

Follow recipe for **Fish in wine sauce**, use trout. Add 1/2 cup (50 g) almond halves at step 4. Garnish with toasted slivers of almonds.

CRAYFISH MEDALLIONS

Follow recipe for **Fish in wine sauce**. Replace fish with 400 g crayfish tail cut into medallions.

FISH IN CREAM CURRY

Follow recipe for **Fish in wine sauce**. Omit cream, add 2 teaspoons (10 g) curry paste at step 2 and 2 tablespoons (40 mL) coconut milk at step 4.

THAI FISH

- *Fish suitable:* flounder, garfish, snapper, silver dory, ling, flathead
- *Serves:* **4**
- *Cooking utensil:* frying pan
- *Preparation time:* **20 minutes and 30 minutes to marinate**
- *Cooking time:* **10–12 minutes**

Ingredients

4 small whole fish
2 tablespoons chopped coriander
1 clove (5 g) garlic, chopped
2 tablespoons (40 mL) lime *or* lemon juice
2 tablespoons (40 mL) sweet chilli sauce
2 tablespoons (40 mL) soy *or* fish sauce
2 tablespoons (20 g) cornflour
1 teaspoon (5 mL) oil *or* spray oil
2 cups cooked noodles (p. 113)

Method

1. Prepare fish: scale and clean, place in dish.
2. Combine coriander, garlic, juice and sauces and pour over fish. Allow to marinate for at least 30 minutes.
3. Remove fish and pat dry. Roll in cornflour.
4. Heat oil and fry fish for 5–6 minutes, turn gently and continue to cook for a further 5–6 minutes.
5. Heat marinade. Serve fish on hot noodles and pour marinade over.

SCALLOPS IN CURRY SAUCE

- *Serves:* **4**
- *Cooking utensil:* small saucepan and large saucepan
- *Preparation time:* **20 minutes**
- *Cooking time:* **15 minutes**

Ingredients

600 g scallops *or* other seafood
Curry sauce
1 tablespoon (20 g) butter
$1\frac{1}{2}$ tablespoons (15 g) plain flour
2 teaspoons (10 g) curry paste
1 cup (250 mL) milk
2 teaspoons (10 mL) lemon juice
$\frac{1}{4}$ teaspoon salt
2 cups cooked rice (p. 113)

Method

1. Prepare scallops: remove dark thread and gristle.
2. Make sauce: melt butter, add flour and curry paste, stir till smooth. Add milk. Stir until boiling.
3. Add scallops, cook for 3 minutes. Add lemon juice, salt and pepper.
4. Serve on a bed of rice.

✦ SCALLOPS IN LEMON SAUCE ✦

Follow recipe for **Scallops in curry sauce**. Omit curry sauce. Use 1 quantity **Lemon sauce** (p. 159).

FISH CAKES

- *Serves:* 4
- *Cooking utensil:* frying pan

Preparation time: **25 minutes**
Cooking time: **5–8 minutes**

Ingredients

425 g can tuna *or* Australian salmon *or* 500 g mullet *or* carp, boned and chopped
1 cup (150 g) cold mashed potato
1 tablespoon chopped parsley
1 tablespoon (20 mL) lemon juice
3 shakes pepper
1 egg
1 tablespoon (20 mL) milk
3 tablespoons (30 g) plain flour
$^{1}/_{3}$ cup (30 g) dried breadcrumbs
2 tablespoons (40 mL) oil
Dipping sauce
2 tablespoons (40 mL) lemon juice
1 teaspoon sugar
2 tablespoons (40 mL) fish sauce
$^{1}/_{2}$ teaspoon chopped chilli *or* sweet chilli sauce

Method

1. Mix together fish, potato, chopped parsley, lemon juice and pepper; may be done in food processor.
2. Spread mixture on plate and divide into 8 or 16 portions.
3. Shape into cakes, croquettes or small balls.
4. Beat egg and milk together.
5. Coat fish in flour, dip in egg and milk mixture, coat in breadcrumbs. Press crumbs on firmly.
6. Heat oil and fry carefully.
7. Turn after 3 minutes and continue to cook gently until golden brown.
8. Lift and drain on absorbent paper.
9. Combine dipping sauce ingredients and serve in a small dish beside fish cakes.

✦ SPICY THAI FISH BALLS ✦

Follow recipe for **Fish cakes**. Omit potato and parsley.
Use 1 cup (40 g) fresh breadcrumbs and 1 tablespoon chopped coriander.
Add 1 tablespoon (20 mL) sweet chilli sauce at step 1. Shape into 16 small balls at step 3.

PRAWNS IN COCONUT CREAM CURRY

- *Serves:* 4
- *Cooking utensil:* frying pan

Preparation time: **10 minutes**
Cooking time: **10–12 minutes**

Ingredients

1 clove (5 g) garlic, crushed
2 teaspoons (10 g) chopped ginger
1/4 teaspoon turmeric
2 teaspoons (10 g) mild spicy curry paste
1 teaspoon (5 mL) oil
400 g shelled green prawns (800 g with shells)
200 mL coconut milk
2 cups cooked rice noodles (p. 113)

Method

1. Blend garlic, ginger, turmeric and curry paste.
2. Heat oil and sauté curry mixture for 1–2 minutes.
3. Add prawns and cook until prawns become opaque (2–3 minutes). Add coconut milk.
4. Cook gently stirring all the time until heated through.
5. Serve on a bed of rice noodles.

TUNA AND NOODLE CASSEROLE

- *Serves:* 4
- *Cooking utensil:* ovenproof dish (2.5 L)

Preparation time: **20 minutes**
Cooking time: **30 minutes**
Oven temperature: **190°C**

Ingredients

425 g can tuna
250 mL (1 quantity) **White sauce** (p. 282)
2 teaspoons chopped parsley
2 teaspoons (10 mL) lemon juice
1 cup cooked noodles (p. 113)
1 tablespoon (5 g) fresh breadcrumbs
4 lemon wedges
4 parsley sprigs

Method

1. Set oven at 190°C. Brush or spray casserole with oil.
2. Combine tuna, **White sauce**, chopped parsley and lemon juice.
3. Place noodles and fish mixture in layers in the casserole.
4. Top with breadcrumbs, spray with oil. Bake at 190°C for 30 minutes.
5. Garnish with lemon and parsley.

Microwave for 10 minutes on medium power.

TUNA AND PINEAPPLE CASSEROLE

Follow recipe for **Tuna and noodle casserole**. Omit noodles.
Use 1 cup cooked rice (p. 113). Drain 440 g can crushed pineapple and add at step 3.

SMOKED FISH

- *Fish suitable:* blue cod, Shetland cod
- *Serves: 4*
- *Cooking utensil:* saucepan

- *Preparation time:* ***20 minutes***
- *Cooking time:* ***15 minutes***

Ingredients

400 g smoked fish
1 teaspoon (5 mL) lemon juice
250 mL (1 quantity) **Parsley sauce** (p. 283) *or* **Lemon sauce** (p. 159)
4 lemon wedges
4 parsley sprigs

Method

1. Cut fish into even pieces.
2. Place in saucepan and add sufficient cold water to cover, add lemon juice.
3. Bring to boil, simmer 5 minutes.
4. Remove saucepan from heat, allow to stand 10 minutes.
5. Lift fish from water. Skin may be removed.
6. Serve on hot dish, pour sauce over. Garnish with lemon and parsley.

SMOKED COD AND CORN CASSEROLE

- *Fish suitable:* blue cod, Shetland cod
- *Serves: 4*
- *Cooking utensil:* ovenproof dish (2.5 L)

- *Preparation time:* ***20 minutes***
- *Cooking time:* ***15 minutes***
- *Oven temperature:* ***180°C***

Ingredients

400 g smoked fish
1 teaspoon (5 mL) lemon juice
Sauce
1 tablespoon (20 g) butter
$1^1/_2$ tablespoon (15 g) plain flour
210 g can sweet corn kernels, drained
1 cup (250 mL) liquid (sweet corn liquid and milk)
1 tablespoon diced capsicum
2 tablespoons (10 g) fresh breadcrumbs
4 parsley sprigs

Method

1. Set oven at 180°C. Brush or spray casserole with oil.
2. Follow method for cooking **Smoked fish** to step 5.
3. Flake fish with fork, remove bones.
4. Make sauce: melt butter, add flour, stirring until smooth.
5. Add liquid. Stir until boiling. Cook 1 minute. Add fish, corn and capsicum.
6. Place in casserole, sprinkle with breadcrumbs, spray with oil. Reheat for 15 minutes at 180°C.
7. Serve garnished with parsley.

CRISPY SHRIMP BASKETS

- *Serves:* 4
- *Cooking utensil:* non-stick muffin pans
- *Preparation time:* **30 minutes**
- *Cooking time:* **10 minutes**
- *Oven temperature:* **200°C**

Ingredients

8 spring roll wrappers, 12 cm square

Filling

1 cup (150 g) shelled shrimps
2 cups (200 g) bean sprouts
100 g snow peas, thinly sliced
$^1/_4$ cup (65 mL) mayonnaise
1 tablespoon (20 mL) yoghurt *or* sour cream
3 teaspoons (15 mL) lemon juice

Method

1. Set oven at 200°C. Brush or spray muffin pans with oil.
2. Place 2 spring roll wrappers together with corners not matching (see diagram).
3. Spray or brush spring roll wrappers and place in muffin pans.
4. Bake at 200°C until golden, about 10 minutes.
5. Combine filling ingredients.
6. Spoon into crisp basket and serve with salad immediately.

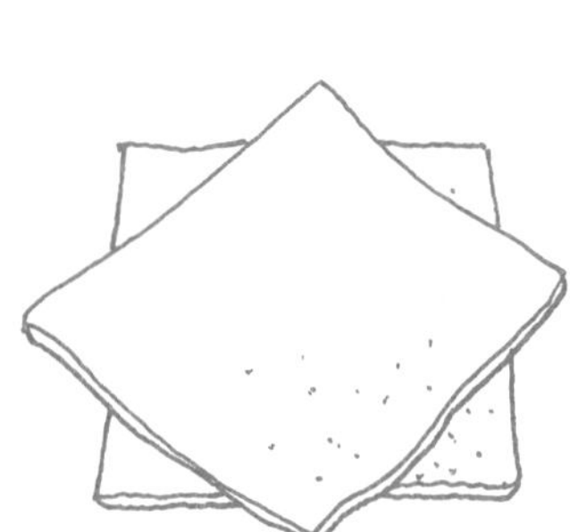

PAELLA

Serves: **4**

Cooking utensil: large frying pan *or* wok

Preparation time: **40 minutes**

Cooking time: **30 minutes**

Ingredients

1 tablespoon (20 mL) oil
1 onion (125 g), chopped
2 cloves (10 g) garlic, crushed
2 tomatoes (250 g), chopped
$^1/_2$ capsicum (65 g), chopped
1 cup (200 g) rice
$^1/_2$ cup (75 g) peas, shelled
$1^1/_2$ cups (375 mL) fish *or* chicken stock
$^1/_8$ teaspoon saffron *or* turmeric
12 prawns (500 g)
12 mussels in shells
1 cup (150 g) chopped cooked chicken
4 black olives

Method

1 Heat oil in frying pan *or* wok and fry onion and garlic for 2 minutes.
2 Add tomatoes, capsicum and rice, mix well.
3 Add the stock and saffron *or* turmeric. Stir until mixture boils. Cover and simmer 20 minutes. Add extra stock if necessary.
4 Shell prawns and remove dark vein.
5 Add prawns, peas, mussels and chicken to rice mixture. Mix gently but thoroughly with a fork while reheating.
6 Garnish with olives. Serve immediately.

SPAGHETTI MARINARA

Serves: **4**

Cooking utensil: saucepan

Preparation time: **15 minutes**

Cooking time: **20 minutes**

Ingredients

150 g spaghetti
1 L (4 cups) boiling water
1 tablespoon (20 mL) olive oil
1 onion (130 g), diced
2 cloves (10 g) garlic, crushed
3 tomatoes (375 g), chopped
1 tablespoon (20 g) tomato paste
3 shakes pepper
2 cups (300 g) cooked seafood, e.g. prawns, scallops, crabmeat, calamari, oysters, mussels, fish
1 tablespoon chopped fresh basil

Method

1 Cook spaghetti in boiling water with $^1/_4$ teaspoon salt for 12–15 minutes. Drain.
2 Fry onion and garlic in oil, add tomato and tomato paste. Cook for 5 minutes then add spaghetti. Shake over heat for $^1/_2$ minute.
3 Add seafood, pepper and basil. Mix gently and reheat.

LITTLE FISH PIES

- *Number:* **8**
- *Cooking utensil:* 8 patty pans, 4-sided oven tray
- *Preparation time:* **20 minutes**
- *Cooking time:* **20 minutes**
- *Oven temperature:* **200°C**

Ingredients

185 g can tuna *or* salmon, drained
2 tablespoons (40 mL) light sour cream
1 tablespoon chopped parsley
250 g (1/2 quantity) **Flaky pastry** (p. 349) *or* **Rough puff pastry** (p. 350)
4 lemon slices
4 parsley sprigs

Method

1. Combine fish, cream and chopped parsley.
2. Set oven at 200°C.
3. Roll out half of pastry large enough to cut 8 rounds for the tops with 6 cm cutter.
4. Place flat pastry scraps evenly on top of other half of pastry.
5. Roll out pastry, cut 8 rounds for the bottoms with 8 cm cutter.
6. Place pastry bottoms in patty pans, place fish mixture in each.
7. Brush lightly around edge with water, place on tops. Press edges gently together.
8. Glaze, slit tops. Place on 4-sided oven tray and bake at 200°C for 10 minutes. Reduce temperature to 180°C if necessary and bake further 10 minutes.
9. Remove from pans and serve garnished with lemon and parsley.

FISH PIE

Follow recipe for **Little fish pies**, using 22 cm pie dish (1 L).

Fish

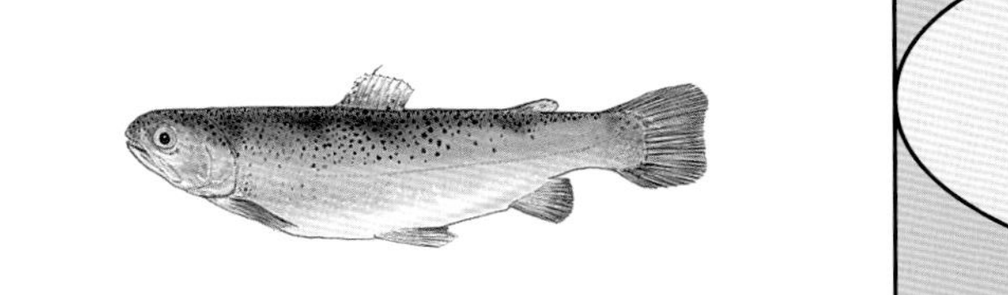
Trout

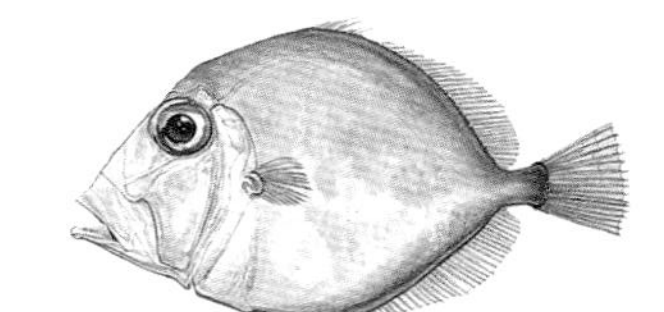
King Dory

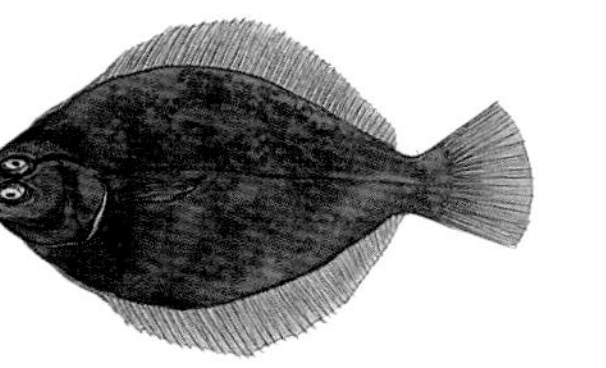
Flounder

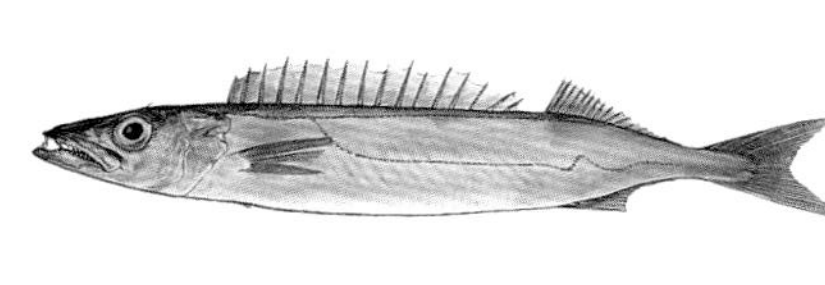
Gemfish

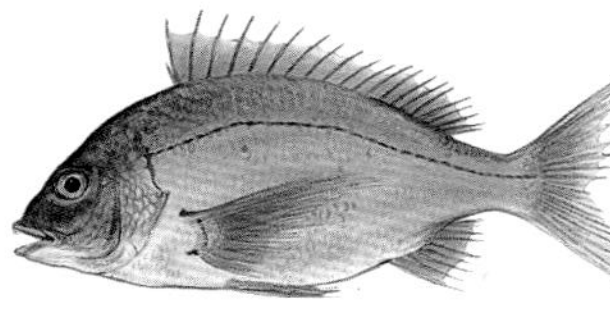

Black bream

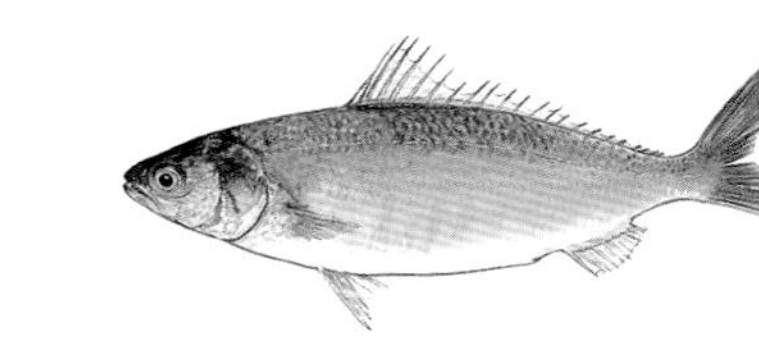
Australian salmon

Blue-eye or Trevalla

Mussels

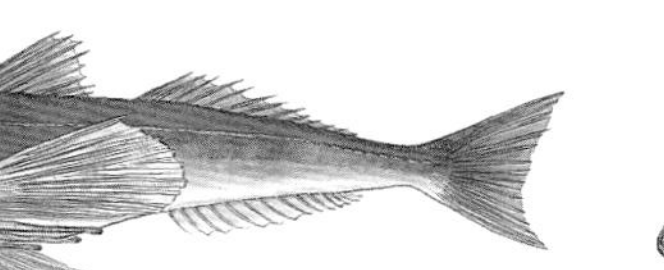
Gurnard

Flathead

Snapper

John Dory

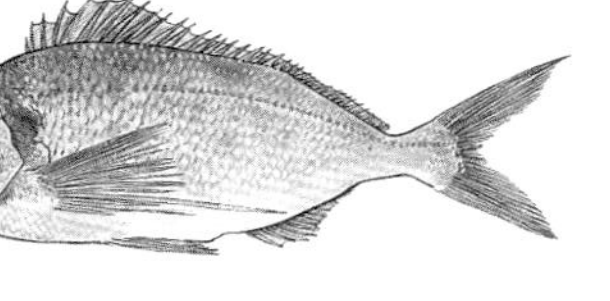
Morwong

Garfish

Scallops

School whiting

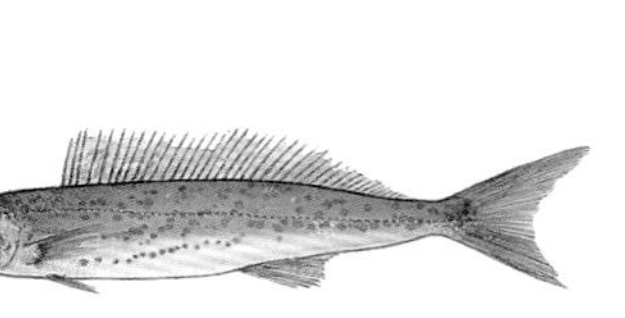

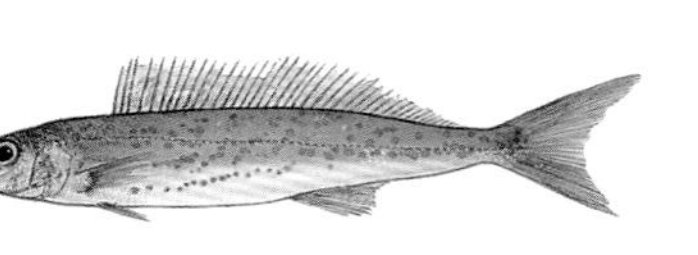
King George Whiting

Crayfish

PLATE 5

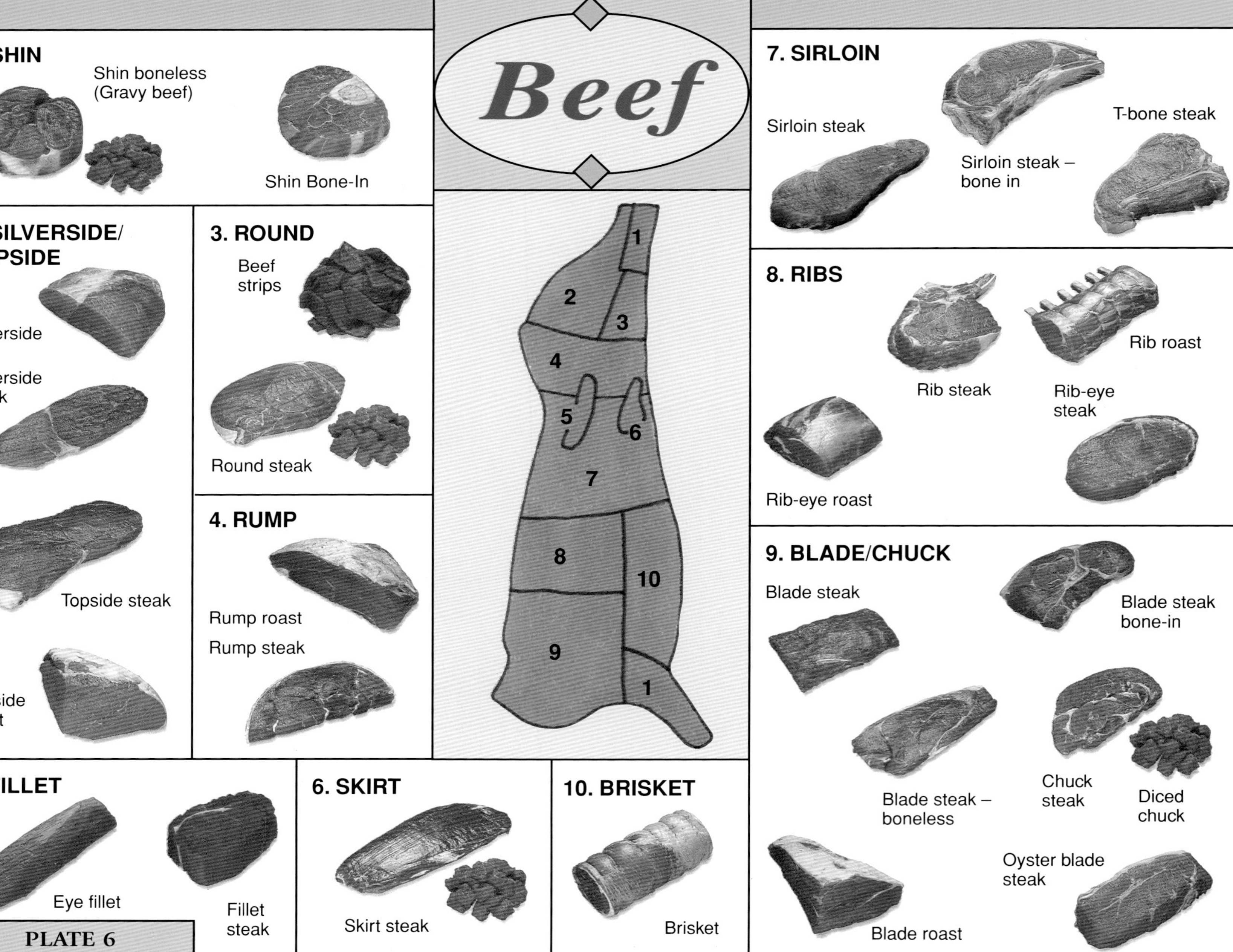

Beef
1. SHIN
Shin boneless (Gravy beef)
Shin Bone-In
2. SILVERSIDE/ TOPSIDE
Silverside
Silverside steak
Topside steak
Topside roast
3. ROUND
Beef strips
Round steak
4. RUMP
Rump roast
Rump steak
5. FILLET
Eye fillet
Fillet steak
6. SKIRT
Skirt steak
7. SIRLOIN
Sirloin steak
Sirloin steak – bone in
T-bone steak
8. RIBS
Rib steak
Rib roast
Rib-eye steak
Rib-eye roast
9. BLADE/CHUCK
Blade steak
Blade steak bone-in
Blade steak – boneless
Chuck steak
Diced chuck
Oyster blade steak
Blade roast
10. BRISKET
Brisket
1
2
3
4
5
6
7
8
9
10
1

PLATE 6

FISH TERRINE

- *Number:* ***8 slices***
- *Cooking utensil:* terrine pan (500 mL) *or* small loaf pan

Preparation time: ***40 minutes***

Ingredients

First layer
105 g can red salmon
1 tablespoon (12 g) gelatine
$^1/_4$ cup (65 mL) hot water
$^1/_2$ cucumber (100 g), diced
1 tablespoon (20 mL) mayonnaise
Second layer
1 smoked trout (250 g)
75 g cream cheese
1 teaspoon gelatine
1 tablespoon (20 mL) hot water
Garnish
4 fresh dill sprigs
1 tablespoon (20 g) caviar

Method

1 Line terrine pan with plastic film.
2 Drain salmon and remove bones.
3 Dissolve gelatine in hot water.
4 Place all first layer ingredients in food processor and blend.
5 Spoon into terrine pan and spread evenly.
6 Remove head, skin and bones from trout. Place flesh in food processor with cream cheese.
7 Dissolve gelatine in hot water, add and blend until smooth. Spoon on top of first layer.
8 Cover, place in refrigerator and allow to chill for 3–4 hours.
9 Turn onto serving plate and remove plastic film. Garnish with caviar and fresh dill or for individual serves, slice into 1.5 cm slices, garnish and serve with crisp bread.

JELLIED SALMON

- *Serves:* ***2***
- *Cooking utensil:* 2 x 125 mL moulds

Preparation time: ***30 minutes***

Ingredients

210 g can pink *or* red salmon
1 tablespoon (12 g) gelatine
2 tablespoons (40 mL) hot water
1 teaspoon lemon juice
1 teaspoon chopped parsley
1 tablespoon (20 mL) mayonnaise
3 shakes cayenne
4 lettuce leaves (mizuna, curly endive)

Method

1 Drain liquid from salmon, make up to $^1/_2$ cup with water.
2 Dissolve gelatine in hot water and add to drained salmon liquid and lemon juice.
3 Flake fish, remove bones and mix with parsley, mayonnaise and cayenne.
4 Combine fish and liquid mixtures and place in mould.
5 Chill until set.
6 Wash and dry lettuce cups and place on serving dish.
7 Unmould jellied salmon onto lettuce cups.

8 Meat and poultry

The emphasis on meat and poultry in our diet has diminished. However, the versatility and nutritional value of these foods means that they are still a focal point in many meals.

Changes in meat production and the methods of butchering provide many quick-cooking meats and a wider range of readily available poultry and game such as pheasant, quail, squab, venison, goat, crocodile and kangaroo. Butchering and breeding techniques have also developed products with a lower fat content, supporting the dietary guideline that encourages us to reduce our fat intake.

Emu and kangaroo meats are low in cholesterol and fat and high in protein. Due to the low fat level these meats are best cooked rare as over-cooking toughens the muscle tissue. Marinades can be used to add extra flavour.

Many retailers partly prepare meat dishes prior to purchase, such as meat and vegetable kebabs, sweet and sour pork, and stir-fry mixes, thereby reducing the amount of time needed to prepare the dish at home.

Composition

Meat consists of muscle tissue, fatty tissue and bone. Muscle tissue is made up of muscle fibres surrounded by connective tissue attaching the fibres to one another and to bone. The muscle fibre proteins, albumen and globulin, give meat its characteristic texture. Fatty tissue is found within the muscle fibres, in connective tissue and in layers around the muscle.

Fine-grained tender meat is cut from the portion of the animal that has the least exercise, and is the most expensive meat to buy. The muscles exercised most yield tougher, less expensive meat, which has the same food value as the more expensive cuts.

When meat is cooked the proteins, albumen and globulin are coagulated and softened at temperatures below the boiling point of water. However, both these and the connective tissue proteins, collagen and elastin, are toughened by high temperatures and dry heat. The less expensive tougher cuts of meat have a high proportion of collagen and elastin and are therefore more tender to eat if cooked at a low temperature in a moist heat, such as in stews and casseroles.

The microwave oven reduces cooking time for stews and casseroles, but does not brown or tenderise meat.

Prepared and cooked stews, casseroles and curries may be refrigerated or frozen. They should be reheated to boiling point before serving.

Food value

Meat and poultry are valuable sources of complete protein as approximately 20% of the muscle tissue is made up of essential proteins. Water makes up 70%, and the remaining 10% is fat, minerals and vitamins. There is comparatively little carbohydrate in meat, most of it in the form of glycogen. Red meat and variety meats such as lamb's fry and kidneys are excellent sources of iron, phosphorus and B complex vitamins.

Effect of heat on meat

- Most bacteria are destroyed.
- Flavour is developed, making meat palatable and appetising.
- Change in colour due to the alteration of colour pigments by heat.
- Browning of outside surface and development of flavour by dry heat.
- Albumen and globulin are coagulated below boiling point, softened at moderate temperatures and toughened at high temperatures.
- Collagen and elastin are toughened by dry heat, therefore cheaper tougher meats containing a high proportion of these proteins need to be cooked by moist heat.
- Collagen is changed to gelatin by long moist gentle heat but elastin is unaltered.
- Meat shrinks in size due to the evaporation of water.
- Fat is melted.

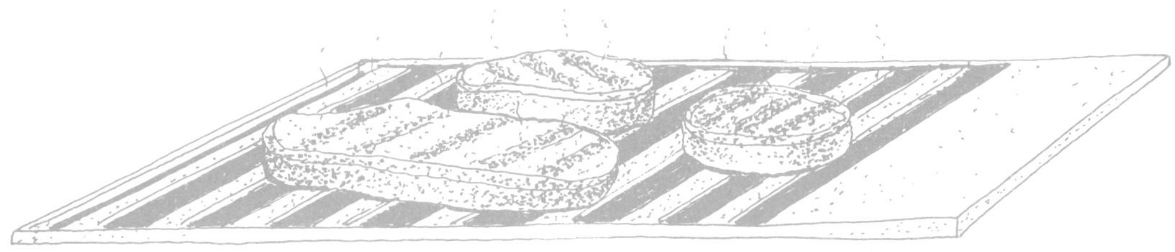

Grilled and barbecued meat and poultry

Grilling and barbecuing are quick methods of cooking small tender pieces of food by dry, radiant heat. Meats may be marinated prior to cooking to enhance flavour and tenderise. If using a marinade that contains sugar or honey, lower the heat to prevent the meat charring. Allow the excess marinade to run off just before cooking or the surfaces will not seal quickly enough to prevent the loss of juices. Suggestions for marinades appear on p. 176–177.

GRILLED STEAK

Grilled steak may be served with a range of condiments including **Savoury butter**, Worcestershire sauce or mustard.

- *Serves:* **1**
- *Cooking utensil:* gas *or* electric griller

Ingredients

100–125 g rump, T-bone, sirloin, fillet, oyster blade, topside steak *or* spare ribs

- *Preparation time:* ***5 minutes***
- *Cooking time:* ***8–14 minutes (see step 5)***

Method

1. Purchase lean meat, well trimmed of excess fat.
2. Heat griller.
3. Seal the surface of the meat quickly under the hot griller to avoid the meat juices being drawn out and evaporated. Use tongs to turn meat. Do not cut or pierce the meat during cooking as this allows the juices to escape, resulting in the meat being tough and dry.
4. Reduce the heat slightly after sealing the meat.
5. Cook 8–14 minutes depending on the thickness of meat and preference of diner. Test to see if cooked by pressing with tongs:
   - rare meat feels 'springy' (8–10 minutes);
   - medium meat feels slightly firm (10–12 minutes);
   - well done meat feels very firm (12–14 minutes).

BARBECUE STEAK

Follow recipe for **Grilled Steak**. Barbecue the meat over a smokeless fire, gas flame or radiant electric hotplate or on a very hot metal plate or griddle over a fire, gas flame or electric hotplate.

✦ SAVOURY BUTTER ✦

Blend 1 tablespoon (20 g) butter, 1/2 teaspoon lemon juice, 2 shakes pepper and 1 teaspoon chopped parsley, shape into 4 balls and refrigerate. Serve one with each serve of meat.

✦ GRILLED LAMB CHOPS ✦

Follow recipe for **Grilled Steak** using 1–2 mid loin, rib, chump *or* forequarter (barbecue) chops per person. Grill 10–12 minutes. May be served with **Savoury butter**.

✦ GRILLED PORK ✦

Follow recipe for **Grilled Steak** using 1 loin *or* forequarter chop, *or* cutlet *or* 100–150 g butterfly, rump *or* loin steak *or* 150 g spare ribs. Cook 15–18 minutes.

✦ BARBECUE SAUSAGES ✦

Follow recipe for **Barbecue Steak** using 2–4 thin sausages per person and cook 8–10 minutes *or* 1–2 thick sausages per person and cook 10–15 minutes.

✦ GRILLED CHICKEN ✦

Follow recipe for **Grilled Steak** using 1–2 pieces chicken per person. Grill 15–20 minutes.

✦ GRILLED BACON ✦

Grill rashers *or* slices 3 minutes.

✦ GRILLED BACON ROLLS ✦

Remove rind from 2 thin rashers (80 g) bacon and cut each rasher into 4. With back of knife, gently stretch each piece of bacon. Roll up and place all on one or two skewers. Grill 3–5 minutes, turning frequently, until fat is transparent. Use as garnish or accompaniment.

PORK SPARE RIBS

- *Serves:* 4
- *Cooking utensil:* griller, barbecue *or* griddle pan

Ingredients

500 g pork spare ribs *or* American-style ribs
2 tablespoons (40 mL) black bean sauce

- *Preparation time:* ***5 minutes and 1 hour to marinate***
- *Cooking time:* ***15–20 minutes***

Method

1. Marinate meat in black bean sauce for 1 hour.
2. Grill or barbeque, turning frequently, for 15–20 minutes.

HONEY MARINADE

► For 400 g meat

Ingredients

1 teaspoon honey
1 teaspoon oil
1 tablespoon (20 mL) soy sauce
3 shakes pepper
1 clove (5 g) garlic, crushed
1/4 teaspoon herbs

Method

1. Mix all ingredients.
2. Marinate meat for 1 hour, turning occasionally.
3. Brush marinade over meat while grilling.

ORANGE MARMALADE MARINADE

► For 400 g meat

Ingredients

1 tablespoon (20 g) butter, melted
2 tablespoons (40 mL) orange juice
2 tablespoons (40 g) marmalade
1 clove (5 g) garlic, crushed

Method

1. Mix all ingredients.
2. Marinate meat for 1 hour, turning occasionally.
3. Brush marinade over meat while grilling.

RED WINE MARINADE

► For 400 g meat

Ingredients

1/4 cup (65 mL) red wine
1 tablespoon (20 mL) oil
1 tablespoon (20 mL) Worcestershire sauce
2 teaspoons (6 g) brown sugar
1 clove (5 g) garlic, crushed

Method

1. Mix all ingredients.
2. Marinate meat for 1 hour, turning occasionally.
3. Brush marinade over meat while grilling.

GINGER MARINADE

For 400 g meat

Ingredients

$^1/_4$ cup (60 mL) soy sauce
$^1/_2$ cup (125 mL) pineapple juice
1 teaspoon (5 g) chopped ginger
2 tablespoons (40 mL) cider vinegar
1 teaspoon (5 g) sugar
2 tablespoons (40 mL) oil
3 shakes pepper

Method

1 Mix all ingredients.
2 Marinate meat for 1 hour, turning occasionally.
3 After meat has been removed for cooking, marinade may be thickened with 1 teaspoon cornflour, brought to the boil and used as a sauce.

SESAME SOY MARINADE

For 400 g meat

Ingredients

2 tablespoons (25 g) sesame seeds
$^1/_4$ cup (65 mL) soy sauce
2 teaspoons (10 mL) sesame oil
1 tablespoon (20 mL) dry sherry
1 tablespoon (20 g) honey
1 clove (5 g) garlic, crushed
1 small red chilli, seeded and finely sliced

Method

1 Mix all ingredients.
2 Marinate meat for 1 hour, turning occasionally.
3 Brush marinade over meat while grilling.

ASIAN MARINADE

For 400 g meat

Ingredients

2 tablespoons (40 mL) soy sauce
1 tablespoon (20 mL) sesame oil
1 tablespoon (20 mL) dry sherry
1 tablespoon (20 mL) honey

Method

1 Mix all ingredients.
2 Marinate meat for 1 hour, turning occasionally.
3 Brush marinade over meat while grilling. Reduce heat if marinade starts to burn.

GRILLED EMU MEDALLIONS

To use our native bush foods, replace the juniper berries with $^1/_2$ cup (65 g) Illawarra plums or $^1/_2$ cup (100 g) riberries. Emu, ostrich and crocodile meats may also be pan-fried.

- *Serves:* *4*
- *Cooking utensil:* griller *or* barbecue
- *Preparation time:* ***20 minutes and overnight to marinate***
- *Cooking time:* ***5–10 minutes***

Ingredients

4 emu medallions *or* fillets (400 g)
1 cup (250 mL) red wine
1 onion (125 g), chopped
1 carrot (130 g), finely chopped
1 cup (120 g) finely chopped leek
1 stalk celery (100 g), chopped
12 juniper berries
1 sprig thyme
grated rind and juice of 1 orange

Method

1. Combine ingredients and marinate overnight in refrigerator.
2. Drain the meat, reserving the marinade.
3. Place marinade in a saucepan, simmer with lid off until thick.
4. Preheat the griller *or* barbecue until very hot.
5. Barbecue *or* grill the meat for 5–10 minutes, turning once.
6. Pour thickened marinade over emu medallions before serving.

GRILLED OSTRICH MEDALLIONS

Follow recipe for **Grilled emu medallions**, using 400 g ostrich medallions *or* fillets.

GRILLED CROCODILE MEDALLIONS

Follow recipe for **Grilled emu medallions**, using 400 g crocodile fillets and I cup (250 g) white wine instead of red wine.

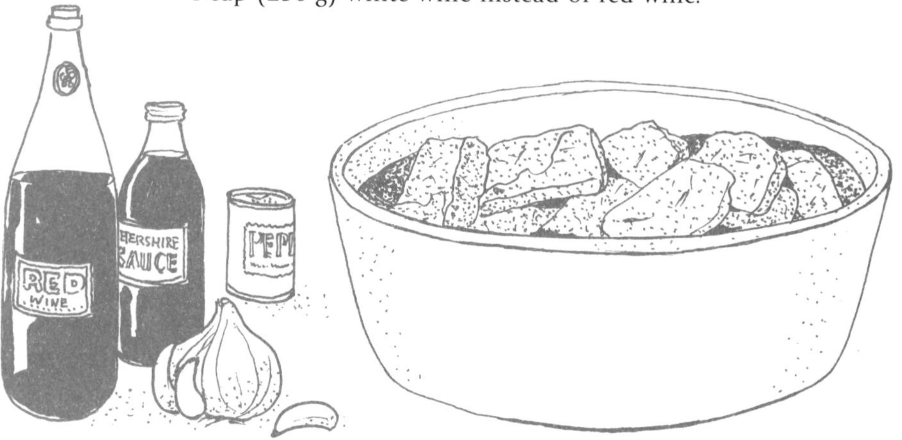

VIETNAMESE PORK SAUSAGES

- *Serves:* 4
- *Cooking utensils:* 8 wooden skewers soaked in water for 1 hour, griller
- *Preparation time:* **20 minutes and 1 hour to marinate**
- *Cooking time:* **8–10 minutes**

Ingredients

250 g finely minced pork
1 clove (5 g) garlic, crushed
1 teaspoon (5 g) chopped ginger
1 teaspoon light soy sauce
2 teaspoons (10 mL) dry sherry
8 lettuce leaves, washed

Dipping sauce

1/4 cup (65 mL) fish sauce
1 teaspoon (5 g) chopped ginger
1 clove (5 g) garlic, crushed
1 tablespoon (20 mL) lemon juice
2 teaspoons (10 g) caster sugar
1 tablespoon (20 mL) water
1 small red chilli, seeded and finely sliced

Method

1. Combine pork, garlic, ginger, soy and sherry. Place in refrigerator for 1 hour.
2. Turn on griller.
3. Divide meat into 8, roll each into sausage shape and slide skewer lengthwise through centre.
4. Cook 8–10 minutes turning several times.
5. Wrap each pork roll into a parcel in a lettuce leaf.
6. Serve with dipping sauce made by combining ingredients.

GRILLED SAVOURY SAUSAGES

- *Serves:* 4
- *Cooking utensil:* griller
- *Preparation time:* **15 minutes**
- *Cooking time:* **10–15 minutes**

Ingredients

8 thick sausages
2 tablespoons (40 mL) chutney
2 rashers (80 g) bacon, cut into 8 pieces
1/2 cup (60 g) grated cheese

Method

1. Split sausages almost in half lengthwise and flatten.
2. Grill 5–7 minutes, turning once.
3. Spread with chutney and place piece of bacon on each.
4. Grill until bacon fat is transparent.
5. Place cheese on each and grill until cheese starts to melt.

SATAYS WITH PEANUT SAUCE

- *Serves:* 4
- *Cooking utensil:* 8 wooden skewers soaked in water for 1 hour, griller

Preparation time: ***20 minutes and 30 minutes to marinate***
Cooking time: ***10–15 minutes***

Ingredients

400 g rump, topside, fillet *or* oyster blade steak
1 teaspoon (5 g) chopped ginger
1 tablespoon (20 g) mild spicy curry paste
1 tablespoon (20 g) peanut butter
1 tablespoon (20 mL) lemon juice
2 cups cooked rice (p. 113)
Peanut sauce
1 tablespoon (20 mL) oil
1/2 onion (65 g), chopped finely
1 clove (5 g) garlic, crushed
2 tablespoons (40 g) peanut butter
2 teaspoons (10 mL) soy sauce
1 teaspoon (5 g) chopped ginger
1 teaspoon (5 g) lemon juice
1 cup (250 mL) coconut milk
1 teaspoon (5 g) chilli sauce

Method

1 Cut meat into 2 cm dice.
2 Mix meat, ginger, curry paste, peanut butter and lemon juice and marinate for 30 minutes.
3 Thread meat on to skewers.
4 Grill for 10–15 minutes, brushing with marinade during cooking.
5 Make sauce: fry onion in oil, add garlic and cook 1 minute longer. Add other ingredients and stir until boiling.
6 Serve satays on bed of rice with sauce poured over them.
7 May be served with **Tomato, onion and cucumber salad** (p. 277) *or* **Gado gado** (p. 271).

MINI SATAYS

Follow recipe for **Satays with peanut sauce**, making 16 small satays.

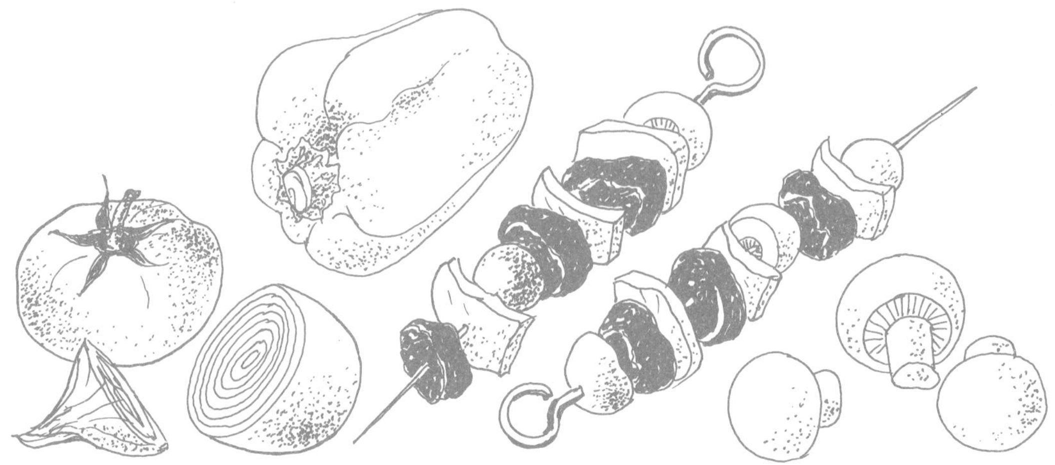

KEBABS

- *Serves:* **4**
- *Cooking utensil:* wooden skewers soaked in water for 1 hour, griller
- *Preparation time:* ***20 minutes and 1 hour to marinate***
- *Cooking time:* ***10–15 minutes***

Ingredients

300 g rump, topside *or* fillet steak
$^{1}/_{4}$ cup (65 mL) soy sauce
3 shakes pepper
1 clove (5 g) garlic, crushed
12 very small (350 g) onions, peeled
12 tiny mushrooms (100 g)
1 green capsicum (125 g)
12 cherry tomatoes (375 g)
2 tablespoons (40 g) butter, melted
2 cups cooked rice (p. 113)

Method

1. Cut meat into 2 cm dice.
2. Mix meat, soy sauce, pepper and garlic and marinate for 1 hour.
3. Remove seeds from capsicum and cut in 3 cm squares.
4. Blanch capsicum and onions *or* microwave for 2 minutes on high power.
5. Place meat and vegetables on skewers, arranging colours attractively. Brush with melted butter.
6. Grill for 10–15 minutes, turning frequently.
7. Place kebabs on a bed of rice to serve.

✦ SHASHLIKS ✦

Follow recipe for **Kebabs**, using lamb fillets.

✦ SOUVLAKI ✦

Follow recipe for **Kebabs**, using lamb fillets cut into thin strips. Omit rice. Serve with salad in pita, souvlaki *or* pocket bread.

Shallow frying, pan-frying and stir-frying

These are quick methods of cooking small portions of meat or poultry at a high temperature in a frying pan or wok containing a small amount of fat or oil. Stir-frying is more successful if a wok is used as the small amount of oil in the base can be kept very hot, sealing the surface of the food and retaining the colour and flavour of the foods. The food may be coated with flour, breadcrumbs or other coating. Turn the food with tongs or large spatula to avoid piercing the surface.

Coatings for fried foods

Seasoned flour Coat in mixture of 2 tablespoons (20 g) plain flour, 1/2 teaspoon salt and 3 shakes pepper. This may be done in a plastic bag.

Flavoured flour mixtures For some stir-fry dishes the flour may be mixed with flavourings, such as curry powder, to give a tasty coating.

Seasoned flour and beaten egg and milk mixture Coat with seasoned plain flour then dip in egg and milk.

Flour, beaten egg and milk mixture, and breadcrumbs Coat in plain flour, then dip in egg and milk and coat with breadcrumbs. Press crumbs on firmly.

Batter

Oils and fats suitable for shallow frying

Butter, margarine, dairy blend and ghee or clarified butter may be used, but will burn if heated to a high temperature.

Olive, sunflower, peanut, soy bean, maize, safflower and canola oils are suitable for shallow frying.

RABBIT IN BASIL SAUCE

- *Serves:* 4
- *Cooking utensil:* large saucepan

Preparation time: **20 minutes**

Cooking time: **1 hour**

Ingredients

1 rabbit (700 g), cut into pieces
4 tablespoons (40 g) plain flour
1 tablespoon (20 g) butter
1 tablespoon (20 mL) oil
1/2 onion (65 g), finely chopped
1/4 cup (65 mL) chicken stock *or* water
1/4 cup (65 mL) white wine
zest and juice of 1/2 lemon
4 shakes black pepper
2 tablespoons chopped parsley
2 tablespoons chopped basil
1 teaspoon thyme leaves
3 tablespoons (60 mL) cream
2 cups cooked noodles (p. 113)

Method

1. Dip the rabbit pieces in flour.
2. Fry rabbit in butter and oil in large saucepan until golden brown. Remove.
3. Fry onion 2 minutes, add stock, wine, lemon juice, pepper and rabbit, simmer 45 minutes.
4. Remove rabbit pieces and place on serving dish, keep warm.
5. Stir in parsley, basil, thyme and cream. Reheat without boiling.
6. Pour over rabbit and serve with noodles.

CRUMBED CUTLETS

► *Serves:* ***4***
► *Cooking utensil:* frying pan

Ingredients
4 lamb *or* pork cutlets
2 tablespoons (20 g) plain flour
1/2 teaspoon salt
3 shakes pepper
1 egg, beaten
1 tablespoon (20 mL) milk
1 cup (90 g) dried breadcrumbs
1/4 cup (65 mL) oil
500 mL (1 quantity) **Fresh tomato sauce** (p. 285) *or* **Espagnol sauce** (p. 285)

Preparation time: ***20 minutes***
Cooking time: ***10–12 minutes***

Method
1 Shape cutlets: flatten and leave 3 cm of cleaned bone.
2 Mix flour, salt and pepper and coat cutlets.
3 Mix egg and milk.
4 Dip cutlets in egg mixture, then coat in breadcrumbs. Press crumbs on firmly.
5 Heat oil and fry cutlets 10–12 minutes, turning once.
6 Drain. May be served with cutlet frill (see below) on bone of each cutlet.

CUTLET FRILLS

Use for covering bones of **Crumbed Cutlets**, **Racks of Lamb** (p. 193), and legs of **Roast Chicken** and **Roast Turkey** (pp. 198, 199).

To make 1 frill, cut a piece of white paper 20 cm long, 6 cm wide. Fold in half lengthwise. Make cuts along the folded edge at 1 cm intervals to a depth of 2 cm. Roll to fit size of bone to be covered and secure. Place over bones of cooked meat just before serving.

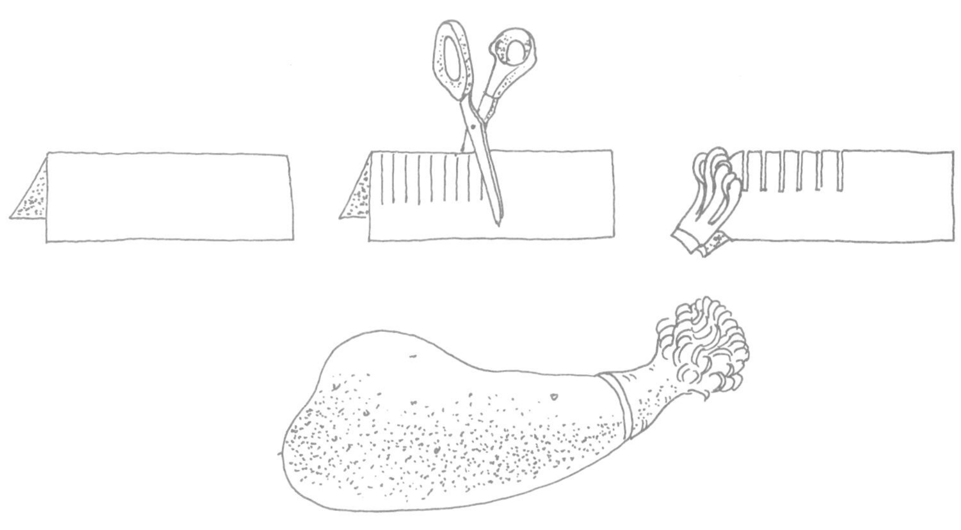

BEEFBURGERS

Beefburgers may be served in a bread roll with grilled rashers of bacon, sliced pineapple, cheese, tomato and gherkin.

- *Serves:* **4**
- *Cooking utensil:* frying pan

Preparation time: ***20 minutes***
Cooking time: ***12–15 minutes***

Ingredients

400 g minced beef
1 tablespoon (20 mL) tomato sauce
2 teaspoons (10 mL) Worcestershire sauce
1/4 cup (10 g) fresh breadcrumbs
1 onion (125 g), grated
1 egg, beaten
6 shakes pepper
1/4 cup (40 g) plain flour
2 tablespoons (40 mL) oil
250 mL (1 quantity) **Barbecue sauce** (p. 284)

Method

1. Place meat, tomato and Worcestershire sauces, breadcrumbs, onion, egg and flavourings in a bowl and mix well.
2. Divide into 8 and shape into rounds 2–3 cm thick.
3. Coat with flour.
4. Heat oil and fry burgers for 12–15 minutes, turning once.
5. Drain on absorbent paper and serve with **Barbecue sauce**.

HAMBURGERS

Follow recipe for **Beefburgers**, using 400 g minced pork.

MICROWAVE BEEFBURGERS

Follow recipe for **Beefburgers**. Omit oil. Place burgers on plate with space between each one. Cover with paper towel and cook for 4 minutes on high power, turn, cook 4 minutes on medium power.

MICROWAVE MEAT BALLS

Follow recipe for **Beefburgers**. Omit oil. Divide mixture into 16. Arrange meat balls on plate with space between each. Do not cover. Microwave for 3 minutes on high power. Turn and cook for 3 minutes on medium power, and serve with **Plum dipping sauce** (p. 482).

WIENER SCHNITZEL

- *Serves:* 4
- *Cooking utensil:* frying pan

Preparation time: ***20 minutes***
Cooking time: ***5 minutes each***

Ingredients

4 slices (400 g) leg *or* fillet of veal
juice of 1 lemon
2 tablespoons (20 g) plain flour
1/2 teaspoon salt
3 shakes pepper
1 egg, beaten
1 tablespoon (20 mL) milk
1 cup (90 g) dried breadcrumbs
2 tablespoons (40 mL) oil
2 tablespoons (40 g) butter
4 lemon wedges

Method

1. Using a meat mallet, beat slices of meat gently until they are half of their original thickness. Allow to stand in lemon juice for 1 hour. Turn meat several times.
2. Coat meat with flour, salt and pepper.
3. Mix egg and milk.
4. Dip meat in egg mixture, then in breadcrumbs. Press crumbs on firmly.
5. Heat butter and oil in pan and fry for 2–3 minutes each side. Drain on absorbent paper.
6. Garnish meat with lemon wedges.

CHICKEN LIVER RISOTTO

- *Serves:* 4
- *Cooking utensil:* frying pan, medium saucepan, large saucepan

Preparation time: ***20 minutes***
Cooking time: ***25 minutes***

Ingredients

250 g chicken livers, chopped
1 onion (125 g), finely chopped
1/2 cup (50 g) sliced mushrooms
1 tablespoon (20 mL) olive oil
1 1/2 cups (375 mL) **Chicken stock** (p. 141)
1/2 cup (100 g) short grain rice *or* arborio rice
1 tablespoon (20 mL) olive oil
1/2 cup (75 g) cooked peas
3 shakes pepper

Method

1. Fry chicken livers, onion and mushrooms in oil for 5 minutes. Remove from heat.
2. Bring chicken stock to boil in medium saucepan.
3. Place rice and oil in large saucepan, stir to coat rice with oil.
4. Add boiling stock 1/2 cup at a time to rice, bringing to boil each time before adding more.
5. Cook until rice is just tender, add chicken livers and peas, reheat and serve.

ORIENTAL BEEF

- *Serves:* **4**
- *Cooking utensil:* wok

Preparation time: ***30 minutes***
Cooking time: ***5–8 minutes***

Ingredients

400 g round steak *or* beef strips
2 teaspoons (10 mL) sesame oil
1 teaspoon (5 g) chopped ginger
1 clove (5 g) garlic, crushed
12 spring onions, cut into 3 cm lengths
1 3/4 cups (200 g) broccoli florets
1 1/2 cups (150 g) snow peas
1 cup (120 g) sliced red capsicum
2 tablespoons (40 mL) soy sauce
2 tablespoons (40 mL) oyster sauce
1 tablespoon (20 mL) dry sherry
1/2 cup (50 g) unsalted cashew nuts
2 cups cooked rice (p. 113)

Method

1. Cut steak into strips.
2. Heat oil in wok. Brown small quantities beef strips for 2–3 minutes stirring continually.
3. Add ginger, garlic, spring onions, broccoli, snow peas and capsicum, stir-fry 2 minutes.
4. Stir in soy and oyster sauces, dry sherry and cashews and stir until heated through.
5. Serve with rice.

SWEET AND SOUR BEEF

Follow recipe for **Oriental beef**. Omit cashew nuts and broccoli. Add 250 g jar sweet and sour sauce *or* 200 g pineapple pieces and 2 tablespoons (40 mL) vinegar at step 4.

STIR-FRY LAMB WITH COUSCOUS

- *Serves:* **4**
- *Cooking utensil:* saucepan, wok

Preparation time: ***15 minutes***
Cooking time: ***10 minutes***

Ingredients

2 cups (500 mL) stock *or* water
1 cup (200 g) couscous
400 g lamb strips
1/4 teaspoon ground cumin
1/4 teaspoon chilli paste
2 tomatoes (250 g), diced
1 zucchini (100 g), diced
1 capsicum (125 g), diced
2 teaspoons (10 mL) olive oil

Method

1. Boil stock, add couscous, bring back to boil, remove from heat, cover and stand.
2. Mix lamb with cumin and chilli paste.
3. Heat oil in wok, add lamb, stir-fry until meat is brown, remove.
4. Add tomato, zucchini and capsicum to wok, cook on high heat for 5 minutes.
5. Return lamb to wok. Stir gently. Reheat couscous. Serve lamb and vegetables on couscous.

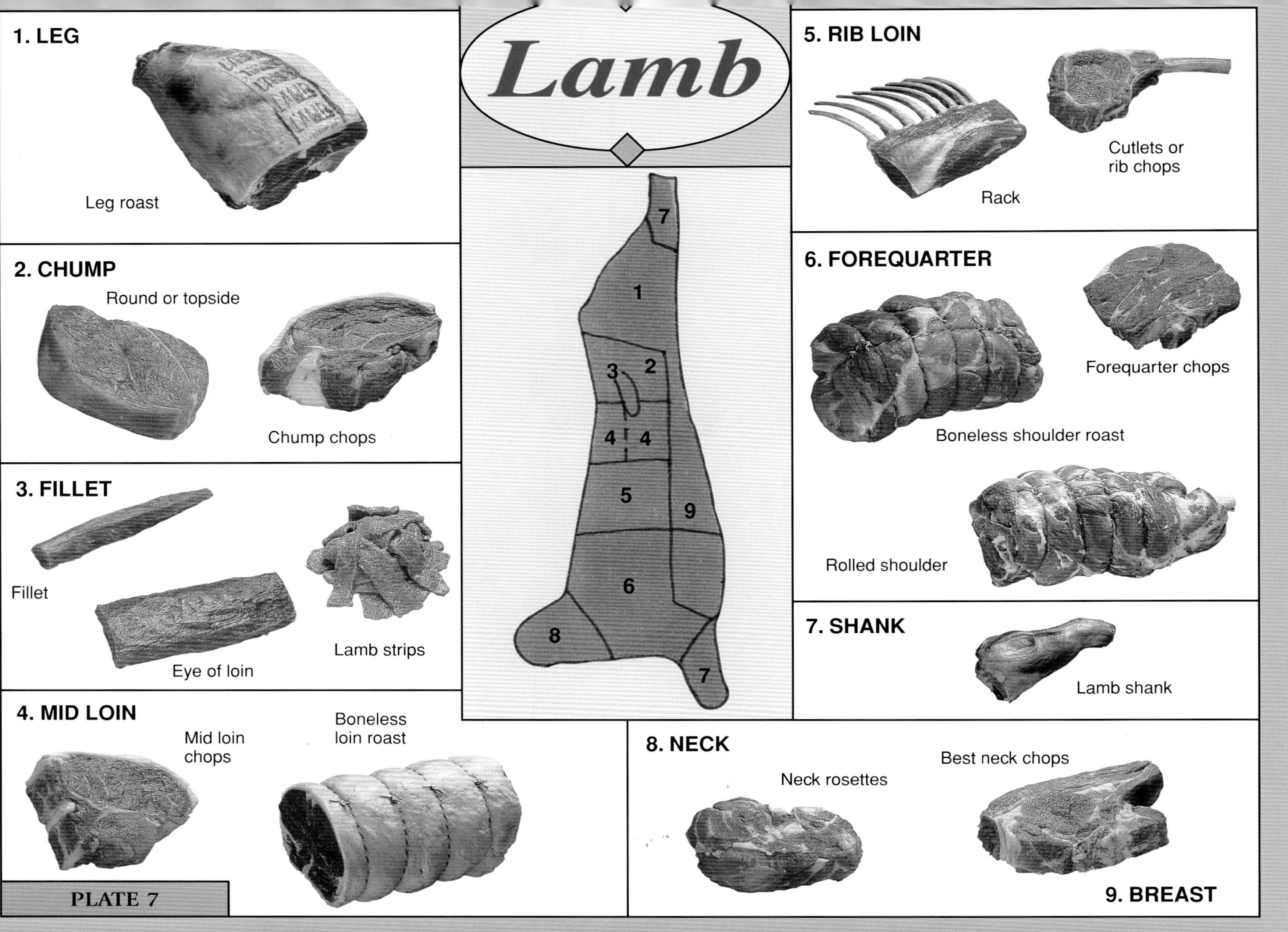
Lamb
1. LEG
Leg roast
2. CHUMP
Round or topside
Chump chops
3. FILLET
Fillet
Eye of loin
Lamb strips
4. MID LOIN
Mid loin chops
Boneless loin roast
5. RIB LOIN
Rack
Cutlets or rib chops
6. FOREQUARTER
Forequarter chops
Boneless shoulder roast
Rolled shoulder
7. SHANK
Lamb shank
8. NECK
Neck rosettes
Best neck chops
9. BREAST
7
1
2
3
4
4
5
9
6
8
7

PLATE 7

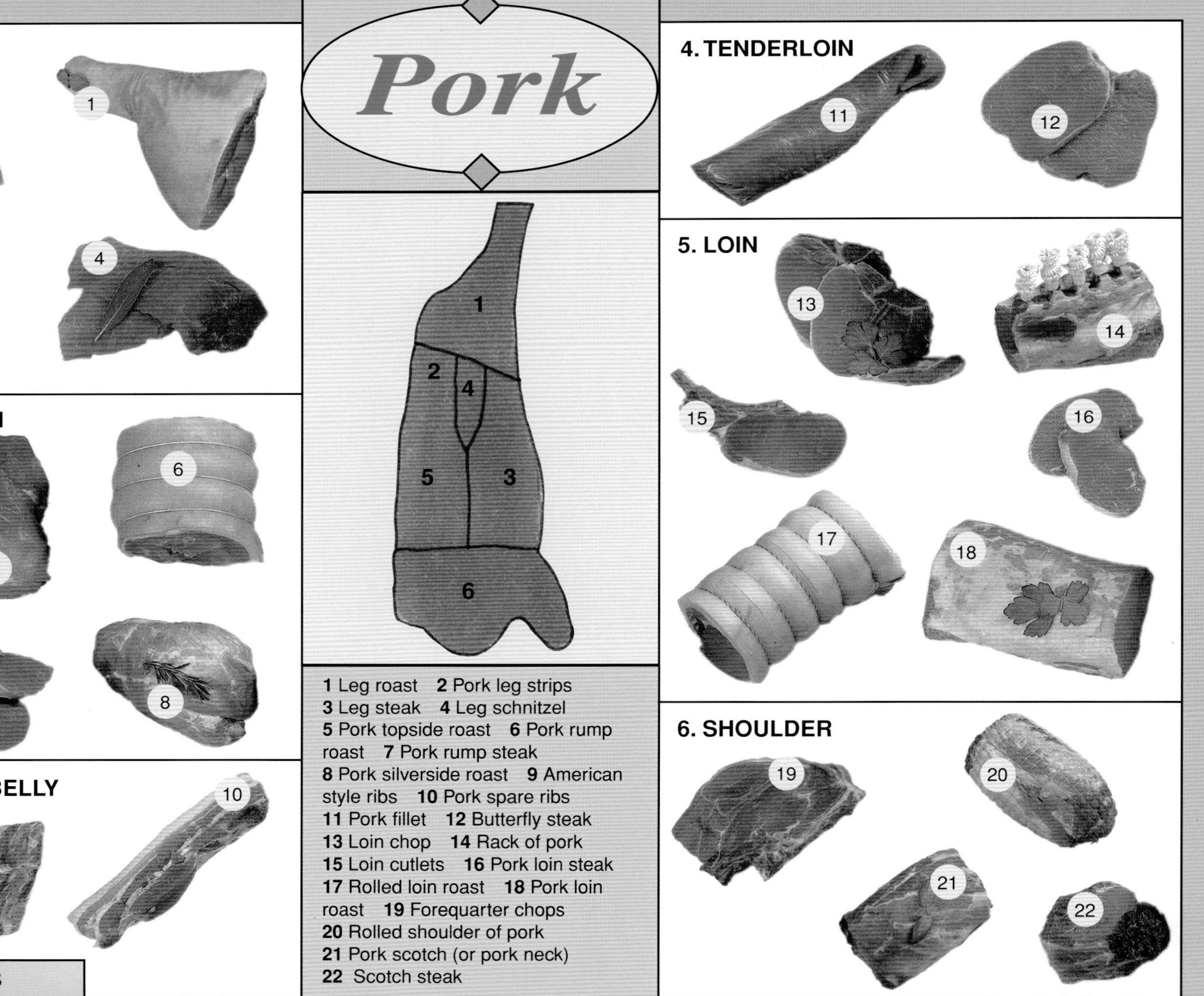

1 Leg roast **2** Pork leg strips
3 Leg steak **4** Leg schnitzel
5 Pork topside roast **6** Pork rump roast **7** Pork rump steak
8 Pork silverside roast **9** American style ribs **10** Pork spare ribs
11 Pork fillet **12** Butterfly steak
13 Loin chop **14** Rack of pork
15 Loin cutlets **16** Pork loin steak
17 Rolled loin roast **18** Pork loin roast **19** Forequarter chops
20 Rolled shoulder of pork
21 Pork scotch (or pork neck)
22 Scotch steak

PLATE 8

BEEF STIR-FRY WITH ASPARAGUS

- *Serves:* 4
- *Cooking utensil:* wok

Preparation time: ***20 minutes***
Cooking time: ***5–10 minutes***

Ingredients

400 g rump steak *or* beef strips
1 tablespoon (20 mL) light soy sauce
1 tablespoon (20 mL) dry sherry
1 teaspoon cornflour
16 asparagus spears
1 tablespoon (20 mL) peanut oil
1/2 clove garlic, crushed
1 teaspoon (5 g) chopped ginger
1 cup (100 g) bean shoots
1/4 cup (65 mL) water
2 cups cooked noodles (p. 113)

Method

1. Cut beef into strips.
2. Mix beef with soy sauce, sherry and cornflour.
3. Wash and trim asparagus and remove hard end portion.
4. Steam asparagus for 2 minutes. Place in cold water 1 minute, drain.
5. Heat oil in wok, add garlic, ginger and meat and stir-fry until meat is brown.
6. Remove meat.
7. Add asparagus, stir-fry 15 seconds, add bean shoots and stir-fry 30 seconds.
8. Add water, stir, cover and cook until asparagus is tender but crisp.
9. Add meat, reheat and serve with noodles.

DEVILLED KIDNEYS

- *Serves:* 2
- *Cooking utensil:* small saucepan

Preparation time: ***10 minutes***
Cooking time: ***7–10 minutes***

Ingredients

4 lamb's kidneys
2 teaspoons (10 g) butter
1/4 teaspoon mustard
1/4 teaspoon salt
2 shakes pepper
1/4 teaspoon curry paste
1 tablespoon (20 mL) vinegar
2 tablespoons (40 mL) water
1 teaspoon plain flour
2 slices hot toast, buttered
1 teaspoon chopped parsley

Method

1. Remove skin and core from kidneys. Dice kidneys.
2. Melt butter in small saucepan, stir in kidneys and other ingredients, except toast and parsley.
3. Sauté for 7–10 minutes, stirring frequently.
4. Serve on buttered toast and garnish with parsley.

BEEF STROGANOFF

Serves: ***4***
Cooking utensil: frying pan *or* saucepan

Preparation time: ***20 minutes***
Cooking time: ***15–20 minutes***

Ingredients

400 g topside *or* fillet steak
1 tablespoon (10 g) plain flour
2 tablespoons (40 g) butter
1/2 cup (75 g) chopped onion
1 cup (100 g) sliced mushrooms
1 clove (5 g) garlic, crushed

Sauce

1 tablespoon (20 g) butter
1 tablespoon (10 g) plain flour
1 tablespoon (20 g) tomato paste
1 1/4 cups (310 mL) stock
1/2 cup (125 mL) sour cream
2 cups cooked rice (p. 113) *or* noodles (p. 113)

Method

1. Cut meat into thin strips across the grain, and roll in flour.
2. Brown meat quickly in butter.
3. Add onions, mushrooms and garlic and cook until onion is brown and tender. Remove mixture from pan.
4. Prepare sauce: melt butter, add flour, blend until smooth, cook 1 minute. Add tomato paste and stock, stir until mixture thickens and boils.
5. Return meat and vegetables to pan, stir in sour cream and heat without boiling. If using topside steak, simmer for 30 minutes. Taste and adjust flavour.
6. Serve at once, accompanied by rice *or* noodles.

MEATBALLS IN STROGANOFF SAUCE ✦

Follow **Beef stroganoff** recipe. Instead of fillet steak use 400 g minced steak formed into 16 balls. Fry for 10 minutes *or* microwave on high power for 3 minutes, turn, then continue cooking on medium power for 3 minutes.

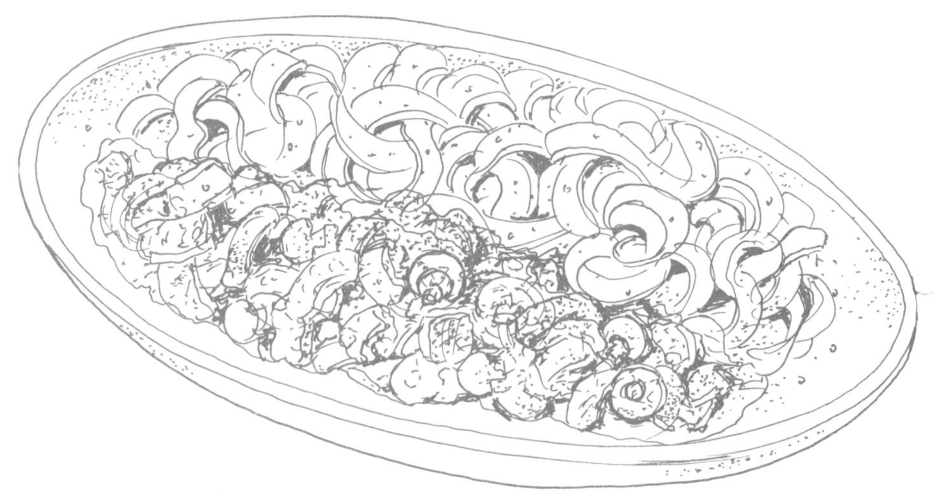

STIR-FRY CHICKEN WITH BOK CHOY

► *Serves:* 4
► *Cooking utensil:* saucepan, wok

🕓 *Preparation time:* **20 minutes**
🕓 *Cooking time:* **10–15 minutes**

Ingredients
400 g chicken, diced
2 teaspoons (10 mL) dry sherry
1 tablespoon (20 mL) light soy sauce
2 teaspoons (5 g) cornflour
4 bok choy (500 g)
1 tablespoon (20 mL) peanut oil
1/2 onion (65 g), diced
1 clove (5 g) garlic, crushed
1 teaspoon (5 g) chopped ginger
1 cup (250 mL) water
400 g can corn kernels, drained
1 tablespoon (20 mL) water
1 small chilli, seeded and finely sliced
2 spring onions, sliced diagonally

Method
1 Mix chicken, sherry, half soy sauce and half the cornflour.
2 Cut each bok choy lengthwise into 4 pieces.
3 Cook bok choy in boiling water for 1 minute and drain.
4 Heat oil in wok, add onion, garlic and ginger, stir fry for 2 seconds. Add chicken and stir-fry for 2 minutes until chicken is brown.
5 Pour 1 cup water into wok, bring to boil, add corn and bok choy.
6 Blend remaining cornflour with 1 tablespoon water, add to wok and stir until boiling.
7 Add remaining soy sauce and chilli.
8 Serve sprinkled with spring onion.

CHICKEN AND ALMONDS

► *Serves:* 4
► *Cooking utensil:* wok *or* deep frying pan

🕓 *Preparation time:* **20 minutes**
🕓 *Cooking time:* **20 minutes**

Ingredients
1 cup (60 g) sliced green beans
1 stalk (100 g) celery, diced
1 tablespoon (20 mL) oil
1/2 cup (60 g) blanched almonds
1 onion (125 g), diced
1 clove (5 g) garlic, crushed
1 cup (100 g) chopped mushrooms
2 tablespoons (20 g) cornflour
1 cup (250 mL) chicken stock
2 cups (300 g) diced cooked chicken
1 teaspoon (5 g) chopped ginger
1 tablespoon (20 mL) soy sauce
50 g almonds for garnish
1 teaspoon oil

Method
1 Cook beans and celery for 1 minute in boiling water. Drain.
2 Heat oil and fry almonds until golden brown. Remove from oil and drain on absorbent paper.
3 Fry onion and garlic 2 minutes. Add mushroom and fry for 1 minute.
4 Blend cornflour with 1/4 cup stock and put aside.
5 Add chicken and other ingredients to mushrooms and cook 5 minutes.
6 Stir in blended cornflour and cook 2 minutes.
7 Sauté almonds for garnish in 1 teaspoon oil, sprinkle over and serve.

PAN-FRIED KANGAROO FILLETS WITH SNOW PEAS

- *Serves:* 4
- *Cooking utensil:* frying pan

Preparation time: **5 minutes**
Cooking time: **5–10 minutes**

Ingredients

4 kangaroo fillet steaks (400 g)
4 shakes black pepper
1 tablespoon (20 g) butter
1 tablespoon (20 mL) olive oil
2½ cups (250 g) snow peas, strings removed

Method

1. Sprinkle fillets with pepper.
2. Heat butter and oil in frying pan.
3. Quickly sear the fillets on both sides, reduce the heat to medium and cook for 3 minutes.
4. Place fillets on hot dish, cover and leave for 3 minutes.
5. Reheat frying pan with remaining oil and juices, stir-fry snow peas quickly for 2 minutes *or* until peas are bright green.
6. Serve immediately with the kangaroo fillets.

CITRUS LAMB'S FRY

- *Serves:* 2
- *Cooking utensil:* frying pan

Preparation time: **15 minutes**
Cooking time: **10 minutes**

Ingredients

250 g lamb's fry (liver)
1 tablespoon (10 g) plain flour
1 orange
½ tablespoon (10 g) butter
1 onion (125 g), diced
1 teaspoon soy sauce
½ cup (125 mL) stock

Method

1. Wash lamb's fry in hot water. Remove skin if necessary. Pat dry using absorbent paper.
2. Slice lamb's fry thinly, removing any large blood vessels. Coat in flour.
3. Cut orange in half and remove 2 very thin slices for garnish. Remove rind and shred finely. Squeeze juice from orange.
4. Heat butter and sauté onion until transparent.
5. Sauté lamb's fry approximately 2 minutes on each side. Add more butter if necessary.
6. Combine orange juice, rind, soy sauce and stock. Add to frying pan and bring to the boil, simmer 2–3 minutes.
7. Serve garnished with orange slices.

CRUMBED BRAINS

- *Serves:* 4
- *Cooking utensil:* frying pan

Preparation time: **15 minutes**
Cooking time: **20 minutes**

Ingredients

4 sets lamb's brains
1/2 teaspoon salt
2 tablespoons (20 g) plain flour
3 shakes pepper
1 egg
2 tablespoons (40 mL) milk
1/2 cup (45 g) dried breadcrumbs
3 tablespoons (60 g) butter
2 rashers (80 g) bacon, fried
2 parsley sprigs

Method

1. Blanch brains: place in saucepan with salt, cover with water and bring to boil. Strain.
2. Remove membrane and blood vessels.
3. Coat with flour and pepper.
4. Dip in beaten egg and milk.
5. Roll in breadcrumbs.
6. Heat butter in frying pan and fry brains for 7–10 minutes. Drain.
7. Serve with bacon, garnished with parsley sprigs.

CRUMBED SWEETBREADS

Follow recipe for **Crumbed brains**, using 300 g sweetbreads.

Roast meat and poultry

Meat to be roasted is placed in a baking dish and cooked using an oven, frying pan or rotisserie. During baking the dry convected and radiated heat browns the outside of the meat and develops the distinctive flavour of roast meat, while muscle fibres in the interior of the meat are softened by the moist heat of their own juices. The meat may be partially cooked on low power in a microwave oven and finished in an oven to develop the flavour and colour of oven roasting.

Oven temperatures and cooking times are related to the size and shape of the meat and the degree of cooking required by individual taste. If cooked at a high temperature until well-done right through, the meat shrinks considerably. High-temperature, short-time cooking produces a meat that is browned on the outside and underdone in the centre and is suited to cooking beef. A moderate or lower temperature with a corresponding increase in cooking time is preferable for lamb and should be used for veal, pork and poultry, all of which, especially poultry, are usually cooked through.

A meat thermometer that indicates the internal temperature of the meat gives a guide to the degree to which the meat has cooked.

General hints for roasting meat and poultry

- Allow 100–125 grams meat or poultry per person, depending on the proportion of bone to flesh.
- Cooking times given are approximate, as factors such as shape and thickness of the meat and personal preference need to be taken into account. Use a meat thermometer if possible. Insert the thermometer at least 10 cm into the thickest part of the meat away from gristle and bone, or into the thigh of poultry. The internal temperature continues to rise for approximately 15 minutes after it has been removed from the oven. Frozen poultry must be completely thawed in the refrigerator before cooking.
- Meat may be wrapped in foil or placed in an oven bag. Place 1 tablespoon flour in bag and shake. Make 4 holes in bag before placing meat in the oven. Meat may be placed on a rack in the baking dish.
- Vegetables suitable for roasting include carrot, choko, marrow, onion, parsnip, potato, pumpkin, kumara, sweet potato. The usual serve per person is 1 piece of potato and 1 piece of another vegetable. Prepare and cut into approximately 100 g pieces. Green or yellow vegetables may be cooked separately and served.
- Meat can be carved more easily if allowed to stand for 15 minutes on a serving plate.
- Meat and poultry may be roasted on a rotisserie or cooked in a frying pan. Follow manufacturers' instructions that come with the appliance.
- Meat left over may be served cold with salad or reheated in gravy and served with vegetables.

ROAST LAMB

- *Meats suitable:* leg, shoulder *or* loin of lamb
- *Serves:* ***6***
- *Cooking utensil:* baking dish

Ingredients

1 kg lamb
fresh sprigs *or* dried rosemary
2 tablespoons (40 mL) water
600 g each vegetable for roasting, cut into 100 g pieces (e.g. potato, pumpkin, onion, marrow)
600 g green vegetables
500 mL (1 quantity) **Brown gravy** (p. 194)
50 mL (1 quantity) **Mint sauce** (p. 194) *or* **Red currant jelly sauce** (p. 194)

- *Preparation time:* ***30 minutes***
- *Cooking time:* ***1 hour per kg*** *lamb*
  1 hour *roast vegetables*
- *Oven temperature:* ***190°C***
- *Internal temperature:* ***80°C***

Method

1. Read General hints for roasting meat and poultry (p. 192). Set oven at 190°C.
2. Insert rosemary into slits in meat.
3. Place meat and water in baking dish, place in oven and cook, basting every 20 minutes.
4. Add roasting vegetables, baste them and turn meat. Insert meat thermometer.
5. After 15 minutes turn vegetables.
6. Cook green vegetables. Make **Mint sauce** *or* **Red currant jelly sauce**.
7. Lift meat and vegetables onto serving dishes and keep hot.
8. Make gravy using liquid from green vegetables as stock.
9. Carve meat and serve with vegetables, **Brown gravy** and **Mint sauce** *or* **Red currant jelly sauce**.

SEASONED ROAST LAMB

Follow recipe for **Roast lamb**. Omit rosemary and **Mint sauce**. Use boneless leg of lamb *or* boneless shoulder of lamb. Fill cavity with 1 quantity **Bread and herb seasoning** (p. 195) *or* **Rice and walnut seasoning** (p. 195), tie into shape using small skewers and string. Remove skewers and string before carving.

RACKS OF LAMB

Follow recipe for **Roast lamb**. Omit rosemary and **Mint sauce**. Allow 1 rack of lamb per person (3 chops in each). Combine 1 cup (40 g) fresh breadcrumbs, 1 clove (5 g) crushed garlic, 1 teaspoon chopped parsley, 2 tablespoons (40 g) melted butter. Spread mixture over the top of each rack and bake for 20–25 minutes. Cover ends of bones with foil during cooking. May be marinated in **Honey marinade** (p. 176) *or* **Orange marmalade marinade** (p. 176) before cooking.

BROWN GRAVY

► *Serves:* 6

► *Cooking utensil:* baking dish in which meat has been cooked

Ingredients

2 tablespoons fat left in baking dish
3 tablespoons (30 g) plain flour
2 cups (500 mL) stock *or* vegetable water
3 shakes pepper

Method

1 Add flour to fat and stir until blended.
2 Stir over low heat until roux is brown.
3 Remove from heat and add liquid gradually, stirring until smooth.
4 Bring to boil, then simmer 1–2 minutes, stirring continuously.
5 Flavour and serve very hot in gravy jug.

MINT SAUCE

► *Serves:* 6

Ingredients

1 tablespoon finely chopped mint leaves
1/2 teaspoon sugar
1 tablespoon (20 mL) boiling water
1 tablespoon (20 mL) vinegar

Method

1 Place mint and sugar in basin, add boiling water and stir until sugar is dissolved.
2 Add vinegar and stand for 15 minutes.
3 Serve in small sauce jug.

REDCURRANT JELLY SAUCE

► *Serves:* 6

Ingredients

2 tablespoons (40 mL) orange juice
2 tablespoons (50 g) red currant jelly
1 tablespoon (20 mL) vinegar
1 tablespoon chopped mint leaves

Method

1 Place orange juice and red currant jelly in saucepan, heat gently until jelly has melted.
2 Add vinegar and mint.
3 Serve in small sauce jug.

BREAD AND HERB SEASONING

Ingredients

1 cup (40 g) fresh breadcrumbs
2 teaspoons chopped parsley
1/4 teaspoon dried thyme *or* 1/2 teaspoon chopped herbs
1/2 onion (65 g), finely chopped
1/4 teaspoon grated lemon rind
1/8 teaspoon nutmeg
1/2 teaspoon salt
3 shakes pepper
1 teaspoon (5 g) butter
2 tablespoons (40 mL) milk

Method

1. Place all dry ingredients in basin.
2. Rub butter into mixture gently.
3. Mix with milk.
4. Makes 1 cup. Use for **Roast lamb**, **Roast chicken**, **Roast beef** and **Roast veal**.

✦ APPLE AND RAISIN SEASONING ✦

Follow recipe for **Bread and herb seasoning**. Add 1/2 cup (65 g) grated apple and 2 tablespoons (30 g) raisins. Use for **Roast turkey**, **Roast pork** and **Roast lamb**.

✦ APRICOT SEASONING ✦

Follow recipe for **Bread and herb seasoning**. Add 2 tablespoons (30 g) chopped dried apricots. Use for **Roast turkey**, **Roast veal** and **Roast pork**.

✦ SAGE AND ONION SEASONING ✦

Follow recipe for **Bread and herb seasoning**. Omit thyme. Add 1/2 teaspoon crushed dried sage *or* 2 teaspoons chopped sage. Use for **Roast pork** and **Roast rabbit.**

✦ RICE AND WALNUT SEASONING ✦

Follow recipe for **Bread and herb seasoning**. Omit breadcrumbs. Add 1/2 stalk (50 g) chopped celery, 1 cup cooked rice (p. 113) and 2 pickled walnuts, chopped, *or* 2 tablespoons (15 g) chopped walnuts. Use for **Roast beef** and **Roast lamb**.

✦ SAUSAGE MEAT SEASONING ✦

Follow recipe for **Bread and herb seasoning**, using 1 finely chopped onion (125 g). Add 500 g sausage meat and 1 chopped apple (150 g) (optional). Use for **Roast turkey** (No. 23 to No. 27 turkey).

ROAST BEEF

- *Meats suitable:* sirloin, topside, ribeye, rump *or* silverside roast
- *Serves:* ***6***
- *Cooking utensil:* baking dish
- *Preparation time:* ***30 minutes***
- *Oven temperature:* ***200°C***

Cooking time and temperature

Cooking	Time per 1 kg	Internal temperature
Rare	30–40 minutes	60°C
Medium	40–50 minutes	70°C
Well-done	40–60 minutes	75°C

Ingredients

1 kg beef
2 tablespoons (40 mL) water
600 g each vegetable for roasting, cut into 100 g pieces (e.g. potato, pumpkin, choko)
600 g green vegetable
500 mL (1 quantity) **Brown gravy** (p. 194)
1 quantity **Yorkshire pudding** (p. 197)

Horseradish sauce

2 teaspoons (10 g) horseradish
1 tablespoon (20 mL) cream
1/4 teaspoon sugar

Method

1. Read General hints for roasting meat and poultry (p. 192).
2. Set oven at 200°C.
3. Place meat and water in baking dish place in oven and cook, basting every 20 minutes.
4. One hour before meat is cooked add roasting vegetables, baste them and turn meat. Insert meat thermometer.
5. Prepare **Yorkshire pudding** (p. 197) and allow mixture to stand for 30 minutes.
6. Turn vegetables after 15 minutes cooking.
7. Bake **Yorkshire pudding**.
8. Cook green vegetables.
9. Make horseradish sauce: combine ingredients.
10. Lift meat and vegetables onto serving dish and keep hot. Allow meat to stand covered with foil for 15 minutes before carving.
11. Make gravy using liquid from green vegetables as stock.
12. Carve meat and serve with vegetables, **Brown gravy**, **Yorkshire pudding** and horseradish sauce.

✦ SEASONED ROAST BEEF ✦

Follow recipe for **Roast beef**. Use boned sirloin *or* topside roast with pocket cut in side. Fill with 1 cup (1 quantity) **Bread and herb seasoning** (p. 195). Skewer and tie into shape with string. Remove skewers and string before carving.

✦ ROAST FILLET OF BEEF ✦

Follow recipe for **Roast beef**. Use 750 g fillet of beef. Before step 3 brown fillet in a hot pan before placing in oven. Cook at 220°C for 20 minutes, depending on thickness.

✦ ROAST VEAL ✦

Follow recipe for **Roast beef**, using leg, shoulder *or* topside of veal. Omit **Yorkshire pudding** and **Horseradish sauce**. Cook 50–60 minutes per kilogram to internal temperature of 77°C. Serve with 500 mL (1 quantity) **Brown gravy** and **Bacon rolls** (p. 175).

✦ SEASONED ROAST VEAL ✦

Follow recipe for **Roast beef** using boned leg, boned shoulder *or* topside of veal with pocket cut in side. Omit **Yorkshire pudding** and **Horseradish sauce**.
Fill with 1 cup (1 quantity) **Apricot seasoning** (p. 195). Skewer and tie into shape with string. Remove skewers and string before carving.

YORKSHIRE PUDDING

- *Serves:* ***6***
- *Cooking utensil:* 6 patty pans
- *Cooking time:* ***20 minutes***
- *Oven temperature:* ***200°C***

Ingredients

$^{1}/_{2}$ cup (75 g) plain flour
$^{1}/_{4}$ teaspoon salt
1 egg (61g), beaten
$^{1}/_{4}$ cup (65 mL) milk
$^{1}/_{4}$ cup (65 mL) water

Method

1. Set oven at 200°C.
2. Brush or spray patty pans with oil.
3. Sift flour and salt and make a well in centre.
4. Place egg in well and, gradually work in the flour and half of liquid.
5. Beat well for 1 minute and stir in remainder of liquid.
6. Allow to stand for 30 minutes before cooking.
7. Pour into patty pans.
8. Bake until golden brown and crisp.
9. Serve with **Roast beef**.

ROAST CHICKEN

Frozen poultry must be completely thawed in the refrigerator before cooking so that the internal temperature is sufficient to prevent microbiological contamination, which may lead to food poisoning.

- *Serves:* ***6***
- *Cooking utensil:* baking dish, baking paper, foil *or* oven bag

- *Preparation time:* ***30 minutes***
- *Cooking time:* ***70 minutes per kg*** *chicken*
  1 hour *roast vegetables*
- *Oven temperature:* ***190°C***
- *Internal temperature:* ***88°C***

Ingredients

1 No. 15 chicken
1 cup (1 quantity) **Bread and herb seasoning** (p. 195)
1 tablespoon (20 mL) oil
600 g each vegetable for roasting, cut into 100 g pieces (e.g. potato, pumpkin, parsnip)
600 g green vegetables
500 mL (1 quantity) **Brown gravy** (p. 143)

Method

1. Read General hints for roasting meat and poultry (p. 192).
2. Set oven at 190°C.
3. Prepare chicken: remove neck, taking care not to damage neck skin. Clean inside. Wash and dry with absorbent paper.
4. To season: with chicken breast resting on board place some seasoning in neck cavity, draw skin over seasoning and secure with skewers. Bend the end section of each wing towards back to rest over end of neck skin flap. Turn bird over, place remaining seasoning in body cavity, skewer cavity edges together. Tie legs together with string.
5. Brush oil over chicken. May be placed in oven bag, with holes to allow steam to escape.
6. Place chicken in baking dish, place in oven and cook. After 30 minutes, turn chicken over. To avoid excessive browning cover breast with baking paper *or* foil.
7. One hour before chicken is cooked add vegetables, baste them and turn chicken.
8. After 15 minutes, turn vegetables.
9. Insert meat thermometer into thigh of chicken.
10. Cook green vegetables.
11. Lift chicken and vegetables onto serving dish and keep hot. Remove skewers and string.
12. Make gravy using liquid from green vegetables as stock.
13. Carve chicken and serve with vegetables and **Brown gravy**.

✦ ROAST DUCKLING ✦

Follow recipe for **Roast chicken**. Omit chicken. Use No. 18 duckling. Season with 1 cup (1 quantity) **Sage and onion seasoning** (p. 195). Remove oil glands from above tail. Cook at 190°C for 70 minutes per kg. Serve with 500 mL (1 quantity) **Brown gravy** (p. 143) flavoured with rind and juice of 1 orange.

✦ ROAST RABBIT ✦

Serves 4. Follow recipe for **Roast chicken**. Omit chicken. Use 1 rabbit and 1 cup (1 quantity) **Sage and onion seasoning** (p. 195).

✦ ROAST TURKEY ✦

Follow recipe for **Roast chicken**. Omit chicken and **Bread and herb seasoning**. To serve 10–12 use No. 23 to No. 27 turkey and 1 cup (1 quantity) **Sausage meat seasoning** (p. 195). Cook for approximately 60 minutes per kg at 160°C. Turkey may be wrapped in foil *or* placed in large oven bag. Insert meat thermometer into thickest part of upper leg. Serve with 500 mL (1 quantity) **Brown gravy** (p. 000) *or* 500 mL (1 quantity) **Espangol sauce** (p. 285) and cranberry sauce *or* **Redcurrant jelly sauce** (p. 194).

ROAST PORK

- *Meats suitable:* loin, rolled loin, shoulder, rolled shoulder
- *Serves:* ***6***
- *Cooking utensil:* baking dish

- *Preparation time:* ***30 minutes***
- *Cooking time:* ***75 minutes per kg*** *meat*
  1 hour *roast vegetables*
- *Oven temperature:* ***190°C***
- *Internal temperature:* ***77°C***

Ingredients

1 kg pork
1 tablespoon (20 mL) oil
600 g each vegetable for roasting, cut into 100 g pieces (e.g. potato, pumpkin, parsnip)
600 g green vegetables
150 g (1 quantity) **Apple sauce** (see below)
500 mL (1 quantity) **Brown gravy** (p. 194)

Method

1. Read General hints for roasting meat and poultry (p. 192).
2. Set oven at 190°C.
3. Prepare meat remove rind, trim fat from underside, tie meat into shape if necessary.
4. Place meat and rind in baking dish with oil, place in oven and cook, basting every 20 minutes.
5. One hour before meat is cooked add vegetables, baste them and turn meat. Insert meat thermometer.
6. After 15 minutes turn vegetables.
7. Cook green vegetables.
8. Make **Apple sauce**.
9. Remove rind from baking dish and grill under hot griller turning occasionally until crisp.
10. Lift meat and vegetables onto serving dishes and keep hot.
11. Make gravy using liquid from green vegetables as stock.
12. Carve meat and serve with vegetables, **Apple sauce** and **Brown gravy**.

✦ APPLE SAUCE ✦

Peel, core and slice 1 cooking apple (150 g). Microwave for 3 minutes on high power in dish with 1 clove, 1 piece of lemon rind and 1 teaspoon water. Serve with **Roast Pork**.

✦ SEASONED ROAST PORK ✦

Follow recipe for **Roast pork**. Use boned loin, boned leg *or* boned shoulder. Fill with 1 cup (1 quantity) **Sage and onion seasoning** (p. 195). Skewer and tie into shape with string. Remove skewers and string before carving.

BAKED HONEY PORK FILLETS

- *Serves:* 4
- *Cooking utensil:* baking dish, saucepan
- *Preparation time:* **20 minutes and 1 hour to marinate**
- *Cooking time:* **25 minutes**
- *Oven temperature:* **200°C**

Ingredients

400 g pork fillets
1 tablespoon (20 mL) tomato puree
2 tablespoons (40 g) honey
1/4 teaspoon five spice powder
2 teaspoons (10 mL) light soy sauce
2 cups cooked rice (p. 113)
Sauce
1/2 cup (125 mL) chicken stock
1 tablespoon (20 mL) dry sherry
2 teaspoons (10 g) honey
1/2 teaspoon oyster sauce

Method

1. Combine tomato puree, honey, five spice powder and soy sauce to make marinade.
2. Add pork fillets, cover and refrigerate for approximately 1 hour.
3. Set oven at 200°C.
4. Lift pork from marinade and place in baking dish, reserve marinade.
5. Bake pork at 200°C for 25 minutes.
6. Place pork on plate, keep warm.
7. Place marinade and sauce ingredients in baking dish, cook over low heat, stirring continuously, for 3 minutes.
8. Cut pork into thick slices, pour sauce over meat and serve with rice.

LEMON GARLIC CHICKEN

- *Serves:* 4
- *Cooking utensil:* casserole (2.5 L)
- *Preparation time:* **25 minutes**
- *Cooking time:* **40 minutes**
- *Oven temperature:* **180°C**

Ingredients

400 g boned chicken pieces
2 tablespoons (20 g) plain flour
2 teaspoons paprika
Lemon garlic sauce
2 teaspoons (10 mL) soy sauce
zest and juice of 2 lemons
1 clove (5 g) garlic, crushed

Method

1. Set oven at 180°C. Brush or spray casserole with oil.
2. Remove skin and toss chicken pieces in flour and paprika.
3. Place pieces in single layer in casserole.
4. Cover and bake at 180°C for 20 minutes.
5. Make sauce: combine ingredients.
6. Turn chicken, spoon sauce over, return to oven and bake 20 minutes, uncovered or until tender, basting occasionally.

BAKED MEAT LOAF

- *Serves:* **4**
- *Cooking utensil:* pyrex loaf pan (1.5 L)
- *Preparation time:* ***20 minutes***
- *Cooking time:* ***1 1/2 hours***
- *Oven temperature:* ***180°C***

Ingredients

250 g minced beef
250 g sausage meat
1/2 cup (45 g) dried breadcrumbs
1 teaspoon salt
6 shakes pepper
1 teaspoon chopped basil
1/8 teaspoon dried thyme
3 shakes nutmeg
1 onion (125 g), grated
1 egg, beaten
500 mL (1 quantity) **Brown gravy** (p. 194)

Method

1. Set oven at 180°C.
2. Place all ingredients except **Brown gravy** in basin and mix well.
3. Spread in loaf pan.
4. Bake at 180°C for 1 1/2 hours.
5. Turn out onto hot serving dish and keep hot.
6. Make **Brown gravy** and serve.

Place mixture in pyrex or microwave loaf pan and cover with plastic food wrap. Microwave for 13–15 minutes on medium power. Check if centre is cooked and cook a further 1–2 minutes if required. Stand 8 minutes before serving.

MEAT LOAF WITH BACON

Follow recipe for **Baked meat loaf**. Add 125 g chopped bacon at step 2.

FRUITY MEAT LOAF

Follow recipe for **Baked meat loaf**. Add 1 grated apple (150 g) and 2 tablespoons (30 g) sultanas at step 2.

CHEESE-TOPPED MEAT LOAF

Follow recipe for **Baked meat loaf**. After cooking sprinkle with 1/2 cup (60 g) grated cheese. Microwave for 1 minute on high power.

POTATO-TOPPED MEAT LOAF

Follow recipe for **Baked meat loaf**. After cooking cover loaf with 2 cups (400 g) mashed potato and sprinkle with 1/2 cup (60 g) grated tasty cheese. Microwave for 1 1/2–2 minutes on high power.

✦ TOMATO-TOPPED MEAT LOAF ✦

Follow recipe for **Baked meat loaf**. After cooking turn onto serving plate and cover with 1 quantity **Fresh tomato sauce** (p. 283) mixed with 1 teaspoon mustard.

CHICKEN TERRINE

- *Serves:* ***6***
- *Cooking utensil:* pyrex loaf pan (1.5 L)
- *Preparation time:* ***20 minutes***
- *Cooking time:* ***$1^1/_2$ hours***
- *Oven temperature:* ***160°C***

Ingredients

400 g chicken, chopped
1 onion (125 g), diced
1 clove (5 g) garlic, crushed
$^1/_4$ cup (65 mL) stock *or* white wine
1 tablespoon (10 g) green peppercorns
1 teaspoon chopped thyme
1 egg
2 rashers (80 g) bacon
6 slices bread

Method

1. Set oven at 160°C.
2. Combine all ingredients except bacon and bread.
3. Line loaf pan with bacon.
4. Place chicken mixture in loaf pan pressing firmly into corners.
5. Cover with foil and place in water-bath in oven. Bake for $1^1/_2$ hours at 160°C.
6. Cool, refrigerate overnight.
7. Turn out, cut into 12 slices. Toast bread and cut into triangles. Serve with terrine slices.

Microwave on high power for 5 minutes then medium power for 8 minutes, covered with plastic film.

✦ VEAL AND PORK TERRINE ✦

Follow recipe for **Chicken terrine**. Replace chicken with 250 g chopped veal and 150 g chopped pork.

✦ TURKEY TERRINE ✦

Follow recipe for **Chicken terrine**. Replace chicken with 400 g chopped turkey.

✦ RABBIT TERRINE ✦

Follow recipe for **Chicken terrine**. Replace chicken with 400 g chopped rabbit.

Boiled meat and poultry

Meats suitable for boiling are the cheaper, tougher cuts that require long slow cooking in moist heat. When served hot, boiled meats are traditionally accompanied by a well-flavoured sauce and root vegetables. Served cold, they are accompanied by salads or used as sandwich fillings. The cooking liquid from boiled fresh meat can be used to make sauces, gravy, soups and stews.

CORNED BEEF

Add a chopped orange to the cooking water to give extra flavour.

- *Meats suitable:* corned silverside, corned brisket
- *Serves:* 6
- *Cooking utensil:* large saucepan *or* pressure cooker

Preparation time: 20 minutes
Cooking time: ***1 1/2–2 hours*** *if under 1.5 kg*
2–2 1/2 hours *if over 1.5 kg*
or ***40 minutes*** *in pressure cooker for 750 g meat*

Ingredients

750 g corned beef
4 peppercorns
1 tablespoon (20 mL) vinegar
2 teaspoons (10 g) brown sugar
2 pimento (allspice berries)
2 cloves
1 bay leaf
4 small (400 g) onions
4 pieces (400 g) carrot
4 pieces (400 g) parsnip *or* swede *or* white turnip

Sauce

2 teaspoons (10 g) grain mustard
1 tablespoon (10 g) cornflour
1 tablespoon (20 g) sugar
1/2 cup (125 mL) vinegar

Method

1. Wash meat in cold water. Trim and tie into shape if necessary.
2. Place meat in saucepan, just cover with cold water, add flavourings and bring slowly to the boil. Simmer for required time with lid on the saucepan.
3. Prepare vegetables, cut into serving pieces and add 30 minutes before serving.
4. Make sauce: Blend dry ingredients with mustard in small saucepan, add 1/2 cup liquid from cooking meat, bring to boil, stirring continuously.
5. Lift meat and vegetables onto hot serving dish. Serve sauce separately.
6. If meat is to be served cold, allow it to cool in cooking water.

✦ PICKLED PORK ✦

Follow recipe for **Corned beef**, using pickled hand, shoulder, leg *or* belly of pork.

✦ PICKLED TONGUE ✦

Follow recipe for **Corned beef**, using 1 ox tongue.

Stews and casseroles

Stewing and casseroling of meat is a method of cooking a tasty dish from the tougher, cheaper cuts of meat that are made tender by moist heat. Fuel is saved, as one container is used for meat and vegetables and only a gentle heat is required to keep the food simmering.

Stews may be cooked in covered saucepan or in a casserole in the oven or microwave. Electric saucepans and frypans are also suitable. Casseroles may be made from ovenproof glass or china or microwave plastic.

Food cooked in a casserole may be served from it to the table, hence the term 'en casserole'.

Main types of stews and casseroles

Stew or casserole Meat, onions and flour are browned in oil or butter and the mixture cooked in stock, often with additional vegetables and spices. If the meat is to be cooked in a casserole omit the fat from ingredients. Coat meat with flour and place it, along with all other ingredients, in the casserole.

Fricassee or white stew Meat and vegetables are simmered in stock until cooked, then thickening, e.g. flour or roux, is added and the fricassee enriched with milk or cream. They may be thickened with potato or cereal such as rice, barley or rolled oats.

Braise Usually left in a large piece, meat is browned, then placed on a bed of vegetables that are just covered with stock, and cooked slowly. When meat is tender the vegetables may be discarded, the gravy strained and thickened. A fresh accompaniment such as fried onions, sautéed mushrooms or tomatoes is cooked separately, then served with the meat.

IRISH STEW

- *Serves:* 4
- *Cooking utensil:* saucepan with tight-fitting lid

Preparation time: ***25 minutes***

Cooking time: ***1¼ hours***

Ingredients

500 g forequarter chops
1 cup (250 mL) water
1 teaspoon salt
3 shakes pepper
2 onions (250 g), diced
1 stalk (100 g) celery, sliced
½ turnip (70 g), diced
500 g potatoes, peeled
1 teaspoon chopped parsley

Method

1. Trim fat from chops and cut chops into pieces.
2. Put water, salt and pepper into saucepan and bring to the boil. Add meat, onion, celery and turnip and half of the potatoes, which have been thinly sliced, cover with lid and simmer for 45 minutes.
3. Remove fat, add remainder of potatoes, which have been cut into chunks. Simmer 30 minutes.
4. Taste and adjust flavour.
5. Serve, garnished with chopped parsley.

BEEF STEW

- *Serves:* **4**
- *Cooking utensil:* saucepan with tight-fitting lid

Preparation time: ***25 minutes***
Cooking time: ***1 1/2 hours***

Ingredients

400 g blade, chuck *or* round steak
1 tablespoon (20 mL) oil
1 1/2 tablespoons (15 g) plain flour
1 onion (125 g), diced
1 carrot (125 g), sliced
1 parsnip *or* turnip (125 g), sliced
1 stalk (100 g) celery, sliced
1 1/2 cups (375 mL) stock
3 shakes pepper

Method

1. Trim fat and sinew from beef, cut into 3 cm dice.
2. Heat oil in saucepan and brown meat quickly on each side.
3. Remove meat.
4. Add flour and mix well. Add vegetables.
5. Return to heat and cook slowly until russet brown. Stir all the time.
6. Add stock and stir while bringing to boil *or* place in a casserole dish and cook in an oven at 180°C for 1 hour.
7. Add pepper and vegetables.
8. Return meat to saucepan and simmer gently for 1 1/4 hours. Stir frequently.
9. Remove fat. Taste stew and adjust flavour if necessary. Garnish with chopped parsley and serve.

Follow recipe for **Beef stew**, using 1 cup stock only. Transfer to microwave dish at step 8 when meat is returned to gravy. Microwave for 8 minutes on high power then for 15–20 minutes on medium power.

✦ OX TAIL STEW ✦

Follow recipe for **Beef stew**, using 800 g ox tail. Cook for 2 1/2 hours.

✦ BRAISED LAMB SHANKS ✦

Follow recipe for **Beef stew**, using 4 lamb shanks.

✦ LAMB SHANKS AND CASHEW NUTS ✦

Follow recipe for **Beef stew**, using 4 lamb shanks. Garnish with 1/2 cup (50 g) cashew nuts.

QUAIL WITH GINGER SAUCE

- *Serves:* 4
- *Cooking utensil:* large saucepan

Preparation time: **30 minutes**
Cooking time: **25 minutes**

Ingredients

4 quail
2 teaspoons (10 g) butter
1 carrot (130 g), diced
1 stalk celery (100 g), diced
1 tablespoon (20 g) golden syrup
2 cloves (10 g) garlic, chopped
1 tablespoon (20 g) chopped ginger
1 tablespoon (20 mL) light soy sauce
3 shakes black pepper
1 cup (250 mL) chicken stock
1 tablespoon chopped parsley

Method

1. Brown quail in butter in saucepan.
2. Add other ingredients except stock and parsley, cover and cook 15 minutes, turning the quail after 8 minutes.
3. Remove the quail from saucepan, keep warm.
4. Add chicken stock to saucepan and heat until liquid is reduced by half.
5. Add parsley and spoon the sauce over the quail.

TRIPE GENOESE

- *Serves:* 4
- *Cooking utensil:* saucepan

Preparation time: **30 minutes**
Cooking time: **1½ hours**

Ingredients

500 g tripe, washed and cut into strips
2 tablespoons (40 mL) olive oil
1 onion (125 g), chopped
1 stalk celery (100 g), chopped
1 carrot (125 g), chopped
1 cup (100 g) chopped mushrooms
425 g can chopped tomatoes
1 cup (250 mL) beef stock
2 cups (300 g) peeled and diced potatoes, cooked

Method

1. Simmer tripe in boiling water for 3 minutes, drain.
2. Heat oil in saucepan, sauté onion for two minutes, add celery, carrots and mushrooms and sauté for 5 minutes.
3. Add tripe, tomatoes and beef stock, cover and simmer for ½ hour.
4. Add potatoes and simmer uncovered until sauce is thick and tripe is tender, stirring occasionally to avoid sticking.

VEAL FRICASSEE

- *Serves:* *4*
- *Cooking utensil:* saucepan with tight-fitting lid

Preparation time: ***30 minutes***
Cooking time: ***1 hour***

Ingredients

500 g veal chops *or* 400 g veal without bone
2 cups (500 mL) stock *or* water
6 peppercorns
1 onion (125 g), sliced
1 turnip (125 g), diced
2 stalks (200 g) celery, sliced
1 tablespoon (20 g) butter
1½ tablespoons (15 g) plain flour
½ cup (125 mL) milk
3 shakes cayenne
8 **Bacon rolls** (p. 175)
1 tablespoon chopped parsley

Method

1. Cut meat into neat pieces.
2. Bring stock and peppercorns to the boil.
3. Add meat and vegetables. Place lid on saucepan.
4. Simmer for 1 hour until tender.
5. Lift meat and vegetables onto serving dish and keep hot. Remove peppercorns and fat, retain liquid.
6. Melt butter, add flour, stir until smooth. Stir in milk, then ½ cup (125 mL) cooking liquid and cayenne. Bring to boil while stirring. Cook 1 minute. Taste and flavour if necessary.
7. Pour sauce over meat and vegetables on serving dish.
8. Serve with grilled **Bacon rolls** and garnish with chopped parsley.

RABBIT FRICASSEE

Follow recipe for **Veal fricassee**, using 1 rabbit.

CHICKEN FRICASSEE

Follow recipe for **Veal fricassee**, using No. 12 chicken.

FRICASSEE OF TRIPE

Follow recipe for **Veal fricassee**, using 400 g tripe. Follow recipe from step 2.

MOROCCAN BEEF

- *Serves:* 4
- *Cooking utensil:* saucepan

Preparation time: **30 minutes**
Cooking time: **1 hour**

Ingredients

400 g blade, chuck *or* round steak, diced
1 (125 g) onion, diced
1 tablespoon (20 mL) olive oil
1/2 teaspoon saffron
3 shakes black pepper
2 teaspoons ground cinnamon
1/4 teaspoon ground ginger
1 cup (250 mL) water
1 cup (200 g) prunes
1 strip lemon rind
1 cup (120 g) roasted almonds
2 sprigs mint

Method

1. Combine meat, onion, olive oil and spices in saucepan.
2. Add water. Cover and simmer for 1 hour or until meat is tender.
3. Remove meat, leaving liquid.
4. Make prune sauce: Add lemon rind and prunes to liquid and cook with lid off for 10 minutes or until soft.
5. Place meat on serving dish, pour prune sauce over meat.
6. Sprinkle with roasted almonds and garnish with mint sprigs.

OSSO BUCCO

- *Serves:* 4
- *Cooking utensil:* saucepan

Preparation time: **20 minutes**
Cooking time: **1 1/4–1 1/2 hours**

Ingredients

1 kg shin of veal sawn into 8 rounds
1 tablespoon (10 g) plain flour
6 shakes pepper
1 tablespoon (20 mL) oil
1 tablespoon (20 g) butter
2 cloves (10 g) garlic, chopped
1 onion (125 g), finely chopped
1 cup (250 mL) stock *or* water
1/4 cup (65 mL) tomato paste
2 cups noodles (p. 113)
1/2 teaspoon grated lemon rind
1 tablespoon chopped parsley

Method

1. Coat meat with flour, salt and pepper.
2. Heat oil and butter in saucepan.
3. Brown meat, add garlic, onion, stock and tomato paste. Bring to the boil.
4. Place lid on saucepan and simmer until tender, approximately 1 1/4 hours.
5. Serve with noodles and sprinkle with lemon rind and parsley.

CHOW MEIN

Serves: 4
Cooking utensil: large saucepan

Preparation time: ***20 minutes***
Cooking time: ***30 minutes***

Ingredients

400 g minced beef
1 packet 2-minute noodles
2 tablespoons (30 g) rice
2 teaspoons (10 mL) soy sauce
2 tablespoons (40 mL) tomato sauce
1 teaspoon curry powder
$1^1/_2$ cups (375 mL) hot water
2 stalks (200 g) celery, sliced
1 onion (125 g), sliced
3 cups (300 g) finely sliced cabbage
$^1/_2$ cup (60 g) sliced green beans

Method

1. Place meat, noodles, rice, sauces, curry powder and hot water in saucepan. Stir well. Cook 15 minutes.
2. Add other ingredients, stir until boiling, and cook for 15 minutes. Stir occasionally. Taste and adjust flavour.

CHILLI CON CARNE

Serves: 4
Cooking utensil: saucepan

Preparation time: ***20 minutes***
Cooking time: ***30 minutes***

Ingredients

250 g minced beef
1 tablespoon (20 mL) oil
1 onion (125 g), chopped
$^1/_8$ teaspoon chilli powder
2 tomatoes (250 g), diced
1 bay leaf, crushed
$^1/_4$ teaspoon ground cumin
$^1/_2$ teaspoon oregano
1 clove (5 g) garlic, crushed
1 cup (250 mL) stock *or* water
310 g can kidney beans

Method

1. Heat oil and fry meat until lightly browned.
2. Add onion and fry until lightly browned.
3. Add other ingredients except beans to saucepan. Bring to the boil and simmer 30 minutes.
4. Heat beans separately, drain and serve around meat *or* add 10 minutes before serving.

✦ TACOS ✦

Follow recipe for **Chilli con carne**. Heat 8 taco shells in oven (180°C) for 5 minutes. Fill shells with 1 cup (100 g) finely sliced lettuce, $^1/_2$ cup (60 g) grated cheese, 1 diced tomato (125 g) and meat. May be served with commercial taco sauce.

APRICOT VEAL

- *Serves:* **4**
- *Cooking utensils:* frying pan, casserole (2.5 L)
- *Preparation time:* **20 minutes**
- *Cooking time:* **45 minutes**
- *Oven temperature:* **180°C**

Ingredients

400 g veal chops
1 tablespoon (20 mL) olive oil
1 teaspoon chopped ginger
2 onions (250 g), finely chopped
1 teaspoon (5 g) tomato paste
1/2 cup (125 mL) red wine
8 apricot halves
3 tablespoons (30 g) dried breadcrumbs

Method

1 Set oven at 180°C.
2 Brown chops in oil in frying pan.
3 Place all ingredients in casserole.
4 Cover casserole, cook at 180°C for 45 minutes.

APPLE PORK

Follow for **Apricot veal**, replacing veal with pork chops, trimmed of fat. At step 4, add 2 peeled and sliced apples (280 g) instead of apricot halves.

SHEPHERD'S PIE

- *Serves:* **4**
- *Cooking utensil:* ovenproof dish (2.5 L), 4-sided oven tray
- *Preparation time:* **15 minutes**
- *Cooking time:* **20 minutes**
- *Oven temperature:* **180°C**

Ingredients

2 cups (300 g) cooked minced beef *or* lamb
1 onion (125 g), grated
1/4 teaspoon mixed herbs
2 tablespoons (40 mL) tomato sauce
1/4 cup (65 mL) stock *or* water
1 1/2 cups (375 g) cooked mashed potatoes
4 parsley sprigs

Method

1 Set oven at 180°C. Brush or spray ovenproof dish with oil.
2 Combine all ingredients except potato and parsley and spoon into dish.
3 Spread potato on the top. Decorate potato with lines drawn with fork. Place dish on 4-sided oven tray.
4 Bake at 180°C for 20 minutes until brown. Serve, garnished with parsley.

CHEESY SHEPHERD'S PIE

Follow recipe for **Shepherd's pie**. Add 1/4 cup (60 g) grated cheese to mashed potato and sprinkle with 1/4 cup (60 g) grated cheese before placing in oven.

MOUSSAKA

- *Serves:* 4
- *Cooking utensil:* saucepan, frying pan, ovenproof dish (2.5 L)
- *Preparation time:* **20 minutes**
- *Cooking time:* **1 hour**
- *Oven temperature:* **180°C**

Ingredients

1 eggplant (300 g)
1 tablespoon (20 g) salt
1 tablespoon (20 g) butter
1 onion (125 g), chopped
250 g minced beef *or* lamb
1/4 cup (65 mL) tomato puree
1/2 cup (125 mL) water
3 shakes pepper
2 tablespoons chopped parsley
2 tablespoons (40 mL) oil
2 potatoes (250 g), par boiled and sliced
2 tomatoes (250 g), sliced
250 mL (1 quantity) **Cheese sauce** (p. 231)

Topping

1/4 cup (10 g) fresh breadcrumbs
1/2 cup (60 g) grated tasty cheese

Method

1. Cut eggplant into 1 cm slices. Sprinkle with salt and allow to stand for 30 minutes. Drain off water and salt. Wash and pat dry.
2. Heat butter in saucepan, fry onion until light brown. Add meat and stir constantly until mixture browns.
3. Add tomato puree, stock, pepper and parsley. Cover pan and cook slowly for 15 minutes. Stir frequently.
4. Set oven at 180°C. Brush or spray ovenproof dish with oil.
5. Heat oil in frying pan and fry eggplant until soft and lightly browned. Drain on absorbent paper.
6. Arrange half of eggplant slices on base and sides of ovenproof dish. Spoon some meat mixture over it. Arrange remainder of eggplant, potato slices, tomato slices and meat mixture in layers. Cover with **Cheese sauce**. Sprinkle with breadcrumbs and grated cheese.
7. Bake at 180°C for 30 minutes.

LAMB PILAF

- *Serves:* 4
- *Cooking utensil:* saucepan
- *Preparation time:* **20 minutes**
- *Cooking time:* **25 minutes**

Ingredients

1 onion (125 g), chopped
1 tablespoon (20 g) butter
1/3 cup (70 g) basmati rice
1 cup (250 mL) stock
1/4 teaspoon oregano
3 shakes pepper
2 tablespoons (40 g) tomato paste
2 tablespoons (30 g) raisins
2 cups (250 g) cooked diced lamb

Method

1. Sauté onion in butter until golden colour.
2. Add rice and stir until it is coated with butter.
3. Add stock, oregano and pepper.
4. Cover and simmer 15 minutes.
5. Stir in tomato paste, raisins and lamb. Reheat and serve.

✦ CHICKEN PILAF ✦

Follow recipe for **Lamb pilaf**, using 2 cups (250 g) cooked diced chicken.

BEEF OLIVES

- *Serves:* **4**
- *Cooking utensil:* ovenproof casserole (2.5 L)
- *Preparation time:* ***20 minutes***
- *Cooking time:* ***$1^1/_2$ hours***
- *Oven temperature:* ***180°C***

Ingredients

1 cup (1 quantity) **Bread and herb seasoning** (p. 195)
4 thin slices (400 g) round steak
1 tablespoon (20 mL) oil
1 onion (125 g), diced
2 tablespoons (20 g) plain flour
1 cup (250 mL) stock *or* water
3 shakes pepper
1 tablespoon chopped parsley

Method

1 Set oven at 180°C.
2 Prepare seasoning.
3 Spread slices of meat with seasoning. Roll up and secure with skewers (*or* toothpicks if using microwave).
4 Heat oil and brown meat. Place in casserole.
5 Brown onion in oil, add flour and mix well. If too dry add 2 teaspoons more oil.
6 Return to heat, add stock and pepper and stir until boiling. Pour into casserole.
7 Cover casserole and cook in oven for approximately $1^1/_2$ hours at 180°C.
8 Remove skewers. Garnish with chopped parsley and serve.

At step 6, place casserole in microwave oven and cook for 5 minutes on high power, stir, then cook for 20 minutes on medium power.

✦ FRUITY BEEF OLIVES ✦

Follow recipe for **Beef olives** using 1 cup (1 quantity) **Apricot seasoning** (p. 195) *or* 1 cup (1 quantity) **Prune seasoning** (p. 195).

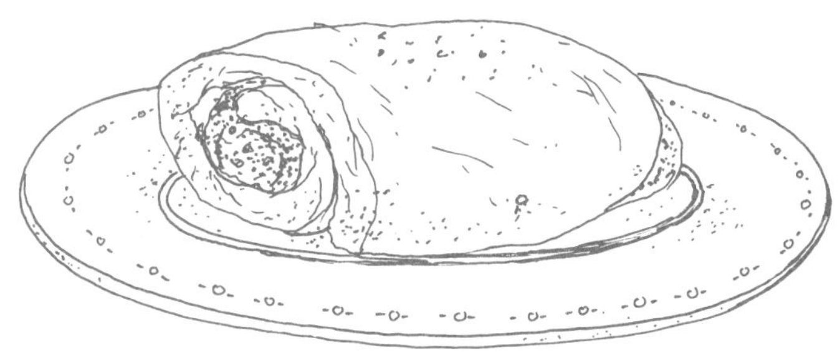

SPAGHETTI BOLOGNAISE

- *Serves:* **4**
- *Cooking utensil:* saucepan
- *Preparation time:* **20 minutes**
- *Cooking time:* **45 minutes**

Ingredients

1 onion (125 g), chopped
1 clove (5 g) garlic, crushed
1 tablespoon (20 mL) oil
250 g minced beef
1/2 cup chopped herbs (oregano, rosemary, basil, thyme, parsley)
2 tomatoes (250 g), chopped
1 tablespoon (20 g) tomato paste
1/2 cup (125 mL) water
200 g spaghetti
1 L (4 cups) boiling water
1/4 teaspoon salt
4 tablespoons (80 g) grated parmesan cheese

Method

1. Fry onion and garlic in oil until light brown.
2. Add meat, fry lightly.
3. Add herbs, tomatoes, tomato paste, water and pepper. Simmer meat sauce at least 30 minutes.
4. Cook spaghetti in boiling water with salt for 15 minutes. Drain, serve onto serving plates, keep warm.
5. Pour sauce over spaghetti, sprinkle with cheese. Serve.

QUICK PASTA SAUCE

Simmer 250 g minced beef with 450 g jar commercial pasta sauce *or* 500 g (1 quantity) **Fresh tomato sauce** (p. 285) for 10 minutes.

LASAGNE

- *Serves:* **4**
- *Cooking utensil:* frying pan, ovenproof dish (2.5 L)
- *Preparation time:* **25 minutes**
- *Cooking time:* **45 minutes**
- *Oven temperature:* **180°C**

Ingredients

1 tablespoon (20 mL) oil
1 onion (125 g), chopped
1 clove (5 g) garlic, crushed
250 g minced beef
2 tomatoes (250 g), chopped
125 g mushrooms, sliced
1 tablespoon (20 g) tomato paste
6 shakes pepper
1/2 cup (125 mL) water
200 g lasagne, instant *or* cooked
250 mL (1 quantity) **Cheese sauce** (p. 231)
1/4 cup (30 g) grated tasty cheese

Method

1. Set oven at 180°C. Brush or spray casserole dish with oil.
2. Heat oil in frying pan. Fry onion and garlic.
3. Add beef, tomatoes, mushrooms, tomato paste, pepper and water. Simmer 10 minutes.
4. Place a thin layer of meat sauce in ovenproof dish, then a layer of lasagne. Repeat these layers. The top layer should be lasagne. Cover top layer with **Cheese sauce**. Sprinkle with grated cheese.
5. Bake at 180°C for 30 minutes until cheese is melted and golden brown. Serve.

Curry

Curry, from the Tamil word 'Kari' meaning 'sauce', is a mixture of many spices. Spices most commonly blended are coriander, cumin, chilli, fennel, fenugreek and turmeric. Other more fragrant spices may be added, including cardamom seeds, cinnamon stick, cloves, nutmeg, lemon grass, fresh ginger and galangal, bay leaves, lime leaves and tamarind. These spice blends are also referred to as 'masalas' and garam masala is a basic blend that is varied to suit different dishes. Masala may be mixed with oil, water or vinegar to make a wet masala or curry paste. Coconut milk or grated fresh coconut is a traditional ingredient of curry. Shredded or desiccated coconut can also be used.

Curry accompaniments

Pappadams are dried wafers made from wheat or lentil flour, usually purchased in packets. To prepare, heat oil in frying pan and fry them for 30 seconds, drain on absorbent paper or place on microwave turntable and microwave 1–2 minutes on high power.

Chutney e.g. mango and paw paw.

Marinated vegetables e.g. cucumber, tomato, onion, celery.

Fresh fruit and vegetables e.g. cucumber, lemon wedges, banana, paw paw, pineapple.

Dried fruits e.g. sultanas, raisins, banana flakes, mango pieces.

Nuts e.g. peanuts, almonds, cashew nuts, macadamia nuts.

Coconut fresh, shredded or desiccated.

Coconut rice Add 2 tablespoons (40 g) coconut milk powder to 1 quantity cooked rice (p. 113).

Bygan dhal See p. 117.

STIR-FRY CURRY

- *Serves:* 4
- *Cooking utensil:* wok

Preparation time: ***20 minutes***
Cooking time: ***10 minutes***

Ingredients

400 g beef *or* lamb strips
2 teaspoons (10 mL) peanut oil
1 tablespoon (20 g) curry powder
1 clove (5 g) garlic, crushed
1 onion (250 g), cut into 8 pieces
1/2 cup (90 g) sultanas
1 tablespoon (15 g) brown sugar
200 g low fat natural yoghurt
2 cups cooked rice (p. 113)

Method

1. Heat oil in wok, brown meat.
2. Stir in curry powder, garlic, onion and sultanas, stir-fry 2 minutes.
3. Reduce heat, add sugar and yoghurt, heat through for 5 minutes.
4. Serve with rice.

CHICKEN CURRY

- *Serves:* 4
- *Cooking utensil:* saucepan

Preparation time: ***20 minutes***
Cooking time: ***1 hour and 40 minutes***

Ingredients

1 kg chicken pieces
1 1/2 tablespoons (30 g) green curry paste
3 shakes black pepper
1 teaspoon sugar
2 tablespoons (40 mL) peanut oil
2 cups (300 g) peeled and diced sweet potato
3 cloves (15 g) garlic, crushed
2 onions (250 g), cut into wedges
1 bay leaf
1 stalk lemon grass, finely chopped
1 cup (250 mL) chicken stock
1/4 cup (65 mL) coconut milk
2 cups cooked rice (p. 113)

Method

1. Mix curry paste, pepper, sugar and rub onto chicken. Refrigerate, covered for 1 hour.
2. Heat oil, add sweet potatoes and brown, turning frequently. Remove.
3. Fry garlic, onions, bay leaf, lemon grass and chicken pieces for 10–12 minutes. Add a little extra oil if necessary.
4. Add stock, simmer gently for 15 minutes or until chicken is nearly tender.
5. Return potatoes to saucepan, add coconut milk, simmer covered for 10 minutes or until both chicken and potato are tender.
6. Serve with rice.

CHICKEN AND SPINACH CURRY

- *Serves:* **4**
- *Cooking utensil:* wok
- *Preparation time:* ***20 minutes***
- *Cooking time:* ***20–30 minutes***

Ingredients

1 bunch spinach
1 tablespoon (20 mL) oil
1/2 onion (65 g), finely diced
1 teaspoon (5 g) chopped ginger
2 cloves (10 g) garlic, crushed
2 teaspoons (10 g) curry paste
2 tomatoes (250 g), chopped
4 chicken thighs, skinned
1 cup (100 g) button mushrooms
1/2 teaspoon hot chilli paste
2 cups noodles (p. 113)

Method

1. Remove spinach leaves from stalks, wash leaves several times in cold water, drain.
2. Heat oil in wok, add onion, ginger and garlic, cook 3 minutes.
3. Add curry paste, tomato, chicken and mushrooms.
4. Bring to boil, cover and cook for 20 minutes.
5. Place spinach leaves on top, cover and cook 3 minutes until spinach has softened.
6. Remove lid, stir spinach through chicken mixture.
7. Season with chilli paste, serve with noodles.

ASIAN-STYLE PORK AND VEGETABLE CURRY

- *Serves:* **4**
- *Cooking utensil:* wok
- *Preparation time:* ***20 minutes***
- *Cooking time:* ***15 minutes***

Ingredients

3 dried mushrooms
400 g leg strips *or* leg, fillet, loin *or* rump of pork
1 tablespoon (20 mL) peanut oil
1 tablespoon (10 g) red curry paste
1 stalk lemon grass, finely chopped
1 1/4 cups (125 g) finely shredded Chinese cabbage
2 carrots (250 g), cut into thin strips
3/4 cup (90 g) green beans, sliced diagonally
1 chilli, seeded and finely chopped
2 tablespoons (40 mL) water
1 tablespoon (20 mL) fish sauce
1 teaspoon sugar
8 Vietnamese mint leaves, chopped

Method

1. Cover mushrooms with hot water, soak for 20 minutes, drain and thinly slice.
2. Cut pork into strips.
3. Heat oil in wok, add curry paste, stir-fry for 1 minute.
4. Add pork, cook 5 minutes.
5. Add vegetables, lemongrass and chilli, stir-fry for 5 minutes.
6. Add water, fish sauce and sugar, stir-fry for 3 minutes. Stir in mint before serving.

BEEF CURRY

- *Serves:* 4
- *Cooking utensil:* saucepan

Preparation time: **25 minutes**
Cooking time: **$1^3/_4$ hours**

Ingredients

300 g blade, chuck, round *or* skirt steak, fat trimmed
1 tablespoon (20 mL) oil
1 onion (125 g), diced
1 tablespoon (10 g) curry powder
1 tablespoon (10 g) coconut
2 tablespoons (20 g) plain flour
1 apple (150 g), diced
1 banana (125 g), diced
1 potato (150 g), diced
1 tomato (125 g), diced
2 tablespoons (40 mL) chutney
1 teaspoon lemon juice
$1^1/_2$ cups (375 mL) stock *or* water
6 shakes pepper
2 tablespoons (30 g) sultanas
2 cups cooked rice (p. 113)

Method

1. Cut steak into 3 cm cubes.
2. Heat oil, brown meat and remove it from the saucepan. Keep hot.
3. Add onion, curry powder and coconut. Fry 2 minutes to develop and mellow the curry powder flavour. Add flour, fry 1 minute.
4. Add all other ingredients and stir until boiling.
5. Add meat, return to boiling point, then simmer until tender, approximately $1^1/_2$ hours.
6. Taste and adjust flavour.
7. Serve with rice and curry accompaniments (p. 215).

PLATE 9

Satays with peanut sauce (p. 180),
Spicy Asian fish soup (p.150),
Stir-fry lamb with couscous (p. 186).

LETTUCE VARIETIES

PLATE 10

Pastries

CORNISH PASTIES

- *Number:* **6**
- *Cooking utensil:* 4-sided oven tray

- *Preparation time:* **30 minutes**
- *Cooking time:* **40–45 minutes**
- *Oven temperature:* **200°C reduced to 180°C**

Ingredients

250 g minced beef
1 onion (125 g), chopped
1 potato (150 g), diced
1/2 carrot (65 g), diced
1/4 turnip (35 g), diced
1/2 teaspoon salt
6 shakes pepper
1 teaspoon chopped parsley
250 g pastry (1 quantity) **Shortcrust pastry** (p. 346)

Method

1. Set oven at 200°C.
2. Combine meat, vegetables, salt, pepper and chopped parsley.
3. Divide pastry into 6 equal parts; knead each into a ball. Roll each piece into a round the size of a saucer.
4. Place an equal portion of prepared mixture on each round, using all of the mixture.
5. Brush half way around the edges of the pastry with water, join edges together over the top of the mixture, pinch a small frill over the join and shape pasties into a crescent.
6. Place on oven tray and pierce top with fork. Glaze with milk.
7. Bake at 200°C for 10 minutes, then at 180°C for 30–35 minutes.

VEGETARIAN PASTIES

Follow recipe for **Cornish pasties**, replacing beef with 250 g mixed vegetables, e.g. peas, sweet potatoes, celery, tomato, swede, parsnip.

KANGAROO PASTIES

Follow recipe for **Cornish pasties** using 250 g kangaroo mince.

MEAT PIE

- *Serves:* **6**
- *Cooking utensil:* 22 cm pie dish (1 L), 4-sided oven tray
- *Preparation time:* ***30 minutes***
- *Cooking time:* ***1 hour*** *meat mixture* ***or 17 minutes*** *microwave* ***or 30–40 minutes*** *in oven*
- *Oven temperature:* ***220°C reduced to 190°C***

Ingredients

750 g blade *or* round steak
1 onion (125 g), diced
2 tablespoons (20 g) plain flour
6 shakes pepper
2 teaspoons chopped parsley
1¼ cups (320 mL) water
125 g (½ quantity) **Flaky pastry** (p. 349) *or* **Rough puff pastry** (p. 350)

Method

1. Cut meat into 2 cm pieces.
2. Place meat, onion, flour, pepper and chopped parsley in saucepan. Mix together.
3. Add stock, bring to the boil and simmer 1 hour. Stir frequently *or* microwave for 5 minutes on high power then 12 minutes on medium power. Place meat mixture in pie dish.
4. Set oven at 220°C.
5. Roll out pastry the shape of the pie dish and 5 cm larger all round. Cut a 2 cm strip from outside edge of pastry. Brush the edge of the pie dish with water. Fit the strip of pastry carefully around the edge without stretching it, cut side out. Join ends neatly and brush strip with water. Using a rolling pin, lift large piece of pastry without stretching it, cover dish and press edges lightly. Trim edge and cut at 3 cm intervals, drawing flakes up with knife.
6. Glaze with milk and slit top of pie to allow steam to escape. Place on 4-sided oven tray.
7. Bake at 220°C for 20 minutes, then at 190°C for further 10–20 minutes, until golden brown.

STEAK AND KIDNEY PIE

Follow recipe for **Meat pie**. At step 2 add 2 lamb's kidneys.

STEAK AND VEGETABLE PIE

Follow recipe for **Meat pie**. At step 2 add ½ diced carrot (65 g), 1 stalk sliced celery, ½ cup (75 g) peas, ½ diced parsnip (65 g).

STEAK AND MUSHROOM PIE

Follow recipe for **Meat pie**. At step 3 add 1¼ cups (125 g) sliced mushrooms after 30 minutes.

CHICKEN PIE

- *Serves:* ***6***
- *Cooking utensil:* 22 cm pie dish (1 L)
- *Preparation time:* ***30 minutes***
- *Cooking time:* ***30 minutes***
- *Oven temperature:* ***220°C***

Ingredients

1 No. 10 chicken, cooked and diced
250 mL (1 quantity) **White sauce** (p. 282)
2 rashers (80 g) bacon, sliced
2 eggs, hard boiled and chopped
1/2 teaspoon lemon juice
1/4 teaspoon grain mustard
3 shakes pepper
1 tablespoon chopped parsley
125 g pastry (1/2 quantity) **Rough puff pastry** (p. 350)

Method

1 Set oven at 220°C.
2 Combine chicken, **White sauce**, bacon, eggs, lemon juice, mustard, pepper and parsley. Place in pie dish.
3 Cover with pastry and cook as in steps 5 to 8, in recipe for **Meat pie** (p. 220).

SAUSAGE ROLLS

- *Number:* ***20 small or 12 large***
- *Cooking utensil:* 4-sided oven tray
- *Preparation time:* ***20 minutes***
- *Cooking time:* ***15–20 minutes***
- *Oven temperature:* ***220°C reduced to 190°C***

Ingredients

250 g (1 quantity) **Flaky pastry** (p. 349) *or* **Rough puff pastry** (p. 350)
500 g sausage meat
1 teaspoon chopped parsley
1/2 teaspoon salt
3 shakes pepper
4 tablespoons (40 g) plain flour

Method

1 Set oven at 220°C.
2 Mix sausage meat, chopped parsley, salt and pepper.
3 Roll out pastry into an oblong 30 cm x 20 cm for large rolls, *or* 40 cm x 18 cm for small rolls. Cut pastry in two lengthwise.
4 Sprinkle board with flour and roll sausage meat into two rolls, the same length as the pastry.
5 Place sausage meat on top of pastry and moisten edges of pastry with water.
6 Fold the pastry over the meat, with the cut edge on the side. Trim cut edges.
7 Cut into suitable sizes and place on oven tray. Mark with a knife.
8 Glaze with milk and bake at 220°C for 10 minutes, then at 190°C for further 10–15 minutes.

SMALL MEAT PIES

- *Number:* ***6***
- *Cooking utensil:* 6 pie pans
- *Preparation time:* ***30 minutes***
- *Cooking time:* ***25–30 minutes***
- *Oven temperature:* ***220°C reduced to 190°C***

Ingredients

400 g minced beef
1 onion (125 g), diced
1 tablespoon (10 g) plain flour
6 shakes pepper
2 teaspoons chopped parsley
1/2 cup (125 mL) stock *or* water
250 g (1 quantity) **Flaky pastry** (p. 349) *or* **Rough puff pastry** (p. 350)

Method

1. Place meat, onion, flour, seasonings and parsley in saucepan and stir well. Add stock.
2. Stir until boiling and simmer for 15 minutes. Cool.
3. Set oven at 220°C.
4. Roll out half of pastry 5 mm thick. Cut 6 rounds for tops.
5. Place flat pastry scraps evenly on top of other half of pastry. Roll out pastry, cut larger rounds to line pie pans.
6. Line the pans with large rounds of pastry, fill with cool meat mixture, moisten the edges of pastry with water and place the tops on. Press lightly. Slit tops.
7. Glaze with milk, place on oven tray and bake at 220°C for 10 minutes, then at 190°C for 15 minutes.
8. Lift pies from pans onto hot serving dish. Garnish with parsley sprigs and serve.

✦ SMALL CURRY PIES ✦

Follow recipe for **Small meat pies**, add 2 teaspoons (5 g) curry powder to the meat mixture.

SAVOURY MINCE TART

- *Serves:* ***6***
- *Cooking utensil:* 22 cm pie dish (1 L)
- *Preparation time:* ***20 minutes***
- *Cooking time:* ***50–55 minutes***
- *Oven temperature:* ***200°C reduced to 180°C***

Ingredients

Filling

400 g minced beef
1 potato (150 g), grated
1 onion (125 g), grated
2 tablespoons (40 mL) tomato sauce
3 shakes pepper
1/8 teaspoon nutmeg
1 egg, beaten
125 g (1/2 quantity) **Shortcrust pastry** (p. 346)

Topping

1/4 cup (65 mL) tomato sauce
1/2 teaspoon honey
1 tablespoon (12 g) sesame seeds

Method

1. Set oven at 200°C.
2. Mix all filling ingredients together.
3. Roll out pastry 3 cm larger than pie dish. Brush edges of plate with water. Using a rolling pin, carefully lift the pastry into the plate. Ease it into place without stretching it. Trim edge. May be decorated by pinching or with fork marks.
4. Spoon mixture into pastry.
5. Prepare topping: combine topping ingredients and spoon over meat mixture.
6. Place on oven tray. Bake at 200°C for 20 minutes, then at 180°C for a further 30–35 minutes. Garnish with parsley and serve.

TOMATO MINCE TART

Follow recipe for **Savoury mince tart**. Omit topping. Cover with 2 tomatoes (250 g), peeled and sliced. Sprinkle with 3 tablespoons (30 g) grated cheese before placing in oven.

CHICKEN IN FILO

- *Serves:* 2
- *Cooking utensil:* 4-sided oven tray
- *Preparation time:* **15 minutes**
- *Cooking time:* **20 minutes**
- *Cooking temperature:* **200°C reduced to 180°C**

Ingredients

4 sheets filo pastry
2 small chicken fillets (75 g)
1 tablespoon (20 g) chutney
2 dried apricots, chopped
4 chives *or* spring onions

Method

1. Set oven to 200°C. Spray or brush oven tray with oil.
2. Spray or brush top surface of pastry with oil.
3. Place fillet of chicken at one end of pastry, spread chutney on fillet and sprinkle with apricot.
4. Roll up in 2 sheets of pastry and gently tie ends with chives *or* spring onion tops to form bon-bon shaped parcel.
5. Spray or brush with oil.
6. Bake at 200°C for 8 minutes then reduce to 180°C for further 8 minutes. May be served with tossed salad.

AUSSIE MEAT STRUDEL

- *Serves:* 4
- *Cooking utensil:* 4-sided oven tray, frying pan
- *Preparation time:* **20 minutes**
- *Cooking time:* **30–40 minutes**
- *Cooking temperature:* **200°C reduced to 170°C**

Ingredients

2 rashers (80 g) bacon, chopped
1/2 onion (125 g), diced
300 g minced beef
1/2 teaspoon thyme
1 teaspoon chopped parsley
1/2 cup (20 g) fresh breadcrumbs
1 tablespoon (20 mL) tomato sauce
1/2 apple (75 g), grated
3 shakes pepper
4 sheets filo pastry

Method

1. Set oven at 200°C. Spray or brush oven tray with oil.
2. Sauté bacon and onion in frying pan for 3 minutes.
3. Add meat, herbs, 1/4 cup breadcrumbs, tomato sauce, apple and pepper.
4. Spray top surface of pastry with oil and sprinkle with remaining breadcrumbs.
5. Form meat mixture into a sausage-shaped roll and place across the centre of the pastry. Fold in narrow ends, then sides. Moisten edges of pastry to make them stick.
6. Place on oven tray with join underneath. Spray or brush top with oil.
7. Bake at 200°C for 10 minutes, reduce temperature to 170°C and cook a further 20–30 minutes.

Deep frying

Deep or French frying is cooking in a large amount of oil, preferably in a thermostatically controlled fryer or deep saucepan. Foods suitable for deep frying include potato chips, fish and fritters as these take a very short time to cook. Most foods should be coated before deep frying and this, combined with a high cooking temperature of 150°C to 180°C, prevents the absorption of fat into the food. A wire basket or tongs should be used to lower foods gently into the oil. When cooked, lift out with slotted spoon and drain on absorbent paper to remove excess oil. Oil may be used several times if care is taken not to overheat during use and to strain when cool.

Oils and fats suitable for deep frying

Sunflower, peanut, maize, grapeseed, safflower and canola oils are suitable for deep frying as they have a smoke point (the temperature at which they start to burn) above 180°C.

Coating of food

Coating for fried foods See p. 182.

Safety hints for frying

- Use a thermostatically controlled fryer if possible. Pan should completely cover electric hotplate or if using gas cooker do not allow gas flame to reach up the sides of the pan.
- The lid should not be placed on pan during heating. Place lid beside fryer.
- Do not overheat the oil. Heat to 180°C - oil ceases to bubble and a small cube of bread browns in 20–30 seconds.
- Moist foods, such as potato chips, should be patted with a paper towel to reduce surface moisture. Water dropped into hot oil may cause an explosion.
- IF OIL CATCHES ALIGHT, SMOTHER IT WITH A LID.
- After use, cool oil slightly then strain into a basin.
- Keep in a cool place.

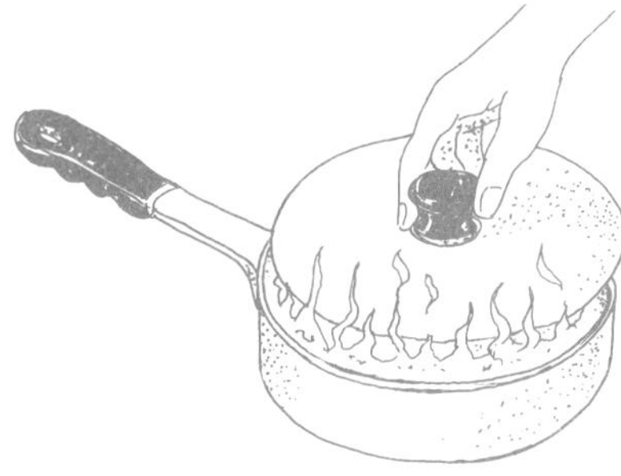

If oil catches alight, smother it with a lid.

SWEET AND SOUR PORK FRITTERS

- *Serves:* **4**
- *Cooking utensil:* deep fryer with 6 cm depth of oil

Preparation time: ***30 minutes***
Cooking time: ***10–12 minutes***

Ingredients

300 g pork fillets
2 teaspoons (10 g) sugar
3 shakes pepper
2 teaspoons (10 mL) soy sauce
1 cup (150 g) self-raising flour
$^3/_4$ cup (190 mL) water
2 spring onions, sliced
2 cups cooked rice (p. 113)
Sweet and sour sauce
1 carrot (125 g)
$^1/_2$ red capsicum (65 g)
$^1/_2$ green capsicum (65 g)
440 g can pineapple pieces *or* 300 g pineapple pieces and 150 mL water
1 tablespoon (20 mL) vinegar
1 tablespoon (10 g) cornflour
1 tablespoon (20 mL) dry sherry

Method

1 See Safety hints for frying (p. 225).
2 Cut pork into 2 cm cubes. Mix with sugar, pepper and soy sauce.
3 Mix the flour and water to a smooth batter consistency.
4 Take meat, batter and tongs to bench next to hotplate.
5 Heat oil slowly to 180°C – oil ceases to bubble and small cube of bread browns in 20–30 seconds.
6 Dip each piece of meat in batter and place carefully in hot oil. Do not overcrowd deep fryer. Cook 5–7 minutes.
7 Lift out with slotted spoon and drain on absorbent paper. Place on serving dish and keep hot.
8 Prepare sauce: cut carrot and capsicum into strips. Cook carrot in pineapple juice for 5 minutes. Add vegetables, pineapple and juice, vinegar and blended cornflour in saucepan. Stir until boiling. Cook 30 seconds, add dry sherry.
9 Pour sauce over meat, sprinkle with spring onions and serve with rice.

9 Vegetables

Vegetables add colour, variety, flavour, interest, nutritional value and versatility to meals. Vegetables, when served with sauces or seasonings, or combined with other selected vegetables, are often used as an accompaniment to meat, poultry and fish dishes. They may also be served as an entree. With the addition of pulses or other protein foods they can be served instead of a meat course.

Food value

Most vegetables are good sources of vitamins, minerals and complex carbohydrates, including fibre. Leaf vegetables are particularly rich in calcium, iron and vitamins A and C. Fruit vegetables are excellent sources of vitamin C, as are most tubers. Seed vegetables are rich in protein.

Prolonged cooking destroys the heat-sensitive vitamins. Water-soluble vitamins are lost if a large amount of cooking water is used and discarded. Eating vegetables raw or cooking them for a short time in little water ensures the maximum nutritional value.

Methods of cooking

Boiling Rapid cooking in a small amount of boiling water conserves vitamins and minerals and retains the colour and flavour of the vegetable.

Microwaving The high water content of vegetables means that they are ideal for this cooking method.

Steaming This method requires a longer cooking time than boiling.

Baking Vegetables dry-baked in their own skins in a moderate oven retain most of their minerals.

Grilling This method is suitable for vegetables that cook quickly, for example, tomatoes and mushrooms. The heat destroys some vitamins, but flavour, colour and minerals are retained.

Braising Vegetables are sautéed with chopped bacon, then cooked slowly in a small amount of stock or water with the lid on.

Roasting Vegetables are roasted in a small amount of oil or in the fat around meat.

Stir-frying Vegetables are stirred rapidly for a very short time in a small quantity of hot oil in a wok or heavy-based frying pan. The high temperature brightens the colour of the vegetables.

Frying Vegetables are cooked by deep or shallow frying in fat or oil.

Classification of vegetables

Edible part of plant	Vegetable	Choice
Leaf	Brussels sprouts, cabbage, Chinese chard, lettuce, watercress, spinach, parsley, endive, chicory or witlof, chives, silver beet, kale, warrigal greens, bok choy	crisp, rich green in colour
Stem	asparagus, celery, silver beet	crisp, free from cracks, even in size
Flower	broccoli, cauliflower, globe artichoke	compact flower, medium in size; cauliflower white
Seeds	(a) fresh: peas, broad beans, borlotti beans, sweet corn	pods crisp, green and full, seeds even; free from impurities and not sprouting
	(b) dried (pulses): peas, beans, lentils	no mould or foreign material
Fruit	cucumber, eggplant or aubergine, pepper or capsicum, pumpkin, squash, marrow, tomato, gherkin, green beans, choko, zucchini, chillies, snow peas, sugar peas, okra, bitter melon	smooth, firm, good shape, medium size; beans crisp, green and seeds not developed
Tuber	potato, Jerusalem artichoke, sweet potato, celeriac	firm and smooth, even size

Edible part of plant	Vegetable	Choice
Bulb	garlic, leeks, onions, shallots, spring onions, water chestnuts, fennel	firm, even in size
Root	carrots, parsnips, radishes, kohlrabi, beetroot, turnip, swede, horseradish, taro	firm crisp tops
Fungi	mushrooms, truffles	firm, free from insects
Sprouts	alfalfa, beanshoots, mung beans, fenugreek, snow pea shoots	firm and crisp

Mixed vegetable dishes

RATATOUILLE

- *Serves:* **4**
- *Cooking utensil:* 2.5 L casserole *or* deep frying pan
- *Cooking time:* **45 minutes**
- *Oven temperature:* **180°C**

Ingredients

1 tablespoon (40 mL) olive oil
1 onion (125 g), sliced
1 eggplant (200 g), sliced
1 capsicum (150 g), sliced
2 tomatoes (250 g), peeled and sliced
1 zucchini (100 g), sliced
1 clove garlic (5 g), crushed
6 shakes pepper
2 tablespoons chopped parsley

Method

1. Set oven at 180°C.
2. Place olive oil in casserole *or* frying pan. Add onion and cook 5 minutes.
3. Layer eggplant and capsicum. Cook 10 minutes, do not stir.
4. Add tomatoes, then zucchini, garlic and pepper.
5. Cover and bake at 180°C for 30 minutes *or* cook over low heat.
6. Add parsley and serve hot or cold.

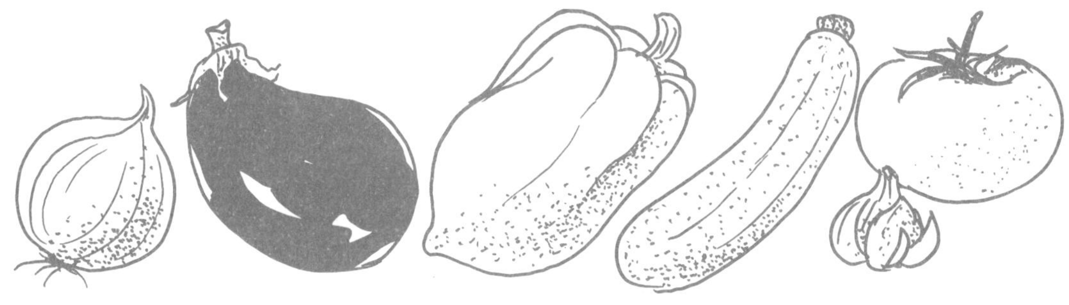

MACEDOINE OF VEGETABLES

- *Serves:* 4
- *Cooking utensil:* saucepan

Cooking time: **12 minutes**

Ingredients

1 carrot (125 g)
1 parsnip (125 g)
250 g shelled peas
100 g cauliflower florets

Method

1. Wash and scrape carrot and parsnip. Cut into 1 cm dice.
2. Cook all vegetables in 3 cm boiling water for 10 minutes.
3. Drain. Add 3 shakes pepper, sauté in 1 teaspoon butter and serve as accompaniment.

ALFALFA

Description: Fine sprouts with small green leaf.
Uses include: Salads, lunch box, garnish.
Preparation: Wash.

ARTICHOKE, GLOBE

Description: Green flowers of which the fleshy base and lower parts of the leaves are eaten.
Uses include: Accompaniment, salads, entree.
Preparation: Wash well, trim base, trim tough leaves from base, trim tops with scissors.

✦ ARTICHOKES AU BEURRE ✦

To serve 4: Cook 4 prepared globe artichokes in 3 cm boiling water with 1 teaspoon lemon juice for 20 minutes *or* steam until just tender. They are cooked when a leaf pulls out easily. Drain and serve with 1 tablespoon (20 g) melted butter poured over.

✦ ARTICHOKES HOLLANDAISE ✦

To serve 4: Cook 4 prepared globe artichokes as above. Drain. Serve with 1/2 cup (1 quantity) **Hollandaise sauce** (p. 232).

✦ CHARGRILLED ARTICHOKE HEARTS ✦

To serve 4: Cook prepared globe artichokes as above. Drain. Spray with olive oil and grill on hot griller until outside layer is dark brown. Marinate in **French dressing** (p. 266) and serve with other salad vegetables.

ARTICHOKE, JERUSALEM

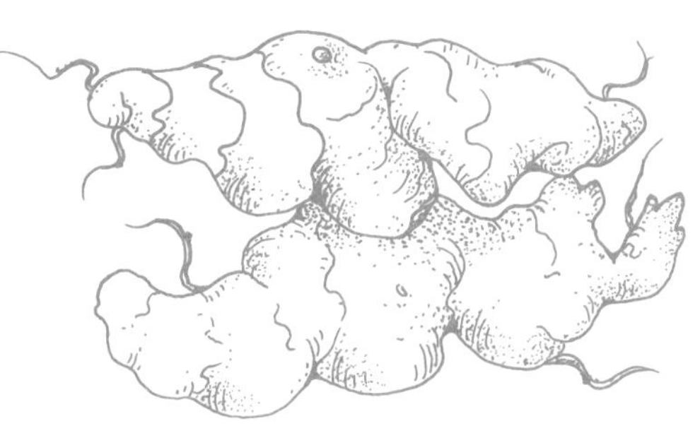

Description: Cream-coloured tuber.
Uses include: Accompaniment, soups.
Preparation: Scrub, peel then place in water with 1 teaspoon lemon juice to prevent discolouration.

✦ ARTICHOKES IN SAUCE ✦

To serve 4: Cook 500 g prepared Jerusalem artichokes in 3 cm boiling water with 1 teaspoon lemon juice for 15 minutes. Drain and serve with 1 cup (1 quantity) **White sauce** (p. 282) *or* **Cheese sauce** (p. 282)

ASPARAGUS

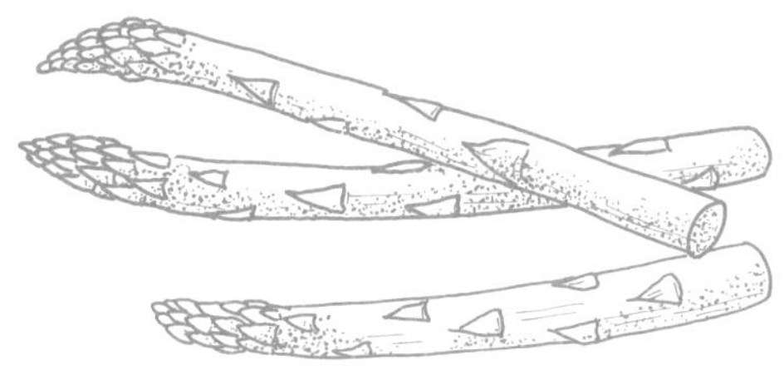

Description: A green or white stem and flower.
Uses include: Accompaniment, salads, soups, entree.
Preparation: Trim, removing hard end portion. Scrape skin from stalk.

Use 1 tablespoon (20 mL) water. Microwave in covered dish for 4 minutes on high power. Turn and cook further 4 minutes on high power.

✦ ASPARAGUS AU BEURRE ✦

To serve 4: Cook 500 g prepared asparagus tied in bundles standing upright in 5 cm boiling water with lid on saucepan for 5–10 minutes. Drain and serve with 1 tablespoon (20 g) melted butter poured over.

✦ ASPARAGUS HOLLANDAISE ✦

To serve 4: Cook 500 g prepared asparagus as above. Drain. Serve with ½ cup (1 quantity) **Hollandaise sauce** (p. 232).

BEANS, BUTTER, GREEN and YOUNG SCARLET RUNNER

Description: Small pods and underdeveloped seeds. The whole fruit is used in cooking.
Uses include: Accompaniment, salads.
Preparation: Wash, top, tail and string beans. Slice diagonally.

✦ SAUTÉED GREEN BEANS ✦

To serve 4: Prepare 375 g beans and cook in 3 cm boiling water for 5–10 minutes. Drain. Add 3 shakes pepper, sauté in 1 teaspoon butter and serve. 1 tablespoon (15 g) pinenuts *or* slivered almonds may be added.

BEANS, BROAD, BORLOTTI and MATURE SCARLET RUNNER

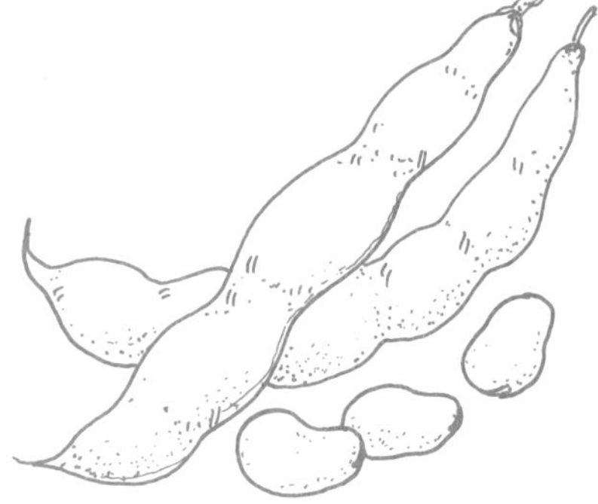

Description: The pods are removed and the seeds only are used.
Uses include: Accompaniment, entree.
Preparation: Remove seeds from pods.

✦ SAUTÉED BROAD BEANS ✦

To serve 4: Pod 1 kg broad beans and cook in 3 cm boiling water for 5–15 minutes. Drain. Add 3 shakes pepper, sauté in 1 teaspoon butter.

✦ BROAD BEANS AND BACON ✦

To serve 4: Pod 1 kg broad beans and cook in 3 cm boiling water for 10 minutes. Drain. Fry 2 tablespoons (30 g) chopped bacon for 30 seconds, add beans and 3 shakes pepper and fry gently for 2 minutes, stirring frequently.

BEANS, SNAKE or LONG

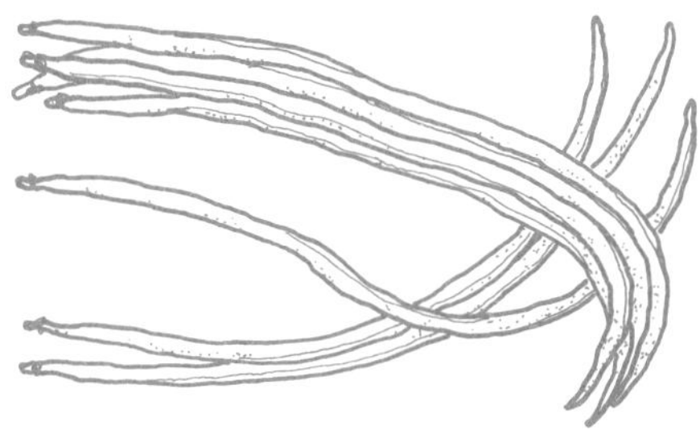

Description: Firm, bright green pods.
Uses include: Meat and fish dishes, Asian dishes.
Preparation: Slice or use whole. Cook as for butter beans.

BEAN SPROUTS (NGA CHOI)

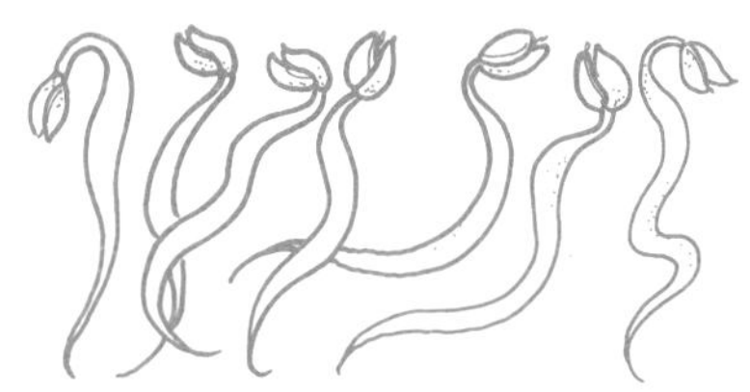

Description: Long white crisp shoots.
Uses include: Salads, Asian dishes, lunch box.
Preparation: Wash.

BEETROOT

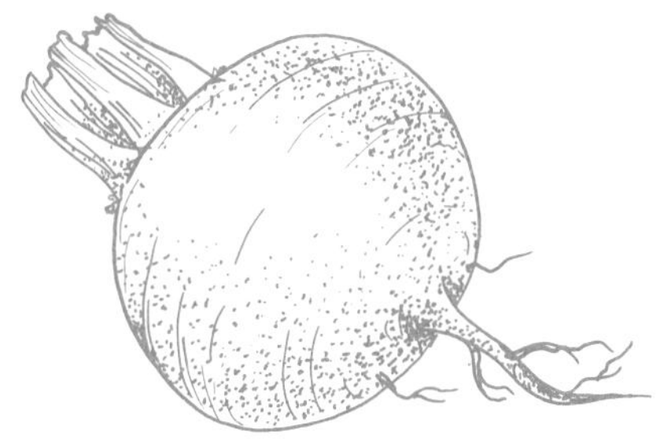

Description: A fleshy red root.
Uses include: Accompaniment, salads, soups.
Preparation: Remove most of the top leaving 3 cm. Wash but do not damage skin or root as colour will be lost. Can be grated raw for use in salads and sandwiches.

✦ BOILED BEETROOT ✦

To serve 4: Place 2 prepared medium beetroot (250 g) in boiling water to cover them. Cook 40–60 minutes or until tender *or* pressure cook 10 minutes. Drain and dice *or* slice to serve hot or cold.

✦ SWEET AND SOUR BEETROOT ✦

To serve 4: Prepare and cook as for **Boiled beetroot**. Cut into 1 cm dice. Heat slowly in a saucepan with 1/2 cup (125 mL) water, 1/4 cup (45 g) brown sugar, 1 tablespoon (20 g) butter, 1/2 cup (125 mL) vinegar and 3 shakes pepper. Blend 1 tablespoon (10 g) cornflour with 2 tablespoons (40 mL) cold water and stir into beetroot. Stir until boiling.

✦ BEETROOT IN VINEGAR ✦

To serve 4: Prepare and cook as for **Boiled beetroot**. Cut into 1 cm dice or slice. Pour 1/2 cup (125 mL) water, 1/3 cup (85 mL) vinegar, 1 tablespoon (20 g) sugar, 1/2 teaspoon salt and 3 shakes pepper over beetroot. Store in refrigerator.

BITTER MELON (FOO GWA)

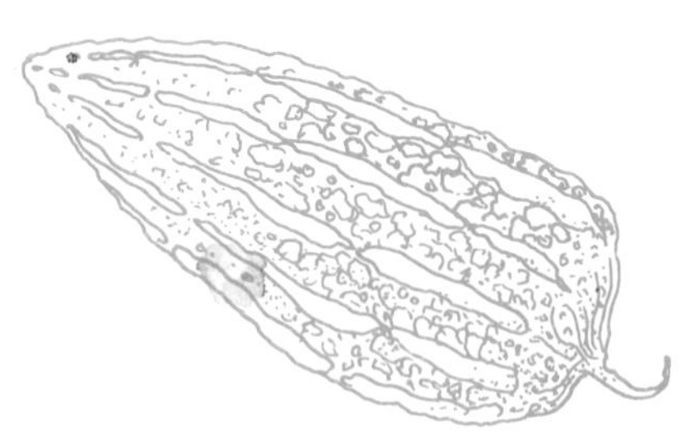

Description: Light green rough surfaced melon with bitter flavour.

Uses include: Asian dishes, stir-fry.

Preparation: Wash, cut in half-lengthwise, remove and discard seeds, blanch and drain, fry or boil for short time.

BOK CHOY (CHINESE CHARD)

Description: Small dark green leaves with white stalks joined at the base to form a small bunch. Has a mild cabbage-like flavour. May be known as bak choy, similar to choi sum.

Uses include: Stir-fry, accompaniment.

Preparation: Wash well. Leaves may be separated or bunch used whole.

PLATE 11

Broad bean and toasted almond salad (p. 268), Greek salad (p. 271), Tortellini salad (p. 277).

ASIAN VEGETABLES

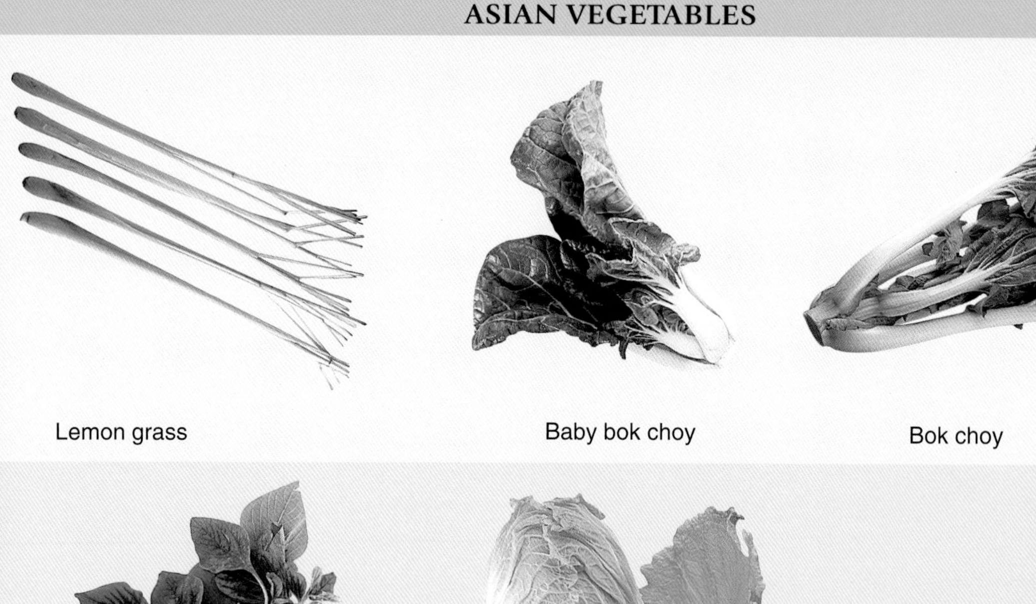

Lemon grass

Baby bok choy

Bok choy

Chinese spinach

Chinese cabbage

Choy sum green

Vietnamese hot mint

Chinese broccoli

Baby choy sum

Shanghai bok choy

Water spinach

Watercress

PLATE 12

BROCCOLI

Description: Green flowers and stem.
Uses include: Accompaniment, salads, crudités.
Preparation: Wash and remove woody stem leaving flower and 10 cm stalk.

✦ HERBED BROCCOLI ✦

To serve 4: Cook 400 g prepared broccoli in 6 cm boiling water for 6–8 minutes. Drain. Combine 2 tablespoons (40 g) butter, 1 teaspoon lemon juice, $^1/_2$ clove crushed garlic, $^1/_8$ teaspoon oregano and 3 shakes pepper and spoon over broccoli.

✦ BROCCOLI MORNAY ✦

To serve 4: Cook 400 g prepared broccoli. Drain. Prepare 1 cup (1 quantity) **Cheese sauce** (p. 282) and pour over broccoli.

✦ BROCCOLI HOLLANDAISE ✦

To serve 4: Cook 400 g prepared broccoli. Drain. Prepare $^1/_2$ cup (1 quantity) **Hollandaise sauce** (p. 232) and pour over broccoli.

BROCCOLI, CHINESE (GAY LUM)

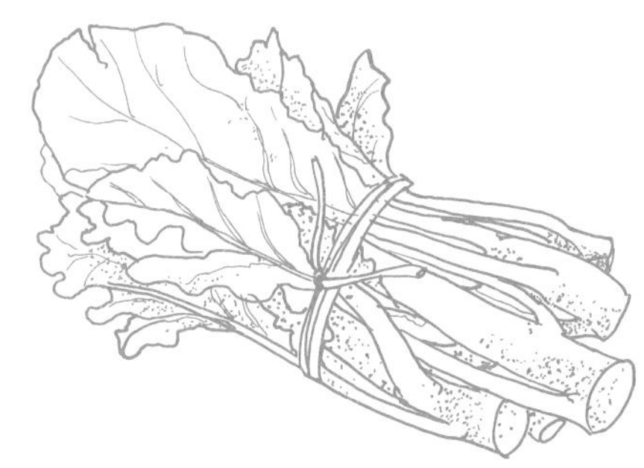

Description: Crisp, dark green leaves with small florets.
Uses include: Soups, meat dishes, Asian dishes.
Preparation: Use leaves and florets, steam or sauté.

BRUSSELS SPROUTS

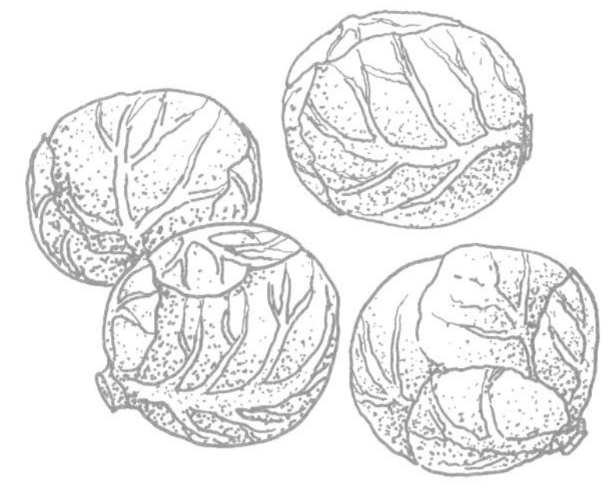

Description: Green leaves forming small heads that grow attached to the stem of the plant. Only the heads are cooked.
Uses include: Accompaniment, salads.
Preparation: Wash, remove discoloured leaves. Trim and cut a cross in base.

✦ SAUTÉED BRUSSELS SPROUTS ✦

To serve 4: Cook 375 g prepared Brussels sprouts in 3 cm boiling water for 5 minutes. Drain, add 3 shakes pepper and sauté in 1 teaspoon butter.

CABBAGE

Description: Green leaves forming large heads. Many varieties are used, for example, Chinese, drumhead, eastern, savoy.
Uses include: Accompaniment, salads, soups.
Preparation: Wash, remove coarse leaves and stems.

✦ SAUTÉED CABBAGE ✦

To serve 4: Cook 1/4 medium-sized prepared and finely shredded cabbage in 3 cm boiling water for 4 minutes. Drain. Add 3 shakes pepper and sauté in 1 teaspoon butter.

✦ BRAISED CABBAGE ✦

To serve 4: Fry 1 rasher (40 g) chopped bacon and 1 chopped onion (125 g) for 3 minutes. Add 1/4 medium-sized cabbage prepared and shredded, 3 shakes pepper and 1 tablespoon (20 mL) water. Place lid on saucepan and simmer 4 minutes.

✦ CABBAGE ROLLS ✦

To serve 4: Wash 4 large, whole cabbage leaves and parboil 2 minutes in boiling water. Drain. Combine 1/2 cup cooked rice, 1 chopped onion (125 g), 125 g minced steak, 1/4 teaspoon oregano, 1 clove (5 g) crushed garlic and 3 shakes pepper. Place some mixture in the centre of each cabbage leaf, fold leaf to form parcel and secure with toothpicks. Place in greased casserole and cover with tomato juice *or* soup and bake for 1 hour at 180°C.

Microwave whole leaves for 1 minute on high power and filled leaves for 10–15 minutes on high power.

✦ RED CABBAGE ✦

To serve 4: Wash and shred 1/4 small red cabbage. Cook in 1/2 cup water and 1/2 cup (125 mL) vinegar for 10 minutes. Add 1/2 cup water, 1 tablespoon (20 g) butter, 3 shakes pepper and 1 teaspoon sugar and boil, stirring continuously, until liquid has evaporated.

CABBAGE, CHINESE (WONG NGA BAAK)

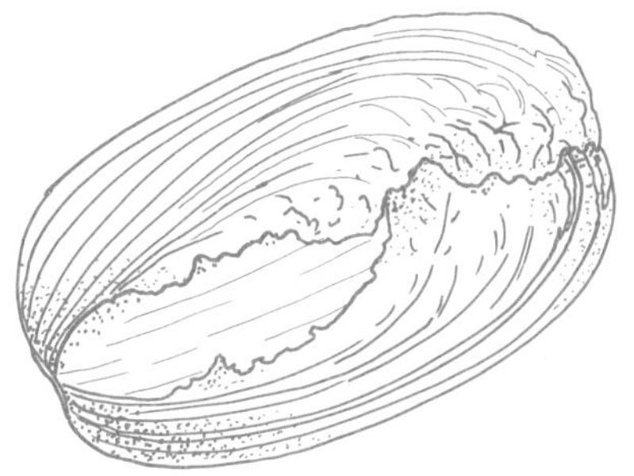

Description: Long, light-green rough leaves.
Uses include: Meat dishes, stir-fry, Asian dishes.
Preparation: Discard coarse leaves and stems, wash, drain, cook quickly.

CABBAGE, CHINESE FLOWERING (CHOY SUM)

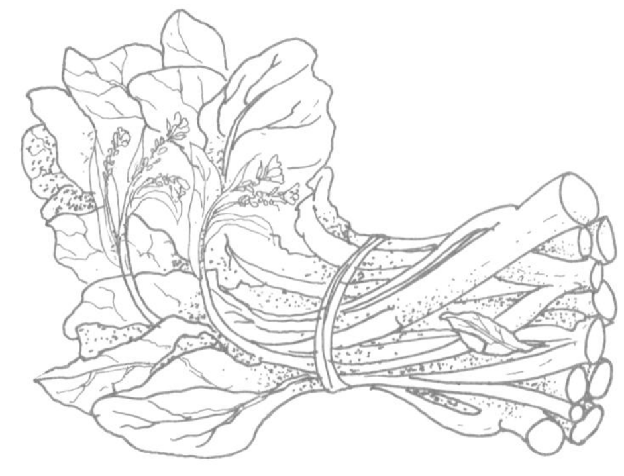

Description: Tender, fleshy stem, bright green leaves, yellow flowers.
Uses include: Meat dishes, stir-fry, Asian dishes.
Preparation: Discard coarse leaves and stems, wash, drain, cook quickly.

CAPSICUM or PEPPER

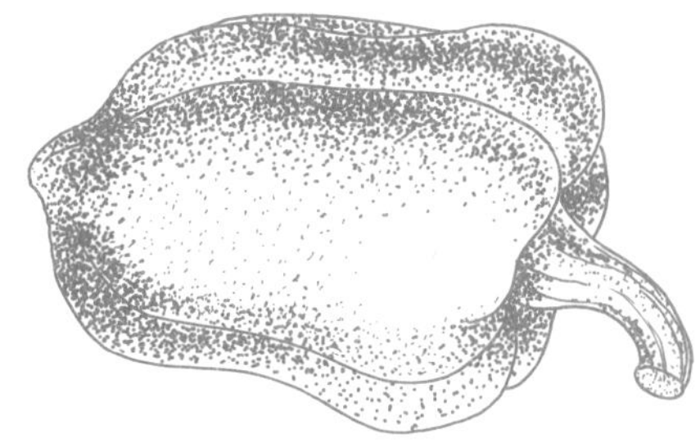

Description: Sweet red, green or yellow fruit.
Uses include: Accompaniment, crudités, soups, salads, casseroles, entree, Asian dishes, lunch box.
Preparation: Wash, remove top and scoop out seeds.

✦ STIR-FRIED CAPSICUM ✦

To serve 4: Prepare 2 capsicum (250 g) and cut into 1 cm pieces. Stir-fry in 1 teaspoon hot oil in a wok *or* heavy-based frying pan. Serve. Can be served with other stir-fried vegetables and rice.

✦ CAPSICUM BOATS ✦

To serve 4: Parboil 4 small prepared capsicum for 5 minutes. Drain. Fill with a mixture of 1/2 cup cooked brown rice, 1 chopped onion (125 g), 2 chopped tomatoes (250 g) and 3 shakes pepper. Sprinkle with 1/4 cup (30 g) grated cheese. Place in pie dish and bake at 180°C for 20–30 minutes.

✦ PEPERONI ✦

To serve 4: Fry 1 chopped onion (125 g) in 1/2 tablespoon (10 g) butter for 2 minutes, add 2 prepared and chopped capsicum (250 g), 1 chopped tomato (125 g) and 3 shakes pepper. Cover and cook 5 minutes. Serve as an accompaniment to grilled meat.

CARROT

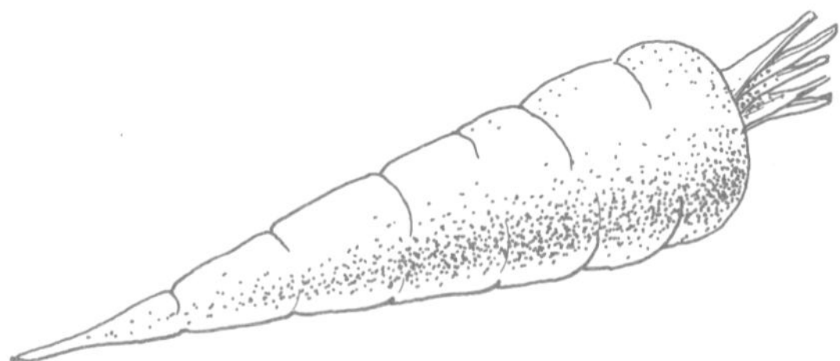

Description: Orange-coloured tap root.
Uses include: Accompaniment, casseroles, crudités, soups, roasts, cakes, carrot sticks in lunch box, grated in sandwiches, rolls and salads.
Preparation: Scrub, trim top and tail.

✦ SAUTÉED CARROTS ✦

To serve 4: Cook 375 g prepared and sliced carrots in 3 cm boiling water for 10 minutes, drain. Add 3 shakes pepper, sauté in 1 teaspoon butter and serve. 1 tablespoon chopped mint *or* parsley may be added before serving.

✦ DEVILLED CARROTS ✦

To serve 4: Prepare 375 g carrots and cut into sticks 6 cm x 5 mm. Sauté in 1 tablespoon (20 g) melted butter for 2 minutes, then add 2 teaspoons brown sugar *or* honey, 1 teaspoon mustard, 3 shakes cayenne and 1 tablespoon (20 mL) water. Simmer 5 minutes.

✦ CARROTS VALENCIA ✦

To serve 4: Prepare 375 g carrots and cut into thin rings. Cook in boiling water for 5 minutes. Drain. Add 1 teaspoon grated orange rind and 2 teaspoons cream *or* yoghurt.

CAULIFLOWER

Description: White or cream-coloured flower and stem.
Uses include: Accompaniment, crudités, entree, lunch box, salads.
Preparation: Wash and cut into florets.

✦ CAULIFLOWER IN CHEESE SAUCE ✦

To serve 4: Cook 1/2 prepared cauliflower in 3 cm boiling water for 10 minutes. Drain and serve with 1 cup (1 quantity) **Cheese sauce** (p. 282).

✦ CAULIFLOWER AU GRATIN ✦

To serve 4: Prepare and cook ½ cauliflower. Arrange in oiled ovenproof dish, cover with 1 cup (1 quantity) **White sauce** (p. 282), sprinkle with 2 tablespoons (20 g) dried breadcrumbs and 2 tablespoons (20 g) grated cheese. Grill until brown. Serve garnished with parsley sprigs. 2 tablespoons (30 g) fried bacon pieces may be added with the sauce.

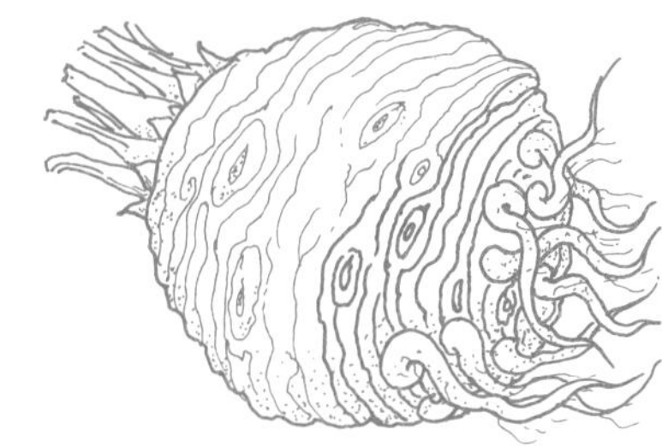

CELERIAC

Description: White tuber with the flavour of celery.
Uses include: Flavouring in soups, casseroles.
Preparation: Wash, trim base and slice.

CELERY

Description: Long white stems joined at base to form head.
Uses include: Accompaniment, soups, casseroles, or raw in crudités, lunch box, salads, rolls and sandwiches.
Preparation: Wash, remove coarse strings.

✦ CELERY IN CHEESE SAUCE ✦

To serve 4: Prepare 4 stalks celery and cut into 3 cm lengths. Cook in boiling water for 7–10 minutes. Drain and serve in 1 cup (1 quantity) **Cheese sauce** (p. 282).

CHICORY (see WITLOF)

CHILLI (LAHT JUI)

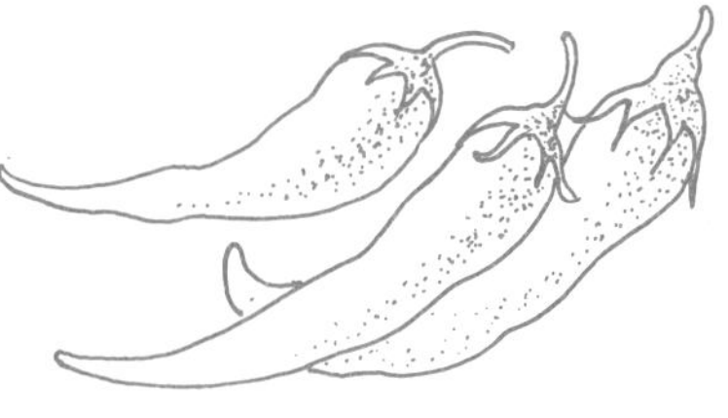

Description: Red, green and yellow fruit with a very hot flavour. The tiny green and red Thai varieties are used in Asian dishes. Jalapeno are very hot and the Habanero are longer and the hottest variety.
Uses include: Flavouring in casseroles, curries and preserves.
Preparation: Wash, use whole or cut off stem, remove seeds.

CHINESE CHARD (see BOK CHOY)

CHIVES

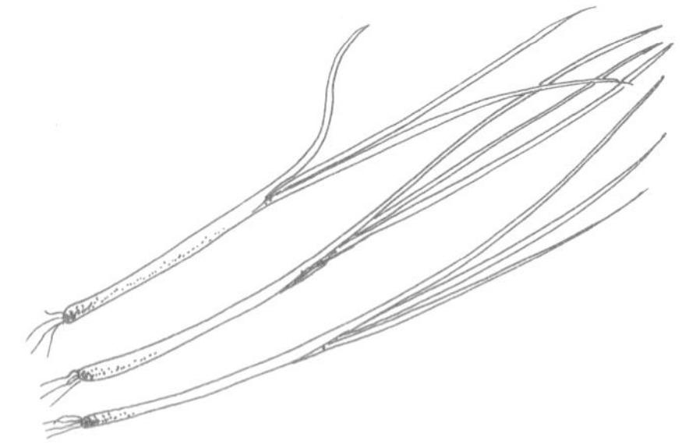

Description: Fine long green leaves with faint onion flavour.

Uses include: Garnish, flavouring in salads, sauces, sandwich fillings.

Preparation: Wash, trim if necessary, snip with scissors.

CHOKO (FAAT SAU GWA)

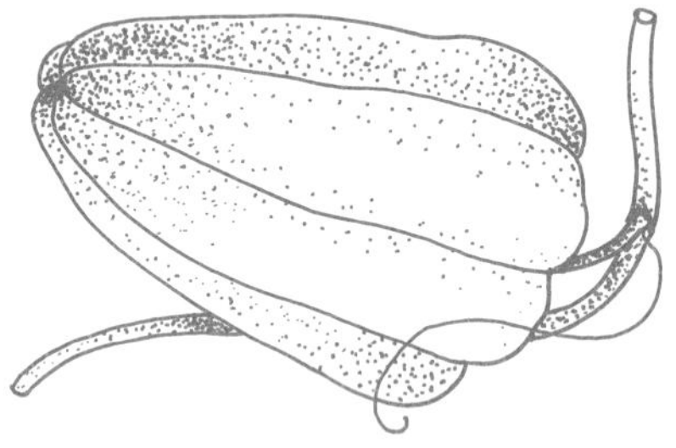

Description: A green, tough-skinned fruit with a centre seed.

Uses include: Accompaniment, roasts (p. 192), Asian dishes.

Preparation: Wash, peel, cut in quarters, remove seed.

✦ CHOKOS IN CHEESE SAUCE ✦

To serve 4: Cook 2 prepared chokos in 3 cm boiling water for 15 minutes. Drain. Serve in 1 cup (1 quantity) **Cheese sauce** (p. 282).

✦ CHOKOS A LA GRÈCQUE ✦

To serve 4: Prepare choko and cut into quarters. Fry 1 chopped onion (125 g) and 1/2 clove crushed garlic in 1 tablespoon (20 mL) oil for 1 minute. Add 1 chopped tomato (125 g), 1/4 cup (65 mL) water, 1 teaspoon lemon juice, 1 teaspoon chopped parsley, 1/2 teaspoon sugar, 3 shakes pepper and choko. Simmer 20 minutes with lid on. Serve hot or cold.

CHRYSANTHEMUM PLANT (TONG HO)

Description: Bright green feathery leaves with an aromatic flavour.

Uses include: Asian dishes.

Preparation: Wash, chop and cook.

CUCUMBER

Description: Green or white-skinned fruit, including short Lebanese or very long continental varieties.
Uses include: Accompaniment, as base for savouries, lunch box, salads, soups.
Preparation: Wash. Peel if necessary.

EGGPLANT or AUBERGINE

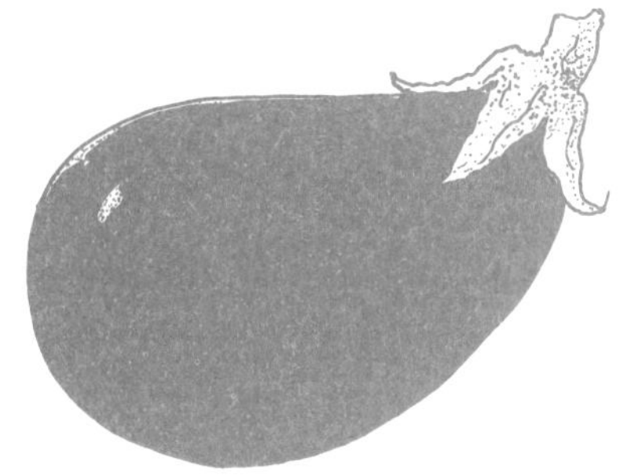

Description: Purple-skinned fruit.
Uses include: Accompaniment, entree.
Preparation: Wash, cut off stem. Cut according to use, sprinkle with salt and leave 30 minutes to extract bitter flavour. Wash well and dry.

SAUTÉED EGGPLANT

To serve 4: Prepare 250 g eggplant, cut into 1 cm slices. Coat with 3 tablespoons (30 g) plain flour and 3 shakes pepper. Sauté in 1 tablespoon (20 g) butter for 5 minutes.

CHARGRILLED EGGPLANT

To serve 4: Prepare 250 g eggplant cut into 1 cm slices. Spray with olive oil. Grill until brown on hot griller. Serve hot *or* marinate in **French dressing** (p. 266) and serve with salads.

BAKED EGGPLANT WITH CHEESE

To serve 4: Prepare 250 g eggplant cut in 1 cm slices. Cook in 3 cm boiling water for 5 minutes. Drain and place in layers in greased ovenproof dish with 1 cup (1 quantity) **Cheese sauce** (p. 282) and 2 tablespoons (20 g) cheese. Sprinkle with 1 tablespoon (5 g) breadcrumbs and bake at 180°C for 40 minutes.

EGGPLANT BOATS

To serve 4: Wash and cut stem off 2 small eggplants. Cut in half lengthwise. Scoop out centre flesh, chop finely and combine with 100 g minced steak, 1 clove (5 g) crushed garlic, 3 shakes pepper and 2 chopped tomatoes (250 g). Place mixture in centre of eggplant shells and bake at 180°C for 40 minutes.

✦ EGGPLANT DIP ✦

To serve 4: Wash and cut stem off 2 small eggplants. Cut in half lengthwise and place on oiled baking tray, cut sides down. Bake at 180°C for 20–25 minutes until tender. Place in blender and blend until smooth. Add 2 tablespoons (20 mL) lemon juice, 2 cloves crushed garlic, 2 teaspoons (10 mL) olive oil and 1 tablespoon (20 mL) tahini. Mix well. Place in serving bowl and serve with crudités.

ENDIVE

Description: Green leaves joined at base to form head. Bitter taste.
Uses include: Accompaniment, salads.
Preparation: Wash, cut off base and wash again.

✦ BRAISED ENDIVE ✦

To serve 4: Prepare 1 head endive and cut into 2 cm lengths. Fry with 2 tablespoons (30 g) chopped bacon for 1 minute. Add 3 shakes pepper and 1 tablespoon (20 mL) water. Cover and simmer 2 minutes.

FENNEL

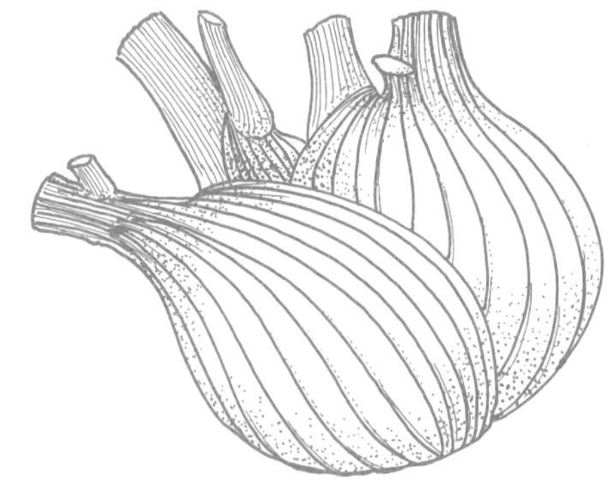

Description: White bulb with pale green stalks and feathery green leaves. Aniseed flavour.
Uses include: Accompaniment, salads, garnish (leaves).
Preparation: Wash and trim.

✦ FENNEL VALENCIA ✦

To serve 4: Prepare 1 medium fennel. Slice the bulb finely crosswise and parboil in boiling water for 2 minutes. Drain. Add 1 cup grated carrot and 1/4 cup (65 mL) orange juice. Chill and serve.

FENUGREEK

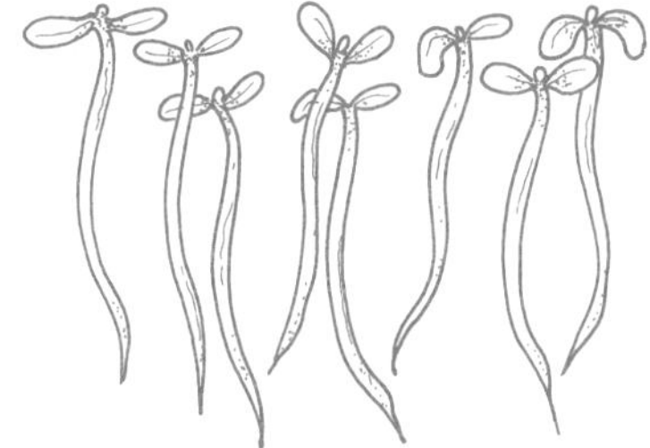

Description: Slight curry flavour.
Uses include: Flavouring in curries, salads.
Preparation: Grind seeds finely or sprout seeds.

GARLIC

Description: Strong-flavoured bulb of the onion family.
Uses include: Flavouring in casseroles, soups, salads.
Preparation: Remove clove from bulb. Trim ends and remove outer skin.

GHERKIN

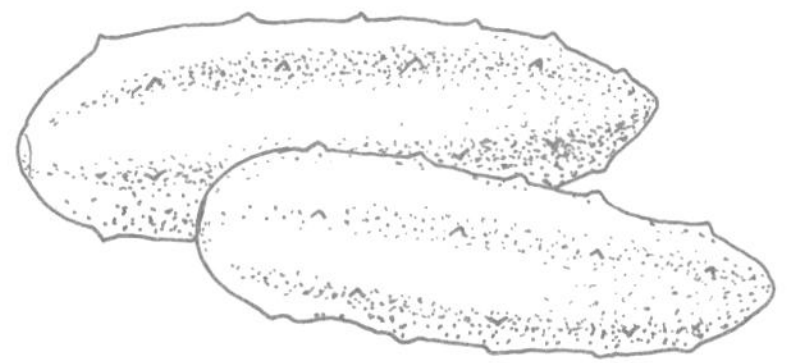

Description: Small type of cucumber.
Uses include: Pickled, then used as garnish or for sandwiches, salads.

HORSERADISH

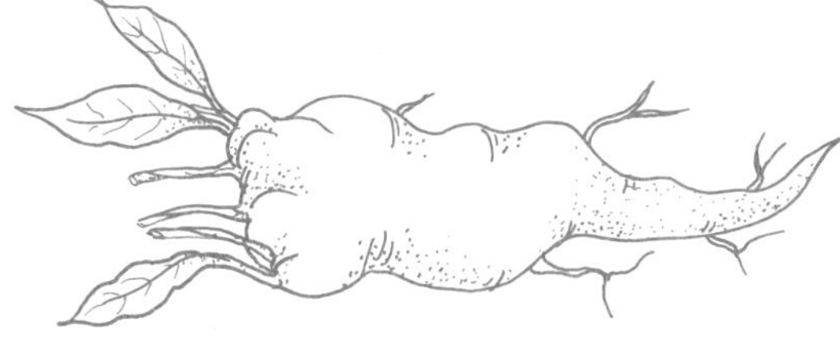

Description: Strongly flavoured root.
Uses include: **Horseradish sauce** (p. 267).
Preparation: Peel and grate.

KALE

Description: Green leafy head with frilled edges. Strong flavour.
Uses include: Garnish, salads.
Preparation: Remove leaves from base, wash well.

KOHLRABI

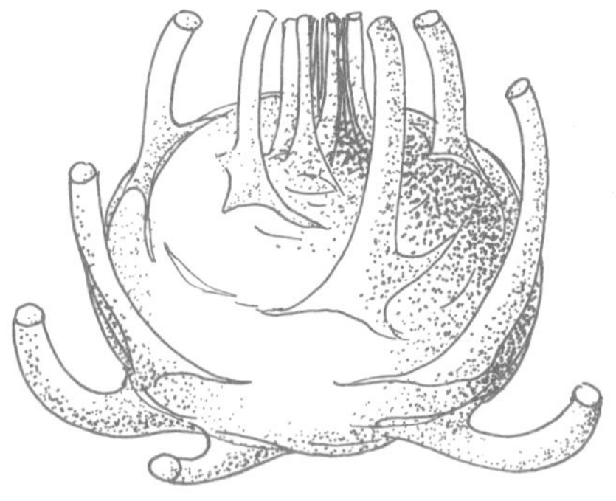

Description: Purple-skinned root similar in flavour and texture to a turnip.

Uses include: Accompaniment.

Preparation: Remove leaves, wash and peel. May be sliced or diced.

KOHLRABI IN LEMON SAUCE

To serve 4: Prepare 2 kohlrabi and cut into 2 cm slices. Cook in 3 cm boiling water for 15–20 minutes. Drain. Serve in 1 cup (1 quantity) **Lemon sauce** (p. 159).

KUMARA (see SWEET POTATO)

LEEK

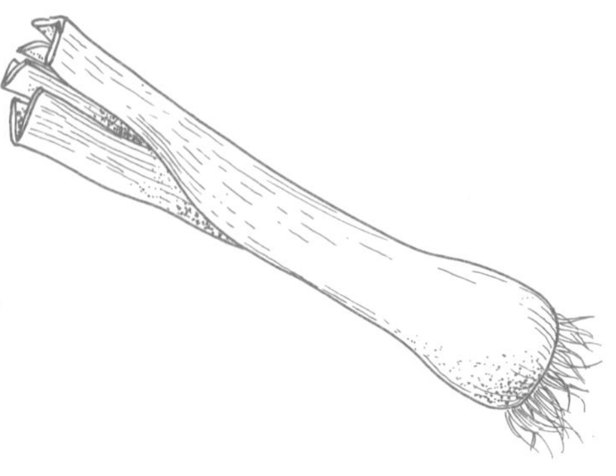

Description: Green leaf and white bulb with onion flavour.

Uses include: Accompaniment, pies, soups, casseroles.

Preparation: Wash very well. Remove base and tops of leaves, slice and wash again.

LEEKS IN CHEESE SAUCE

To serve 4: Slice 1 leek and cook in 3 cm boiling water for 5 minutes. Drain. Serve in 1 cup (1 quantity) **Cheese sauce** (p. 282).

BRAISED LEEKS

To serve 4: Prepare and slice 1 leek. Fry with 2 tablespoons (30 g) chopped bacon for 1 minute. Add 3 shakes pepper and 1 tablespoon (20 mL) water. Cover and simmer 4 minutes.

LETTUCE

Description: Leafy head. Varieties include crisp green iceberg and frill ice; soft green cos; soft red and green butterheads; coral, oakleaf and mignonette. A mix of leaves may be sold as salad mix or mesclun.
Uses include: Lunch box, salads, sandwiches and rolls. Often used as garnish for salads and platters of sandwiches.
Preparation: Cut out base. Wash well through hole in base. Separate leaves and wash again. Drain in colander. To keep crisp, seal in plastic bag or container in refrigerator.

MARROW

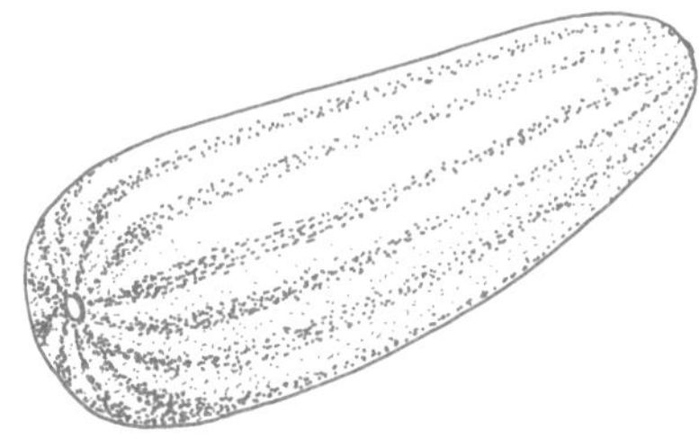

Description: Green or yellow-skinned, white to cream flesh.
Uses include: Accompaniment, entree, roasts.
Preparation: Wash.

✦ MARROW IN CHEESE SAUCE ✦

To serve 4: Prepare 375 g marrow, peel if necessary and cut into 4 pieces. Cook in boiling water for 8 minutes. Drain. Serve in 1 cup (1 quantity) **Cheese sauce** (p. 282).

 Microwave for 5 minutes on high power. Turn and continue to microwave for 10 minutes on medium power.

MUNG BEANS

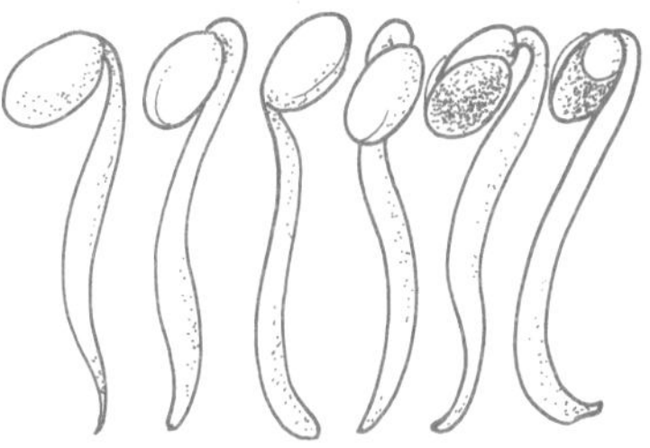

Description: Small green seeds, firm white sprouts with green leaf.
Uses include: Asian cooking, lunch box, salads.
Preparation: Wash.

MUSHROOM, FIELD or CULTIVATED

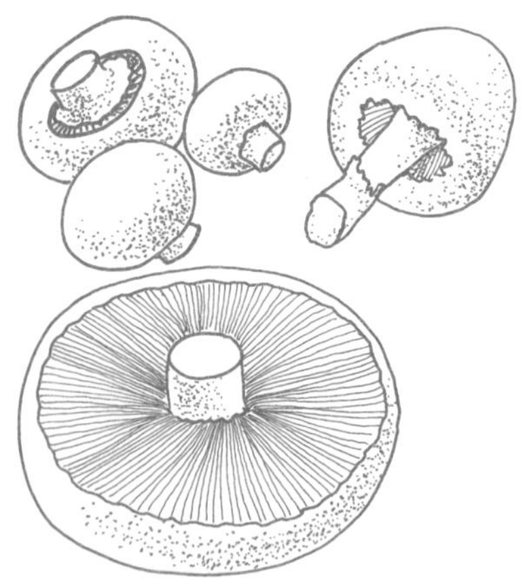

Description: Edible fungi. Field and cultivated types are used. Sold in three sizes: button (small, closed), caps (slightly open, darker), and flat (open with dark underside, rich in flavour).

Uses include: Accompaniment, entree, lunch box, salads, soups, casseroles.

Preparation: Peel and wash if field mushrooms. Wipe cultivated mushrooms if necessary.

✦ SAUTÉED MUSHROOMS ✦

To serve 4: Sauté 375 g prepared mushrooms in 1 tablespoon (20 g) butter and 3 shakes pepper for 5–7 minutes. Serve. May be thickened with 1 tablespoon (10 g) flour blended with $^1/_4$ cup (65 mL) milk.

✦ GRILLED MUSHROOMS ✦

To serve 4: Prepare 4 large mushrooms, brush with 1 tablespoon (20 g) melted butter and grill 5–7 minutes. Sprinkle with 3 shakes pepper.

✦ PICKLED MUSHROOMS ✦

To serve 4: Make 2 cups ($^1/_2$ quantity) **Spiced vinegar** (p. 479), bring to boil, add 250 g button mushrooms and simmer 3 minutes. Add $^1/_4$ cup (65 mL) olive oil, cool and bottle. Store in refrigerator.

MUSHROOM, ENOKI

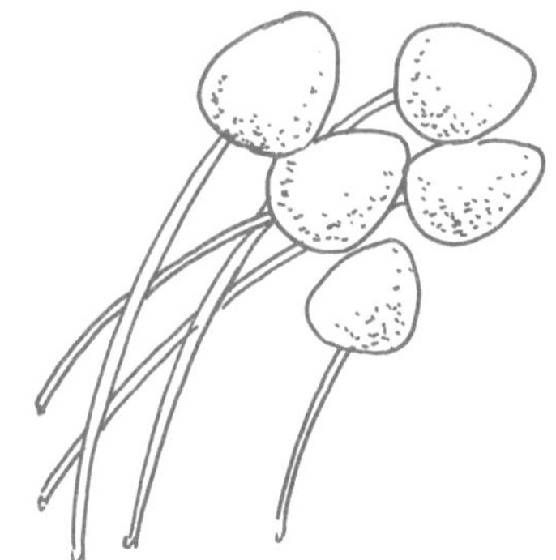

Description: Long, thin-stemmed white mushrooms with tiny caps.

Uses include: Stir-fry, Asian dishes, seafood dishes, raw in salads.

Preparation: Use whole, cook quickly.

MUSHROOM, OYSTER (SYN TUNG KOO)

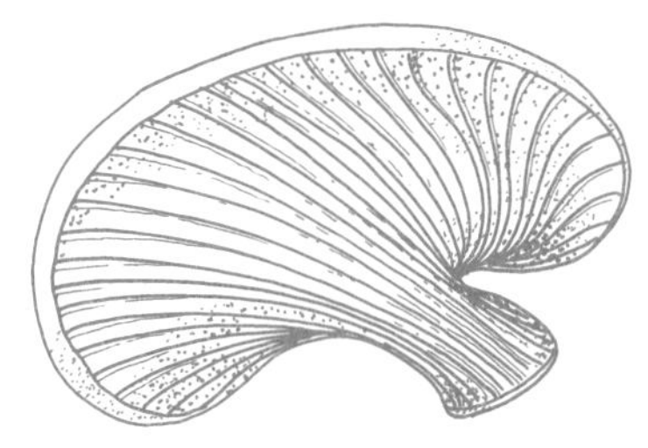

Description: Fresh mushrooms with delicate oyster flavour.
Uses include: Stir-fry, Asian dishes, seafood, raw in salads.
Preparation: Slice or use whole. Cook quickly.

MUSHROOM, PORTABELLO

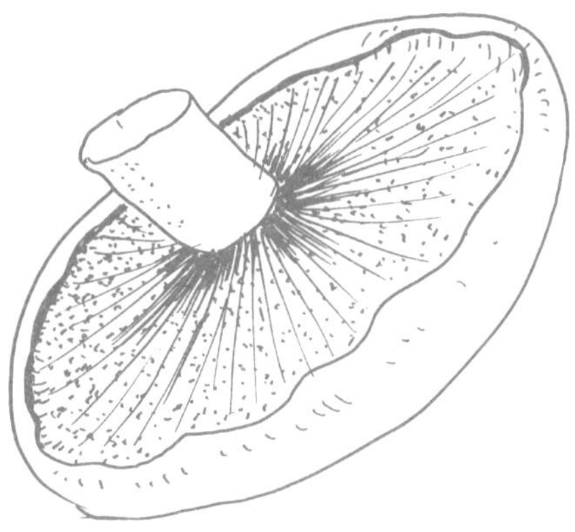

Description: Very large, dry texture with full robust flavour.
Uses include: Barbecue, casseroles, soups, raw.
Preparation: Wipe, peel, slice or use whole.

MUSHROOM, SHITAKE (TUNG KOO)

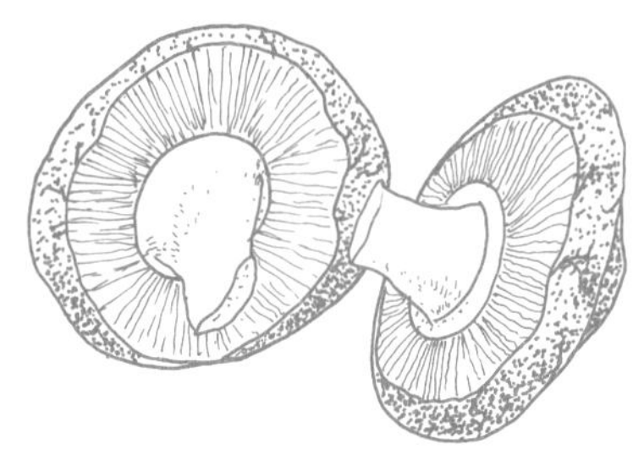

Description: Golden brown cap with cream underside. May be dried.
Uses include: Stir-fry, Asian dishes, salads, risotto, pasta.
Preparation: Slice or use whole. Cook quickly. Soak in hot water if dried.

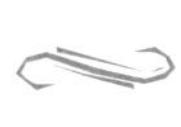

MUSHROOM, SWISS BROWN

Description: Light brown with rich nutty flavour.
Uses include: Meat and fish dishes casseroles, soups and sauces.
Preparation: Wipe, slice or use whole.

OKRA

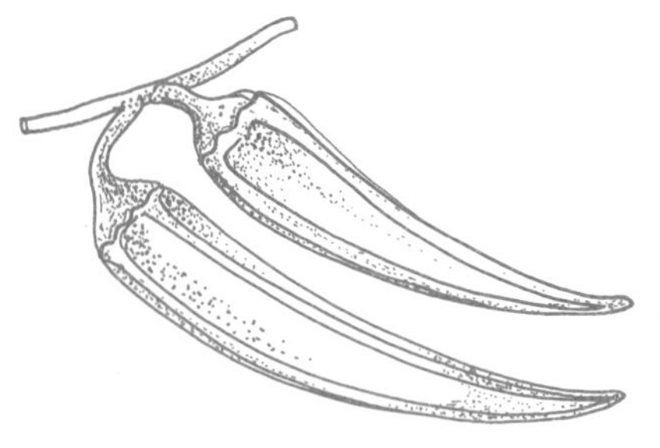

Description: Elongated green pod with pale flesh. Bitter flavour. May be called 'ladies fingers'.
Uses include: Accompaniment, soups.
Preparation: Wash and trim, blanch to remove bitter flavour.

✦ SAUTÉED OKRA ✦

To serve 4: Prepare 375 g okra. Cook in 3 cm water for 5 minutes. Drain. Sauté in 1 teaspoon butter.

ONION

Description: Bulb with a distinctive flavour. May be strong-flavoured brown onion, milder white onion or small spring onion where green tops are used as well as the bulb, or dark red Spanish onion.
Uses include: Accompaniment, casseroles, salads, soups, pickles, roasts.
Preparation: Remove skin and base.

✦ ONIONS IN SAUCE ✦

To serve 4: Prepare 4 onions and cut into 1 cm slices. Cook in 3 cm boiling water for 5 minutes. Drain. Serve in 1 cup (1 quantity) **White sauce** (p. 282) made using $^{1}/_{2}$ cup (125 mL) cooking liquid. If onions are small they can be left whole.

✦ SAUTÉED ONIONS ✦

To serve 4: Prepare 4 onions and cut into 5 mm slices. Sauté in 1 tablespoon (20 g) butter with 3 shakes pepper for 7–10 minutes until golden.

✦ ONIONS MONAGUESQUES ✦

To serve 4: Prepare 400 g very small onions. Cook onions with 1 cup (25 mL) water, 1/2 teaspoon salt. 1 tablespoon tomato (20 g) paste, 1 tablespoon (20 g) sugar, 2 tablespoons (40 mL) vinegar, 2 tablespoons (40 mL) olive oil, 2 tablespoons (30 g) sultanas, sprigs of thyme and parsley and a bay leaf. Simmer 45 minutes. Serve hot or cold.

PARSLEY

Description: Green leafy herb.
Uses include: Garnish, flavourings in casseroles, salads and soups.
Preparation: Wash, chop if necessary.

PARSLEY, CHINESE or CORIANDER (IN SIE)

Description: Bright green, soft leaves, roots attached.
Uses include: Soups, meat dishes, Asian dishes.
Preparation: Chop leaves and stems. Roots may be used.

PARSNIP

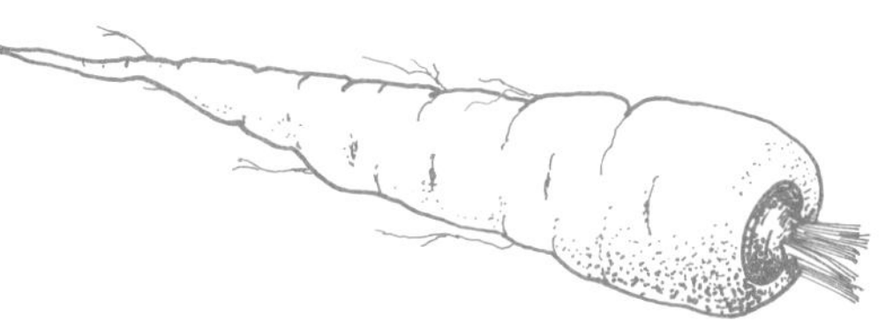

Description: Cream-coloured tap root.
Uses include: Accompaniment, soups, casseroles, roasts, cooked and served with boiled meat.
Preparation: Wash, peel, remove top and tail.

✦ MASHED PARSNIPS ✦

To serve 4: Prepare 375 g parsnips and cut into 3 cm slices. Cook in 3 cm boiling water for 10–15 minutes. Drain. Mash. Add 1 tablespoon (20 g) butter and 3 shakes pepper.

PEAS

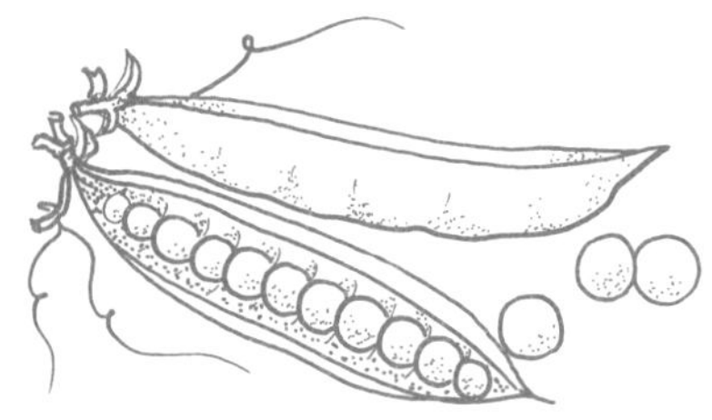

Description: Green seeds removed from pods.
Uses include: Accompaniment, casseroles, salads.

✦ SAUTÉED PEAS ✦

To serve 4: Prepare 500 g peas and cook in 3 cm boiling water with a sprig of mint for 7–10 minutes. Drain, remove mint. Sauté in 1 teaspoon butter.

POTATO

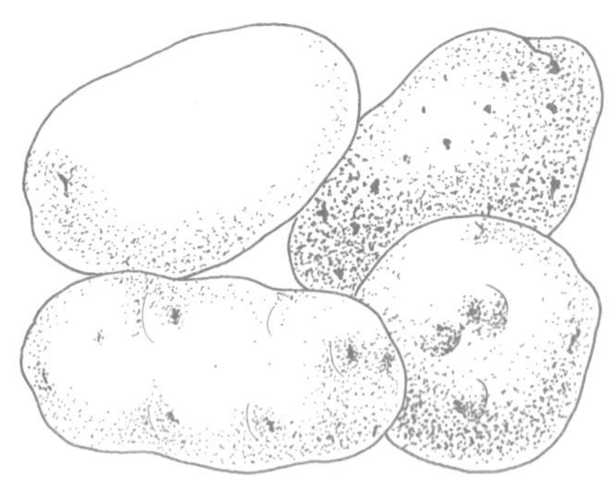

Description: There are many varieties of this tuber, each with a distinctive flavour, colour and texture. The skin varies from transparent to brown to reddish-purple. The tuber may be smooth or pitted with 'eyes'. Some varieties are elongated, e.g. klipfer or pink fir apple. For frying and roasting choose potatoes with a waxy flesh (see **Potato chips**). Those best for dry baking, boiling and mashing are 'floury' in texture (see **Mashed potatoes**). Those recommended for **Potato salad** (p. 273) keep their shape after cooking. Potatoes are now sold by varietal name, with recommended cooking methods. Varieties are suggested in each of the following recipes.
Uses include: Accompaniment, salads soups, casseroles, roasts, fried.
Preparation: Wash and scrub. Peel if necessary, and cut into quarters if large.

✦ MASHED or CREAMED POTATOES ✦

To serve 4: Cook 400 g prepared and peeled 'floury' potatoes (nicola, pontiac, Toolangi delight, desiree) in 3 cm boiling water for 20–25 minutes. Drain. Mash. Add 1 tablespoon (20 g) butter, 3 shakes pepper and sufficient milk to moisten. Beat until fluffy.

✦ POTATO AND CORN PATTIES ✦

To serve 4: Prepare 2 cups (300 g) mashed potato (see above). Combine with 1/2 cup (130 g) corn kernels, 1 tablespoon chopped parsley, 1/4 teaspoon caraway seeds, 1/2 grated onion (65 g), a beaten egg and 1 cup (30 g) fresh breadcrumbs. Mix well. Divide into 8 and shape into patties. Heat 2 tablespoons (40 mL) olive oil and 1 tablespoon (20 g) butter in a frying pan and brown patties on each side.

✦ POTATO AND PARSNIP PATTIES ✦

To serve 4: Prepare 1 1/2 cups (225 g) mashed potato and 1 1/2 cups (225 g) mashed parsnip, add 1 stock cube and 1/2 cup (60 g) grated cheese and mix well. Heat 2 tablespoons (40 mL) oil in a frying pan. Place 8 spoonsful of mixture into pan and brown on each side.

✦ POTATO WEDGES ✦

To serve 4: Prepare 400 g potatoes (Idaho, spunta, russet, burbank, kennebec). Cut into thick wedges and place on baking paper on an oven tray. Sprinkle with flour, then salt, chopped herbs and pepper or a seasoned salt. Spray with oil. Bake at 200°C for 30–45 minutes, until golden brown and crisp.

✦ ANNA POTATOES ✦

To serve 4: Prepare 400 g potatoes (patrone, bintje, Toolangi delight). Cut into 1 cm slices and place layer in base of casserole dish brushed or sprayed with oil. Combine 3 tablespoons (60 g) melted butter, 1/2 teaspoon oregano *or* thyme and 3 shakes pepper and pour a little over first potato layer. Continue potato and butter layers. Cover and bake 1 hour at 180°C. Remove cover after 30 minutes of baking.

 Microwave for 10 minutes on high power for 5 minutes on medium power.

✦ SCALLOPED POTATOES ✦

To serve 4: Prepare potatoes as for **Anna potatoes**. Using 3 tablespoons (30 g) flour, sprinkle some between each potato layer. Before baking, heat 1 cup (250 mL) milk and pour it over potatoes. Herbs may be omitted.

✦ DUCHESS POTATOES ✦

To serve 4: Prepare 1 quantity **Mashed potatoes**. Use 1 beaten egg instead of milk, reserving 1 teaspoon for glaze. Pipe potato into 8 high mounds. Glaze and bake 10 minutes at 200°C.

✦ NEW POTATOES ✦

To serve 4: Wash 375 g small new potatoes (snow gems, chats) and cook in 3 cm boiling water for 10–15 minutes. Drain. Toss in 1 tablespoon (20 g) butter, 2 teaspoons chopped mint and 3 shakes pepper.

✦ POTATO CHIPS ✦

To serve 4: See Safety hints for frying (p. 225). Prepare and peel 500 g 'waxy' potatoes (kennebec, russet burbank, sebago) and cut into chips 1 cm thick. Soak in cold water, rinse, drain and dry. Place 6 cm oil into thermostatically controlled fryer. Heat to 180°C (oil ceases to bubble and small cube of bread browns in 20 seconds). Place half of the chips in frying basket and lower gently into oil. Fry until golden brown. Repeat with remaining chips. Drain on absorbent paper.

✦ JACKET POTATOES ✦

To serve 4: Scrub and dry 4 medium potatoes (spunta, pink-eye, patrone, bintji, russet burbank). Pierce with fork and bake at 180°C for 1 hour. Cut cross in top and serve with yoghurt, butter *or* sour cream.

Microwave for 10 minutes on high power.

✦ CHEESY POTATOES ✦

To serve 4: Prepare 1 quantity **Jacket potatoes**. When cooked, cut in half, scoop out centres, mash with sufficient milk, 1 teaspoon butter, 3/4 cup (90 g) grated cheese, 3 shakes pepper and fill potato cases. Sprinkle with 1/4 cup (30 g) cheese and reheat under griller or in oven 7–10 minutes.

POTATO, SWEET

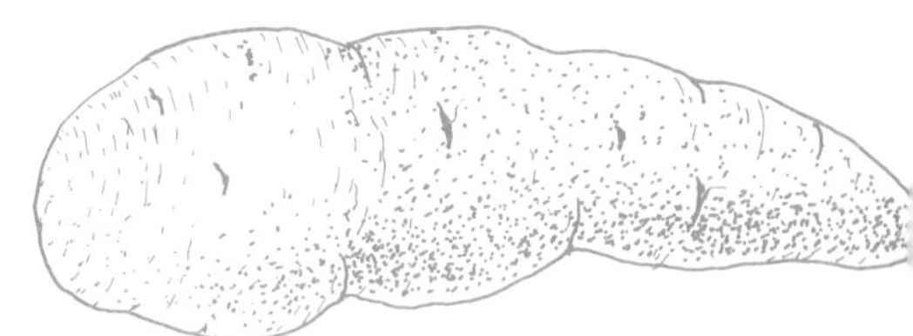

Description: Tuber with sweet taste. May have purple skin and white flesh or orange skin with orange flesh. The orange variety may also be called 'kumara'.

Uses include: Accompaniment, roasts.

Preparation: Wash, scrub, peel and rinse.

✦ MASHED SWEET POTATO ✦

Follow recipe for **Mashed potato** (p. 250).

PUMPKIN

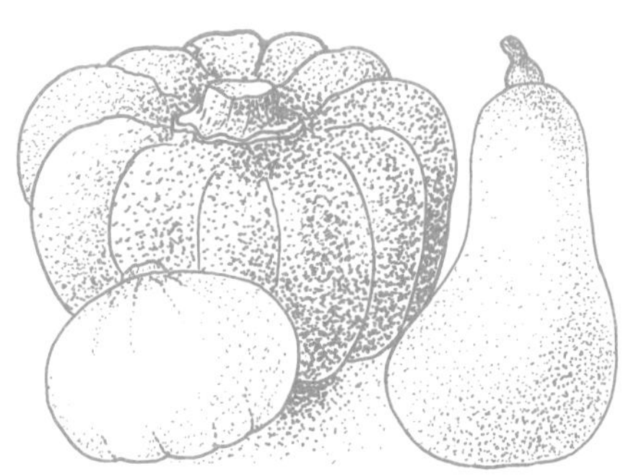

Description: Large, hard-skinned fruit with yellow to orange flesh. There are many varieties including the butternut (bell-shaped with gold skin and orange flesh), golden nugget (small, round shape with bright orange skin and orange flesh), Queensland blue (large flat shape with dusty blue skin and yellow flesh).

Uses include: Accompaniment, salads, soups, roasts, scones, desserts.

Preparation: Remove skin, cut into serving-size pieces, remove seeds and pith.

✦ PUMPKIN AU GRATIN ✦

To serve 4: Cook 375 g prepared and sliced pumpkin in 3 cm boiling water for 10 minutes. Drain and cool. Fry 1 onion (125 g), 2 tablespoons (30 g) bacon pieces and 1 clove (5 g) crushed garlic in saucepan. Add 2 chopped tomatoes (300 g), $^1/_4$ cup (65 mL) water, $^1/_8$ teaspoon nutmeg, 3 shakes pepper and simmer 5 minutes. Layer pumpkin and tomato mixture in greased ovenproof dish. Sprinkle with $^1/_2$ cup (20 g) breadcrumbs and $^1/_4$ cup (30 g) grated cheese. Bake at 180°C for 25–30 minutes.

✦ MASHED PUMPKIN ✦

To serve 4: Cook 375 g prepared pumpkin in 3 cm boiling water for 15–20 minutes. Drain. Mash. Add 1 tablespoon (20 g) butter and 3 shakes pepper.

 GOLDEN NUGGET DELIGHT ✦

To serve 4: Wash 1 medium *or* 4 small golden nugget pumpkins and slice across top to form lids. Cover and microwave base for 6 minutes and lid for 3 minutes on medium power. Scoop out seeds. Sauté 1 small onion (125 g) in 1 teaspoon butter, add $^1/_3$ cup (70 g) brown rice, 1 cup (125 mL) water, 1 tablespoon (20 g) tomato paste, 1 teaspoon cumin and simmer until rice is tender, stirring every 5 minutes, adding extra water if necessary. Fill pumpkin with rice mixture, replace lid and reheat.

RADISH

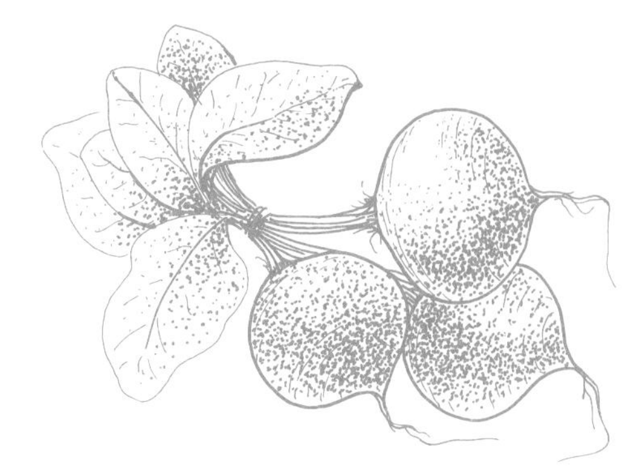

Description: Red or white-skinned root.
Uses include: Garnish, lunch box, salads.
Preparation: Wash and cut off top and tail if necessary.

RADISH, WHITE (LOH BAAK)

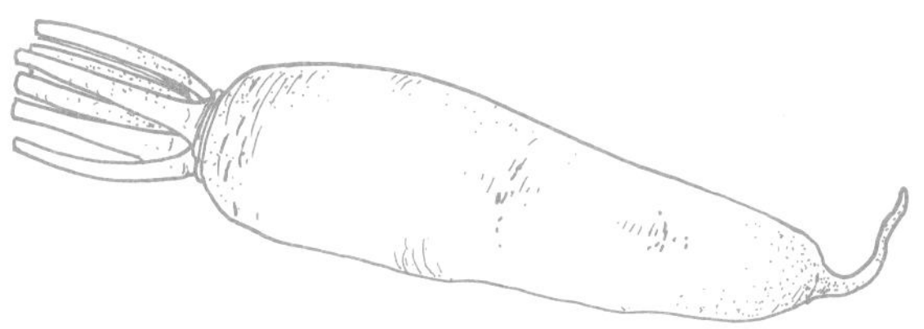

Description: White tap root with bright green leaves.
Uses include: Salads, pickles, meat dishes.
Preparation: Wash, peel thinly and slice.

SHALLOTS

Description: Bulb of the onion family.
Uses include: Flavouring in soups and casseroles.
Preparation: Wash, remove skin and trim base.

SILVER BEET

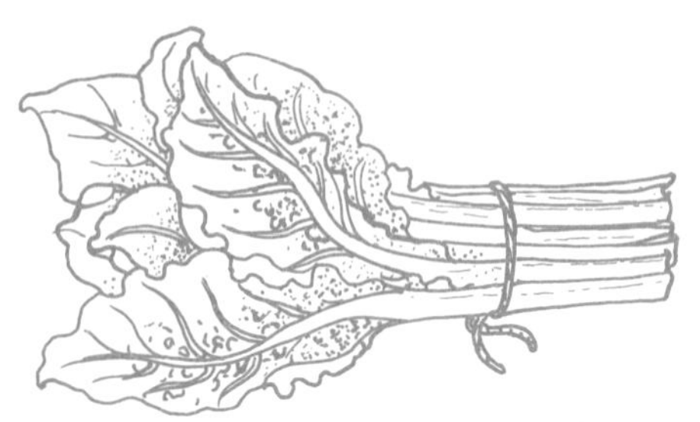

Description: Large dark green leaves with white stalks.
Uses include: Accompaniment, Asian dishes, entree.
Preparation: Wash well, cut stalks from leaves.

✦ SAUTÉED SILVER BEET ✦

To serve 4: Prepare $^{1}/_{2}$ bunch silver beet, shred leaves and slice stalks. Cook sliced stalks in boiling water for 5 minutes, add leaves and cook further 3 minutes. Drain. Add 3 shakes pepper, sauté in 1 teaspoon butter.

✦ GARLIC SILVER BEET ✦

To serve 4: Prepare $^{1}/_{2}$ bunch silver beet and shred leaves. Sauté 1 clove (5 g) garlic in 1 teaspoon butter for 30 seconds, add silver beet leaves and sauté 2 minutes.

SNOW PEA (HOLONDOW)

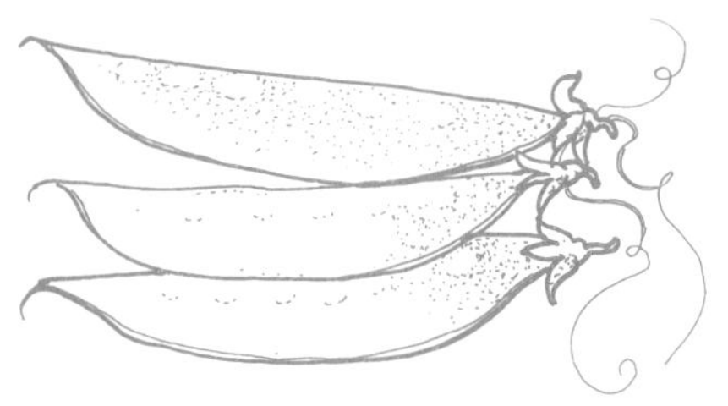

Description: Bright green, tender edible pod, with small seeds.
Uses include: Accompaniment, Asian dishes, salads, stir-fry, soups.
Preparation: Wash, remove strings. Blanch and use in salads.

✦ SAUTÉED SNOW PEAS ✦

To serve 4: Cook 200 g prepared snow peas in 3 cm water for 2 minutes. Drain. Sauté in 1 teaspoon butter. Serve.

SPINACH

Description: Green leaves with thin stem attached to root. Sorrell is a variety of spinach with a sharp lemon flavour.

Uses include: Accompaniment, entree, soups.

Preparation: Wash well removing root and cut into 3 cm pieces, and wash again.

✦ SAUTÉED SPINACH ✦

To serve 4: Cook a bunch of prepared spinach in 3 cm boiling water for 3 minutes. Drain. Add 3 shakes pepper, sauté in 1 teaspoon butter.

✦ CREAMED SPINACH ✦

To serve 4: Cook a bunch of prepared spinach in 3 cm boiling water for 3 minutes. Drain. Add 3 shakes pepper, 1 tablespoon (20 g) butter, 2 tablespoons (40 mL) sour *or* fresh cream *or* yoghurt and 1/4 teaspoon nutmeg. Mix well and serve.

SPINACH, CHINESE (IN CHOY)

Description: Bright green leaves and green stems.

Uses include: Steam, boil, stir-fry, Asian dishes.

Preparation: Wash well, discard roots and stem ends, chop.

SPRING ONION (JSUNG) (see ONION)

SQUASH

Description: Small fruit with green or yellow skin, pale flesh and seeds in centre.
Uses include: Accompaniment, salads, soups.
Preparation: Wash and trim.

✦ SAUTÉED SQUASH ✦

To serve 4: Cook 8 small prepared squash in 3 cm boiling water for 5–8 minutes. Drain. Sprinkle with chopped parsley, sauté in 1 teaspoon butter.

SQUASH, SPAGHETTI

Description: Large oval golden yellow squash.
Preparation: Boil whole for 30–40 minutes, then pull out spaghetti-like strands with fork. Serve with **Fresh tomato sauce** (p. 283).

SWEDE

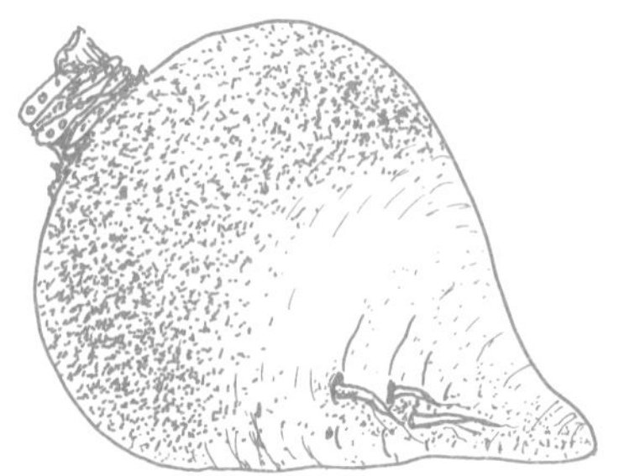

Description: Large yellow root. May also be called 'rutabago'.
Uses include: Accompaniment.
Preparation: Wash, peel thickly and cut up as required.

✦ MASHED SWEDE ✦

To serve 4: Cook 375 g prepared swede in 3 cm boiling water for 15–20 minutes. Drain, mash with 3 shakes pepper and 1 tablespoon (20 g) butter.

SWEET CORN

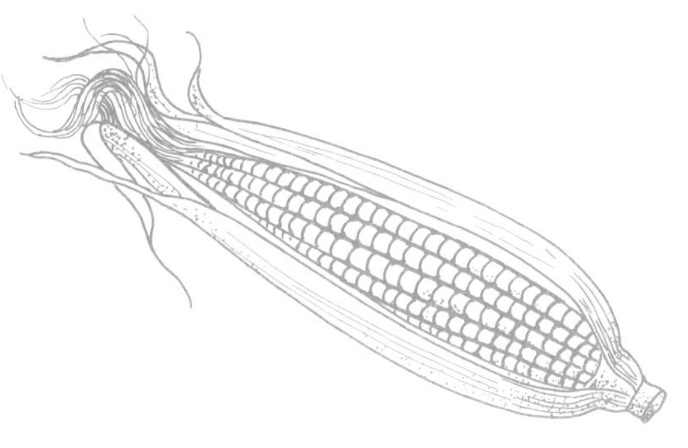

Description: Cob consists of green husk enveloping yellow seeds or kernels. New varieties include those with red or blue kernels.
Uses include: Accompaniment, entree, soups, salads.
Preparation: Remove husks and silk. Wash. Trim top and tail if necessary.

SWEET CORN AU BEURRE

To serve 4: Cook 4 prepared cobs in boiling water to cover for 10–15 minutes. Drain. Serve with pepper and 2 tablespoons (40 g) melted butter. May be served as an entree.

Place cob of sweet corn (with husk and silk intact) in microwave oven for 2 minutes on high power, turn and cook after 2 minutes. Serve as for **Sweet corn au beurre** (p. 257) after removing husk and silk.

CREAM OF SWEET CORN

To serve 4: Cook 4 prepared cobs in boiling water to cover, for 10–15 minutes. Drain. Cut kernels off cobs. Combine kernels with 1 cup (1 quantity) **White sauce** (p. 282). A 300 g can sweet corn kernels may be used instead of cooked kernels. May be served 'en croute' as entree.

TARO ROOT (WOO TAU)

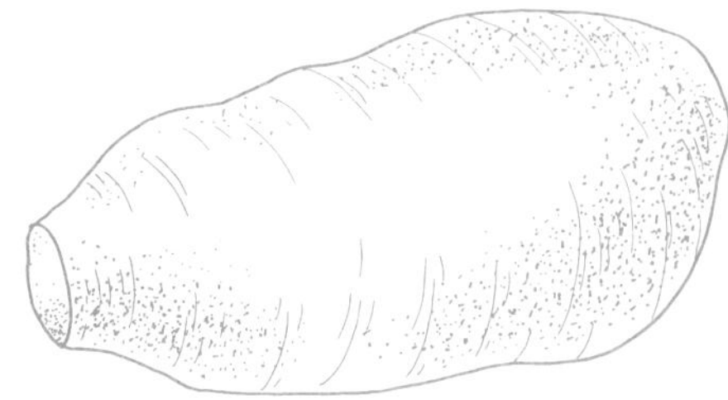

Description: Light brown-coloured tuber.
Uses include: Boiled, mashed, roasts.
Preparation: Peel and slice or cut into pieces.

TOMATO

Description: A pulpy fruit containing seeds, usually red, but can be yellow, green or purple.
Uses include: Accompaniment, casseroles, entree, lunch box, salads, soups.
Preparation: Wash and remove stem scar. Remove skin if necessary by dipping in hot water or holding over flame for 3 seconds and peeling.

✦ SAVOURY-FILLED TOMATOES ✦

To serve 4: Wash and dry 4 tomatoes (500 g). Cut slice from bottom of each tomato and put aside. Scoop out centre of each tomato and chop. Fry 1 tablespoon (15 g) bacon pieces with 1 small chopped onion (125 g). Cook 1 minute, add 1 tablespoon (5 g) breadcrumbs, 1 tablespoon chopped parsley, 3 shakes pepper, 2 teaspoons (10 g) butter and chopped tomato centres. Mix and refill tomato cases. Replace bottom slices as lids, place in ovenproof dish and bake at 180°C for 15–20 minutes.

 Microwave for 4 minutes on medium power.

✦ TOMATO AND ONION PIE ✦

To serve 4: Wash and peel 375 g tomatoes. Cut into 1 cm slices. Peel and thinly slice 1 medium white onion (125 g). Brush or spray ovenproof dish with oil. Arrange tomato and onion in layers, sprinkling with 3 shakes pepper between layers and 1/4 cup (10 g) breadcrumbs on top. Bake for 1 hour at 180°C. Serve garnished with parsley. If onion is sautéed first, the cooking time can be reduced.

 Microwave for 5 minutes on high power and 5 minutes on medium power.

✦ BAKED TOMATOES ✦

To serve 4: Wash and dry 4 tomatoes (500 g). Score skin to prevent splitting, place on oven tray and bake for 20 minutes at 180°C. Serve garnished with parsley sprigs.

 Microwave for 5 minutes on high power.

✦ GRILLED TOMATOES ✦

To serve 4: Wash and dry 2 tomatoes (250 g). Cut in half and sprinkle with pepper. Grill cut surface for 5–7 minutes. Serve garnished with fresh basil.

✦ SAUTÉED TOMATOES ✦

To serve 4: Cut 375 g prepared and peeled tomatoes into 2 cm slices. Sauté 5 minutes in 1 tablespoon (20 g) butter and 3 shakes pepper.

TRUFFLE

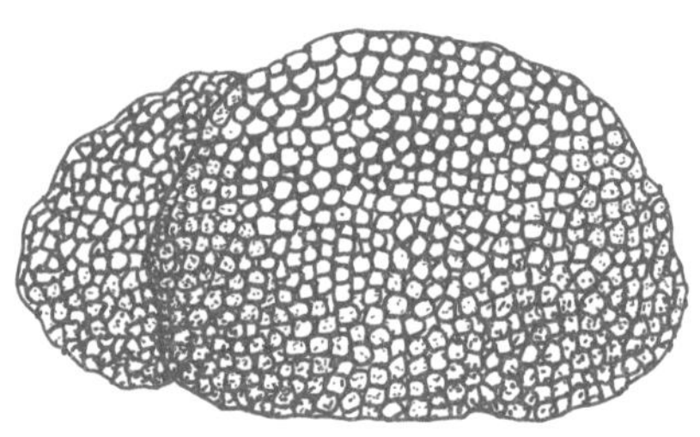

Description: A fungus found by specially bred and trained pigs in certain parts of France. An expensive delicacy available fresh or in cans.

TURNIP

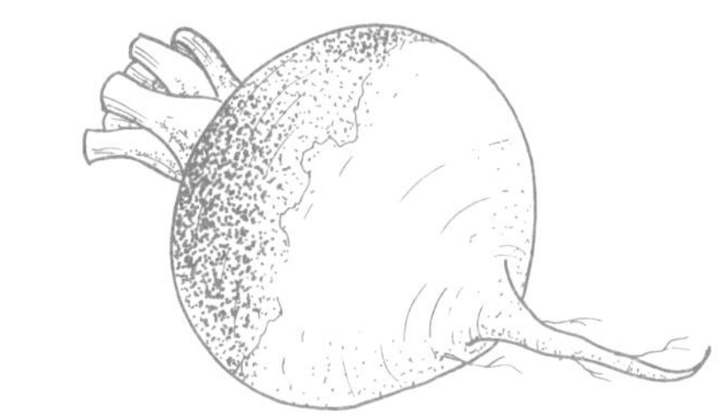

Description: White root.
Uses include: Flavouring in soups and casseroles.
Preparation: Wash, peel thickly and cut as required.

TURNIP, JAPANESE (KOKABU)

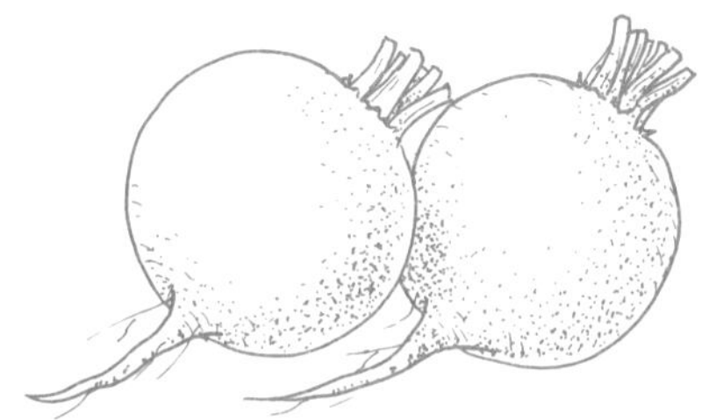

Description: Small white radishes
Uses include: Stir-fry.
Preparation: Wash, discard leaves.

WARRIGAL GREENS

Description: Indigenous plant widely grown in Australia. The plant has large bright green leaves and tiny yellow flowers, and grows most vigorously in spring and summer.
Uses include: In similar ways to spinach or silver beet.
Preparation: Wash then blanch to remove excess oxalates.

WATERCRESS (SAI YEUNG CHO)

Description: Small green leaves.
Uses include: Salads, sandwiches, garnish soups and stocks. Adds a peppery taste to dishes.
Preparation: Wash.

WITLOF or CHICORY

Description: Pale greenish-white leaves joined at base to form head. Bitter flavour.
Uses include: Accompaniment, salads.
Preparation: Wash, chop, blanch to reduce bitter flavour.

✦ BRAISED WITLOF or CHICORY ✦

To serve 4: Fry 400 g prepared witlof with 2 tablespoons (30 g) chopped bacon for 3 minutes. Add 3 shakes pepper and 1 tablespoon (20 mL) water. Cover and simmer 2 minutes.

ZUCCHINI

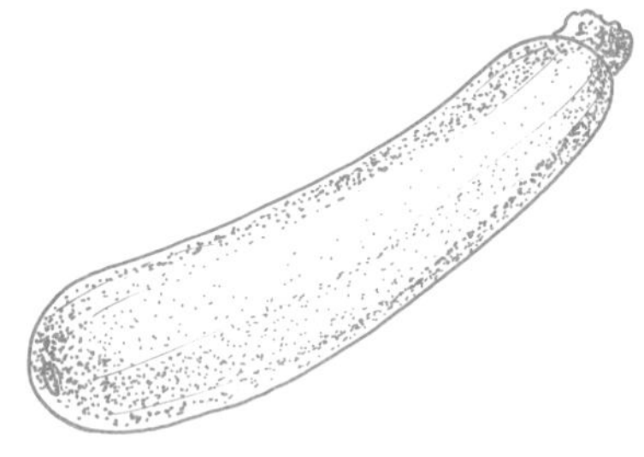

Description: Small green or golden marrow. May be called 'courgette'. The yellow flowers are used in salads and as a vegetable.
Uses include: Accompaniment, crudités, casseroles, entree, salads, soups, cakes.
Preparation: Wash, trim ends, may be sliced.

✦ BAKED ZUCCHINI ✦

To serve 4: Prepare 4 zucchini (400 g). Brush with butter and bake 30 minutes at 180°C. Serve.

✦ GRILLED ZUCCHINI ✦

To serve 4: Cut zucchini in half lengthwise, brush cut surface with butter and grill 5–10 minutes.

ZUCCHINI, CHINESE (CHIT KOU)

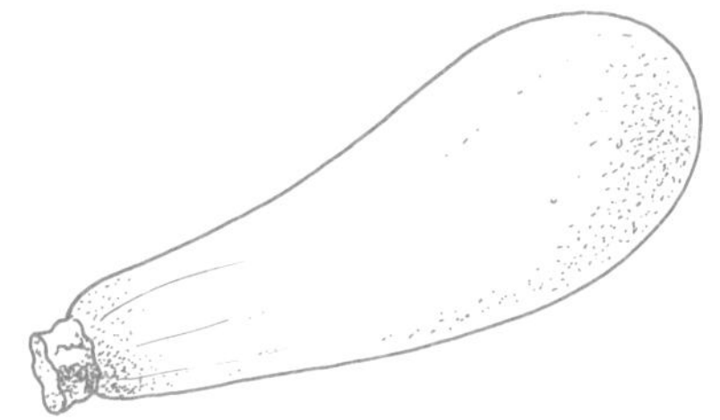

Description: Bright green skin.
Uses include: Steamed, boiled, stir-fry.
Preparation: Wash and slice.

10 Salads

A freshly prepared salad provides variety in colour, flavour and texture, adds interest to a menu and enhances the nutritive value of a meal.

Food Value

Salads made from raw vegetables and fruits provide vitamins, minerals and fibre. Salads containing meat, fish, eggs, cheese or legumes and soy bean products add protein. Oil-based salad dressings increase the fat content of the salad.

Preparation of salad ingredients

Blanched vegetables

Vegetables such as asparagus, cauliflower, broccoli, green beans, snow peas and zucchini may be placed in boiling water for 30 seconds to 1 minute, and then refreshed in iced water for 30 seconds. Blanching stops enzyme action and enhances the colour while still retaining the crispness of the vegetable.

Cooked vegetables

Vegetables such as beetroot, potato, pumpkin, parsnip and artichoke hearts may be prepared (see **Chapter 9 Vegetables**) and cooked to use in salads.

Avocado

The Hass variety has purple-black knobbly skin and a creamy texture. The Fuerte has smooth shiny green skin and a deeper green-yellow flesh. Cut in half lengthwise and twist to separate.

The stone may be lifted out with the point of a sharp knife. In some varieties the skin peels easily, or may be removed with a knife. The flesh may be sliced and served, or mashed and combined with other ingredients.

Beetroot

Wash, peel and grate. May be combined with **French dressing** (p. 266) and other salad ingredients.

Cabbage

Tender leaves may be finely shredded and served in **Coleslaw** (p. 270), or combined with other ingredients to form a variety of salads.

Capsicum or pepper

Cut off top, remove seeds and cut into rings or cut in half, remove seeds and cut into strips or dice finely. To enhance the flavour cut in half or quarters and place under a hot griller and brown. The skin is then easily removed if placed in a plastic bag for 10 minutes to steam.

Carrot

Peel, and using a vegetable peeler, slice thin, lengthwise strips from the carrot. Roll up the long strips and secure with a toothpick. Chill in ice-cold water for 30 minutes, remove toothpicks and serve. Carrot may be grated and combined with other ingredients.

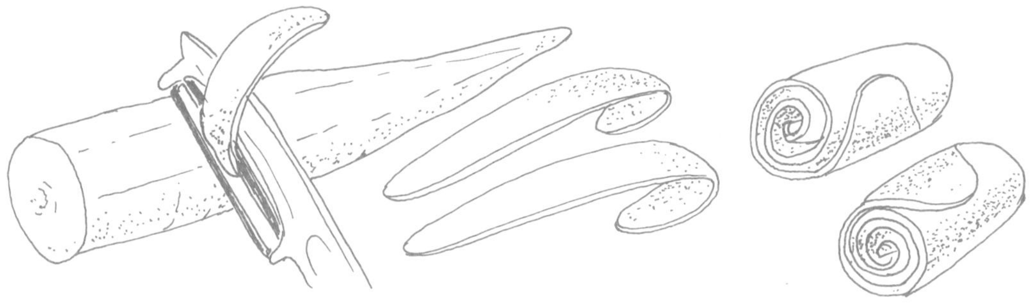

Celery

May be made into celery curls. Cut into 6 cm lengths, and then cut into thin parallel strips to within 2 cm of the end of each stick. The strips curl when placed in ice-cold water for about 30 minutes. Celery may be finely diced and combined with other ingredients.

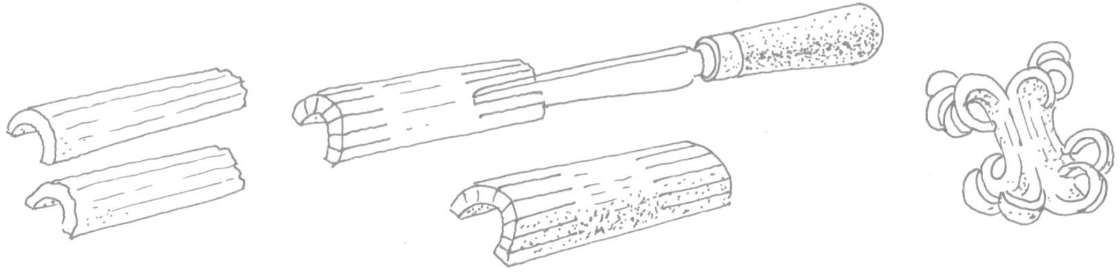

Cucumber

Score lengthwise with a fork and slice thinly. May be cut into small dice and combined with other ingredients.

Endive

Prepare and use in a similar manner to lettuce.

Fennel

Wash and slice thinly. Has a mild aniseed flavour.

Flowers

Marigold, nasturtium, viola pansies and violets are edible and add zest and colour to a green salad.

Garlic

This is used as a flavouring in salads. Peel a clove of garlic, cut in half and rub the cut edge around the inside of the salad bowl or for a more robust flavour chop finely and add to other ingredients.

Gherkin

Slice or dice finely. Gherkins may be cut into fancy shapes by slicing lengthwise into 3 cm strips, almost to the stem end. Spread into a fan, and press the uncut end lightly so that the fan holds its shape.

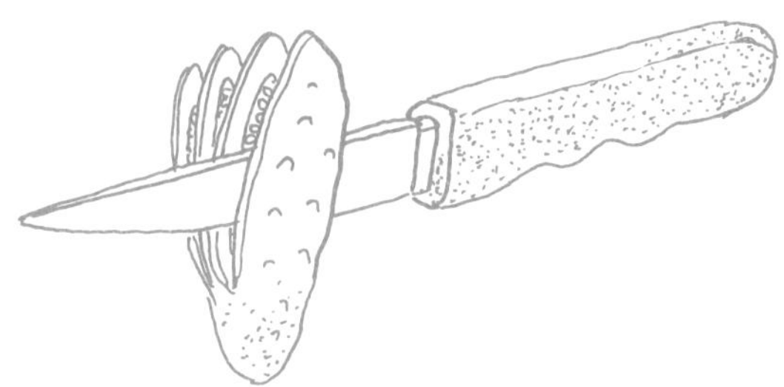

Lettuce

To prepare lettuce, remove outer leaves, cut out centre stem, run water into cavity, turn over and allow to drain, then refrigerate to chill. Lettuce may be finely shredded or it may be torn into neat pieces and tossed in **French dressing** (p. 266) or other salad dressing. Lettuce leaves may be used to line salad bowls, platters or individual plates. There are many types of lettuce, including: crisp, e.g. iceberg and frill-ice; soft, e.g. mignonette and butter; green and red varieties such as coral and oak leaf. Flavour varies from the slightly bitter taste of endive and radicchio to the sweet taste of cos and romano. A mixture of salad greens, which may include rocket, arugula, sorrell, mizuna, chicory or witlof, endive and edible flowers, is sold as mesclun or gourmet salad.

Mushroom

Wipe and use whole, sliced or chopped as required.

Onions

Red Spanish and white odourless onions may be diced or thinly sliced.

Parsley

Wash and chop, use as garnish or combine with other vegetables.

Radish, long

Trim root and stalk and cut into quarters, leaving 2 cm uncut at the stalk end. Place in ice-cold water for 30 minutes to open and curl slightly.

Radish, round

These may be cut into roses. Trim root and stalk, and using the tip of a vegetable knife mark six petals from root end to stalk. With the point of the knife gently lift the skin back to form petals, taking care to leave the petals joined at the stalk end. Place in ice-cold water for 30 minutes to open and curl slightly.

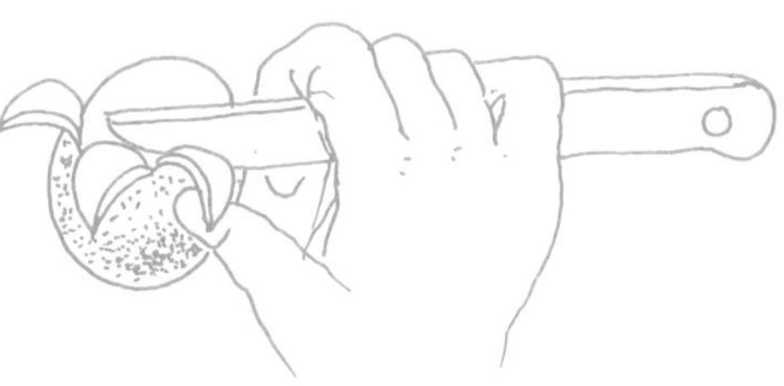

Rocket

A spicy-flavoured type of cress used in mixed salads.

Snow peas

Wash, remove string from both sides, serve whole or sliced. May be blanched.

Sprouting vegetables

Alfalfa, mung beans or fenugreek may be sprouted in about five days. Place one tablespoon of seeds in a sprouter or jar covered with gauze. Twice each day rinse water through the seeds. Leave in a warm place to sprout. Use as a garnish or combine with other vegetables.

Spinach

Wash, use whole or torn into small pieces. Sorrell is a variety of spinach that has a sharp lemon flavour.

Spring onion

Trim the green tops to within 4 cm of the white, and cut the remaining green section into parallel strips. These form curls when placed in ice-cold water for approximately 30 minutes. Spring onions may be finely sliced and combined with other ingredients.

Tomato

Remove stalk, and slice thinly crosswise, or cut into wedges. May be cut in a decorative manner, for example, Vandyke style, shown below. To do this, remove the stalk, and insert the point of a vegetable knife on a slant through the side of the tomato, into the centre. Insert the blade again on the opposite slant, forming a V with the previous cut. Cut completely around the tomato in this zigzag manner, and the halves should lift apart. Roma tomatoes can be semi-dried in the oven at 100°C for 4 hours. Cool and add to salads.

Cherry tomatoes may be used whole.

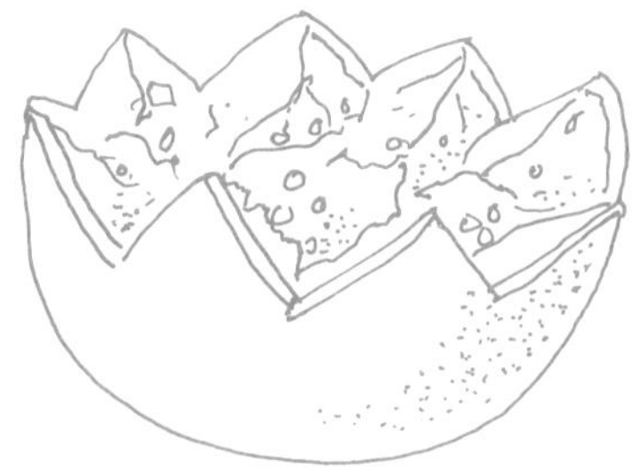

Watercress

Wash and dry. Use as a garnish.

Zucchini

Slice thinly or dice finely. The yellow flowers may also be used.

Salad dressings

Salad dressings add flavour and enhance the appearance of a salad. There is a wide variety of dressings from the rich egg and oil-based mayonnaise to the lighter vinegar and oil mixtures. The kilojoule value can be reduced by choosing a lower oil content dressing or a commercially prepared no-oil dressing. The amount of dressing to add to a salad depends on personal taste and the type of salad prepared. The guideline should be less rather than more dressing, with the option to add more at the table.

Dressings should be added to a salad immediately prior to serving to prevent the wilting of the salad greens.

Vinegar See p. 479.

Oils See p. 44.

Vinaigrette This is a mixture of vinegar and oil in the proportions of one part oil to one part vinegar. Crushed garlic, mustard or chopped herbs may be added.

QUICK SALAD DRESSING

Ingredients

1 tablespoon (20 g) mustard
1/2 teaspoon salt
1 can (400 g) condensed skim milk
3/4 cup (190 mL) vinegar

Method

1. Blend mustard, salt and condensed milk, gradually stir in vinegar.
2. Store in refrigerator. Use as required.

This is quickly and easily made in a food processor or blender.

Ingredients

2 egg yolks
1/4 teaspoon salt
3 shakes cayenne
1/2 teaspoon mustard
1/2 teaspoon sugar
3/4 cup (185 mL) light olive oil
2 tablespoons (40 mL) wine vinegar

Method

1. Place egg yolks in basin with flavourings and beat slightly.
2. Add oil a drop at a time, beating until thick and creamy.
3. Add vinegar a drop at a time, beating well. Extra vinegar *or* lemon juice can be added to obtain desired consistency.
4. Use as required. Will keep several weeks in refrigerator. Chopped herbs such as basil, chives, parsley *or* tarragon can be added just before use.

FRENCH DRESSING

Ingredients

1/2 cup (125 mL) olive *or* canola oil
1/2 cup (125 mL) wine vinegar, cider vinegar *or* herb vinegar
1/2 teaspoon salt
1 teaspoon grain mustard
1 teaspoon sugar
1 clove (5 g) garlic, chopped (optional)

Method

1. Combine all ingredients in a screw-top jar.
2. Add 1–2 tablespoons to salad just prior to serving.
3. Will keep several weeks in refrigerator.

YOGHURT DRESSING

Ingredients

1 cup (250 mL) natural yoghurt (low-fat yoghurt can be used to reduce fat content)
1 teaspoon lemon juice
½ teaspoon sugar
¼ teaspoon salt

Method

1. Combine all ingredients.
2. Add 1–2 tablespoons to salad just prior to serving.
3. Will keep 1–2 weeks in refrigerator.

✦ YOGHURT HORSERADISH DRESSING ✦

Follow recipe for **Yoghurt dressing**.
Add 1 tablespoon (20 g) horseradish cream *or* grated horseradish.

✦ YOGHURT GINGER DRESSING ✦

Follow recipe for **Yoghurt dressing**. Add 1 teaspoon chopped ginger *or* galangal and 1 tablespoon (20 g) chopped preserved ginger.

✦ FRUITY YOGHURT DRESSING ✦

Follow recipe for **Yoghurt dressing**. Add 2 tablespoons (40 g) fruit chutney.

✦ YOGHURT MUSTARD DRESSING ✦

Follow recipe for **Yoghurt dressing**. Add 1 tablespoon (40 g) French mustard.

✦ YOGHURT GREEN HERB DRESSING ✦

Follow recipe for **Yoghurt dressing**. Add 1 tablespoon chopped parsley and 2 teaspoons fresh lemon thyme.

BROAD BEAN AND TOASTED ALMOND SALAD

► *Serves:* 4

Ingredients

2 cups (240 g) cooked broad beans
2 tablespoons (40 mL) **Mayonnaise** (p. 266) *or* **French dressing** (p. 266)
2 tablespoons chopped chives *or* spring onions
1/2 cup (50 g) toasted *or* smoked almonds

Method

1 Combine broad beans and **Mayonnaise** *or* **French dressing**.
2 Add chives or spring onions and almonds, mix through. Place in salad bowl.
3 Chill and serve.

BROCCOLI SALAD

► *Serves:* 4

Ingredients

12 cherry tomatoes
2 cups (240 g) blanched broccoli florets
3 tablespoons (60 mL) **French dressing** (p. 266)

Method

1 Wash tomatoes.
2 Place broccoli in dish, arrange tomatoes around.
3 Add dressing, serve immediately in salad bowl.

CAESAR SALAD

► *Serves:* 4

Ingredients

4 slices bread, 2 cm thick
2 tablespoons (40 mL) olive oil
1 teaspoon (5 g) chopped garlic
1 cos lettuce
2 eggs, boiled 2 minutes
125 g parmesan cheese, shaved
12 anchovy fillets
juice of 1 lemon
3 shakes black pepper
1 tablespoon (20 mL) olive oil

► *Cooking utensil:* frying pan

Method

1 Cut bread into 2 cm dice. Heat oil in frying pan. Fry bread with garlic to make garlic croutons.
2 Wash lettuce and tear large leaves into pieces.
3 Chop eggs.
4 Place all ingredients in salad bowl and mix gently.

CHICKEN SALAD

► *Serves: 4*

Ingredients

2 cups (300 g) diced cooked chicken
2 stalks (200 g) celery, sliced
6 shakes pepper
1 tablespoon chopped parsley
1/4 cup (65 mL) light sour cream *or* **Yoghurt dressing** (p. 267)
1/3 cup (40 g) chopped toasted almonds

Method

1 Combine all ingredients except almonds. Mix well.
2 Chill and serve in salad bowl with almonds sprinkled on top.

✦ CHICKEN AND GREEN BEAN SALAD ✦

Follow recipe for **Chicken salad**. At step 1, add 1 cup (120 g) blanched sliced green beans.

✦ CHICKEN AND MANDARIN SALAD ✦

Follow recipe for **Chicken salad**. At step 1, add 1 can (240 g) drained mandarin segments. Garnish with 2 teaspoons (10 g) capers.

✦ CHICKEN AND MANGO SALAD ✦

Follow recipe for **Chicken salad**. At step 1, add 1 teaspoon curry paste and 1 peeled and diced mango.

CUCUMBER AND YOGHURT SALAD

► *Serves: 4*

Ingredients

1 cucumber (200 g)
1/2 teaspoon salt
3 shakes pepper
1/2 cup (125 mL) natural yoghurt
juice of 1/2 lemon
1 teaspoon chopped parsley *or* dill

Method

1 Wash cucumber and slice very finely.
2 Combine all ingredients, except parsley *or* dill.
3 Chill thoroughly.
4 Serve in salad bowl and sprinkle with parsley *or* dill.

COLESLAW

▶ *Serves:* 4

Ingredients

2 cups (200 g) finely shredded cabbage
1/2 cup (75 g) finely diced cucumber
1/2 cup (75 g) finely diced celery
1/4 cup (30 g) diced capsicum
1/4 teaspoon paprika
1 teaspoon mixed mustard
3 tablespoons (60 mL) mayonnaise
3 tablespoons (60 mL) **French dressing** (p. 266)

Method

1 Combine all ingredients.
2 Toss lightly and serve in salad bowl.

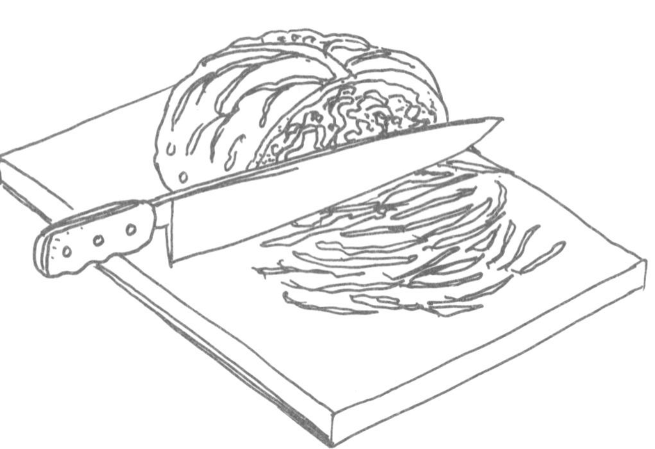

✦ TROPICAL COLESLAW ✦

Follow recipe for **Coleslaw**. Add one *or* more of: 1/2 cup (75 g) pineapple pieces, 1/2 cup (75 g) grated carrot, 1/2 cup (90 g) sultanas, 1/2 cup (75 g) diced apple, 1/2 cup (75 g) diced orange.

✦ RED COLESLAW ✦

Follow recipe for **Coleslaw**. Replace 1 cup (100 g) cabbage with 1 cup (100 g) red cabbage.

FRENCH SALAD

▶ *Serves:* 4

Ingredients

8 prepared lettuce leaves, e.g. iceberg, cos *or* butter lettuce
3 tablespoons (60 mL) **French dressing** (p. 266)
1/2 teaspoon finely chopped parsley

Method

1 Tear lettuce into small pieces and place in salad bowl.
2 Sprinkle with parsley and dressing.
3 Toss and serve immediately in salad bowl.

GADO GADO

- *Serves:* **6**
- *Cooking utensils:* 1 small and 1 large saucepan
- *Cooking time:* **20 minutes**

Ingredients

Peanut sauce

2 teaspoons (10 mL) oil
1 onion (125 g), finely chopped
1 clove (5 g) garlic, crushed
1 teaspoon chilli powder
1 teaspoon curry powder
1/2 cup (60 g) chopped peanuts
1/4 cup (65 mL) brown vinegar
2 tablespoons (40 g) peanut butter
1 cup (250 mL) water
2 teaspoons (10 mL) soy sauce

Vegetables

1 cup (100 g) bean shoots
1/2 cup (60 g) green beans, blanched
1 carrot (125 g), sliced and blanched
1 cucumber (200 g), sliced
1 cup (120 g) cauliflower florets, blanched
2 eggs, hard boiled and sliced

Method

1. Heat oil in small saucepan, add onion and garlic. Sauté for 2 minutes.
2. Add chilli and curry powder. Cook 1 minute.
3. Add peanuts, vinegar, peanut butter, water and soy sauce.
4. Bring to the boil, simmer 10 minutes. Allow to cool.
5. Prepare vegetables and place in groups on serving plate.
6. Serve with peanut sauce and sliced egg on top.

GREEK SALAD

- *Serves:* **6**

Ingredients

8 lettuce leaves, e.g. iceberg, endive *or* mizuna
1/2 red capsicum (60 g)
1/2 green capsicum (60 g)
1 white onion (125 g)
2 stalks (200 g) celery
2 tomatoes (250 g)
1/2 cucumber (100 g)
12 black olives
125 g fetta cheese
3 tablespoons (60 mL) **French dressing** (p. 266)

Method

1. Tear lettuce into small pieces and place in a bowl.
2. Slice capsicums, onion, celery, tomatoes and cucumber. Combine and add olives.
3. Just before serving, dice cheese and place on top of vegetables.
4. Add dressing. Serve immediately in salad bowl.

MEAT AND SALAD PLATTER

► *Serves:* 4

Ingredients

4 lettuce leaves, e.g. coral, oakleaf *or* iceberg
375 g cold cooked sliced meat, e.g. corned beef, salami, ham, pork, beef, pressed meats, chicken
selection of salad vegetables, e.g. vandyke tomatoes, radish roses, spring onion curls, celery curls, carrot strips, capsicum rings, gherkin fans

Method

1 Place lettuce leaves on a large platter and arrange meat on lettuce.
2 Arrange salad vegetables around the meat.
3 Mayonnaise and pickles may be served separately.

MUSHROOM SALAD

► *Serves:* 4

Ingredients

250 g mushrooms, e.g. enoki, oyster *or* shitake
1 cup chopped parsley
3 tablespoons (60 mL) **French dressing** (p. 266)

Method

1 Wipe mushrooms and cut into thin slices, except for enoki.
2 Combine mushrooms, parsley and dressing. Chill and serve in a salad bowl.

POTATO SALAD

► *Serves:* 4

► *Cooking utensil:* saucepan
Cooking time: ***15 minutes***

Ingredients

3 potatoes (450 g), e.g. pink eye, patrone, nicola *or* bintji
2 tablespoons chopped spring onions *or* chives
2 teaspoons chopped fresh mint *or* fresh basil
3 tablespoons (60 mL) **Mayonnaise** (p. 266)
2 tablespoons (40 mL) **French dressing** (p. 266)
4 lettuce leaves, e.g. cos *or* curly endive

Method

1 Scrub potatoes and cut into 1 cm dice.
2 Place in saucepan, cover with cold water and bring to boil. Turn off heat and allow to stand 5 minutes.
3 Drain and cool.
4 Add onions and mint to potatoes.
5 Mix **Mayonnaise** and **French dressing** and pour over to bind the vegetables. Chill.
6 Serve on lettuce leaves in salad bowl *or* platter.

MICROWAVE POTATO SALAD ✦

Follow recipe for **Potato salad**, cooking for 5 minutes on high power at step 2.

✦ CREAMY POTATO SALAD ✦

Follow recipe for **Potato Salad**. Omit mint and **Mayonnaise**. Add 3 tablespoons sour cream and 1 tablespoon grain mustard.

✦ ITALIAN POTATO SALAD ✦

Follow recipe for **Potato Salad**. Omit mint. Add 4 sliced stuffed olives and 1 clove (5 g) crushed garlic. Garnish with anchovy fillets *or* **Croutons** (p. 153).

✦ GOLD AND GREEN POTATO SALAD ✦

Follow recipe for **Potato salad**. Omit mint, add 130 g can corn kernels and 1/2 cup (60 g) chopped green capsicum.

NICOISE SALAD

► *Serves:* 6

► *Cooking utensil:* saucepan

Ingredients

1 1/2 cups (180 g) baby beans, tailed
500 g new potatoes
4 tomatoes, chopped
100 g baby spinach leaves
1 cos lettuce
100 g black olives
4 eggs, hard boiled and halved
185 g can Italian-style tuna, drained and broken into small chunks
1 tablespoon finely chopped flat-leaf parsley
1 tablespoon finely chopped basil
8 anchovy fillets in oil, drained and halved crosswise

Dressing

1/2 cup (125 mL) olive oil
1 tablespoon (20 mL) lemon juice
1 tablespoon (20 mL) red wine vinegar
1 clove (5 g) garlic, crushed

Method

1. For the dressing, combine all ingredients and whisk well.
2. Cook beans and potatoes separately in boiling water until just tender, drain and rinse under cold water.
3. Halve potatoes.
4. Place lettuce and spinach leaves on large platter and top with potato, beans, tomato, eggs, tuna and anchovies.
5. Sprinkle with parsley and basil and scatter olives.
6. Drizzle dressing over salad. Serve immediately in salad bowl or platter.

PASTA SALAD

Serves: 4

Cooking utensil: saucepan

Cooking time: **12 minutes**

Ingredients

1 cup (100 g) pasta
125 g ham
1 stalk (100 g) celery, diced
2 spring onions, sliced
3 tablespoons (60 mL) mayonnaise
1/2 teaspoon prepared horseradish
3 shakes pepper
4 lettuce leaves, e.g. red oakleaf, cos
1 tomato (125 g)
1/2 capsicum (60 g)

Method

1. Cook pasta in boiling, salted water 12 minutes. Strain and rinse.
2. Cut ham into julienne strips.
3. Combine pasta, ham, celery, onion, mayonnaise, horseradish, gherkin and pepper.
4. Chill and place mixture into lettuce leaves in salad bowl *or* platter. Garnish with tomato wedges and finely sliced capsicum and serve.

RICE AND EGG SALAD

Serves: 4

Cooking utensil: saucepan

Cooking time: **12 minutes** *white rice*
45 minutes *brown rice*

Ingredients

1/2 cup (100 g) jasmine, basmati *or* brown rice
2 eggs, hard boiled and chopped
2 spring onions, sliced
1 stalk (100 g) celery, diced
1/2 capsicum (60 g), diced
1/4 cup (40 g) grated carrot
2 tablespoons (40 mL) **French dressing** (p. 266)
3 tablespoons (60 mL) **Quick salad dressing** (p. 266) *or* **Yoghurt dressing** (p. 267).

Method

1. Cook rice in boiling salted water.
2. Combine all ingredients and mix lightly. Chill well and serve in salad bowl *or* platter.

FRUIT AND NUT RICE SALAD

Follow recipe for **Rice and egg salad**. Omit egg. Add 1/2 cup (90 g) sultanas, 1/3 cup (40 g) pine nuts and 2 teaspoons chopped preserved ginger. Garnish with 1 tablespoon (15 g) chopped walnuts.

SUMMER SALAD

Serves: 4

Ingredients

$^{1}/_{2}$ cup (50 g) sultana grapes
$^{1}/_{2}$ cup (75 g) orange *or* mandarin segments
$^{1}/_{2}$ cup (50 g) bean sprouts *or* alfalfa
$^{1}/_{2}$ cup (75 g) diced cucumber
$^{1}/_{2}$ cup (75 g) diced celery
1 avocado, sliced
1 cup (100 g) sliced snow peas
3 tablespoons (60 mL) **French Dressing** (p. 266)
$^{1}/_{4}$ cup (25 g) toasted almonds

Method

1. Combine fruits and vegetables.
2. Pour dressing over just before serving in salad bowl.
3. Garnish with toasted almonds.

TABOULI

Serves: 4

Ingredients

$^{1}/_{2}$ cup (45 g) burghul *or* cracked wheat
1 cup (250 mL) boiling water
2 cups chopped parsley
2 tomatoes (250 g), diced
2 cloves (10 g) garlic, crushed
2 tablespoons chopped mint
$^{1}/_{2}$ cup (75 g) spring onion, sliced
2 tablespoons (40 mL) lemon juice
2 tablespoons (40 mL) oil
$^{1}/_{2}$ teaspoon salt
6 lettuce leaves, e.g. iceberg, rocket *or* green oakleaf

Method

1. Wash burghul and place in the boiling water for 5 minutes. Drain.
2. Combine burghul with prepared vegetables.
3. Mix lemon juice, oil and salt and stir through burghul mixture.
4. Serve in lettuce leaves in salad bowl.

THAI SALAD WITH HERB CROUTONS

► *Serves:* 4

► *Cooking utensil:* frying pan, griller

Ingredients

2 small bok choy, chopped
1/2 yellow capsicum, cut into julienne strips
1/2 red capsicum, cut into julienne strips
1/2 cup (40 g) mung beans
1/2 cup (40 g) bean sprouts
1/2 zucchini, grated
1 tablespoon chopped coriander

Dressing

1/2 cup (65 mL) coconut cream
2 teaspoons lime juice
1/4 teaspoon sesame oil
1/4 teaspoon honey
1/4 teaspoon fish sauce

Croutons

1 slice bread, toasted on one side
1 teaspoon chopped coriander
1 teaspoon sesame seeds
1 teaspoon butter, softened

Method

1. To make dressing: shake all ingredients together in a screw-top jar.
2. To make croutons: combine coriander, sesame seeds and butter. Spread mixture on untoasted side of bread. Toast under a griller. Cut into cubes.
3. Combine vegetables and dressing in salad bowl.
4. Sprinkle croutons over salad and toss.

TOMATO AND CHEESE SALAD

► *Serves:* 4

Ingredients

4 lettuce leaves, e.g. green oak leaf *or* butter lettuce
2 firm tomatoes (250 g)
2 spring onions
125 g cheddar cheese
2 tablespoons (40 mL) **French dressing** (p. 266)
1 teaspoon chopped parsley

Method

1. Line bowl *or* platter with lettuce leaves.
2. Cut tomatoes into 1 cm dice. Slice spring onion. Cut cheese into 1 cm dice. Combine with dressing.
3. Spoon into lettuce leaves, sprinkle with parsley and serve in salad bowl *or* platter.

TOMATO AND MINT SALAD

► *Serves:* 6

Ingredients
4 tomatoes (500 g)
6 spring onions, chopped
1/2 cup chopped mint
juice and zest of 2 limes
2 teaspoons (10 g) sugar
1/4 chilli, finely chopped

Method
1 Combine all ingredients.
2 Serve in salad bowl.

TOMATO, ONION AND CUCUMBER SALAD

► *Serves:* 4

Ingredients
2 tomatoes (250 g)
1 cucumber (200 g)
1/2 white onion (65 g)
1/4 teaspoon salt
3 shakes pepper
1 teaspoon sugar
1 tablespoon (20 mL) malt vinegar
1 teaspoon chopped parsley

Method
1 Wash tomatoes and cut thinly.
2 Peel, score and cut cucumber thinly.
3 Remove skin and cut onion thinly.
4 Arrange tomatoes, onion and cucumber in layers in salad bowl, sprinkling with salt, pepper and sugar.
5 Pour vinegar over and serve garnished with parsley.

TORTELLINI SALAD

► *Serves:* 6

► *Cooking utensil:* saucepan
Cooking time: ***12 minutes***

Ingredients
500 g tortellini
2 red capsicums (250 g)
1/2 cup (75 g) sun-dried tomatoes
340 g can artichoke hearts
4 spring onions, chopped
1/4 cup basil leaves
1 tablespoon (20 mL) lemon juice
2 teaspoons (10 g) grain mustard
1 tablespoon (20 mL) balsamic vinegar
1/4 cup (65 mL) olive oil
6 shakes pepper

Method
1 Cook tortellini in boiling salted water for 12 minutes. Drain and refrigerate for 1 hour.
2 Slice capsicums thinly. Blanch and drain.
3 Add capsicum, tomatoes, artichoke hearts and onions to tortellini.
4 Chop basil leaves and mix with lemon juice, vinegar and mustard *or* mix all in blender, adding oil slowly.
5 Pour over salad and serve in salad bowl.

TOSSED GREEN SALAD

Serves: 4

Ingredients

1 clove (5 g) garlic
200 g mesclun *or* salad mix
1/2 cucumber (100 g)
2 spring onions
1 stalk (100 g) celery
1/2 capsicum (60 g)
2 radishes
3 tablespoons (60 mL) **French dressing** (p. 266)
1 tomato (125 g)
2 teaspoons chopped parsley

Method

1 Cut garlic and rub over inside of salad bowl. Discard garlic.
2 Tear lettuce into small pieces and place in bowl.
3 Finely slice cucumber, onions, celery, capsicum and radishes. Add to bowl.
4 Sprinkle with dressing and toss lightly.
5 Garnish with tomato wedges and chopped parsley. Serve immediately.

WALDORF SALAD

Serves: 4

Ingredients

1 green apple (150 g)
1 red apple (150 g)
1 cup (150 g) finely diced celery
2 tablespoons (40 mL) mayonnaise
2 tablespoons (30 g) walnut *or* pecan pieces
4 lettuce leaves, e.g. radicchio *or* frill ice

Method

1 Core and cut apples into 1 cm dice *or* fine slices.
2 Combine with mayonnaise and celery.
3 Spoon into lettuce leaves, garnish with walnut *or* pecan pieces.
4 Serve immediately in salad bowl *or* platter.

WARM CHICKEN SALAD

Serves: **4**

Cooking utensil: frying pan
Cooking time: ***10 minutes***

Ingredients

2 chicken breasts (400 g), cut into strips
1 tablespoon (20 g) green curry paste
2 red capsicums (250 g), sliced into thin strips
2 cups (200 g) snow peas
1 1/2 cups (180 g) broccoli florets
1 1/4 cups (150 g) green beans, cut in 5 cm lengths
1/2 cup (125 mL) stock
1 teaspoon (5 g) chopped ginger
4 coriander sprigs

Method

1. Coat chicken in green curry paste. Marinate for 2 hours *or* microwave on defrost for 2 minutes.
2. Blanch capsicum, snow peas, broccoli and green beans.
3. Fry chicken in frying pan until brown (approximately 5 minutes). Remove from pan and cool.
4. Add stock and ginger to the pan and boil for 3 minutes to reduce the liquid.
5. Arrange the vegetables on platter and place the chicken on top. Pour the warm liquid over and serve garnished with coriander.

WARM BEEF SALAD

Follow recipe for **Warm chicken salad**. Replace chicken with 400 g rump steak. Grill steak, in one piece, until rare. Cool 10 minutes and slice thinly. Serve as for chicken.

WARM POTATO SALAD

Serves: **4**

Cooking utensil: saucepan
Cooking time: ***10 minutes***

Ingredients:

2 potatoes (300 g), pink eye, patrone, nicola *or* bintji
1 rasher (40 g) bacon, diced
1 stalk (100 g) celery, sliced
1 white onion (125 g), sliced finely
1/2 red capsicum (60 g), sliced
1 tablespoon chopped parsley
2 tablespoons (40 mL) natural yoghurt *or* light sour cream
3 shakes pepper

Method

1. Scrub potatoes, cut into 1 cm dice. Place in cold water in saucepan and bring to boil. Remove from heat, allow to stand 5 minutes. Drain, keep warm.
2. Fry bacon lightly.
3. Place potato, bacon, vegetables and parsley in a warm dish.
4. Combine yoghurt *or* sour cream and pepper and pour over vegetables.

ZUCCHINI SALAD

Serves: 4

Ingredients

2 zucchini (200 g), sliced
1 clove (5 g) garlic, crushed
1/4 teaspoon salt
3 shakes cayenne
1/4 cup (65 mL) sour cream *or* natural yoghurt

Method

1 Blanch zucchini. Strain and cool.
2 Combine all ingredients and chill.
3 Serve in salad bowl.

ZUCCHINI AND APPLE SALAD

Follow recipe for **Zucchini salad**. Add 1 apple (150 g), cored and cut into thin slices at step 2.

VIETNAMESE COLESLAW

Serves: 4

Ingredients

2 cups (200 g) finely shredded cabbage
1/4 cup chopped Vietnamese mint
1/4 cup (40 g) chopped peanuts
1 cup (200 g) finely sliced rare beef *or* cooked chicken
juice and zest of 2 limes
1 teaspoon (5 g) sugar
1/4 teaspoon (5 g) garlic
3 shakes pepper
1/2 teaspoon salt

Method

1 Mix all ingredients thoroughly in salad bowl.

11 Sauces

Sauces add flavour and colour to sweet and savoury dishes. They moisten dry ingredients, for example, custard sauce with steamed puddings, and add flavour to foods, for example, mint sauce with roast lamb.

Thickening agents

Roux Consists of flour and melted fat (butter, margarine, dairy blend or oil) blended to a smooth paste and then cooked over a low heat to burst the starch grains, e.g. **White sauce**.

Starch A starch, such as cornflour, mixed to a paste with a small amount of liquid (blending) before being combined with the rest of the liquid, e.g. **Sweet cornflour sauce**.

Egg yolk May be used in cooked sauce, as in **Custard sauce**, or in an uncooked sauce such as **Mayonnaise**.

Butter May be melted to combine with other ingredients, e.g. **Hollandaise sauce**, or used without melting, as in **Brandy sauce**.

Beurre manié A butter paste used to thicken sauces and gravies when the consistency needs adjusting after cooking has finished. Blend 3 tablespoons (60 g) butter with 3 tablespoons (30 g) plain flour. Store in a covered jar in refrigerator. To use: add $^1/_2$ teaspoon at a time, stir until melted and reheat after each addition to cook the starch.

Savoury sauces

WHITE SAUCE

This is a basic white sauce that can be used with additional flavourings.

Serves: 4

Ingredients

1 tablespoon (20 g) butter
$1^1/_2$ tablespoons (15 g) plain flour
1 cup (250 mL) milk
$^1/_2$ teaspoon salt
6 shakes white pepper

Cooking utensil: small saucepan

Method

1. Melt butter in small saucepan and remove from heat.
2. Add flour. Stir with a wooden spoon.
3. Cook slowly for 30 seconds, stirring continuously. Do not allow to brown. Remove from heat. (This cooked butter/flour mixture is called a 'roux'.)
4. Add the liquid gradually and stir until smooth.
5. Return to heat and stir until boiling. Reduce heat and stir 1 minute.
6. Flavour and use as required.

Melt butter, add flour. Cook on medium power for 30 seconds. Add milk gradually, stirring continuously. Cook on high power for 1 minute. Stir. Cook for further $1^1/_2$ minutes, add other ingredients and cook for further 30 seconds.

CHEESE SAUCE

Follow recipe for **White sauce**. Add 3 tablespoons (30 g) grated tasty cheese and $^1/_4$ teaspoon mustard after adding milk.

CURRY SAUCE

Follow recipe for **White sauce**. Add 1 teaspoon curry paste and $^1/_2$ teaspoon lemon juice. Fry curry paste in butter when making roux.

✦ MUSTARD SAUCE ✦

Follow recipe for **White sauce**. Add 1 teaspoon mustard, 1 tablespoon (20 mL) vinegar and 1 teaspoon sugar after adding milk.

✦ ONION SAUCE ✦

Follow recipe for **White sauce**. Sauté $^{1}/_{4}$ diced onion (30 g) in 1 teaspoon butter for 2 minutes, add with 1 tablespoon chopped parsley after adding milk.

✦ PARSLEY SAUCE ✦

Follow recipe for **White sauce**. Add 1 tablespoon chopped parsley.

✦ THICK WHITE SAUCE ✦

Follow recipe for **White sauce** using 2 tablespoons (40 g) butter and 3 tablespoons (30 g) plain flour.

✦ BECHAMEL SAUCE ✦

Follow recipe for **White sauce**, replacing half the milk with vegetable cooking liquid *or* stock.

CORNFLOUR SAUCE

► *Serves:* 4

Ingredients

$1^{1}/_{2}$ tablespoons (15 g) cornflour
1 cup (250 mL) milk
$^{1}/_{2}$ teaspoon salt
3 shakes pepper

► *Cooking utensil:* saucepan

Method

1. Blend cornflour with $^{1}/_{4}$ cup of milk.
2. Heat remainder of milk in small saucepan until almost boiling.
3. Pour over the blended cornflour, stirring with a wooden spoon.
4. Return to saucepan. Stir over heat until boiling, reduce heat and simmer 30 seconds.
5. Add salt and pepper.

Blend cornflour with milk, cook on high power for 1 minute. Stir and cook for further 1 minute on high power. Stir again and cook for further 1 minute. Add salt and pepper.

BROWN SAUCE

This basic brown sauce can be flavoured and used with savoury dishes.

Serves: 4

Ingredients

2 tablespoons (40 g) butter
1 onion (125 g), diced
2 tablespoons (20 g) plain flour
1 cup (250 mL) stock *or* water
1 teaspoon Worcestershire sauce

Cooking utensil: small saucepan

Method

1. Using a small saucepan, fry onion in butter until light brown.
2. Add flour and stir with wooden spoon, cooking until mixture is light brown.
3. Remove from heat. Add the liquid gradually, stirring continuously.
4. Return to heat and stir until boiling. Add remaining ingredients, reduce heat and simmer 1 minute.
5. Flavour and use as required.

BARBECUE SAUCE

Follow recipe for **Brown sauce**. Add 1 clove (5 g) crushed garlic with onion at step 1. Add 1 tablespoon (20 mL) vinegar, 1 teaspoon grain mustard and 1 teaspoon brown sugar at step 3.

MUSHROOM SAUCE

Follow recipe for **Brown sauce**. Add $^1/_2$ cup (50 g) chopped and sautéed mushrooms *or* 200 g can mushrooms in butter sauce.

ONION SAUCE

Follow recipe for **Brown sauce**. Use 1 extra diced onion (125 g).

ESPAGNOLE SAUCE

Serves: 4

Cooking utensil: saucepan

Ingredients

2 tablespoons (40 g) butter
2 tablespoons (20 g) plain flour
$1\frac{1}{2}$ cups (375 mL) stock
$\frac{1}{2}$ cup (75 g) chopped carrot
1 onion (125 g), chopped
bouquet garni (p. 487)
1 tablespoon (20 g) tomato paste
1 tablespoon (15 g) chopped bacon
2 shakes pepper

Method

1. Melt butter, add flour.
2. Stir with wooden spoon until light brown.
3. Remove from heat. Add stock gradually, stirring continuously.
4. Return to heat, stir until boiling. Add remaining ingredients, reduce heat and simmer 30 minutes.
5. Strain through sieve, reheat, flavour and use as required.

FRESH TOMATO SAUCE

A quickly made tomato sauce to serve with meat, fish and pasta dishes.

Serves: 4

Cooking utensil: saucepan

Ingredients

1 tablespoon (20 g) butter
1 onion (125 g), chopped
1 clove (5 g) garlic, chopped
4 tomatoes (500 g)
1 tablespoon chopped basil *or* parsley
6 shakes black pepper

Method

1. Melt butter, fry onion and garlic lightly in saucepan.
2. Remove skin from tomatoes and dice.
3. Add tomatoes, basil *or* parsley and pepper, simmer 15 minutes.

TARTARE SAUCE

A tasty sauce to serve with grilled and fried fish dishes.

Serves: 4

Ingredients

$\frac{1}{2}$ cup (125 mL) **Mayonnaise** (p. 266)
1 teaspoon vinegar
1 teaspoon chopped gherkins
1 teaspoon chopped capers
1 teaspoon chopped parsley

Method

1. Combine all ingredients.
2. Serve with fish, as required.

HOLLANDAISE SAUCE

A sharp, buttery sauce to serve with vegetables such as asparagus and green beans.

Serves: 4

Ingredients

1/4 cup (65 g) butter
2 egg yolks, beaten
1 tablespoon (20 mL) lemon juice
2 teaspoons water
1/4 teaspoon salt
3 shakes pepper

Cooking utensil: double saucepan

Method

1 Melt butter in top of double saucepan over simmering water in base.
2 Allow butter to cool then mix in egg yolks, lemon juice, water, salt and pepper.
3 Place over simmering water and stir with a wooden spoon until thickened.

Melt butter on medium power for 30 seconds, mix in other ingredients. Cook for 30 seconds on medium power, stir, cook for further 30 seconds.

BEARNAISE SAUCE

A sharp, buttery sauce to serve with grilled meat and fish.

Serves: 4

Ingredients

1 quantity **Hollandaise sauce** (see above)
4 spring onions, finely chopped
1 teaspoon chopped fresh tarragon

Cooking utensil: double saucepan

Method

1 Mix all ingredients.

Sweet sauces

CUSTARD SAUCE

► *Serves:* 4

► *Cooking utensil:* double saucepan

Ingredients

1 cup (250 mL) milk
2 eggs *or* 3 egg yolks
1 tablespoon (20 g) sugar
1/4 teaspoon vanilla

Method

1. Warm milk in top of double saucepan. Remove from heat.
2. Mix eggs and sugar and add to warmed milk.
3. Return to heat and cook over simmering water, stirring with a wooden spoon until the mixture coats the back of the spoon.
4. Remove from heat, add sugar and vanilla.

Note: If sauce curdles, remove from heat at once, pour into cold basin and beat well with a whisk or beater.

CUSTARD POWDER SAUCE

► *Serves:* 4

► *Cooking utensil:* small saucepan

Ingredients

1 1/2 tablespoons (15 g) custard powder
1 cup (250 mL) milk
1 egg, beaten (optional)
1 tablespoon (20 g) sugar

Method

1. Blend custard powder with 1/4 cup of milk.
2. Heat remainder of milk in small saucepan until almost boiling.
3. Pour over the blended custard powder, stirring with a wooden spoon.
4. Return to saucepan. Stir over heat until boiling, reduce heat and simmer 30 seconds.
5. Stir in egg and sugar.

Blend custard powder with milk, cook on high power for 1 minute. Stir and cook for further 1 minute on high power. Stir again and cook for further 1 minute or until boiling. Add egg and sugar.

CHOCOLATE SAUCE

Serves: 4–6

Cooking utensil: saucepan

Ingredients

$^1/_2$ cup (55 g) cocoa
$^1/_2$ cup (125 g) sugar
1 cup (250 mL) water
1 tablespoon (20 g) butter

Method

1 Blend cocoa, sugar and water to a paste in small saucepan. Stir until boiling, simmer 3 minutes.
2 Add butter, stir until blended, bring to boil again. Simmer 4 minutes.
3 Serve hot or cold. Will keep well in refrigerator.

Blend cocoa and water, cook on medium power for 30 seconds. Stir. Cook for further 1 minute on high power, add sugar and butter. Cook for further 1 minute on high power.

FRUIT SAUCE

Serves: 4

Cooking utensil: small saucepan

Ingredients

1 tablespoon (10 g) arrowroot
$^1/_2$ cup (125 mL) water
$^1/_2$ cup (125 mL) fruit juice *or* pureed fruit
1 tablespoon (20 mL) lemon juice
1 tablespoon (20 g) sugar

Method

1 In small saucepan blend arrowroot with water.
2 Add fruit juice *or* fruit and lemon juice, bring to the boil, stirring continuously. Simmer 30 seconds.
3 Reheat, add sugar to taste.

Blend arrowroot with water, cook on medium power 30 seconds. Stir. Cook further 1 minute on high power. Add other ingredients. Reheat for 10 seconds.

✦ PASSIONFRUIT SAUCE ✦

Follow recipe for **Fruit sauce** using pulp and juice of 2 passionfruit.

✦ ORANGE FRUIT SAUCE ✦

Follow recipe for **Fruit sauce** using $^1/_2$ cup (125 mL) orange juice and 2 teaspoons grated orange rind.

✦ LEMON FRUIT SAUCE ✦

Follow recipe for **Fruit sauce**. Use extra 1/4 cup (65 mL) water, 1/4 cup (65 mL) lemon juice and 1 teaspoon grated lemon rind.

✦ JAM SAUCE ✦

Follow recipe for **Fruit sauce**. Use extra 1/2 cup (125 mL) water and replace fruit juice and sugar with 3 tablespoons (60 g) jam.

CONFECTIONERS' CUSTARD

A filling for tarts and profiteroles. For meringue-topped dishes use 2 egg yolks in custard and 2 egg whites in meringue.

► *Serves:* 4

Ingredients

2 tablespoons (40 g) butter
1/4 cup (40 g) plain flour
3/4 cup (190 mL) milk
2 egg yolks *or* 1 egg, beaten
1 tablespoon (20 g) sugar
1/2 teaspoon vanilla

► *Cooking utensil:* saucepan

Method

1 Melt butter in saucepan, add flour, stir until smooth.
2 Add milk, stir until boiling, cook 1 minute, cool slightly.
3 Add egg, beat well. Add sugar and vanilla. Cool.

CARAMEL SAUCE

► *Serves:* 4

Ingredients

1/4 cup (60 g) butter
1 cup (200 g) brown sugar
1 tablespoon (20 mL) golden syrup
1/3 cup (85 mL) evaporated milk
1/4 teaspoon vanilla

► *Cooking utensil:* small saucepan

Method

1 Combine all ingredients except vanilla in small saucepan and bring slowly to boil, stirring continuously. Simmer for 1 minute.
2 Allow to cool, add vanilla and use as required.

STRAWBERRY COULIS

Serves: 6

Cooking utensil: saucepan

Ingredients

1 punnet (250 g) strawberries
1 tablespoon (20 mL) water
2 tablespoons (40 g) sugar

Method

1 Warm strawberries and water in saucepan, stirring all the time. Bring to boil, immediately remove from heat.
2 Add sugar.
3 Push through sieve, cool and serve.

MANGO COULIS

Use 250 g sliced mango instead of strawberries.

CINNAMON HONEY CREAM

Delicious served with stewed fruit.

Serves: 4

Ingredients

1/2 cup (125 mL) cream, whipped
1/2 cup (125 mL) natural yoghurt
1 tablespoon (20 g) honey
1/2 teaspoon cinnamon

Method

1 Fold cream into yoghurt, add honey and cinnamon, mix until blended.

12 Desserts and fruits

Hot and cold desserts are traditionally served after the main course of a dinner or a formal lunch. Because of changing lifestyles, many people only serve desserts on special occasions. Select a dessert that complements the previous courses and provides contrast in colour, texture and flavour.

Fruit is often served as the final course of a meal and in Australia we are fortunate to have a wide selection of local, tropical and bush fruits available all year round. (For a listing of Australian bush fruits, see **Chapter 2 Ingredients and equipment**.)

Food value

Fresh fruit and fruit-based desserts are comparatively high in fibre, vitamins and minerals and may be low in fat if not made with pastry. Desserts that are high in carbohydrates, such as steamed and baked puddings, may be made with wholemeal flour to increase the fibre content.

Low-fat desserts can be made with fat-reduced dairy products such as cottage or ricotta cheese instead of cream cheese, and low-fat yoghurt can be used instead of cream or ice-cream. These desserts are good sources of calcium and protein. Desserts made with fruit contain fructose, a sugar, and many desserts have added sugar.

Fruits

ABIUS

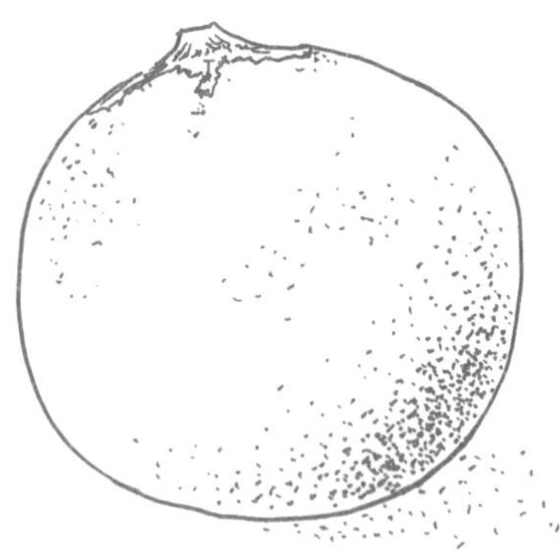

Description: Tropical fruit about the size of a small apple with bright yellow glossy skin.
Uses include: Eat fresh by removing the seeds and spooning out the flesh, use in fruit salads and puree in drinks.

APPLE

Description: A core surrounded by crisp, juicy white flesh. The skin may vary between red, green or yellow according to the variety. Apples are picked between February and May for most varieties but are available all year round with the use of controlled-atmosphere storage.

Varieties

Granny Smith

Description: Bright green in colour, firm and juicy, from sweet to tart in taste.
Uses include: Use for cooking, eating fresh, juicing, canning and drying.

Jonathon

Description: Bright to a dull-deep red, white, juicy flesh, crisp and fragrant.
Uses include: Choice eating fresh.

Delicious

Description: Red or golden in colour, mildly aromatic and sweet. The five bumps around the base distinguish it from other varieties.
Uses include: Excellent for eating fresh but not generally used for cooking.

Fuji

Description: Round and red with a crisp texture and sweet flavour.
Uses include: Eat fresh, suitable to serve with cheese due to its crispness. Texture is maintained after cooking.

Pink Lady

Description: Golden colour with streaks of red, crisp texture.
Uses include: Excellent for eating fresh.

Bonza

Description: Red skin with a crisp texture and exceptional keeping qualities.
Uses include: Excellent for eating fresh.

APRICOT

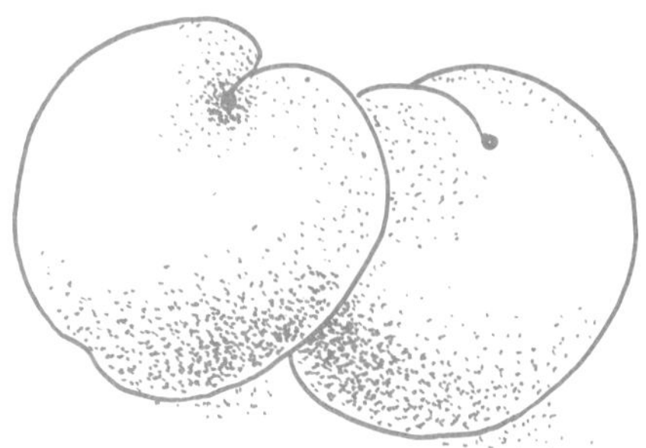

Description: Fleshy one-seed stone fruit, pale orange colour.
Uses include: Eat fresh, or may be stewed, poached, dried or brandied. Use in cakes, desserts, pastries, chutneys and jams.

BANANA

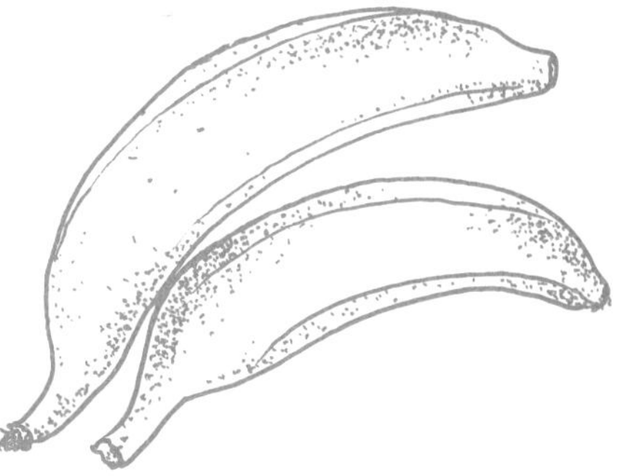

Description: Green (starchy taste) ripening to yellow (sweet taste). The lady finger or sugar banana has a sweeter flavour than common varieties.
Uses include: Eat fresh, or use in cakes, desserts and fruit salads. May be baked, fried, poached, grilled or dried. Serve as an accompaniment to curry.

BLACKBERRY

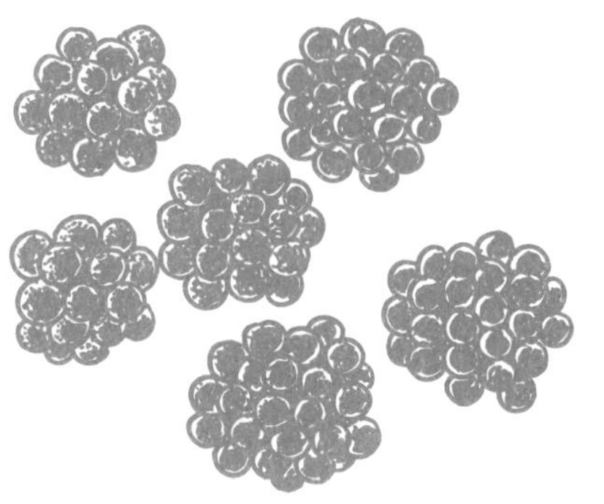

Description: A shiny black fruit made up of a collection of drupelets.
Uses include: Eat fresh, use in jams, cakes and desserts.

BLACKCURRANT

Description: Very small juicy black berries.
Uses include: Eat fresh, use in cheese platters, fruit salads, pies, tarts and jellies. May be served as a sauce with meats and desserts. Juice used as a drink.

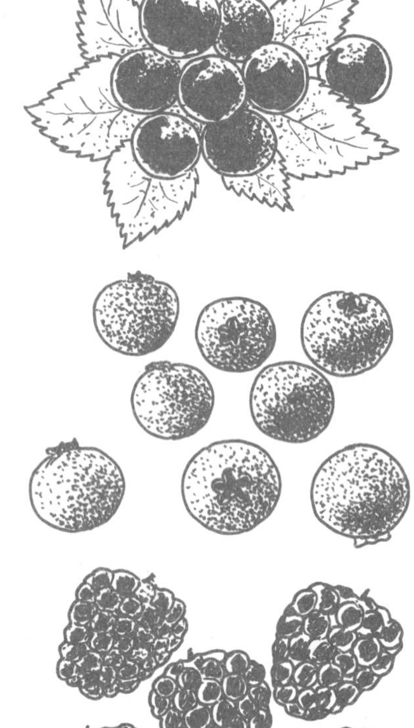

BLUEBERRY

Description: Small, spherical, smooth-skinned blue-black fruit.
Uses include: Eat fresh, use in cakes, pies, desserts, jams and muffins.

BOYSENBERRY

Description: A cross between a blackberry and a raspberry.
Uses include: Eat fresh, use in cakes, pies, desserts and jams.

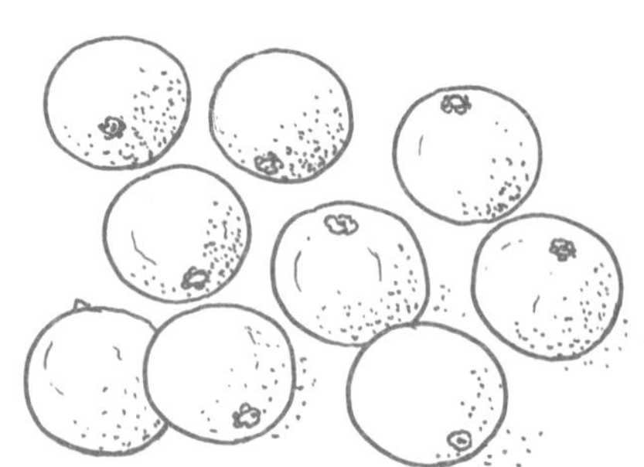

CAPE GOOSEBERRY

Description: Fruit is contained in a papery husk with one fruit inside each shell – ripe fruit is a greenish yellow and has a slight cherry taste.
Uses include: Eat fresh, use in jams and preserves.

CARAMBOLA (STAR FRUIT or FIVE CORNER FRUIT)

Description: Five-angled fruit with a star shape in cross section with a waxy yellow skin.
Uses include: Eat fresh, use in jams, jellies and fruit salads. An attractive garnish when sliced.

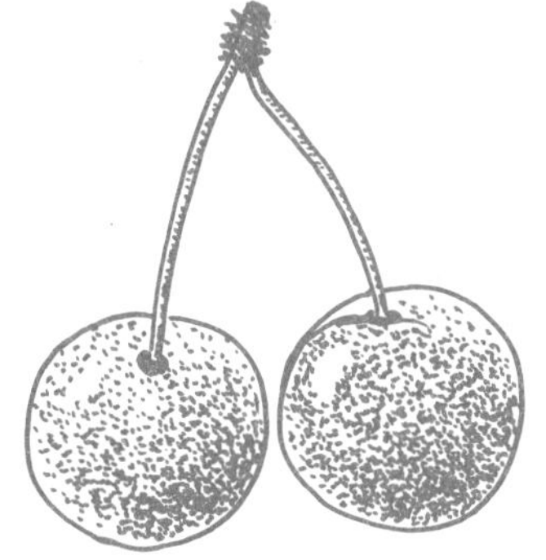

 CHERRIES

Description: Shiny fruit formed in clusters, bright red in colour, ripening to a deep-red colour.
Uses include: Eat fresh, may be canned, stewed, brandied. Use in fruit salad, cakes, desserts. Glacé cherries are used as a garnish.

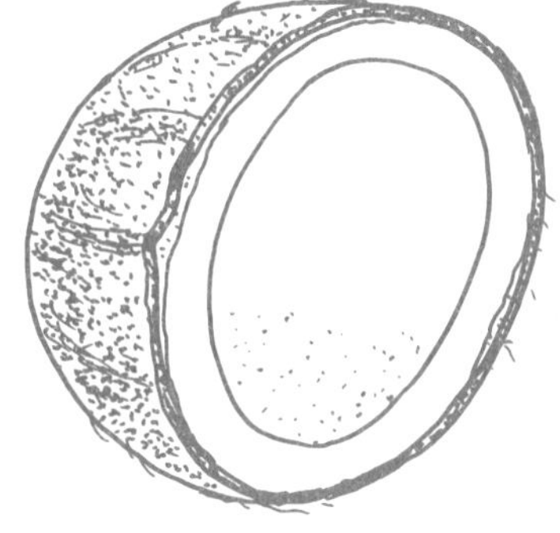

 COCONUT

Description: Fruit of the coconut palm: the large fruit is covered by a thick layer of fibrous husks, inside the husk is a thin white fleshy layer ('meat') and the hollow is filled with liquid.
Uses include: Can be dried, desiccated, shredded, flaked and cubed. Use in cakes, biscuits, curries, ice-cream, desserts, confectionery.

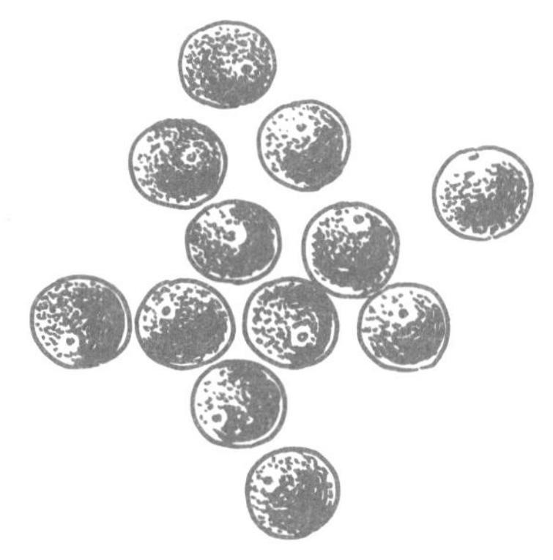

 CRANBERRY

Description: Small round red fruit with a pleasant acidic taste.
Uses include: Juice used as a drink. Use in sauces, relishes, sandwiches, desserts and cakes. Cranberry jelly or sauce is a traditional accompaniment with turkey.

CUMQUAT

Description: Sometimes spelt kumquat. Looks like a miniature orange, with a tart flavour.
Uses include: Use in marmalade, cakes, biscuits, brandied liqueur fruit.

CUSTARD APPLE

Description: Smooth-skinned fruit with a netted pattern and a dull yellow to red skin. Ripe flesh is sweet with a granular texture.

Uses include: Eat fresh, use in fruit salads, ice-cream and desserts.

DATE

Description: Fruit of the date palm, oval russet brown-coloured fruit, available fresh or dry.

Uses include: Use in both sweet and savoury dishes, added to breads, cakes, scones, muffins and muesli. Soft or fresh dates can be served with cheese platters.

DURIAN

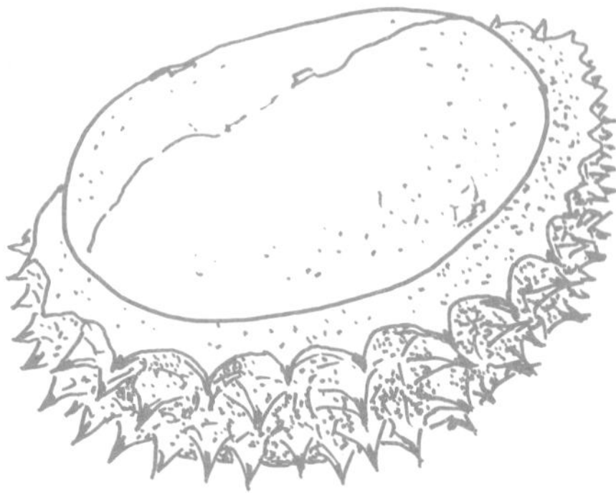

Description: Large fruit weighing up to 4 kg with a yellow woody outer layer and hard sharp spines. Has offensive, slightly sickening aroma when overripe. The custard-like flesh is pale yellow with large brown seeds and has an aromatic, sweet flavour. A delicacy in Asian countries.

Uses include: Eat fresh, use in cakes and jams. May be served with Asian rice and meat dishes.

FEIJOA

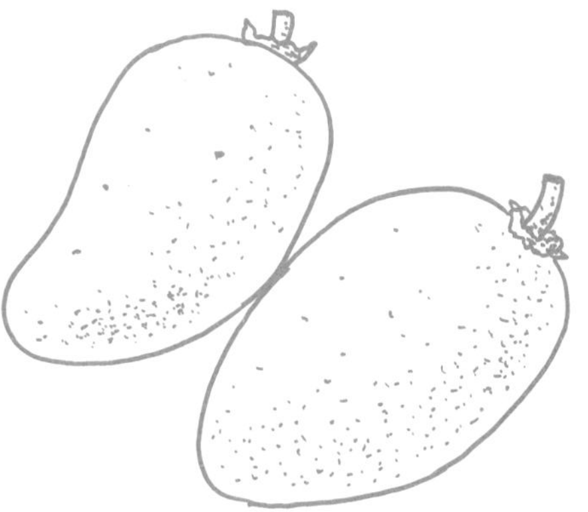

Description: Oval berries, dark green to yellow when ripe with a tough skin. Flesh is white or yellow around a jelly-like pulp.

Uses include: Use in jellies and preserves.

FIG

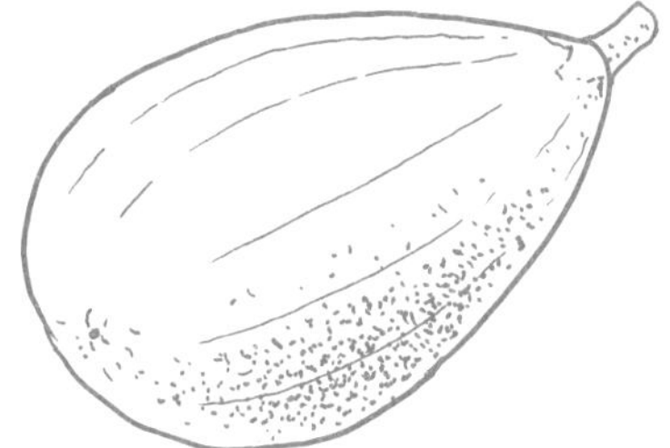

Description: Purple, green or red pear-shaped fruit, available fresh and dried.
Uses include: Use fresh in a cheese platter, dried in preserves, cakes, desserts and breads.

GOOSEBERRY

Description: Small oval green to purple berries, particularly high in vitamin C.
Uses include: Use in fruit compotes, salads, pies, tarts, desserts and preserves.

GRAPE

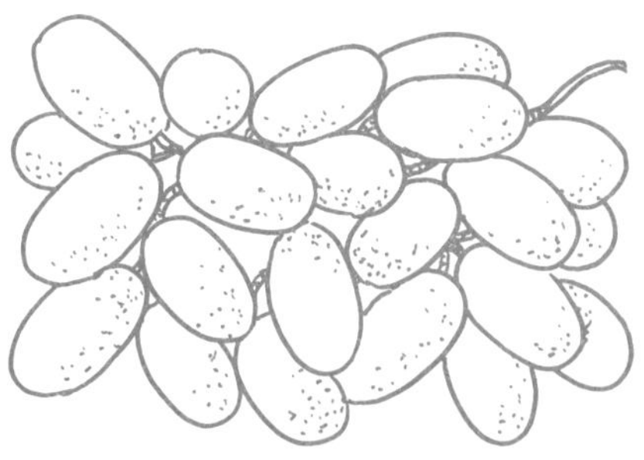

Description: Bunches or clusters of small white, black, red, purple or green fruit. The size of the fruit and colour vary according to the variety, available fresh and dried.
Uses include: Eat fresh, use in desserts, cheese and fruit platters and preserves. Used in wine making. May be dried (sultanas and currants) and used in cakes, desserts, breads, muffins and muesli.

GRAPEFRUIT

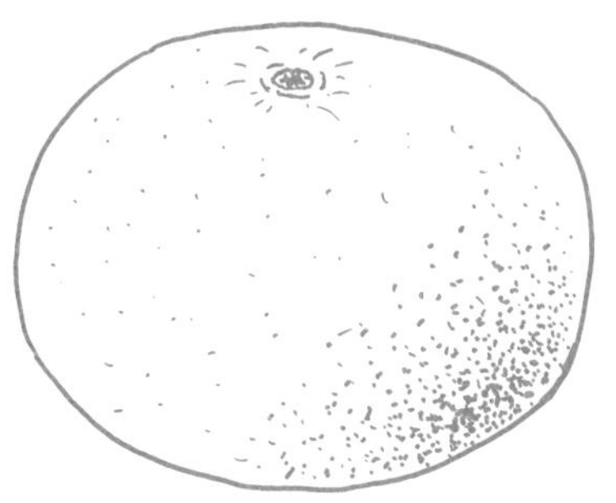

Description: Large yellow to pink citrus fruit with segmented flesh containing juice and surrounded by pith and skin, sour-sweet flavour.
Uses include: Cut in half and separate into segments to eat fresh. Use in drinks and marmalade.

GUAVA

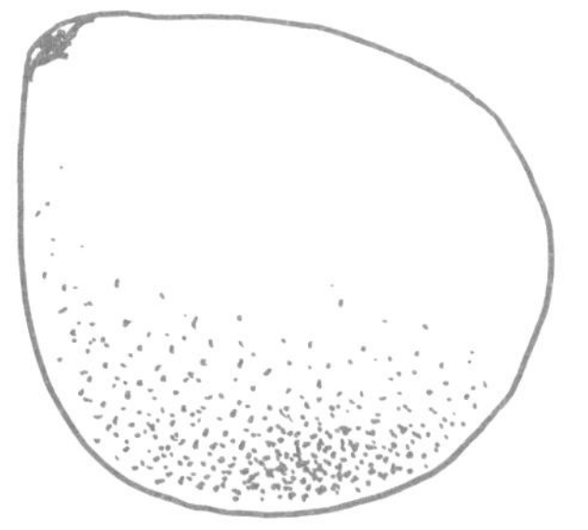

Description: Fruit is green, turning yellow when ripe with flesh colour ranging from white to deep pink, one of the richest sources of vitamin A.
Uses include: Serve fresh with cheese and in fruit salad. May be poached and stewed. Use in jellies, preserves and fruit juice.

HONEY DEW

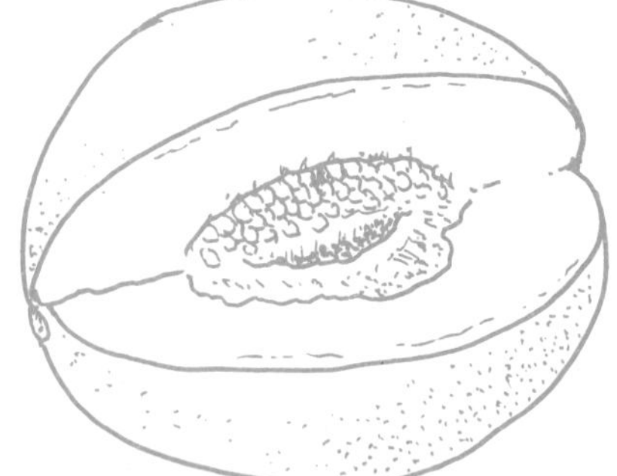

Description: Round melon with smooth white-green skin. The pale to darker green flesh is fine textured, sweet and juicy.

Uses include: Eat fresh and use in fruit platters and fruit salads.

JACKFRUIT

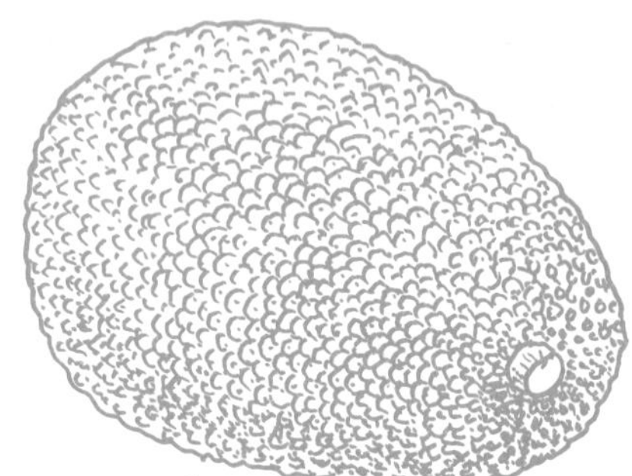

Description: Very large oval fruit with a rough green rind composed of hexagonal fleshy spines, weighing 4–23 kg. Flesh is soft and juicy with a pungent odour and contains 100–500 large white seeds.

Uses include: Eat fresh and cooked, use in chutneys, ice-cream and jams.

KIWIFRUIT

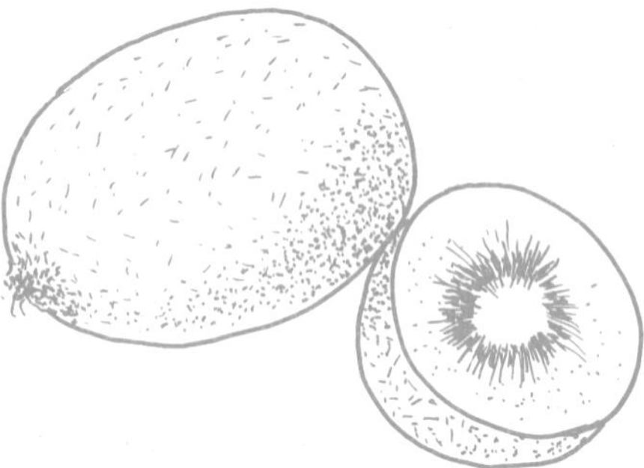

Description: Light brown furry skin, green pulp with many tiny black seeds around the centre, rich source of vitamin C.

Uses include: Use in fruit salads, desserts, pies, cakes, ice-cream, sorbets, chutneys and pickles and in fruit and cheese platters.

LEMON

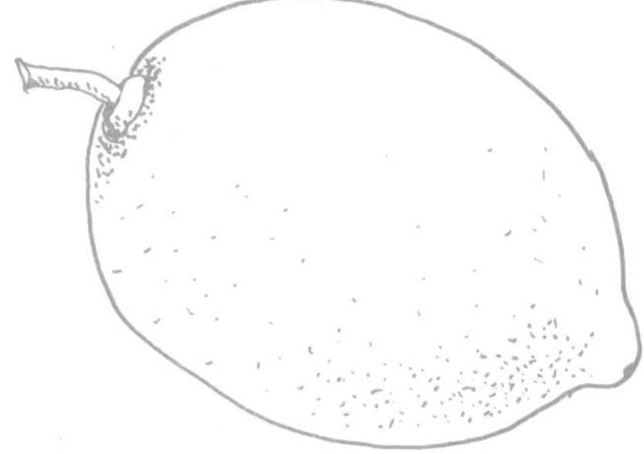

Description: Oval citrus fruit with yellow skin and acidic flavour.

Uses include: Use to flavour and garnish sweet and savoury dishes.

LIME

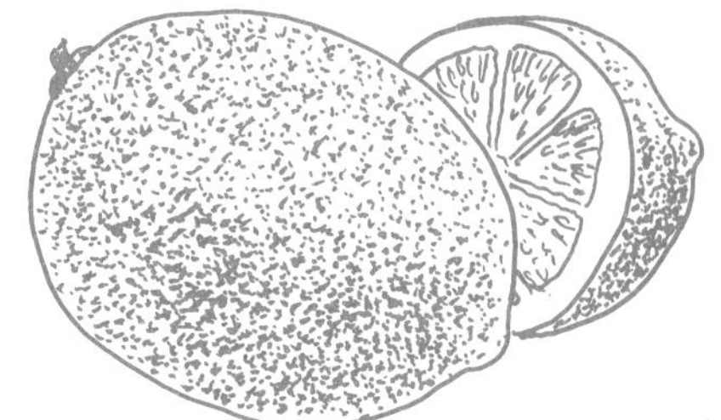

Description: Similar to lemon, with a bright green, thin rind and green juicy pulp.
Uses include: Use in a similar manner to lemon.

LYCHEE

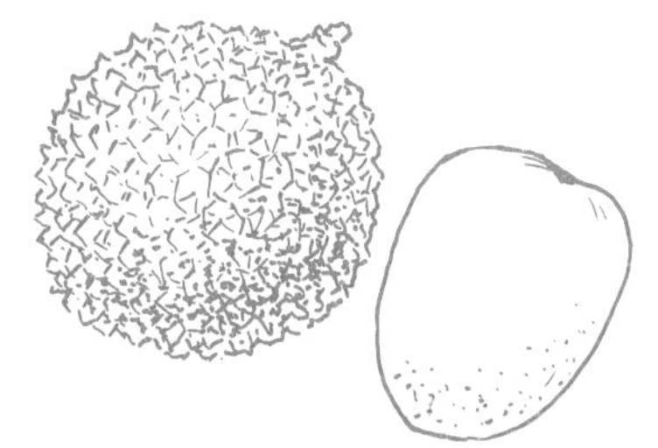

Description: Small and round with a rough leathery red skin. The flesh is translucent and pearly white, surrounding a hard shiny brown seed. The flavour is sweet.
Uses include: Eat fresh, use in fruit salads. May be served with ice-cream, ham, chicken and pork.

LOGANBERRY

Description: Small dull red fruit, cylindrical in shape, made up of a group of drupelets. Strong, slightly tart flavour.
Uses include: Use in desserts, pancakes, muffins, fruit salad and puddings.

LOQUAT

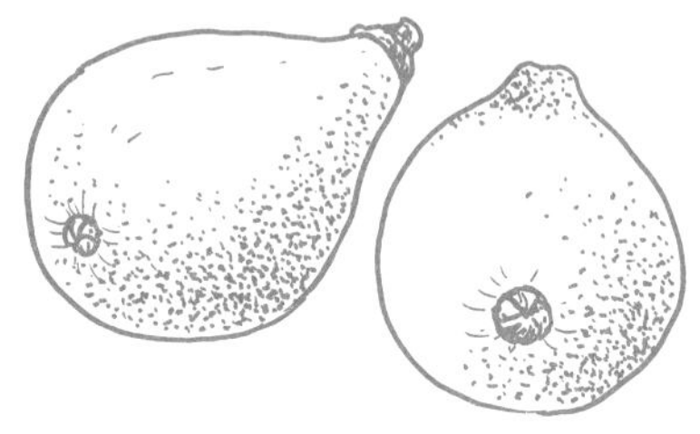

Description: Round with a yellow furry thin skin. The flesh is white to yellow, firm with a tangy sweet flavour. One or two large seeds in each fruit.
Uses include: Eat fresh, use in fruit salads.

MANDARIN

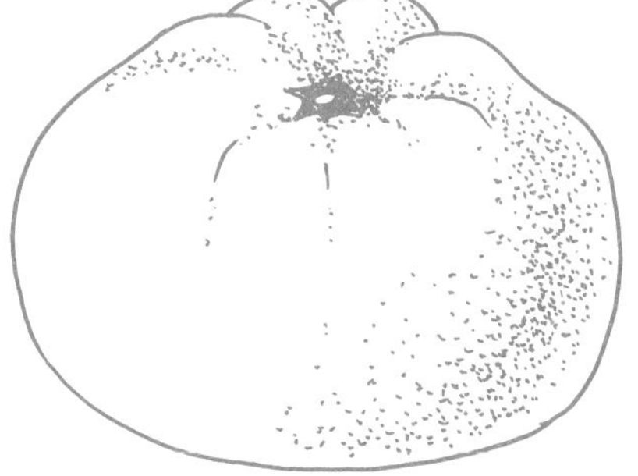

Description: Smaller than an orange, with a deep orange-coloured skin that peels easily. The flesh is in segments.
Uses include: Eat fresh, use in desserts and salads.

MANGO

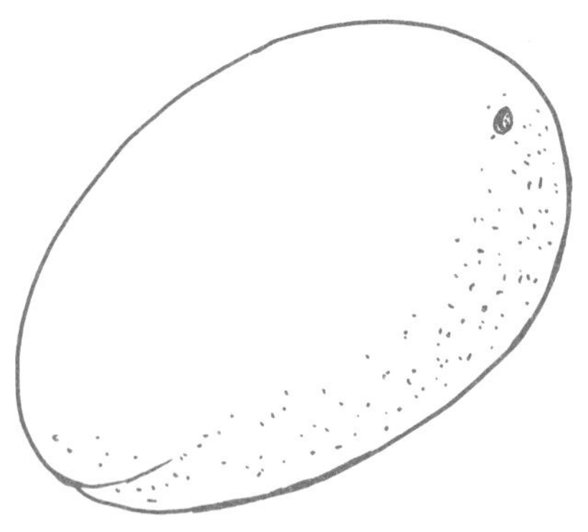

Description: Oval fruit with yellow to green or orange to red skin, with an inedible tough skin and large flat stone to which the fibrous flesh adheres. Excellent source of vitamin A.

Uses include: Eat fresh, use in ice-cream, fruit salads, cakes, pies, puddings, jams, chutneys and sauces. May be served as an accompaniment to curries.

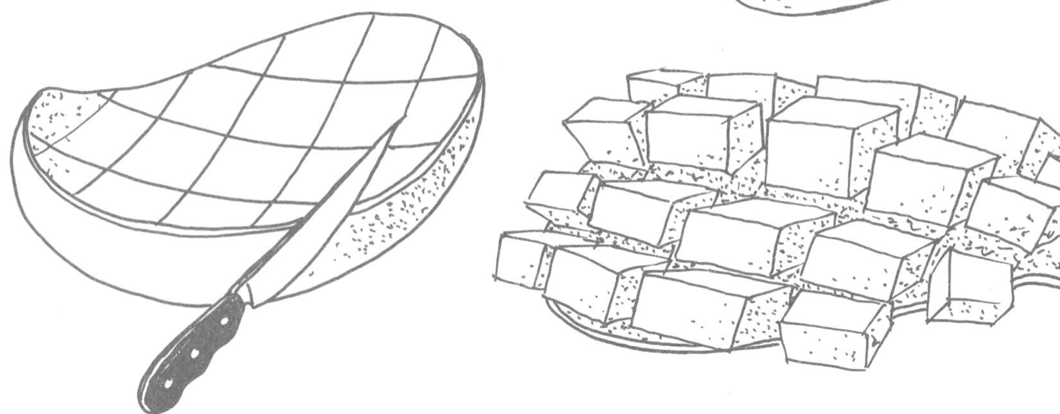

MULBERRY

Description: Not a true berry but a multiple fruit, shiny deep purple colour, 2–3 cm in size. The leaves are used as a food for silkworms.

Uses include: As for berries.

NASHI

Description: Asian variety of fruit resembling an apple with green to brownish textured skin. Flesh is crisp, white and juicy.

Uses include: Eat fresh.

NECTARINE

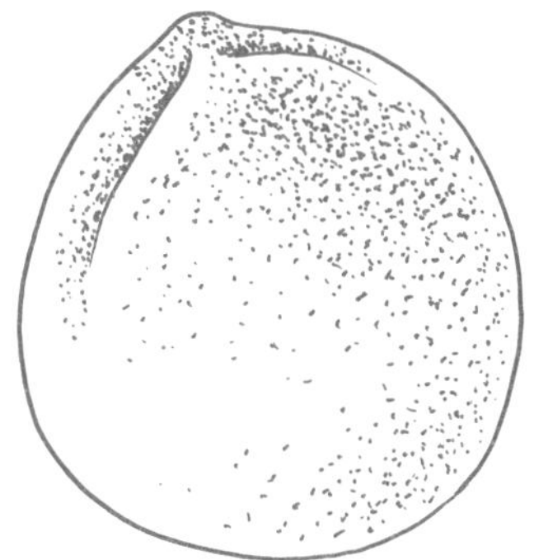

Description: Stone fruit with a yellow to red smooth skin and white to yellow flesh.
Uses include: Eat fresh, use in compotes, salads, desserts, cakes and preserves.

ORANGE

Description: Orange-coloured citrus fruit with white pith surrounding orange segments.

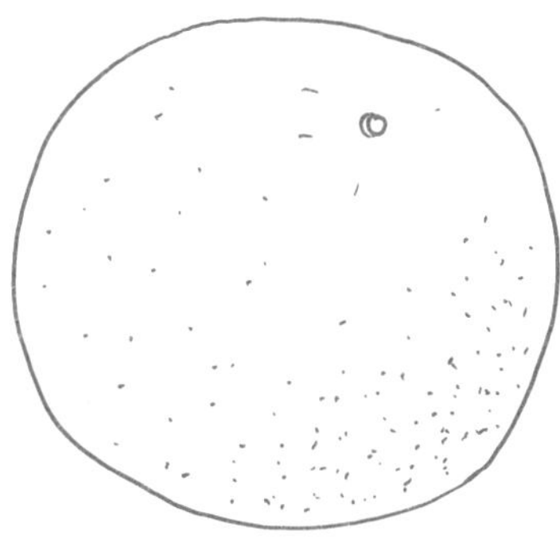

Varieties

Navel (winter)

Description: Thick and pebbly skin, easy to peel and divide into segments, seedless.
Uses include: Eat fresh, use in marmalade, desserts and cakes.

Valencia (summer)

Description: Smooth, thin skin with a few seeds.
Uses include: Eat fresh, use in salads, desserts and cakes. Mainly used for juice. Skin may be finely grated (rind or zest) and used as a flavouring.

PAPAYA

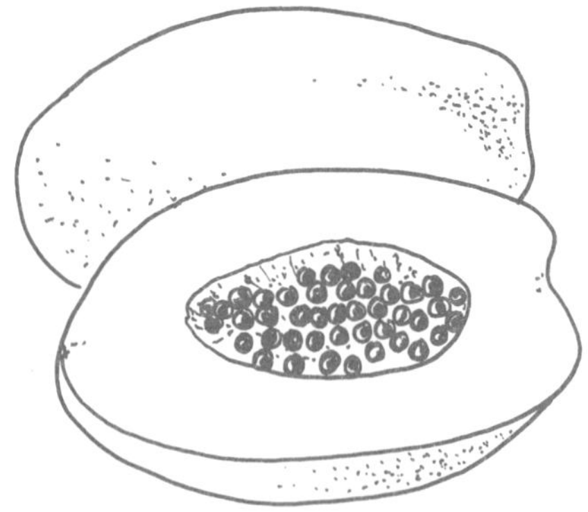

Description: Oval-shaped green to yellow to orange in colour with pink to orange flesh. Centre is filled with edible brown-black round seeds.

Uses include: Eat fresh, use in fruit platters, preserves, fruit salads and desserts. Fresh papaya tenderises meat.

PASSIONFRUIT

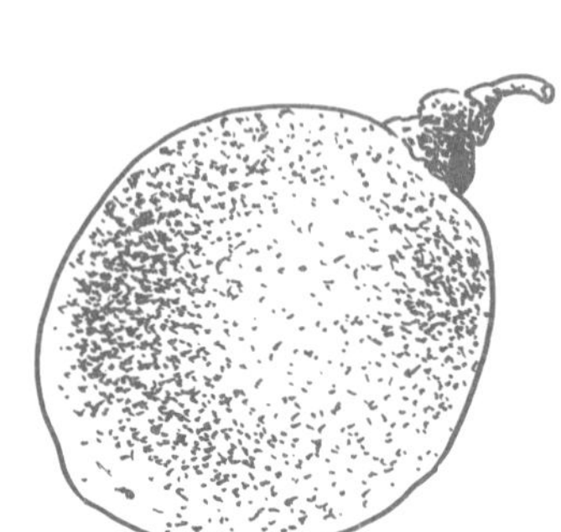

Description: Egg-shaped fruit with a thick purple skin, the cavity is filled with sweet juicy yellow pulp containing small black seeds.

Uses include: Eat fresh, use in fruit juices, on pavlova, ice-cream, icing, fillings, jams, fruit salads, gelatine desserts and sauces.

PEACH

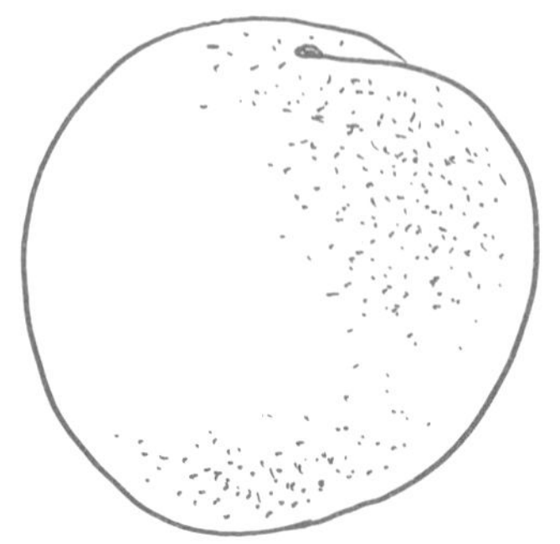

Description: Stone fruit with a velvety white, yellow or red skin. The white or yellow flesh may be attached to the stone (clingstone) or separated (slipstone).

Uses include: Eat fresh, use in salads, compotes, fruit platters, pies, sauces and preserves.

PEAR

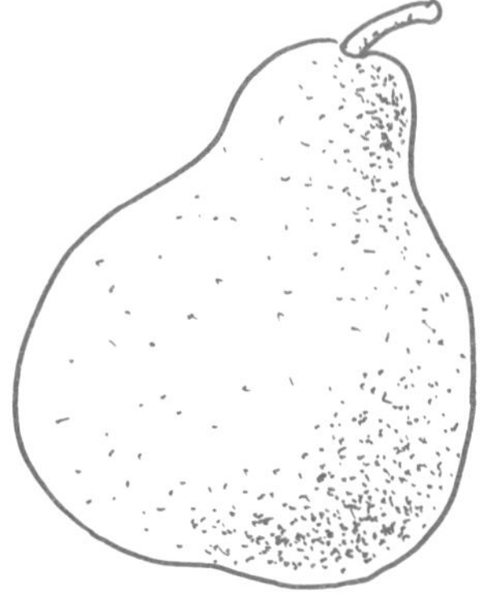

Description: Most varieties are the traditional pear shape with white flesh, and with a slightly acid but sweet taste. Skin colour varies according to variety.

Uses include: Eat fresh, use in cheese platters, fruit and vegetable salads, compotes, desserts, cakes and preserves.

Varieties

Beurre Bosc

Description: Elongated shape with a long tapering neck, flesh is firm, white and juicy with an aromatic flavour, skin is a russet brown changing to dark cinnamon brown when mature. Keeps well, available late March through to the end of June.

Corello

Description: Small pear with an attractive red blush, crisp texture and a sweet flavour.

Packham

Description: Medium to large with a short neck, green skin changing to light yellow when ripe, with a white juicy sweet flesh, available mid-February to July.

Williams

Description: Medium to large regular shape, light green skin changing to light yellow when ripe, white sweet flesh with an aromatic flavour, mainly used for canning and drying, available late January to end of February.

PEPINO (TREE MELON)

Description: Small melon-shaped fruit with a satin-like green to yellow skin with vivid purple stripes. The flesh is pale yellow with a delicate sweet flavour resembling a mixture of lemon, pineapple and melon.
Uses include: Eat fresh, use in fruit salads, marinades and liqueur.

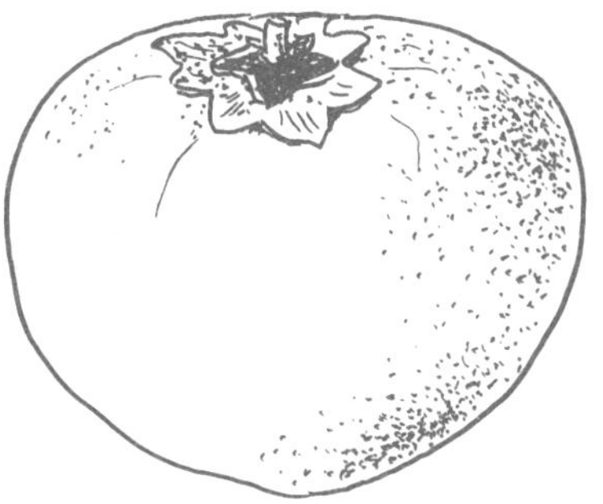

PERSIMMON (FUJI FRUIT)

Description: Round orange to red-coloured fruit 5–8 cm in size.
Uses include: Eat fresh, use in jams, cakes and salads.

PINEAPPLE

Description: Large cylindrical fruit with a tuft of narrow pointed leaves at the top and diamond patterned rough skin that is green to yellow in colour. The flesh is fibrous, radiating from a hard central core and is sweet but slightly acidic in flavour. As the pineapple ripens the flesh becomes deeper yellow, softer and sweeter.

Uses include: Eat fresh, use in desserts, jams, salads, fruit drinks, cakes and biscuits.

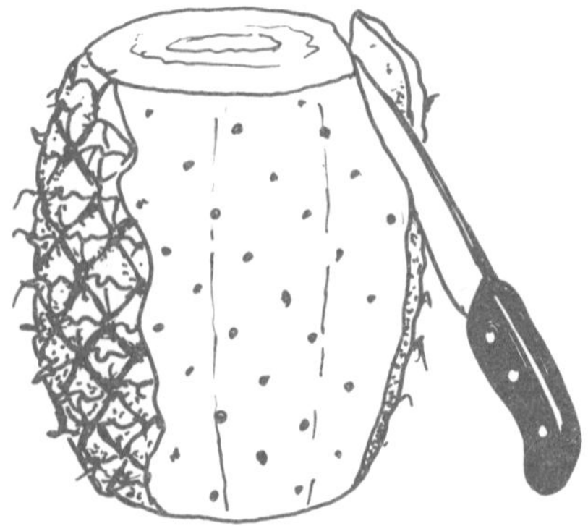

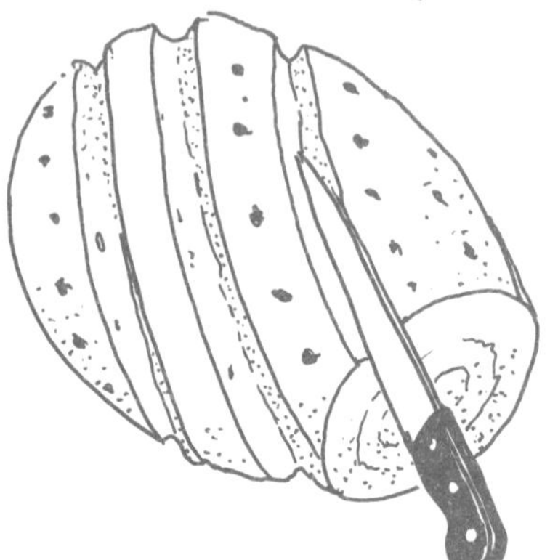

PLUM

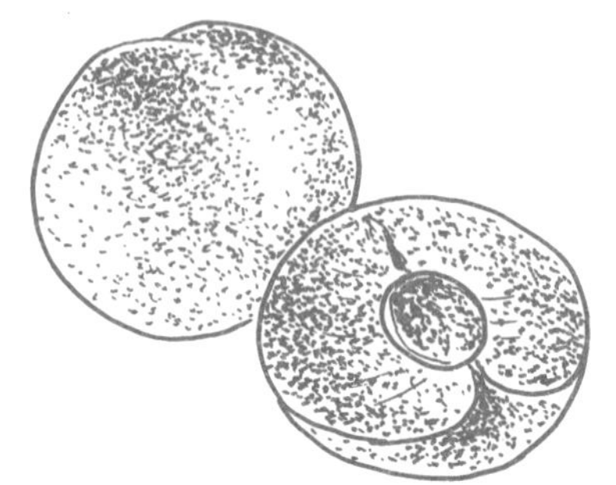

Description: Stone ovoid fruit with many varieties, distinguishable by skin and flesh colours. Dried plums are called prunes.

Uses include: Eat fresh, use in fruit salads, compotes, pies, cakes, fillings, desserts, jams and preserves.

POMEGRANATE

Description: Orange to red spherical fruit. The fruit is crowned with a permanent calyx and divided by walls of pith into several cells containing many seeds surrounded by pink sweet-acid pulp.

Uses include: Eat fresh, use in Turkish dishes and as a garnish for fruit salads. The juice may be used in drinks and jellies.

QUINCE

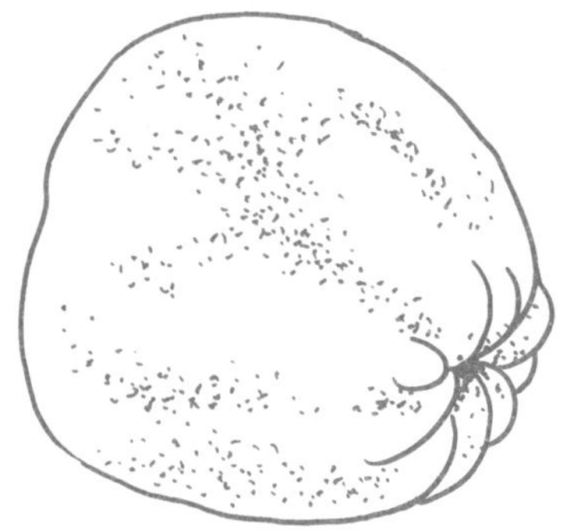

Description: Hard, yellow fruit, oblong in shape with a small crown at the stalk end.

Uses include: Must be cooked, developing a pink colour. Use in desserts, preserves, jams, jellies and paste. May be oven-roasted to serve with meats.

RAMBUTAN (HAIRY LYCHEE)

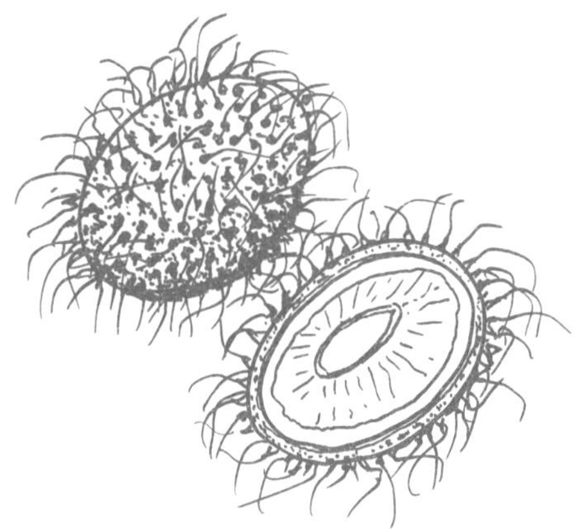

Description: Bright red or orange skin covered with soft spines or hairs. The fruit contains a single seed with juicy, sweet-acid flesh, resembling a grape in flavour.

Uses include: Eat fresh, use in the same way as a lychee. Serve with cheese and meat platters, use in jams and jellies.

RASPBERRY

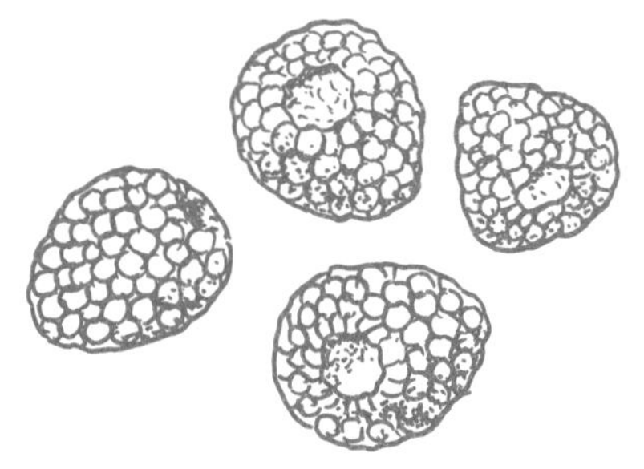

Description: One-seeded drupe, red fruit conical in shape and approximately 2.5 cm in length.

Uses include: Use in fruit salads, desserts, sauces, coulis, sorbets and jams.

REDCURRANT

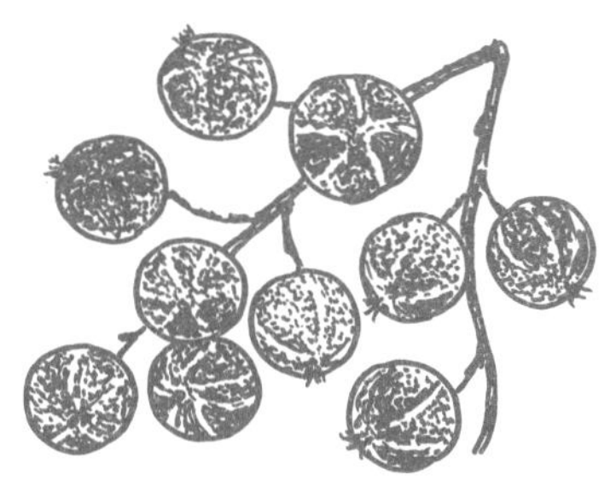

Description: Small juicy red berries. Very short summer season.

Uses include: Eat fresh, use in fruit salads, cheese platters, pies, tarts and jellies. Serve as a sauce with meats and desserts and in small bundles as a garnish.

RHUBARB

Description: Long fleshy stalks green and red in colour. Strong acid flavour.

Uses include: Use in soufflés, jams, ice-cream, cakes, puddings and pies, often combined with apple.

ROCKMELON (CANTALOUPE)

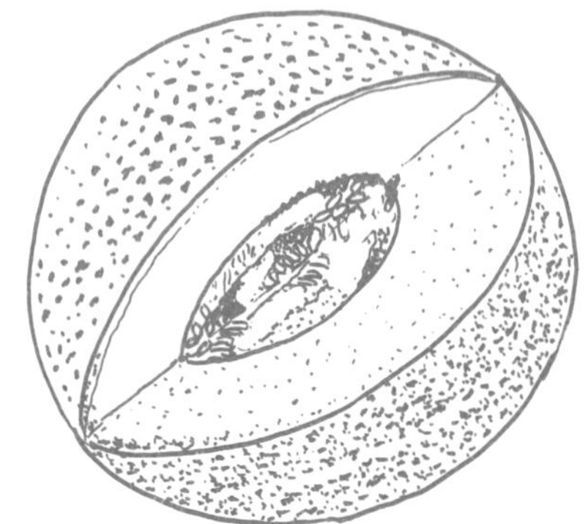

Description: There are several varieties of rockmelon, of which cantaloupe is one. They have a hard-ribbed scaly rind and orange flesh that is sweet and aromatic.

Uses include: Eat fresh, use in desserts and salads.

STRAWBERRY

Description: Many varieties, all red externally, some red and some white inside. The larger varieties tend to have less flavour than others.

Uses include: Eat fresh, use in fruit salad, desserts, sorbets, ice-cream, mousses, pies, tarts, jams, glazes, coulis and sauces.

TAMARILLO

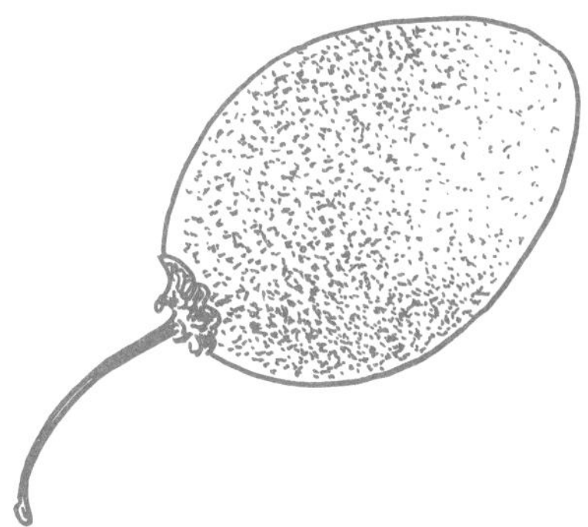

Description: Ovoid in shape with a bright orange to red skin and orange flesh with centre seeds. The skin is bitter and flesh has a slightly acid flavour.

Uses include: Eat fresh with a sprinkling of sugar, use in stuffing for roast lamb, jams and chutneys.

TAMARIND

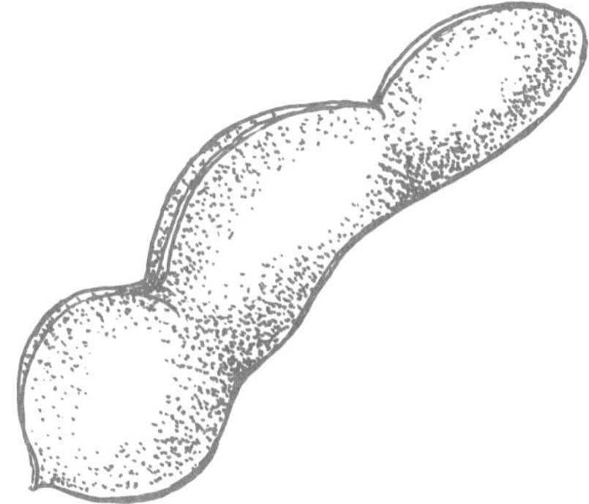

Description: A flat pod 7–15 cm long containing black seeds. When ripe the pods are dark brown and sweet.

Uses include: Use the young pod to season meat and rice dishes and, when fully grown with open pods, eat the fresh pulp.

WATERMELON

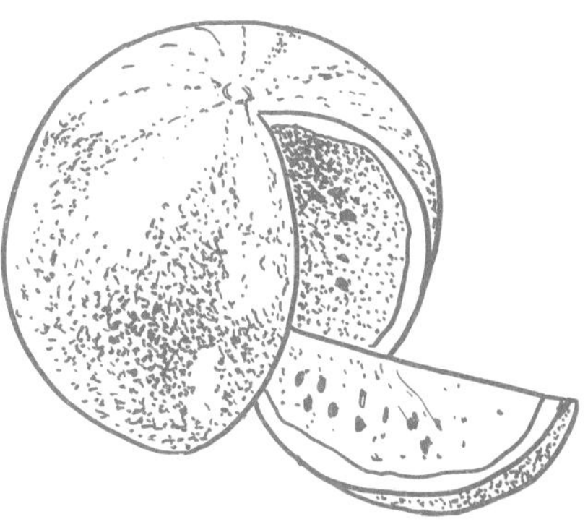

Description: Large round or oblong melon with a rich deep green variegated skin. Flesh is soft, sweet, juicy and a deep pink to red in colour, some with black seeds throughout.

Uses include: Eat fresh, use in fruit platters, fruit salads sorbet and ice-cream. The shell can be scooped out to hold salads.

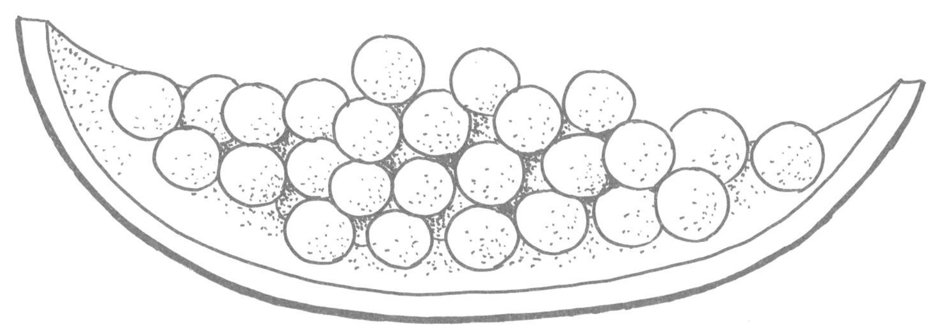

WHITECURRANT

Description: Small juicy white/slightly green, transparent berry. Short summer season.
Uses include: Eat fresh, use in fruit salads, cheese platters, desserts, pies, tarts and jellies.

Fruit-based desserts

APPLE PUREE

This makes 2 cups apple puree, which can be used for fillings and as a base for other desserts.

- *Serves:* *4*
- *Cooking utensil:* saucepan

Preparation time: ***20 minutes***

Ingredients

500 g apples
grated rind 1/2 lemon
4 cloves
1/4 cup (65 mL) water
1 tablespoon (20 g) sugar

Method

1. Peel apples thinly, quarter, core and slice.
2. Place all ingredients except sugar in saucepan. Cook apples gently until soft. Stir in sugar. Remove cloves and rind.
3. To puree: rub through a sieve, mix in an electric blender *or* mash with a fork.

Reduce water to 1 tablespoon (20 mL). Microwave for 8 minutes on high power.

✦ APRICOT PUREE ✦

Follow recipe for **Apple puree**, omitting apples, cloves and lemon rind. Use 500 g apricots.

APPLE SNOW

Serves: **4**

Preparation time: ***15 minutes***

Ingredients

500 g (1 quantity) **Apple puree** (p. 308), cooled
2 egg whites (61 g)
2 glacé cherries

Method

1 Whip egg whites until stiff and fold into **Apple puree**.
2 Spoon into serving dish (1 L) and refrigerate. Decorate with cherries.
3 May be served with **Custard sauce** (p. 287) prepared from the leftover yolks of eggs.

APRICOT SNOW

Follow recipe for **Apple snow**, using **Apricot puree**.

BAKED PEAR AND RHUBARB SOUFFLÉ

Serves: **4**
Cooking utensil: saucepan, 14 cm soufflé dish (1 L) *or* 4 individual 8 cm soufflé dishes (250 mL), baking tray

Preparation time: ***30 minutes***
Cooking time: ***12–15 minutes***
Oven temperature: ***180°C***

Ingredients

1 teaspoon butter
2 teaspoons (10 g) caster sugar
1 pear (125 g), peeled, cored and diced
1 cup (150 g) peeled sliced rhubarb
1 teaspoon lemon juice
1 teaspoon grated orange rind
2 tablespoons (40 mL) caster sugar
1 tablespoon (20 mL) water
4 egg whites (61 g)
1 tablespoon (20 g) icing sugar mixture

Method

1 Butter soufflé dishes and dust with caster sugar.
2 Cook pear, rhubarb, lemon juice, orange rind, 1 tablespoon sugar and water in saucepan.
3 Sieve fruit *or* puree in blender or food processor.
4 Beat egg whites until stiff, add remaining caster sugar and beat until stiff.
5 Mix $^{1}/_{3}$ of the egg white into the fruit mixture, fold in the remaining egg white.
6 Spoon mixture into the soufflé dishes and place dishes on baking tray.
7 Bake at 180°C for 12–15 minutes, until risen and golden brown.
8 When cooked, dust with icing sugar mixture and serve immediately.

FRESH FRUIT PLATTER

Serves: 4

Ingredients

choose a variety of fruits

Method

1 Select fruits to give variety of colour, flavour, texture and shape.
2 Peel if necessary, remove stones or seeds and cut into suitably sized pieces.
3 Dip fruit that browns easily (e.g. apple, banana, carambola) in lemon juice to prevent oxidation.
4 Arrange prepared fruit on platter *or* individual plates.
5 Refrigerate and serve.

FRESH FRUIT SALAD

Follow recipe for **Fresh fruit platter**. Cut prepared fruit into bite-sized pieces and place in a serving dish. Chill and serve.

FRUIT DIP

Serves: 8

Preparation time: 15 minutes

Ingredients

400 g natural yoghurt
2 passionfruit
500 g diced fresh fruit

Method

1 Cut the passionfruit in half and scoop out the pulp.
2 Mix pulp into the yoghurt.
3 Place dip in a bowl, place in centre of **Fresh fruit platter**.

FRUIT GELATO

- *Serves:* **8**
- *Cooking utensil:* saucepan
- *Preparation time:* ***20 minutes***

Ingredients

1/2 cup (125 g) sugar
1 cup (250 mL) hot water
juice of 1/2 orange
juice of 1/2 lemon
1 ripe banana (125 g), mashed
1 egg (61 g), separated

Method

1. Dissolve sugar in hot water. Cool.
2. Add orange and lemon juice.
3. Combine banana and egg yolk, mix well.
4. Add to juice and water mixture.
5. Pour into plastic container and place in freezer for 2 hours.
6. Beat mixture until just smooth.
7. Beat egg white until stiff.
8. Fold egg white into mixture. Refreeze overnight.

PASSIONFRUIT GELATO

Follow recipe for **Fruit gelato**. Add pulp of two passionfruit after step 7.

FRUIT JELLY

- *Serves:* **4**
- *Cooking utensil:* small saucepan, medium mould (1 L) *or* 4 individual moulds (250 mL)
- *Preparation time:* ***15 minutes and 4 hours setting time***

Ingredients

1 tablespoon (12 g) gelatine
1 cup (250 mL) water
rind of 2 lemons, thinly peeled
rind of 1 orange, thinly peeled
1/2 cup (125 g) sugar
3/4 cup (190 mL) orange *or* other fruit juice

Method

1. Put gelatine in the water, add rind and sugar. Bring to boil.
2. Add fruit juice. Strain through a fine strainer.
3. Pour into a mould. Refrigerate for 4 hours, until set.
4. When set, dip mould into sufficient hot water to almost reach the top, turn onto serving dish.

FRUIT IN JELLY

Follow **Fruit jelly** recipe. Add 1 cup (250 g) fresh, stewed *or* canned fruit.

Note: Fresh pineapple cannot be used in a jelly as it contains the enzyme papain, which denatures the protein in the gelatine and prevents it from setting. Cooking fresh pineapple before using destroys the enzyme.

LEMON PANCAKES

Number: ***10–15***

Preparation time: ***30 minutes***

Ingredients

10–15 **Pancakes** (p. 368)
juice of 2–3 lemons
2 tablespoons (40 g) caster sugar
½ cup (250 mL) cream

Method

1. Sprinkle each pancake with lemon juice and caster sugar.
2. Fold into quarters *or* roll and serve with cream.

FRUIT PANCAKES

Follow recipe for **Lemon pancakes**, using 1 cup (250 g) cooked, canned *or* fresh fruit as the filling.

RICOTTA FRUIT PANCAKES

Follow recipe for **Lemon pancakes**, using 250 g smooth ricotta cheese, 1 cup (180 g) sultanas, 1 teaspoon cinnamon and 1 tablespoon (15 g) icing sugar mixture as the filling.

STRAWBERRY LIQUEUR PANCAKES

Number: ***10–15***

Cooking utensil: flame-proof pan, saucepan

Preparation time: ***30 minutes and 3 hours to marinate***

Ingredients

10–15 **Pancakes** (p. 368)
250 g strawberries, quartered
¼ cup orange liqueur
1 tablespoon (20 g) caster sugar
2 tablespoons (40 mL) extra orange liqueur
½ cup (250 mL) whipped cream

Method

1. Marinate strawberries in liqueur and sugar for 3 hours.
2. Spread strawberries on pancakes and fold into quarters.
3. Place in flame-proof pan.
4. Heat extra orange liqueur very carefully in small long-handled saucepan.
5. Take liqueur to flame-proof dish, light liqueur and immediately pour over pancakes to 'flame' them.
6. Serve with whipped cream.

MELON SORBET

▶ *Serves:* ***6***
▶ *Cooking utensil:* saucepan

Preparation time: ***20 minutes***

Ingredients

2 cups (500 mL) water
$^1/_2$ cup (125 g) sugar
750 g melon (rockmelon or cantaloupe, honey dew, watermelon)
2 tablespoons (30 g) chopped glacé ginger

Method

1. Stir water and sugar over low heat until sugar dissolves.
2. Boil 1 minute. Cool.
3. Sieve melon flesh *or* use food processor.
4. Add cooled syrup and ginger.
5. Pour into plastic container and place in freezer for 2 hours.
6. Beat mixture until just smooth. Refreeze overnight.

MELON TRIO

▶ *Serves:* ***6***

Preparation time: ***30 minutes***

Ingredients

500 g watermelon
1 small rockmelon (cantaloupe)
1 small honeydew melon
1 tablespoon (20 mL) lemon juice

Method

1. Cut melons into small balls with ball cutter.
2. Sprinkle with lemon juice. Refrigerate for 30 minutes.

✦ MELON PLATTER ✦

Follow recipe for **Melon delight**. Cut prepared fruit into slices and arrange on serving dish. Refrigerate for 30 minutes.

RASPBERRY MOUSSE

- *Serves:* **6**
- *Cooking utensil:* saucepan
- *Serving dish:* 6 individual serving dishes (200 mL)

Preparation time: ***40 minutes and 1 hour refrigeration time***

Ingredients

250 g fresh *or* frozen raspberries
2 eggs (61 g), separated
1/4 cup (65 g) sugar
1/2 cup (125 mL) milk
3 teaspoons (9 g) gelatine
1/4 cup (65 mL) hot water
200 mL cream, whipped
6 raspberries for decoration

Method

1. Sieve raspberries *or* use food processor.
2. Beat together egg yolks and sugar.
3. Bring milk to boil, add to egg yolk mixture, return to heat for 1 minute. Stir this custard rapidly. Do not boil.
4. Dissolve gelatine in hot water, add to raspberries. Allow to cool.
5. Beat egg whites until stiff.
6. Fold raspberry mixture, custard, cream and egg whites together.
7. Pour into serving dishes. Refrigerate until set.
8. Decorate with raspberries.

STRAWBERRY MOUSSE

Follow recipe for **Raspberry mousse**, using 250 g strawberries.

STEWED APRICOTS

- *Serves:* **4**
- *Cooking utensil:* saucepan

Preparation time: ***10 minutes***
Cooking time: ***5–10 minutes***

Ingredients

500 g apricots
1/4 cup (65 g) sugar
1 cup (250 mL) water

Method

1. Wash apricots, cut in half and remove stone.
2. Place in saucepan with sugar and water, bring to the boil and cook gently until tender, approximately 5–10 minutes.
3. Cool. Serve or use as required.

For all stewed fruit recipes, microwave on high power for approximately 3/4 of the cooking time. Turn fruit during cooking.

✦ PEACH COMPOTE ✦

Follow recipe for **Stewed apricots**, using peeled peaches, halved and stone removed. Cook for 10–15 minutes or until tender.

✦ POACHED CHERRIES ✦

Follow recipe for **Stewed apricots** using whole cherries.

✦ POACHED PEARS ✦

Follow recipe for **Stewed apricots**, using peeled pears, halved and cored using a teaspoon. Add 4 cloves *or* 3 cm cinnamon stick at step 2. Cook for 20–30 minutes or until tender. Remove flavourings at step 3.

✦ STEWED APPLE ✦

Follow recipe for **Stewed apricots** using cored and sliced apples. Add 4 cloves *or* strip of lemon rind at step 2, remove at step 3.

✦ STEWED PLUMS ✦

Follow recipe for **Stewed apricots**, using whole plums *or* halved and stone removed.

✦ STEWED QUINCES ✦

Follow recipe for **Stewed apricots**, using peeled quartered, cored and sliced quinces. Use 1/2 cup (125 g) sugar and add 4 cloves at step 2. Cook for 30–40 minutes. Remove cloves at step 3.

✦ STEWED RHUBARB ✦

Follow recipe for **Stewed apricots**, using trimmed and washed rhubarb cut into 3 cm lengths and 1/2 cup (125 g) sugar. At step 2 add lemon rind. 1/2 teaspoon powdered ginger *or* 1 tablespoon (15 g) chopped glacé ginger may be added.

✦ WINTER FRUIT SALAD ✦

Follow recipe for **Stewed apricots**, using 125 g dried fruit soaked 30 minutes or more in 1 cup (250 mL) extra water. 1 tablespoon (20 mL) brandy may be added at step 3. Serve with **Cinnamon honey cream** (p. 290).

PEACH MELBA

► *Serves:* ***6***

🕓 *Preparation time:* ***20 minutes***

Ingredients

6 rounds sponge cake (6 cm diameter)
3 tablespoons (60 mL) peach syrup *or* sherry
6 halves canned peaches
6 scoops ice-cream
3 tablespoons (60 mL) raspberry syrup
$^{1}/_{2}$ cup (125 mL) cream, whipped
1 tablespoon (15 g) chopped nuts

Method

1 Place rounds of sponge cake in 6 individual glass dishes and soak with peach syrup *or* sherry.
2 Place a peach half on sponge, with hollow side uppermost. Place a scoop of ice-cream on each peach.
3 Pour raspberry syrup over ice-cream. Decorate with whipped cream and chopped nuts.

SUMMER PUDDING

A popular summer dessert made from berries in season. Other berries may be used when they are in season or replace up to 150 g berries with 425 g can berries, drained.

► *Serves:* ***4***
► *Cooking utensil:* saucepan, medium mould (1 L) *or* 4 individual moulds (250 mL)

🕓 *Preparation time:* ***45 minutes and overnight for setting***

Ingredients

150 g fresh *or* frozen raspberries
150 g fresh *or* frozen boysenberries *or* blackberries
150 g fresh *or* frozen redcurrants *or* blueberries
1 Granny Smith apple (150 g), peeled and grated
$^{1}/_{4}$ cup (65 g) caster sugar
8 slices bread, 1 cm thick
200 mL cream

Method

1 Place fruit and sugar in saucepan. Bring slowly to boil. Remove from heat.
2 Line moulds using 5–6 slices of bread, cutting bread to fit exactly.
3 Spoon in fruit, filling to the top.
4 Pour in juice to top of moulds.
5 Fit remaining bread to cover fruit and cover with plate so that it presses on to the bread.
6 Place a weight on the plate and leave overnight in refrigerator.
7 Turn out just before serving and serve with cream.

Frozen desserts

CASSATA

- *Serves:* ***8***
- *Cooking utensil:* 3 medium loaf pans (1 L each), double saucepan

Preparation time: ***30 minutes and freezing time***

Ingredients

50 g chocolate
1/4 cup (65 mL) cream
1 tablespoon (10 g) cocoa, sifted
1 L vanilla ice-cream
1/3 cup (60 g) chopped red and green glacé cherries
1/3 cup (60 g) chopped glacé ginger
1/2 cup (60 g) flaked almonds
1/2 teaspoon almond essence

Method

1. Melt chocolate over hot water. Beat in cream and cocoa.
2. Divide ice-cream into 3 bowls.
3. Fold chocolate mixture into first bowl of ice-cream and spread evenly in the first loaf pan. Freeze.
4. Fold cherries and ginger into second bowl of ice-cream. Spread evenly in second loaf pan. Freeze.
5. Fold almonds and almond essence into remaining bowl of ice-cream. Spread evenly in third pan. Freeze.
6. When ice-cream is solid, unmould by quickly dipping each pan base into hot water and invert on to a plate. Place one layer on top of the next with the chocolate layer in the middle.
7. Smooth edges with spatula. Refreeze.
8. Serve in slices.

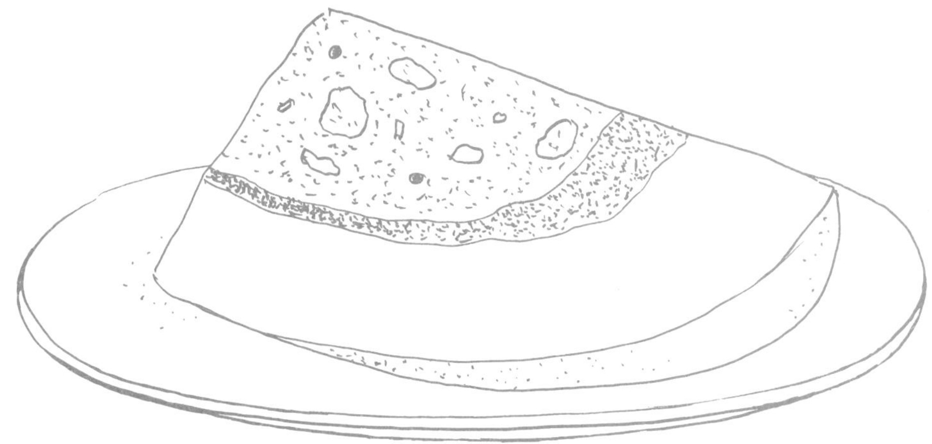

FROZEN CHRISTMAS PUDDING

- *Serves:* **8**
- *Cooking utensil:* large mould (2 L)

Preparation time: ***40 minutes, overnight and 1 week freezing time***

Ingredients

1/2 cup (90 g) chopped raisins
1/2 cup (90 g) sultanas
1/2 cup (90 g) currants
1/4 cup (45 g) chopped glacé cherries
1/4 cup (45 g) mixed peel
1/4 cup (65 mL) fruit juice *or* brandy
1 teaspoon cinnamon
1 teaspoon grated nutmeg
1/2 cup (60 g) blanched almonds
1/2 cup (125 mL) cream
1 L chocolate ice-cream

Method

1. Combine fruits with fruit juice and spices. Cover and allow to stand overnight.
2. Mix together soaked fruits, almonds, cream and ice-cream.
3. Pour into mould, cover with foil and freeze at least one week to allow flavour to develop.
4. Unmould by quickly dipping into hot water and inverting onto a serving plate.

ICE-CREAM

- *Serves:* **6–8**
- *Cooking utensil:* double saucepan

Preparation time: ***20 minutes and freezing time***

Ingredients

5 egg yolks
1 cup (250 g) caster sugar
2 cups (500 mL) cream
1 vanilla bean *or* 1/2 teaspoon vanilla essence

Method

1. Beat together yolks and sugar.
2. Place cream and vanilla bean in a saucepan. Bring slowly to the boil. Cool slightly. Remove bean.
3. Pour cream over yolk mixture, stirring continuously in top of double saucepan over simmering water.
4. Cook until mixture coats the back of the spoon.
5. Pour into plastic container and freeze, *or* use an ice-cream churn.

BANANA ICE-CREAM

Follow recipe for **Ice-cream**. Add 3 pureed bananas (375 g) after step 4.

BERRY ICE-CREAM

Follow recipe for **Ice-cream**. Add 1 punnet (250 g) mixed berries, chopped strawberries *or* raspberries *or* blackberries after step 4.

Custard-based desserts

Custards are cooked mixtures of milk, eggs, sugar and flavouring. The consistency and richness of a custard depends on the proportion of eggs to milk. The richness of flavour and smoothness of texture are determined by the egg yolk, and the albumen in the egg white influences the consistency. Fat-reduced milk does not set to a firm custard.

Custards require gentle heat and slow cooking to coagulate the egg proteins that thicken and set the mixture. Egg proteins coagulate between 65°C and 70°C. Above this temperature the protein hardens. In baked custards this causes the texture to be porous and tough. With custard sauce, if the mixture curdles remove from heat at once, pour into a cold basin and beat well with a whisk or rotary beater. To maintain an even temperature, custards should be cooked over water in the top of a double saucepan or steamer, or baked in a pie dish standing in a baking dish containing 3 cm of water, called a 'water bath'.

Custard uses a proportion of one egg to 175–200 mL of milk, with extra eggs giving a richer custard. Two egg yolks can replace a whole egg in custard, giving a similar result.

BAKED CUSTARD

- *Serves:* 4
- *Cooking utensil:* ovenproof dish (2 L), baking dish with 3 cm water for water bath, saucepan
- *Preparation time:* **15 minutes**
- *Cooking time:* **40–45 minutes**
- *Oven temperature:* **180°C**

Ingredients

2 eggs (61 g)
2 tablespoons (40 g) sugar
1 1/2 cups (375 mL) milk
1/2 teaspoon vanilla essence
1/4 teaspoon grated nutmeg

Method

1. Set oven at 180°C. Brush or spray ovenproof dish with oil.
2. Beat eggs and sugar lightly.
3. Warm milk and vanilla essence, stir into eggs and sugar.
4. Pour into ovenproof dish, sprinkle with nutmeg.
5. Stand ovenproof dish in water bath and bake at 180°C for 40–45 minutes until set.
6. To test: slip a knife into custard about 3 cm from edge. If custard shows a cut when knife is drawn to the side, it is cooked, if liquid, continue cooking.

BREAD AND BUTTER CUSTARD

Follow recipe for **Baked custard**, using 2 thin slices of buttered bread and 2 tablespoons (35 g) sultanas. Cut bread into squares and arrange in ovenproof dish. Sprinkle with sultanas. Pour custard over bread and bake.

BANANA CUSTARD

- *Serves:* 4
- *Cooking utensil:* saucepan
- *Serving dish:* serving bowl (1 L)

Preparation time: ***20 minutes and 1 hour refrigeration time***

Ingredients

2 tablespoons (20 g) custard powder
1 cup (250 mL) milk
1 tablespoon (20 g) sugar
1 banana (125 g)

Method

1. Blend custard powder with $^1/_4$ cup milk.
2. Heat remainder of milk until almost boiling.
3. Pour hot milk over blended custard.
4. Return to saucepan. Stir until boiling.
5. Add sugar and allow to cool down a little.
6. Peel and slice bananas, add to custard.
7. Pour into serving bowl. Refrigerate for 1 hour.

Blend custard powder with $^1/_4$ cup milk, add remainder of milk. Cook on high power for 1 minute, stir and cook for further 1 minute. Stir and cook for 1 minute more on high power.

DATE AND CHOCOLATE CUSTARD

- *Serves:* 6
- *Cooking utensil:* ovenproof dish (2 L), baking dish with 3 cm water for water bath

Preparation time: ***20 minutes***
Cooking time: ***30–40 minutes***
Oven temperature: ***180°C***

Ingredients

4 thick slices date bread *or* raisin bread
3 tablespoons (30 g) chopped roasted hazelnuts
$^1/_2$ cup (30 g) grated chocolate
2 tablespoons (40 g) butter
3 eggs (61 g)
$^1/_4$ cup (65 g) sugar
$1^1/_2$ cups (375 mL) milk
1 teaspoon vanilla essence
1 tablespoon (20 mL) orange liqueur
Glaze
1 tablespoon (20 g) orange marmalade
1 tablespoon (20 mL) orange liqueur

Method:

1. Set oven at 180°C. Toast bread slices on both sides.
2. Combine nuts, chocolate and butter and spread over toasted slices.
3. Beat milk, eggs, sugar, vanilla essence and orange liqueur.
4. Pour into ovenproof dish and carefully float toasted slices, topping side down.
5. Stand ovenproof dish in water bath and bake at 180°C for 30–40 minutes until set.
6. Make glaze: warm marmalade and orange liqueur in saucepan.
7. Brush glaze over top of custard.

CREME CARAMEL

These may be cooked in the oven or in an electric frypan.

- *Serves:* 4
- *Cooking utensil:* 4 individual ovenproof moulds (250 mL), saucepan

Preparation time: ***35 minutes***
Cooking time: ***15–20 minutes***
Oven temperature: ***160°C***

Ingredients

Caramel
1/4 cup (65 g) sugar
1 tablespoon (20 mL) water

Custard
2 eggs (61 g)
1 tablespoon (20 g) sugar
1 cup (250 mL) milk
1/2 cup (125 mL) cream

Method

1. Prepare caramel: dissolve 1/4 cup sugar in water in saucepan, then boil for a short time without stirring, until mixture is an amber colour. Immediately pour into moulds coating the bases.
2. Set oven at 150°C. Beat eggs and sugar lightly.
3. Warm the milk and cream in the saucepan and whisk into the eggs and sugar.
4. Pour into moulds.
5. To cook in oven: place in baking dish with 3 cm water, cook at 160°C for 15–20 minutes, until just set. To cook in frypan: stand in 3 cm water at 150°C for 15–20 minutes, cover with foil so that water does not drip into custard and cook until just set.
6. Turn out into individual serving dishes. May be served hot or cold with cream.

✦ BAKED CARAMEL CUSTARD ✦

Follow recipe for **Creme caramel**, using ovenproof dish (2 L) brushed or sprayed with oil. Set oven at 180°C. Stand pie dish in baking dish with 3 cm water and bake in oven at 180°C for 30–40 minutes until set. May be turned out onto platter.

LEMON DELICIOUS

- *Serves:* **4**
- *Cooking utensil:* ovenproof dish (2 L), baking dish with 3 cm water for water bath
- *Preparation time:* ***25 minutes***
- *Cooking time:* ***45 minutes***
- *Oven temperature:* ***190°C***

Ingredients

1 tablespoon (20 g) butter
1/4 cup (65 g) caster sugar
2 eggs (61 g), separated
rind and juice of 2 lemons
1 tablespoon (10 g) plain flour
2 tablespoons (20 g) self-raising flour
1 cup (250 mL) milk

Method

1. Set oven at 190°C. Brush or spray ovenproof dish with oil.
2. Beat butter and sugar until light and creamy.
3. Stir in egg yolks, lemon juice and rind.
4. Stir in sifted flours and milk alternately.
5. Beat egg whites until stiff. Fold into mixture and pour into pie dish.
6. Stand pie dish in water bath. Bake at 190°C for 45 minutes until set and lightly browned.
7. May be served with cream or ice-cream.

Pastry desserts

APPLE PIE

This recipe is for a double-crust pie, with apple encased in pastry layers.

- *Serves:* ***6***
- *Cooking utensil:* saucepan, 22 cm pie dish (1 L), 4-sided oven tray

- *Preparation time:* ***30 minutes***
- *Cooking time:* ***30 minutes***
- *Oven temperature:* ***200°C reduced to 180°C***

Ingredients

250 g (1 quantity) **Rich shortcrust pastry** (p. 347) *or* **Biscuit pastry** (p. 347)
4 cooking apples (600 g), peeled, cored and quartered
2 tablespoons (40 g) sugar
2 tablespoons (40 mL) water
3 cloves *or* 2 strips lemon rind
1 teaspoon milk

Method

1. Place apples, sugar, water and cloves or lemon rind in saucepan and bring to boil. Cool.
2. Set oven at 200°C.
3. Divide pastry into 2 portions: $^2/_3$ and $^1/_3$.
4. Roll out $^2/_3$ portion of pastry to shape of pie dish and 3 cm larger all round.
5. Brush edge of dish with water.
6. Lift pastry into dish. Ease pastry into place without stretching it. Pastry should come just over top of the rim.
7. Place apples in pastry base.
8. Roll out the $^1/_3$ pastry top and cover pie.
9. Press edges together lightly, trim with a sharp knife and pinch into frill or mark with a teaspoon or fork.
10. Glaze with 1 teaspoon milk. Stand on 4-sided oven tray for baking.
11. Bake at 200°C for 10 minutes, lower temperature to 180°C and continue cooking for about 20 minutes.

FRUIT MINCE PIE

Follow recipe for **Apple pie** using 400 g (1 quantity) **Fruit mince** (p. 327) as filling.

FRUIT PIE

Follow recipe for **Apple pie** using 500 g of stewed, canned *or* fresh fruit as filling.

TRADITIONAL APPLE PIE

The traditional apple pie is made with a flaky type pastry on the top of the apples.

- *Serves:* **6**
- *Cooking utensil:* saucepan, 22 cm pie dish (1 L), 4-sided oven tray
- *Preparation time:* ***30 minutes***
- *Cooking time:* ***25–30 minutes***
- *Oven temperature:* ***200°C reduced to 180°C***

Ingredients

4 cooking apples (600 g)
2 tablespoons (40 g) sugar
2 tablespoons (40 mL) water
3 cloves *or* 2 strips lemon rind
125 g (1/2 quantity) **Rough puff pastry** (p. 350) *or* **Flaky pastry** (p. 349)
1 teaspoon milk

Method

1. Set oven at 200°C.
2. Peel, quarter, core and slice apples. Bring apples, sugar, water and cloves to boil. Cool slightly.
3. Place apples in pie dish.
4. Roll pastry to the shape of pie plate *or* dish, 5 cm larger all round and 5 mm thick.
5. Cut a 2 cm strip from outside edge of pastry.
6. Brush the edge of pie dish with water.
7. Fit the strip of pastry carefully around the edge without stretching it, cut side out. Join ends neatly and brush strip with water.
8. Lift large piece of pastry onto pie dish. Press edges together lightly.
9. Trim edges with a sharp knife. Cut the edge at 3 cm intervals drawing up flakes lightly with knife.
10. Glaze top with milk. Make several cuts in top of pastry.
11. Place pie dish on 4-sided oven tray and bake at 200°C for 10 minutes, then at 180°C for 15–20 minutes.
12. May be served with **Custard sauce** (p. 287), yoghurt *or* ice-cream.

APPLE STRUDEL

- *Serves:* **6**
- *Cooking utensil:* 4-sided oven tray

- *Preparation time:* ***30 minutes***
- *Cooking time:* ***30 minutes***
- *Oven temperature:* ***200°C reduced to 180°C***

Ingredients

4 sheets filo pastry
3 tablespoons (60 g) butter, melted
Filling
3 apples (450 g), cored and finely diced
1/2 cup (90 g) sultanas
1/2 teaspoon cinnamon
grated rind of 1/2 lemon
2 tablespoons (30 g) chopped walnuts
1/2 cup (15 g) fresh breadcrumbs
1 tablespoon (15 g) icing sugar mixture

Method

1. Set oven at 200°C. Cover base of oven tray with baking paper.
2. Place 2 sheets of filo pastry on a clean tea towel and lightly brush pastry with melted butter. Place remaining sheets of pastry on top and brush again with melted butter.
3. Mix filling ingredients and place onto the pastry, spreading out to 5 cm from each edge.
4. Roll pastry over the filling, and continue to roll as for **Egg sponge** (p. 396).
5. Place strudel, join down, on 4-sided oven tray and tuck the ends of the pastry underneath.
6. Brush with remaining butter and make several shallow slits on top of pastry to allow any excess moisture to escape.
7. Bake at 200°C for 10 minutes, then at 180°C for 20 minutes.
8. Lift onto a cake cooler and dust with sifted icing sugar mixture.
9. Serve sliced, either hot or cold with ice-cream or cream.

APPLE BERRY STRUDEL

Follow recipe for **Apple strudel**, replacing 1 apple with 1 cup (150 g) raspberries and 1 tablespoon (20 g) sugar.

CHERRY AND APPLE STRUDEL

Follow recipe for **Apple strudel**, replacing 1 apple with 425 g can pitted black cherries, drained. Replace walnuts with pecans.

CUSTARD TART

Tarts are pastry cases or bases, filled with custard or fruit and usually served hot, with cream or custard.

- *Serves:* **6**
- *Cooking utensil:* 22 cm pie dish (1 L), saucepan
- *Preparation time:* ***30 minutes***
- *Cooking time:* ***40–45 minutes***
- *Oven temperature:* ***200°C reduced to 180°C***

Ingredients

125 g (1/2 quantity) **Shortcrust pastry** (p. 346)
2 eggs (61 g)
2 tablespoons (40 g) sugar
1 cup (250 mL) milk
1/2 teaspoon grated nutmeg

Method

1 Set oven at 200°C.
2 Roll pastry out to shape of pie dish or flan ring and 3 cm larger all round. Place in pie dish without stretching. Trim edge with sharp knife. Flute edge to level of dish.
3 Beat eggs and sugar.
4 Warm milk and pour over egg mixture.
5 Pour warm custard mixture gently into pastry case. Sprinkle with nutmeg.
6 Bake at 200°C for 10 minutes then at 180°C for 35 minutes until custard is set.
7 Serve warm with cream or cool and decorate with whipped cream and strawberries.

✦ FRUIT CUSTARD TART ✦

Follow recipe for **Custard tart**. Spread 1 cup (200 g) **Apricot puree** (p. 308) on pastry case before pouring in custard.

FRUIT FLAN

Flans are pastry cases with sweet fillings, decorated with fruit, cream or chocolate and usually served cold.

Serves: ***6***

Ingredients

125 g ($^1/_2$ quantity) **Rich shortcrust pastry** (p. 347), made into 22 cm flan *or* tart case and 'baked blind' (p. 352) *or* 22 cm flan pastry case.
200 mL (1 quantity) **Confectioners' custard** (p. 000), cooled
250 g fruit, e.g. mandarin segments, canned sliced peaches, apricot halves, strawberries, kiwi fruit, cherries
125 mL ($^1/_2$ quantity) **Fruit sauce** (p. 289) *or* 125 mL whipped cream

Preparation time: ***30 minutes***

Method

1. Place pastry case on serving dish.
2. Spread custard in pastry case.
3. Arrange fruit to form decorative pattern.
4. Glaze with **Fruit sauce** *or* decorate with whipped cream.

FRUIT MINCE

This makes 400 g fruit mince, which can be used to fill tarts, pies and slices.

Ingredients

1 apple (125 g), peeled, cored and grated
$^1/_3$ cup (60 g) currants
$^1/_3$ cup (60 g) sultanas
$^1/_3$ cup (60 g) raisins
1 tablespoon (15 g) mixed peel
1 teaspoon mixed spice
1 tablespoon (20 mL) lemon juice *or* brandy
$^1/_3$ cup (85 g) caster sugar

Preparation time: ***25 minutes***

Method

1. Mix all ingredients.
2. Will keep for 3 months in refrigerator. Scald washed jars and lids by dipping in boiling water and drain dry. Place fruit mince in jars, cover and store in refrigerator.

LEMON MERINGUE TART

- *Serves:* **6**
- *Cooking utensil:* saucepan, 4-sided oven tray
- *Preparation time:* **30 minutes**
- *Cooking time:* **5 minutes**
- *Oven temperature:* **180°C**

Ingredients

125 g (1/2 quantity) **Shortcrust pastry** (p. 346) *or* **Rich shortcrust pastry** (p. 347), made into 22 cm flan or tart case and 'baked blind' (p. 352) *or* 22 cm tart *or* flan pastry case
4 tablespoons (40 g) arrowroot
1 cup (250 mL) water
1/2 cup (125 g) butter
3/4 cup (190 g) sugar
4 eggs (61 g), separated
grated rind and juice of 4 lemons
3 tablespoons (60 g) caster sugar

Method

1 Set oven at 180°C. Place pastry case on ovenproof serving plate on oven tray.
2 Blend arrowroot with water and place it in saucepan with butter, sugar, yolks, lemon rind and juice. Stir until boiling, cook 1 minute. Cool slightly.
3 Pour filling into pastry case.
4 Beat egg whites stiffly and fold in caster sugar gradually. Pile or pipe meringue on top of filling. Brown lightly in oven at 180°C for approximately 5 minutes.
5 Serve with cream or ice-cream.

APPLE MERINGUE TART

Follow recipe for **Lemon meringue tart**, using 500 g **Stewed apples** (p. 315) as filling.

SMALL FRUIT MINCE PIES

- *Number:* **18**
- *Cooking utensil:* patty pans
- *Preparation time:* **30 minutes**
- *Cooking time:* **15–20 minutes**
- *Oven temperature:* **180°C**

Ingredients

125 g (1/2 quantity) **Biscuit pastry** (p. 347)
200 g (1/2 quantity) **Fruit mince** (p. 327)
1 teaspoon milk

Method

1 Set oven at 180°C. Brush or spray patty pans with oil.
2 Roll out pastry to 5 mm thickness. Cut pastry into 18 rounds x 8 cm diameter for bases and 18 rounds x 6 cm diameter for tops.
3 Line patty pans with large rounds of pastry and fill with fruit mince.
4 Moisten edges of pastry with water and place the tops on. Press lightly.
5 Glaze with milk. Place on oven tray and bake at 180°C for 15–20 minutes.

Baked and steamed puddings

APPLE AND RICE DESSERT

- *Serves:* **6**
- *Cooking utensil:* ovenproof dish (2 L)
- *Preparation time:* ***30 minutes***
- *Cooking time:* ***50 minutes***
- *Oven temperature:* ***180°C***

Ingredients

2 cups cooked rice (p. 113)
2 tablespoons (40 g) caster sugar
1 tablespoon (10 g) custard powder
2 eggs (61 g)
400 g (1 quantity) **Apple puree** (p. 308) *or* 410 g can pie apples
1 teaspoon cinnamon
1 teaspoon mixed spice
1 teaspoon grated lemon rind
1/2 cup (125 mL) cream

Method

1. Combine all ingredients. Brush or spray ovenproof dish with oil.
2. Pour into dish.
3. Bake at 180°C for 50 minutes until set.
4. Cool before serving. May be dusted with icing sugar mixture and served with cream or ice-cream.

APPLE CHARLOTTE

- *Serves:* **4**
- *Cooking utensil:* ovenproof dish (2 L)
- *Preparation time:* ***25 minutes***
- *Cooking time:* ***30 minutes***
- *Oven temperature:* ***190°C***

Ingredients

8 thin slices of stale bread
2 tablespoons (40 g) butter, melted
400 g (1 quantity) **Apple puree** (p. 308) *or* 410 g can pie apples
1 teaspoon cinnamon
2 teaspoons (10 g) caster sugar

Method

1. Set oven at 190°C.
2. Cut bread to fit base, sides and top of ovenproof dish.
3. Dip one side of bread in melted butter and place the buttered side to the dish, making a complete lining.
4. Fill with **Apple puree** and cover with bread, buttered side up.
5. Bake at 190°C for 30 minutes until light brown and crisp.
6. Sprinkle with mixed cinnamon and sugar.
7. May be served with **Custard sauce** (p. 287) or cream.

APPLE CRUMBLE

- *Serves:* *4*
- *Cooking utensil:* ovenproof dish (2 L)

- *Preparation time:* ***20 minutes***
- *Cooking time:* ***30 minutes***
- *Oven temperature:* ***190°C***

Ingredients

3–4 cooking apples (500 g)
3 tablespoons (60 mL) water
3 cloves
2 tablespoons (40 g) butter
1/4 cup (40 g) self-raising flour
2 tablespoons (30 g) brown sugar
2 tablespoons (16 g) coconut
2 tablespoons (20 g) rolled oats *or* bran buds

Method

1 Set oven at 190°C.
2 Peel, core and slice apples. Place in ovenproof dish with water and cloves.
3 Rub butter into flour until mixture is crumbly. Mix in brown sugar, coconut and rolled oats *or* bran buds. Sprinkle over apples.
4 Bake at 190°C for 30 minutes.
5 May be served with **Custard sauce** (p. 287).

Microwave at step 2 for 8 minutes on high power and then at step 4 for 6 minutes on high power.

✦ FRUIT CRUMBLE ✦

Follow recipe for **Apple crumble**, using fruits such as peaches, gooseberries, rhubarb *or* apricots. If stewed or canned fruit is used, reduce cooking time to 20 minutes.

APPLE SPONGE

- *Serves:* *6*
- *Cooking utensil:* ovenproof dish (2 L)

- *Preparation time:* ***30 minutes***
- *Cooking time:* ***30–45 minutes***
- *Oven temperature:* ***190°C***

Ingredients

1/4 cup (65 g) butter
1/4 cup (65 g) caster sugar
1 egg, beaten
1 cup (150 g) wholemeal self-raising flour
1/3 cup (85 mL) milk
400 g (1 quantity) **Apple puree** (p. 308), hot

Method

1 Set oven at 190°C. Brush or spray ovenproof dish with oil.
2 Cream butter and sugar until light and fluffy.
3 Add egg, mix well.
4 Stir in flour and milk alternately.
5 Place hot apple in ovenproof dish.
6 Spread cake mixture over apples.
7 Bake at 190°C for 30–45 minutes.
8 May be served with **Custard sauce** (p. 287) or cream.

✦ FRUIT SPONGE ✦

Follow recipe for **Apple sponge**, using fruit such as rhubarb, apricots *or* berry fruits.

BAKED CHEESECAKE

- *Serves:* ***8–10***
- *Cooking utensil:* 20 cm springform cake pan (1.75 mL), oven tray
- *Preparation time:* ***45 minutes***
- *Cooking time:* ***50 minutes***
- *Oven temperature:* ***150°C***

Ingredients

Base

1 cup (120 g) plain sweet biscuit crumbs
1/4 cup (65 g) melted butter

Filling

2 1/2 cups (625 g) cream cheese
1/2 cup (125 g) caster sugar
3 eggs
grated rind of 1 lemon
1/2 cup (125 mL) lemon juice
1/2 teaspoon grated nutmeg
200 mL cream, whipped

Method

1 Set oven at 150°C.
2 Brush or spray springform pan with oil and line base with baking paper.
3 Place biscuits in a plastic bag and roll with a rolling pin to crush finely.
4 Place crushed biscuits in a bowl and stir in butter.
5 Place biscuit mixture in the bottom of pan, press down and level with a flat-bottomed glass. Chill for 30 minutes.
6 Place the springform pan on oven tray.
7 Beat the cream cheese and sugar until smooth.
8 Add the eggs one at a time, beating well in between.
9 Mix in the lemon rind and juice, and beat until the mixture is smooth and creamy.
10 Pour the mixture into the springform pan and bake at 150°C for 50 minutes.
11 Cool the cheesecake and refrigerate for several hours or overnight.
12 Sprinkle with nutmeg and serve with whipped cream.

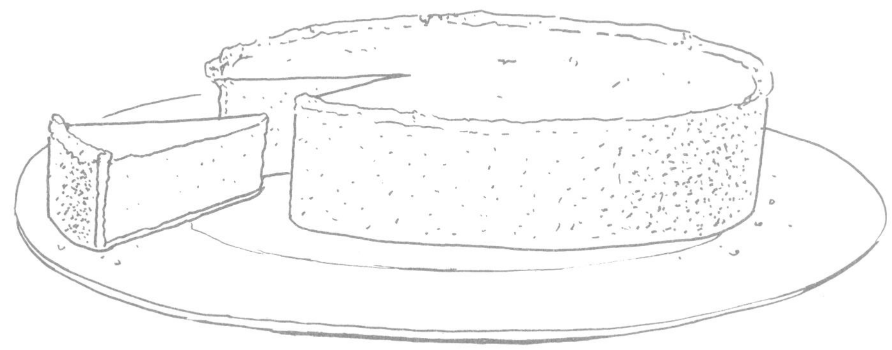

STEAMED PUDDING

- *Serves:* ***6***
- *Cooking utensil:* large saucepan *or* steamer, medium pudding basin (1.5 L). May also be cooked in 6 individual moulds (250 mL) in a frypan with 2 cm simmering water

Cooking time: ***1 1/2 hours** medium pudding basin*
***30 minutes** individual moulds*
Preparation time: ***30 minutes***

Ingredients

1/2 cup (125 g) butter
1/2 cup (125 g) caster sugar
1 egg (61 g), beaten
1/2 teaspoon vanilla essence
1 1/2 cups (225 g) self-raising flour
1/2 cup (125 mL) milk

Method

1 Place water in saucepan to come 3/4 up side of pudding basin or nearly fill base of steamer with water. Heat water.
2 Brush or spray basin or moulds with oil.
3 Cream butter and sugar until light and fluffy.
4 Add egg and vanilla essence, mix well.
5 Stir in flour and milk alternately, 1/3 at a time. Mix thoroughly.
6 Place mixture in basin or moulds, cover with foil or oiled paper and tie firmly with string to keep out water, making a handle with string across top of pudding to use in lifting pudding out of saucepan.
7 Place in top of steamer *or* in saucepan of boiling water. Do not immerse completely. Water must remain boiling. Check every 30 minutes and add water to retain level. If cooking individual moulds in frypan, ensure water does not enter moulds. Boil for times as above.
8 Turn onto warm plate. May be served with **Custard sauce** (p. 287) or **Fruit sauce** (p. 289), and cream or ice-cream.

✦ CHOCOLATE STEAMED PUDDING ✦

Follow recipe for **Steamed pudding**. Add 2 tablespoons (20 g) sifted cocoa with flour. Add 1 tablespoon extra milk.

✦ COLLEGE STEAMED PUDDING ✦

Follow recipe for **Steamed pudding**. Place 1/4 cup (65 g) jam in base of basin. Cover with mixture.

✦ GINGER STEAMED PUDDING ✦

Follow recipe for **Steamed pudding**. Add 1 teaspoon bicarbonate of soda and 2 teaspoons ground ginger at step 3. Add 1 tablespoon (20 g) golden syrup to milk in step 3.

STICKY DATE PUDDING

- *Serves:* **6**
- *Cooking utensil:* small saucepan, 20 cm round cake pan, baking paper
- *Preparation time:* ***30 minutes***
- *Cooking time:* ***50 minutes***
- *Oven temperature:* ***180°C***

Ingredients:

1 1/4 cups (200 g) chopped dates
1 1/4 cups (315 mL) water
1 teaspoon bicarbonate of soda
3 tablespoons (60 g) butter
3/4 cup (190 g) caster sugar
2 eggs (61 g), beaten
1 cup (150 g) self-raising flour
Butterscotch sauce
1 cup (200 g) brown sugar
1 cup (250 mL) cream
3/4 cup (190 g) butter

Method

1. Set oven at 180°C. Brush or spray cake pan with oil and line base with baking paper.
2. Combine dates and water in saucepan, bring to the boil.
3. Remove saucepan from heat, add bicarbonate of soda, stand 5 minutes.
4. Place in blender or food processor until smooth.
5. Cream butter and sugar until light and creamy.
6. Beat in eggs a little at a time.
7. Fold in flour, then date mixture.
8. Pour mixture into cake pan, bake at 180°C for 50 minutes.
9. To make sauce: stir ingredients over heat, boil 3 minutes.
10. Turn pudding onto a warm plate, cut into wedges and pour sauce over. Serve with cream or ice-cream.

FRUIT STEAMED PUDDING

- *Serves:* **6**
- *Cooking utensil:* steamer *or* large saucepan, medium pudding basin (1.5 L), small saucepan

Preparation time: ***30 minutes***
Cooking time: ***1 hour***

Ingredients

1 tablespoon (40 g) butter
1 cup (250 mL) milk
1/3 cup (60 g) sultanas
1/3 cup (60 g) raisins
1/3 cup (60 g) currants
1/4 cup (30 g) chopped pecan nuts
1 cooking apple (125 g), peeled, cored and diced
2 tablespoons (40 g) sugar
1 teaspoon bicarbonate soda
1 cup (150 g) self-raising flour
1/2 teaspoon mixed spice
1 teaspoon cinnamon

Method:

1. Place water in saucepan to come 3/4 up side of pudding basin *or* nearly fill base of steamer with water. Heat water.
2. Brush or spray basin with oil.
3. Place butter, milk, fruit, nuts, diced apple and sugar in a saucepan and bring to the boil.
4. Remove saucepan from heat, add bicarbonate of soda, stir well and allow to fizz.
5. Sift flours and spices, add and mix well.
6. Place mixture in basin, cover with foil or oiled paper and tie firmly with string to keep out water, making a handle with string across top of pudding to use in lifting pudding out of saucepan.
7. Place in top of steamer *or* in saucepan of boiling water. Do not immerse completely. Water must remain boiling. Check every 30 minutes and add water to retain level. Boil for 1 hour.
8. Turn pudding onto serving plate, cut into wedges.
9. May be served with **Custard sauce** (p. 287) or cream.

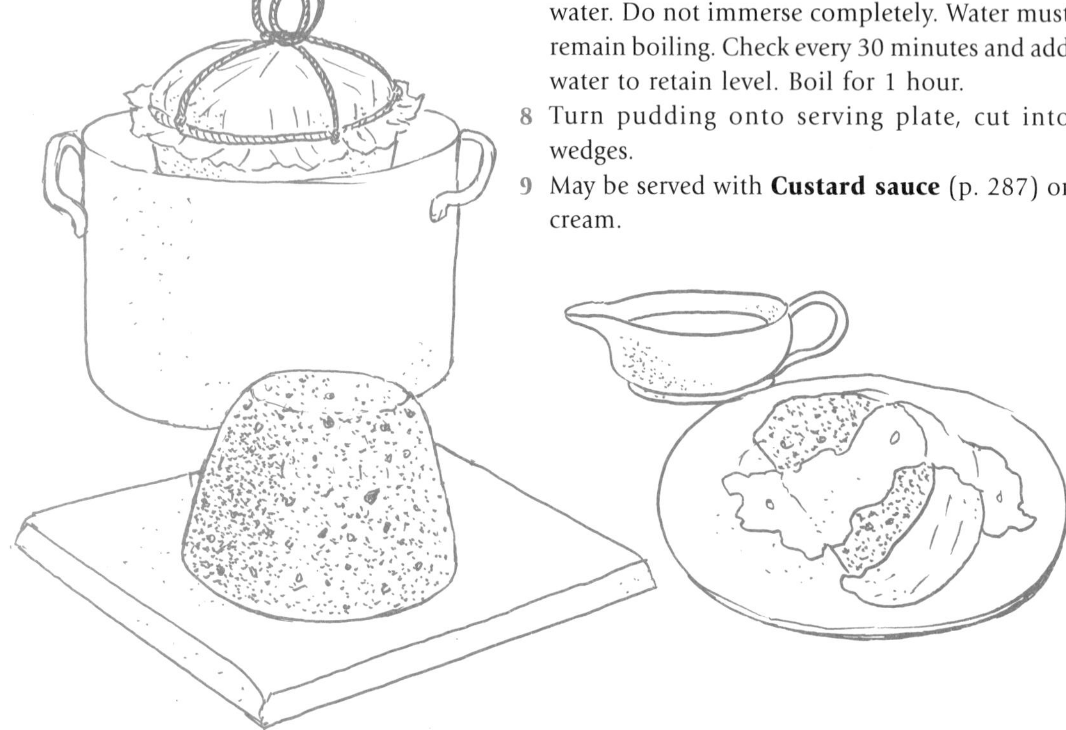

CHRISTMAS PUDDING

This pudding matures well if made at least 4 weeks in advance, then reheated to serve. Allow 1$^{1}/_{2}$ hours for reheating in boiling water.

- *Serves:* 8
- *Cooking utensil:* steamer *or* large saucepan of boiling water, large pudding basin (2 L)

Preparation time: **1 hour**
Cooking time: **3 hours**

Ingredients

$^{3}/_{4}$ cup (135 g) sultanas
$^{3}/_{4}$ cup (135 g) raisins
$^{3}/_{4}$ cup (135 g) chopped dates
$^{1}/_{3}$ cup (60 g) currants
$^{1}/_{3}$ cup (60 g) mixed peel
$^{1}/_{2}$ cup (50 g) chopped blanched almonds
$^{3}/_{4}$ cup (110 g) plain flour
$^{1}/_{4}$ teaspoon bicarbonate of soda
$^{1}/_{4}$ teaspoon cinnamon
1 cup (40 g) fresh breadcrumbs
$^{1}/_{2}$ cup (125 g) butter
$^{1}/_{2}$ cup (90 g) brown sugar
3 eggs (61 g), beaten
2 tablespoons (40 mL) fruit juice *or* brandy
Brandy sauce
$^{1}/_{2}$ cup (125 g) butter
1$^{1}/_{2}$ cups (270 g) icing sugar mixture
$^{1}/_{4}$ cup (65 mL) brandy
nutmeg in shaker

Method

1. Place water in saucepan to come $^{3}/_{4}$ up side of pudding basin *or* nearly fill base of steamer with water. Heat water.
2. Brush or spray basin *or* moulds with oil.
3. Mix fruit, peel and almonds.
4. Sift flour, bicarbonate soda, cinnamon and add to fruit. Add breadcrumbs.
5. Beat butter and sugar until light and creamy.
6. Add eggs gradually, mix well, add fruit juice *or* brandy then flour and fruit mixture. Mix thoroughly.
7. Place mixture in basin, cover with foil *or* oiled paper and tie firmly with string to keep out water, making a handle with string across top of pudding to use in lifting pudding out of saucepan.
8. Place in top of steamer *or* in saucepan of boiling water. Do not immerse completely. Water must remain boiling. Check every 30 minutes and add water to retain level. Boil for 3 hours.
9. Make brandy sauce: beat butter and sugar until light and creamy. Mix in brandy. Place in small dish and dust with nutmeg.
10. Turn pudding onto serving plate, cut into wedges. Serve with brandy sauce.

GOLDEN SYRUP DUMPLINGS

These may be cooked in the oven or by boiling the dumplings in the saucepan of syrup.

- *Serves:* 4
- *Cooking utensil:* large saucepan *or* ovenproof dish (2 L)
- *Preparation time:* ***20 minutes***
- *Cooking time:* ***20–30 minutes***
- *Oven temperature:* ***190°C***

Ingredients

2 tablespoons (40 g) butter
1 cup (150 g) self-raising flour
1 egg (61 g), beaten
3 tablespoons (60 mL) milk
Syrup
$1\frac{1}{2}$ cups (375 mL) water
$\frac{1}{3}$ cup (85 g) golden syrup
1 tablespoon (20 mL) lemon juice
$1\frac{1}{2}$ tablespoons (30 g) butter

Method

1. Set oven at 190°C. Rub butter into flour. Add egg and milk and mix into a dough.
2. Place syrup ingredients in a saucepan and stir until dissolved. Bring to the boil.
3. *To boil*: when syrup is boiling, drop in spoonfuls of dough, simmer for 30 minutes.
   To bake: place spoonfuls of dough in ovenproof dish (2 L), pour in boiling syrup and bake at 190°C for 30 minutes.
4. May be served with **Custard sauce** (p. 287), cream or ice-cream.

PINEAPPLE UPSIDE-DOWN PUDDING

- *Serves:* 6
- *Cooking utensil:* 20 cm round cake pan (1.5 L)
- *Preparation time:* ***35 minutes***
- *Cooking time:* ***35–40 minutes***
- *Oven temperature:* ***180°C***

Ingredients

$\frac{1}{2}$ cup (125 g) butter
$\frac{1}{2}$ cup (90 g) brown sugar
6 slices canned *or* fresh pineapple
$\frac{1}{2}$ cup (125 g) butter
$\frac{1}{2}$ cup (125 g) caster sugar
1 teaspoon vanilla essence
2 eggs (61 g)
1 cup (150 g) self-raising flour
$\frac{1}{4}$ cup (40 g) plain flour
$\frac{1}{4}$ cup (65 mL) milk

Method:

1. Set oven at 180°C. Brush or spray cake pan with oil and line base with baking paper.
2. Cream butter and brown sugar until light and fluffy.
3. Spread over the base of cake pan.
4. Arrange pineapple slices on base of pan.
5. Cream butter and caster sugar until light and fluffy.
6. Beat in eggs one at a time, add vanilla essence.
7. Mix sifted flours and milk alternately into mixture.
8. Spread the mixture over the pineapple.
9. Bake at 180°C for 35–40 minutes.
10. Serve upside-down. May be served with **Custard sauce** (p. 287) or cream.

✦ APPLE UPSIDE-DOWN PUDDING ✦

Follow recipe for **Pineapple upside-down pudding**, using 2 peeled, cored and quartered Granny Smith apples (300 g). At step 7 add 1 teaspoon of cinnamon.

✦ APRICOT UPSIDE-DOWN PUDDING ✦

Follow recipe for **Pineapple upside-down pudding**, using 12 canned *or* fresh apricot halves.

✦ PEAR AND GINGER UPSIDE-DOWN PUDDING ✦

Follow recipe for **Pineapple upside-down pudding**, using 6 canned *or* fresh pear halves. At step 7 add 1 teaspoon ground ginger.

SAGO PLUM PUDDING

- *Serves:* 6
- *Cooking utensil:* steamer *or* large saucepan, medium pudding basin (1.5 L)

Cooking time: **2½ hours**
Preparation time: **30 minutes**

Ingredients

½ cup (90 g) sago *or* seed tapioca
1¼ cups (315 mL) milk
1½ cups (45 g) fresh breadcrumbs
1 egg (61 g), beaten
½ cup (125 g) sugar
1 cup (180 g) raisins
1 tablespoon (20 g) butter, melted
1 teaspoon bicarbonate soda

Method

1. If possible, soak sago in milk overnight. If sago is not soaked, cook pudding for an extra 30 minutes.
2. Place water in saucepan to come ¾ up side of pudding basin *or* nearly fill base of steamer with water. Heat water.
3. Brush or spray basin with oil.
4. Add all ingredients to sago and milk. Blend thoroughly.
5. Place mixture in basin, cover with foil *or* oiled paper and tie firmly with string to keep out water, making a handle with string across top of pudding to use in lifting pudding out of saucepan.
6. Place in top of steamer *or* in saucepan of boiling water. Do not immerse completely. Water must remain boiling. Check every 30 minutes and add water to retain level. Boil for 2½ hours.
7. Turn onto warm plate. May be served with **Custard sauce** (p. 287) or cream.

SELF-SAUCING CHOCOLATE PUDDING

► *Serves:* ***6***
► *Cooking utensil:* ovenproof dish (2 L)

Preparation time: ***25 minutes***
Cooking time: ***40–45 minutes***
► *Oven temperature:* ***175°C***

Ingredients

1 cup (150 g) self-raising flour
2 teaspoons (5 g) cocoa
1/4 cup (65 g) butter
1/2 cup (125 g) caster sugar
1 egg, beaten
1/2 cup (60 g) chopped walnuts
1/2 cup (125 mL) milk

Sauce

1/2 cup (90 g) brown sugar
1 tablespoon (10 g) cocoa
1 1/2 cups (315 mL) boiling water

Method

1. Set oven at 175°C. Brush or spray ovenproof dish with oil.
2. Sift flour and cocoa.
3. Cream butter and caster sugar until light and creamy.
4. Add egg and walnuts, mix well.
5. Stir in flour and milk alternately. Pour into ovenproof dish.
6. Make sauce: combine brown sugar and cocoa. Sprinkle on top of mixture in dish, and pour boiling water gently over all this.
7. Bake at 175°C for 40–45 minutes.
8. May be dusted with icing sugar mixture and served with **Custard sauce** (p. 287) or ice-cream.

 Microwave on medium power for 8 minutes.

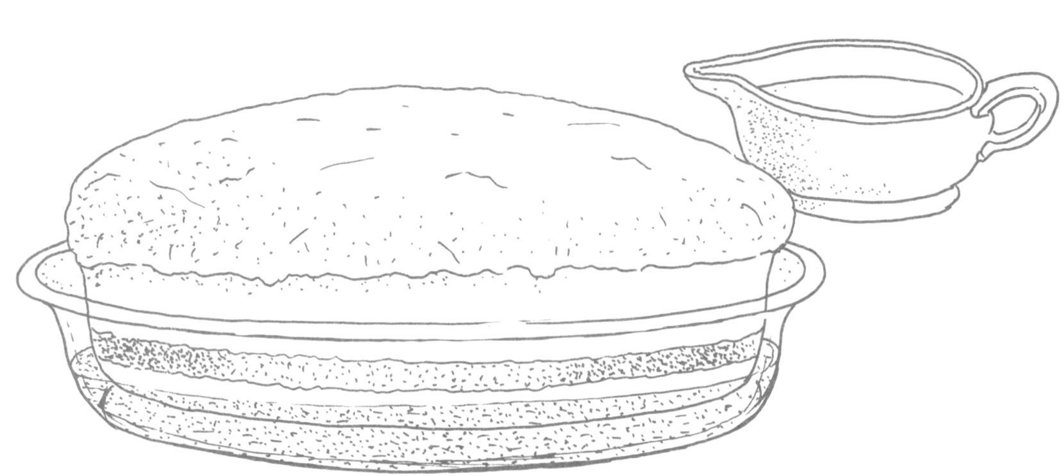

Other desserts

CHOCOLATE BLANCMANGE

These may be sprinkled with coconut or decorated with glacé cherries or other decorations after turning out of the mould.

- *Serves:* 4
- *Cooking utensil:* saucepan, medium mould (1 L) *or* 4 individual moulds (250 mL)

Preparation time: ***20 minutes and setting time***

Ingredients

4 tablespoons (40 g) cornflour
1 tablespoon (10 g) cocoa
2 tablespoons (40 g) sugar
2 cups (500 mL) milk
1/2 teaspoon vanilla essence

Method

1 Blend cornflour, cocoa and sugar with 1/4 cup of the milk.
2 Heat remainder of milk with lemon rind until almost boiling.
3 Remove lemon rind and pour milk over blended cornflour mixture, stirring constantly.
4 Return to saucepan and stir over heat until boiling. Reduce heat and cook for 1 minute, stirring all the time.
5 Add vanilla essence and pour into mould.
6 When cold and set, turn out onto serving dish.

CHOCOLATE MOUSSE

- *Serves:* 6
- *Cooking utensil:* double saucepan
- *Serving dish:* 6 individual (200 mL) serving dishes

Preparation time: ***30 minutes and 2 hours refrigeration time***

Ingredients

200 g dark chocolate
300 mL cream, semi-whipped
1 tablespoon (20 g) sugar
3 eggs (61 g), separated
1 teaspoon vanilla essence
6 teaspoons grated chocolate for decoration

Method

1 Break up chocolate and melt over hot water *or* in microwave oven (p. 73).
2 Rapidly whisk *or* blend in processor egg yolks, chocolate and vanilla essence until mixture is smooth, fold in semi-whipped cream.
3 Beat egg whites until stiff.
4 Fold egg whites into chocolate mixture.
5 Pour into serving dishes and refrigerate for 2 hours until firm.
6 Decorate with grated chocolate and serve.

✦ CHOCOLATE LIQUEUR MOUSSE ✦

Follow recipe for **Chocolate mousse**. At step 3 add 2 teaspoons kirsch or other liqueur. At step 5 decorate with glacé *or* preserved cherries.

✦ MOCHA MOUSSE ✦

Follow recipe for **Chocolate mousse**. At step 3 add 2 teaspoons instant coffee dissolved in 2 teaspoons water.

LEMON CHEESECAKE

- *Serves:* ***8***
- *Cooking utensil:* 20 cm springform pan (1.75 mL), double saucepan

Preparation time: ***30 minutes and 2 hours setting time***

Ingredients

Base

1 cup (120 g) plain sweet biscuits
1/4 cup (65 g) melted butter

Filling

2 eggs (61 g), separated
1/2 cup (125 g) caster sugar
3/4 cup (190 mL) milk
1 tablespoon (12 g) gelatine
2 tablespoons (40 mL) hot water
1/2 cup (125 mL) lemon juice
1 tablespoon grated lemon rind
1 cup (250 g) cream cheese
1 cup (250 mL) cream, whipped
6–8 glacé cherries

Method

1. Place biscuits in a plastic bag and roll with a rolling pin to crush finely.
2. Place crushed biscuits in a bowl and stir in butter.
3. Place biscuit mixture in the bottom of pan, press down and level with a flat-bottomed glass. Chill for 30 minutes.
4. Beat yolks and sugar.
5. Heat milk and pour over yolks and sugar.
6. Cook in top of double saucepan over water until custard thickens. Cool.
7. Dissolve gelatine in hot water, add lemon juice and rind.
8. Beat custard, cream cheese, sugar and gelatine mixture.
9. Beat egg whites until stiff, then fold into cheese mixture.
10. Pour into base and refrigerate 2 hours.
11. Decorate with whipped cream and cherries. Serve.

LEMON SAGO

- *Serves:* 4
- *Cooking utensil:* saucepan

Preparation time: ***20 minutes***

Ingredients

2 cups (500 mL) water
1/2 cup (100 g) sago *or* seed tapioca
2 tablespoons (40 g) sugar
1 tablespoon (20 g) golden syrup
grated rind and juice of 1 lemon

Method

1. Bring water to the boil. Add sago to water, stir well.
2. Cook until clear, stirring frequently.
3. Add sugar, syrup, lemon rind and juice.
4. Cook 1 minute. Cool slightly and pour into serving dish (1.5 L).
5. May be served with **Custard sauce** (p. 287) or cream.

Microwave at step 1 for 6–8 minutes on high power, and at step 4 for 1 minute on high power.

LEMON SOUFFLÉ

- *Serves:* 6
- *Cooking utensil:* double saucepan, 14 cm soufflé dish (1 L) *or* 6 individual 8 cm soufflé dishes (250 mL)

Preparation time: ***40 minutes and 2 hours refrigeration time***

Ingredients

2 teaspoons grated lemon rind
3/4 cup (190 mL) lemon juice, strained
4 eggs (61 g), separated
1/2 cup (125 g) caster sugar
1 tablespoon (12 g) gelatine
1/2 cup (125 mL) hot water
1 cup (250 mL) cream, semi-whipped
1/2 cup (60 g) finely chopped nuts
1/4 cup (65 mL) cream, whipped
6 lemon slices

Method

1. Attach a strip of baking paper around each soufflé dish to form collar 3 cm above edge.
2. Place lemon rind, juice, egg yolks and sugar in the top of a double saucepan.
3. Stir over boiling water for 5 minutes until thick. Cool.
4. Dissolve gelatine in hot water, cool and fold into custard mixture with the semi-whipped cream.
5. Beat egg whites until stiff.
6. Fold whites into mixture until evenly mixed.
7. Pour into soufflé dish. Refrigerate for 2 hours, until set.
8. Carefully remove paper collar and cover sides with nuts.
9. Decorate with piped whipped cream and lemon slices.

PAVLOVA

► *Serves:* **6**
► *Cooking utensil:* oven tray *or* 20 cm springform pan (1.75 L), baking paper

◷ *Preparation time:* ***30 minutes***
◷ *Cooking time:* ***1¼–1½ hours***
► *Oven temperature:* ***110°C***

Ingredients

4 egg whites
1 cup (250 g) caster sugar
1 tablespoon (10 g) cornflour
1 teaspoon vanilla essence
2 teaspoons vinegar
1 cup (250 mL) cream, whipped
1 banana (125 g), sliced
¼ cup (40 g) pineapple pieces
1 passionfruit
1 kiwi fruit (80 g), sliced
4 glacé cherries

Method

1 Set oven at 110°C. Line oven tray *or* springform pan with baking paper.
2 Beat egg whites until stiff. Add sugar gradually and continue to beat until mixture is stiff.
3 Fold in 1 tablespoon cornflour and add vanilla essence and vinegar.
4 Pile on oven tray *or* place in springform pan.
5 Bake at 110°C for 1¼–1½ hours, until firm, without allowing pavlova to colour.
6 Cool on oven tray *or* base of springform pan.
7 Place pavlova on serving plate and spread with half the whipped cream. Cover this with fruit. Decorate with remaining whipped cream and cherries.

200 F
1 1/2 - 2 hrs.
beat eggs whites to consistancy of marshmallos

► *Serves:* **6**
► *Serving dish:*
20 cm x 10

Ingredients

18–20 sponge
100 mL strong
3 tablespoons
4 eggs (61 g),
3 tablespoons
400 g mascar
300 mL crear
3 tablespoon

me: ***40 minutes and 2 hours***
time

ge fingers in serving dish,
covering the base.
coffee and marsala over the
ers.
yolks and sugar until light and

mascarpone cheese and semi-
eam.
g whites until stiff and fold into
mixture.
6 Pour over sponge fingers.
7 Refrigerate for 2 hours before serving. Dust with sifted cocoa.

PARFAIT

These colourful desserts are a variation of the trifle and are traditionally served in tall glass dishes or parfait glasses.

- *Serves:* ***1***
- *Serving dish:* 200 mL tall parfait glass

Preparation time: ***10 minutes***

Ingredients

Choose 3–4 of the following: ice-cream, fruit pieces, jelly, sweet sauce, e.g. chocolate, custard, fruit
whipped cream
nuts
glacé cherries

Method

1. Arrange layers of food in parfait glass to provide attractive colour combinations.
2. Top with whipped cream, nuts and glacé cherry.

TRIFLE

- *Serves:* ***6***
- *Serving dish:* glass serving bowl (1 L)

Preparation time: ***40 minutes***

Ingredients

250 mL (1 quantity) **Custard sauce** (p. 287)
1 sponge cake (175 g)
1/3 cup (85 g) jam
1 tablespoon (15 g) chopped glacé ginger
2 tablespoons (30 g) chopped nuts
1/4 cup (65 mL) fruit juice *or* sherry
1/2 cup (125 mL) cream, whipped
1/2 cup (125 mL) red jelly, chopped
1/2 cup fruit pieces, e.g. pulp of 1 passionfruit, 1 kiwi fruit (80 g), sliced, 1 banana (125 g), chopped, 6 strawberries, halved

Method

1. Cut sponge into small slices, spread with jam and sandwich together.
2. Arrange in serving bowl and sprinkle with ginger and half of the nuts.
3. Pour fruit juice *or* sherry over sponge.
4. Cover with custard. Decorate with whipped cream, jelly and fruit pieces.

13 Pastry

Pastry is used as a case or cover for sweet or savoury mixtures for pies, pasties, tarts, flans, rolls, dumplings and fruit slices. Good pastry is light and crisp. The crisp texture is due to the high proportion of fat to flour and the small amount of liquid used for mixing.

Commercially prepared or packaged mixes may be bought and stored for use when time is limited.

Food value

As pastry consists chiefly of flour and fat it is an energy-dense food. The high percentage of fat slows down the rate of digestion, therefore, pastry should not be served frequently, especially if a reduction in dietary fat intake is required.

Varieties of pastry

Shortcrust pastries

- **Shortcrust pastry** for sweet and savoury pies, tarts, turnovers and pasties.
- **Rich shortcrust pastry** for tarts, flans and pies when a richer, crisper result is desired.
- **Cheese pastry** for small cases and biscuits with savoury fillings.
- **Biscuit pastry** for sweet biscuits, small tarts and slices.

Flaky and puff pastries

Made using a process of rolling and folding, thereby producing many layers of dough and fat.

- **Flaky pastry** for sausage rolls, savoury and fruit pies, meat and fish patties, jam tarts or tartlets.

- **Rough puff pastry** is a little richer than flaky pastry and is often used as a substitute when making savoury and fruit pies, meat and fish patties, sausage rolls and apple pie. This pastry may be served cold.
- **Puff pastry** for elaborate pastries, patties and vol-au-vents. Because it is expensive and time consuming to make, it is not used extensively unless bought commercially prepared.

Filo or strudel pastry

From the Greek word 'phyllo', meaning a leaf. Use three or four paper thin layers and brush between each layer with butter or oil for a crisp finish or every second layer to reduce the fat content. The recipe for filo pastry is not given in this book as commercially prepared filo pastry is usually used.

Choux pastry

French in origin meaning cabbage, as the puffs can be likened to little cabbages. When a thick mixture of flour, water, butter and beaten eggs is baked, it swells forming puffs. Attractive sweets and savouries can be made with choux pastry.

Commercially prepared pastries

- Precooked pastries: flans, vol-au-vents, patty cases and choux pastry cases are available.
- Packaged shortcrust pastry mixes: after the addition of liquid this pastry is ready for use.
- Ready-to-use frozen pastry may be purchased in sheets or rolls.

Ingredients for pastry making

Flour Generally plain flour is used. **Shortcrust pastry** requires a raising agent, such as using a mixture of plain and self-raising flour or by adding baking powder. No chemical raising agent is necessary for flaky pastries as the air enclosed between the layers acts as the raising agent.

Fat This term refers to all types of fats and oils used in baking. For pastry making fat should be firm. Butter, margarine, lard, clarified fat or a mixture of these are used. Butter gives the best flavour and should be used for elaborate pastries. The inclusion of a small amount of lard gives crispness to pastry.

Liquid Water is generally used and should be cold. Less water is required when egg yolk and lemon juice are used. The quantity of water required may vary because of differing moisture content in flour.

Glaze Pastry, except **Choux pastry**, is glazed before it is baked to give a glossy finish. Care must be taken to glaze only the top surface as glaze on the cut side surfaces prevents the separation of layers of flaky pastries.

- **Savoury glaze:** beaten egg and milk, or milk only, is used for meat and savoury pastries.
- **Sweet glaze:** beaten egg white and sugar or equal quantities of water and sugar, dissolved, is used for sweet pastries. Honey, warmed in a microwave oven, may also be used.

Guidelines for pastry making

- Handle pastry as little as possible and use the fingertips only for rubbing in the fat. Do not roll out more than is necessary.
- Add liquid gradually as an excess causes a sticky unmanageable dough, and the addition of extra flour results in tough pastry. Sprinkle the board and rolling pin very lightly with flour.
- Coolness is the key to good results. Pastries are improved by being cooled in a refrigerator between rollings. Allow pastry to 'rest' by placing it in the refrigerator for a short time before using.
- Roll pastry to required size and shape on non-stick baking paper and use the paper to transfer pastry to baking pan or top of pie.
- Most pastries are baked in a hot oven to cause a sudden expansion of enclosed air and to rupture the starch grains quickly to ensure rapid absorption of fats.
- After the pastry is lightly … the oven temperature should be reduced to allow the … ome crisp.

…CRUST PASTRY

…nts may be combined in a food processor.

¹/₂ teaspoon salt
¹/₂ cup (125 g) margarine, butter *or* dairy blend
¹/₃–¹/₂ cup (85–125 mL) water
¹/₄ teaspoon lemon juice

Method

1. Mix flours and salt.
2. Add fat, rub into the flour using fingertips until mixture resembles breadcrumbs.
3. Gradually add sufficient water and lemon juice to mix to a firm dough, leaving the basin clean.
4. Sprinkle board lightly with flour, turn dough onto board and knead lightly until smooth.
5. Sprinkle flour on rolling pin, roll pastry to size and shape as required:
   - Lining a tart plate or flan ring (p. 352)
   - Covering a pie with pastry (p. 352)
   - Preparing double-crust pies (p. 353).

✦ WHOLEMEAL SHORTCRUST PASTRY ✦

Follow recipe for **Shortcrust pastry**. Replace $^1/_2$ cup (75 g) plain flour with $^1/_2$ cup (75 g) wholemeal plain flour.

RICH SHORTCRUST PASTRY

For quick mixing, all ingredients may be combined in a food processor.

Ingredients

1$^1/_2$ cups (225 g) plain flour
$^1/_4$ teaspoon salt
1 egg yolk
1 tablespoon (20 mL) water
$^1/_4$ teaspoon lemon juice
$^1/_2$ cup (125 g) butter

Method

1. Mix flour and salt.
2. Mix yolk, water and lemon juice together.
3. Lightly rub butter into flour.
4. Add liquid and carefully combine ingredients into a ball, leaving the basin clean.
5. Turn onto floured board and knead lightly. Refrigerate 5 minutes. Roll out as required:
   - Lining a tart plate or flan ring (p. 352)
   - Covering a pie with pastry (p. 352)
   - Preparing double-crust pies (p. 353).

BISCUIT PASTRY

For quick mixing, all ingredients may be combined in a food processor.

Ingredients

1 cup (150 g) plain flour
1 cup (150 g) self-raising flour
$^1/_2$ cup (125 g) caster sugar
$^1/_2$ cup (125 g) butter, margarine *or* dairy blend
1 egg (61 g), beaten

Method

1. Mix flours. Add sugar.
2. Rub butter into dry ingredients.
3. Add egg and mix into a firm dough, leaving the basin clean.
4. Lift onto a lightly floured board, knead lightly. Refrigerate 5 minutes.
5. Roll out and use as required:
   - Lining a tart plate or flan ring (p. 352)
   - Covering a pie with pastry (p. 352)
   - Preparing double-crust pies (p. 353).

CHEESE PASTRY

For quick mixing, all ingredients may be combined in a food processor.

Ingredients

1 cup (150 g) plain flour
$^{1}/_{4}$ teaspoon salt
$^{1}/_{8}$ teaspoon cayenne
$^{1}/_{4}$ teaspoon mustard
1 egg yolk
2–3 tablespoons (40–60 mL) water
$^{1}/_{4}$ teaspoon lemon juice
2 tablespoons (40 g) butter
$^{1}/_{3}$ cup (40 g) grated cheese

Method

1 Mix flour, salt, cayenne and mustard.
2 Mix egg yolk, water and lemon juice.
3 Rub butter into flour. Add cheese.
4 Add liquid and lightly combine ingredients into a ball, leaving basin clean.
5 Turn onto floured board, knead lightly. Refrigerate 5 minutes.
6 Roll out and use as required:
   - Lining a tart plate or flan ring (p. 352)
   - Covering a pie with pastry (p. 352)
   - Preparing double-crust pies (p. 353).

Shortcrust pastries: tips for product quality

Quality criteria

- crisp and light texture
- golden-brown colour
- even shape, not shrinking at edges.

Poorly textured pastry:

- wrong proportion of fat added
- slow handling when rubbing in fat caused it to melt
- too much water added or unevenly mixed
- pastry handled too much when being kneaded and rolled
- too much flour used on the pastry board
- oven temperature too low
- pastry may tend to be flaky if fat insufficiently rubbed in.

Pastry breaks and crumbles easily:

- too much fat used
- insufficient water added
- pastry not kept cool.

Shrinkage of pastry:

- pastry overstretched when being rolled out or when being shaped
- pastry insufficiently rested after kneading.

Poor appearance in cheese pastries:

- coarsely grated cheese used
- mixture over-handled after the addition of the cheese
- oven too hot causing the cheese to melt too quickly.

Flaky pastries

FLAKY PASTRY

Ingredients

2 cups (300 g) plain flour
$^{1}/_{4}$ teaspoon salt
$^{1}/_{2}$–$^{2}/_{3}$ cup (125–165 mL) water
$^{1}/_{4}$ teaspoon lemon juice
$^{2}/_{3}$ cup (160 g) margarine, butter *or* dairy blend

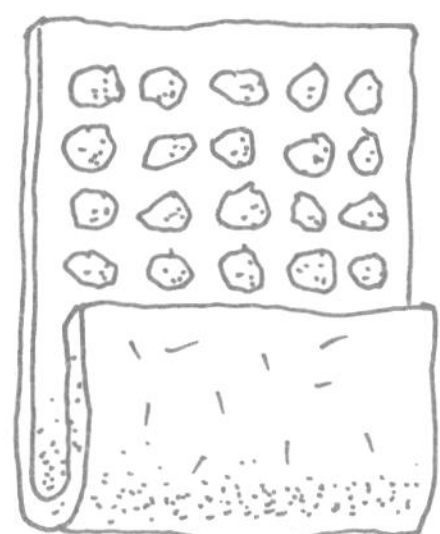

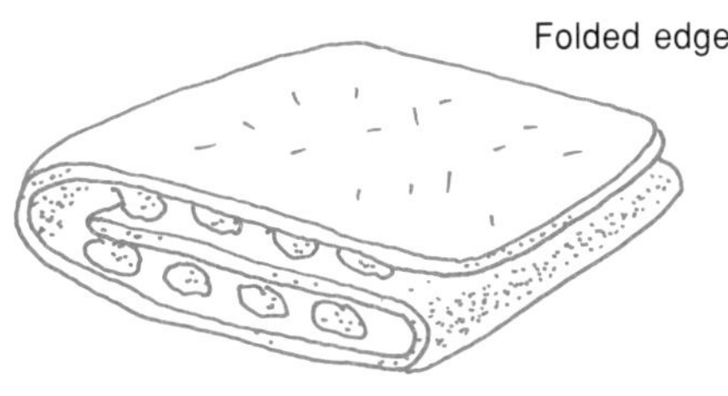

Method

1 Mix flour and salt. Combine water and lemon juice.
2 Soften fat slightly with a knife and divide into four.
3 Rub one portion of fat into flour.
4 Mix into a dough with the water and lemon juice.
5 Turn onto floured board and knead lightly until pastry is smooth and pliable.
6 Roll pastry into a rectangular shape.
7 Spread one portion of fat on top two-thirds of pastry as in diagram.
8 Fold in three by placing the lower third over centre third and top third over lower third. Rest pastry in refrigerator 5 minutes.
9 Turn pastry so that the folded edge is to the left. Press rolling pin at intervals along pastry thus evenly distributing the fat. Roll out again, rolling away from you to keep the layers of flakes even in the pastry. Use short light strokes and keep pastry in good rectangular shape. Rest pastry in refrigerator 5 minutes between each rolling and folding.
10 Proceed as before until the remaining portions of fat have been used.
11 Cover and place pastry in refrigerator until required:
- Lining a tart plate or flan ring (p. 352)
- Covering a pie with pastry (p. 352)
- Preparing double-crust pies (p. 353).

ROUGH PUFF PASTRY

Ingredients

2 cups (300 g) plain flour
$^{1}/_{4}$ teaspoon salt
1 egg yolk
$^{1}/_{2}$ cup (125 mL) water
$^{1}/_{4}$ teaspoon lemon juice
$^{3}/_{4}$ cup (185 g) butter, margarine *or* dairy blend

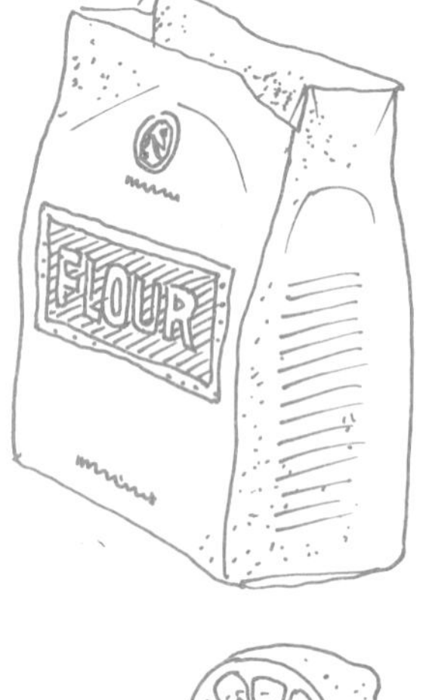

Method

1. Mix flour and salt.
2. Beat yolk, add water and lemon juice.
3. Cut butter into pieces the size of a walnut and add to flour. Do not rub in.
4. Add liquid to flour and mix to a soft dough without breaking pieces of butter.
5. Turn onto floured board, shape into rectangle.
6. Roll pastry lightly, keeping rectangular shape.
7. Sprinkle lightly with flour and fold in three by placing the lower third over centre third and top third over lower third. Rest pastry in refrigerator 5 minutes.
8. Turn pastry so that the folded edge is to the left. Press rolling pin at intervals along pastry to evenly distribute the butter. Roll out again, rolling only away from you to keep the layers of flakes even in the pastry. Use short light strokes and keep pastry in good rectangular shape.
9. Proceed as before, sprinkling with flour and rolling and folding until pastry has been rolled and folded three times. Rest pastry in refrigerator 5 minutes after each folding.
10. Cover and place pastry in refrigerator until required:
    - Lining a tart plate or flan ring (p. 352)
    - Covering a pie with pastry (p. 352)
    - Preparing double-crust pies (p. 353).

Flaky pastries: tips for product quality

Quality criteria

- evenly risen
- crisp and light texture
- golden-brown colour.

Pastry not sufficiently flaky:

- different fats not blended sufficiently before being added to flour
- pastry not kept cool, therefore warm fat blended with flour instead of remaining in layers.

Poorly textured pastry:

- pastry over-handled or rolled too much
- too much water added
- pastry not kept sufficiently cool
- dough kneaded too much
- too much flour used on pastry board
- oven temperature too low to burst starch grains quickly and absorb fat.

Pastry hard on outside and heavy inside:

- pastry under-cooked
- temperature too high causing outside of pastry to brown before it was cooked through.

Shrinkage of pastry:

- dough over-stretched during rolling process
- insufficient time allowed for relaxation of dough between rollings and before cooking
- pastry not kept cool during preparation
- oven temperature too low.

Uneven rising of pastry:

- fat unevenly distributed
- uneven pressure during rolling
- pastry not kept with squared corners during rolling and folding
- pastry not turned in correct direction during rolling and folding
- dough over-stretched during the rolling process
- all of the edges not cut
- insufficient time allowed for the relaxation of dough between rollings and before cooking.

Lining a tart plate or flan ring

Use 125 g (1/2 quantity) of **Shortcrust pastry** or **Rich shortcrust pastry**.

1. Roll out pastry on baking paper to shape of tart plate or flan ring and 3 cm larger all round. If ring is used place it on oven tray.
2. Brush the edge of the plate or ring with water.
3. Lift pastry on paper and invert into plate or ring. Carefully peel paper away and ease pastry into place without stretching it. Trim edge with sharp knife. Flute edge to level of plate for shortcrust pastries.

Baking tart cases ('baking blind')

1. To retain shape of unfilled flans or cases during baking, press a piece of foil in the case, large enough to cover edge of pastry to prevent excess browning.
2. Bake at 190–200°C for 10 minutes. Remove foil, reduce temperature to 180°C and continue baking for further 20 minutes until pastry is pale fawn and crisp.
3. Tart cases may be stored in an airtight container and used as required.
4. Small tart cases may be baked in patty pans. Pierce bottom of pastry. Bake at 190°C for 5 minutes, reduce temperature to 180°C and continue cooking for further 10 minutes until pastry is pale fawn and crisp.

Covering a pie with pastry

Use 125 g (1/2 quantity) of **Shortcrust pastry**, **Flaky pastry** or **Rough puff pastry**.

1. Roll pastry on baking paper to the shape of pie plate or dish, 5 cm larger all round and 5 mm thick.
2. Cut a 2 cm strip from outside edge of pastry.
3. Place filling in pie dish and use a pie funnel if required.
4. Brush the edge of pie dish with water.
5. Fit the strip of pastry carefully around the edge without stretching it, cut side out. Join ends neatly and brush strip with water.
6. Lift large piece of pastry on baking paper and invert over pie dish. Carefully peel paper away and press edges together lightly.
   - Shortcrust pastries: trim edges with a sharp knife and pinch into frill or mark with a teaspoon or fork.
   - Flaky pastries: trim edges with a sharp knife. Cut the edge at 3 cm intervals drawing up flakes lightly with knife.
7. Slit top of pie to allow steam to escape and decorate as desired.
8. Glaze. Stand on 4-sided oven tray for baking.

Preparing double-crust pies

Use 250 g (1 quantity) of **Shortcrust pastry**, **Flaky pastry** or **Rough puff pastry**.

1 Divide pastry into 2 portions – usually $^2/_3$ and $^1/_3$.
2 Roll out $^2/_3$ portion of pastry on baking paper to shape of dish or plate and 3 cm larger all round.
3 Brush edge of dish with water.
4 Lift pastry on paper and invert into dish. Carefully peel paper away and ease pastry into place without stretching it. Pastry should come just over top of the rim.
5 Arrange filling in lined dish.
6 Brush edges with water.
7 Roll out the small portion of pastry on baking paper to fit top, lift pastry on paper and invert into position to cover pie. Carefully peel paper away and press edges together lightly.
8 Trim edges and pinch frill for **Shortcrust pastry** or **Rough puff pastry**, or cut edges at 3 cm intervals drawing up flakes lightly with knife for **Flaky pastry**.
9 Slit top to allow steam to escape and decorate as desired.
10 Glaze with **Sweet glaze** (p. 345) or **Savoury glaze** (p. 345). Stand tart on 4-sided oven tray for baking.

CHOUX PASTRY

► *Cooking utensil:* medium-sized saucepan

Ingredients

$^3/_4$ cup (115 g) plain flour
$^3/_4$ cup (190 mL) water
$^1/_4$ cup (60 g) butter
3 eggs (61g)

Method

1 Place flour onto a piece of paper.
2 Put water and butter into saucepan, stir until butter is melted and bring to boil.
3 Remove from heat immediately, add flour all at once.
4 Stir vigorously with a wooden spoon until mixture leaves the sides of the saucepan and forms a smooth ball.
5 Allow to cool for 2 minutes.
6 Add eggs one at a time, beating thoroughly after each addition. (Electric beater may be used). Beat well until the mixture is smooth and glossy.
7 Cool thoroughly before using. May be refrigerated.

CHOUX PASTRY PUFFS

- *Number:* ***16 large puffs*** *or* ***24 small puffs***
- *Cooking utensil:* wet oven trays, piping bag fitted with 2 cm plain pipe
- *Cooking time:* ***45–50 minutes*** *large puffs* ***30–40 minutes*** *small puffs*
- *Oven temperature:* ***220°C reduced to 180 °C***

Ingredients

1 quantity **Choux pastry** (p. 353)

Method

1. Set oven at 220°C.
2. Fill piping bag with mixture and pipe it onto the trays, cut off mixture with a wet knife and leave space between each puff. Pipe 16 large puffs (approximately 1 tablespoon each), *or* 24 small puffs (approximately 1 teaspoon each).
3. Bake at 220°C, reducing to 180°C after 15 minutes. Cook until puffs are golden brown in colour with a definite sheen, and no beads of moisture are visible.
4. Cool on cake cooler.
5. Partly split puffs to release steam and ensure crispness. Remove any soft mixture if necessary.
6. Fill with sweet or savoury mixture or store in an airtight container until required.

✦ CREAM PUFFS ✦

Follow recipe for **Choux pastry puffs**. Using 1 cup (250 mL) whipped cream, fill puffs and dust with 2 tablespoons (30 g) icing sugar mixture just before serving.

✦ CHOCOLATE ECLAIRS ✦

Follow recipe for **Choux pastry puffs**, piping mixture onto trays in 8 cm lengths (making 18 eclairs). Using 1 cup (250 mL) whipped cream, fill puffs. Ice with 1 quantity **Chocolate icing** (p. 395).

✦ PROFITEROLES ✦

Follow recipe for **Choux pastry puffs**, making 30 small puffs. Using 1 cup (250 mL) smooth ricotta, mixed with 1 tablespoon (15 g) icing sugar mixture *or* 200 mL (1 quantity) **Confectioners' custard** (p. 289), fill puffs. Serve as dessert with **Fruit sauce** (p. 289).

CROQUEMBOUCHE

► *Serves:* ***12–15***

► *Serving utensil:* 43 cm diameter semi-circle of cardboard formed into a cone, covered with foil, standing on serving dish

Ingredients

2 quantities **Choux pastry** (p. 353) made into 60 small puffs
200 mL (1 quantity) **Confectioners' custard** (p. 289) *or* 1 cup (250 mL) cream, whipped
2 tablespoons (40 g) caster sugar
1 teaspoon finely grated orange rind
1/2 teaspoon orange essence
Caramel
1/2 cup (125 mL) water
2 cups (500 g) sugar

Method

1 Combine cream, sugar, rind and essence.
2 Make a small hole in the base of each puff and pipe in a little cream *or* **Confectioners' custard**.
3 Prepare caramel: dissolve sugar in the water over low heat. Boil rapidly without stirring until the mixture just begins to turn light golden, remove from heat.
4 Place one row of puffs around the base of the cone. Quickly dip a small part of each remaining puff in the caramel so they stick together to form a tower around the cone. If caramel sets, gently reheat to melt.
5 To make fine threads of caramel, dip wooden spoon into remaining caramel, and quickly pull up and down the tower. These strands will hold the puffs in place.
6 Allow to cool before serving.

Choux pastry: tips for product quality

Quality criteria

- evenly risen
- crisp and light texture
- golden-brown colour.

Puffs did not rise:

- too much liquid
- flour added before water boiled
- oven too cool.

Soggy puffs:

- inaccurately measured ingredients
- mixture insufficiently beaten
- puffs not sufficiently cooked
- oven door opened too soon.

Puffs do not hold shape:

- mixture not cooled before adding eggs
- insufficient beating between additions of eggs
- mixture not cooled sufficiently before being piped onto tray.

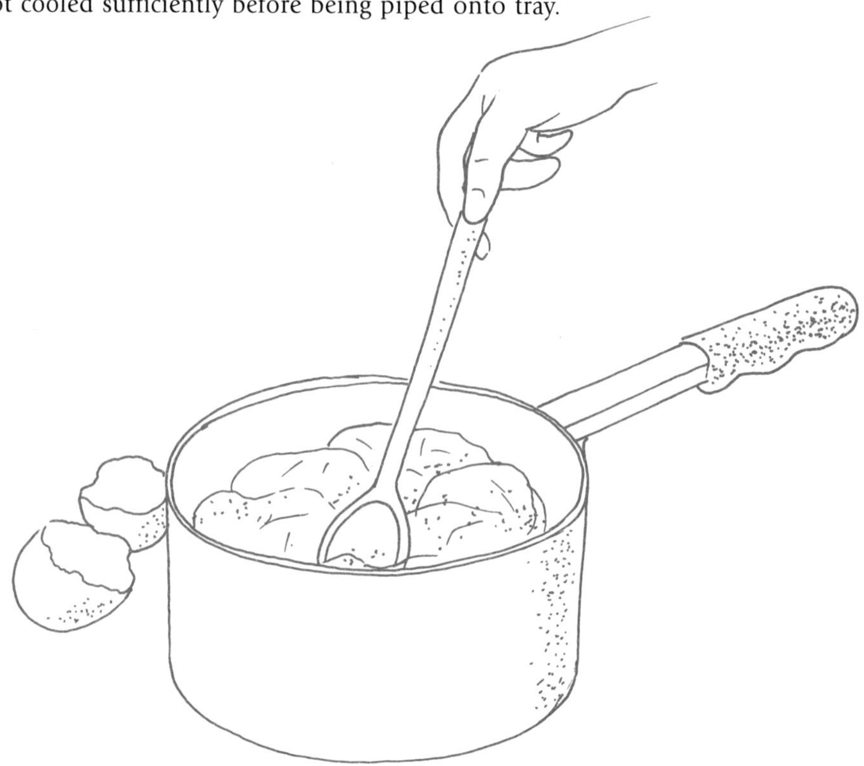

Crumb crusts and shells

Although these crusts and shells are not strictly a pastry they are used for baked and refrigerated cheesecakes and similar desserts.

BISCUIT CRUMB CRUST

► *Utensil:* 20 cm springform pan (1.75 L) *or* sponge pan (1 L) lined with foil

Ingredients

2/3 cup (160 g) butter
2 cups (240 g) sweet biscuit crumbs
1 teaspoon cinnamon

Method

1. Melt butter and stir in crumbs and cinnamon.
2. Press evenly into pan using a straight-sided glass to form a right angle between sides and base of crust.
3. Refrigerate for 30 minutes, then use as required.

COCONUT PIE SHELL

► *Utensil:* 20 cm springform pan (1.75 L) *or* sponge pan (1 L) lined with foil

Ingredients

1/2 cup (125 g) butter
1 1/2 cups (135 g) toasted coconut
1 tablespoon (15 g) icing sugar mixture

Method

1. Melt butter and stir in coconut and sugar.
2. Press mixture evenly around sides and base of pan.
3. Refrigerate for 30 minutes, then use as required.

14 Scones, muffins and pancakes

Scones, muffins and pancakes are quickly made mixtures of flour and liquid, cooked and served as a snack or light meal, for example, **Apple muffins**, **Savoury ham scone rolls** and **Scones** served with jam and cream.

Scones are made from flour, raising agent and milk mixed to a soft dough, which gives a light flaky texture and crisp crust when baked for a short time in a hot oven. They may be served as a snack or for lunch. Plain, cheese or savoury scone dough may also be used as a base for **Pizza** and for dumplings in an oven-baked casserole.

Muffins are made from a self-raising flour mixture. They are baked in the oven and are often classified as quickbreads as they may be used as a substitute for bread. Muffins can be made with sweet or savoury fillings and may be served for breakfast, lunch or as a snack.

Pancakes are thin flat cakes made from a batter of flour, egg and milk, which is cooked in a small amount of butter or oil in a frying pan. They may be served with sweet or savoury fillings and eaten for breakfast, lunch, as a snack or as a dessert.

Scones, muffins and pancakes are best eaten soon after cooking, however, they may be frozen for up to 1 month. Cool and wrap in freezer wrap. To use, remove from freezer (do not thaw) and warm for 2 minutes in microwave oven on defrost setting.

Food value

As the main ingredient is flour, scones, muffins and pancakes are high in carbohydrates. Using wholemeal flour increases the fibre content. Other nutrients depend on the flavourings used, for example, serving with cream and jam increases the fat and sugar content, as does adding chocolate. The addition of cheese increases fat and protein, and fruits and vegetables add fibre.

GEM SCONES

Gem irons are heavy cast iron patty pan trays, traditionally used for gem scones. Shallow patty pan trays can be used, which do not require preheating.

- *Number:* ***24***
- *Cooking utensil:* gem irons
- *Preparation time:* ***20 minutes***
- *Cooking time:* ***10–12 minutes***
- *Oven temperature:* ***180°C***

Ingredients

2 tablespoons (40 g) butter
$^{1}/_{3}$ cup (85 g) caster sugar
1 egg (61g), beaten
$1^{1}/_{2}$ cups (225 g) self-raising flour
$^{1}/_{2}$ cup (125 mL) milk

Method

1. Set oven at 180°C and heat gem irons for 10 minutes.
2. Cream butter and sugar. Add egg, mix well.
3. Add flour and milk alternately, $^{1}/_{3}$ at a time. Stir gently and thoroughly.
4. Spray or brush gem irons with oil. Quickly half fill with mixture.
5. Bake at 180°C for 10–12 minutes.
6. Cool on cake cooler and serve with butter, margarine or dairy blend.

Suitable for freezing for up to 1 month. Warm frozen gem scones for 2 minutes on defrost in microwave oven before serving.

SCONES

The traditional 'Devonshire tea' is freshly baked scones served with berry jam and thick whipped cream.

- *Number:* **12**
- *Cooking utensil:* non-stick oven tray

Preparation time: ***15 minutes***
Cooking time: ***10–12 minutes***
- *Oven temperature: 220°C*

Ingredients

1 tablespoon (20 g) butter, margarine *or* dairy blend
2 cups (300 g) self-raising flour
1/4 teaspoon salt
1 cup (250 mL) milk

Suitable for freezing for up to 1 month. Warm frozen scones for 2 minutes on defrost in microwave oven before serving.

Method

1 Set oven at 220°C.
2 Rub butter into flour and salt, using fingertips.
3 Mix into a soft dough using most of the milk. Add a little more of the milk if required.
4 Turn onto a lightly floured board and knead for a short time, until smooth.
5 Roll out 2 cm thick and cut into 12 shapes using a 6 cm round cutter or a knife.
6 Arrange on oven tray and glaze tops with milk.
7 Bake at 220°C for 10–12 minutes until golden brown. To test: sides of scone should be set.
8 Cool on cake cooler.
9 When cool break in half and butter lightly. Serve.

✦ CHEESE SCONES ✦

Follow recipe for **Scones**. Sift 1/4 teaspoon cayenne and 1/4 teaspoon mustard with flour and add 2/3 cup (80 g) grated tasty cheese to flour.

✦ FRESH HERB SCONES ✦

Follow recipe for **Scones**. After step 2 add 2 tablespoons snipped chives, 2 tablespoons chopped dill and 2 tablespoons chopped parsley *or* other fresh herbs.

✦ FRUIT SCONES ✦

Follow recipe for **Scones**. At step 2 add 1/2 cup (90 g) dried fruit, e.g. sultanas, currants, raisins *or* dates, and 1 tablespoon (20 g) caster sugar.

✦ BUTTERMILK SCONES ✦

Follow recipe for **Scones**. Replace 1 cup (250 mL) milk with 1 cup (250 mL) buttermilk.

✦ RICH SCONES ✦

Follow recipe for **Scones**. Replace 1/4 cup (65 mL) milk with 1/4 cup (65 mL) cream.

✦ PIZZONES ✦

Follow recipe for **Scones**. Roll scone dough out to 5 mm thick. Cut into 10 cm rounds. Spread with tomato paste, and a selection of chopped mushrooms, chopped capsicums, pineapple pieces, ham and salami strips, tomato slices, anchovies, olives or prawns. Top with grated cheese. Cook at 180°C for 7–10 minutes.

✦ DAMPER ✦

Damper was one of the main staple foods eaten by early migrant Australian settlers. It was made from cheap and readily available ingredients and cooked over hot coals. To make damper follow the recipe for **Scones**, **Fresh herb scones** or **Cheese scones** and bake in one large round, marked into 8 wedges. After baking, break into wedges for serving. The dough may also be shaped into a loaf and cut into slices after baking.

WHOLEMEAL SCONES

Uncooked scone dough may be placed on the top of a casserole or hotpot 30 minutes before the end of cooking, to make a tasty topping.

- *Number:* **12**
- *Cooking utensil:* non-stick oven tray
- *Preparation time:* ***15 minutes***
- *Cooking time:* ***12–15 minutes***
- *Oven temperature:* ***220°C***

Ingredients

1 tablespoon (20 g) butter, margarine *or* dairy blend
1½ cups (225 g) wholemeal self-raising flour
½ cup (75 g) self-raising flour
1 cup (250 mL) milk

Method

1. Set oven at 220°C.
2. Rub butter into flour and salt, using fingertips.
3. Mix into soft dough using most of the milk. Add a little more of the milk if required.
4. Turn onto a lightly floured board and knead for a short time, until smooth.
5. Roll out 2 cm thick and cut into 12 rounds with 6 cm cutter.
6. Arrange on oven tray.
7. Glaze with milk.
8. Bake at 220°C for 12–15 minutes until golden brown.
9. Lift onto cake cooler. Serve warm.

Suitable for freezing for up to 1 month. Warm frozen scones for 2 minutes on defrost in microwave oven before serving.

WHOLEMEAL DATE SCONES

Follow recipe for **Wholemeal scones**. After step 2 add ½ cup (90 g) chopped dates and 1 tablespoon (20 g) caster sugar.

WHOLEMEAL FRESH HERB SCONES

Follow recipe for **Wholemeal scones**. After step 2 add 2 tablespoons snipped chives, 2 tablespoons chopped dill and 2 tablespoons chopped parsley *or* other fresh herbs.

Illawarra plum
Riberry
Warrigal greens
Wild rosella
Muntries
Davidson plum
Bunga nuts
Wild lime
PLATE 13

PLATE 14

Summer pudding (p. 316),
Sticky date pudding (p. 333),
Tiramisu (p. 342),
Fresh fruit platter (p. 310).

FRUIT SCONE ROLLS

A quickly made popular morning tea, with many variations. All the variations can also be made replacing half the flour with wholemeal self-raising flour.

- *Number:* ***12***
- *Cooking utensil:* non-stick oven tray *or* non-stick 22 cm round cake pan (2.5 L)
- *Preparation time:* ***15 minutes***
- *Cooking time:* ***15–20 minutes***
- *Oven temperature:* ***200°C reduced to 180°C***

Ingredients

2 cups (300 g) self-raising flour
2 tablespoons (40 g) butter, margarine *or* dairy blend
1 cup (250 mL) milk
Filling
1/4 cup (45 g) sultanas
1/4 cup (45 g) currants
1 tablespoon (15 g) mixed peel
1 tablespoon (20 g) caster sugar
1/2 teaspoon mixed spice
1/2 teaspoon cinnamon

Method

1. Set oven at 200°C.
2. Mix flours, rub in butter using fingertips.
3. Mix into a soft dough with most of the milk. Add more of the milk if necessary.
4. Turn onto lightly floured board and knead for a short time, until smooth.
5. Roll out into an oblong 30 cm x 20 cm and spread with softened butter.
6. Mix filling ingredients together and sprinkle over dough. Roll up as for **Egg sponge roll** (p. 396).
7. Spray or brush oven tray *or* cake pan with oil.
8. Cut into 12 slices, arrange closely together on oven tray *or* in cake pan and glaze with milk.
9. Bake at 200°C for 10 minutes, then 180°C for further 5–10 minutes until golden brown.
10. Cool on cake cooler. Serve with butter, margarine or dairy blend.

Suitable for freezing for up to 1 month. Warm frozen rolls for 2 minutes on defrost in microwave oven before serving.

BUTTERSCOTCH SCONE ROLLS

Follow recipe for **Fruit scone rolls**. Omit filling. Cream 3 tablespoons (60 g) softened butter and 3 tablespoons (45 g) brown sugar, and spread on dough at step 6.

SAVOURY HAM SCONE ROLLS

Follow recipe for **Fruit scone rolls**, replacing filling with 1 tablespoon (20 g) seed mustard, 3 tablespoons (45 g) chopped ham, 1 tablespoon grated onion and 1 tablespoon chopped parsley.

✦ CHUTNEY AND HAM SCONE ROLLS ✦

Follow recipe for **Fruit scone rolls**, replacing filling with 3 tablespoons (45 g) chopped ham, 1 tablespoon grated onion, 1 tablespoon chopped parsley and 3 tablespoons (60 g) fruit chutney.

PUMPKIN SCONES

To save time, cook the chopped pumpkin for 5–7 minutes on high power in microwave oven.

- *Number:* **12**
- *Cooking utensil:* non-stick oven tray
- *Preparation time:* **25 minutes**
- *Cooking time:* **10–15 minutes**
- *Oven temperature:* **220°C**

Ingredients

2 cups (300 g) self-raising flour
1 tablespoon (20 g) butter, margarine *or* dairy blend
1 tablespoon (20 g) sugar
3/4 cup (150 g) cooked mashed pumpkin
1 egg, beaten
1 tablespoon (20 mL) milk

Method

1. Set oven at 220°C.
2. Rub butter into flour using fingertips.
3. Stir in sugar, pumpkin and egg. Mix with sufficient milk to form a soft dough.
4. Turn onto lightly floured board and knead for a short time, until smooth.
5. Roll out 2 cm thick. Using a knife cut into 12 scones.
6. Arrange on oven tray and glaze tops with milk.
7. Bake at 220°C for 10–15 minutes until golden brown.
8. Lift onto cake cooler. Serve with butter.

Suitable for freezing for up to 1 month. Warm frozen scones for 2 minutes on defrost in microwave oven before serving.

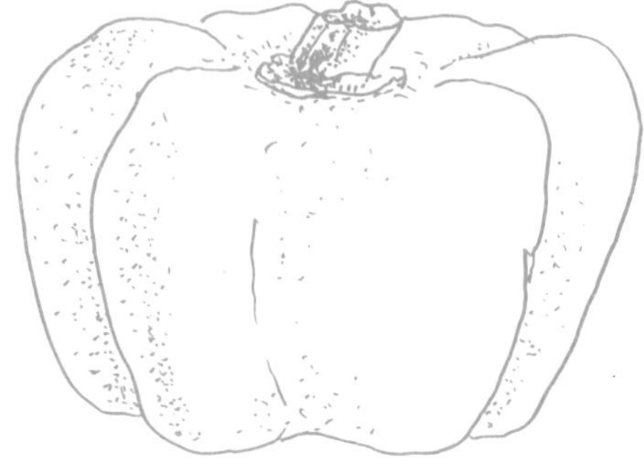

APPLE MUFFINS

Muffins are mixed quickly just to the stage where the mixture is still lumpy and then baked in deep-sided muffin pans. Muffins cooked in the microwave oven are a speedy and nutritious after-school snack.

- *Number:* ***6 large, 12 small***
- *Cooking utensil:* non-stick muffin pans
- *Preparation time:* ***15 minutes***
- *Cooking time:* ***15–20 minutes***
- *Oven temperature:* ***200°C***

Ingredients

1 1/2 cups (225 g) self-raising flour
1/2 teaspoon cinnamon
2 tablespoons (40 g) caster sugar
1 apple (150 g), grated
2 tablespoons (40 g) butter, margarine *or* dairy blend, melted
3/4 cup (190 mL) milk
1 egg (61 g), beaten

Method

1. Set oven at 200°C. Brush or spray pans with oil.
2. Mix flour, cinnamon and sugar. Mix in grated apple.
3. Melt butter, add milk and egg, mix well.
4. Using a knife, stir milk mixture into flour until just mixed, but still lumpy.
5. Place mixture in muffin pans and bake at 200°C for 15–20 minutes.
6. Serve warm with butter, margarine or dairy blend.

MICROWAVE APPLE MUFFINS

Using microwave muffin pans, cook on high power for 4 minutes.

WHOLEMEAL APPLE MUFFINS

Follow recipe for **Apple muffins**, replacing 3/4 cup (110 g) self-raising flour with 3/4 cup (110 g) wholemeal self-raising flour.

BANANA BRAN MUFFINS

Follow recipe for **Apple muffins**, replacing 1/2 cup (75 g) self-raising flour with 1/2 cup (45 g) bran and 1 teaspoon baking powder. Replace apple and cinnamon with 2 mashed bananas.

BLUEBERRY MUFFINS

Follow recipe for **Apple muffins**. Omit apple and cinnamon. At step 4 add 100 g fresh *or* frozen blueberries.

APRICOT AND ALMOND MUFFINS

Follow recipe for **Apple muffins**. Omit apple and cinnamon. At step 4 add 1/2 cup fresh *or* canned chopped apricots, and 1/2 cup (60 g) chopped *or* flaked almonds.

CHEESE AND CHIVE MUFFINS

Savoury muffins can be quickly made for the lunch box.

- *Number:* **6 large, 12 small**
- *Cooking utensil:* non-stick muffin pans
- *Preparation time:* **15 minutes**
- *Cooking time:* **15–20 minutes**
- *Oven temperature:* **200°C**

Ingredients

$1^1/_2$ cups (225 g) self-raising flour
$^1/_2$ cup (60 g) grated tasty cheese
2 tablespoons snipped chives *or* chopped spring onions
2 tablespoons (40 mL) oil
$^3/_4$ cup (190 mL) milk
1 egg (61g), beaten

Method

1. Set oven at 200°C. Brush or spray muffin pans with oil.
2. Mix flour, cheese and chives.
3. Beat oil, milk and egg.
4. Using a knife, stir milk mixture into flour until just mixed, but still lumpy.
5. Place mixture in muffin pans and bake at 200°C for 15–20 minutes.
6. Serve warm with butter, margarine or dairy blend.

MICROWAVE CHEESE AND CHIVE MUFFINS

Using microwave muffin pans, cook on high power for 4 minutes.

WHOLEMEAL CHEESE AND CHIVE MUFFINS

Follow recipe for **Cheese and chive muffins**, replacing $^3/_4$ cup (110 g) self-raising flour with $^3/_4$ cup (110 g) wholemeal self-raising flour.

PUMPKIN MUFFINS

Follow recipe for **Cheese and chive muffins**. Omit cheese and chives. At step 4 add $^1/_2$ cup (100 g) cooked mashed pumpkin and $^1/_2$ teaspoon mixed spice.

CORN MUFFINS

Follow recipe for **Cheese and chive muffins**. Omit cheese and chives. Replace $^1/_2$ cup (75 g) self-raising flour with $^1/_2$ cup (75 g) polenta (cornmeal) and 1 teaspoon baking powder. Add $^1/_2$ cup (75 g) cooked corn kernels at step 3.

SALMON AND DILL MUFFINS

Follow recipe for **Cheese and chive muffins**. Omit cheese and chives. At step 4 add $^1/_2$ can (75 g) salmon, drained, and 2 tablespoons chopped dill.

Scones and muffins: tips for product quality

Quality criteria

- Golden-brown crust.
- Well-shaped and evenly risen.
- Light cream-coloured crumb.
- Fine, flaky soft texture.

Heavy and not well-risen:

- proportion of liquid too low
- dough not handled lightly, especially during kneading
- oven not hot enough
- oven temperature too high; gluten set before the carbon dioxide expanded.

Loss of shape:

- dough too soft; too much liquid used
- not cleanly cut with scone-cutter or knife
- careless handling
- scraps from the first rolling not well kneaded
- glaze allowed to run down the sides of scones
- oven tray too heavily greased
- incorrect positioning of oven tray causing uneven oven heat.

Rough surface on baked scones:

- mixture too dry
- uneven or insufficient mixing and kneading.

Too pale on top and too dark on base:

- incorrect size of oven tray – too large to allow heat to circulate
- oven temperature too low, requiring longer cooking time
- positioned too low in oven.

PANCAKES

Pancakes may be made in advance, cooled, stacked, wrapped tightly in freezer wrap and placed in freezer for up to 1 month. Warm frozen pancakes for 2 minutes on defrost in microwave oven before serving.
For sweet pancake fillings see p. 312.

► *Number:* ***12–15***

Ingredients

1 cup (150 g) plain flour
$^1/_2$ teaspoon salt
1 egg (61 g), beaten
$1^1/_2$ cups (375 mL) milk

► *Cooking utensil:* 16 cm frying pan

Method

1. Sift flour and salt and make a well in the centre of the mixture.
2. Place egg in well and use a wooden spoon to gradually work in the flour and half of the milk. A blender may be used.
3. Beat well for 1 minute and stir in remainder of the milk.
4. Allow to stand for $^1/_2$ hour before cooking. This softens the cellulose of the starch grains producing a lighter batter.
5. Brush frying pan with oil. Place on heat.
6. When hot, use a $^1/_4$ cup measure to pour in sufficient batter to just cover the base of the pan. Cook until set and lightly browned on the base of the pancake.
7. Turn pancake with a spatula or by tossing; cook until brown on other side.
8. Turn onto plate and keep warm.
9. Repeat steps 6 to 8 to make 10–15 pancakes.
10. Serve with savoury filling (see over the page) or sweet fillings (see p. 312).

✦ WHOLEMEAL PANCAKES ✦

Follow recipe for **Pancakes**, replacing $^1/_2$ cup (75 g) flour with $^1/_2$ cup (75 g) self-raising wholemeal flour.

✦ BUTTERMILK PANCAKES ✦

Follow recipe for **Pancakes**. Replace milk with $1^1/_2$ cups (375 mL) buttermilk. Use any of the savoury fillings over the page.

✦ MEXICAN CORNMEAL PANCAKES ✦

Follow recipe for **Pancakes**. Replace 1/2 cup (75 g) flour with 1/2 cup (75 g) polenta and 1 teaspoon baking powder. Make 1 quantity **Savoury mince** (p. 223) and place 3 tablespoons on each pancake, fold in half. Serve as a light meal.

✦ HAM AND MUSTARD PANCAKES ✦

Follow recipe for **Pancakes**. Use a very thin slice of ham for each pancake. Spread each pancake with 1/2 teaspoon seed mustard, cover with ham, roll up and serve garnished with parsley.

✦ CHICKEN AND HAM PANCAKES ✦

Follow recipe for **Pancakes**. Make 2 quantities (500 mL) **White sauce** (p. 282) and add 2 cups (300 g) cooked, chopped chicken and ham combined, 2 tablespoons chopped parsley and 1 teaspoon seed mustard. Reheat mixture and spread on pancakes. Roll up and serve.

✦ SEAFOOD PANCAKES ✦

Follow recipe for **Pancakes**. Make 2 quantities (500 mL) **White sauce** (p. 282) and add 500 g cooked seafood, 1 tablespoon chopped parsley and juice of 1 lemon. Reheat mixture and spread on pancakes. Roll up and serve.

✦ VEGETABLE PANCAKE STACKS ✦

Follow recipe for **Pancakes**. Make 2 quantities (500 mL) **White sauce** (p. 282) *or* use 500 g cottage cheese. Add 2 cups (300 g) cooked, chopped vegetables, e.g. asparagus, cauliflower, broccoli, zucchini or spinach. Reheat, spoon on pancake, stack pancakes 3 high and cut into 4 wedges. Serve garnished with parsley.

✦ SPINACH AND CHEESE PANCAKES ✦

Follow recipe for **Pancakes**. Add 125 g spinach to the uncooked batter at step 2. Roll pancakes lightly after cooking and keep warm. Make 2 quantities (500 mL) **Cheese sauce** (p. 282) and pour over pancakes before serving.

✦ SAVOURY CREPES ✦

Follow recipe for **Pancakes**. Add extra 1/4 cup (65 mL) milk and make 20 thin crepes. Crepes may be served with fillings similar to those above.

DROP SCONES or PIKELETS

- *Number:* ***24 to 30***
- *Cooking utensil:* frying pan

Preparation time: ***10 minutes***

Cooking time: ***3–4 minutes for each panful***

Ingredients

1 cup (150 g) self-raising flour
2 tablespoons (40 g) caster sugar
1 egg (61g), beaten
$^2/_3$ cup (165 mL) milk
1 tablespoon (20 g) butter, margarine *or* dairy blend

Method

1. Mix flour and sugar. Make a well in the centre of mixture.
2. Add milk to egg and pour into well. Using a wooden spoon, gradually beat in the flour.
3. Brush frying pan with a little of the butter. Place over heat.
4. When hot, place spoonfuls of mixture in frying pan. When bubbles appear on surface of drop scones, turn with a spatula. Allow to brown on other side and cook through.
5. Brush frying pan with butter between batches of drop scones.
6. Lift onto cake cooler covered with a clean cloth. Cover drop scones to keep them soft.
7. Drop scones may be served buttered *or* with jam and whipped cream.

APPLE PIKELETS

Follow recipe for **Drop scones**. Add 1 grated apple (150 g), to batter before cooking.

FLAPJACKS

These are an American version of **Drop scones**, larger in size and served with maple syrup. Follow recipe for **Drop scones**. Omit sugar. Use $^1/_3$ cup (185 mL) batter for each flapjack. Makes 10. Serve as a dessert, breakfast dish or snack, topping each flapjack with 1 teaspoon butter and 1 tablespoon (20 mL) maple syrup.

BLINI

These are a Russian version of **Drop scones**, smaller in size and made with sour cream. In Russia they are often made with buckwheat. Follow recipe for **Drop scones**. Omit sugar and replace $^2/_3$ cup (165 mL) milk with $^2/_3$ cup (185 mL) light sour cream. Use 1 tablespoon (20 mL) batter for each blini. Makes 25–30. Serve as a base for savouries and hors d'oeuvres (p. 82).

15 Cakes and cake presentation

Cake making provides an opportunity to be creative and to add a touch of individuality. Some cakes may be quickly and easily prepared for family snacks, and others, such as rich fruit cakes, may be prepared and decorated for special occasions.

Food value

Cakes supply mainly carbohydrate and fat, with a small amount of protein from eggs. To reduce saturated fat in the diet, use oils with a high ratio of polyunsaturated fats, such as canola oil. Cakes with low fat and high fibre provide a nutritious snack.

Processes used in cake making

Stirring or mixing Ingredients are combined with a circular motion, using a spoon.

Creaming The sugar is mixed with the butter, margarine or dairy blend until the mixture resembles stiffly beaten cream. A wooden spoon, whisk, electric beater or food processor may be used.

Beating or whipping Ingredients are blended rapidly, enclosing as much air as possible. An electric beater, rotary beater or whisk may be used.

Folding Two mixtures are combined, retaining as much air as possible. The lighter mixture is placed on the heavier one, e.g. flour on beaten eggs and sugar. A metal spoon is used to gently cut down through the mixtures, folding the heavier over the lighter mixture. Using as few strokes as possible, folding continues until blending is complete. It is important to retain air already beaten into the mixture.

Methods used in cake making

Rubbing-in method

The butter, margarine or dairy blend is rubbed into the flour with the fingertips, pastry blender or food processor until the mixture resembles breadcrumbs. Other dry ingredients are added, then moist ingredients. Cakes and loaves made by this method tend to be drier than those mixed by other methods and will keep for only 3–4 days.

Creaming method

Butter, margarine or dairy blend is creamed with the sugar until the mixture resembles whipped cream. This may be done with a wooden spoon, whisk, food processor or electric beater. The eggs are then added and the mixture beaten, then the flour and milk folded in alternately. Cakes made by the creaming method contain a higher proportion of butter, margarine or dairy blend to flour than cakes made by other methods and they have a richer flavour and will remain moist for up to 1 week.

Beating method

The eggs or egg whites and sugar are beaten until thick, then the dry ingredients carefully folded in. The beating method produces a light textured cake. The lightness depends on the amount of air incorporated. Sponges should be served within 1–2 days as they do not remain moist for as long as cakes made with butter.

Melt and mix method

Some of the ingredients, including the butter, margarine or dairy blend, are melted and the other moist ingredients are added and then dry ingredients and then they are mixed well. Cakes made by this method usually have a close texture and will stay moist if kept in an airtight container for up to 1 week.

Quick-mix method

This method has one or two steps, with all or most of the ingredients placed in a bowl, mixed together and then cooked, often in the microwave oven. The texture of the cakes is usually coarser, causing them to become dry within 3–4 days, or a little longer if they contain fruit or vegetables such as apple or carrot.

Commercial cake mixes

A wide variety of cake mixes is available. They are valuable as time savers and emergency foods. They usually require the addition of one or more of the following: egg, butter, margarine or dairy blend, milk or water.

Choice of ingredients

The quality of the ingredients used in making cakes influences the final result. Further information on basic ingredients can be found in **Chapter 2 Ingredients and equipment**.

Flour Cake flours are fine in texture with a low gluten content giving a soft texture. Mixtures with cream of tartar must be baked immediately, but those with phosphate aerators can stand before baking without deteriorating. The amount of liquid absorbed by flour may vary.

Butter, margarine, dairy blend or oil The fat or oil used in cakes is often referred to as shortening. Butter, margarine or dairy blend may be used interchangeably. Oil gives a coarser texture and should only be used if specifically called for in a recipe.

Sugars These vary in texture. In cake making, caster sugar blends readily. Brown sugar may be used to vary the flavour and colour.

Eggs These should be fresh. The size of the eggs may affect the result. Recipes in this book are given for 61g and should be adjusted if eggs are not this size.

Milk Usually fresh milk is used. Reconstituted powdered milk may be substituted.

Measuring ingredients for cake making

All ingredients should be measured accurately.

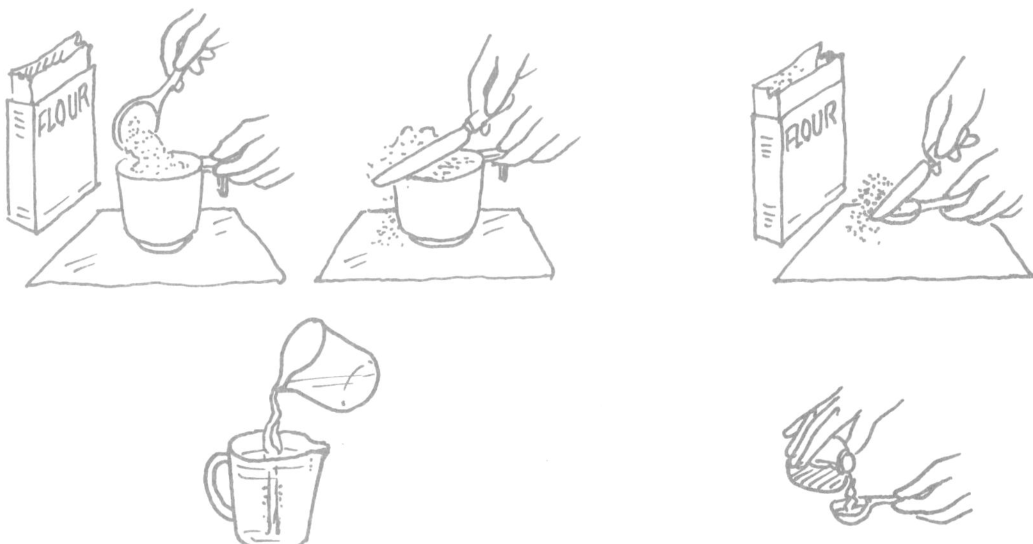

Choice of cake pans

There is a large range of cake pans available. Cakes will be easier to turn out of the pan if a non-stick surface is used. Volume is given in litres (L).

The following pans are used in this book. Others with slightly different dimensions, but holding the same volume, will produce satisfactory results. The volume of cake pans may be compared by measuring the amount of water each will hold.

Round cake pans

Size	Volume	Diameter	Serves
Round 18 cm	1 L	18 cm	8
Round 20 cm	1.5 L	20 cm	8–10
Round 22 cm	2.25 L	22 cm	12–14
Ring 22 cm	1.75 L	22 cm	12
Ring 24 cm	2.5 L	24 cm	16
Deep springform 20 cm	1.75 L	20 cm	10–12
Deep springform 22 cm	2.5 L	22 cm	12–14
Deep springform 24 cm	3.25 L	24 cm	18–20
Sponge	1 L	20 cm	8
Patty pans	65 mL (1/8 cup) each		12 to tray
Small muffin pans	125 mL (1/4 cup) each		12 to tray
Large muffin pans	185 mL (3/4 cup) each		6 to tray

Rectangular cake pans

Size	Volume	Length	Width	Serves
Square 18 cm	1.5 L	18 cm	18 cm	10
Square 20 cm	2.5 L	20 cm	20 cm	16
Medium loaf	1 L	22 cm	10 cm	10
Large loaf	1.5 L	23 cm	13 cm	14
Nut loaf (cylinder)	1 L	22 cm	10 cm	10
Swiss roll	1 L	30 cm	24 cm	10

Preparation of cake pans

Cake pans should be brushed or sprayed with oil. Cakes cooked in pans with a non-stick surface or with the base lined with baking paper will be easier to turn out.

Lining square or oblong pans

Cut paper large enough to cover the pan and extend 3 cm above the top of the pan. Mark size and shape of the base in the centre of the paper, and cut from the edges down to each corner. Fold, and place paper in the pan.

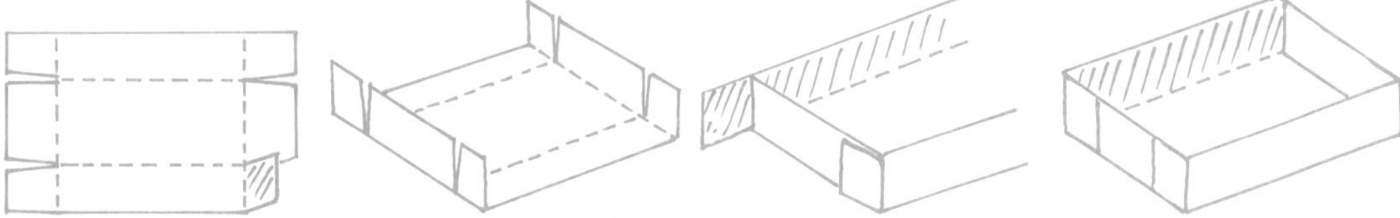

Lining round pans

Cut a base 1 cm smaller than the pan. Cut a straight strip 3 cm longer than the circumference, and 3 cm deeper than the side of the pan. Fold 2 cm strip along one edge of straight piece and make cuts in this from edge to fold at 2 cm intervals. Fit this strip into the pan with folded cut edge on the base. Place round base paper over this. Grease the paper.

Oven management

Oven temperatures and cooking times are given for each recipe, but every oven varies slightly. Use the given temperature and cooking time as a guide. Temperatures may need to be lowered by up to 10°C if using a fan-forced oven.

The effect of dry heat on flour mixtures

1. Fat and sugar are melted.
2. Starch grains burst and absorb the melted fat, sugar and other liquids.
3. The raising agent gives off carbon dioxide, which, when heated, expands and stretches the 'gluten' (a protein formed in flour), causing the cake to rise as the carbon dioxide expands.
4. As the temperature of the cake increases, the heat sets the proteins and the cake retains its shape.
5. The golden brown surface of the cake is formed by caramelisation (the effect of heat on sugar) and by the 'Maillard reaction' (the effect of sugars on amino acids).

Microwave cakes

Cakes cook very quickly in the microwave and it is easy to over-cook them – one minute can make a lot of difference. As the air temperature reaches only 100°C, browning does not occur during cooking by microwaves, thus colour and flavour are different from traditional baking. To obtain a golden appearance, ingredients such as brown sugar, spices and cocoa are often used.If necessary, ovenproof glass, ceramic and microwave plastic are suitable for the microwave oven. Cakes cook more evenly if placed in a ring cake pan or in a dish with an oiled glass in the centre.

APPLE COFFEE CAKE

This may be served as a delicious dessert with whipped cream dusted with cinnamon.

- *Number:* ***16 slices***
- *Cooking utensil:* 24 cm non-stick ring cake pan (2.5 L)

Ingredients

2 teaspoons instant coffee
2 tablespoons (40 mL) boiling water
1/2 cup (125 mL) milk
2 cups (300 g) plain flour
3 teaspoons baking powder
1/3 cup (85 g) butter, margarine *or* dairy blend
1 cup (250 g) sugar
2 eggs (61 g), beaten
2 Granny Smith apples (300 g), peeled and grated
1/3 cup (85 g) brown sugar
1 teaspoon cinnamon

- *Preparation time:* ***25 minutes***
- *Cooking time:* ***60 minutes***
- *Oven temperature:* ***180°C***

Method

1. Set oven at 180°C. Brush or spray cake pan with oil.
2. Dissolve instant coffee in boiling water. Add milk.
3. Sift flour and baking powder into a large bowl.
4. Rub butter into flour mixture with the fingertips until it resembles breadcrumbs.
5. Stir in sugar, coffee mixture and eggs.
6. Pour into cake pan. Spread grated apple evenly over the surface and sprinkle with brown sugar and cinnamon.
7. Bake at 180°C for 60 minutes. To test if cooked: cake will shrink slightly from sides of pan and a fine skewer inserted in cake comes out clean and dry.
8. Cool in cake pan before turning onto a cake cooler.

Will keep for 3–4 days in an airtight container. Suitable for freezing for up to 3 months.

MICROWAVE APPLE COFFEE CAKE ✦

Follow recipe for **Apple coffee cake**. Place in oiled 22 cm microwave ring pan. Cook for 6 minutes on high power. Stand for 3 minutes before turning out.

APRICOT AND ALMOND CAKE

A low-fat cake that could be served as a snack or dessert.

- *Number:* ***8–10 slices***
- *Cooking utensil:* 20 cm round cake pan (1.5 L)

Ingredients

1 cup (150 g) plain flour
1 1/2 teaspoons baking powder
2 eggs (61 g)
3/4 cup (190 g) sugar
1/4 cup (65 mL) milk

Filling

1 cup (180 g) chopped dried apricots
1/2 cup (60 g) chopped almonds
1/4 cup (65 g) marmalade

- *Preparation time:* ***25 minutes***
- *Cooking time:* ***50–55 minutes***
- *Oven temperature:* ***180°C***

Method

1. Set oven at 180°C. Brush or spray cake pan with oil and line base with baking paper.
2. Sift flour and baking powder.
3. Beat eggs and sugar, add milk.
4. Fold flour into egg mixture.
5. Pour half of the mixture into the cake pan.
6. Mix filling ingredients and place in spoonfuls over mixture.
7. Spread remaining cake mixture over the top.
8. Bake at 180°C for 50–55 minutes. To test if cooked: cake will shrink slightly from sides of pan and a fine skewer inserted in cake comes out clean and dry.
9. Cool for 15 minutes before turning onto a cake cooler.

Will keep for up to 1 week in an airtight container. Suitable for freezing for up to 3 months.

✦ FIG AND PECAN CAKE

Follow recipe for **Apricot and almond cake**. Use 1 cup (180 g) chopped dried figs instead of apricots and 1/2 cup (60 g) chopped pecans instead of almonds.

BUTTER CAKE

The basic butter cake can be flavoured and decorated for birthdays, parties and other special occasions. Choose from the 3 basic recipes below and follow the method on p. 380.

PLAIN BUTTER CAKE

Ingredients	***Cooking utensil***	***Time/Temperature/Number***
$^{1}/_{2}$ cup (125 g) butter, margarine *or* dairy blend	20 cm round cake pan (1.5 L) *or*	*Preparation time:* ***20 minutes***
$^{1}/_{2}$ cup (125 g) caster sugar	22 cm ring cake pan (1.75 L) *or*	*Cooking time:* ***35–40 minutes***
2 eggs (61 g), beaten	large loaf cake pan (1.5 L)	*Oven temperature:* ***180°C***
$1^{1}/_{4}$ cups (190 g) self-raising flour		*Number:* ***8–10 slices***
$^{1}/_{3}$ cup (85 mL) milk		

MEDIUM BUTTER CAKE

Ingredients	***Cooking utensil***	***Time/Temperature/Number***
$^{3}/_{4}$ cup (185 g) butter, margarine *or* dairy blend	20 cm round cake pan (1.5 L) *or*	*Preparation time:* ***25 minutes***
$^{3}/_{4}$ cup (190 g) caster sugar	18 cm square cake pan (1.5 L) *or*	*Cooking time:* ***45–60 minutes***
3 eggs (61 g), beaten	large loaf cake pan (1.5 L)	*Oven temperature:* ***180°C, decrease to 160°C during cooking***
$1^{3}/_{4}$ cups (265 g) self-raising flour		*Number:* ***8–10 slices***
3 tablespoons (60 mL) milk		

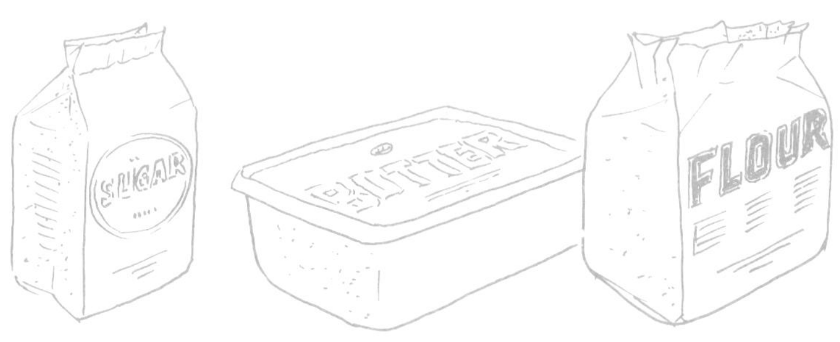

RICH BUTTER CAKE

To make a cake to cut into 20–22 serves, make double quantity **Rich butter cake** and cook for 1 1/2 to 1 3/4 hours in a 24 cm, deep springform pan.

Ingredients	*Cooking utensil*	*Time/Temperature/Number*
1 cup (250 g) butter, margarine *or* dairy blend 1 cup (250 g) caster sugar 4 eggs (61 g), beaten 2 cups (300 g) self-raising flour 2 tablespoons (40 mL) milk	22 cm round cake pan (2.25 L) *or* 20 cm square cake pan (2.5 L) *or* 22 cm springform cake pan (2.5 L)	*Preparation time:* ***30 minutes*** *Cooking time:****1–1 1/4 hours*** *Oven temperature:* ***180°C, decrease to 160°C during cooking*** *Number:* ***12–14 slices***

Method for Plain butter cake, Medium butter cake and Rich butter cake

1 Set oven at 180°C. Brush or spray cake pan with oil and line base with baking paper.
2 Cream butter and sugar until light and fluffy.
3 Gradually add eggs, beating well.
4 Stir in flour and milk alternately, about 1/3 at a time. Stir gently, but thoroughly.
5 Place in cake pan and bake at 180°C for time indicated in table. To test if cooked: cake will shrink slightly from sides of pan and a fine skewer inserted in cake comes out clean and dry.
6 Cool on a cake cooler. Ice with 1/2 cup (1 quantity) **Butter icing** (p. 383) *or* **Melted butter icing** (p. 384).

Will keep for up to 1 week in an airtight container. Suitable for freezing for up to 3 months (without icing).

Follow the **Plain butter cake**, **Medium butter cake** or **Rich butter cake** recipe to make variations.

BANANA BUTTER CAKE

Add 3 mashed bananas after step 2. Sift 1 teaspoon bicarbonate of soda with flour. Ice with 1/2 cup (1 quantity) **Cream cheese icing** (p. 384). Decorate with small bananas moulded from **Almond paste** (p. 414) *or* **Fondant icing** (p. 418) and tinted with food colour.

✦ CHERRY AND ALMOND BUTTER CAKE ✦

Add 1/2 cup (90 g) chopped glacé cherries and 1/2 cup (60 g) chopped almonds after step 2. Decorate icing with cherries and almonds.

✦ CHOCOLATE BUTTER CAKE ✦

Sift 2 tablespoons (20 g) cocoa with the flour. Add 2 tablespoons (40 mL) extra milk, and 1/2 teaspoon vanilla essence. Flavour icing with chocolate and decorate with cherries and almonds.

✦ COFFEE AND PECAN BUTTER CAKE ✦

Add 2 teaspoons instant coffee and 1/2 cup (60 g) chopped pecans after step 2. Flavour icing with coffee and decorate with pecans.

✦ DATE AND WALNUT BUTTER CAKE ✦

Add 1/2 cup (90 g) chopped dates and 1/2 cup (60 g) chopped walnuts after step 2. Flavour icing with lemon.

✦ MARBLE BUTTER CAKE ✦

Follow **Medium** *or* **Rich butter cake** recipe. Divide mixture into three parts. Add 1 tablespoon (10 g) cocoa to 1/3, add 1/4 teaspoon pink colouring to 1/3, and leave 1/3 plain. Place spoonfuls into cake pan, alternating the colours. Mix lightly to give streaky appearance. Flavour icing with chocolate *or* colour pink.

✦ ORANGE BUTTER CAKE ✦

Add 1 tablespoon grated orange rind after step 2. Flavour icing with orange juice and decorate with mandarin segments.

✦ SULTANA BUTTER CAKE ✦

Add 1 cup (180 g) sultanas after step 2. Sift 1 teaspoon mixed spice with flour. Decrease oven temperature during cooking if necessary.

Decorating butter cakes

Butter cakes may be decorated by:

- covering with **Butter icing** (p. 383), **Melted butter icing** (p. 384) *or* **Cream cheese icing** (p. 384)
- covering with **Almond paste** (p. 414) *or* **Fondant icing** (p. 418)
- covering with **Chocolate glaze** (p. 386)
- piping with **Melted chocolate** (p. 385)
- using **Almond paste** (p. 414) *or* **Fondant icing** (p. 418) in shapes such as flowers, fruit and vegetables
- using **Modelling chocolate** (p. 387)
- covering sides with a wide ribbon
- placing on a doily or presentation board (p. 416).

✦ CELEBRATION BUTTER CAKES ✦

For a birthday or nameday a butter cake could be iced and decorated. Brush top of cake with 2 tablespoons (50 g) jam, boiled and sieved. Roll 300 g white **Fondant icing** (p. 418) *or* **Soft icing** (p. 416) to a circle slightly larger than top of cake. Place onto cake and trim level with top edge. Pinch edge or scallop with icing tongs and decorate top with 12 small fruits and leaves modelled from **Almond paste** (p. 414) *or* **Fondant icing** (p. 418) and painted with food colouring. Tie a wide coloured ribbon around cake and place on a doily. For Easter, the **Fondant icing** (p. 418) could be coloured pale lemon. Decorate with 12 small coloured chocolate eggs around edge and a fluffy chicken in a nest of shredded coconut in the centre. Tie a yellow ribbon around cake and place on a doily. Other special occasion suggestions: cover cake with 175 g (1 quantity) **Chocolate glaze** (p. 387) and decorate with 100 g **Modelling chocolate** (p. 386) and dust with icing sugar mixture.

✦ TORTE ✦

Cut one **Plain** *or* **Medium butter cake** (p. 378) into three layers. Place bottom layer on serving plate or board. Using 1/4 cup (65 g) apricot jam, spread half on bottom layer. Place middle layer on top and cover with remaining jam. Place top layer on and ice with 1/2 cup (1 quantity) **Butter icing** (p. 383) flavoured with chocolate, coffee *or* vanilla. Decorate with **Chocolate leaves** (p. 386), blanched almonds, half dipped in chocolate, *or* 100 g **Modelling chocolate** (p. 387).

✦ CHOCOLATE TORTE ✦

Cut one **Plain** *or* **Medium butter cake** into three layers. Place bottom layer on serving plate or board. Using 1/4 cup (65 g) apricot jam, spread half on bottom layer. Place middle layer on top and cover with remaining jam. Place top layer on and cover with 1/2 cup (1 quantity) **Chocolate glaze** (p. 386). Decorate with **Modelling chocolate** (p. 386), silver cachous, almonds or other contrasting decoration.

✦ HOUSE CAKE ✦

1 Use one **Rich butter cake** cooked in a 20 cm square cake pan.
2 Cut cake in two parts (diagram 1: A is base, B is roof).
3 Place the base on a board 20 cm x 30 cm covered with foil.
4 Cut roof piece diagonally (diagram 2).
5 Make two quantities **Melted butter icing** (p. 384).
6 Join roof pieces with a thin layer of icing (diagram 3).
7 Attach roof to base with icing (diagram 4).
8 Trim cake if necessary.
9 Spread icing over top and sides of cake.
10 Using a fork, mark icing to represent bark or use a knife to mark ridges for weatherboards. Other utensils can be used to mark bricks and other features.
11 Use confectionery (e.g. jelly beans, licorice, mint leaves) to make tiles, windows, door, path, flowers and garden.

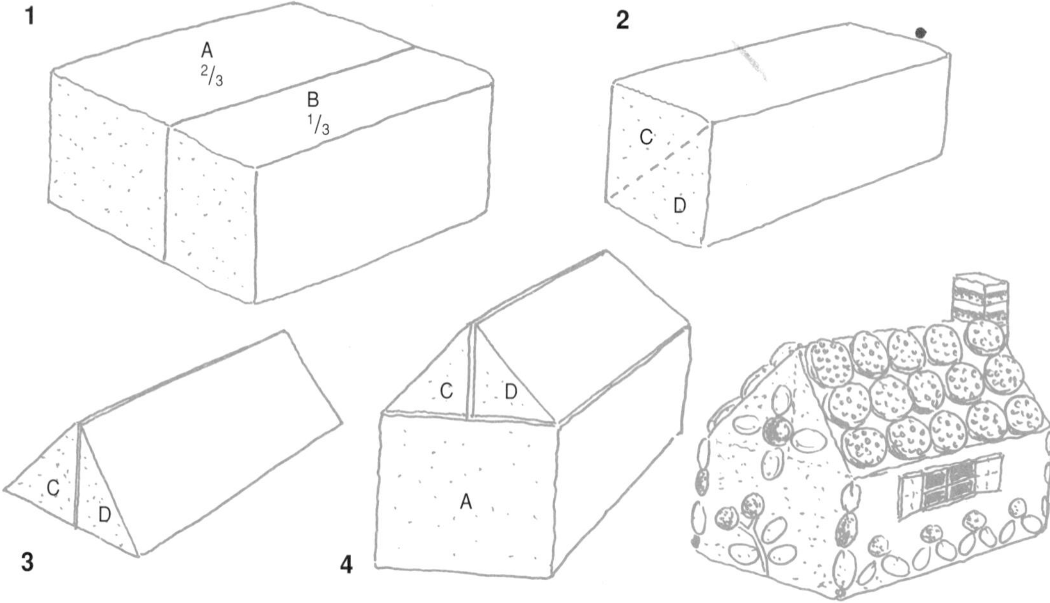

Fig. 15.6

✦ LAMINGTONS ✦

Cook 1 quantity **Rich butter cake** *or* $1^1/_2$ quantities **Plain butter cake** in 20 cm square cake pan (2.5 L). Prepare $1^1/_2$ cups (3 quantities) **Chocolate glacé icing** (p. 395) and $1^1/_2$ cups (135 g) coconut. Cut cake into 25 blocks (each 4 cm square) and spread icing on all sides, roll in coconut. Allow to dry on a cake cooler.

BUTTER ICING

Use as a filling for biscuits or to ice and fill butter cakes.
Also called 'Vienna icing'.

Ingredients

$^1/_2$ cup (90 g) icing sugar mixture
2 tablespoons (40 g) butter
4 drops vanilla *or* other essence
2 teaspoons (10 mL) water *or* other liquid

Method

1. Sift icing sugar mixture.
2. Cream butter, adding icing sugar gradually.
3. Add vanilla essence and mix thoroughly. Liquid may be added if softer icing is required.

✦ CHOCOLATE BUTTER ICING ✦

Melt 100 g chocolate over hot water and add to the mixture at step 3 *or* blend 2 teaspoons cocoa in 1 tablespoon (20 mL) boiling water and stir into mixture at step 3.

✦ COFFEE BUTTER ICING ✦

Add 1 teaspoon instant coffee powder at step 2.

✦ LEMON BUTTER ICING ✦

Omit vanilla essence. Add 2 teaspoons finely grated lemon rind and 2 teaspoons (10 mL) lemon juice to the mixture at step 3.

✦ ORANGE BUTTER ICING ✦

Omit vanilla essence. Add 3 teaspoons finely grated orange rind and 2 teaspoons (10 mL) orange juice to the mixture at step 3.

✦ APRICOT BUTTER ICING ✦

Omit vanilla essence. Add 2 tablespoons (40 g) apricot puree to the mixture at step 3.

MELTED BUTTER ICING

Use as a filling for biscuits or to ice and fill butter cakes.

Ingredients

$^{2}/_{3}$ cup (120 g) icing sugar mixture
1 tablespoon (20 g) butter
2–3 teaspoons hot water
colouring
flavouring

Method

1 Sift icing sugar mixture.
2 Add butter to hot water, allow to melt.
3 Add sufficient butter and hot water to make icing the consistency of treacle.
4 Colour and flavour as in **Butter icing** variations.

CREAM CHEESE ICING

Use for icing cakes containing fruit and vegetables, e.g. carrot, banana and zucchini cakes.

Ingredients

125 g cream cheese *or* smooth ricotta cheese
2 tablespoons (30 g) icing sugar mixture
1–2 teaspoons orange *or* lemon juice

Method

1 Beat cheese, gradually add icing sugar mixture.
2 Add juice and beat well.
3 Spread or pipe as required.

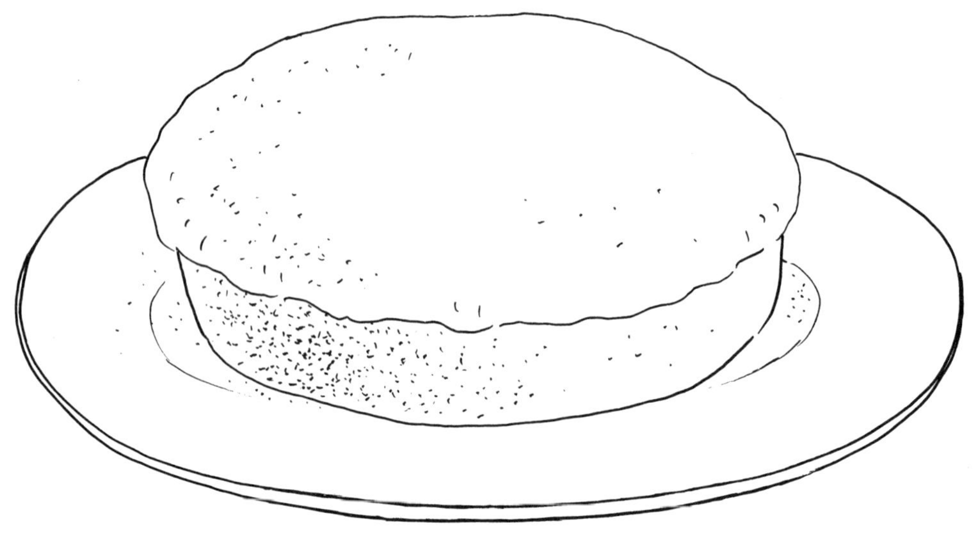

Decorating with chocolate

Melting chocolate

Chocolate may be melted over hot water or in the microwave. Compound or cooking chocolate in blocks or buttons melts readily when warmed and sets quickly. Chocolate must be melted using gentle heat or it will burn and become bitter.

To melt chocolate over hot water Break chocolate into small pieces and place in top of double boiler or small heatproof bowl over gently simmering water.

To melt chocolate in microwave oven Place 100 g chocolate in microwave-safe container. Heat on medium power for 1 minute, stir, then continue heating with 20 second bursts and stirring until chocolate is melted. Note that the chocolate will appear to hold its shape even though it is melted.

Chocolate leaves

1 Brush melted chocolate onto the veined side of non-toxic leaves, e.g. rose, camellia, being careful not to let chocolate go over the edge.
2 Place leaves, chocolate side up, on a tray lined with baking paper.
3 Refrigerate until set.
4 Carefully peel away green leaf and handle chocolate leaf by edge.
5 Store in an airtight container in a cool place until required.

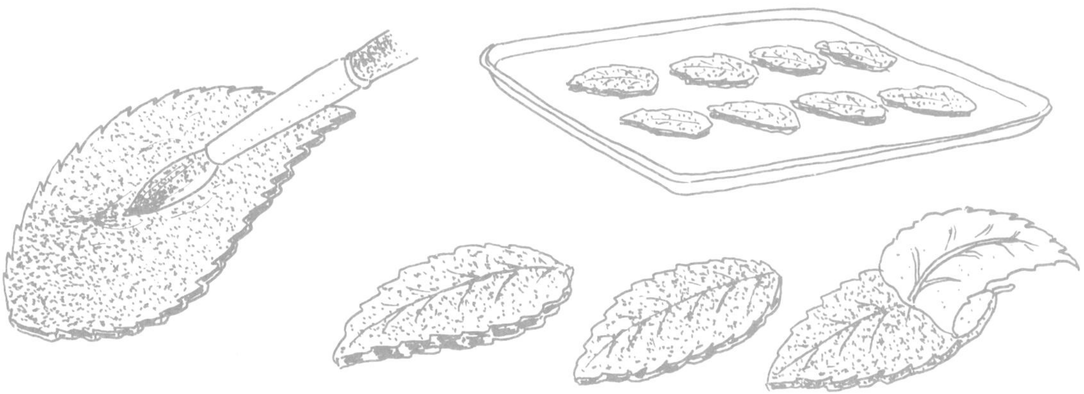

Piped chocolate shapes

1 Draw leaves, shapes, outlines or lace on white paper.
2 Place a sheet of baking paper over white paper.
3 Place a small quantity of melted chocolate into a paper piping bag and carefully follow outlines, then fill in spaces with melted chocolate as appropriate.
4 When chocolate has set, peel away paper and store in an airtight container in a cool place.

Chocolate curls

1 Spread 60 g melted chocolate in a thick layer over flat surface such as laminated board, marble slab or back of oven tray.
2 When almost set use a long sharp knife at a slight angle and draw across chocolate to make curls.
3 Allow to harden before piling in centre of cake or storing in an airtight container in a cool place.

Chocolate glaze

1 Melt 100 g chocolate in microwave on medium power for 1 minute or until melted, or over simmering water.
2 Add 75 g softened unsalted butter and beat well using whisk, electric beater or wooden spoon.
3 Stand until the glaze starts to thicken then spread the mixture quickly over the cake.

Modelling chocolate

1 Melt 150 g compound chocolate and add 1/2 cup warmed liquid glucose.
2 Mix well and leave to set at least 1 hour.
3 Knead well before each use.

BOILED FRUIT CAKE

This cake keeps moist for 4 weeks.

- *Number:* ***20 slices***
- *Cooking utensils:* 20 cm square cake pan (2.5 L), saucepan
- *Preparation time:* ***40 minutes***
- *Cooking time:* ***1 hour***
- *Oven temperature:* ***180°C***

Ingredients

3/4 cup (190 g) sugar
1 cup (250 mL) water
2 1/2 cups (450 g) mixed dried fruit
1/3 cup (60 g) mixed peel
1 teaspoon nutmeg
1 teaspoon bicarbonate of soda
1/2 cup (125 g) butter
2 eggs (61 g), beaten
1 cup (150 g) self-raising flour
1 cup (150 g) plain flour

Method

1. Set oven at 180°C. Brush or spray cake pan with oil and line base with baking paper.
2. In saucepan place sugar, water, dried fruit, mixed peel, nutmeg, bicarbonate of soda and butter. Stir until boiling. Allow to cool for 5 minutes.
3. Add eggs.
4. Sift flours, add to other ingredients and mix thoroughly.
5. Place in cake pan and bake at 180°C for 1 hour. To test if cooked: cake will shrink slightly from sides of pan and a fine skewer inserted in cake comes out clean and dry.
6. Allow to stand in cake pan for 15 minutes then turn onto cake cooler.

Will keep for up to 4 weeks in an airtight container. Suitable for freezing for up to 3 months.

Decorating boiled fruit cakes

Using approximately 80 g **Almond paste** (p. 414) *or* **Fondant icing** (p.418), shape 12 small fruits such as apples, orange and plums. Cut leaf shapes and mark veins with back of knife. Paint with food colouring and leave to dry. Space evenly around edge of cake and attach with a small amount of jam. Tie a coloured ribbon around cake and place on a doily or presentation board (p. 416).

CARROT AND PUMPKIN CAKE 

A moist loaf with a touch of ginger, suitable for packed lunches.

- *Number:* ***14 slices***
- *Cooking utensil:* large loaf cake pan (1.5 L)
- *Preparation time:* ***25 minutes***
- *Cooking time:* ***30–35 minutes***
- *Oven temperature:* ***180°C***

Ingredients

3/4 cup (110 g) wholemeal plain flour
1 cup (150 g) plain flour
1 teaspoon bicarbonate of soda
1 teaspoon mixed spice
2 teaspoons grated fresh ginger
3 tablespoons (60 mL) oil
3 tablespoons (45 g) brown sugar
1 egg (61 g)
1 carrot (125 g), grated
1 cup (300 g) cooked mashed pumpkin
1/2 cup (90 g) sultanas

Method

1. Set oven at 180°C. Brush or spray cake pan with oil and line base with baking paper.
2. Sift wholemeal flour, plain flour, bicarbonate of soda and mixed spice.
3. Mix ginger, oil, sugar, egg, carrot, pumpkin and sultanas.
4. Fold in flour mixture.
5. Place into cake pan and bake at 180°C for 30–35 minutes. To test if cooked: cake will shrink slightly from sides of pan and a fine skewer inserted in cake comes out clean and dry.
6. Cool in cake pan, then turn onto a cake cooler.
7. May be iced with 1/2 cup (1 quantity) **Cream cheese icing** (p. 384). May be decorated with moulded carrots made from **Almond paste** (p. 414) *or* **Fondant icing** (p. 418), tinted with food colouring.

Will keep for up to 1 week in an airtight container. Suitable for freezing for up to 3 months (without icing).

MICROWAVE CARROT AND PUMPKIN CAKE ✦

Follow recipe for **Carrot and pumpkin cake**. Place mixture in 22 cm microwave ring pan (1.75 L). Cook for 6 minutes on high power. Stand for 3 minutes to allow to cool, then turn onto cake cooler.

CARROT CAKE

- *Number:* ***14 slices***
- *Cooking utensil:* large loaf cake pan (1.5 L)
- *Preparation time:* ***20 minutes***
- *Cooking time:* ***50–60 minutes***
- *Oven temperature:* ***190°C***

Ingredients

1/3 cup (85 mL) oil
2 eggs (61 g)
1 cup (180 g) brown sugar
1 1/2 carrots (225 g), grated
1 cup (150 g) self-raising flour
1/2 cup (60 g) chopped nuts
1/2 teaspoon vanilla essence
1/2 teaspoon cinnamon

Method

1. Set oven at 190°C. Brush or spray cake pan with oil and line base with baking paper.
2. Combine oil, eggs and sugar, add all other ingredients and mix well.
3. Place in cake pan and bake at 190°C for 50–60 minutes. To test if cooked: cake will shrink slightly from sides of pan and a fine skewer inserted in cake comes out clean and dry.
4. Cool for 15 minutes, then turn onto cake cooler. May be iced with 1/2 cup (1 quantity) **Cream cheese icing** (p. 384). May be decorated with moulded carrots made from **Almond paste** (p. 414) *or* **Fondant icing** (p. 418), tinted with food colouring.

Will keep for up to 1 week in an airtight container. Suitable for freezing for up to 3 months (without icing).

ZUCCHINI CAKE

Follow recipe for **Carrot cake**. Use 2 (200 g) grated zucchini instead of carrots.

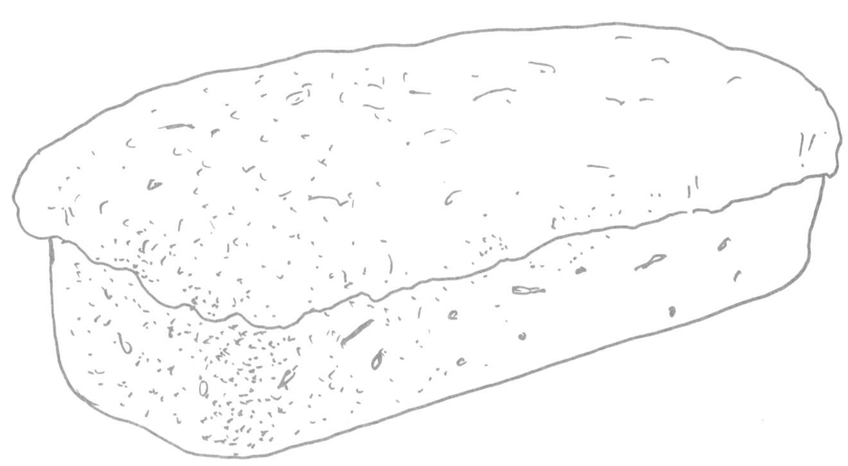

CHOCOLATE QUICK-MIX CAKE 

- *Number:* ***8–10 slices***
- *Cooking utensil:* 20 cm round cake pan (1.5 L)
- *Preparation time:* ***15 minutes***
- *Cooking time:* ***40–45 minutes***
- *Oven temperature:* ***180°C***

Ingredients

1 cup (150 g) self-raising flour
2 tablespoons (20 g) cocoa
3/4 cup (190 g) caster sugar
3 tablespoons (60 g) soft butter, margarine *or* dairy blend
1/2 cup (125 mL) milk
2 eggs (61 g)

Method

1. Set oven at 180°C. Brush or spray cake pan with oil and line base with baking paper.
2. Place all ingredients in bowl, beat for 3 minutes using an electric beater, food processor or wooden spoon.
3. Pour into cake pan and bake at 180°C for 40–45 minutes. To test if cooked: cake will shrink slightly from sides of pan and a fine skewer inserted in cake comes out clean and dry.
4. Cool on cake cooler. May be iced using 1/2 cup (1 quantity) **Cream cheese icing** (p. 384) *or* 175 g (1 quantity) **Chocolate glaze** (p. 386).

Will keep for up to 1 week in an airtight container. Suitable for freezing for up to 3 months (without icing).

COFFEE NUT QUICK-MIX CAKE

Follow recipe for **Quick-mix cake**. Add 2 teaspoons instant coffee. Fold in 1/3 cup (40 g) chopped nuts after mixing.

BLACK FOREST CAKE

1. Cut one **Chocolate quick-mix cake** into three layers.
2. Drain 425 g can pitted black cherries and reserve 8 for decoration. Reserve 1/4 cup (65 mL) juice and combine with 1 tablespoon (20 mL) kirsch.
3. Whip 300 mL cream until stiff and mix 1/3 with cherries.
4. Place bottom layer of cake on serving plate.
5. Sprinkle with 1/2 juice and kirsch, spread with 1/2 cherries and cream mixture.
6. Place middle layer of cake on top and repeat step 5.
7. Place top layer on and cover top and sides with cream, reserving some for piping.
8. Using a spatula, press 60 g grated chocolate around side of cake.
9. Using reserved cream, pipe a decorative edge around top of cake and decorate with remaining cherries and **Chocolate curls** (p. 386).
10. Refrigerate until ready to serve.

DUTCH ORANGE SYRUP CAKE

Add 1 tablespoon of orange or almond flavoured liqueur to the syrup to make a delicious dessert. Serve with cream.

- *Number:* ***12 slices***
- *Cooking utensil:* 22 cm ring cake pan (1.75 L)
- *Preparation time:* ***20 minutes***
- *Cooking time:* ***30–35 minutes***
- *Oven temperature:* ***180°C***

Ingredients

$^{1}/_{2}$ cup (125 g) butter, margarine *or* dairy blend
$^{1}/_{2}$ cup (125 g) caster sugar
2 eggs (61 g), beaten
$1^{1}/_{4}$ cups (190 g) self-raising flour
rind of 1 lemon, grated
rind of 1 orange, grated

Topping

$^{1}/_{3}$ cup (80 g) caster sugar
juice of 1 lemon
juice of 2 oranges
$^{3}/_{4}$ cup (185 mL) water

Method

1. Set oven at 180°C. Brush or spray cake pan with oil.
2. Cream butter and sugar until light and fluffy.
3. Add eggs gradually and mix well. Add lemon and orange rind.
4. Sift in flour. The mixture should be firm.
5. Place in cake pan and bake at 180°C for 30–35 minutes. To test if cooked: cake will shrink slightly from sides of pan and a fine skewer inserted in cake comes out clean and dry.
6. Combine topping ingredients in saucepan. Stir until sugar has melted, but do not boil.
7. Turn cake onto cake cooler, leave upside down.
8. Place a large plate under cake cooler. Spoon hot topping over hot cake. Repeat process with topping collected on plate until all is absorbed.

Will keep for up to 1 week in an airtight container. Suitable for freezing for up to 3 months.

EGG SPONGE

A basic egg sponge, sometimes called a sponge sandwich as the two cakes may be sandwiched together with whipped cream. Check the tips for product quality of sponges on p. 398.

- *Number:* ***8–10 slices***
- *Cooking utensils:* two 20 cm round sponge pans (1 L each)

Ingredients

$^2/_3$ cup (100 g) plain flour
4 tablespoons (40 g) custard powder *or* cornflour
1 teaspoon baking powder
4 eggs (61 g)
$^2/_3$ cup (165 g) caster sugar
1 tablespoon (20 mL) water, if required

Will keep for 2 days in refrigerator with icing and cream. Will keep for up to 1 week (without cream) in an airtight container. Suitable for freezing (without icing and cream) for up to 3 months.

- *Preparation time:* ***25 minutes***
- *Cooking time:* ***20 minutes***
- *Oven temperature:* ***190°C***

Method

1 Set oven at 190°C. Brush or spray cake pans with oil and line bases with baking paper.
2 Sift flour, custard powder *or* cornflour and baking powder.
3 Separate eggs, placing whites into a mixing bowl.
4 Beat egg whites until stiff, using an electric or rotary beater or whisk.
5 Gradually add sugar, while continuing to beat, until very stiff.
6 Add egg yolks and continue beating until mixture forms a figure '8' and resembles thick cream.
7 Using a tablespoon, fold in sifted flour very lightly. If very thick add water. Do not overmix.
8 Pour into cake pans and bake at 190°C for 20 minutes. To test if cooked: press lightly with the finger in the centre of the cake – the impression should disappear at once.
9 When cooked, remove from cake pans immediately and place right-side up to cool on a flat surface.
10 To make two single layer sponges, cut each sponge into two layers, cover each bottom layer with 1 cup (250 mL) whipped cream and cover with top layers. Ice each top with $^1/_2$ cup (1 quantity) **Glacé icing** (p. 395). For flavoured icings and **Feather icing** see p. 395.
11 To make a double layer cake, place one sponge bottom-side up, spread with 1 cup (250 mL) whipped cream, cover with other sponge bottom side down, and ice top with $^1/_2$ cup (1 quantity) **Glacé icing** (p. 395). For flavoured icings and **Feather icing** see p. 395.

✦ CHOCOLATE EGG SPONGE ✦

Follow recipe for **Egg sponge**. Add 1$^1/_2$ tablespoons (15 g) cocoa to flour before sifting. Add extra $^1/_2$–1 tablespoon of water if required. Ice with $^1/_2$ cup (1 quantity) **Chocolate glacé icing** (p. 395), which may be flavoured with lemon juice *or* peppermint. Decorate with almonds *or* walnuts.

✦ GINGER EGG SPONGE ✦

Follow recipe for **Egg sponge**. Add 2 teaspoons ground ginger and $^1/_2$ teaspoon mixed spice to flour before sifting. Ice with $^1/_2$ cup (1 quantity) **Lemon glacé icing** (p. 395). Decorate with chopped glacé ginger and walnuts.

✦ LEMON CREAM EGG SPONGE ✦

Join cooled sponge cakes with 2 tablespoons (40 mL) **Lemon spread** (p. 489) *or* commercial lemon butter combined with 1 cup (250 mL) whipped cream. Dust with icing sugar.

✦ PASSIONFRUIT EGG SPONGE ✦

Join or fill sponge cake with 1 cup whipped cream (250 mL). Ice with passionfruit **Glacé icing**: follow recipe for **Glacé icing** (p. 395), using 1 tablespoon (20 mL) passionfruit pulp as liquid.

✦ RASPBERRY CREAM EGG SPONGE ✦

Spread one cooled sponge cake with 2 tablespoons (40 g) raspberry jam. Using 1 cup (250 mL) whipped cream, spread half on jam. Place second layer on top and spread remaining cream. Decorate with fresh raspberries.

✦ SMALL SPONGE CAKES 

1 To make 24, follow recipe for **Egg sponge**. Use patty pan trays brushed or spread with oil, or paper patty pans on oven tray.
2 Place mixture into patty pans.
3 Bake at 180°C for approximately 10 minutes. To test if cooked: press lightly with the finger in the centre of a cake – the impression should disappear at once.
4 Cool on a cake cooler.
5 Whip 1 cup (250 mL) cream. Cut each cake in half, place 2 teaspoons cream in each, replace tops.
6 Ice tops with $^1/_2$ cup (1 quantity) **Glacé icing**.

Will keep for up to 1 week in airtight container (without cream). Suitable for freezing for up to 3 months (without icing or cream).

✦ SNOWBALLS ✦

1 To make 24, follow recipe for **Egg sponge** (p. 392). Use patty pan trays brushed or spread with oil, or paper patty pans on oven tray.
2 Place mixture into patty pans.
3 Bake at 180°C for approximately 10 minutes. To test if cooked: press lightly with the finger in the centre of a cake – the impression should disappear at once.
4 Cool on a cake cooler.
5 Ice tops and sides with 1 cup (2 quantities) **Chocolate glacé icing** (p. 395).
6 Sprinkle with 1 cup (90 g) coconut.
7 Whip 1 cup (250 mL) cream and cut part way through each cake. Fill with cream.

Will keep for up to 1 week in airtight container (without cream). Suitable for freezing for up to 3 months (without icing or cream).

✦ STRAWBERRY CREAM EGG SPONGE ✦

Use 1 cup (250 mL) whipped cream and 1 punnet (250 g) strawberries. Slice half the strawberries and mix with half the cream. Spread on the cooled sponge cake. Place second layer on top, spread remaining cream. Decorate with remaining strawberries.

Decorating egg sponges

Egg sponges may be decorated by:

- covering with **Glacé icing** (p. 395)
- covering top *or* joining with whipped cream and fresh fruit, e.g. strawberries
- dusting top with icing sugar mixture
- dusting top with icing sugar mixture using a doily *or* cut out to create a silhouette effect
- using a **Feather icing** effect (p. 398)
- piping with **Melted chocolate** (p. 385).

PLATE 15

Chocolate torte (p. 380), Nectarine cake (p. 405), Black Forest roll (p. 390).

PLATE 16

Right

1 round cake pan
2 casserole with lid
3 small muffin pan
4 deep round cake pan
5 medium loaf pan
6 large loaf pan
7 black bread pan
8 Swiss roll pan
9 square cake pan
10 spring form pan
11 patty pan tray
12 large muffin pan
13 ring cake pan
14 flan or quiche pan
15 pie dish

Above **1** sieve **2** rotary beater **3** whisk **4** wok and stirrer **5** $^1/_4$, $^1/_3$, $^1/_2$ cup measures **6** 1 cup measure **7** measuring jug **8** measuring spoons **9** melon baller **10** zester **11** spatula **12** small vegetable knife **13** 28 cm chefs' knife **14** serrated edge knife **15** filleting knife **16** egg lifter **17** 26 cm non-stick frying pan **18** wooden spoon **19** colander

GLACÉ ICING

Use to ice biscuits and egg sponges.

Ingredients

3/4 cup (135 g) icing sugar mixture
1 tablespoon (20 mL) water *or* fruit juice
colouring
flavouring

Method

1. Sift icing sugar mixture into basin.
2. Add half the liquid and mix. Add colouring and flavouring.
3. Continue to add sufficient of the remaining liquid, beating well, until icing runs smoothly and slowly.
4. Pour over surface of cake or biscuits.

LEMON OR ORANGE GLACÉ ICING

Use 1 tablespoon (20 mL) orange *or* lemon juice as liquid.

CHOCOLATE GLACÉ ICING

Use 1 tablespoon (20 mL) boiling water as liquid, blended with 2 teaspoons cocoa. Add 4 drops vanilla essence and a little more water if necessary.

COFFEE GLACÉ ICING

Use 1 tablespoon (20 mL) boiling water as liquid, blended with 1 teaspoon instant coffee powder.

FEATHER ICING CAKE

This effect is produced by piping contrasting lines of icing on an iced cake (p. 398). Place filling between layers of sponge before icing.

1. Using 1/2 cup (1 quantity) **Glacé icing**, remove 1 tablespoon icing, add colouring to it and thin slightly with water to the consistency of honey.
2. Place in a piping bag. Ice top of cake with remaining icing and immediately pipe parallel lines of contrasting colour 1–2 cm apart across surface of cake.
3. Using a skewer or satay stick, score quickly and lightly through the piped lines to give the effect of a feather. Icing must still be wet when this is done to gain full effect.
4. Score between these strokes in the opposite direction to produce a zigzag effect.

EGG SPONGE ROLL

Check the tips for product quality of sponges on p. 398.

- *Number:* ***10 slices***
- *Cooking utensil:* Swiss roll cake pan (24 cm x 30 cm - 1L)

Preparation time: ***20 minutes***
Cooking time: ***12–15 minutes***
- *Oven temperature:* ***190°C***

Ingredients

1 tablespoon (20 g) caster sugar
1/2 cup (75 g) plain flour
3 tablespoons (30 g) cornflour
1 teaspoon baking powder
3 eggs (61 g)
1/2 cup (125 g) caster sugar
2 teaspoons (10 mL) water, if required
filling (see variations below)

Method

1. Set oven at 190°C. Brush or spray Swiss roll cake pan with oil and line base with baking paper. Spread out clean tea towel, sprinkle with 1 tablespoon caster sugar.
2. Sift flours and baking powder.
3. Separate eggs, placing whites into mixing bowl.
4. Beat egg whites until stiff, gradually add sugar while continuing to beat. Add egg yolks and beat until mixture forms a figure '8' and resembles thick cream.
5. Using a tablespoon, fold in sifted flour very lightly. If very thick add water. Do not overmix.
6. Pour into Swiss roll cake pan and bake at 190°C for 12–15 minutes. To test if cooked: press lightly with the finger in the centre of the cake – the impression should disappear at once.
7. Turn baked sponge onto tea towel, remove paper, quickly trim side edges to remove crust and immediately roll up tea towel and cake together.
8. Allow to stand for 2 minutes.
9. Unroll when cool, spread sponge with filling, and reroll.

Will keep for 1–2 days in airtight container (without cream). Suitable for freezing for up to 3 months (without cream).

SWISS ROLL

Follow recipe for **Egg sponge roll**, using 4 tablespoons (80 g) warm jam, e.g. raspberry, as filling.

✦ FRUIT SPONGE ROLL ✦

Follow recipe for **Egg sponge roll**. Fill with 250 g chopped strawberries *or* other fruit mixed with $^3/_4$ cup (190 mL) whipped cream. Dust with icing sugar and serve.

✦ CHOCOLATE SPONGE ROLL ✦

Follow recipe for **Egg sponge roll**. Add $1^1/_2$ tablespoons (15 g) cocoa to flour before sifting. Add extra $^1/_2$–1 tablespoon water if required. Fill with 1 cup (250 mL) whipped cream *or* $^1/_2$ cup (1 quantity) **Chocolate butter icing** (p. 383). Decorate with piped **Chocolate shapes** (p. 385).

✦ GINGER SPONGE ROLL ✦

Follow recipe for **Egg sponge roll**. Add 2 teaspoons ground ginger and $^1/_2$ teaspoon mixed spice to flour before sifting. Fill with 1 cup (250 mL) whipped cream *or* $^1/_2$ cup (1 quantity) **Butter icing** (p. 383) to which 2 tablespoons (40 g) finely chopped glacé ginger has been added.

✦ BLACK FOREST ROLL ✦

Follow recipe for **Chocolate sponge roll**. Drain 425 g can pitted dark cherries, reserve juice. Whip 300 mL cream. Add cherries (reserve some for decoration) to cream (reserve some for decoration). Brush sponge roll with 2 tablespoons (40 mL) cherry juice, fill with cream and cherries, roll up and decorate top with piped cream, remaining cherries and **Chocolate leaves** (p. 385), piped **Chocolate shapes** (p. 385) *or* **Modelling chocolate** shapes (p. 386).

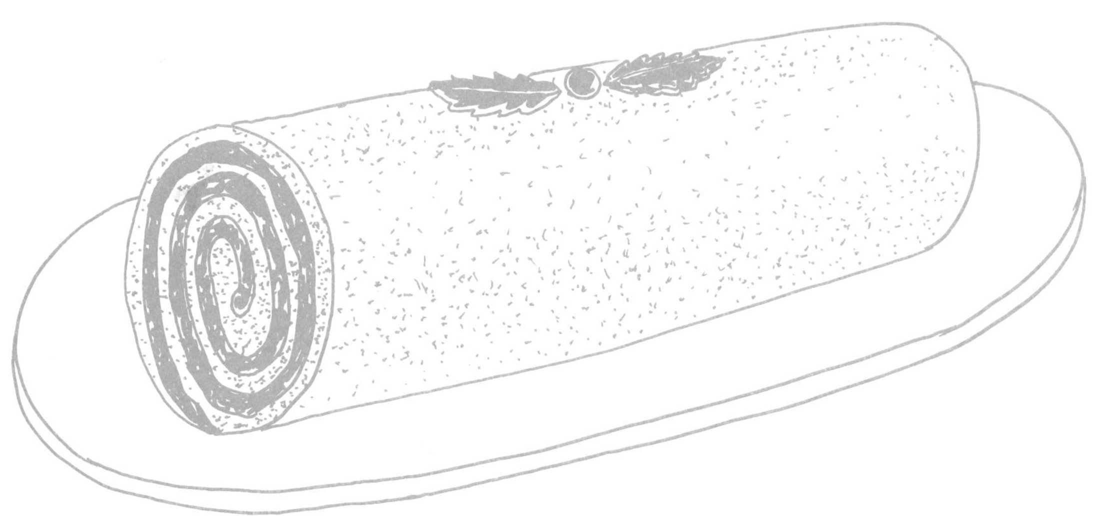

Sponges: tips for product quality

Quality criteria

- light, even, spongy texture
- flat, smooth top
- light brown, even surface.

Close and heavy texture:

- too much sugar or flour
- eggs and sugar not beaten sufficiently
- beating of flour instead of folding, thus releasing air
- too much flour added at one time, forcing out air
- oven too hot; mixture set before gas from raising agent has expanded
- oven too cool; not enough heat to expand gas from raising agent
- oven door opened too soon, too often or slammed
- cake moved before it had set.

Lumps in texture:

- insufficient mixing.

Sunk in centre:

- excess of sugar or liquid
- oven too hot causing gas to expand too quickly and to over stretch and weaken gluten, which then collapses
- cake moved before it had set, or taken from oven before cooked
- oven door opened too soon, too often or slammed.

Sticky top:

- oven temperature too low
- stored before cold.

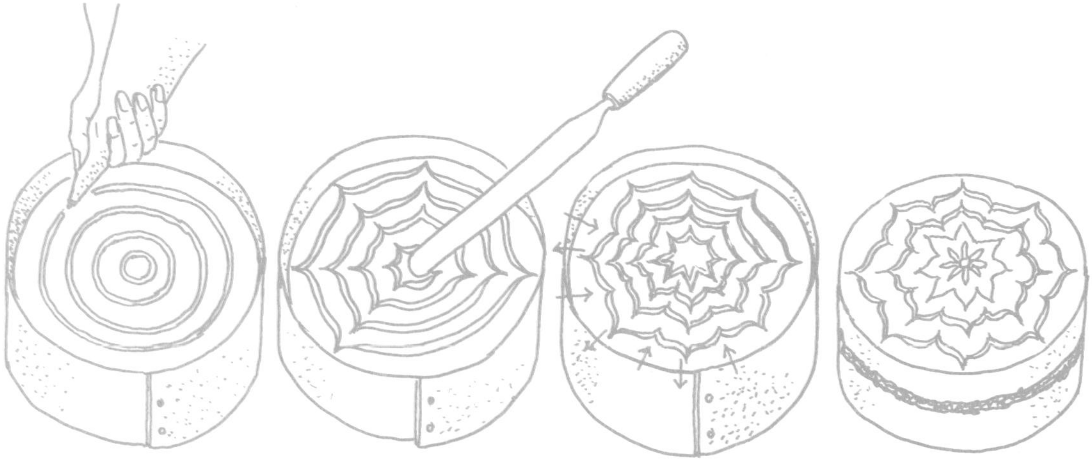

EGGLESS APPLE AND RAISIN CAKE 

A tasty, moist cake suitable for those wishing to reduce their intake of eggs.

- *Number:* ***12–14 slices***
- *Cooking utensil:* 22 cm round cake pan (2.25 L)
- *Preparation time:* ***20 minutes***
- *Cooking time:* ***1 hour***
- *Oven temperature:* ***180°C***

Ingredients

1/2 cup (125 g) butter, margarine *or* dairy blend
1/2 cup (90 g) brown sugar
1 teaspoon bicarbonate of soda
1 teaspoon hot water
1 1/2 cups (300 g) cooked apple
2 cups (300 g) wholemeal self-raising flour
1 cup (180 g) chopped raisins
1 teaspoon cinnamon
2 tablespoons (30 g) almond slivers

Method

1. Set oven at 180°C. Brush or spray cake pan with oil and line with baking paper.
2. Cream butter and sugar until light and fluffy.
3. Mix bicarbonate of soda and water. Stir in all other ingredients except almonds and mix well.
4. Place in cake pan. Sprinkle almond slivers on top and bake at 180°C for 1 hour. To test if cooked: cake will shrink slightly from sides of pan and a fine skewer inserted in cake comes out clean and dry.
5. Cool on a cake cooler.

Will keep for up to 1 week in an airtight container. Suitable for freezing for up to 3 months.

EGGLESS APPLE, DATE AND WALNUT CAKE

Follow recipe for **Eggless apple and raisin cake**, replacing raisins with 1/2 cup (60 g) chopped walnuts and 1/2 cup (90 g) chopped dates.

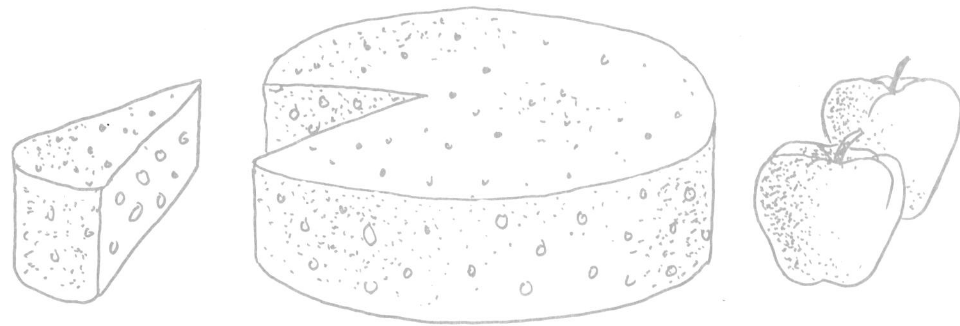

FRESH FRUIT CAKE

A moist almond cake with the flavour of fresh fruit.

- *Number:* **10 slices**
- *Cooking utensil:* medium loaf cake pan (1 L)
- *Preparation time:* **20 minutes**
- *Cooking time:* **25 minutes**
- *Oven temperature:* **180°C**

Ingredients

$^{1}/_{4}$ cup (45 g) brown sugar
2 eggs (61 g)
2 tablespoons (20 g) plain flour
$^{3}/_{4}$ cup (75 g) ground almonds
1 cup (250 g) diced pineapple, apricots *or* peaches

Method

1. Set oven at 180°C. Brush or spray cake pan with oil and line base with baking paper.
2. Beat sugar and eggs until mixture is thick.
3. Fold in flour and ground almonds.
4. Mix 2 tablespoons mixture with fruit.
5. Place remaining mixture into cake pan, cover with fruit.
6. Bake at 180°C for 25 minutes. To test if cooked: cake will shrink slightly from sides of pan and a fine skewer inserted in cake comes out clean and dry.
7. When cooked, allow cake to cool in cake pan for a few minutes then carefully turn onto a cake cooler.
8. Gently turn right side up onto a serving dish.

Will keep for up to 1 week in an airtight container. Suitable for freezing for up to 3 months.

GLACÉ FRUIT CAKE

A rich, colourful cake that could be wrapped in clear cellophane for an attractive gift.

- *Number:* ***20–25 thin slices***
- *Cooking utensil:* large loaf cake pan (1.5 L)

Ingredients

$^1/_2$ cup (75 g) plain flour
$^1/_4$ teaspoon baking powder
2 tablespoons (40 g) butter, margarine *or* dairy blend
$^1/_4$ cup (45 g) brown sugar
1 egg (61 g), beaten
1 tablespoon (20 mL) fruit juice *or* brandy
$^1/_2$ cup (90 g) chopped glacé pineapple
$^1/_2$ cup (90 g) chopped glacé apricots
$^1/_2$ cup (90 g) chopped red and green glacé cherries
$^1/_2$ cup (60 g) chopped almonds *or* macadamia nuts
$^1/_2$ cup (60 g) chopped brazil nuts
$^1/_2$ cup (90 g) mixed dried fruit

- *Preparation time:* ***30 minutes***
- *Cooking time:* ***1–1$^1/_2$ hours***
- *Oven temperature:* ***150°C***

Method

1. Set oven at 150°C. Brush or spray cake pan with oil and line base and sides with baking paper.
2. Sift flour and baking powder.
3. Cream butter and sugar until light and fluffy.
4. Add eggs gradually, mix well.
5. Stir in flour and fruit juice *or* brandy.
6. Add fruit and nuts, retaining a few for top of cake.
7. Place mixture into cake pan, putting remaining fruit and nuts on top.
8. Bake at 150°C for 1–1$^1/_2$ hours. To test if cooked: cake will shrink slightly from sides of pan and a fine skewer inserted in cake comes out clean and dry.
9. Allow to cool slightly in cake pan before turning onto cake cooler.
10. Slice very thinly to serve.

Will keep for up to 3 months in an airtight container. Not suitable for freezing.

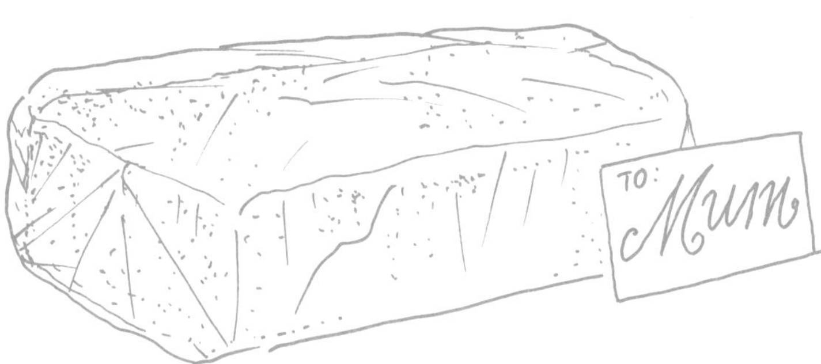

HONEY SPONGE ROLL 

Check the tips for product quality of sponges on p. 398.

- *Number:* ***10–12 slices***
- *Cooking utensil:* Swiss roll cake pan (24 cm x 30 cm – 1 L)
- *Preparation time:* ***25 minutes***
- *Cooking time:* ***14–18 minutes***
- *Oven temperature:* ***190°C***

Ingredients

1 tablespoon (20 g) caster sugar
1 cup (150 g) self-raising flour
1 teaspoon cinnamon
4 eggs (61 g)
1/4 cup (65 g) caster sugar
1 tablespoon (20 mL) honey
1/2 teaspoon bicarbonate of soda
2 teaspoons (10 mL) hot water

Filling

1/4 cup (65 g) butter, margarine *or* dairy blend
3/4 cup (135 g) icing sugar mixture
2 teaspoons (10 g) honey

Method

1. Set oven at 190°C. Brush or spray Swiss roll cake pan with oil and line base with baking paper. Spread out clean tea towel sprinkled with 1 tablespoon caster sugar.
2. Sift flour and cinnamon.
3. Separate egg whites from yolks, placing whites in mixing bowl.
4. Beat egg whites until stiff using an electric or rotary beater or whisk.
5. Gradually add sugar while continuing to beat, until very stiff.
6. Add egg yolks and honey and continue beating until mixture forms a figure '8' and resembles thick cream.
7. Add bicarbonate of soda dissolved in hot water. Using a tablespoon lightly fold in flour.
8. Pour into Swiss roll cake pan and bake at 190°C for 14–18 minutes. To test if cooked: press lightly with the finger in the centre of the cake. The impression should disappear at once.
9. Turn sponge onto prepared tea towel. Remove paper, quickly trim side edges to remove crust and immediately roll up tea towel and cake together. Allow to cool.
10. Prepare filling: cream butter and sugar, add honey and beat until thoroughly blended.
11. Unroll, spread sponge with honey filling and re-roll.

Will keep for 1–2 days in an airtight container. Suitable for freezing for up to 3 months.

MACADAMIA CAKE

- *Number:* ***8–10 slices***
- *Cooking utensil:* 20 cm round cake pan (1.5 L)
- *Preparation time:* ***25 minutes***
- *Cooking time:* ***40–45 minutes***
- *Oven temperature:* ***180°C***

Ingredients

1/2 cup (125 g) butter, margarine *or* dairy blend
1/2 cup (125 g) caster sugar
1 teaspoon cinnamon
2 eggs (61 g), beaten
1 1/2 cups (225 g) self-raising flour
1 1/2 teaspoons bicarbonate of soda
1/2 cup (125 mL) natural yoghurt
1/2 cup (65g) chopped macadamia nuts

Method

1. Set oven at 180°C. Brush or spray cake pan with oil and line base with baking paper.
2. Cream butter, sugar and cinnamon until light and fluffy.
3. Gradually add eggs and mix well.
4. Sift flour and bicarbonate of soda.
5. Add flour and yoghurt alternately, about 1/3 at a time.
6. Stir in macadamia nuts.
7. Place in cake pan and bake at 180°C for approximately 40–45 minutes. To test if cooked: cake will shrink slightly from sides of pan and a fine skewer inserted in cake comes out clean and dry.
8. Cool in cake pan then turn onto a cake cooler.

Will keep for up to 1 week in an airtight container. Suitable for freezing for up to 3 months.

MERINGUES

May be used as 'mushrooms' to decorate cakes.

- *Number:* ***24–30 single***
- *Cooking utensil:* oven tray
- *Preparation time:* ***10 minutes***
- *Cooking time:* ***1–1½ hours***
- *Oven temperature:* ***110°C, reduce during cooking***

Ingredients

2 egg whites (61 g)
¼ teaspoon salt
½ cup (125 g) caster sugar
½ teaspoon vanilla essence

Method

1. Set oven at 110°C. Lightly brush or spray oven tray with oil or cover base with baking paper.
2. Add salt to egg whites and beat until stiff.
3. Add sugar gradually and continue to beat until very thick.
4. Stir in vanilla essence.
5. Pipe into shapes on oven tray.
6. Bake at 110°C for 1–1½ hours reducing temperature during cooking. Meringues should not colour.
7. Cool on cake cooler. May be sandwiched into pairs with whipped cream.

Will keep for up to 2 weeks in an airtight container (without cream). Not suitable for freezing.

MACAROONS

- *Number:* ***24***
- *Cooking utensil:* oven tray
- *Preparation time:* ***20 minutes***
- *Cooking time:* ***15 minutes***
- *Oven temperature:* ***160°C***

Ingredients

2 egg whites (61 g)
¾ cup (135 g) icing sugar mixture
1½ cups (135 g) coconut
1 teaspoon vanilla essence

Method

1. Set oven at 160°C. Cover base of oven tray with baking paper.
2. Beat egg whites until stiff.
3. Add sugar gradually and continue beating until thick.
4. Stir in coconut and vanilla.
5. Pile in teaspoonfuls onto oven tray and bake at 160°C for 15 minutes until slightly coloured.
6. Cool on cake cooler.

Will keep for up to 2 weeks in an airtight container. Not suitable for freezing.

NECTARINE CAKE

- *Number:* ***14–16 slices***
- *Cooking utensil:* 22 cm deep springform cake pan (2.5 L)
- *Preparation time:* ***35 minutes***
- *Cooking time:* ***60–70 minutes***
- *Oven temperature:* ***180°C***

Ingredients

500 g nectarines
1 tablespoon (20 g) sugar
1½ cups (225 g) self-raising flour
1 teaspoon baking powder
¾ cup (185 g) butter, margarine *or* dairy blend
¾ cup (190 g) caster sugar
2 eggs (61 g), beaten
grated rind and juice of 1 orange
½ cup (125 mL) milk

Method

1. Set oven at 180°C. Brush or spray cake pan with oil and line base with baking paper.
2. Cut each nectarine in half, remove stone and cut each half into eight slices. Place in a bowl and sprinkle with 1 tablespoon sugar.
3. Sift flour and baking powder.
4. Cream butter and sugar until light and fluffy.
5. Gradually add eggs, then orange rind and juice.
6. Add flour and milk alternately, ⅓ at a time. Stir gently and thoroughly.
7. Spoon mixture into cake pan.
8. Place nectarines evenly over top of the mixture.
9. Bake at 180°C for 60–70 minutes. To test if cooked: cake will shrink slightly from sides of pan and a fine skewer inserted in cake comes out clean and dry. Nectarines sink during cooking.
10. When cooked, stand for 10–15 minutes before removing from the cake pan onto a cake cooler.

Will keep for up to 1 week in an airtight container. Suitable for freezing for up to 3 months.

✦ PLUM CAKE ✦

Follow recipe for **Nectarine cake**, using plums instead of nectarines.

ONE-BOWL ORANGE CAKE

- *Number:* ***10 slices***
- *Cooking utensil:* 20 cm round cake pan (1.5 L) *or* 22 cm non-stick ring cake pan (1.75 L)
- *Preparation time:* ***10 minutes***
- *Cooking time:* ***30–35 minutes***
- *Oven temperature:* ***180°C***

Ingredients

2 eggs (61 g)
1/2 cup (125 g) soft butter
3/4 cup (190 g) caster sugar
1 1/2 cups (225 g) self-raising flour
1/4 cup (65 mL) milk
grated rind and juice of 1 orange

Method

1. Set oven at 180°C. Brush or spray cake pan with oil and line base with baking paper.
2. Place all ingredients in bowl and beat for 3 minutes using an electric beater or wooden spoon.
3. Pour into pan and bake at 180°C for 30–35 minutes. To test if cooked: cake will shrink slightly from sides of pan and a fine skewer inserted in cake comes out clean and dry.
4. Cool on a cake cooler. May be iced with 1/2 cup (1 quantity) **Orange glacé icing** (p. 395).

Will keep for up to 1 week in an airtight container. Suitable for freezing for up to 3 months.

NUT AND DATE LOAF

- *Number:* ***14 slices***
- *Cooking utensil:* large loaf cake pan (1.5 L)
- *Preparation time:* ***30 minutes***
- *Cooking time:* ***45 minutes***
- *Oven temperature:* ***180°C***

Ingredients

1 cup (250 mL) water
3 tablespoons (60 g) butter, margarine *or* dairy blend
1 1/2 cups (225 g) wholemeal self-raising flour
1/2 cup (125 g) honey
1 teaspoon cinnamon
1/2 cup (60 g) chopped walnuts, pecans *or* hazelnuts
1/2 cup (90 g) chopped dates
2 apples (300 g), peeled and grated

Method

1. Set oven at 180°C. Brush or spray cake pan with oil and line base with baking paper.
2. Place water and butter in a saucepan and bring to the boil.
3. Remove from heat, stir in all other ingredients. Mix well.
4. Place mixture in loaf cake pan and bake at 180°C for 45 minutes. To test if cooked: cake will shrink slightly from sides of pan and a fine skewer inserted in cake comes out clean and dry.
5. Cool in cake pan and then turn onto a cake cooler.

Will keep for up to 1 week in an airtight container. Suitable for freezing for up to 3 months.

NUT LOAF

- *Number:* ***10 slices***
- *Cooking utensil:* 1 nut loaf pan (1 L) *or* medium loaf cake pan (1 L)
- *Preparation time:* ***25 minutes***
- *Cooking time:* ***50–60 minutes***
- *Oven temperature:* ***180°C***

Ingredients

$1^1/_2$ cups (225 g) self-raising flour
$^1/_2$ teaspoon mixed spice
1 tablespoon (20 g) butter, margarine *or* dairy blend
$^1/_2$ cup (125 g) caster sugar
$^3/_4$ cup (90 g) chopped walnuts
1 egg (61 g), beaten
$^1/_2$ cup (125 mL) milk

Method

1. Set oven at 180°C. Brush or spray cake pan (and lid if nut loaf pan) with oil.
2. Sift flour and mixed spice.
3. Rub butter into flour, add sugar and nuts.
4. Mix into a soft dough with egg and milk.
5. Place mixture in cake pan. If using nut loaf pan fill to $^2/_3$, place lid on and stand upright on an oven tray.
6. Bake at 180°C for 50–60 minutes. To test if cooked: cake will shrink slightly from sides of pan and a fine skewer inserted in cake comes out clean and dry.
7. Cool on a cake cooler. Slice and serve with butter, margarine or dairy blend.

Will keep for 3–4 days in an airtight container. Suitable for freezing for up to 3 months.

NUT AND FRUIT LOAF

Follow recipe for **Nut loaf**. Replace $^1/_4$ cup walnuts with $^1/_4$ cup (45 g) sultanas.

MARMALADE POLENTA CAKE 

- *Number:* ***10–12 slices***
- *Cooking utensil:* 20 cm springform cake pan (1.75 L)
- *Preparation time:* ***25 minutes***
- *Cooking time:* ***60–70 minutes***
- *Oven temperature:* ***180°C***

Ingredients

1 cup (150 g) self-raising flour
2/3 cup (100 g) polenta
1/2 cup (50 g) ground almonds
1/2 cup (125 g) butter
1/2 cup (125 g) caster sugar
1/2 cup (150 g) marmalade
2 eggs (61 g)
1/2 cup (125 mL) milk
1 orange, thinly sliced

Will keep for up to 1 week in an airtight container. Suitable for freezing for up to 3 months.

Method

1. Set oven at 180°C. Brush or spray cake pan with oil and line base with baking paper.
2. Mix flour, polenta and almonds.
3. Cream butter and sugar until light and fluffy.
4. Gradually add eggs, beating well. Add marmalade.
5. Add flour and milk alternately, about 1/3 at a time.
6. Place mixture into cake pan. Arrange orange slices over top of mixture and bake at 180°C for 60–70 minutes. To test if cooked: cake will shrink slightly from sides of pan and a fine skewer inserted in cake comes out clean and dry.
7. Cool in cake pan for 10 minutes before turning onto a cake cooler.

PATTY CAKES

- *Number:* ***12***
- *Cooking utensil:* patty pan tray *or* paper patty pans on oven tray
- *Preparation time:* ***20 minutes***
- *Cooking time:* ***12–15 minutes***
- *Oven temperature:* ***200°C***

Ingredients

1/4 cup (65 g) butter, margarine *or* dairy blend
1/4 cup (65 g) caster sugar
1 egg (61 g), beaten
1/2 teaspoon vanilla essence
3/4 cup (110 g) self-raising flour
3 tablespoons (60 mL) milk

Will keep for up to 1 week in an airtight container. Suitable for freezing for up to 3 months (without icing).

Method

1. Set oven at 200°C. Brush or spray patty pan tray with oil.
2. Cream butter and sugar until light and fluffy.
3. Add egg and vanilla essence, mix well.
4. Add flour and milk alternately, about 1/3 at a time. Stir gently and thoroughly.
5. Place mixture into pans, half-filling each one. Bake at 200°C for 12–15 minutes until golden brown and shrinking slightly from sides of pans.
6. Cool in patty pans for 2 minutes then lift onto cake cooler.
7. May be iced with 1/2 cup (1 quantity) **Glacé icing** (p. 395) *or* **Melted butter icing** (p. 384).

✦ APPLE CAKES ✦

Follow recipe for **Patty cakes**. Place 1 teaspoon cake mixture in each patty pan, add 1 teaspoon **Apple puree** (p. 308) and cover with 1 teaspoon cake mixture.

✦ CHERRY AND NUT CAKES ✦

Follow recipe for **Patty cakes**. Add 2 tablespoons (30 g) chopped glacé cherries and 1 tablespoon chopped almonds *or* walnuts to mixture at step 4. Decorate before cooking with a piece of cherry *or* nut, *or* ice after cooking with 1/2 cup (1 quantity) pink **Glacé icing** (p. 395) *or* **Melted butter icing** (p. 384) and decorate with a piece of cherry.

✦ CHOCOLATE CAKES ✦

Follow recipe for **Patty cakes**. Add 2 teaspoons (30 g) cocoa sifted with flour. Ice with 1/2 cup (1 quantity) **Chocolate butter icing** (p. 383) *or* **Melted butter icing** (p. 384). Decorate with nuts.

✦ DATE AND WALNUT CAKES ✦

Follow recipe for **Patty cakes**. Add 2 tablespoons chopped dates and 1 tablespoon chopped walnuts at step 4. Place piece of walnut on mixture in each patty pan before cooking.

✦ CITRUS CAKES ✦

Follow recipe for **Patty cakes**. Add grated rind of 1 orange *or* 1/2 lemon at step 4. Ice with 1/2 cup (1 quantity) **Orange butter icing** *or* **Lemon butter icing** (p. 383) *or* **Glacé icing** (p. 395).

✦ FACE CAKES ✦

Make 12 **Patty cakes**, cooked at 180°C to ensure a flat top. When cool, ice tops of cakes with 1/2 cup (1 quantity) skin-coloured (e.g. beige, brown, pink) **Melted butter icing** (p. 384). Make faces using chocolate sprinkles or coconut for hair and other sweets for nose, mouth and eyes.

✦ LEMON BUTTERFLIES ✦

Use 12 **Patty cakes**, 1 cup (250 mL) whipped cream, 4 tablespoons (80 mL) lemon butter, 2 tablespoons (30 g) icing sugar. Using a small sharp knife remove a circle from top of each cake. Place 1/2 teaspoon lemon butter and 1 teaspoon cream in each hollow. Cut removed circle in two and place on cream to resemble wings. Dust with icing sugar mixture.

QUICK FRUIT LOAF

- *Number:* ***14 slices***
- *Cooking utensil:* large loaf cake pan (1.5 L)
- *Preparation time:* ***overnight and 10 minutes***
- *Cooking time:* ***40 minutes***
- *Oven temperature:* ***180°C***

Ingredients

250 g dried fruit, e.g. apricots, apple, figs, prunes
2 cups (500 mL) water
1 large ripe banana, mashed
$1\frac{1}{2}$ cups (225 g) wholemeal self-raising flour
grated rind and juice of 1 orange

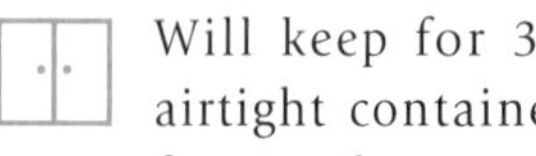

Will keep for 3–4 days in an airtight container. Suitable for freezing for up to 3 months.

Method

1 Roughly chop dried fruit into large pieces. Soak in water in covered dish overnight.
2 Set oven at 180°C. Brush or spray cake pan with oil and line base with baking paper.
3 Mix soaked fruit and liquid, banana, flour, orange juice and rind.
4 Place mixture into cake pan and bake at 180°C for 40 minutes. To test if cooked: cake will shrink slightly from sides of pan and a fine skewer inserted in cake comes out clean and dry.
5 Cool in cake pan, then turn onto a cake cooler.

QUICK-WHIP GINGER CAKE

- *Number:* ***8–10 slices***
- *Cooking utensil:* 20 cm round cake pan (1.5 L)
- *Preparation time:* ***20 minutes***
- *Cooking time:* ***20–25 minutes***
- *Oven temperature:* ***180°C***

Ingredients

$1\frac{1}{2}$ cups (225 g) self-raising flour
1 teaspoon cinnamon
1 teaspoon ground ginger
3 tablespoons (60 g) soft butter, margarine *or* dairy blend
$\frac{1}{2}$ cup (125 g) sugar
$\frac{1}{2}$ cup (125 g) golden syrup
$\frac{1}{2}$ cup (125 mL) milk
1 egg (61 g)
$\frac{1}{2}$ teaspoon bicarbonate of soda
$\frac{1}{4}$ cup (65 mL) boiling water

Will keep for up to 1 week in an airtight container. Suitable for freezing for up to 3 months (without icing).

Method

1 Set oven at 180°C. Brush or spray cake pan with oil and line base with baking paper.
2 Sift flour, cinnamon and ginger into a large bowl.
3 Add butter, sugar, golden syrup, egg and milk.
4 Beat with an electric beater for 3 minutes. Remove beaters.
5 Dissolve bicarbonate of soda in boiling water and pour into mixture. Mix with spoon.
6 Place mixture into cake pan and bake at 180°C for 20–25 minutes. To test if cooked: cake will shrink slightly from sides of pan and a fine skewer inserted in cake comes out clean and dry.
7 Cool on a cake cooler and ice with $\frac{1}{2}$ cup (1 quantity) **Glacé icing** (p. 395) and decorate with glacé ginger.

ROCK CAKES

- *Number:* ***24***
- *Cooking utensil:* oven tray
- *Preparation time:* ***15 minutes***
- *Cooking time:* ***10–15 minutes***
- *Oven temperature:* ***200°C***

Ingredients

2 cups (300 g) self-raising flour
$\frac{1}{4}$ teaspoon mixed spice
$\frac{1}{3}$ cup (85 g) butter, margarine *or* dairy blend
$\frac{1}{3}$ cup (85 g) caster sugar
2 tablespoons (30 g) sultanas
2 tablespoons (30 g) currants
1 tablespoon (15 g) mixed peel
1 egg (61 g), beaten
$\frac{1}{2}$ cup (125 mL) milk

Method

1. Set oven at 200°C. Brush or spray oven tray with oil or cover with baking paper.
2. Sift flour and mixed spice.
3. Rub butter into flour with fingertips.
4. Add sugar, fruit and mixed peel.
5. Mix with egg and sufficient milk to form a stiff dough.
6. Place spoonfuls of mixture on oven tray.
7. Bake at 200°C until golden brown, 10–15 minutes.
8. Cool on a cake cooler.

Will keep for 3–4 days in an airtight container. Suitable for freezing for up to 3 months.

MICROWAVE ZUCCHINI CAKE

- *Number:* ***12 slices***
- *Cooking utensil:* 22 cm microwave ring cake pan (1.75 L)
- *Preparation time:* ***20 minutes***
- *Cooking time:* ***6 minutes***
- *Standing time:* ***3 minutes***

Ingredients

1$\frac{1}{4}$ cups (190 g) plain flour
1 teaspoon baking powder
2 teaspoons cinnamon
2 teaspoons mixed spice
2 eggs (61 g)
$\frac{3}{4}$ cup (190 g) caster sugar
$\frac{3}{4}$ cup (185 mL) oil
3 zucchini (300 g), grated

Should be eaten within 24 hours.

Method

1. Sift together flour, baking powder and spices. Brush or spray cake pan with oil.
2. Beat eggs, sugar and oil.
3. Stir in flour and zucchini.
4. Pour into microwave cake pan.
5. Microwave for 6 minutes on high power.
6. Allow to stand 3 minutes.
7. Turn onto a cake cooler.
8. When cool ice with $\frac{1}{2}$ cup (1 quantity) **Cream cheese icing** (p. 384).

MICROWAVE CARROT CAKE

Follow recipe for **Microwave zucchini cake**. Replace zucchini with 2 cups (300 g) grated carrot and $\frac{1}{2}$ cup (90 g) sultanas.

TEACAKE

- *Number:* ***8–10 slices***
- *Cooking utensil:* 20 cm round cake pan (1.5 L)
- *Preparation time:* ***25 minutes***
- *Cooking time:* ***30–35 minutes***
- *Oven temperature:* ***190°C***

Ingredients

1/4 cup (65 g) butter, margarine *or* dairy blend
1/2 cup (125 g) caster sugar
1 egg (61 g), beaten
1/3 cup (85 mL) milk
1 1/3 cups (200 g) self-raising flour

Method

1. Set oven at 190°C. Brush or spray cake pan with oil and line base with baking paper.
2. Cream butter and sugar until light and fluffy.
3. Mix in egg.
4. Add flour and milk alternately, one-third at a time, mixing lightly.
5. Place in cake pan and bake at 190°C for 30–35 minutes. To test if cooked: cake will shrink slightly from sides of pan and a fine skewer inserted in cake comes out clean and dry.
6. Cool on a cake cooler. Serve with butter.

Will keep for 2–3 days in an airtight container. Suitable for freezing for up to 3 months.

✦ CINNAMON TEACAKE ✦

Follow recipe for **Teacake**. Before baking, sprinkle with a mixture of 2 teaspoons caster sugar and 1 teaspoon cinnamon.

✦ CINNAMON TOPPING TEACAKE ✦

Follow recipe for **Teacake**. After baking, while still hot, spread with 1 teaspoon melted butter and sprinkle with mixture of 1 teaspoon cinnamon and 2 teaspoons caster sugar.

✦ LITTLE TEACAKES ✦

Follow recipe for **Teacake** to end of step 3. Use patty pans trays brushed or sprayed with oil or paper patty pans on oven tray. Makes 15–18 cakes. Bake at 180°C for 15–20 minutes.

✦ SPICED APPLE TEACAKE ✦

Follow recipe for **Teacake**. Place mixture in cake pan and cover with thinly sliced apples. Sprinkle apples with cinnamon and caster sugar and bake.

RICH FRUIT CAKE

May be decorated for special occasions, such as weddings, parties and birthdays (see pp. 414–18).

- *Number:* ***30 slices***
- *Cooking utensil:* 22 cm round cake pan (2.25 L) *or* 20 cm square cake pan (2.5 L)
- *Preparation time:* ***overnight and 45 minutes***
- *Cooking time:* ***2 hours***
- *Oven temperature:* ***160°C reduced to 130°C for 1 hour***

Ingredients

1½ cups (270 g) sultanas
1½ cups (270 g) currants
1½ cups (270 g) chopped raisins
⅓ cup (60 g) chopped glacé cherries
⅓ cup (60 g) mixed peel
⅓ cup (60 g) chopped dates *or* prunes
¼ cup (65 mL) fruit juice *or* brandy
⅓ cup (40 g) halved blanched almonds
2 cups (300 g) plain flour
½ cup (75 g) self-raising flour
1 teaspoon cinnamon
1 teaspoon mixed spice
¼ teaspoon nutmeg
1 cup (250 g) butter
1 cup (180 g) brown sugar
5 eggs (61 g), beaten

Method

1. Add prepared fruit to fruit juice *or* brandy. Cover and leave overnight.
2. Brush or spray cake pan with oil. Cut lengths of newspaper to go around outside of cake pan twice, 3–4 cm higher than sides of cake pan. Tie or pin the paper on the cake pan. Stand cake pan on two layers of newspaper on oven tray.
3. Set oven at 160°C.
4. Sift flours, mixed spice and nutmeg.
5. Cream butter and sugar until light and fluffy.
6. Add eggs gradually. Mix well.
7. Add fruit, nuts, flour and liquid. Stir gently and thoroughly.
8. Place mixture in cake pan and hollow out centre slightly, to allow for rising.
9. Place just below centre of oven.
10. Bake at 160°C for 1 hour. Reduce oven temperature to not less than 130°C for a further 1 hour. To test if cooked: cake will shrink slightly from sides of pan and a fine skewer inserted in cake comes out clean and dry.
11. When baked, leave in cake pan until cold.

Will keep for up to 6 months in an airtight container. Not suitable for freezing.

Decorating rich fruit cakes

Cake decorating is a creative art and the fundamental processes are discussed only briefly in this book. It must be remembered that practice is required to fully develop these skills.
Rich fruit cakes may be decorated by:

- covering with a layer of **Almond paste**, then a layer of **Fondant icing** (p. 418), decorating with piped **Royal icing** (p. 416), **Almond paste** *or* **Fondant icing** (p. 418) shapes and placing decorated cake on presentation board.
- covering with a layer of **Almond paste**, then a layer of **Frosting** (p. 417), decorating with **Almond paste** *or* **Fondant icing** (p. 418) shapes and placing decorated cake on presentation board (p. 416).

ALMOND PASTE

This may be called marzipan and is also used for modelling fruits, vegetables and other shapes to decorate cakes.

Ingredients

$2^1/_2$ cups (450 g) icing sugar mixture
1 cup (100 g) ground almonds
2 egg yolks
$^1/_4$ teaspoon almond essence
2 tablespoons (40 mL) orange juice, strained

Method

1. Sift icing sugar into a basin, add almonds, mix well.
2. Beat egg yolks lightly, add almond essence and orange juice.
3. Stir liquid into dry ingredients and mix to a stiff dough.
4. Turn on to a board lightly dusted with icing sugar and knead lightly.

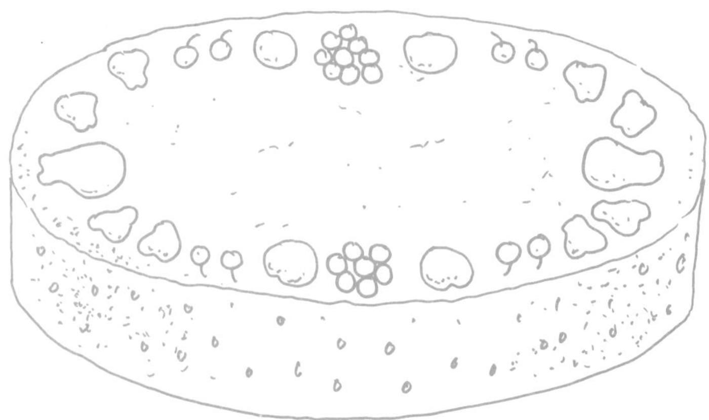

Covering a cake with Almond paste

Ingredients

1 **Rich fruit cake**
1 quantity **Almond paste** *or* 500 g almond paste *or* marzipan
2 tablespoons (40 g) jam, boiled and sieved
½ cup (90 g) icing sugar mixture, sifted

Method

1. Level top surface of cake with a sharp knife, remove loose crumbs or invert cake to ice bottom surface. Place on board or turntable.
2. Brush lightly with jam.
3. Fill cracks or build up uneven surface with **Almond paste**. Roll **Almond paste** on clean board dusted with icing sugar to the same shape as the top of the cake, and large enough to cover the top and almost all of the sides of the cake.
4. Using rolling pin, carefully lift **Almond paste** onto cake.
5. Lightly roll the top surface and sides.
6. Dust palms of hands with icing sugar and mould **Almond paste** over the corners and down to base of the sides.
7. If the cake is square, the corners may be carefully pleated out and cut away cleanly to leave a neat join.
8. Using a clean rolling pin dusted with icing sugar, lightly roll top edge and sides of cake to obtain a perfectly smooth surface.
9. Corners may be rounded or squared according to design.
10. If necessary, carefully trim away the surplus **Almond paste** at the bottom of the cake with a sharp knife.
11. Allow to dry for 1–2 days.

Cake presentation

Requirements

wooden board *or* thick cardboard, 8–10 cm larger in size than the cake
white paper *or* foil
gold *or* silver doily
1 teaspoon jam

Method

1 Cover board with white paper *or* foil.
2 Attach doily to paper *or* foil, using small amount of jam.
3 Place jam in the centre of the doily.
4 Place cake in position, press down firmly.
5 Decorate with piped decorations made from **Royal icing** or moulded decorations.

ROYAL ICING

Pure icing sugar must be used. Icing sugar mixture contains a small quantity of starch, which prevents the icing sugar forming hard lumps when stored. This starch prevents royal icing from holding its shape.

Test for pure icing sugar

Place 1 teaspoon icing sugar in a glass containing 3–4 tablespoons cold water and mix with a spoon. Allow to stand 1–2 minutes. If starch is present it will settle to the bottom of the glass.

Ingredients

2 cups (360 g) pure icing sugar
1/2 teaspoon lemon juice, strained
1 egg white

Method

1 Sift icing sugar.
2 Place egg white in a basin, beat until stiff.
3 Add icing sugar slowly, beating well.
4 Add lemon juice and beat icing until it holds in stiff peaks.
5 Keep basin covered with damp cloth to prevent drying out.

May be kept in an air-tight container in the refrigerator for several days. Beat well before use.

Colouring Royal icing

Use either powder or liquid food colouring. Follow instructions on packet. Add colouring a drop at a time until desired shade is obtained. A wide range of shades can be obtained by blending colours.

Making a paper icing bag

If icing tube is to be used, cut approximately 1–2 cm off the pointed end of the bag and insert the tube. Half fill the bag with **Royal icing**. Fold the front lower edge of the bag flat across the top of the icing. Fold each side across. Fold the remaining pointed edge over twice, giving the flat surface on which the thumb rests while piping.

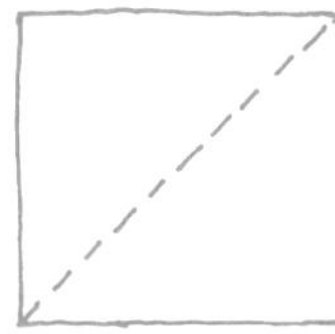

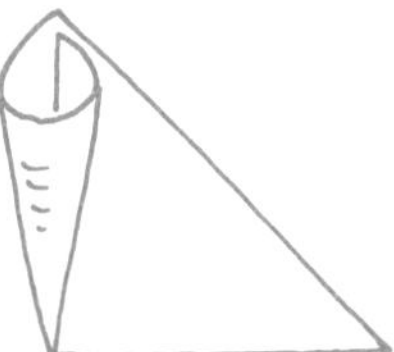

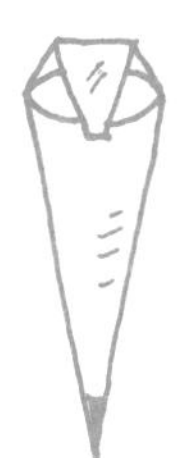

FROSTING

Ingredients

2 egg whites
1 cup (250 g) sugar
4 tablespoons (80 mL) water

Method

1. Place all ingredients in top of double saucepan.
2. Place over boiling water and beat constantly for 12–15 minutes until mixture thickens and will hold its shape.
3. Spread quickly over cake, using spatula to achieve a swirling effect.

FONDANT ICING

This may be used to cover cakes and to shape into flowers, fruits and figures for decorating cakes.

Ingredients

$2\frac{1}{2}$ cups (450 g) icing sugar mixture
2 tablespoons (40 g) liquid glucose
1 egg white
flavouring *or* essence
colouring

Method

1 Sift icing sugar into basin, make a well in the centre.
2 Soften liquid glucose over hot water.
3 Place glucose, egg white and flavouring in the well of icing sugar.
4 Beat the mixture with a wooden spoon drawing the icing sugar into centre until ingredients form a stiff paste.
5 Turn onto a board lightly dusted with sifted icing sugar, knead well.
6 If colouring is to be added, work it in one or two drops at a time while kneading.

Covering a cake with Fondant icing

Ingredients

1 **Rich fruit cake**
1 quantity **Fondant icing** *or* 500–750g commercial soft icing
$\frac{1}{2}$ cup (90 g) icing sugar mixture, sifted

Method

1 Dust pastry board lightly with icing sugar. Roll icing to the same shape as top of cake and large enough to cover the top and almost all of the sides.
2 Brush cake surface with water.
3 Using a rolling pin, carefully lift icing onto cake.
4 Lightly roll the top surface.
5 Dust palms of hands with icing sugar and mould paste over the corners and down the sides of the cake.
6 Lightly roll top and sides of cake with clean rolling pin to obtain a smooth surface.
7 Edges and corners may be rounded or squared according to design of cake.
8 If necessary use a sharp knife to trim away surplus icing from the base of the cake.
9 Allow to dry for 2–3 days.

Cakes: tips for product quality

Quality criteria

- golden brown surface
- smooth, slightly rounded top
- even, light, moist texture
- fruit and other ingredients evenly distributed.

Close and heavy texture:
- too large a proportion of flour
- fat was over-heated during mixing
- excess of liquid
- fat and sugar over-creamed
- over-mixing while adding flour and liquid
- oven temperature too low or cake insufficiently cooked.

Coarse and open texture:
- fat and sugar insufficiently creamed
- insufficient mixing when combining flour with moist ingredients
- oven temperature too high.

Uneven texture:
- insufficient blending of fat – small lumps melt leaving holes
- mixture scraped from sides of basin and left in centre of cake
- over mixing while adding flour and liquid
- air trapped by placing small spoonfuls of mixture in cake pan.

Dry:
- too small a quantity of eggs or liquid
- cooked too long or at too low a temperature.

Risen unevenly or in centre:
- oven had not reached required temperature or initial oven temperature too high.

Cracked surface:
- initial oven temperature too high
- if oven temperature is not sufficiently reduced, mixture may ooze through crack.

Sunk in centre:
- excess sugar or liquid
- oven temperature too low or oven door open too soon, too often or slammed
- cake moved before it has set, or taken from oven before cooked.

Fruit unevenly distributed:
- uneven mixing of fruit into mixture or mixture too thin to support fruit
- oven temperature too low.

Sugary crust:
- cake cooked too long at too low a temperature
- type of sugar too coarse for mixture.

16 Biscuits and slices

The aroma of freshly baked biscuits is long remembered and there is a feeling of satisfaction in being able to serve homemade biscuits made with spices, fruits, nuts and other flavours. The basic biscuit mixture can be made with many variations and will keep well for several weeks. Slices tend to be more moist, with ingredients that make them suitable for the lunch box. Uncooked biscuits are quickly made and often served on festive occasions. Homemade biscuits are an ideal gift with a personal touch. The notes about choice of ingredients and methods given at the beginning of **Chapter 15 Cakes and cake presentation** apply also to the biscuits and slices in this chapter.

When cooling, biscuits remain crisper if they are not stacked one on another until they are completely cold. Biscuits without filling which have softened may be crisped by placing them on an oven tray and warmed at 100°C for 3–5 minutes and then cooled on a cake cooler. Store each type of biscuit in a separate airtight container so that the flavours do not mix.

Biscuits can be stored unfilled, then iced and filled as required.

ALMOND BREAD

Gift idea: place in cellophane bag and tie with a bright ribbon.

- *Number:* ***36 slices***
- *Cooking utensil:* medium loaf pan (1 L)
- *Preparation time:* ***20 minutes and 1–3 days storage time***
- *Cooking time:* ***50–60 minutes***
- *Oven temperature:* ***180°C***

Ingredients

4 egg whites (61 g)
$^1/_2$ cup (125 g) caster sugar
1 cup (150 g) plain flour
1 cup (125 g) whole almonds with skins on

Method

1. Set oven at 180°C. Line loaf pan with baking paper.
2. Beat egg whites until stiff. Gradually add sugar and continue beating until mixture is stiff.
3. Fold in flour and almonds.
4. Place in pan and bake at 180°C for 50–60 minutes.
5. Cool on cake cooler.
6. Wrap in foil and store for 1–3 days.
7. Slice very thinly, place slices on oven tray and dry in oven at 130°C for about 10 minutes, until crisp and dry.

HAZELNUT BREAD

Follow recipe for **Almond bread**.
Use 1 cup (100 g) whole hazelnuts with skins on instead of almonds.

PISTACHIO NUT BREAD

Follow recipe for **Almond bread**.
Use 1 cup (100 g) whole pistachio nuts instead of almonds.

BISCUITS

Many variations can be made from this basic biscuit mixture.
Some examples follow the recipe.

- *Number:* **48**
- *Cooking utensil:* oven trays
- *Preparation time:* **20 minutes**
- *Cooking time:* **10–15 minutes**
- *Oven temperature:* **160°C**

Ingredients

1 cup (150 g) plain flour
1 cup (150 g) self-raising flour
1/2 cup (125 g) butter, margarine *or* dairy blend
1/2 cup (125 g) caster sugar
1 egg (61 g), beaten
1/2 teaspoon vanilla essence
2 tablespoons (40 mL) milk

Method

1. Set oven at 160°C. Brush or spray oven trays with oil or cover base with baking paper.
2. Sift flours.
3. Cream butter and sugar. Add egg and vanilla essence, mix well.
4. Add flour and mix into a firm dough.
5. Lift onto lightly floured surface, knead until smooth.
6. Roll to 5 mm thickness.
7. Cut into 48 shapes and place on tray. Glaze with milk.
8. Bake at 160°C for 10–15 minutes, until pale biscuit colour.
9. Cool on cake cooler. Leave plain, ice or fill with **Butter icing** (p. 383).

ALMOND BISCUITS

Follow recipe for **Biscuits**. Add 3 drops of almond essence with egg. Before baking, glaze and place 1/2 a blanched almond on each biscuit.

CHOCOLATE BISCUITS

Follow recipe for **Biscuits.** Replace 3 tablespoons (30 g) flour with 3 tablespoons (30 g) cocoa. Roll out and cut with biscuit cutter, or shape into balls and flatten with a fork. After baking may be iced or joined with **Butter icing** (p. 383).

CHOCOLATE-DIPPED BISCUITS

Follow recipe for **Biscuits**. Use a star or heart-shaped cutter at step 7. After baking and cooling, melt 200 g white, milk *or* dark chocolate over hot water or in a microwave oven (see p. 385). Dip half of each biscuit into chocolate and place on baking paper to set. The chocolate may also be placed in a piping bag and lines piped on each biscuit.

✦ COFFEE BISCUITS ✦

Follow recipe for **Biscuits.** Add 1 teaspoon instant coffee powder to butter and sugar. After baking join with **Coffee butter icing** (p. 383).

✦ DATE BISCUITS ✦

Follow recipe for **Biscuits** to step 6. Cut rolled dough into strips approximately 3 cm x 8 cm. Using 1 1/3 cups (240 g) whole pitted dates, roll each date in a strip of dough. Glaze and bake.

✦ FINGER BISCUITS ✦

Follow recipe for **Biscuits** to step 6. Cut rolled dough into fingers approximately 2 cm x 7 cm and bake at 160°C for 15–20 minutes, until pale fawn in colour. Beat 1 egg white until stiff and mix in 1 cup (180 g) icing sugar mixture to make a smooth, thick paste. Spread some on each biscuit. Using 1/2 cup (60 g) chopped almonds *or* 1/2 cup (45 g) coconut, sprinkle some on each biscuit and return to oven at 160°C for approximately 3 minutes, until topping is lightly browned.

✦ LEMON BISCUITS ✦

Follow recipe for **Biscuits**. Add grated rind of 1 lemon with sugar. Glaze and decorate with mixed peel before baking, or join with **Lemon butter icing** (p. 383) after baking.

✦ PINWHEEL COOKIES ✦

Follow recipe for **Biscuits** to step 5. Divide mixture and work 1 tablespoon (10 g) cocoa into one half. Roll each piece of dough into an oblong approximately 24 cm x 12 cm. Place one piece on top of the other and roll into a firm roll. Cut in slices 5 mm thick. Place on tray and bake.

ANZACS

The name originated when these biscuits were sent to Australian soldiers during World War I.

- *Number:* **30**
- *Cooking utensil:* oven trays
- *Preparation time:* ***20 minutes***
- *Cooking time:* ***15–18 minutes***
- *Oven temperature:* ***160°C***

Ingredients

$^3/_4$ cup (75 g) rolled oats
$^1/_2$ cup (125 g) sugar
$^3/_4$ cup (70 g) desiccated coconut
$^3/_4$ cup (110 g) wholemeal plain flour
2 tablespoons (40 mL) golden syrup
1 teaspoon bicarbonate of soda
2 tablespoons (40 mL) boiling water
$^1/_2$ cup (125 g) butter, melted

Method

1. Set oven at 160°C. Brush or spray oven tray with oil or cover base with baking paper.
2. Mix oats, sugar, coconut and flour.
3. Mix golden syrup, soda and boiling water. While frothing, add melted butter then pour into dry ingredients. Mix thoroughly.
4. Drop spoonfuls of mixture onto tray allowing room for mixture to spread.
5. Bake at 160°C for 15–18 minutes.
6. Cool on cake cooler.

APRICOT MUESLI SLICE

A high-energy slice, good for the lunch box or a picnic.

- *Number:* **25**
- *Cooking utensil:* 20 cm square cake pan (2.5 L)
- *Preparation time:* ***20 minutes***
- *Cooking time:* ***20 minutes***
- *Oven temperature:* ***180°C***

Ingredients

$1^1/_2$ cups (150 g) toasted muesli
1 cup (90 g) desiccated coconut
1 cup (150 g) wholemeal self-raising flour
$^1/_2$ cup (90 g) brown sugar
$^1/_2$ cup (125 g) honey
$^1/_2$ cup (90 g) chopped dried apricots
$^1/_4$ cup (30 g) flaked almonds
$^1/_2$ cup (125 g) butter, melted
$^1/_2$ cup (125 g) peanut butter

Method

1. Set oven at 180°C. Brush or spray cake pan with oil and line base with baking paper.
2. Combine all ingredients. Mix well.
3. Press into cake pan.
4. Cook at 180°C for 20 minutes.
5. Cool in cake pan. Cut into 25 (each 4 cm square).

BROWNIES

- *Number:* ***16***
- *Cooking utensil:* 18 cm square cake pan (1.5 L), saucepan
- *Preparation time:* ***20 minutes***
- *Cooking time:* ***30 minutes***
- *Oven temperature:* ***180°C***

Ingredients

$^1/_2$ cup (125 g) butter, margarine *or* dairy blend
125 g chocolate
1 cup (180 g) brown sugar
2 eggs (61 g), beaten
1 cup (150 g) plain flour
$^3/_4$ cup (90 g) chopped walnuts

Method

1. Set oven at 180°C. Brush or spray cake pan with oil and line base with baking paper.
2. Melt butter and chocolate over low heat or in microwave oven on low power (see p. 385).
3. Add sugar and stir until dissolved.
4. Mix in eggs, flour and walnuts.
5. Pour into cake pan.
6. Cook for 30 minutes at 180°C.
7. Cool in pan. Cut into 16 (each 4.5 cm square).

BURNT BUTTER BISCUITS

- *Number:* ***48***
- *Cooking utensil:* oven trays, saucepan
- *Cooking time:* ***10–12 minutes for each tray***
- *Oven temperature:* ***180°C***

Ingredients

$^1/_2$ cup (125 g) butter
$^1/_2$ cup (125 g) sugar
1 egg (61 g), beaten
1 teaspoon vanilla essence
$1^1/_2$ cups (225 g) self-raising flour
24 blanched almonds

Method

1. Set oven at 180°C. Brush or spray oven trays with oil or cover base with baking paper.
2. Melt butter in saucepan and cook until it is a light brown colour.
3. Cool slightly and add sugar. Beat well.
4. Stir in egg and vanilla essence.
5. Add flour and mix to a stiff dough.
6. Roll mixture into 48 balls and place on tray, allowing room for mixture to spread. Place half an almond on each biscuit.
7. Bake at 180°C for 10–12 minutes until golden brown.
8. Cool on cake cooler.

✦ CITRUS DROPS ✦

Follow recipe for **Burnt butter biscuits**. Add 1 teaspoon grated orange rind and 1 teaspoon grated lemon rind at step 3. Place piece of walnut on each biscuit at step 6.

CARAMELS

- *Number:* ***36***
- *Cooking utensil:* 18 cm square cake pan (1.5 L), saucepan

Ingredients

$^1/_2$ cup (125 g) butter
$1^1/_2$ cups (375 g) brown sugar
400 g can sweetened condensed milk
3 tablespoons (60 g) golden syrup

Method

1. Brush or spray cake pan with oil.
2. Melt butter.
3. Add other ingredients, stir over low heat until dissolved.
4. Boil without stirring to 118°C (firm ball consistency).
5. Pour into pan. Allow to set and cut into 36 (each 3 cm square).

CARAMEL SQUARES

- *Number:* ***16***
- *Cooking utensil:* 18 cm square cake pan (1.5 L)
- *Preparation time:* ***20 minutes***
- *Cooking time:* ***25–30 minutes***
- *Oven temperature:* ***180°C***

Ingredients

1 cup (150 g) wholemeal self-raising flour
2 teaspoons cinnamon
$^1/_2$ cup (125 g) butter, melted
$^3/_4$ cup (185 g) sugar
1 egg (61 g), beaten
1 teaspoon vanilla essence
1 cup (180 g) chopped dates *or* raisins
$^1/_2$ cup (60 g) chopped walnuts

Method

1. Set oven at 180°C. Brush or spray cake pan with oil and line base with baking paper.
2. Mix flour and cinnamon.
3. Mix butter and sugar. Add egg and beat well.
4. Add all other ingredients, mix well.
5. Spread into cake pan and bake at 180°C for 25–30 minutes.
6. Cut into 16 (each 4.5 cm square) while still warm, cool in pan.
7. Lift onto cake cooler when cool.

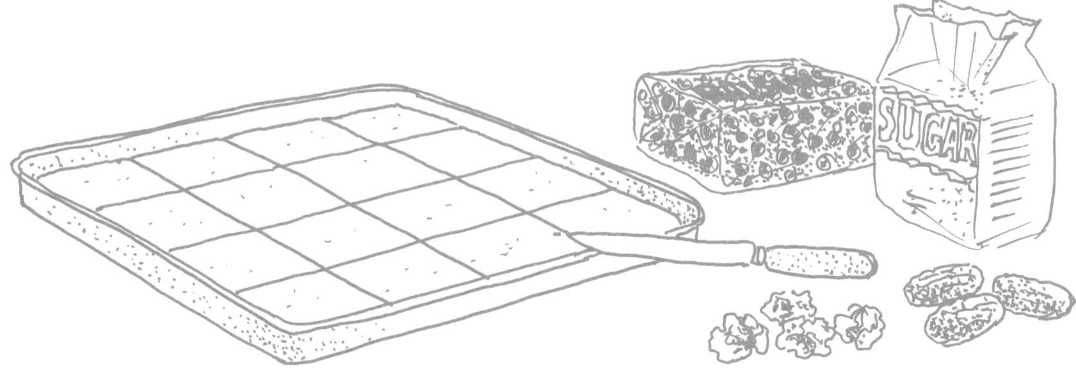

CHEESE STRAWS

- *Number:* ***18 bundles***
- *Cooking utensil:* oven trays
- *Preparation time:* ***20 minutes***
- *Cooking time:* ***12–15 minutes***
- *Oven temperature:* ***160°C***

Ingredients

1 cup (150 g) plain flour
1/2 teaspoon salt
1/8 teaspoon cayenne
1/4 teaspoon mustard
1/4 cup (60 g) butter, margarine *or* dairy blend
2/3 cup (80 g) grated tasty cheese
1 egg yolk (61 g)
1/4 teaspoon lemon juice
1 tablespoon (20 mL) water, if required

Method

1. Set oven at 160°C. Brush or spray oven trays with oil or cover base with baking paper.
2. Sift flour, salt, cayenne and mustard.
3. Rub butter into flour, add cheese and mix into a stiff dough with egg yolk and lemon juice. Add water if necessary.
4. Knead lightly and roll out to 5 mm thick.
5. Make rings: cut 18 rings, using two round scone cutters of different sizes (2 cm and 3 cm diameter) to give rings of pastry. Place on oven tray.
6. Make straws: knead pastry again and roll out to 5 mm thick. Cut into strips 5 mm x 6 cm. Place carefully on oven tray.
7. Bake at 160°C for 12–15 minutes, until slightly coloured. Allow to cool on tray.
8. Place cheese straws in rings to serve.

CHEESE BISCUITS

Follow recipe for **Cheese straws** to step 4. At step 5 use 4 cm round scone cutters to cut out shapes. Place on oven tray, brush with milk and sprinkle each with 1/4 teaspoon parmesan cheese. Bake at 160°C for 12–15 minutes, until slightly coloured. Allow to cool on tray.

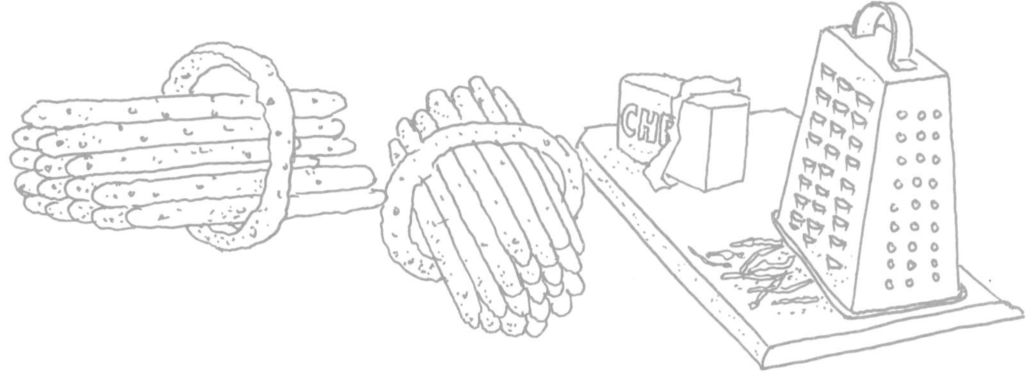

CHERRY ROUNDS

- *Number:* ***30***
- *Cooking utensil:* oven trays
- *Preparation time:* ***20 minutes***
- *Cooking time:* ***12–15 minutes***
- *Oven temperature:* ***180°C***

Ingredients

1/2 cup (125 g) butter, margarine *or* dairy blend
1/2 cup (90 g) brown sugar
1/4 teaspoon vanilla essence
1 egg yolk (61 g)
1 1/4 cups (190 g) self-raising flour
Topping
1 egg white (61 g), slightly beaten
3/4 cup (90 g) finely chopped walnuts
5 glacé cherries

Method

1. Set oven at 180°C. Brush or spray oven trays with oil or cover base with baking paper.
2. Cream butter, sugar and vanilla essence, mix in egg yolk.
3. Add flour and mix thoroughly. Chill for 30 minutes if possible.
4. Shape into 30 balls, dip each in egg white and then into nuts. Decorate each biscuit with a piece of cherry and place on tray.
5. Bake at 180°C for 12–15 minutes.
6. Allow to cool slightly before removing from tray. Cool on cake cooler.

CHOCOLATE NUT COOKIES 

- *Number:* ***24***
- *Cooking utensil:* oven trays, saucepan
- *Preparation time:* ***20 minutes***
- *Cooking time:* ***10–15 minutes***
- *Oven temperature:* ***180°C***

Ingredients

1 cup (150 g) plain flour
2 tablespoons (20 g) cocoa
1/2 cup (125 g) butter, margarine *or* dairy blend
1/4 cup (60 g) caster sugar
1/4 teaspoon vanilla essence
1/4 cup (40 g) chopped almonds
1 tablespoon (15 g) icing sugar mixture

Method

1. Set oven at 180°C. Brush or spray oven trays with oil or cover base with baking paper.
2. Sift flour and cocoa.
3. Cream butter, sugar and vanilla essence. Add almonds.
4. Add flour and cocoa and mix thoroughly.
5. Roll into 24 balls and place on tray.
6. Bake at 180°C for 10–15 minutes.
7. Cool on cake cooler. May be rolled in icing sugar before serving.

COCONUT ICE

Gift idea: wrap in cellophane and tie with a ribbon.

Number: 36

Cooking utensil: 18 cm square cake pan (1.5 L)

Ingredients

1 cup (250 g) milk
4 cups (1 kg) sugar
$^1/_4$ teaspoon cream of tartar
2 cups (180 g) desiccated coconut
pink colouring

Method

1. Brush or spray cake pan with oil.
2. Heat milk, sugar and cream of tartar. Stir until sugar is dissolved.
3. Boil approximately 10 minutes, to 114°C (soft ball consistency).
4. Remove from heat, divide mixture into two.
5. Add 1 cup (90 g) coconut and pink colouring (very little) to half, stir quickly until thick and creamy. Pour into pan.
6. Add 1 cup (90 g) coconut to other half, stir until thick and creamy, pour over pink layer.
7. Allow to set and cut into 36 (each 3 cm square).

FUDGE

Number: 36

Cooking utensil: 18 cm square cake pan (1.5 L), saucepan

Ingredients

$^1/_4$ cup (65 g) grated dark chocolate
2 cups (500 g) sugar
1 teaspoon glucose
$^3/_4$ cup (375 mL) milk
1 tablespoon (20 g) butter
1 teaspoon vanilla essence

Method

1. Brush or spray cake pan with oil.
2. Dissolve chocolate, sugar and glucose in milk.
3. Add butter, boil to 116°C (soft ball consistency), stirring all the time. Remove from heat.
4. Add vanilla essence, beat with wooden spoon until creamy.
5. Pour into pan. Allow to set and cut into 36 (each 3 cm square).

GINGER CREAMS

- *Number:* **30**
- *Cooking utensil:* oven trays

- *Preparation time:* **20 minutes**
- *Cooking time:* **10–15 minutes**
- *Oven temperature:* **160°C**

Ingredients

1/2 cup (75 g) plain flour
1 1/2 cups (225 g) self-raising flour
1 1/2 teaspoons ground ginger
1/2 teaspoon mixed spice
1/2 cup (125 g) butter, margarine *or* dairy blend
1/2 cup (125 g) caster sugar
1 egg (61 g), beaten
1 teaspoon golden syrup
2 tablespoons (40 mL) milk
1/2 cup (1 quantity) **Butter icing** (p. 383)
1/4 cup (30 g) chopped glacé ginger

Method

1. Set oven at 160°C. Brush or spray oven trays with oil or cover base with baking paper.
2. Sift flours, ground ginger and spices.
3. Cream butter and sugar. Add egg and golden syrup and mix well.
4. Add flour and mix into firm dough.
5. Lift onto lightly floured surface, knead until smooth.
6. Roll to 5 mm thickness, cut into 60 rounds and place on trays. Glaze with milk.
7. Bake at 160°C for 10–15 minutes, until pale biscuit colour.
8. Cool. Join with **Butter icing** mixed with chopped glacé ginger.

GINGER NUTS

- *Number:* **48**
- *Cooking utensil:* oven trays

- *Preparation time:* **20 minutes**
- *Cooking time:* **12–15 minutes**
- *Oven temperature:* **180°C**

Ingredients

2 cups (300 g) self-raising flour
2 tablespoons (20 g) ground ginger
1 teaspoon bicarbonate of soda
1/2 cup (125 g) butter, margarine *or* dairy blend
2/3 cup (120 g) brown sugar
1 tablespoon (20 g) golden syrup
1 egg (61 g), beaten
2 tablespoons (40 g) sugar

Method

1. Set oven at 180°C. Brush or spray oven trays with oil or cover base with baking paper.
2. Sift flour, ginger and soda.
3. Cream butter, brown sugar and golden syrup. Add egg and mix well.
4. Add flour and mix thoroughly.
5. Roll into 48 balls and dip in sugar. Place on trays, sugar side up, allowing room for biscuits to spread.
6. Bake at 180°C for 12–15 minutes.
7. Allow to cool slightly before removing from tray. Cool on cake cooler.

GINGER SHORTCAKE

- *Number:* **16**
- *Cooking utensil:* 22 cm round cake pan (1.75 L)
- *Preparation time:* **20 minutes**
- *Cooking time:* **45 minutes**
- *Oven temperature:* **175°C**

Ingredients

$\frac{1}{2}$ cup (125 g) butter, melted
1 egg (61 g), beaten
$1\frac{1}{2}$ cups (225 g) plain flour
$\frac{1}{2}$ cup (125 g) caster sugar
$\frac{1}{2}$ cup (90 g) chopped glacé ginger
$\frac{1}{4}$ cup (30 g) slivered almonds
1 teaspoon milk

Method

1. Set oven at 175°C. Brush or spray cake pan with oil and line base with baking paper.
2. Mix butter, egg, flour, caster sugar and ginger.
3. Press into cake pan.
4. Decorate with almonds. Brush top with milk.
5. Bake at 175°C for 45 minutes.
6. Allow to cool in cake pan.
7. Cut into 16 wedges and serve.

CHERRY SHORTCAKE

Follow recipe for **Ginger shortcake**. Omit ginger and almonds. Add $\frac{2}{3}$ cup (120 g) chopped glacé cherries at step 2. Decorate with 16 walnut pieces.

HEDGEHOG

- *Number:* 24
- *Cooking utensil:* 18 cm square cake pan (1.5 L), saucepan

Ingredients

$\frac{2}{3}$ cup (160 g) butter, margarine *or* dairy blend
$\frac{1}{2}$ cup (125 g) caster sugar
2 tablespoons (20 g) cocoa
2 tablespoons (20 g) desiccated coconut
1 egg (61 g), beaten
$\frac{1}{2}$ cup (60 g) chopped walnuts
$\frac{1}{2}$ cup (90 g) glacé cherries
$\frac{1}{2}$ teaspoon vanilla essence
2 cups (240 g) crushed sweet biscuits

Method

1. Line cake pan with baking paper.
2. Melt butter and sugar, add cocoa and mix well.
3. Remove from heat and stir in coconut and egg.
4. Add walnuts, cherries and vanilla essence.
5. Stir in crushed biscuits and mix well.
6. Press into pan and chill.
7. Cut into 24 (each 3 cm x 4.5 cm).

LEMON SLICE

- *Number:* **25**
- *Cooking utensil:* double saucepan, 20 cm square cake pan (2.5 L), 2 x 20 cm squares baking paper
- *Preparation time:* **35 minutes**
- *Cooking time:* **25 minutes**
- *Oven temperature:* **190°C**

Ingredients

Filling

3/4 cup (185 g) sugar
2 eggs (61 g), beaten
rind and juice of 2 lemons

Pastry

1 cup (150 g) plain flour
1 cup (150 g) self-raising flour
1/2 cup (125 g) butter, margarine *or* dairy blend
1/2 cup (125 g) caster sugar
1 egg (61 g), beaten

Decoration

13 blanched almonds, halved

Method

1. Prepare filling: mix sugar and eggs in top of double saucepan. Blend in lemon juice and rind. Place over water simmering in the base of the double saucepan. Stir until mixture thickens, approximately 20 minutes. Cool.
2. Set oven at 190°C.
3. Prepare pastry: sift flours, add sugar. Rub butter into dry ingredients, add egg and mix into a firm dough.
4. Lift onto lightly floured surface, knead until smooth.
5. Divide into two. Roll out half onto baking paper and place in cake pan, with the baking paper side down.
6. Spread lemon filling over pastry base.
7. Roll out other half of pastry on baking paper, roll both onto rolling pin. Unroll onto lemon filling, remove paper.
8. Brush lightly with milk. Place almonds so that one half will be in the centre of each piece when cut *or* sprinkle with chopped almonds.
9. Bake at 190°C for 25 minutes.
10. Allow to stand in pan until almost cold. Cut into 25 (each 4 cm square) and place on cake cooler.

APPLE SLICE

Follow recipe for **Lemon slice** using 1 cup (200 g) **Apple puree** (p. 308) for filling.

BAKEWELL SLICE

Follow recipe for **Lemon slice**. Omit filling. At step 5 roll full quantity of pastry onto baking paper and lift into cake pan. Spread with 2 tablespoons (40 g) apricot jam. Cover with topping made by creaming 1/4 cup (60 g) butter with 1/4 cup (60 g) caster sugar, add egg then stir in 1/2 cup (45 g) desiccated coconut. Bake at 180°C for 25–30 minutes. Cut into 25 squares when cold.

RASPBERRY SLICE

Follow recipe for **Lemon slice**. Omit filling. At step 5 roll full quantity of pastry to fit cake pan. Spread with 3 tablespoons (60 g) raspberry jam. Cover with topping made by beating 1 egg with 1/2 cup (125 g) caster sugar and 1/2 cup (45 g) coconut. Bake at 180°C for 30 minutes. Cut into 25 squares when cold.

MARSHMALLOW

- *Number:* 36
- *Cooking utensil:* 18 cm square cake pan (1.5 L)

Ingredients

1 cup (250 mL) water
1 cup (250 g) sugar
2 tablespoons (24 g) gelatine
1/4 teaspoon cream of tartar
1 tablespoon (20 mL) lemon juice
1/2 cup (45 g) coconut, toasted

Method

1. Brush or spray cake pan with oil.
2. Heat water, sugar, gelatine and cream of tartar, stir until sugar is dissolved.
3. Boil quickly for 15 minutes.
4. Cool, add lemon juice.
5. Beat with electric beater on high speed until white and creamy.
6. Pour into pan. Allow to set and cut into 36 (each 3 cm square). Roll in toasted coconut.

MELTING MOMENTS

- *Number:* 24
- *Cooking utensil:* oven trays
- *Preparation time:* **20 minutes**
- *Cooking time:* **15–20 minutes**
- *Oven temperature:* **160°C**

Ingredients

1/2 cup (75 g) self-raising flour
1/2 cup (65 g) cornflour
1/2 cup (125 g) butter, margarine *or* dairy blend
1/4 cup (45 g) icing sugar mixture

Method

1. Set oven at 160°C. Brush or spray oven tray with oil or cover base with baking paper.
2. Sift flour and cornflour.
3. Cream butter and sugar. Add flour and mix thoroughly.
4. Place 24 spoonfuls on tray, or pipe onto tray with a star pipe and bag.
5. Bake at 160°C for 15–20 minutes.
6. Cool on cake cooler.

REFRIGERATOR NUTTIES 

The uncooked mixture may be frozen, then thawed, cut into slices and baked as needed.

- *Number:* 60
- *Cooking utensil:* oven trays
- *Preparation time:* **20 minutes**
- *Cooking time:* **10–15 minutes**
- *Oven temperature:* **160°C**

Ingredients

1/2 cup (125 g) butter, margarine *or* dairy blend
2/3 cup (120 g) brown sugar
1 egg (61 g), beaten
1/2 teaspoon vanilla essence
1/4 cup (30 g) chopped nuts
1/2 cup (90 g) chopped glacé cherries
1/4 cup (30 g) chopped glacé ginger
2 cups (300 g) self-raising flour

Method

1. Cream butter and sugar. Add egg and vanilla essence, mix well.
2. Add nuts and fruit then flour. Mix well.
3. Turn onto lightly floured surface and shape into a roll 3 cm in diameter. Wrap in plastic film. Refrigerate for up to a week or freeze.
4. When required cut into 60 slices approximately 5 mm thick. Place on oven trays that have been brushed or sprayed with oil or the base covered with baking paper.
5. Bake at 160°C for 10–15 minutes.
6. Cool on cake cooler.

RUM TRUFFLES

- *Number:* 24

Ingredients

1/4 cup (60 g) butter, margarine *or* dairy blend
1/2 cup (90 g) mixed dried fruit
1/2 cup (90 g) icing sugar mixture
1 cup (60 g) chocolate cake crumbs
2 tablespoons (16 g) coconut
2 tablespoons (40 mL) rum *or* orange juice
1/4 cup (30 g) chocolate sprinkles

Method

1. Mix all ingredients except chocolate sprinkles (the dried fruit may be soaked in the rum *or* juice overnight. If so, the mixture may need a little more liquid).
2. Roll into 24 balls.
3. Roll in chocolate sprinkles.

✦ PLUM PUDDING TRUFFLES ✦

Follow recipe for **Rum truffles**. Melt 250 g white chocolate over hot water or in microwave oven (see p. 385). Spread baking paper on tray, make 24 circles, each with 1 teaspoon of white chocolate. Place truffle on each circle before it sets, top each with a drizzle of white chocolate and a piece of red or green cherry or coloured almond paste (p. 414) cut to represent holly and berries. Place in gift box or on festive table.

SHORTBREAD

These can be cut into a variety of shapes and gift-wrapped for festive occasions.

- *Number:* ***24 or 32***
- *Cooking utensil:* oven trays
- *Preparation time:* ***20 minutes***
- *Cooking time:* ***20–25 minutes***
- *Oven temperature:* ***160°C***

Ingredients

1¼ cups (190 g) plain flour
1 tablespoon (10 g) rice flour
2 tablespoons (40 g) caster sugar
½ cup (125 g) butter at room temperature
½ teaspoon vanilla essence

Method

1. Set oven at 160°C. Brush or spray oven tray with oil or cover base with baking paper.
2. Sift flours, add sugar and rub in butter. Add vanilla essence. Work into a stiff dough. Turn onto a lightly floured board and knead well.
3. Divide mixture into 3 or 4 portions. Roll each into round 1 cm thick and the size of a saucer. Pinch edges. Lift onto oven tray. Cut each round into 8 pieces and mark with fork.
4. Bake at 160°C for 20–25 minutes, until pale fawn colour.
5. Cool on cake cooler.

YO-YOS

- *Number:* ***36 single, 18 pairs***
- *Cooking utensil:* oven trays
- *Preparation time:* ***20 minutes***
- *Cooking time:* ***10–15 minutes***
- *Oven temperature:* ***170°C***

Ingredients

1 cup (150 g) self-raising flour
½ cup (65 g) custard powder
⅓ cup (60 g) icing sugar mixture
⅔ cup (160 g) butter, margarine *or* dairy blend

Method

1. Set oven at 170°C. Brush or spray oven tray with oil or cover base with baking paper.
2. Sift flour, custard powder and sugar.
3. Rub in butter and work into a stiff dough.
4. Roll in 36 balls and place on oven tray. Using a fork, flatten each ball a little.
5. Bake at 170°C for 15–20 minutes, until pale fawn colour.
6. Cool on cake cooler and join together in pairs with jam *or* **Butter icing** (p. 383).

WHITE CHRISTMAS

► *Number:* **36**

► *Cooking utensil:* 18 cm square cake pan (1.5 L)

Ingredients

1 cup (100 g) powdered non-fat milk
1 cup (90 g) desiccated coconut
1 cup (180 g) mixed dried fruit
2 cups (60 g) rice bubbles
$^1/_2$ cup (90 g) icing sugar mixture
250 g copha

Method

1 Mix all ingredients except copha.
2 Melt copha slowly and pour over mixture, blend well.
3 Press into pan.
4 Cool and allow to set.
5 Cut into 36 (each 3 cm square).

Cooked biscuits: tips for product quality

Quality criteria

- even, golden-brown colour
- crisp surface
- even in size.

Spread on tray:

- too much liquid or insufficient flour
- baking tray too heavily greased, allowing the soft biscuit mixture to spread before it had set
- oven too cool.

Too dark on base and too pale on top:

- baking tray too large or incorrectly positioned, preventing circulation of heat.

Biscuits too pale:

- oven temperature too low
- insufficient cooking time.

Biscuits too dark:

- oven temperature too high
- over-cooked.

Soft biscuits:

- insufficient cooking
- not removed from oven tray as soon as taken from oven
- not placed separately on cake cooler
- placed in storage container before quite cold
- storage container not airtight.

17 Yeast breads and buns

Bread, historically considered to be the staff of life, is found in different forms in every country and culture. Most breads are leavened, for example, pumpernickel, croissants, focaccia and dark rye, and use yeast as the raising agent. Unleavened breads, for example, matzo and mountain bread, are flat breads with no raising agent.

There are many different yeasts that have been used for thousands of years to prepare fermented foods and drinks. Yeast is a single-celled living organism. When moist and heated to a temperature between 30°C and 37°C, it converts carbohydrates to alcohol and carbon dioxide gas. This action is called fermentation. The carbon dioxide gas bubbles expand on heating and this makes the mixture rise.

Flour and water are mixed with yeast to form a basic bread dough. Gliadin and glutenin are two proteins found in wheat, rye, barley and oat flour, and when these proteins are mixed with water, gluten is formed. Gluten is a strong, elastic protein that stretches as the carbon dioxide gas bubbles expand in the bread dough during fermentation. During proving, the bubbles are caught in the web of gluten within the dough. The dough expands and rises to twice its original size. The alcohol produced during fermentation gives the distinctive 'fresh bread' aroma and evaporates during baking.

Food value

As flour is the major ingredient of all breads, the main food nutrient is carbohydrate with some protein and fibre. Yeast is a source of vitamins from the B group. Ingredients such as eggs and milk supply small amounts of other food nutrients.

Bread-making utensils and ingredients

Warm utensils and ingredients promote optimum yeast fermentation.

Bread pans

A medium-size bread pan (23 cm long x 10 cm wide and 9 cm deep, 2 L) is required for a 3 cup (450 g) flour recipe. A loaf cake pan of similar capacity is satisfactory. Regular baking of bread may justify the expense of purchasing a special bread pan with black painted sides which absorb heat quickly and help to produce a crisp crust.

Flour

Plain flour is used in breadmaking. Flour milled from 'hard' wheat is rich in the proteins gliadin and glutenin. When mixed with water these proteins together form gluten, another protein, which has the effect of increasing the strength and elasticity of the dough, thus trapping more gas during proving and increasing the volume of the loaf. Gluten flour may be added to flour to make a 'stronger' flour. Unbleached plain flour may be used instead of plain flour. Wholemeal flour increases the nutritive and fibre content of the loaf and usually requires additional liquid for mixing.

Commercial bread improver

This improves the texture and gives a crumb that remains fresh for a longer period after baking.

Yeast

Yeast acts as the raising agent in breadmaking. Dried yeast or compressed yeast may be used in any of the recipes in this chapter. Double the amount by weight of compressed yeast is needed compared to dried yeast.

Dried yeast granules, sold in vacuum-sealed foil packs, retain freshness and are easy to use.

Compressed yeast is a creamy grey colour, has a smooth texture, is cool and moist to the touch and breaks sharply. It keeps for 1–2 weeks in plastic food wrap or in an airtight container in the refrigerator. It contains approximately 70% water.

Yeast is most active between 30°C and 37°C. Below 30°C the yeast is not activated and above 40°C it deteriorates rapidly and dies.

Sugar

A little sugar stimulates yeast fermentation and improves the brown colour of the crust. Increased amounts change the flavour and texture.

Fat

Butter, margarine and oils improve the flavour and crust, but too much may reduce the activity of the yeast.

Liquid

Skim milk powder, fresh milk and water are used in the recipes in this chapter. Water makes a lighter dough than milk.

Bread-making processes

Mix Combine ingredients by hand or in an electric mixer with a dough hook.

Knead Dough is sticky when mixed but becomes easier to handle as it is kneaded on a lightly floured surface. Kneading develops gluten, making the dough elastic, and distributes the bubbles of carbon dioxide formed by the yeast, thus producing a fine, even texture. To knead bread, fold the far edge of the dough to the centre and push it with the knuckles or heel of the hand. Turn dough slightly and repeat the process until the surface is smooth.

Prove After kneading, the dough is warmed and doubles in size through the production and expansion of carbon dioxide gas. Place dough in a warm basin, cover closely with plastic food wrap, and keep in a warm place (basin may be placed in 6 cm of hot water in a sink or large bowl), keeping the dough between 30°C and 37°C. During proving, check the temperature, which should be comfortably warm to the touch. Avoid over-proving (dough increases to more than double size), as this gives a coarse texture and a yeasty, fermenting flavour to the loaf.

Bake Changes that occur when yeast doughs are baked:

- The high temperature destroys the yeast and fermentation ceases.
- Heat penetrates the dough, setting the gluten, thus forming the shape of the loaf.
- Starch grains burst and absorb most of the moisture.
- The alcohol and some of the moisture evaporates.
- Some of the starch is converted to dextrin, thus forming the golden-brown crust.
- Yeast mixtures are cooked when the loaf shrinks slightly from the sides of the pan and a hollow sound is produced by gently tapping the knuckles on the underside of the loaf.

Glaze Milk or syrup glaze may be brushed on the loaf before baking or during the final 5 minutes of cooking to give a shiny appearance.

Cool Turn out of pan onto cake cooler to ensure a crisp crust.

See tips for product quality (p. 448) for the features of a good quality loaf and the possible causes of problems.

QUICK BREAD

- *Number:* ***1 loaf***
- *Cooking utensil: bread pan (2 L)*
- *Preparation time:* ***50 minutes***
- *Cooking time:* ***30 minutes***
- *Oven temperature:* ***220°C reduced to 200°C***

Ingredients

3 cups (300 g) plain flour
1 teaspoon salt
2 teaspoons (7 g) dried yeast
1 tablespoon (20 g) skim milk powder *or* milk
1 teaspoon oil
1 teaspoon milk
$1^1/_2$ cups (375 mL) hot water
Glaze
1 tablespoon (20 mL) milk

Method

1. Brush or spray bread pan with oil.
2. Mix all dry ingredients together.
3. Add oil, milk and hot water, mix to a soft dough.
4. Cover closely with plastic food wrap. Allow to prove in warm place (basin may be placed in 6 cm hot water in a sink or bowl) until double in size, approximately 20 minutes.
5. Turn onto lightly floured surface and knead 3–5 minutes, until just smooth.
6. Set oven to 220°C.
7. Shape into loaf and place into bread pan.
8. Brush top with water and prove in warm place until dough doubles in size, approximately 20 minutes.
9. Glaze with milk, place in oven and bake 20 minutes at 220°C. Reduce temperature to 200°C and bake 10 minutes until golden brown and sounds hollow when tapped.
10. Cool 5 minutes in bread pan before turning onto cake cooler.

QUICK LIGHT WHOLEMEAL BREAD

Follow recipe for **Quick bread**, replacing 1 cup (150 g) plain flour with 1 cup (150 g) wholemeal plain flour.

GOLDEN CORN LOAF

Follow recipe for **Quick bread**. Replace $^1/_2$ cup (75 g) wholemeal flour with $^1/_2$ cup (75 g) polenta. Brush or spray bread pan with oil and sprinkle 3 tablespoons (30 g) extra polenta into pan. At step 9 glaze with milk and sprinkle with 2 teaspoons extra polenta.

WALNUT BREAD

Follow recipe for **Quick bread**. Add $^2/_3$ cup (80 g) chopped walnuts and 1 tablespoon (20 g) sugar at step 2.

✦ HERB AND GARLIC BREAD ✦

Follow recipe for **Quick bread**. Add 1 clove (5 g) crushed garlic and 1 cup chopped mixed fresh herbs (chives, parsley, basil, sage, marjoram) at step 2. At step 9 glaze with milk and sprinkle with 2 teaspoons sesame seeds.

✦ SUN-DRIED TOMATO AND OLIVE BREAD ✦

Follow recipe for **Quick bread**. At step 2 add 1/4 cup (40 g) sliced sun-dried tomatoes, 8 sliced pitted olives, 2 tablespoons chopped chives, 2 tablespoons chopped parsley and 2 tablespoons chopped basil.

✦ FRUIT LOAF ✦

Follow recipe for **Quick bread**. At step 2 add 1 teaspoon mixed spice, 1/2 teaspoon cinnamon, 1/4 teaspoon nutmeg, 3/4 cup (135 g) mixed dried fruit and 1 tablespoon (20 g) sugar. At step 3 add an extra 2 tablespoons (40 mL) hot water. At step 9 glaze with milk and sprinkle with 2 teaspoons poppy seeds.

✦ FOCCACIA ✦

Follow recipe for **Quick bread** to step 6. At step 7 divide dough in half, roll each piece into an oblong approximately 24 cm x 16 cm. Place on oiled trays. Cover with plastic food wrap and prove in warm place until double in size. Brush top of each with 1 tablespoon (20 mL) olive oil and sprinkle with lemon pepper, mixed herbs, and 1 tablespoon (10 g) grated parmesan cheese. Bake 15 minutes at 220°C, reduce to 200°C and bake for a further 5 minutes.

✦ COTTAGE LOAVES ✦

Follow recipe for **Quick bread** to step 6. At step 7 divide dough in half. Shape each portion into a round and cut each into 6 pieces. Re-form each into a round and arrange in 2 oiled 18 cm pans. Glaze with milk and sprinkle with sesame seeds. Bake 15 minutes at 220°C, reduce to 200°C and bake for a further 5 minutes.

✦ SOURDOUGH BREAD ✦

Follow recipe for **Quick bread**, using 1/2 cup sourdough starter, instead of yeast. Shape dough into round, place on oiled oven tray and slash across centre with knife before cooking. Dust lightly with flour after cooking.

Sourdough starter must be started 2–3 days before making the bread. To make sourdough starter: mix 1/2 cup (125 mL) warm water, 1/2 cup (65 g) plain flour, 1/2 teaspoon (2 g) dried yeast and 2 tablespoons (40 mL) natural yoghurt *or* buttermilk and allow to stand 24 hours in warm place in a covered glass container. Add 1/2 cup (65 g) plain flour and 1/4 cup (65 mL) warm water and continue to stand in warm place for a further 24 hours until it has a sour, fermenting odour. Place in refrigerator. This starter keeps indefinitely in the refrigerator; 1 cup (125 g) plain flour and 1/2 cup (125 mL) water must be added weekly.

POCKET BREAD

- *Number:* ***4 pockets***
- *Cooking utensil:* hot griller

Preparation time: ***25 minutes***
Cooking time: ***3–4 minutes***

Ingredients

1 cup (150 g) plain flour
1 teaspoon (4 g) dried yeast
1/2 teaspoon salt
1/2 teaspoon sugar
100 mL hot water

Method

1. Mix dry ingredients, add water and mix to a soft dough. If too sticky add 1–2 tablespoons (10–20 g) extra flour.
2. Cover with plastic food wrap, pushed down to completely cover the dough. Prove in a warm place for 15 minutes.
3. Turn dough onto floured board and knead until smooth.
4. Cut into 4 portions. Knead each until smooth and roll out to the size of a large saucer.
5. Turn on griller.
6. Allow the dough to prove in warm place for 5 minutes.
7. Place under hot griller. It should balloon in about 1 minute. Turn and cook second side 1–2 minutes, turn again and cook a further 1 minute.
8. Allow to cool, open pocket and fill with shredded lettuce, grated carrot, sliced tomato, sliced onion, alfalfa sprouts, grated cheese and a little mayonnaise.

PIZZA

Follow recipe for **Pocket bread** to step 3. Set oven at 220°C. An unglazed tile may be placed in the oven for the pizza to stand on during cooking, as this gives a crisper base. At step 4 roll out dough to the size of a 22 cm pizza pan. Brush or spray pizza pan with oil, place mixture on pan and cover with plastic film. Stand in warm place for 10 minutes to rise. Top with 1/2 cup **Fresh tomato sauce** (p. 283) and one or more of the following: sardines, prawns or other seafood, capsicum rings, mushrooms, salami, anchovies, olives, semi-dried tomatoes, chargrilled artichokes. Top with 1/2 cup (65 g) grated cheese such as mozzarella. Bake at 220°C for 20 minutes. Serve hot.

INVOLTINIS

Follow recipe for **Pocket bread** to step 3. Set oven at 210°C. At step 4 divide mixture into 4 and roll each piece out to a 12 cm square. Across the diagonal of each square spread 2 tablespoons **Fresh tomato sauce** (p. 283) and add one or more of the pizza toppings listed above. Moisten uncovered corners and fold across filling. Stand in warm place for 10 minutes to rise. Brush tops with a little milk and bake at 220°C for 20 minutes. Serve hot.

CHEESE AND HERB BREAD RING

- *Number:* ***1 loaf***
- *Cooking utensil:* 22 cm ring pan *or* oven tray
- *Preparation time:* ***40 minutes***
- *Cooking time:* ***35–40 minutes***
- *Oven temperature:* ***200°C reduced to 180°***

Ingredients

2 teaspoons (7 g) dried yeast
1 tablespoon (20 g) sugar
1 cup (250 mL) warm water
2½ cups (375 g) plain flour
1 teaspoon salt
2 tablespoons chopped fresh herbs (parsley, chives, lemon thyme)
1 tablespoon (20 mL) oil
1 cup (125 g) grated tasty cheese
Glaze
1 tablespoon (20 mL) milk

Method

1. Brush or spray ring pan *or* oven tray with extra oil.
2. Mix yeast with sugar and warm water. Cover and allow to stand until frothy, approximately 10 minutes.
3. Mix flour, salt and herbs.
4. Add yeast mixture and oil, mix into a soft dough.
5. Turn onto a lightly floured surface and knead until dough is smooth and elastic.
6. Return dough to mixing bowl, cover and prove in warm place until double in size, approximately 20 minutes.
7. Turn onto floured surface, knead and then roll into an oblong about 30 cm x 25 cm.
8. Sprinkle cheese on dough and roll up as for **Egg sponge roll** (p. 396).
9. Place roll in ring pan *or* on oven tray, seal ends together. With sharp knife make 8–10 cuts in top of ring.
10. Prove in warm place until double in size, approximately 20 minutes.
11. Set oven at 200°C.
12. Glaze loaf with milk, and bake at 200°C for 20 minutes. Reduce temperature to 180°C and continue cooking for 15–20 minutes until golden brown and sounds hollow when tapped.
13. Cool on cake cooler.

BACON, CHEESE AND HERB BREAD RING

Follow recipe for **Cheese and herb bread ring**. Sprinkle 1 rasher (40 g) chopped bacon with the cheese at step 8.

SUN-DRIED TOMATO AND HERB BREAD RING

Follow recipe for **Cheese and herb bread ring**, replacing cheese with ½ cup (125 g) sun-dried tomatoes.

WHITE BREAD

▶ *Number:* ***1 loaf***
▶ *Cooking utensil:* bread pan (2 L)

Preparation time: ***1 hour***
Cooking time: ***25 minutes***
▶ *Oven temperature:* ***220°C reduced to 190°C***

Ingredients

1 tablespoon (14 g) dried yeast
2 teaspoons sugar
1 1/2 cups (375 mL) warm water
3 cups (450 g) plain flour
2 teaspoons salt
1 tablespoon (20 mL) oil
1 tablespoon (10 g) skim milk powder *or* milk
2 teaspoons bread improver (optional)

Glaze

1 egg white
1 tablespoon (20 mL) water

Method

1. Brush or spray bread pan with oil.
2. Mix yeast with sugar and warm water. Cover and allow to stand until frothy, approximately 10 minutes.
3. Mix dry ingredients.
4. Add yeast mixture, oil and milk, mix into a soft dough.
5. Turn onto a lightly floured surface and knead until dough is smooth and elastic.
6. Return dough to mixing bowl. Cover and prove in warm place until double in size, approximately 20 minutes.
7. Turn onto floured surface, knead and shape into loaf, place in pan and press into corners.
8. Prove in warm place until double in size, approximately 20 minutes.
9. Set oven at 220°C.
10. Bake loaf for 10 minutes at 220°C. Reduce temperature to 190°C, cook for a further 10 minutes.
11. Combine bread glaze ingredients and brush over top of loaf. Cook for a further 5 minutes or until golden brown and sounds hollow when tapped.
12. Remove from pan immediately and cool on cake cooler.

✦ LIGHT WHOLEMEAL BREAD ✦

Follow recipe for **White bread**. Replace 1 cup (150 g) plain flour with 1 cup (150 g) wholemeal plain flour. Use 1 2/3 cups (415 mL) warm water.

✦ WHOLEMEAL BREAD ✦

Follow recipe for **White bread**. Use 3 cups (450 g) wholemeal plain flour instead of plain flour. Use 1 3/4 cups (440 mL) warm water.

✦ SQUARE LOAF ✦

Follow recipe for **White bread**. At step 9, invert pan onto oiled oven tray and bake.

✦ RAISIN BREAD ✦

Follow recipe for **White bread**. At step 3 add 2 teaspoons cinnamon and 1/2 cup (90 g) raisins.

✦ FRENCH BREAD STICKS ✦

Follow recipe for **White bread**. At step 6 divide dough into two and shape each half to fit oiled French bread pans.

✦ HERBED FRENCH BREAD ✦

Cut 1 cooked **French bread stick** into 2 cm slices. Combine 1/3 cup (80 g) butter, 1 teaspoon chopped fresh herbs and 1 teaspoon lemon juice. Spread each slice with butter mixture and reform into a loaf. Wrap loaf in foil and place in oven at 200°C for 5 minutes. Serve hot to accompany barbecue meals and salads.

✦ GARLIC FRENCH BREAD ✦

Follow recipe for **Herbed French bread**. Add 2 cloves (10 g) crushed garlic to butter mixture.

✦ MIXED GRAIN BREAD ✦

Follow recipe for **White bread**. Replace 3 cups (450 g) plain flour with 1 1/2 cups (225 g) wholemeal plain flour, 1 cup (150 g) plain flour, 1/4 cup (50 g) kibbled wheat and 1/4 cup (20 g) bran.

BREAD ROLLS

- *Number:* **8–10**
- *Cooking utensil:* oven tray
- *Preparation time:* ***1 hour***
- *Cooking time:* ***15–20 minutes***
- *Oven temperature:* ***200°C reduced to 190°C***

Ingredients

2 teaspoons (7 g) dried yeast
1 tablespoon (20 g) sugar
$^{2}/_{3}$ cup (165 mL) warm water
1 tablespoon (20 g) butter
2 cups (300 g) plain flour
1 teaspoon salt
2 tablespoons (20 g) skim milk powder *or* milk
1 egg (61 g), beaten
Glaze
1 egg white
1 tablespoon (20 mL) water
2 teaspoons sesame *or* poppy seeds

Method

1 Brush or spray oven tray with oil.
2 Mix yeast with sugar and warm water. Cover and allow to stand until frothy, approximately 10 minutes.
3 Rub butter into flour, add salt.
4 Combine all ingredients except glaze and mix to a soft dough, adding extra water if necessary.
5 Turn onto a lightly floured surface and knead until dough is smooth and elastic.
6 Return dough to mixing bowl, cover and prove in a warm place until double in size, about 20 minutes.
7 Set oven at 200°C.
8 Knead dough, divide into 8 or 10 pieces and shape into rolls, e.g. horseshoe, twist, knot, cross, plait, roll, or 3 small rounds placed together to form cloverleaf. Place on tray, cover and prove in warm place for 10–15 minutes.
9 Make glaze: beat egg white, add water. Brush glaze on rolls and sprinkle with seeds.
10 Bake at 200°C for 10 minutes. Reduce temperature to 190°C and cook further 5–10 minutes until golden brown.
11 Cool on cake cooler.

SWEET YEAST BUNS

- *Number:* **12**
- *Cooking utensil:* oven tray, small saucepan
- *Preparation time:* ***1½ hours***
- *Cooking time:* ***15 minutes***
- *Oven temperature:* ***200°C reduced to 180°C***

Ingredients

2 teaspoons (7 g) dried yeast
2 tablespoons (40 g) sugar
⅔ cup (165 mL) warm water
2 cups (300 g) plain flour
1 teaspoon salt
2 tablespoons (40 g) butter, melted
2 tablespoons (20 g) skim milk powder *or* milk
1 egg (61g), beaten

Glaze

¼ cup (65 g) sugar
¼ cup (65 mL) water
1 teaspoon gelatine
1 teaspoon mixed spice

Method

1. Brush or spray oven tray with oil.
2. Mix yeast with sugar and warm water. Cover and allow to stand until frothy, approximately 10 minutes.
3. Sift flour and salt.
4. Make a well in centre of flour, pour in yeast, add butter, milk and egg. Mix into a soft dough.
5. Turn onto slightly floured surface and knead until smooth and elastic.
6. Return dough to basin, cover and prove in warm place until double in size, approximately 20 minutes.
7. Divide dough into 12 pieces and shape each into a bun. Place on tray.
8. Cover and prove in warm place for 20 minutes.
9. Set oven at 200°C.
10. Bake at 200°C for 10 minutes. Reduce temperature to 180°C and continue cooking for further 5 minutes, until golden brown.
11. Make glaze: combine ingredients in a small saucepan. Stir over heat, bring to boil.
12. Place buns on cake cooler, glaze and cool.

SPICY YEAST BUNS

Follow recipe for **Sweet yeast buns**. At step 3 add 1 teaspoon mixed spice to flour. At step 4 add ¾ cup (135 g) dried fruit.

HOT CROSS BUNS

Follow recipe for **Sweet yeast buns**. At step 3 add ¼ teaspoon cinnamon and ½ teaspoon mixed spice. At step 4 add ½ cup (90 g) mixed sultanas and currants and 1 tablespoon (15 g) mixed peel. Just before placing in oven to cook, mix 3 tablespoons (30 g) plain flour, 2 tablespoons (20 g) caster sugar and 1½ tablespoons (30 mL) water and, using a piping bag and plain tube, pipe a cross on each bun.

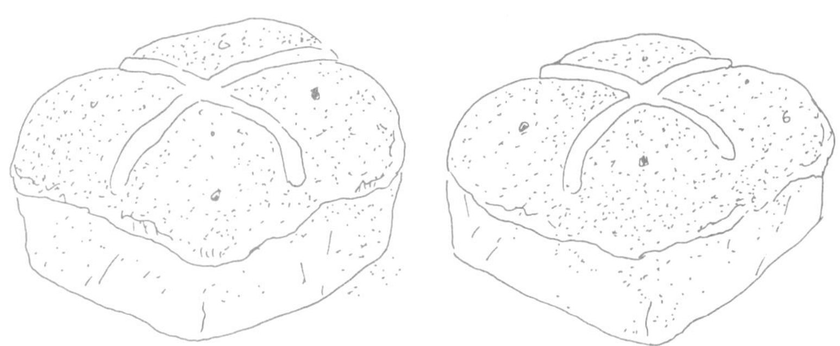

✦ CINNAMON SCROLLS ✦

Follow recipe for **Sweet yeast buns**. At step 7, roll dough into a rectangle approximately 20 cm x 30 cm. Spread dough with 2 tablespoons (40 g) brown sugar and 1 tablespoon (10 g) cinnamon. Roll up as for **Egg sponge roll** (p. 396) and cut into 12 slices.

✦ APPLE PLAIT ✦

Follow recipe for **Sweet yeast buns**, reserving 1 teaspoon egg for glaze. At step 7, roll dough into a rectangle approximately 20 cm x 30 cm on baking paper. Mix 1 diced Granny Smith apple, 1/2 cup (90 g) sultanas, 2 tablespoons (40 g) brown sugar and 1 teaspoon cinnamon, and spread down the centre of the dough leaving 5 cm dough around the filling on all sides. Using scissors, cut out corners of dough and cut strips 3 cm apart on the long side. Tuck in end pieces of dough and plait the strips across the loaf covering the filling. Place plait and baking paper on oven tray. Combine the reserved teaspoon of egg with 1 teaspoon water and brush plait. Bake at 220°C for 10 minutes then reduce to 200°C for 15–20 minutes, until golden brown. May be dusted with icing sugar.

Yeast breads and buns: tips for product quality

Quality criteria

- golden brown crust, crisp, and even thickness
- well-shaped loaf with a smooth, crisp surface
- light cream-coloured crumb, fine and even in texture, soft and spongy to touch
- sweet nutty flavour.

Texture open and uneven:

- too much liquid
- excess kneading
- over-proving.

Grey crumb, pale crust, sour taste:

- over-proving.

Strong smell of yeast in baked loaf:

- too much yeast
- over-proving.

Small dense loaf with close crumb:

- kneaded insufficiently to develop the gluten
- proving temperature too low
- proving time too short
- poor quality or old yeast.

18 Beverages

Beverages can be served as a summer cooler or a winter warmer, as a welcome on a social occasion or when taking a relaxing break from work.

A beverage is any liquid taken into the body to quench thirst, nourish, stimulate or refresh. Liquids are essential to the body as they help to regulate bodily processes and maintain good health. Water lost through excretion, including perspiration, must be replaced. The climate influences our need for fluid, causing us to drink more during the hot weather.

Types of beverages

Refreshing These are used to quench thirst and are mainly fruit and vegetable juices and drinks, aerated waters and cordials.

Nourishing These include milk drinks and thick soups. These may be quickly prepared with an electric blender.

Stimulating These include clear soups, tea, coffee and cocoa.

Food value

Refreshing beverages, if made from fresh fruit or vegetables, supply vitamin C, minerals, fibre, and carbohydrate from any sugar used for sweetening. Some commercial drinks have a high sugar content. Electric juice extractors may remove fibre from fruit and vegetables and for maximum vitamin retention the juices should be served as soon as they are extracted.
Nourishing beverages supply the body with vitamins, minerals, protein, carbohydrate and fat. They are often served to people who find it difficult to swallow and digest solid food.
Stimulating beverages have very little food value but stimulate the nervous system. Caffeine is the stimulant present in tea and coffee. Theobromine, present in cocoa, is a very mild stimulant, and for this reason cocoa is a satisfactory beverage for children.

FRUIT CORDIAL

Serves: ***about 50***

Ingredients

3 cups (750 g) sugar
1 tablespoon (20 g) citric acid
1 tablespoon (20 g) tartaric acid
3 lemons
3 oranges
1.5 L (6 cups) boiling water

Method

1. Place sugar and acids in a large basin.
2. Grate rind from lemons and oranges and add to sugar mixture.
3. Squeeze juice from lemons and oranges and add to mixture.
4. Pour boiling water over and stir until sugar is dissolved. Cool and bottle.
5. Before serving, dilute with iced water in the proportion of 1 part cordial to 4 parts water (1:4).

Will keep for 3–4 weeks in bottles in refrigerator.

ORANGE AND APRICOT PUNCH

► *Serves:* ***16***

Ingredients

2 cups (500 mL) orange juice
2 cups (500 mL) apricot nectar
1/2 cup (125 mL) lemon juice
1 L (4 cups) tea
1 L (4 cups) mineral water
1 orange, sliced

Method

1 Chill all ingredients.
2 Mix all ingredients together.
3 Serve cold.

CIDER CUP

► *Serves:* ***12***

Ingredients

2.5 L (10 cups) unsweetened cider
1 teaspoon (5 g) crushed fresh ginger
1/2 teaspoon cinnamon
juice of 1 lemon
1 apple

Method

1 Chill cider.
2 Mix cider, ginger, cinnamon and lemon juice.
3 Core apple, slice thinly and add to mixture.
4 Serve cold.

FRUIT CUP

► *Serves:* ***20***

Ingredients

1 L (4 cups) pineapple juice
2 L (4 cups) dry ginger ale
6 sprigs of mint
juice of 6 lemons
juice of 6 oranges
pulp of 6 passionfruit
1/2 cup diced fruit

Method

1 Chill all ingredients.
2 Mix all ingredients together.
3 Serve cold.

MULLED PINEAPPLE JUICE

Serves: 4

Ingredients

3 cups (750 mL) pineapple juice
5 cm cinnamon stick
1 tablespoon (20 mL) lemon juice

Method

1 Place pineapple juice and cinnamon stick in a saucepan and simmer for 2 minutes.
2 Remove cinnamon stick and add lemon juice.
3 Serve hot in warmed glasses.

HOT CHOCOLATE DRINK

Serves: 2

Ingredients

1 tablespoon (10 g) cocoa
2 teaspoons (10 g) brown sugar
2 cups (500 mL) low-fat milk

Method

1 Mix cocoa, sugar and 2 tablespoons (40 mL) milk.
2 Heat remaining milk in microwave oven (low power for 2 minutes).
3 Pour milk onto cocoa mixture. Mix well and serve.

✦ BANANA CHOCOLATE DRINK ✦

Follow recipe for **Hot chocolate drink**. Mash 1 ripe banana with the cocoa and sugar or place all ingredients in blender after heating milk. Reheat after blending.

FRUIT SMOOTHIE

Serves: 4

Ingredients

$1^3/_4$ cups (440 mL) milk
$^3/_4$ cup (190 mL) yoghurt
$1^1/_2$ cups (225 g) chopped fruit, e.g. strawberries, banana

Method

1 Chill all ingredients.
2 Mix all ingredients in blender.
3 Serve cold.

EGG FLIP

Serves: **1**

Ingredients

1 egg
$^1/_2$ teaspoon sugar (optional)
$^3/_4$ cup (190 mL) warm *or* cold milk
4 drops vanilla essence
nutmeg

Method

1 Beat egg, sugar, milk and vanilla essence in basin or electric blender.
2 Strain, pour into glass, sprinkle nutmeg on top, and serve.

BANANA FLIP

Follow recipe for **Egg flip**, adding 1 mashed banana in step 1. Do not strain.

BANANA NOG

Follow recipe for **Banana flip**, adding 2 tablespoons (40 g) ice-cream *or* yoghurt.

Tea

Tea is obtained from the *Thea sinesis* tree. The young leaves and shoots are used. Most tea is made from leaves that are allowed to ferment before being roasted and dried. Green tea is made from leaves that have been dried only.

Making tea

1 Bring water to boil.
2 Heat teapot with small amount of water and pour out.
3 Place 1 teaspoon of tea per cup in pot.
4 Pour boiling water over. Stand 3–4 minutes to extract flavour and colour (infusion).

Service

Black tea can be served with slice of lemon and sugar offered separately. White tea has a little milk added and sugar offered separately. Iced tea is strained and served chilled with a slice of lemon and a mint leaf.

Herbal infusions

Herbal infusions are made from dried herbs and spices and are infused in a similar way to tea. The herbs and spices are free from caffeine and provide an alternative to tea and coffee. Examples include cinnamon, chamomile, rose hip, lemon myrtle, clove, wattle seed, peppermint and mixtures of these. They may be served hot or iced.

Coffee

Coffee beans are obtained from the fruit of the evergreen shrub *Coffea arabica*. The flavour and strength of coffee beans differ considerably according to the variety of beans and time of roasting. Because of this, and individual preference, quantities given are for the average taste.

Making coffee

1 Select the variety of coffee beans and the grind (fine, medium, coarse) to suit your needs.
2 Keep ground coffee in an airtight container in refrigerator or grind beans as needed.
3 Do not boil coffee as an unpleasant bitter flavour develops.
4 Allow 2 teaspoons ground coffee per cup.

Coffee can be made using the following methods:

Plunger Measure finely ground coffee and place in coffee plunger, pour boiling water over, mix and cover. Stand 3–5 minutes. Push plunger down and serve.

Dripolator Water drips on to ground coffee and then through a fine filter.

Percolator Water below boiling point cycles through coffee in filter basket for 10 minutes.

Espresso Steam is forced through finely ground coffee to extract the flavour.

Service

Long black Made without milk.

Short black Highly concentrated black coffee made using less water.

Flat white Cold milk is added to strong black coffee.

Cappuccino Half black coffee and half milk that has been frothed by forcing steam through it.

Caffe latte or macchiato Hot milk is added to strong coffee.

Instant coffee Use 1 teaspoon instant coffee per cup. Decaffeinated instant coffee is available.

Coffee substitutes Contain no caffeine and may be made from a blend of chicory, barley or beetroot.

► *Serves:* **1**

Ingredients

1/3 cup (85 mL) strong black coffee (chilled)
1/2 cup (125 mL) milk
1/2 teaspoon sugar
1 ice cube
2 tablespoons (40 g) cream *or* ice-cream

Method

1 Pour coffee, milk and sugar in glass with ice cube.
2 Spoon cream *or* ice-cream on top. Serve.

19 Preserving fruits and vegetables

Home preserving foods when they are plentiful, less expensive and at peak quality can provide variety in the household menu and the opportunity to give gifts with a personal touch. Small jars of jam, pickles and bottled summer fruits can be quickly made using the microwave oven and decorated with colourful labels and cloth covers. Vinegars, with sprigs of aromatic herbs packed into tall bottles, make attractive gifts.

Seasonal fruit guide

Use fruit at the peak of the season for maximum flavour and cost efficiency. Controlled-atmosphere storage and refrigerated transport has extended the time when many fruits are available.

Stone fruits e.g. cherries, apricots, peaches, nectarines, plums. Different varieties of each stone fruit ripen at different times between November and March.

Berry fruits e.g. strawberries, raspberries, blackberries, blueberries. The locally grown season is November to late March. Strawberries and some other berry fruits are available at other times of the year, and are more expensive.

Pommes e.g. apples, pears, quinces, ripen during late summer but controlled-atmosphere storage extends their season.

Citrus e.g. locally grown oranges, lemons, grapefruit, cumquats, mandarins, are in season from late April to September. Imported fruits increase availability.

Tropical and other warm-climate fruits e.g. rockmelon (cantaloupe), paw-paw and mango, figs, feijoas, guavas, persimmons, tamarillos, passionfruit, grapes, bananas, pineapple, have a limited local season from November to March. They keep well under controlled conditions, which extends their availability.

Tomatoes are available all year but are cheapest and have maximum flavour from December to March, during their locally grown peak season. The low-acid varieties are not suitable for bottling, sauces or chutneys.

Fruit bottling

Bottling fruits when they are cheapest is an economical way of providing variety in the menu. Leftover fruits may be bottled in small amounts using the microwave oven. Fruit may be home-bottled using a preserving unit or microwave oven or by using boiled stewed fruit.

During the process of home bottling, spoilage organisms causing fermentation and putrefaction are destroyed. Most yeasts and moulds that cause fermentation, leading to off-flavour, are destroyed if subjected to a temperature of 82°C. Bacteria that cause putrefaction of food and pathogenic bacteria, e.g. *Clostridium botulinum*, cause food poisoning. Bacteria are not destroyed at temperatures that can be reached with home bottling unless a combination of heat and acid is used. For this reason only medium to high acid foods, that is fruits and tomatoes, should be preserved by home bottling. VEGETABLES HAVE A LOW ACID CONTENT AND MUST NOT BE HOME BOTTLED. Jars must be completely sealed to maintain the sterile state of the contents.

Equipment

Preserving unit Use any vessel with a lid that is deep enough to take the bottles. Units with an electric element and thermostatic control or intended for heating over a hot plate are available, e.g. Fowler's Vacola Preserving Outfit. A microwave oven may also be used (p. 000).

Bottles, rings and clips Glass bottles or jars with tightly fitting lids, sealed with an airtight ring between the jar and the lid, must be used. The jars, lids and rings must be unaffected by food acids, so that they do not corrode and allow the entry of air. Jars, rings and stainless steel lids manufactured especially for home bottling are recommended. Some types of bottles need clips to hold the lid and ring in position during processing, while others have screw lids to hold a metal and ring insert until sealed. The jars, lids and clips should be washed and completely dried after use and stored in a dry place. The rings should be replaced after each use.

Reusing jars Screw-top glass food jars, of the type in which sauces and pickles (such as the popular brands of pasta sauces, jams, tomato chutneys) are purchased, may be reused. These have metal lids with an attached sealing ring and a food acid resistant lacquer coating on the inside surface of the lid. Check that the sealing ring and lacquer coating are undamaged so that the jar seals on cooling. Wash jars and lids before use, scald by dipping in boiling water then drain just before filling. These jars are particularly successful in the microwave oven.

Other equipment A wooden spoon and spatula can be used for packing the fruit. Cherry and peach stoners and pear and pineapple corers are obtainable, or a teaspoon can be used to remove peach stones and pear cores.

Choice of fruit

- Fruit must be fresh with a well-developed colour and flavour and have firm-ripe flesh with minimum blemishes.
- Medium-acid fruits such as tropical fruits (e.g. rockmelon, paw-paw, mango) and figs should have 1/4 teaspoon citric acid *or* 1 tablespoon (20 mL) lemon juice added to each 500 g fruit to raise the acid content to a safe level.
- Choose fruit of an even size as the bottles are easier to pack, look more attractive and all of the fruit cooks at the same time.

Preserving liquids

MEDIUM SYRUP

Ingredients

1/2 cup (125 g) sugar
2 cups (500 mL) water

Method

1. Put sugar and water into saucepan. Cook over medium heat, stirring until sugar is dissolved. May be heated in microwave oven on high power, stirring regularly.
2. Bring to the boil and boil for 3 minutes.

Note: This makes a syrup in the proportions of 1 sugar:4 water.

✦ HEAVY SYRUP ✦

Follow recipe for **Medium syrup**, using 1 cup (250 g) sugar to 2 cups (500 mL) water (1 sugar:2 water).

✦ LIGHT SYRUP ✦

Follow recipe for **Medium syrup**, using 1/4 cup (65 g) sugar to 2 cups (500 mL) water (1 sugar:8 water).

Preserving unit fruit bottling

1. Prepare fruit. (See specific bottled fruit recipes beginning p. 460.)
2. Prepare preserving liquid. (See specific bottled fruit recipes beginning p. 460.)
3. Wash bottles, rings and lids or jars. (See note on reusing jars p. 457.)
4. Check that sealing rings are undamaged.
5. Using tongs, scald one batch of bottles, rings and lids by dipping in boiling water. Drain quickly so that bottles remain hot. Where necessary, place rings in position on bottles ensuring that they are not twisted.
6. Immediately pack fruit firmly into bottles.
7. Fill bottles with syrup. Tap bottles to ensure that there are no air pockets.
8. Place lids in position, attaching with clips or screwing on tightly.
9. Repeat steps 5–8 with each batch of bottles. Place bottles in preserving unit.
10. Pour in cold water to come just below lids.
11. Place thermometer in position if there is no thermostat. Place lid on preserving unit.
12. Heat slowly for approximately 45 minutes to 92°C.
13. MAINTAIN WATER TEMPERATURE AT 92°C FOR 45 MINUTES.
14. Remove bottles from preserving unit, stand on towel or several thicknesses of newspaper and immediately tighten screw-on lids.
15. When cold, wipe bottles clean. Remove clips if necessary.
16. Test the seal by turning upside down. If liquid escapes the bottle it is not sealed and must be reprocessed.
17. Label and store in a cool, dry place.
18. Store in refrigerator after opening. Best used within 12 months.

Stewed fruit bottling

Fruits may be bottled after stewing, although the result may not be as attractive as other methods.

1. Wash bottles, rings and lids or jars. (See note on reusing jars p. 457.)
2. Check that sealing rings are undamaged.
3. Prepare fruit. (See specific bottled fruit recipes beginning p. 460.)
4. Add other ingredients:

   Tomatoes Stir 1 tablespoon (20 g) salt into each kg of tomatoes.

   Berry fruits Stir $^{1}/_{4}$ cup (65 g) sugar into each 500 g fruit.

   Other fruits Add 1 cup (250 mL) water and $^{1}/_{4}$ cup (65 g) sugar or 1 cup (250 mL) ***Medium syrup*** (p. 457) to each 500 g fruit.
5. Cook fruit in saucepan or cook in covered dish in microwave oven on high power for 8–10 minutes until very soft.
6. Scald one bottle, ring and lid by dipping in boiling water. Drain quickly so that bottle remains hot. Where necessary, place ring in position on bottle, ensuring that it is not twisted.
7. Immediately fill the bottle with boiling fruit. Seal immediately with lid and clips or screw on lid tightly.

8 Repeat steps 5 and 6 with each bottle, standing filled bottles on towel or several thicknesses of newspaper.
9 Follow steps 15 to 18 for Preserving unit fruit bottling.

Microwave fruit bottling

1 Prepare fruit. (See specific bottled fruit recipes beginning p. 460.)
2 Prepare preserving liquid. (See specific bottled fruit recipes beginning p. 460.).
3 Wash bottles, rings and lids or jars. (See note on reusing jars p. 457.)
4 Check that sealing rings are undamaged.
5 Scald one bottle, ring and lid by dipping in boiling water. Drain quickly so that bottle remains hot. Where necessary, place ring in position on bottle, ensuring that it is not twisted.
6 Immediately pack fruit firmly into bottle.
7 Fill bottle with hot syrup. Tap bottle to ensure that there are no air pockets.
8 Place lid in position, attaching with clips or screwing on tightly.
9 Repeat steps 5–8 in batches of up to four bottles.
10 Place maximum of four bottles evenly spaced on ovenproof dish with handles or rim so that it can be easily lifted in and out of the microwave oven and the dish will catch the syrup overflow. Place in microwave oven. Do not allow bottles to touch each other or side of oven.
11 Cook on medium power as indicated in instructions for individual fruits.
12 Remove bottles from microwave oven. (If too much syrup has overflowed from jars, leaving fruit exposed, remove lid, top up with boiling syrup and reprocess for 1 minute.)
13 Stand on towel or several thicknesses of newspaper and immediately tighten screw-top lids.
14 When cold, wipe bottles clean. Remove clips if necessary.
15 Test for seal by turning upside down. If liquid escapes the bottle is not sealed and must be reprocessed.
16 Label and store in a cool, dry place.
17 Store in refrigerator after opening. Best used within 12 months.

Bottled apples

Varieties Cooking varieties, such as Granny Smith, retain their shape.

Preparation Peel, core and cut into even-sized pieces. Place in salted water to prevent discolouration, drain and rinse before placing in bottles. Use **Medium syrup** (p. 457) (1 sugar: 4 water).

Cooking Suitable for **Preserving unit fruit bottling, Microwave fruit bottling** and **Stewed fruit bottling**.

Microwave times for four bottles:

Bottles 300–500 mL: 12 minutes on medium power (6 minutes for one bottle and 2 minutes for each additional bottle).

Bottles 500–750 mL: 15 minutes on medium power (9 minutes for one bottle and 2 minutes for each additional bottle).

Bottles 750 mL–1 L: 18 minutes on medium power (12 minutes for one bottle and 2 minutes for each additional bottle).

Variations

Bottled apples and cinnamon Follow recipe for **Bottled apples**, adding 1/2 teaspoon cinnamon and juice and grated rind of 1/2 lemon to each 500 mL syrup.

Bottled apricots

Preparation Wash, cut in half and remove stone. Use **Light syrup** (p. 457) (1 sugar:8 water).

Cooking Suitable for **Preserving unit fruit bottling**, **Microwave fruit bottling** and **Stewed fruit bottling**.

Microwave times for four bottles:

Bottles 300–500 mL: 11 minutes on medium power (5 minutes for one bottle and 2 minutes for each additional bottle).

Bottles 500–750 mL: 14 minutes on medium power (8 minutes for one bottle and 2 minutes for each additional bottle).

Bottles 750 mL–1 L: 16 minutes on medium power (10 minutes for one bottle and 2 minutes for each additional bottle).

Variations

Bottled brandied apricots Follow recipe for **Bottled apricots**, adding 1/4 cup (65 mL) brandy to each 500 mL syrup.

Bottled berry fruits

Varieties Blackberries, blackcurrants, blueberries, boysenberries, loganberries, raspberries, strawberries.

Preparation Remove stem or calyx. If washed, drain well.

Cooking Add $^1/_4$ cup (65 g) sugar to 500 g berries and cook in covered bowl in microwave oven on high power, *or* in saucepan until sugar is dissolved, stirring at 1 minute intervals. Follow **Stewed fruit bottling** method (p. 458) from step 3, *or* **Microwave fruit bottling** method (p. 459) from step 3 using the following microwave times.

Microwave times for four bottles:

Bottles 300–500 mL: 5 minutes on medium power (2 minutes for one bottle and 1 minute for each additional bottle).

Bottles 500–750 mL: 9 minutes on medium power (3 minutes for one bottle and 2 minutes for each additional bottle).

Bottles 750 mL–1 L: 10 minutes on medium power (4 minutes for one bottle and 2 minutes for each additional bottle).

Variations

Bottled berries and pears Cook 250 g pears (peeled, cored and diced) with $^1/_2$ cup (125 mL) water and $^1/_2$ cup (125 g) sugar until soft in saucepan or microwave oven on high power for 5 minutes. Add 250 g berries and bring to boil. Follow **Stewed fruit bottling** method (p. 458) from step 3, *or* the **Microwave fruit bottling** method (p. 459) from step 3 using the microwave times given above.

Bottled cherries

Preparation Wash, remove stone if desired. Use **Medium syrup** (p. 457) (1 sugar:4 water).

Cooking Suitable for **Preserving unit fruit bottling**, **Microwave fruit bottling** and **Stewed fruit bottling**.

Microwave times for four bottles:

Bottles 300–500 mL: 9 minutes on medium power (3 minutes for one bottle and 2 minutes for each additional bottle).

Bottles 500–750 mL: 12 minutes on medium power (6 minutes for one bottle and 2 minutes for each additional bottle).

Bottles 750 mL–1 L: 14 minutes on medium power (8 minutes for one bottle and 2 minutes for each additional bottle).

Bottled cumquats

Preparation Wash and drain. Use **Heavy syrup** (p. 457) (1 sugar:2 water).

Cooking Suitable for **Preserving unit fruit bottling** and **Microwave fruit bottling**.

Follow microwave times for ***Bottled apricots***.

Variations

Bottled cumquats and brandy Follow recipe for **Bottled cumquats**. Add $^1/_4$ cup (65 mL) brandy to each 500 mL syrup.

Bottled nectarines

Preparation Wash, cut in half and remove stone. Use **Light syrup** (p. 457) (1 sugar:8 water).

Cooking Suitable for **Preserving unit fruit bottling**, **Microwave fruit bottling** and **Stewed fruit bottling**.

 *Follow microwave times for* ***Bottled apricots.***

Bottled passionfruit

Preparation Cut in half and remove pulp.

Cooking Add 1/4 cup (65 g) sugar to 500 g pulp and cook in covered bowl in microwave oven on high power for 2 minutes (stir at 1 minute) *or* in saucepan until sugar is dissolved. Pour into scalded bottles and follow **Stewed fruit bottling** method (p. 458) from step 3, *or* **Microwave fruit bottling** method (p. 459) from step 3.

 *Follow microwave times for* ***Berry fruits.***

Bottled peaches

Varieties Clingstone (e.g. Golden Queen) or Freestone.

Preparation Wash, cut in half and remove stone. Use **Medium syrup** (p. 457) (1 sugar:4 water).

Cooking Suitable for **Preserving unit fruit bottling**, **Microwave fruit bottling** and **Stewed fruit bottling**.

 *Follow microwave times for* ***Bottled apples.***

Bottled pears

Varieties Cooking varieties such as Williams, Beurre Bosc or Bartlett retain their shape.

Preparation Peel, core and cut into even-sized pieces. Place in salted water to prevent discolouration, drain and rinse before placing in bottles. Use **Medium syrup** (p. 457) (1 sugar:4 water).

Cooking Suitable for **Preserving unit fruit bottling**, **Microwave fruit bottling** and **Stewed fruit bottling**.

 *Follow microwave times for* ***Bottled apples.***

Variations

Bottled pears and cinnamon Follow recipe for **Bottled pears**, adding 1/2 teaspoon cinnamon and juice and grated rind of 1/2 lemon to each 500 mL syrup.

Bottled pineapple

Preparation Peel, cut and core pineapple. Cut into wedges *or* dice. Use **Light syrup** (p. 457) (1 sugar:8 water).

Cooking Suitable for **Preserving unit fruit bottling**, **Microwave fruit bottling** and **Stewed fruit bottling**.

 *Follow microwave times for* ***Bottled cherries.***

Bottled plums

Preparation Wash, cut in half and remove stone. Use **Medium syrup** (p. 457) (1 sugar:4 water).

Cooking Suitable for **Preserving unit fruit bottling**, **Microwave fruit bottling** and **Stewed fruit bottling**.

 *Follow microwave times for* ***Bottled apricots***.

Bottled quinces

Preparation Peel, core and cut into even-sized pieces. Place in salted water to prevent discolouration, drain and rinse before placing in bottles. Use **Heavy syrup** (p. 457) (1 sugar:2 water).

Cooking Suitable for **Preserving unit fruit bottling**, **Microwave fruit bottling** and **Stewed fruit bottling**.

 *Microwave times for four bottles:*

Bottles 300–500 mL: 16 minutes on medium power (7 minutes for one bottle and 3 minutes for each additional bottle).

Bottles 500–750 mL: 19 minutes on medium power (10 minutes for one bottle and 3 minutes for each additional bottle).

Bottles 750 mL–1 L: 25 minutes on medium power (13 minutes for one bottle and 4 minutes for each additional bottle).

Bottled tomatoes

Preparation Wash and drain. Remove core and cut small cross in round end. Dip into boiling water and remove skin. Cut in quarters. Stir 1 tablespoon (20 g) salt into 1 kg tomatoes. No preserving liquid is required.

Cooking Suitable for **Preserving unit fruit bottling**, **Microwave fruit bottling** and **Stewed fruit bottling**.

 *Follow microwave times for* ***Bottled apples***.

Jams, marmalades and jellies

Jams, marmalades and jellies should be clear and bright in colour with the consistency of a lightly set jelly and should be well-coloured and flavoured by the fruit used. They can be used as spreads on bread, toast and scones, and for fillings in pastry cases. The setting of jams, jellies and marmalades is dependent on the amount of pectin and acid in the fruit, and the amount of water and sugar added.

Equipment

Use a large, heavy-based saucepan or an ovenproof container in the microwave oven for making jams, jellies and marmalades. Glass jars may be used and covered after filling with paraffin wax, cellophane jam covers or plastic food wrap and screw-on lids. Screw-top glass food jars may be reused (see p. 457).

The jars and lids must be washed before use, scalded by dipping in boiling water and then drained just before filling. This ensures that they are clean and warm.

Choice of fruit

- Choose fruit that is in season, so that it is rich in colour and flavour. Fruit is well-matured and cheaper in the middle of the season (see seasonal fruit guide p. 455). Choose about half the fruit at the firm ripe stage to provide sufficient pectin for setting.
- If using medium-acid fruit, such as tropical fruits (e.g. rockmelon, paw-paw, mango, melons and figs), add 1/4 teaspoon citric acid or 1 tablespoon (20 mL) lemon juice to each 500 g fruit to provide the correct ratio of acid to pectin for setting.
- If using low-pectin fruit, such as kiwifruit, pineapple, cherries, tamarillos, figs, guavas, peaches, pears and persimmons, add commercial pectin during cooking. Pectin is a carbohydrate found in the cell wall of plants, which is released during cooking. It assists the preserve to set or form a 'gel' on cooling. If there is insufficient pectin the result is runny. It is present in the greatest proportion in fruits at the firm ripe stage.

Pectin test

The pectin content may be checked during cooking using the pectin test.

1. Remove 1 teaspoon of the cooked fruit pulp, cool and add to 1 tablespoon (20 mL) methylated spirits.
2. Shake gently, stand for 1 minute.
3. If the clot formed is in large pieces, there is sufficient pectin. If the clots are broken into many small pieces, commercial pectin mixture must be added. Follow instructions on the packet.

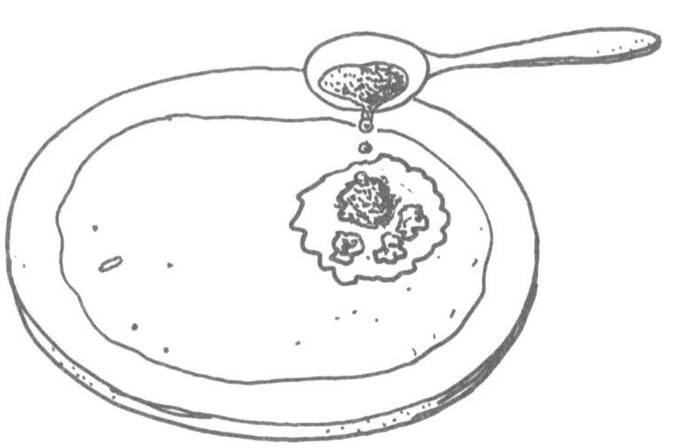

Gel test

This is used to test if the jam, jelly or marmalade is sufficiently cooked to set or 'gel'.

1 Dip wooden spoon in cooked mixture. When mixture drops (not runs) from the wooden spoon, place 1 teaspoon on plate.
2 Cool rapidly, such as over ice.
3 Tilt plate – if surface of mixture wrinkles it is cooked sufficiently to set.
4 A jam or confectionery thermometer may also be used. When mixture reaches 105°C it is cooked sufficiently to set.

Jams

Jam is made by boiling fruit pulp with sugar. Fresh fruit, preserved fruit pulp and some types of dried fruits such as apricots, may be used. If fruit is cut into small pieces the resulting mixture is called jam, but if fruit is left whole or in large pieces, it is called conserve. Fruits commonly used are apricots, plums, peaches, apples, pears, quinces, blackberries, gooseberries, raspberries, strawberries, black and red currants, melons and figs.

Cooking methods

If a recipe for a specific fruit is not included in this book then choose the method appropriate for the fruit:

- Most fruits used for jam making, particularly the firmer varieties, are cooked in water until soft, then equal amounts of cooked fruit and sugar, both measured by cup, are brought to the boil and cooked rapidly to 105°C.
- Soft fruits with a high water content, such as berry fruits, are added to an equal weight of sugar and cooked rapidly for a short time to retain their colour.
- Where the fruit is to remain in large pieces in the jam, called a conserve, the fruit and sugar are allowed to stand overnight and then cooked rapidly with the water. The cell walls of the fruit absorb the sugar through osmotic pressure and this prevents the fruit from breaking up while cooking.

APRICOT JAM

Ingredients

1 kg apricots
1 cup (250 mL) water
juice of 1 lemon
approximately 3 cups (750 g) sugar

Method

1 Prepare apricots; wash, drain, cut in half and remove stones.
2 Place water and apricots in saucepan, add lemon juice, bring to boil and cook for 5–10 minutes until cooked. Test for pectin (p. 464) and add 1 tablespoon (15 g) commercial pectin if necessary.
3 Measure cooked apricot pulp in cups. For every cup of pulp add 3/4 cup (190 g) sugar.
4 Bring quickly to boil, stirring continuously while sugar is dissolving.
5 Boil for 25–30 minutes, until gel test (p. 465) is satisfactory.
6 Scald washed jars and lids by dipping in boiling water and drain dry before bottling jam.
7 Cool jam slightly, pour into jars and cover.
8 Allow to become cold then wipe clean, label and store in a cool, dry place.

✦ NECTARINE JAM ✦

Follow recipe for **Apricot jam**, using 1 kg nectarines.

MICROWAVE APRICOT JAM

Ingredients

1 kg apricots
juice of 1 lemon
1/2 cup (125 mL) water
approximately 3 cups (750 g) sugar

Method

1 Prepare apricots: wash, drain, cut in half and remove stones.
2 Place apricots, lemon juice and water in covered dish and microwave on high power for 8 minutes. Test for pectin (p. 464) and add 1 tablespoon (15 g) commercial pectin if necessary.
3 Measure cooked apricot pulp in cups.
4 Reheat apricot pulp on high power.
5 For every cup of apricot pulp add 3/4 cup (190 g) sugar.
6 Microwave in uncovered dish on high power for 10–15 minutes, until gel test (p. 465) is satisfactory.
7 Scald washed jars and lids by dipping in boiling water and drain dry before bottling jam.
8 Cool jam slightly, pour into jars and cover.
9 Allow to become cold then wipe clean, label and store in a cool, dry place.

MICROWAVE NECTARINE JAM ✦

Follow recipe for **Microwave apricot jam**, using 1 kg nectarines.

PLUM JAM

Ingredients

1 kg plums
1 cup (250 mL) water
approximately 4 cups (1 kg) sugar

Method

1. Prepare plums; wash, drain, cut in half and remove stones.
2. Place water and plums in saucepan, bring to boil and cook for 5–10 minutes until cooked.
3. Measure cooked plum pulp in cups. For every cup of pulp add 1 cup (250 g) sugar.
4. Bring quickly to boil, stirring continuously while sugar is dissolving.
5. Boil for 15–20 minutes, until gel test (p. 465) is satisfactory.
6. Scald washed jars and lids by dipping in boiling water and drain dry before bottling jam.
7. Cool jam slightly, pour into jars and cover.
8. Allow to become cold then wipe clean, label and store in a cool, dry place.

✦ PLUM AND RASPBERRY JAM ✦

Follow recipe for **Plum jam**. Use 750 g plums, washed, drained and stones removed, and 250 g raspberries.

✦ FEIJOA JAM ✦

Follow recipe for **Plum jam**, using 1 kg feijoas.

✦ TAMARILLO JAM ✦

Follow recipe for **Plum jam**, using 1 kg tamarillos.

MICROWAVE PLUM JAM

Ingredients

1 kg plums
$^{1}/_{2}$ cup (125 mL) water
approximately 4 cups (1 kg) sugar

Method

1 Prepare plums: wash, drain, cut in half and remove stones.
2 Place plums and water in covered dish and microwave on high power for 8 minutes.
3 Measure cooked plum pulp in cups.
4 Reheat plum pulp on high power.
5 For every cup of plum pulp add 1 cup (250 g) sugar.
6 Microwave in uncovered dish on high power for 10–15 minutes, until gel test (p. 465) is satisfactory.
7 Scald washed jars and lids by dipping in boiling water and drain dry before bottling jam.
8 Cool jam slightly, pour into jars and cover.
9 Allow to become cold then wipe clean, label and store in a cool, dry place.

MICROWAVE PLUM AND RASPBERRY JAM ✦

Follow recipe for **Microwave plum jam**. Use 750 g plums, washed, drained and stones removed, and 250 g raspberries.

MICROWAVE FEIJOA JAM ✦

Follow recipe for **Microwave plum jam**, using 1 kg feijoas.

MICROWAVE TAMARILLO JAM ✦

Follow recipe for **Microwave plum jam**, using 1 kg tamarillos.

FIG JAM

Ingredients

1 kg figs
1 cup (250 mL) water
grated rind and juice of 2 lemons
approximately 3 cups (750 g) sugar
1 tablespoon (15 g) commercial pectin mixture

Method

1. Prepare figs: wash, drain, remove stalks and slice.
2. Place water, lemon juice and figs in saucepan, bring to boil and cook for 5–10 minutes, until cooked.
3. Measure cooked fig pulp in cups. For every cup of pulp add 3/4 cup (190 g) sugar. Add pectin and lemon rind.
4. Bring quickly to boil, stirring continuously while sugar is dissolving.
5. Boil for 25–30 minutes, until gel test (p. 465) is satisfactory. During cooking, remove scum containing seed as it rises.
6. Scald washed jars and lids by dipping in boiling water and drain dry before bottling jam.
7. Cool jam slightly, pour into jars and cover.
8. Allow to become cold then wipe clean, label and store in a cool, dry place.

FIG AND GINGER JAM

Follow recipe for **Fig jam**, adding 2 tablespoons (50 g) grated fresh ginger.

MICROWAVE FIG JAM

Ingredients

1 kg figs
1/2 cup (125 mL) water
grated rind and juice of 2 lemons
approximately 3 cups (750 g) sugar
1 tablespoon (15 g) commercial pectin mixture

Method

1. Prepare figs: wash, drain, remove stalks and slice.
2. Place figs, lemon juice and water in covered dish and microwave on high power for 5 minutes.
3. Measure cooked fig pulp in cups.
4. Reheat fig pulp on high power.
5. For every cup of fig pulp add 3/4 cup (190 g) sugar. Add pectin and lemon rind.
6. Microwave in uncovered dish on high power for 10–15 minutes, until gel test (p. 465) is satisfactory.
7. Scald washed jars and lids by dipping in boiling water and drain dry before bottling jam.
8. Cool jam slightly, pour into jars and cover.
9. Allow to become cold then wipe clean, label and store in a cool, dry place.

RASPBERRY JAM

Ingredients

500 g raspberries
2 cups (500 g) sugar

Method

1. Prepare raspberries: remove stems. Wash only if necessary and drain well.
2. Place raspberries and sugar in saucepan. Stir continuously while bringing rapidly to boil.
3. Cook rapidly for 6 minutes until gel test (p. 465) is satisfactory.
4. Scald washed jars and lids by dipping in boiling water and drain dry before bottling jam.
5. Cool jam slightly, pour jam into jars and cover.
6. Allow to become cold then wipe clean, label and store in a cool, dry place.

✦ BLACKBERRY JAM ✦

Follow recipe for **Raspberry jam**, using 500 g blackberries. At step 2 cook for 8 minutes.

✦ STRAWBERRY JAM ✦

Follow recipe for **Raspberry jam**, using 500 g strawberries. At step 2 add juice of 1 lemon and 1 tablespoon (15 g) commercial pectin mixture and at step 3 cook for 8 minutes.

MICROWAVE BERRY JAM ✦

Follow recipe for **Raspberry jam**, **Blackberry jam** or **Strawberry jam**. At step 2, place berries and sugar in uncovered dish and microwave on high power for 8–10 minutes, stirring every 2 minutes, until gel test (p. 465) is satisfactory. If using strawberries, add juice of 1 lemon and 1 tablespoon (15 g) commercial pectin mixture.

PEACH AND PINEAPPLE CONSERVE

A conserve is jam where the fruit remains in firm large pieces.

Ingredients

2 cups (300 g) diced pineapple
2 cups (300 g) diced yellow peaches
2 cups (500 g) sugar
1 cup (250 mL) water
1 tablespoon (15 g) commercial pectin mixture

Method

1 Cover peeled and diced fruit with sugar and allow to stand overnight.
2 Place fruit, water and pectin in saucepan and bring quickly to boil, stirring continuously. Boil for 30–35 minutes, until gel test (p. 465) is satisfactory.
3 Scald washed jars and lids by dipping in boiling water and drain dry before bottling jam.
4 Cool conserve slightly, pour in jars and cover.
5 Allow to become cold then wipe clean, label and store in a cool, dry place.

✦ APRICOT AND PINEAPPLE CONSERVE ✦

Follow recipe for **Peach and pineapple conserve**, using 300 g apricots instead of peaches.

✦ DRIED APRICOT AND PINEAPPLE CONSERVE ✦

Follow recipe for **Peach and pineapple conserve**, using 100 g diced dried apricots, soaked in 2 cups (500 g) warm water for 2 hours instead of peaches.

MICROWAVE PEACH AND PINEAPPLE CONSERVE ✦

Follow recipe for **Peach and pineapple conserve**, using 1/2 cup (125 mL) water only. At step 2 place fruit and pectin in covered dish in microwave oven on high power for 10 minutes, stirring every 2 minutes, until gel test (p. 465) is satisfactory.

Marmalade

The name 'marmalada' is of Portuguese origin from the word 'marmelo', a quince, which was, in the 15th century, the most common fruit used in jam making. The name is now used only for preserves made from citrus fruits. Fruit used for marmalade include grapefruit, Poor-man's oranges, Seville oranges and other sweet oranges, cumquats, lemons and limes.

Preparation of fruit

If a recipe for a specific fruit is not included in this book then choose the method appropriate for the fruit:

Slice finely skin, pith and pulp. Use for fruits with a transparent pith after cooking: grapefruit, cumquat, Poor-man's orange, Seville orange.

Peel and slice rind, slice thinly. Remove pith and chop. Slice pulp thinly. Tie pith and pips in muslin bag. Use for fruits with cloudy, opaque pith after cooking: Navel and Valencia oranges, lemon, lime.

Mince for a quick, but less attractive result, remove pips then mince skin, pith and pulp.

Ingredients

500 g grapefruit
500 g Seville *or* Poor-man's oranges
1 L (4 cups) water
approximately 4 cups (1 kg) sugar

Method

1. Wash and dry fruit.
2. Halve fruit horizontally and remove pips and centre pith. Soak pips in some of the water to extract pectin. Strain and add liquid to fruit at step 4.
3. Prepare fruit by finely slicing the skin, pith and pulp.
4. Cover with the water and stand for 2–3 hours to extract pectin.
5. Simmer this mixture until skins are soft and pith is transparent, about 45 minutes. If skins are not soft, they will be tough in the finished marmalade.
6. Measure cooked pulp in cups. For every cup of pulp add 1 cup (250 g) sugar.
7. Bring to boil and stir until sugar has dissolved.
8. Boil rapidly for about 20 minutes, until gel test (p. 465) is satisfactory.
9. Scald washed jars and lids by dipping in boiling water and drain dry before bottling marmalade.
10. Cool marmalade slightly, pour into jars and cover.
11. Allow to become cold, then wipe clean, label and store in a cool, dry place.

✦ ORANGE MARMALADE ✦

Follow recipe for **Marmalade**, using 1 kg Valencia *or* Navel oranges. At step 3 peel rind, slice thinly, remove pith and chop, slice pulp thinly and tie pith and pips in muslin bag. The pith remains cloudy and opaque. Grated rind and juice of 1 lemon may be used.

MICROWAVE MARMALADE

Ingredients

250 g grapefruit
250 g Seville *or* Poor-man's oranges
2 cups (500 mL) water
approximately 3 cups (750 g) sugar

Method

1. Wash and dry fruit.
2. Halve fruit horizontally and remove centre pith and pips. Soak pips in some of water to extract pectin. Strain and add liquid to fruit at step 4.
3. Prepare fruit by finely slicing the skin, pith and pulp. Cover with the water and stand for 2–3 hours to extract pectin.
4. Cook in covered dish in microwave oven on high power for 5–10 minutes, until skins are soft and pith is transparent. If skins are not soft, they will be tough in the finished marmalade.
5. Measure cooked marmalade pulp in cups.
6. Reheat marmalade pulp on high power.
7. For every cup of marmalade pulp add 1 cup (250 g) sugar.
8. Microwave in uncovered dish on high power for 15–18 minutes, until gel test (p. 465) is satisfactory.
9. Scald washed jars and lids by dipping in boiling water and drain dry before bottling marmalade.
10. Cool marmalade slightly, pour into jars and cover.
11. Allow to become cold, then wipe clean, label and store in a cool, dry place.

MICROWAVE CUMQUAT MARMALADE ✦

Follow recipe for **Microwave marmalade**, using 500 g cumquats.

MICROWAVE ORANGE MARMALADE ✦

Follow recipe for **Microwave marmalade**, using 500 g Valencia *or* Navel oranges. At step 3 peel rind, slice thinly, remove pith and chop, slice pulp thinly and tie pith and pips in muslin bag. The pith remains cloudy and opaque. Grated rind and juice of 1 lemon may be used.

Jelly

Jellies are made by boiling the strained extract of well-cooked fruit with sugar. Fruits that can be used for jelly making include apples, crab apples, japonica fruits, quinces, citrus fruits (e.g. cumquats and lemons), blackberries and raspberries. Fruits can also be combined, for example, blackberry and apple, raspberry and apple.

APPLE JELLY

Ingredients

2 kg apples (e.g. Granny Smith)
1.5 L (6 cups) water
approximately 4 cups (1 kg) sugar

Method

1. Wash fruit and cut up roughly without peeling or coring.
2. Cover fruit with water, bring to the boil and cook until fruit is soft, approximately 45 minutes.
3. Make extract by allowing apple pulp to strain through scalded jelly bag over a basin, to catch extract. (Jelly bags made from a fine material attached to a frame on a stand may be purchased *or* use a fine cotton tea towel in a colander or large strainer.) Do not squeeze the bag or the result will be cloudy.
4. Measure extract. Allow 1 cup (250 mL) extract to 1 cup (250 g) sugar
5. Bring extract to the boil, remove from heat and add sugar. Stir over low heat until dissolved then boil rapidly, until gel test (p. 465) is satisfactory.
6. Scald washed jars and lids by dipping in boiling water and drain dry before bottling jelly.
7. Cool slightly, then bottle. Pour jelly slowly into jars from a height of not more than 3 cm above the top of the jar. This prevents the intake of air that may cloud the jelly. Cover.
8. Allow to become cold, then wipe clean, label and store in a cool, dry place.

✦ QUINCE JELLY ✦

Follow recipe for **Apple jelly**, using 2 kg quinces. Longer cooking time may be required.

✦ BERRY AND APPLE JELLY ✦

Follow recipe for **Apple jelly**, using 1.5 kg apples and 500 g berries.

✦ CUMQUAT JELLY ✦

Follow recipe for **Apple jelly**, using 2 kg cumquats.

✦ GUAVA JELLY ✦

Follow recipe for **Apple jelly**, using 2 kg guavas.

✦ CRAB APPLE JELLY ✦

Follow recipe for **Apple jelly**, using 2 kg crab apples.

✦ PERSIMMON JELLY ✦

Follow recipe for **Apple jelly**, using 2 kg persimmons.

✦ MINT JELLY ✦

Follow recipe for **Apple jelly**, using 1.25 L (5 cups) water.
After gel test (p. 465) is satisfactory add 1/2 cup (125 mL) vinegar and 1 cup chopped mint.
Boil 2 minutes, cool and bottle.

MICROWAVE APPLE JELLY

Ingredients

1 kg cooking apples (e.g. Granny Smith)
2 cups (500 mL) water
approximately 4 cups (1 kg) sugar

Method

1 Wash fruit and cut up roughly without peeling or coring.
2 Cook fruit and water in covered dish in microwave oven on high power for 5–10 minutes, until very soft.
3 Make extract by allowing apple pulp to strain through scalded jelly bag over a basin, to catch extract. (Jelly bags made from a fine material attached to a frame on a stand may be purchased *or* use a fine cotton tea towel in a colander or large strainer.)
4 Measure extract in cups.
5 Reheat extract on high power.
6 For every cup of extract add 1 cup (250 g) sugar.
7 Microwave in uncovered dish on high power for 20–25 minutes, until gel test (p. 465) is satisfactory.
8 Scald washed jars and lids by dipping in boiling water and drain dry before bottling jam.
9 Cool jelly slightly, pour into jars and cover.
10 Allow to become cold then wipe clean, label and store in a cool, dry place.

MICROWAVE FRUIT JELLY ✦

Follow recipe for **Microwave apple jelly**, using different fruits to make **Quince jelly**, **Berry and apple jelly**, **Cumquat jelly**, **Guava jelly**, **Crab apple jelly**, **Persimmon jelly** or **Mint jelly**.

Jams, marmalades and jellies: tips for product quality

Quality criteria

- full flavour of fruit
- free from mould
- free from sugar crystals
- firm and set – holds shape on spoon
- bright colour, jellies should be clear
- fruit evenly distributed
- free from air bubbles.

Dull cloudy appearance:
- under-ripe fruit
- overripe fruit
- too much pectin in proportion to acid and sugar
- insufficient acid present in fruit
- badly strained extract
- poured into jars from too great a height above rim of jar.

Unsatisfactory gel test:
- insufficient pectin present
- insufficient sugar used in proportion to the amount of pectin present
- too much sugar
- insufficient cooking after sugar was added
- overcooked: dark in colour, especially marmalade, with a syrupy consistency.

Crystallisation:
- covering fruit with too much sugar when allowed to stand overnight
- too much sugar
- allowed to boil before all sugar is dissolved
- overcooking
- jelly stirred after it has boiled.

Mould on surface:
- fruit mushy because it was overripe or picked in damp weather
- insufficient sugar, also gives a tough rubbery consistency to jelly
- jam not cooked sufficiently to evaporate excess water
- containers were not dry
- left too long before sealing
- insufficient care when sealing
- place of storage not suitable.

Fermentation:
- insufficient sugar used
- insufficient cooking of jam.

Shredded skin tough:
- insufficient boiling of marmalade before sugar is added.

Poor colour and flavour:
- under-ripe fruit.

Pickles, sauces, relishes and chutneys

Pickles, sauces, relishes and chutneys are preserved fruits and vegetables in vinegar and served as an accompaniment to savoury dishes. They give variety to the menu and stimulate the appetite. Many pickles, sauces, relishes and chutneys have a strong flavour so they should be served in small quantities.

Herbs, garlic or other foods which have not been dried should not be added to oils and then stored as food-poisoning bacteria will develop in the food.

Ingredients

Vegetables and fruits commonly used include beans, beetroot, red and green cabbage, carrots, cauliflower, celery, red and green tomatoes, Chinese radish, cucumber, capsicums or peppers, chillies, gherkins, black and green olives, apricots, apples, gooseberries, grapes, green walnuts, plums, dried fruits, e.g. sultanas and currants.

Vinegar is used as the main preservative. Hot vinegar softens the cellulose of vegetables and under-ripe fruits. Cold vinegar retains the crispness of the pickled vegetables. Use vinegar of the best available quality, either white or brown according to preference. Cider vinegar, made from apples, and malt vinegar, made from malted cereals, are usually fermented and matured in vats before being bottled. Herbs, such as tarragon, may be added to vinegar to give particular flavours.

Spices used include cayenne, cloves, cinnamon, ginger, mace, mustard, nutmeg, pepper, pimento or allspice and turmeric. Turmeric is also used as a colouring agent. Mixtures of pickling spices are available.

Sugar is used in varying proportions to give slightly sweet flavours, and to soften the sharpness of vinegar. It also acts as a preservative.

Salt may be used dry, or as a solution called brine. Salt is used as a preservative and as a seasoning. Soaking pickling vegetables and fruits in brine or salt allows some of the liquid and bitter flavours to be drawn out. After soaking they should be thoroughly rinsed in several changes of cold water to remove excess salt.

Brine is made by dissolving 1 cup (250 g) salt in 4 cups (1 L) water.

Utensils

Metal utensils, except stainless steel, should be avoided as much as possible, because vinegar and brine both attack metal surfaces, causing corrosion. This may flavour the food, and causes rust and pitting on the surface of the utensils. Stainless steel, plastic, china, wood or enamel utensils should be used. Use glass or earthenware jars for bottling. Plastic food wrap, cork or cellophane covers may be used for sealing. Screw-top glass food jars may be reused (see p. 457).

Pickles

These are usually uncooked fruits and vegetables preserved in vinegar which may be flavoured with salt and spices or sugar and spices.

SPICED VINEGAR

Spiced vinegar may be used to pickle mixed vegetables, onions, zucchini and other vegetables.

Ingredients

1 L (4 cups) vinegar
1/4 cup (65 g) sugar
1 teaspoon chopped fresh ginger
1 clove (5 g) garlic, minced
2 teaspoons peppercorns
1 teaspoon pimento (allspice)
1 teaspoon cloves
1 teaspoon mustard seeds
1 teaspoon nutmeg
1 teaspoon salt

Method

1. Place all ingredients in saucepan and bring to the boil.
2. Simmer for 5 minutes and strain before using.
3. Sufficient for 2 kg prepared vegetables.

VEGETABLE PICKLES

Ingredients

1 cup (250 g) salt
1 L (4 cups) water
approximately 1 kg vegetables,
e.g. cabbage, cauliflower, carrots, red capsicum, green tomatoes, onions
1/2 quantity **Spiced vinegar**

Method

1. Make brine by dissolving salt in water.
2. Prepare vegetables: wash, peel if necessary, cut into small pieces.
3. Soak vegetables in brine for 1 day.
4. Drain and wash salt from vegetables.
5. Place vegetables and spiced vinegar in saucepan and bring to the boil. Immediately remove from heat.
6. Scald washed jars and lids by dipping in boiling water and drain dry before bottling pickles.
7. Allow to cool. Pour into jars and cover.
8. Allow to become cold, then wipe clean, label and store in a cool, dry place.

ZUCCHINI PICKLES

Ingredients

1 kg zucchini, sliced
1 kg onions, sliced
2 tablespoons (40 g) salt
1 cup (250 g) sugar
2 teaspoons mustard seeds
1 teaspoon celery seeds
1/2 teaspoon turmeric
2 cups (500 mL) cider vinegar

Method

1. Place zucchini and onions in large bowl, sprinkle with salt and cover with water. Allow to stand for 2 hours.
2. Drain and rinse well.
3. Add sugar, mustard seeds, celery seeds and turmeric. Add vinegar and stand for 2 hours.
4. Place in pan, bring to the boil, stirring occasionally. Cook for 5 minutes.
5. Scald washed jars and lids by dipping in boiling water and drain dry before bottling pickles.
6. Allow to cool. Pour into jars and cover.
7. Allow to become cold, then wipe clean, label and store in a cool, dry place.

SPICED PLUMS

Ingredients

350 g small firm red plums
2 cups (500 mL) vinegar
1 1/2 cups (375 g) sugar
3 cm cinnamon stick
3 cloves
1/8 teaspoon nutmeg

Method

1. Wash plums and place in basin.
2. Combine all other ingredients in saucepan, bring to the boil and simmer for 15 minutes.
3. Pour mixture over plums immediately and allow to stand for 3 days.
4. Place plums and vinegar mixture in pan, bring slowly to the boil and simmer gently for 5 minutes.
5. Scald washed jars and lids by dipping in boiling water and drain dry before bottling plums.
6. Cool, pack plums into jars, being careful not to break skins. Add vinegar mixture to cover plums. Cover jars.
7. Allow to become cold, then wipe clean, label and store in a cool, dry place.

PICKLED ONIONS

Pickled onions are made with small brown onions, known as pickling onions.

Ingredients

1 cup (250 g) salt
1 L (4 cups) water
1 kg pickling onions
3 cups (750 mL) **Spiced vinegar** (p. 479)

Method

1 Prepare brine by dissolving salt in water.
2 Peel onions, place in brine and allow to stand for 1–2 days. Turn occasionally with a wooden spoon.
3 Wash onions thoroughly, removing all traces of salt.
4 Place onions and spiced vinegar in a pan and bring to the boil and immediately remove from heat.
5 Scald washed jars and lids by dipping in boiling water and drain dry before bottling onions.
6 Allow to cool. Pack onions into jars, fill with vinegar and cover.
7 Allow to become cold, then wipe clean, label and store in a cool dry place.

MIXED MUSTARD PICKLES

Ingredients

1 cup (250 g) salt
1 L (4 cups) water
approximately 1 kg vegetables, e.g. cabbage, cauliflower, carrot, beans, green tomatoes, onions
$^1/_4$ teaspoon ground allspice
4 shakes cayenne
1 tablespoon (10 g) ground mustard
1 cup (250 g) sugar
1 teaspoon turmeric
1 teaspoon curry powder
3 cups (750 mL) vinegar

Method

1 Make brine by dissolving salt in water.
2 Prepare vegetables: wash, peel if necessary, cut into small pieces.
3 Soak vegetables in brine for 1 day.
4 Drain and wash salt from vegetables.
5 Blend dry ingredients with a small amount of vinegar.
6 Combine with vegetables and remainder of vinegar. Bring to boil in saucepan, stirring all the time. Remove from heat immediately.
7 Scald washed jars and lids by dipping in boiling water and drain dry before bottling pickles.
8 Pour into jars and cover.
9 Allow to become cold, then wipe clean, label and store in a cool, dry place.

Sauces

These are made from fruit and vegetables that have been cooked until very soft, and then strained. The consistency of the usual varieties made in the home should be that of a pouring sauce or thick gravy.

TOMATO SAUCE

Ingredients

5 kg tomatoes (not low-acid variety)
1 clove (5 g) garlic, chopped
6 pimento (allspice)
2 teaspoons mustard seeds
12 cloves
1/8 teaspoon cayenne
2 1/2 cups (625 mL) vinegar
2 tablespoons (20 g) salt
1 1/2 cups (375 g) sugar

Method

1. Wash and drain tomatoes. Cut each in half.
2. Cook tomatoes, spices and garlic in saucepan until tomatoes are very soft. Stir frequently.
3. Strain pulp through sieve or colander.
4. Return to saucepan, add remaining ingredients and cook, stirring frequently for 1 1/2 hours until correct consistency, when a small quantity of sauce placed on a plate has no liquid separating from solids.
5. Scald washed jars by dipping in boiling water and draining just before bottling sauce.
6. Pour into three 750 mL bottles and cover.
7. Allow to become cold, then wipe clean, label and store in a cool, dry place.

PLUM SAUCE

Ingredients

1 kg plums
3 cups (750 mL) vinegar
2 cups (500 g) sugar
2 teaspoons salt
1 1/2 tablespoons (45 g) cloves
1/8 teaspoon cayenne
2 teaspoons ground ginger

Method

1. Wash and drain plums. Remove stones.
2. Place in saucepan with vinegar, bring to boil and cook for 45 minutes.
3. Add all other ingredients and cook rapidly for 1 hour. Stir frequently.
4. Strain through a colander or sieve.
5. Scald washed jars and lids by dipping in boiling water and drain dry before bottling sauce.
6. Bring sauce to boil, pour into bottles and cover.
7. Allow to become cold, then wipe clean, label and store in a cool, dry place.

Relishes

These are cooked for only a short time and are thickened with flour.

APRICOT RELISH

Ingredients

1.5 kg apricots
500 g onions, diced
1 tablespoon (10 g) salt
6 cloves
6 pimento (allspice)
1/8 teaspoon cayenne
2 1/2 cups (625 mL) vinegar
1/2 cup (125 g) golden syrup
1 cup (250 g) sugar
2 teaspoons turmeric
2 teaspoons plain flour

Method

1. Wash and drain apricots. Remove stones and cut up roughly.
2. Sprinkle apricots and onions with the salt.
3. Place cloves, pimento and cayenne in saucepan with vinegar, golden syrup and sugar and bring to the boil.
4. Add apricots and onions and cook 45 minutes.
5. Blend turmeric and flour with a little cold water and stir into mixture. Bring to the boil again and cook for 3 minutes.
6. Scald washed jars by dipping in boiling water and drain dry before bottling relish.
7. Allow to cool. Pour into jars and cover.
8. Allow to become cold, then wipe clean, label and store in a cool, dry place.

GREEN TOMATO RELISH

Ingredients

500 g green tomatoes
650 g onions, sliced
2 teaspoons salt
$^1/_4$ teaspoon ground allspice
4 shakes cayenne
1 tablespoon (10 g) ground mustard
1 cup (250 g) sugar
$^1/_4$ cup (40 g) plain flour
1 teaspoon turmeric
1 teaspoon curry powder
3 cups (750 mL) vinegar

Method

1. Wash and slice tomatoes.
2. Sprinkle tomatoes and onions with the salt. (May be left overnight.)
3. Mix other dry ingredients with a little of the vinegar.
4. Place remainder of vinegar and vegetables in a saucepan, and heat until boiling, stirring frequently. Cook 1 minute.
5. Add blended ingredients and stir until boiling. Cook 2 minutes and remove from heat.
6. Scald washed jars by dipping in boiling water and drain dry before bottling relish.
7. Allow to cool. Pour into jars and cover.
8. Allow to become cold, then wipe clean, label and store in a cool dry place.

TOMATO RELISH

Ingredients

1.5 kg tomatoes (not low-acid variety)
500 g onions, sliced
2 teaspoons salt
$2^1/_2$ cups (625 mL) vinegar
2 cups (500 g) sugar
1 tablespoon (10 g) cloves
1 tablespoon (10 g) ground mustard
1 tablespoon (10 g) plain flour
$^1/_8$ teaspoon cayenne

Method

1. Wash, peel and chop tomatoes.
2. Sprinkle tomatoes and onions with the salt. (May be left overnight.)
3. Place 2 cups vinegar in saucepan, add sugar and cloves, bring to the boil and cook 5 minutes.
4. Add tomatoes and onions, bring to the boil again and cook for 20 minutes. Stir frequently.
5. Blend mustard, flour and cayenne with remaining vinegar. Add to tomato mixture, stir until boiling and cook 5 minutes.
6. Scald washed jars and lids by dipping in boiling water and drain dry before bottling.
7. Pour into jars and cover.
8. Allow to become cold, then wipe clean, label and store in a cool, dry place.

Chutneys

The name comes from the Indian word 'chutnee'. Chutneys were originally introduced from India, where mango is the basic ingredient. Chutney may be served as an accompaniment to curried meats and vegetables and with cold cooked meat and poultry. Chutney is made by cooking fruits and vegetables for a long time in flavoured vinegar. The consistency should be similar to a jam or conserve.

APPLE CHUTNEY

Ingredients

1 kg apples
500 g onions, sliced
2 cups (500 mL) vinegar
12 pimento (allspice)
1 tablespoon (30 g) cloves
2 teaspoons salt
$^{1}/_{8}$ teaspoon cayenne
$1^{1}/_{2}$ cups (375 g) sugar
1 cup (180 g) sultanas

Method

1. Peel, core and dice apples.
2. Put all ingredients in saucepan, cook $1^{1}/_{2}$ hours, stirring frequently.
3. Scald washed jars and lids by dipping in boiling water and draining just before bottling chutney.
4. Pour into jars and cover.
5. Allow to become cold, then wipe clean, label and store in a cool, dry place.

PLUM CHUTNEY

Ingredients

1 kg plums
250 g onions, sliced
12 cloves
1 teaspoon mustard seeds
$^{1}/_{8}$ teaspoon cayenne
2 teaspoons chopped fresh ginger
1 small chilli
$2^{1}/_{2}$ cups (625 mL) vinegar
$^{3}/_{4}$ cup (190 g) sugar

Method

1. Wash plums and remove stones.
2. Put all ingredients except sugar in saucepan, cook 45 minutes, stirring frequently.
3. Add sugar, stir until boiling and cook 20 minutes. Stir frequently. Remove chilli.
4. Scald washed jars and lids by dipping in boiling water and drain dry before bottling chutney.
5. Pour into jars and cover.
6. Allow to become cold, then wipe clean, label and store in a cool, dry place.

TOMATO CHUTNEY

Ingredients

1.5 kg tomatoes (not low-acid variety)
250 g onions, diced
1 clove (5 g) garlic, chopped
$2^{1}/_{2}$ cups (625 mL) vinegar
$1^{1}/_{2}$ cups (270 g) sultanas
6 cloves
$^{1}/_{8}$ teaspoon cayenne
1 tablespoon (10 g) salt
$1^{1}/_{2}$ cups (375 g) sugar

Method

1. Peel and chop tomatoes.
2. Put all ingredients except sugar in saucepan, stir until boiling and cook until mixture thickens, about $1^{1}/_{2}$ hours.
3. Add sugar, stir until boiling and cook for a further 30 minutes, stirring frequently until mixture does not separate. To test correct consistency, a small quantity of sauce placed on a plate has no liquid separating from solids.
4. Scald washed jars and lids by dipping in boiling water and drain dry before bottling chutney.
5. Pour into jars and cover.
6. Allow to become cold, then wipe clean, label and store in a cool, dry place.

MICROWAVE TOMATO CHUTNEY ✦

Follow recipe for **Tomato chutney**, using 2 cups (500 mL) vinegar. At step 2 cook all ingredients in covered dish in microwave oven on high power for 10 minutes. At step 3 cook in uncovered dish in microwave oven on medium power for 15–20 minutes. Stir occasionally.

Other preserves

DRIED HERBS

Ingredients

100 g fresh herbs

Method

1 Tie stems in small bunches and place in paper bags with the opening firmly tied around the stems.
2 Dry in a current of air, in residual heat in oven *or* on low power in microwave oven.
3 When dry strip the leaves from stems and store in airtight container.

CANDIED PEEL

Ingredients

400 g citrus fruit skins with pith, e.g. 1 grapefruit, 1 orange, 2 lemons, cut into 1 cm wide strips
2 teaspoons bicarbonate soda
1 cup (250 mL) water
$1^1/_2$ cups (375 g) sugar

Method

1 Wash and dry skins.
2 Dissolve bicarbonate of soda in 1 L boiling water. Add skins and soak for 20 minutes. Drain and rinse.
3 Place skins in fresh water, bring to the boil and simmer until tender. Drain.
4 Make a syrup of 1 cup (250 mL) water and 1 cup (250 g) sugar, bring to the boil. Soak skins in syrup for 2 days.
5 Add $^1/_2$ cup (125 g) sugar to syrup and skins and bring to the boil. Simmer until skins become clear. Lift from syrup, reserving it.
6 Place skins on cake cooler over tray overnight.
7 Bring syrup back to the boil, dip skins into it and place on cake cooler over tray to dry.
8 Cut peel finely for cakes and puddings or in strips for dipping in chocolate.
9 Store in refrigerator for up to 4 weeks.

✦ CHOCOLATE CANDIED PEEL ✦

Follow recipe for **Candied peel**. When peel is dry, melt 150 g chocolate. Dip each piece of peel into chocolate, being careful to completely cover it. Allow to dry on waxed or baking paper. Re-dip if peel is not completely covered.

HERB VINEGAR

Ingredients

1–2 cups herbs, e.g. tarragon, thyme, chives, sage, basil, rosemary
2 cups (500 mL) cider vinegar

Method

1. Crush herbs to release flavouring oils, place in glass jar.
2. Cover with vinegar, seal and allow to stand for 2–3 weeks.
3. Scald washed jars and lids by dipping in boiling water and drain dry just before bottling vinegar.
4. Strain into bottles. Add a sprig of herb used. Seal.

OVEN-DRIED TOMATOES

Ingredients

2 kg small tomatoes

Method

1. Wash and drain tomatoes.
2. Cut each in half and place cut side up on oven tray.
3. Place in oven at 120°C for 4 hours or until quite dry.
4. Store in airtight jar.
5. May be covered with spiced vinegar and a little olive oil and stored in refrigerator.

✦ OVEN-DRIED CAPSICUMS ✦

Follow recipe for **Oven-dried tomatoes**, using 250 g capsicums, seeded and cut into strips.

MUSTARD

Ingredients

$^{3}/_{4}$ cup (125 g) yellow mustard seeds
1 teaspoon sugar
$^{3}/_{4}$ cup (165 mL) white wine vinegar *or* cider vinegar
$^{1}/_{2}$ cup (125 mL) olive oil
1 teaspoon salt

Method

1. Mix all ingredients and refrigerate overnight.
2. Mix in food processor for 30 seconds, until blended, but not smooth.
3. Place in sterilised jars. Keep in refrigerator.

LEMON BUTTER

Ingredients

$^1/_3$ cup (85 g) butter
1 cup (250 g) sugar
2 eggs (61 g), beaten
rind and juice of 2 lemons

Method

1 Place butter and sugar in top of double saucepan, mix. Blend in eggs, then add lemon rind and juice.
2 Place over water simmering in base of the double saucepan. Stir occasionally until mixture thickens, approximately 20–30 minutes.
3 Scald small washed jars and lids by dipping in boiling water and drain dry.
4 Cool lemon butter, place in jars and seal. Keeps for 2–3 weeks.

PASSIONFRUIT BUTTER

Follow recipe for **Lemon butter**. Omit lemon rind. Add pulp of 4 passionfruit. Store in refrigerator.

LEMON SPREAD

Follow recipe for **Lemon butter**. Omit butter. Store in refrigerator.

FROZEN VEGETABLES

Requirements

Vegetables, e.g. green beans, green peas, broad beans, cauliflower florets, broccoli
plastic freezer bags
ties
labels

Method

1 Wash and prepare vegetables as for cooking.
2 Bring large saucepan of water to the boil. Place 1 cup of vegetables in sieve, dip into boiling water, bring water back to boiling point. Remove vegetables.
3 Plunge vegetables immediately into cold water. Drain. Pack into bags in quantity sufficient for a family meal. Repeat steps 2 and 3 until all vegetables are used.
4 Expel as much air as possible from the bag, tie and seal. Label and date.
5 Turn freezer to lowest setting and freeze vegetables as rapidly as possible. Return to normal setting after freezing is complete.

Appendix 1

Glossary

Accompaniment Sauce or side dish that is traditionally served with a specific food.

Adzuki beans Small red-brown legume used in Asian cakes. Also called feijao beans.

Agar Extract from sea plant. Similar to gelatine, although gel is more stable.

Aioli A mayonnaise made from garlic, olive oil, lemon juice and egg yolk.

À la carte Menu where dishes are individually priced.

Al dente Italian term that translates to 'on the teeth', referring to the texture of cooked pasta, meaning cooked through, but firm.

Allergies Adverse reaction to protein foods by the body's immune system. See also Sensitivities.

Andouille sausage French sausage made with tripe.

Angostura bitters West Indian mixture of herbs and spices including quinine, which gives a bitter flavour. Used in drinks.

Aspic Stock with high gelatine content that sets and is used to glaze savoury foods.

Au gratin Cooked food covered with sauce, breadcrumbs, and butter, browned under a griller.

Au naturel Food served raw.

Baba Yeast cake from Russia, also known as savarin.

Bagel Donut-shaped bread roll. The dough is boiled before being baked.

Baguette Long thin bread stick, also known as French stick.

Bain-marie Heated serving table or vessel for keeping food hot.

Baklava Middle Eastern or Greek pastry made from filo filled with nuts, sugar and cinnamon, then soaked in a sugar syrup.

Ballotine Meat boned, stuffed and cooked whole. May be sliced for serving.

Beignet Deep fried fritter.

Besan flour See Chickpea flour.

Bierwurst German smoked sausage.

Bijon noodles Noodles made from corn.

Bilton Dried beef strips, also known as beef jerky.

Biryani Spicy rice dish with meat or fish, from India.

Black pudding English sausage, made from pig's blood, oatmeal and spices.

Black-eyed beans Quick-cooking small white legume with black spot.

Blanquette White stew of veal or other white meat.

Bleached flour Flour whitened by oxidising agents to remove the yellow pigment.

Boiling point Water reaches boiling point at 100° C. Boiling liquid bubbles briskly.

Bombay duck Salted and dried bummaloe fish, crumbled over curry.

Bonito Tuna used for Japanese dishes.

Borlotti beans Speckled brown-pink legume, used in Italian dishes.

Bouillabaisse Mediterranean fish stew.

Bourguignon Stew of meat cooked with red wine, onions and mushrooms, from France.

Brandade Pounded salt cod mixed with olive oil and garlic.

Bratwurst German sausage of pork, veal, bacon and spices.

Brawn Variety of meats and seasonings cooked, chopped and allowed to set in their own jelly.

Brewer's yeast Yeast used in the brewing of beer.

Brioche Small yeast bun made with egg. May be filled with sweet or savoury filling.

Bromelin Enzyme from pineapple that breaks down protein and is used to tenderise meat.

Burrito See Tortilla.

Cabanossi Russian smoked spicy sausage.

Calvados Apple brandy.

Canellini beans White oval legume that needs to be soaked and well cooked.

Capers Unopened buds of a Mediterranean shrub that are pickled and served with savoury dishes.

Carnauba wax From Brazilian wax palm. Hardest wax known and used in food glazes.

Carob Cocoa substitute from the carob tree.

Carpaccio Finely sliced raw beef with olive oil, served as an entree.

Cassava Root of tropical plant; starchy extract is made into tapioca.

Cassoulet Stew of meat, beans, garlic and onions from the south of France.

Caul Lacy fat membrane that lines abdomen of lamb, used to wrap meat dishes.

Caviar Eggs or roe of sturgeon fish caught in the Black and Caspian seas. Beluga (large, black) is the best. Others include Oseitra (smaller, grey-brown) and Sevruga (green-black).

Cellophane noodles Thin transparent noodles made from ground mung bean starch paste. Used in Asian cookery and may be fried or boiled.

Chanterelle Wild orange or yellow mushroom from France.

Chantilly cream Whipped cream with sugar and vanilla essence.

Chapatti Indian flat bread often made from chickpeas.

Chaud-froid sauce White sauce or mayonnaise with gelatine, used for decorating savoury foods.

Chianti Italian table wine.

Chickpeas Light brown, round legume. Soak for 24 hours before cooking. Also known as garbanzos.

Chickpea flour Flour ground from chickpeas, also known as besan flour and gram flour.

Chiffonnade Very finely sliced leaf vegetables, such as lettuce.

Chinois Conical strainer with fine mesh.

Chipolata Small sausage.

Chorizo Hot, smoked Spanish pork sausage flavoured with chilli.

Cioppino Italian seafood and tomato stew.

Clafouti Dessert of fruit covered with cake mixture then baked.

Cochineal Red colouring extracted from the dried bodies of the female insect *Dactylopius coccus*.

Cocoa butter Fat from roasted cocoa nibs, hard at room temperature.

Condiment Spice, seasoning or highly flavoured sauce, usually served at the table.

Cornichon Tiny pickled gherkin.

Coulibiac Russian fish pie, served hot.

Coulis Puree of a fruit or vegetable, used as a sauce.

Court bouillon Water, lemon and herbs used for cooking fish.

Crème brûlée Rich custard covered with caramelised sugar.

Crème fraiche Cream with bacterial culture to make it thick, with a tart taste. Can be made using 1 cup cream and 1 tablespoon natural yoghurt, keeping it at room temperature overnight.

Crème patisserie Thick, rich custard, used as a filling in pastries.

Creole Cooking style from New Orleans, usually containing tomatoes and capsicum.

Croquette Ball or roll of minced food, coated with breadcrumbs and fried.

Croustade Case made of bread, pastry or other food and deep-fried before filling.

Croute Slice of bread, fried or toasted.

Csabai Spicy Hungarian sausage, made from pork and red wine.

Cuisine French word for cookery.

Damper Scone dough made from flour, water and salt, traditionally baked in hot coals by early European settlers in Australia.

Dariole mould Small deep cylindrical container used for cooking food.

Daube Stew of meat braised in red wine and herbs or spices, in a sealed casserole.

Demerara sugar A light-brown crystallised cane sugar, originally from Demerara, Guyana.

Dhal Indian legume puree eaten with rice.

Dolmades Vine leaves wrapped around a rice, lamb and herb mixture, from Greece and Turkey.

Duxelles Finely chopped mushrooms sauteed with onions and herbs.

En casserole Foods cooked and served in a casserole.

Enchiladas Mexican spicy bean, meat, onion and tomato mixture wrapped in cornmeal pancakes.

Entree Course that precedes the main course.

Escalope Thin slice of meat cut from leg, flattened and fried.

Farce Mixture of finely chopped foods used as filling or stuffing to flavour foods.

Fava beans Broad beans.

Feijao beans See adzuki beans.

Fines herbes Mixture of fresh herbs.

Five-spice powder Mixture of ground spices, usually star anise, pepper, cinnamon, cloves and fennel, used in Asian cooking.

Flageolet beans Small, green quickly cooked legume, used in salads.

Foie gras Pâté made from livers of geese fed large quantities of fat.

Fondue Dish prepared from melted cheese into which food on skewers is dipped, then eaten.

Forcemeat Finely chopped meat used as stuffing or seasoning.

Frankfurt Smoked sausage, usually with red skin.

French toast Sliced bread dipped in an egg and milk mixture and fried in butter.

Fritter Food dipped in batter and deep fried.

Fritto misto Small pieces of several different foods dipped in batter and fried.

Galantine Dish of meat rolled, cooked, pressed, glazed and served cold.

Galette Flat sweet or savoury food made with a pastry, meringue or potato base, with a topping.

Garbanzos See Chickpeas.

Gari Japanese pickled ginger.

Gateau Rich cake, elaborately decorated.

Gefillte fish Jewish dish made from minced fish, matzo meal and egg.

Glacé fruit Fruit preserved in sugar solution.

Glutamic acid An amino acid from which MSG is derived. See Monosodium glutamate (MSG).

Gougere Choux pastry cooked in a ring and filled with a savoury or sweet mixture.

Gougon Small strips of fish, crumbed and deep fried.

Goulash Thick meat stew, flavoured with vegetables and paprika, of Hungarian origin.

Gnocchi Italian pasta style dish, made using a potato and egg mixture which is then boiled and served in a sauce.

Gram flour See Chickpea flour.

Gravlax Raw salmon cured with salt and sugar.

Gremolata Chopped lemon, garlic and parsley, sprinkled over food to add flavour.

Griddle cakes Batter cooked on flat iron griddle pan.

Grissini Thin, crisp Italian bread sticks.

Gumbo Stew based on the vegetable okra, from southern America.

Haggis Scottish dish made from oatmeal, chopped heart and liver, placed in sheep's stomach and boiled.

Halal Method of slaughtering animals in accordance with Muslim rites.

Halva Sweet Middle Eastern dish made from spices, semolina and nuts or seeds.

Hangi Maori feast or Maori oven in which food is steamed over hot coals in the ground.

Haricot beans Small white oval legume, also called navy beans.

Hash browns Grated potato made into patties and fried.

Hearts of palm Stem of the cabbage tree palm.

Hijike Dried, black seaweed used in Japanese dishes.

Hoisin sauce Savoury sauce made from soy beans, used in Asian dishes.

Hummus See **Hommus** (p. 81).

Hush puppies Fried patties made from cornmeal and onions. Originally from southern America.

Hydrolysed vegetable protein Flavour enhancer from vegetable proteins, contains MSG.

Infusion Flavoured liquid produced by soaking a substance in boiling liquid.

Jerky Sun-dried meat strips.

Julienne Food, usually vegetables, cut to match-size pieces.

Junket Dessert made by setting milk with rennet.

Jus lie Gravy made from pan juices, thickened.

Kedgeree Indian dish of rice, smoked fish and hard-boiled eggs.

Kefir Fermented camels' milk.

Kibbeh Middle Eastern dish made from minced meat and cracked wheat.

Kidney beans Dull red, kidney-shaped legume, used in chilli con carne.

Kilocalorie Old unit used to express the energy value of foods – we now use kilojoule.

Kimchi Fermented vegetables served in Korea.

Kirsch Liqueur distilled from cherries.

Kobe beef Top grade of beef produced in Japan from cattle that are fed sake and beer.

Kombu Dark green seaweed used in Japanese dishes. Soak 30–40 minutes before using.

Kosher foods Foods produced to the dietary laws of the Jewish faith. Includes ritual slaughtering methods, and no contact between meat and dairy products in food preparation.

Legumes Dried peas and beans, also known as pulses. Rich in protein, therefore popular for vegetarian dishes.

Lentils Small, dried seeds of peas. Quickly cooked and good source of protein.

Lima beans Small, green-white legume, originating in Peru, used in salads, soups and casseroles.

Liverwurst Liver and pork pâté.

Loading Cereals or dried beans used in pastry cases during cooking. See baking blind p. 352.

Maître d'Hôtel butter See **Savoury butter** (p. 175).

Manioc See Cassava.

Maraschino Distilled liqueur from fermented maraschino cherries.

Marron Freshwater crayfish found in Western Australia.

Marzipan Mixture of ground almonds, sugar and egg white, used in cakes and confectionery.

Mascarpone Fresh unripened Italian cheese with slightly sweet taste, used in desserts.

Matzo Unleavened bread eaten during the Jewish feast of Passover.

Mead Wine made from honey.

Melba toast Thinly sliced bread, baked to golden brown and served with soups, pâtés.

Meringue Beaten egg white and sugar.

Mille feuilles Layers of puff pastry with sweet or savoury filling.

Mirepoix Chopped vegetables used as base for cooking pot roasts or braise.

Mirin Japanese fermented rice wine.

Mise en place Preparation of food and equipment prior to meal service.

Miso Fermented soya bean product, used in Japanese dishes.

Mocha Coffee flavour, or a combination of coffee and chocolate used as flavouring.

Modified starch Starch treated chemically to increase solubility, stability and texture.

Monosodium glutamate or MSG A salt derived from glutamic acid, found naturally in many foods, such as tomatoes. Some people may have a reaction or sensitivity to MSG when used as an added flavour enhancer.

Mortar Small, heavy bowl in which foods are pounded with a pestle.

Mulligatawny Spicy curry-flavoured Indian soup.

Mung beans Tiny green legume which may be eaten in sprouted form.

Naan Indian flat bread made with yeast and yoghurt.

Nachos Mexican dish made from corn chips and melted cheese.

Nasi goreng Indonesian dish of fried rice with meat, fish, onion, egg and garlic.

Navarin French stew of lamb, potatoes, onions and root vegetables.

Navy beans See Haricot beans.

Nitrous oxide gas Gas used as a propellant in some canned whipped toppings.

Nori Seaweed dried into flat sheets, used for making sushi rolls.

Nuoc mam Vietnamese fish sauce, made from dried, salted fermented fish.

Okara By-product from making tofu, used in a similar way to tofu.

Ouzo Greek distilled spirit flavoured with anise.

Panada *or* ***panade*** Thick binding sauce.

Pancetta Italian bacon cured with salt and spices.

Panettone Sweet Italian cake made with yeast, sultanas and candied peel.

Papain Protein-digesting enzyme from papaya fruit, used as a meat tenderiser.

Pappadams Indian lentil flat bread, cooked in oil.

Parma ham Salt-cured ham from Parma region, Italy.

Passover Annual Jewish celebration of deliverance from Egypt, during which leavened foods are forbidden.

Pastrami Beef cured with spices and salt, often used in sandwiches.

Pastis Aniseed-flavoured alcoholic drink from France.

Paupiette Thin slice of meat, spread with stuffing, rolled and fried or simmered in liquid.

Pemmican Dried and pounded buffalo or deer meat, made into cakes with fat and dried fruit, originally by the American Indians.

Peperoni Spicy pork and beef sausage, flavoured with garlic, often used in pizzas.

Pepitas Roasted pumpkin seeds.

Pesto Paste of basil, olive oil, garlic, pine nuts and dry grated cheese.

Petit fours Tiny cakes, iced and decorated.

Piccalilli East Indian spiced vegetable and mustard pickle.

Pide Flat Turkish bread.

Pinto beans Pale yellow speckled pink-beige legume, turning deep pink on cooking. Must be well cooked. Used mainly in Mexican dishes.

Piperade French dish of tomatoes, capsicum and eggs beaten over heat to aerate.

Piroshki Small savoury filled cases of pastry originating in Russia.

Pistou Mixture of basil, garlic and olive oil, used to flavour savoury dishes.

Poi Hawaiian dish fermented from the taro root.

Powdered sugar Finely ground sugar, called icing sugar or confectioners' sugar.

Praline Caramelised sugar and almond mixture.

Pregelatinised starch Starch that has been processed to allow swelling and absorption in cold liquid.

Pressure cooker Vessel for cooking food under pressure, so that it cooks more quickly.

Prosciutto High quality, very lean cured ham.

Quenelle Light dumpling made from egg and seafood or poultry.

Quinine Bitter flavour from the cinchona tree, often used in drinks such as tonic water.

Quorn Fungi-based textured vegetable protein, used as a meat substitute.

Ragoût French stew.

Ramadan Annual fast for Muslims, during which no food is consumed between dawn and dusk.

Remoulade Mayonnaise mixed with herbs and pickled vegetables.

Rennet Milk coagulant extracted from the enzyme rennin in the stomach of cows. Used in cheese and junket making.

Rhum baba Yeast cakes from Russia, soaked in rum after cooking.

Rice noodles Noodles made from rice flour, used in Asian dishes.

Rice paper Edible paper made from rice flour, used to wrap sticky confectionery and Asian foods.

Rillettes Meat and spices cooked, then pressed in bowl to set in refrigerator. Served cold, sliced.

Rosti Swiss national dish of crisp potato cake.

Sabayon Sweet, foamy sauce made from egg yolks, sugar and wine, served with desserts.

Sake Japanese fermented rice wine.

Salpicon Mixture of finely diced vegetables or fruit used as filling or topping.

Salami Sausage made from pork, beef and spices and hung to dry.

Salsa Mexican spicy sauce consisting of finely chopped raw vegetables with flavourings.

Sambal Hot spicy sauce used as an accompaniment to curries.

Samosa Tiny Indian pasties filled with spicy meat or vegetables.

Sashimi Japanese dish of raw fish and wasabi.

Sauerkraut Fermented cabbage.

Savarin See Baba.

Scallion Variety of small onion.

Scaloppine Thin slice of veal, fried and served with a tomato or wine sauce.

Scampi Very small lobster that live in the sand at the bottom of the sea.

Sensitivities Adverse reaction to non-protein-based foods by the body's immune system. See also Allergies.

Silicon dioxide Anti-caking agent used in foods. It can absorb up to 120% of its weight and remain free flowing.

Sippets Dry toast cut into neat pieces.

Skordalia Mixture of sieved, cooked potato, crushed garlic, lemon juice and olive oil, used as accompaniment to foods.

Sliver Long thin strip of food.

Slivovitz Dry plum brandy from Hungary.

Soba Japanese noodles made from buckwheat.

Soya beans Small, light brown legume, made into many soy-based products. Contains over 40% protein, all the essential amino acids and 18% polyunsaturated oil.

Spanikopita Greek filo pastry filled with spinach and fetta cheese.

Succotash North American Indian dish of sweet corn and lima beans.

Sudza Traditional African dish made of cornmeal.

Sushi Japanese dish using cooked rice and other ingredients wrapped in nori.

Tabasco Mexican sauce made of fermented capsicums.

Table d'hôte Set price menu, sometimes with choices for each course.

Taco Mexican fried cornmeal pancake, or tortilla, often filled with spicy kidney beans, chilli and other fillings.

Tahine Paste made from ground sesame seeds, used in Middle Eastern dishes; may be called tahini.

Tallow Animal fat from mutton and beef.

Tandoori Indian blend of spices including garam masala used to flavour food.

Tandoor oven Cylindrical clay oven heated by a wood or charcoal fire used in Indian cooking.

Tandoori paste Yoghurt and spicy sauce spread over foods before cooking in tandoor oven.

Tapas Savoury snacks, originating in Spain.

Tapenade Paste of black olives, garlic, and lemon juice.

Tapioca Starchy grains from the root of the cassava plant, used in desserts and as a thickener.

Taramasalata Greek mixture of cod roe (tarama), garlic and lemon.

Taro Tuber used to make poi.

Tempeh Firm-textured block of partially cooked, fermented soya beans. Can be marinated and roasted, grilled, fried or steamed.

Tempura Japanese dish of meat, seafood or vegetables fried in a special light batter.

Tepid Lukewarm, the same temperature as blood (37° C).

Textured Vegetable Protein (TVP) Processed vegetable protein usually from soya beans.

Timbale Food cooked in a small deep mould.

Tofu Curd formed when soya beans are soaked, ground, heated and coagulant added. Has a bland taste that will readily take up other flavours.

Tortellini Small pasta pouches filled with cooked meat, seafood or vegetables.

Tortilla Mexican pancake made from ground white corn, fried to make tacos.

Truffles Edible fungi which is very expensive, used in savoury dishes.

Verjuice Sour juice of unripe fruits, used in salad dressing.

Vermouth Italian wine flavoured with herbs and spices.

Vindaloo Indian meat curry in which vinegar is used to give a slightly sour taste.

Wasabi Green-coloured hot horseradish paste, served with Japanese dishes.

Zabaglione Italian dish made by whisking egg yolks, marsala and sugar over hot water.

Zest Thin outside skin of citrus fruits.

Appendix 2

Weights and measures

Commodity (whole in brackets)	1 Tablespoon	1 cup	¾ cup	⅔ cup	½ cup	⅓ cup	¼ cup
almonds, ground	10 g	100 g	75 g	65 g	50 g	40 g	25 g
apple (125 g), purée	20 g	200 g	150 g	135 g	100 g	70 g	50 g
arrowroot	10 g	130 g	100 g	90 g	65 g	45 g	35 g
bacon (80 g), chopped	15 g	180 g	135 g	120 g	90 g	60 g	45 g
baking powder	10 g	130 g	100 g	90 g	65 g	45 g	35 g
beans, dried	15 g	200 g	150 g	135 g	100 g	70 g	50 g
beans, fresh	10 g	120 g	90 g	80 g	60 g	40 g	30 g
beanshoots	10 g	100 g	75 g	65 g	50 g	40 g	25 g
bicarbonate of soda	10 g	130 g	100 g	90 g	65 g	45 g	35 g
biscuit crumbs	10 g	120 g	90 g	80 g	60 g	40 g	30 g
bran	10 g	90 g	65 g	60 g	45 g	35 g	25 g
breadcrumbs, dried	10 g	90 g	65 g	60 g	45 g	35 g	25 g
breadcrumbs, fresh	5 g	40 g	30 g	25 g	20 g	12 g	10 g
butter	20 g	250 g	190 g	165 g	125 g	85 g	65 g
cabbage, shredded		100 g	75 g	65 g	50 g	40 g	25 g
cake crumbs	5 g	60 g	45 g	40 g	30 g	20 g	15 g
capsicum (125 g), diced	10 g	120 g	90 g	80 g	60 g	40 g	30 g
carrot (125 g), diced	12 g	150 g	110 g	100 g	75 g	50 g	40 g
cauliflower, florets		120 g	90 g	80 g	60 g	40 g	30 g
celery (125 g), sliced	12 g	150 g	110 g	100 g	75 g	50 g	40 g
cheese	20 g	250 g	190 g	165 g	125 g	85 g	65 g
cheese, grated	10 g	120 g	90 g	80 g	60 g	40 g	30 g

Commodity (whole in brackets)	1 Table-spoon	1 cup	3/4 cup	2/3 cup	1/2 cup	1/3 cup	1/4 cup
chicken, cooked, chopped	12 g	150 g	110 g	100 g	75 g	50 g	40 g
chicken, uncooked, chopped	20 g	220 g	165 g	160 g	110 g	80 g	55 g
chocolate, grated	8 g	90 g	65 g	60 g	45 g	35 g	25 g
chutney	20 g	250 g	190 g	165 g	125 g	85 g	65 g
citric acid	10 g	130 g	100 g	90 g	65 g	45 g	35 g
cocoa	10 g	130 g	100 g	90 g	65 g	45 g	35 g
coconut	8 g	90 g	70 g	60 g	45 g	30 g	25 g
coconut milk powder	10 g	100 g	75 g	65 g	50 g	40 g	25 g
coffee, instant	5 g	60 g	45 g	40 g	30 g	25 g	15 g
corn, kernels	12 g	150 g	110 g	100 g	75 g	50 g	40 g
cornflakes	5 g	30 g	25 g	20 g	15 g	10 g	8 g
cornflour	10 g	130 g	100 g	90 g	65 g	45 g	35 g
couscous	15 g	200 g	150 g	135 g	100 g	70 g	50 g
cracked wheat	8 g	90 g	65 g	60 g	45 g	35 g	25 g
cream	20 mL	250 mL	190 mL	165 mL	125 mL	85 mL	65 mL
cream cheese	20 g	250 g	190 g	165 g	125 g	85 g	65 g
cream of tartar	10 g	130 g	100 g	90 g	65 g	45 g	35 g
cucumber, (125 g) diced	12 g	150 g	110 g	100 g	75 g	50 g	40 g
custard powder	10 g	130 g	100 g	90 g	65 g	45 g	35 g
dried fruit	15 g	180 g	135 g	120 g	90 g	60 g	45 g
egg white (40 g)	20 g	250 g	190 g	165 g	125 g	85 g	65 g
egg yolk (20 g)	20 g	250 g	190 g	165 g	125 g	85 g	65 g
flour	10 g	150 g	110 g	100 g	75 g	50 g	40 g
fruit puree	20 g	200 g	150 g	135 g	100 g	70 g	50 g
gelatine	12 g	150 g	110 g	100 g	75 g	50 g	40 g
ginger, fresh, chopped	20 g	150 g	110 g	100 g	75 g	50 g	40 g
glucose, liquid	25 g	330 g	250 g	220 g	165 g	110 g	80 g
golden syrup	20 g	250 g	190 g	165 g	125 g	85 g	65 g

Commodity (whole in brackets)	1 Table-spoon	1 cup	3/4 cup	2/3 cup	1/2 cup	1/3 cup	1/4 cup
honey	20 g	250 g	190 g	165 g	125 g	85 g	65 g
jam	20 g	250 g	190 g	165 g	125 g	85 g	65 g
leek (100 g), diced	10 g	120 g	90 g	80 g	60 g	40 g	30 g
lentils	15 g	200 g	150 g	135 g	100 g	70 g	50 g
mayonnaise	20 mL	250 mL	190 mL	165 mL	125 mL	85 mL	65 mL
meat, cooked, chopped	12 g	150 g	110 g	100 g	75 g	50 g	40 g
meat, uncooked, chopped	20 g	220 g	165 g	160 g	110 g	80 g	55 g
milk	20 mL	250 mL	190 mL	165 mL	125 mL	85 mL	65 mL
milk powder	10 g	100 g	75 g	65 g	50 g	40 g	25 g
mushrooms, sliced	10 g	100 g	65 g	75 g	50 g	40 g	25 g
nuts, chopped	15 g	120 g	90 g	80 g	60 g	40 g	30 g
nuts, whole	10 g	100 g	75 g	65 g	50 g	40 g	25 g
oil	20 mL	250 mL	190 mL	165 mL	125 mL	85 mL	65 mL
onion (125 g), diced	12 g	150 g	110 g	100 g	75 g	50 g	40 g
parsnip (125 g), diced	12 g	150 g	110 g	100 g	75 g	50 g	40 g
pasta, uncooked	10 g	100 g	75 g	66 g	50 g	33 g	25 g
pasta, cooked	20 g	200 g	150 g	135 g	100 g	70 g	50 g
peas, dried	15 g	200 g	150 g	135 g	100 g	70 g	50 g
peas, fresh	12 g	150 g	110 g	100 g	75 g	50 g	40 g
peel, mixed	12 g	150 g	110 g	100 g	75 g	50 g	40 g
polenta	12 g	150 g	110 g	100 g	75 g	50 g	40 g
potato (125 g), diced	12 g	150 g	110 g	100 g	75 g	50 g	40 g
pumpkin, diced	12 g	150 g	110 g	100 g	75 g	50 g	40 g
rice, uncooked	15 g	200 g	150 g	135 g	100 g	70 g	50 g
riceflour	10 g	130 g	100 g	90 g	65 g	45 g	35 g

Commodity (whole in brackets)	1 Tablespoon	1 cup	¾ cup	⅔ cup	½ cup	⅓ cup	¼ cup
rolled oats	10 g	100 g	75 g	65 g	50 g	40 g	25 g
salt	20 g	250 g	190 g	165 g	125 g	85 g	65 g
seafood, cooked, chopped	12 g	150 g	110 g	100 g	75 g	50 g	40 g
seafood, uncooked, chopped	20 g	220 g	165 g	160 g	110 g	80 g	55 g
sesame seeds	12 g	150 g	110 g	100 g	75 g	50 g	40 g
snow peas		100 g	75 g	65 g	50 g	40 g	25 g
spices	10 g	130 g	100 g	90 g	65 g	45 g	35 g
sugar	20 g	250 g	190 g	165 g	125 g	85 g	65 g
sugar, brown	15 g	180 g	135 g	120 g	90 g	60 g	45 g
sugar, caster	20 g	250 g	190 g	165 g	125 g	85 g	65 g
sugar, icing	15 g	180 g	135 g	120 g	90 g	60 g	45 g
sweet potato, diced	12 g	150 g	110 g	100 g	75 g	50 g	40 g
tartaric acid	10 g	130 g	100 g	90 g	65 g	45 g	35 g
tomato (125 g), diced	20 g	200 g	150 g	135 g	100 g	70 g	50 g
tomato paste	20 g	250 g	190 g	165 g	125 g	85 g	65 g
tomatoes, sun-dried	12 g	150 g	110 g	100 g	75 g	50 g	40 g
turnip, diced	12 g	150 g	110 g	100 g	75 g	50 g	40 g
vegetables, chopped	12 g	150 g	110 g	100 g	75 g	50 g	40 g
vegetables, mashed	20 g	250 g	190 g	165 g	125 g	85 g	65 g
wheatgerm	10 g	90 g	65 g	60 g	45 g	35 g	25 g
yeast, compressed	15 g	180 g	135 g	120 g	90 g	60 g	45 g
yeast, dried	14 g	180 g	135 g	120 g	90 g	60 g	45 g
yoghurt	20 mL	250 mL	190 mL	165 mL	125 mL	85 mL	65 mL
zucchini (100 g), diced	10 g	120 g	90 g	80 g	60 g	40 g	30 g

Linking Cookery the Australian Way to the

Health and Physical Education — Strand: Self and relationships

Suggested activities to address the learning outcomes.

Level 5

5.1 Describe hereditary and environmental factors that affect human development.

Nutrition as an environmental factor affecting development (Chapter 1). Students prepare any recipe from *Cookery the Australian Way* (e.g. **Bircher-style Muesli** p. 111) and evaluate it in terms of nutritional quality using the food selection models (pp. 3–7).

Foods as a social factor affecting development, and a tool for promoting social and emotional development. Students prepare food(s) from *Cookery the Australian Way* suitable for celebrations (e.g. **Baked Cheesecake** p. 331). Discuss why we eat these types of foods and the needs they fulfil.

5.2 Describe the effect of family and community expectations on the development of personal identity and values.

Students use *Cookery the Australian Way* to find a recipe that their family consumes often. It is then prepared by the student and 'shared' among the class. Do other students consume this food? Why/why not? The teacher might also prepare a selection of foods that are not popularly consumed in the group (e.g. **Tripe Genoese** p. 207, **Osso Bucco** p. 209). Why aren't these consumed? Who may consume them? How might the family play a role in the meals a person consumes regularly?

Look at the role of the family in developing individual values and how it can develop good health values relating to food. A range of meals that are nutritionally adequate yet popular can be prepared by the students (e.g. **Vegetable Lasagne** p. 123, **Polenta Pizza with Vegetable Topping** p. 118, **Mini Pizzas** p. 91, **Shepherd's Pie** p. 211 etc.).

Level 6

6.1 Evaluate a specific intervention designed to enhance human development.

Background of food models and dietary guidelines is outlined (pp. 3–7). Students survey how widely these nutrition tools are used and evaluate the success of their introduction.

Students prepare a meal and evaluate it in relation to the food models (pp. 3–7) and/or dietary guidelines.

Technological advances in food production:
- Students investigate the methods of food cooking available, including the microwave.
- Students prepare a microwave dish (see the comprehensive list on p. 515).
- Students visit the supermarket to investigate the range of microwave products available.
- Students prepare a commercially available microwave product and a similar homemade product. Compare quality and palatability. Suggest reasons why the microwave product is available.

6.2 Identify the major tasks involved in establishing personal identity.

Survey teenagers' meal patterns: what they eat, where they eat, reasons for eating meals away from the family. Compare to the results from a similar survey of younger children. Suggest reasons for the differences, including increasing independence.

Using *Cookery the Australian Way* students plan a lunch suitable for a 3-year-old child and one suitable for an adolescent. Suggest reasons for the differences in the meals planned. How may increasing independence lead to a change in meals planned?

Health and Physical Education — Strand: Health of individuals and populations

Suggested activities to address the learning outcomes.

Level 5

5.1 Describe health issues about which young people make decisions, and strategies that are designed to maintain or improve their health.

Look at and prepare foods that are low in fat and high in fibre and yet popular with teenagers.
- Low fat foods/cookery: suggestions on reducing fat intake in diet (p. 32). Students plan foods to reduce fat intake based on these suggestions. Prepare low-fat foods (e.g. **Low-fat Muesli** p.111).
- High fibre foods, especially snack foods. Use *Cookery the Australian Way* to plan meals that are high in vegetables, fruits and cereals.

Look at the dietary guidelines for children and adolescents (pp. 3–4). Compare these to the guidelines for the rest of the population. Why is there a difference? Using *Cookery the Australian Way* plan meals that support the guidelines.

5.2 Describe health resources, products and services available to individuals and groups in Australia and consider how they could be used to improve health.

Collect information from community groups (e.g. the Heart Foundation, the Diabetes Foundation) which suggests how to improve the nutritional health of the population. Use *Cookery the Australian Way* to practice implementing the strategies suggested by these groups. Recipes may be used as is or modified.

Level 6

6.1 Analyse the positive and negative health outcomes of a range of personal behaviours and community actions

Students choose and prepare their favourite recipe from *Cookery the Australian Way*. Teacher may need to limit the choice – e.g. savoury only, or time/cost limit. Evaluate the nutritional content of this food. How could it be improved? Why might a diet consisting entirely of a person's personal favourites affect his or her long-term health?.

Technology — *Strand: Materials* — **Level 4**

Learning outcome 4.1 Explain how the specific characteristics of materials affect functional and aesthetic design requirements.

Suggested activities to address the learning outcome.

Investigating	Designing	Producing	Evaluating
1 Students are to design a fruit salad. They are provided with a selection of different fruits (including exotic ones) of which they are to use a selected number. Using *Cookery the Australian Way* (pp. 292–308) students find out about the fruits chosen. They may also find out about how these fruits can be prepared.	**1** Students design their fruit salad by planning how they will prepare their fruits, how they will present them and what accompaniment they could serve with the salad.	**1** Students use a range of tools including knives, apple corers, chopping boards etc. to prepare the fruit salad. The teacher may have to demonstrate: • correct and safe use of a knife • correct food handling techniques.	**1** Students evaluate their fruit salad. They decide if the fruit was prepared in the best way, if the combination of fruits was appropriate (including taste, texture), if the look of the salad was optimal.
2 Students research the classification of vegetables using *Cookery the Australian Way* (pp. 228–9). They investigate the prices, seasonable availability and signs of freshness of a selected number of vegetables. Students can also refer to the food value of vegetables (p. 227). Students investigate the variety of Asian vegetables using Chapter 9.	**2** Students design a vegetarian platter. Constraints may include availability of certain vegetables and that students are to use a variety of cooking methods. Ideas can be generated from *Cookery the Australian Way* (e.g. **celery curls** p. 262, **Zucchini Slice** p. 132, **Spanish Omelette** p.108, **Summer Salad** p. 275). OR Students design a stir-fry dish using **Bok Choy and Ginger Noodle** recipe (p. 124). Other vegetables to be used are Asian. Develop criteria for evaluation. Justify preferred option and prepare a detailed work plan that notes safety features to be followed.	**2** Students produce their preferred option ensuring they meet the constraints of the design brief. The teacher may have to demonstrate: • correct and safe use of equipment • correct procedures for cooking methods. Students use *Cookery the Australian Way* (Chapters 9 and 10) to discuss or demonstrate techniques when preparing vegetables for salads and/or stir-fries.	**2** Evaluate the product commenting on the appearance, taste and texture. Prepare an evaluation report that comments on: • student work practices • techniques used • ability to work safely.

Learning outcome 4.2 Prepare designs for products, organise and undertake a range of production processes and evaluate against the design specifications.

Suggested activities to address the learning outcome.

Investigating	Designing	Producing	Evaluating
1 Students are to make a chocolate cake for an afternoon tea. They investigate the different techniques (creaming, melt and mix, and sponge making) for preparing a chocolate cake using *Cookery the Australian Way*.	**1** Students choose the cake they will make. They should consider the time available to them, the skills they are familiar with, the characteristics of a quality cake (p. 419 – tips for product quality).	**1** Students produce the cake chosen. The teacher may have to demonstrate the different methods of preparation: • creaming method • melt and mix method • sponge making.	**1** Students evaluate the cake they made in terms of the design specifications given.
2 Students decide which type of chocolate cake should be made for a surprise visitor who will arrive that afternoon. They have 90 minutes to prepare the cake ready for consumption. They are to investigate by preparing the different chocolate cakes that appear in *Cookery the Australian Way*.	**2** Working in groups, students plan which cake-mixing methods they will follow, and develop a detailed work plan. The skill level of each student will need to be considered. Design an evaluation sheet that will assist in the selection of a chocolate cake recipe, it could include: the time it takes to make from start to being ready for consumption; preferred flavour, texture and appearance.	**2** Students make the different chocolate cakes, practising the different techniques of preparation: melt and mix; microwave; packet mix; sponge; and creaming.	**2** Evaluate the cake using the designed sheet. Students decide which is most suitable for the design brief given, and justify their decision.

Learning outcome 5.1 Explain some of the social and environmental implications of using particular materials in products.

Suggested activities to address the learning outcome.

Investigating	Designing	Producing	Evaluating
1 Students investigate the production of soy and soy products, including genetically engineered soy beans. Include reasons for the increase in the use of soy-based products, their advantages (i.e. nutritional), and the potential advantages and disadvantages of genetically modified food products on world food production.	1 Students design a vegetarian meal. Constraints may be that the meal must include a soy-based product such as tofu or soy milk or cheese. Students design an evaluation sheet for taste, appearance and texture.	1 Students produce a meal using a soy-based product, (e.g. **Tofu Sesame Sticks** p. 118, **Sweet and Sour Tofu** p. 118, or **Vegetable Lasagne** p. 123).	1 Students use their evaluation sheet to evaluate the meal. Students evaluate the potential for the use of soy-based products in world food production including the possible social and environmental advantages and disadvantages.
2 Students investigate packaging of food products, e.g. types and uses. Students investigate the cost of pre-cooked packaged foods in relation to the same product when homemade.	2 Students design a menu/recipe that mirrors a packaged menu/recipe. Its design must allow for storage so it can be used later – as is a packaged product. Students design an evaluation sheet that considers the packaging materials used for the homemade and packaged product. It should also evaluate flavour, texture, cost and appearance.	2 Students prepare their chosen menu/recipe (e.g. **Custard Tart** p. 326, **Sausage Rolls** p. 221, **Self saucing Chocolate Pudding** p. 338, **Macaroni Cheese** p. 120).	2 Students use their evaluation sheet to assess the menu/recipe. They make judgements regarding the cost of the product and the quantity of waste each product generates. They comment on the environmental friendliness of the production of each product.

Learning outcome 5.2 Justify, develop and implement design ideas, using some complex equipment and processes, and evaluate the efficiency of the processes used.

Suggested activities to address the learning outcome.

Investigating	Designing	Producing	Evaluating
1 Students investigate mechanical/electrical equipment available for use in the kitchen. They investigate their correct and safe use, and what they are used for.	1 Students design a menu that uses a number of different pieces of the equipment they investigated. Use *Cookery the Australian Way* to find suitable recipes.	1 Students produce the menu. The teacher may need to demonstrate the safe and appropriate use of the equipment.	1 Students evaluate the use of the tools in preparing the menu, in terms of: ease of use; success of product; time saved by using equipment rather than doing the same process by hand (students can use the preparation time in each recipe in *Cookery the Australian Way* as a guide).
2 Students investigate the melt and mix method versus rubbing in or creaming methods for preparing biscuits and slices. The investigation should include how these methods are performed and the relative advantage of using each for biscuit/slice preparation.	2 Students choose two recipes from Chapter 16 of *Cookery the Australian Way*. One must use the melt and mix method, the other either the creaming or rubbing in method. Design evaluation criteria, including: time taken; texture of finished product; ease of preparation; possible uses of each method of preparation.	2 Suggested recipes include: **Anzacs** p. 424, **Cherry Rounds** p. 428, **Lemon Slice** p. 432, **Hedgehog** p. 431.	2 Students evaluate and compare the recipes produced.

Technology Strand: *Materials* **Level 6**

Learning outcome 6.1 Analyse the appropriateness of using particular materials, including emerging materials, for specific purposes.

Suggested activities to address the learning outcome.

Investigating	Designing	Producing	Evaluating
1 Investigate the different grains/seeds that can be used in food preparation and how this varies in different countries (e.g. Middle Eastern cuisine). Students should find and read the following recipes: • **Tabouli** (p. 275) • **Hommus** (p. 87). Students should visit a supermarket and investigate the different ingredients and costs e.g. chickpeas, tahini, and burghul.	**1** Using *Cookery the Australian Way* design a Middle Eastern dish, using grains and cereals. Justify the preferred option. Prepare a detailed work plan showing time, processes and equipment, and include a shopping list. Develop criteria for the evaluation of the product, e.g. taste, colour, nutritional value.	**1** Produce the preferred option that meets the needs of the design brief. The teacher may need to demonstrate the following: • crushing garlic • correct and safe use of cook's knife • use of a processor or blender and safety precautions • adjusting seasoning • presentation techniques and use of garnishes • blanching vegetables • processes related to seeds and grains.	**1** Students use predetermined criteria for evaluation. Discuss visual appeal and flavour. Students look at the colour of dishes – green of tabouli, effects of blanching on vegetables. Evaluate nutritional value and compare to food selection models (pp. 3–7).
2 Students investigate the properties of various flours, e.g. rice, wheat, corn etc. Students investigate where each of these flours is used in recipes using *Cookery the Australian Way.*	**2** Students design a practical that examines the effect of the different types of flours on a baked product. They design an evaluation sheet to look at the quality, taste, texture and appearance of the finished product.	**2** Students complete the practical as designed.	**2** Students evaluate the practical using the designed evaluation sheet.

Learning outcome 6.2 Prepare detailed design proposals, make products using some complex equipment, and analyse the effectiveness of the products with reference to specified criteria.

Cookery the Australian Way *can be used in the planning and implementation of design briefs for learning outcome 6.2.*

Index

D

G

L

M

N

O

P